GROWING OLD IN AMERICA

GROWING OLD IN AMERICA

New Perspectives on Old Age
Third Edition

Edited by

Beth B. Hess and Elizabeth W. Markson

Transaction Books
New Brunswick (U.S.A.) and Oxford (U.K.)

Library of Congress Catalog Number: 84-28040
ISBN: 0-87855-998-1 (Paper)
Printed in the United States of America

Library of Congress Cataloging in Publication Data
Main entry under title:

Growing old in America.

Includes index.
1. Aged—United States—Addresses, essays, lectures. 2. Aging—Addresses, essays, lectures 3. Gerontology—United States—Addresses, essays, lectures. I. Hess, Beth B., 1928–   . II. Markson, Elizabeth Warren.
HQ1064.U5G75   1985   305.2′6′0973   84-28040
ISBN 0-87855-998-1 (pbk.)

Contents

List of Tables

List of Figures

Acknowledgments

The editors gratefully acknowledge the following publishers and publications for permission to use previously published materials:

Jill Quadagno, "Old Age in Industrializing England," was originally published in *Aging in Early Industrial Society*, pp. 13-22, New York: Academic Press, 1982. Reprinted with the permission of Academic Press, Inc. The author has provided a new conclusion for this chapter, prepared especially for the present volume.

Corinne N. Nydegger, "Family Ties of the Aged in Cross-Cultural Perspective," from *The Gerontologist* Vol. 23, No. 1, 1983, pp. 26-31. Reprinted by permission of the Gerontological Society of America, Washington, D.C.

Linda Cool and Justine McCabe, "'The Scheming Hag' and the 'Dear Old Thing': The Anthropology of Aging Women," from *Growing Old in Different Societies, Cross-Cultural Perspectives*, ed. Jay Sokolovsky. Copyright © 1983 by Wadsworth, Inc. Reprinted by permission of Wadsworth Publishing Company, Linda Cool, and Justine McCabe.

Kyriakos S. Markides, "Minority Aging," originally appeared in *Leading Edges: Recent Research on Psychosocial Aging*, pp. 189-230, ed. B.B. Hess and K. Bond. NIH Publication No. 81-2390, November 1981, Washington, D.C.: U.S. Government Printing Office.

Charlotte Ikels, "The Process of Caretaker Selection," originally published in *Research on Aging*, Vol. 5, No. 4 (December 1983), pp. 491-509. Copyright © 1983 by Sage Publications, Inc. Reprinted by permission of Sage Publications, Inc., Beverly Hills, Calif.

Arnold Arluke and Jack Levin, "'Second Childhood': Old Age in Popular Culture," from *Public Communications Review*, Vol. 1, No. 2, Winter, 1982, pp. 21-25. Reprinted by permission of the publisher.

Lois M. Verbrugge, "Women and Men: Mortality and Health of Older People," originally appeared in *Leading Edges: Recent Research in Psychosocial Aging*, pp. 231-286, ed. B.B. Hess and K. Bond. NIH Publication No. 81-2390, November 1981, Washington, D.C.: U.S. Government Printing Office.

Ruth B. Weg, "Beyond Babies and Orgasm," from *Educational Hori-*

zons, Vol. 60, No. 1, Summer 1982, pp. 161-170. Reprinted by permission of Pi Lamda Theta, National Honor and Professional Asssociation in Education, Bloomington, Ind.

Jabar F. Gubrium and Robert J. Lynott, "Rethinking Life Satisfaction," from *Human Organization*, Vol. 42, No. 1, 1983, pp. 30-38. Reprinted by permission of the Society for Applied Anthropology.

David A. Karp and William C. Yoels, "Work, Careers, and Aging," from *Qualitative Sociology*, Vol. 4, No. 2, Summer 1981, pp. 145-165. Reprinted by permission of Human Sciences Press, New York, N.Y.

Matilda White Riley, "Aging, Social Change, and the Power of Ideas," is reprinted by permission of *Daedalus*, Journal of the American Academy of Arts and Sciences, "Generations," Vol. 107, No. 4, 1978, pp. 39-52, Boston, Mass.

Maximiliane E. Szinovacz, "Beyond the Hearth: Older Women and Retirement," is reprinted by permission of the publisher from *Older Women*, ed. Elizabeth W. Markson, Lexington, Mass.: Lexington Books, D.C. Heath and Company, Copyright © 1983, D.C. Heath and Company. This project was supported by a grant from the NRTA-AARP Andrus Foundation, Washington, D.C.

Gary R. Lee, "Marriage and Aging," is reprinted from *Society*, January/February 1981, Transaction: New Brunswick, N.J.

Charles H. Mindel, "The Elderly in Minority Families," originally appeared in *Family Relationships in Later Life*, pp. 193-208, ed. T.H. Brubaker. Copyright © 1983 by Sage Publications, Inc. Reprinted by permission of Sage Publications, Inc. Beverly Hills, Calif.: Sage.

Nancy Foner, "Caring for the Elderly: A Cross-Cultural View," is an expanded and revised version of "Care for the Aged in Nonindustrial Cultures," originally appeared in the *Hastings Center Report*, Vol. 15, No. 1, April 1985. Reprinted by permission of The Hastings Center, Hastings-on-Hudson, N.Y.

Claire Pedrick-Cornell and Richard J. Gelles, "Elder Abuse: The Status of Current Knowledge," from *Family Relations*, Vol. 31, 1982, pp. 457-465. Copyright © 1982 by the National Council on Family Relations, 1219 University Avenue Southeast, Minneapolis, Minn. Reprinted by permission.

Jeffrey P. Rosenfeld, "To Heir Is Human," from *American Demographics*, September 1983, pp. 19ff. Reprinted by permission of American Demographics, Inc., Ithaca, N.Y.

Anne Woodward, "Housing the Elderly," is reprinted from *Society*, January/February 1982, pp. 52-57, Transaction: New Brunswick, N.J.

Deborah A. Sullivan and Sylvia A. Stevens, "Snowbirds: Seasonal

Preface

The third edition of *Growing Old in America* is a very different volume from its predecessors. Our earlier goal had been to introduce students to the newly emerging discipline of social gerontology as it was. Over the past eight years, however, the field has become saturated with introductory textbooks and readers that effectively cover the basic ground. In this book, subtitled *New Perspectives on Old Age*, we want to take instructors and students to the leading edges of contemporary gerontological thinking, introduce a "second generation" of talent, and in the process indicate new directions of research and theory.

Thus, there will be very few "golden oldies" of the gerontological literature included in this volume. Many pieces have been specially written, others have only recently been presented at professional meetings; and, with one exception, all have been written or published in the 1980s. In addition to their recency, the chapters of this book are characterized by a reformulation of basic assumptions in social gerontology. This thrust goes beyond simple debunking, as each author attempts to illuminate our understanding of current trends through a critical assessment of taken-for-granted beliefs. Each essay has something new to say either by presenting new evidence or by looking at existing data in a new way.

We hope that you will find this collection as stimulating and provocative as we did when putting it together. Our thanks are due to all the authors for their willingness (eagerness, in many cases) to allow us to use their material. Indeed, our friendship with many of the authors is one of the latent benefits of being in this field today. We are grateful also to Irving Louis Horowitz and the Transaction staff for their encouragement and assistance in all phases of this enterprise. And, as always, we acknowledge the support and affection of our families.

INTRODUCTION

1

America's Elderly:
A Demographic Overview

Beth B. Hess

As we compiled the data for this third version of the demographic essay that opens each edition of *Growing Old in America,* we were struck both by how little has changed in the ten years since the first edition and by the tenacity of a range of myths about aging in America. Despite two decades of increasingly high levels of research activity and academic instruction in the fields of aging and gerontology, the lives of the elderly seem little affected, while the views of the general public remain locked into inaccurate stereotypes. After reviewing the most recent data on the status of the elderly, we will attempt to explain this apparent lack of change.

How Many Elderly?

There are today approximately 27 million persons aged 65+ in the United States, composing 11.5 percent of our population. Since the proportion of elderly in any society depends upon the numbers of persons in younger age brackets, we must examine the entire age structure in order to predict the relative size of the oldest age groups in the decades ahead. As Table 1.1 shows, the secular trend since 1900 is toward a progressively "older" society, rising slowly until the 1940s, jumping upward and then stabilizing throughout the "baby boom" years, increasing more sharply in the 1980s, reaching a plateau for the remainder of this century, and then surging ahead in 2020 as the birth cohorts of the baby boom reach old age. By 2030, over one in five Americans will be 65+, a proportion that should remain stable until the middle of the twenty-first century, barring any unforeseen dramatic change in birth rates.

The proportion of elderly varies by race, ethnicity, and sex. People age 65+ make up 12 percent of all Whites, 8 percent of Blacks, 6 percent of

TABLE 1.1
Actual and Projected Growth of U.S. Population 65 + , 1900-2050

Year	Number	Percent
1900	3,084,000	4.0
1910	3,950,000	4.3
1920	4,933,000	4.7
1930	6,634,000	5.4
1940	9,019,000	6.8
1950	12,270,000	8.1
1960	16,560,000	9.2
1970	19,980,000	9.8
1980	25,554,000	11.3
1990	31,799,000	12.7
2000	35,036,000	13.1
2010	39,269,000	13.9
2020	51,386,000	17.3
2030	64,345,000	21.1
2040	66,643,000	21.6
2050	67,061,000	21.7

Source: Bureau of the Census, Current Population Reports, Series P-23, No. 128, September 1983: 3.

Asians, and 5 percent each of the Hispanic and American Indian populations. The low proportion of elderly in minority populations is largely due to higher birth rates and younger ages of Asian and Hispanic immigrants. Nonetheless, over the past 15 years the rate of increase of minority elderly has been higher than that for Whites.

Today's older population also contains a large number of foreign-born persons, the last of the great waves of immigration between 1880 and 1920. The proportion of foreign-born will, of course, steadily decline as members of these cohorts die off. Since 1920, migration to America has been more limited and controlled and is not expected to have a major effect on the age structure of the society.

Life Expectancy

Whilst the proportion of elderly in the population is a function of changing fertility rates, the growth in absolute numbers of old people reflects factors that determine life expectancy, i.e. the average number of years that members of a given birth group (cohort) can expect to live at particular ages (e.g. at birth, at age 40, or at age 65). Table 1.2 shows the dramatic gains in average life expectancy at birth for both Blacks and Whites, and women and men, in the United States over this century:

TABLE 1.2
U.S. Life Expectancy at Birth by Race and Sex, 1900-82

	White		Black	
	Female	*Male*	*Female*	*Male*
1900-2	51.1	48.2	35.0	32.5
1982	78.7	71.4	73.8	64.8

Sources: Siegel and Davidson, forthcoming; Table 5.1, Department of Health and Human Services, National Center for Health Statistics, Monthly Vital Statistics Report, Vol. 31, No. 13, October 5, 1983: p. 4.

As you can see, life expectancy has increased by almost one-half for Whites and has doubled for Blacks in the past 80 years. Most of this increase is due to the control of infectious diseases that once killed large numbers of infants and children. Having survived childhood many people in the past lived to a "ripe old age"; the great change has been in the proportion of each birth cohort that avoided early death. For example, as late as 1930, only 54 percent of all newborns could expect to live to age 65 compared to almost 80 percent today.

There have also been gains in life expectancy at the older age levels, but these have been minimal compared to those of childhood. Between 1940 and 1982, remaining life expectancy at age 65 for men increased by two and one-half years, from 12 to 14.5, and for women by over five years, from 13.6 to 19 (American Council of Life Insurance, 1982). The proportion surviving from age 65 to age 80 increased during these decades from roughly one-third to three-fifths, but most of these gains occurred before 1954 and have only recently begun to rise again (Siegel and Davidson, forthcoming, Table 5.2). Major increases in life expectancy in the United States do not appear likely over the rest of this century. At most, female life expectancy at birth may increase to 82 years and that for males to 76.

After age 75, life expectancy for Blacks is actually greater than that for Whites, reflecting the higher Black mortality rates at earlier ages that remove the less robust, leaving the most biologically fit to survive to very old ages (Manton, 1982; Markides, 1983). Since death rates vary by education, income, and occupational status, the favored position of Whites reduces mortality at earlier ages, leaving Whites more vulnerable than Blacks to the death-producing conditions of very old age.

Despite frequent news stories heralding an approaching "breakthrough" in extending life, the prospect appears unlikely. The human life span is a species-specific characteristic—slightly over 100 years. The variable that changes over time is the probability of living close to that limit. According to the 1980 Census there were 32,000 persons aged 100 or older in the United States, two-thirds of whom were women. These numbers are what one would expect on the scientific estimate of two or three centenarians (people over 100 years old) per 100,000 population (Hayflick, n.d.). Claims of the existence of extremely long-lived populations in parts of Ecuador and the Soviet Union are wildly out of line with such estimates, and, upon closer inspection, turn out to be wildly inaccurate (Medvedev, 1974; Mazess and Forman, 1979). Yoghurt commercials notwithstanding, most of the people portrayed as being 120 or 140 years old are actually in their eighties and nineties. The difficulties in reckoning age among illiterate populations with poor or nonexistent birth records are often compounded by the fact that the same name recurs among members of different generations. In any event, there is little evidence to support the claims of extreme long life in these isolated areas.

Sex Differences in Life Expectancy

As the data in Table 1.2 indicate, female life expectancy in the United States is higher than that of males, and this relative advantage has grown larger over this century, a pattern found in other modern industrial societies (or any society with low mortality rates in general). There is no simple explanation for these sex differences. Verbrugge (chapter 13) points to three separate sets of causal variables: (1) genetic risks that vary by sex (e.g. men's greater vulnerability to "killer" heart conditions) ; (2) acquired risks having to do with exposure to death-producing environments or behaviors (e.g. smoking and occupational accidents for men, pregnancy and childbearing for women); and (3) gender differences in perceiving symptoms and seeking health care (i.e. women are more likely than men to recognize symptoms, to seek out help, and to reduce their activity level when ill). All three factors combine to increase life expectancy for American women in this century: until late adulthood, they are hormonally protected against heart attacks; the probability of death in childbirth or from the negative effects of multiple pregnancies has been greatly reduced; and the fact that women more often report illness and do something about it may actually lengthen their lives.

In addition, there is little evidence that this sex difference in life expectancy will narrow in the near future, although it will not increase either (Siegel and Davidson, in press). Possibly, male death rates will decline as men adopt more healthful behaviors, but the natural biological superiority of women will continue to manifest itself under conditions of modern life. As a consequence, there are and will continue to be many more older women than older men. Sixty percent of all Americans age 65 and over are women, an increase of 5 percent since 1960. The *sex ratio*—the number of males for every hundred women—declines directly with age: from a slight excess at birth (104 male babies for every hundred females) to 80 per 100 for persons age 65-69, and only 42 per 100 at age 85+ (Bureau of the Census, 1983g: 4-5). These data mean that most old women will outlive their husbands, live alone or in the home of an adult child, and suffer from the chronic illnesses of extreme age.

Marital Status and Living Arrangements

As seen in Table 1.3, the majority of old men, even at age 75 and older are married and living with their wife. In contrast, the majority of older women are not currently married.

TABLE 1.3
Marital Status of Older Americans, 1983 (in percents)

	Age 65-74		Age 75 +	
	Male	*Female*	*Male*	*Female*
Never married	5.6	5.1	3.1	6.0
Married, spouse present	79.8	48.8	70.8	23.9
Married, spouse absent	2.0	1.8	1.7	1.0
Widowed	9.0	39.2	21.7	66.6
Divorced	3.7	5.2	2.6	2.6

Source: Bureau of the Census, Current Population Reports, Series P-20, No. 389, June 1984: 8.

The proportions of both older men and women who are not married is even higher in the Black population, reaching 78 percent widowed for Black women aged 75+.

The very high probability of an older man having a wife to attend to his needs is due to several factors: the longer life expectancy of women, the fact that men typically marry women younger than themselves, and the much higher remarriage rates of older men compared to women. For example, in 1980, among nonmarried persons aged 45-64 men were three-and-a-half times more likely to remarry than were women, and at ages 65+, men remarried at *nine* times the rate of women (U.S. Department of Health and Human Services, 1983b:7).

These data on marital status are reflected in Table 1.4 on living arrangements. Table 1.4 also reflects the most striking change in living arrangements of any age/sex group over the past two decades: the decline in older women who live with other relatives (from 19 to 10 percent between 1965 and 1981) and the commensurate rise in proportions living alone (from 31 to 40 percent during the same time period). This shift is largely due to the enhanced ability of older women to afford independent residence, thanks

TABLE 1.4
Living Arrangements of Persons 65 + , 1982 (in percents)

	Women		Men	
	65-74	75 +	64-75	75 +
In Households:				
With Spouse	49	19	79	65
With Others	16	24	8	9
Alone	34	45	11	19
Not in Household:	2	12	2	7

Sources: Bureau of the Census, Current Population Reports, Series P-20, No. 380, May 1983: 22; Siegel and Davidson, forthcoming, Table 7.3.

to liberalization of Social Security benefits and the introduction of Medicare in 1965.

In the future, it is expected that increases in the numbers of divorced persons will be offset by smaller increases in the number of widowed elderly, leaving the percentage of households maintained by an older couple relatively stable. But there will also continue to be increases in single-person households maintained by older women, particularly at ages 75+ (Siegel and Davidson, forthcoming, Table 7.6).

In addition, there were about 120,000 households in 1983 in which a nonmarried couple, one of whom was 65+, lived together (Bureau of the Census, 1983d:4)—in the inimitable language of officialdom, "persons of the opposite sex sharing living quarters," or POSSLQs. This figure may be lower than a decade ago when many older POSSLQs did not marry for fear of losing the pension rights of one spouse, leading to a change in Social Security regulations allowing remarried elderly to retain full benefits.

Institutionalized Elderly

An additional 5 percent of all people aged 65 and over live in nursing homes or mental hospitals. In 1982, 1.3 million elderly were residents of nursing homes. The risk of institutionalization rises with age, from 1.5 percent of people age 65-74 to 6 percent of those 75-84, and 23 percent of those age 85+ (Bureau of the Census, 1983g:17). The typical nursing home resident is a widow, over age 80, with few, if any, surviving children, and suffering from health problems that limit their ability to care for themselves.

As will become evident in several of the selections of this volume, it is simply not true that large numbers of older people are "dumped" into nursing homes by uncaring offspring. This is one of those myths that no amount of data can dislodge from the public mind. Most institutional placements occur after all other alternatives have been tried, and particularly after a major health setback to the older person or some change in the ability of adult children to provide care. In fact, at least 80 percent of all home care needed by the elderly is already being given by family members (spouses, children, other relatives), at great personal cost and sacrifice (Soldo and Myllylouma, 1983; Cantor, 1983; Hess and Soldo, 1984).

There are undoubtedly many frail elderly whose institutionalization could have been avoided or delayed if there were a range of community services available to assist family caregivers. But at this moment few communities have established this kind of home care system, and few elderly or their children can afford to pay for private health care services over a long period. One major problem is that most of such services are not covered by the health insurance programs established by Congress in 1965: Medicare for all elderly and some disabled persons (funded by payroll taxes and individual payments for extra insurance), and Medicaid for the poor of any age, 16 percent of whom are over age 65 (jointly funded by the federal government and the various states, with the exception of Arizona). These programs are biased toward institutional care, in contrast to preventive and community-based services. As hospital and nursing home costs outstrip the amounts of money going into these programs, there is a growing perception of "crisis" in the Medicare/Medicaid programs.

In any event, the great majority of nursing home residents do not qualify for Medicare reimbursement, which is given only for cases requiring constant skilled nursing care. An older person could "spend down", i.e. use up all personal assets, and thus qualify for Medicaid. Yet, most nursing home residents or their children are paying in full for health-related care, at an average of $20,000 per year. Indeed, there are not enough nursing home beds for all those who could use continual care, especially in light of the growing population of persons age 85 and older, most of whom will be widowed women.

Nonetheless, 95 percent of all elderly do live in the community and most are in their own households. How do they fare?

Labor Force Participation

As seen in Figure 1.1, the long-term (secular) trend for men has been toward *reduced* rates of employment. For men age 65 and over, labor force participation has declined from 46 percent in 1950 to 18 percent in the early 1980s; and for men age 55-64, there has been a steady decrease since 1965, from roughly 87 percent to about 71 percent. The primary factors here, contrary to another myth about forced (mandatory) retirement, are the availability of retirement income from the Social Security system or other pension plan, and the health status of the worker.

Social Security was enacted as a "stop gap" measure in 1935 to provide income for older workers willing to leave the labor force, thus making room for younger workers during the Great Depression. By 1950, some older workers had paid into the system for enough years to provide an assured retirement income, and as the years went by, more and more men choose to leave the labor force as soon as they were entitled to benefits (partial at age 62, full at age 65). In many cases, such "voluntary" retirees

FIGURE 1.1
Labor Force Participation of Persons Aged 55-64 and 65+, by Sex, 1950-81

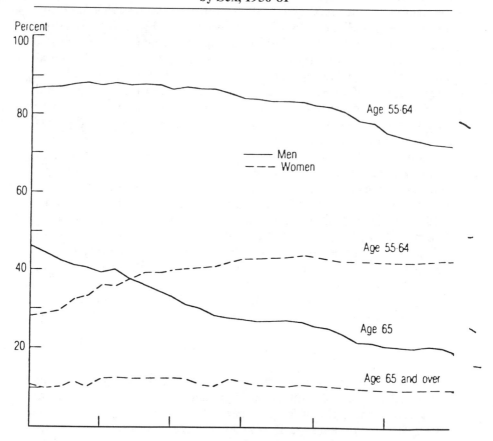

Sources: U.S. Bureau of the Census, Current Population Reports, P-23, No. 128, 1983, p. 17; *Statistical Abstract of the United States,* 1982-83, p. 377.

also received retirement income from savings, investments, or private pension plans.

Voluntary retirement, however, is very uncommon among men who leave the labor force *before* age 62. For four-fifths of Black men and two-thirds of White men retiring before age 62, the primary reason was poor health. Many were disabled (though not seriously enough to qualify for full Social Security disability benefits), and a small proportion had been laid off and unable to find employment because of their age (U.S. House of Representatives, 1981). These "involuntary" retirees will receive reduced benefits for the remainder of their lives; reduced, that is, from already low entitlements.

Older Female Workers

In contrast to the pattern for men, Figure 1.1 shows a relatively slow decline in labor force participation for women age 65+, approximately 11 percent of whom were in the labor force in 1950 compared to 8 percent in 1981. Among women aged 55-64, however, the trend has been upward, from 28 percent in 1950 to over 41 percent in 1981. Clearly, it is not retirement income that accounts for older women's employment decisions. Some will leave the work force when their husband retires, and many (especially in the oldest age groups) will not have been in paid employment following their marriage or childbearing years. But increasingly, women have either remained in the labor force throughout most of their adulthood or have reentered once their children are in school. Labor force participation rates at all adult ages have risen with each new cohort of women, thus making it likely that the curve for female workers age 55-64 will continue to approach that for men.

Increasingly, also, older (65+) men and women in the work force are on part-time schedules: 48 percent of the men and 60 percent of the women in 1981 in contrast to 30 percent and 43 percent in 1960 (Bureau of the Census, 1983g). Most part-time workers report that they choose their reduced schedules when offered rather than find themselves forced back on the job market out of economic necessity.

Unemployment

Unemployment rates refer to persons who are actively seeking jobs or who consider themselves in the labor force although recently laid off. For workers age 65+, the unemployment rate in 1982 was about half of that of younger workers (higher for women than for men). For workers aged 55-64, unemployment rates were also lower than for younger people but higher than they had been since 1945 (Bureau of the Census, 1983g). In comparison with younger unemployed people, older workers take longer to find a new job, receive lower wages when reemployed, and are more likely to become discouraged and stop looking for work. Thus, periods of high unemployment have a disproportionate effect on older job-seekers, many of whom will become the "involuntary" retirees described earlier.

Employment status is important largely through its effects on income, and not, as another myth has it, because work is essential to a man's sense of self-worth. As mandatory retirement rules cover only a small fraction of American workers, the dramatic drop-off in labor force participation at age 65 suggests that people retire as soon as they are assured of income maintenance. In 1965 and again in 1972, the Social Security Act was amended to expand benefits; particularly important was the coupling of benefits to the cost-of-living index. In 1982, however, the Act was amended to reduce the range and extent of benefits and to raise the age at which future pensioners qualify for full entitlements. In addition, the disability regulations were tightened. It is too early to tell whether the new changes will make retirement a less attractive alternative to older workers, forcing some people in ill health or low wage occupations to remain on the job, and blocking paths of upward mobility for younger workers. In times of high inflation rates and general economic uncertainty, older workers may postpone retirement.

In general, older employed workers have higher incomes than retired persons, but most older people in the labor force are relatively young (65-69). The vast majority of elderly in America depend on Social Security and other pensions for their retirement income.

Income

Comparing income *medians* (the point at which 50 percent of the cases fall above and 50 percent below) for persons 65+ with those of all American adults, old people receive roughly two-thirds the overall median and one-half the median for people in the peak earnings years, 45-54 (Bureau of the Census, 1983e; 1984c). But this simple comparison obscures enormous variation by age within the older strata, by sex, race, marital status, and employment. Indeed, just looking at the medians might lead to the conclusion that the economic status of old people is relatively secure, especially since many older people own their homes free of mortgage debt. A survey of elderly homeowners (Rabushka and Jacobs, 1980) concluded that a majority of older Americans are not ill-housed, ill-fed, or poor. Elderly homeowners, however, are likely to be under age 69, to be married, relatively healthy, and to have accumulated assets in addition to Social Security.

TABLE 1.5
Median Income of Persons 65 +, by Sex and Race, 1982 (in dollars)

	Men		Women	
	65-69	*70 +*	*65-69*	*70 +*
White	11,890	8,488	5,710	5,554
Black	5,866	4,906	3,865	3,533

Source: Bureau of the Census, Current Population Reports, Series P-60, No. 142, February 1984, pp. 151-55.

Income declines directly with age, and varies greatly by race and sex as seen in Table 1.5.

In 1983, older people who live in families (defined by the Bureau of the Census as living with at least one other person related by marriage, birth, or adoption) had median incomes almost three times higher than people classified as "unrelated individuals": $16,868 compared to $6,938 (Bureau of the Census, 1984c). Most of the latter, as noted earlier, will be widows living alone. Clearly, these are not the old women that many believe control America's wealth. To the contrary, at least 90 percent of persons age 65+ with incomes of $75,000 and over in 1982 were White males. With respect to race, the income difference between White and Blacks in old age is more extreme than that for younger people, roughly 44 percent the median income of White persons age 65+, in part because elderly Blacks are less likely than Whites to be living in families.

It should be noted, however, that because households headed by older people typically have only one or two members, the difference between *per person* median income for older and younger households is less than that for families in general.

Sources of Income

These differentials by race and sex also reflect generally higher life-time earnings and savings of White males, who are far more likely than women or Blacks and Hispanics to have been employed in firms with private pension plans. Thus, in retirement they have more, and more varied, sources of income than other workers: interest-bearing securities, second pensions, and savings, in addition to top level social security benefits.

Of the total income received by older people in 1981, Social Security accounted for 37 percent, earnings for 25 percent, savings and property income for 23 percent, and private pensions for 13 percent. However, the proportions of old people receiving significant amounts from assets, earnings, or second pensions are quite low. For example, the income from private pensions averages a bit over $2000 per year, and only 2 percent of the elderly receive more than half their income from such pensions. Income from property is, on average, similarly low. In fact, the most common and substantial asset of most older persons is the home in which they are currently living.

In addition, the likelihood of having earnings is directly related to age; while 10 percent of people aged 65-69 worked year-round full-time in 1981, only 2 percent of those age 70 and over did so. For most elderly, Social Security is the primary source of old-age income. Over 91 percent of older Americans now receive some benefits, and for over half of these recipients, their Social Security payments account for more than half their yearly income. Again, there are marked differences by sex and race in dependency upon income from Social Security. In 1981, these benefits provided 47 percent of the income of all Black households, 46 percent of the total income of older persons living alone, and 62 percent of the income of older Black unrelated individuals (Bureau of the Census, 1983g: 9-10). The older the person, the more dependent upon Social Security. Older widows are especially vulnerable; of the 3 million older persons receiving a minimum social security benefit of $122 per month in 1981, over 85 percent were women. This is the benefit that the Reagan administration has sought to eliminate in order to "save money" and "avoid double dipping" by people who also receive other pensions.

As these data indicate, the income distributions of older people reflect their earlier placement in the social stratification system. Although Social Security does provide a higher "replacement ratio" (the proportion of pre-retirement income represented by the benefit) to people who had been low wage earners, the relative income status of individuals is not greatly changed. Poverty in old age is distributed in much the same way as at younger ages.

Poverty

In 1959, before the "war on poverty" and major amendments to the Social Security Act, including Medicare, over one-third of all elderly fell below the poverty threshold, half again as high as the poverty rate for all persons. By 1978, the poverty rate for older persons had fallen to 14 percent, only a few points higher than the overall level of 11.4. In 1980 and 1981 poverty among the elderly rose to over 15 percent, but declined to slightly over 14 percent in 1983 (Bureau of the Census, 1983e, 1984b). In 1983 the poverty threshold for one person age 65+ was about $4,775 ($6,023 for a 2-person household). If one included the "near poor," i.e.

persons within 125 percent of the poverty line, almost one-fourth of all elderly Americans could still be considered in great need.

As poverty is the other side of the income coin, rates vary greatly by age, sex, race, and marital status. In terms of age, only 10 percent of persons in their early 60s are poor compared to 18 percent of people age 72 and over. With respect to minority group status, in 1982, for example, while the poverty rate for all elderly was 14.6, the percentage for Whites was 12.4 compared to 38.2 for Blacks and 26.6 for Hispanic elderly. By sex, the poverty rate for older women was almost 60 percent higher than that of older men, rising to over 25 percent of all female householders (and over half of Black female householders).

Thus, while old age poverty was cut in half by the introductions of Medicare in 1965 and the liberalization of Social Security benefits in 1972, many old people—those who are not White male family householders—remain among the most economically deprived of Americans, as seen in Table 1.6:

TABLE 1.6
Family Householders and Unrelated Individuals 65 + below
the Poverty Level, by Race and Sex, 1982 (in percents)

	White		Black	
	Male	*Female*	*Male*	*Female*
Family Householder	6.6	11.3	26.8	34.9
Unrelated Individual	16.9	25.4	50.2	66.3

Sources: Siegel and Davidson, forthcoming, Table 8.8; Bureau of the Census, Current Population Reports, P-60, No. 144, March 1984: 13-14.

Benefits

In addition to Social Security, the elderly benefit from a number of special programs, some targeted to all people over age 65, others to the poor (many of whom are elderly). There is a growing debate, among gerontologists and within the federal government, on the relative value of using age or need as the major criterion for designing benefit programs (see Neugarten, 1982). A number of articles in this book (Chapters 33-37) deal in greater detail with public policy matters. In this introductory essay, however, we shall present only the relevant data on benefit programs in which older people participate.

As noted, over 90 percent of older Americans receive some income from Social Security, either as a retired worker, the spouse of a retiree, the widow/widower of a beneficiary, or as a disabled person. Over 90 percent of the elderly are also covered by the Medicare program for health care reimbursements. Both Social Security and Medicare are open to all who qualify regardless of income or need. Other benefit programs involve a means test; that is, applicants must show that they do not have the resources to meet their needs. The major means-tested programs for older people are food stamps (used by 6.5 percent of elderly households), housing subsidies (used by 5.5 percent), and Medicaid (13.3 percent). As these low percentages suggest, not all eligible elderly participate—only half the households that could meet the means test receive any of these benefits (Bureau of the Census, 1983f). Many do not know about the programs or are unaware of their eligibility; others prefer to avoid the stigma of being a welfare recipient, particularly when there is a strong current of anti-welfarism generated by political leaders.

The most stigmatizing of all programs is called Supplemental Security Income (SSI), a name chosen in 1972 for a Federal program designed to replace a variety of state-run public assistance programs for the aged, blind, and disabled. The change in name was cosmetic only; SSI payments are minimal and rarely matched by the various states. The average monthly SSI benefit to an older person in 1982 was under $150, and the elderly make up almost 60 percent of all SSI recipients (two-thirds of whom are women). Maximum SSI payments remain below the poverty level; even so, recent federal budget proposals seek to save money by delaying SSI cost-of-living adjustments and by making a greater effort to weed out aged, blind, and disabled "cheaters." Other means-tested programs are also subject to cutbacks and tightened eligibility rules, although such benefits account for roughly 2 percent of the entire 1984 budget (U.S. Senate, 1983).

These budget cuts are often rationalized on the basis of the claim that programs for old people account for one-fourth of all government expenditures. This claim is accurate only if one includes Social Security and Medicare, but both these programs are largely self-financed by the recipients themselves, through payroll taxes and employer contributions (in lieu of higher wages). It is not quite fair, therefore, to suggest that Social Security and Medicare payments are budget outlays in the same sense as defense spending or interest on the national debt. When self-funded programs are excluded, only 4 percent of the federal budget is devoted to assistance to the nation's elderly. Further, as the U.S. Senate Special Committee on Aging (1983:3) points out, the yearly dollar increases look large in part because of *underfunding* in previous decades. Furthermore, since about 11-12 percent of federal income tax revenues come from elderly taxpayers, a figure identical to their proportion of the population, receiving 4 percent of revenue outlays can hardly be considered greedy or unfair.

Reagan administration cost-cutters have also suggested that means-tested benefits be counted as income to the recipients, in which case the percentage of Americans, young or old, who live below the poverty level would be drastically lowered. In addition, the revised income level could be used to reduce eligibility for means-tested programs, a type of catch-22 for those who depend upon such entitlements. It should be noted, however, that Medicaid and housing subsidies are paid directly to the service providers, and therefore are not quite the same as disposable income.

Health

The health status of the elderly will be explored in several chapters in part II of this book. Here we would note only that the overall level of health of America's aged has not changed greatly since 1970: while there are proportionately more chronically ill very old people, the younger aged are in better health than in the past. Nine-tenths of the elderly describe their health as fair or better compared with other people their age (Bureau of the Census, 1983g), and over half report no limits on any major activity because of health considerations. By age 85+, these figures shift, with half reporting themselves unable to carry out a major activity because of poor health. In 1980, as in 1965, four out of five older people reported having at least one chronic condition, although in most cases this did not interfere with major activities.

What has changed, however, is the cost of health care. Even with Medicare to cover hospital bills, 20 percent of the yearly income of older persons is spent on health care—all the expenses not covered by Medicare such as regular check-ups, eyeglasses, canes, and the like. In fact, old people today pay out-of-pocket for over one-third of their annual health costs, a fraction actually higher than before the enactment of Medicare in 1965.

Contrary to popular opinion, old people do not utilize ordinary medical services much more than do younger adults—an average of six visits to physicians to every five by the general population. Compared with younger people, however, the elderly are hospitalized twice as often, for twice as long, and receive twice the volume of prescription drugs. As a consequence, per person health care expenditures for persons over age 65 are three times higher than for younger patients (Siegel and Davidson, forthcoming). In part, these data reflect more severe medical needs, but also the fact that hospital bills are covered by Medicare whereas outpatient treatment is an out-of-pocket expense, so that hospitalization is the "cheaper" alternative for an ill older person.

Although it had been hoped by many in the mid-1960s that Medicare legislation would gradually lead to a more comprehensive system of health insurance for all Americans, the trend has been otherwise. The enormous yearly increases in the costs of medical treatment have led to a reduction in coverage and reimbursement formulas as well as increases in the premiums paid by older people and in the deductible portion of their bills. At this writing, the "Medicare crisis" is receiving the same kind of attention that was given to the "Social Security crisis" in 1983, and with the same probable outcome: a further reduction in the scope of the program and additional financial burdens placed upon the elderly users of health services (Rosen, 1983).

Once again, it is important to bear in mind that any decreases in government-supported programs will have a disproportionate impact on the very oldest strata, and thus upon widowed women already living at the edge of poverty.

Housing

One of the few assets owned by most old people is their home. Home ownership among the elderly is far higher than for younger people. Not only do 70 percent of older people own their own homes, but four-fifths of the homes are free of any mortgage debt. However, homes owned by the elderly tend to have a lower market value than that of homes owned by younger persons: only 11 percent were built after 1970, and are, on average, of lower quality than more recently built houses (U.S. Senate, 1982: 18-20). In many cases, needed repairs have been delayed; plumbing and electrical systems have not been replaced; and the normal wear and tear of use have eroded the basic structure. In addition, the neighborhoods in which older people own their homes may have undergone great change and even decay, particularly in the central cities. For all these reasons, then, home ownership data can lead to an exaggerated picture of elderly assets.

Because of their favorable mortgage situation, the absolute cost of owning a home is lower for the elderly than for younger owners. As a proportion of their total income, however, the costs are higher for the elderly — over 25 percent of total household income compared to 16 percent for household heads age 35-64 (U.S. Senate, 1982, p. 18). A small fraction of elderly homeowners live in mobile homes (7 percent of homeowners and 5 percent of all old people), but the trend is up: twice as many new mobile homes in 1980 were occupied by older owners than by younger ones.

Of the remaining 29 percent of older people, 5 percent are in institutions, one percent in single-room occupancy hotels, another 5 percent in subsidized housing units, and the remainder in nonsubsidized rental apartments or in the home of relatives. The cost of shelter to older renters is also relatively high, at least 30 percent of total income. The basic government

programs to meet the need for safe and affordable housing for the elderly
— to encourage the construction of low-income housing units and to sub-
sidize rental payments — have been largely abandoned by the current
administration in favor of a system of rental vouchers for which tenants'
contribution would remain at roughly 30 percent. The administration's
1984 budget, in addition, contained no funding for social or nutritional
services to the impaired residents of congregate housing (U.S. Senate,
1983).

Geographic Distribution

Two-thirds of our older population live in or near large cities, and most
of the remainder live in very small towns and rural areas. In contrast to
1970, when most of the urban elderly lived within the central city, only
about half do today. This population shift is probably not due to older
people moving out of central cities, but to the "aging in place" of persons
outside the inner city. That is, people who were in their 50s in 1970 and
living on the outer edges of large cities are now in their 60s, while the very
oldest of inner city aged have died off, thus leading to a more even distribution of elderly across the metropolitan area. However, Black and Hispanic
elderly remain heavily concentrated in the central core of older cities — 68
percent and 82 percent respectively in 1980.

Aging in place will gradually raise the proportion of old people living in
suburbs, as those who bought homes as young adults in the 1950s reach old
age. In other words, people do not have to change residence in order to
bring about shifts in the distribution of old people (Heaton, 1983). And
contrary to popular belief, large numbers of retired people do *not* pack up
and leave for warmer places; indeed, the older the person, the less likely to
experience geographic mobility. Between 1980 and 1981, for example, only
4.5 percent of persons 65+ changed residence (compared to 16.6 percent for
all Americans), and almost half of these moves were within the same
county (U.S. Census, 1983a, p. 15). About 1 percent of older movers will go
to another state, but when they do it is typically to the "sunbelt," Florida
and the Southwest states. Movers are more likely than nonmovers to be
unmarried, nonworking, to have higher educational levels, and not be
receiving income assistance. People move not only for reasons of health
and comfort, but often to be near other relatives or to return to where one
grew up. In general, however, old people remain where they have lived as
adults, in the same homes in which they raised families, and in the neighborhoods that, for all the changes wrought over time, remain familiar.

This then is a brief demographic portrait of America's aged. To understand the world of the elderly, however, requires going beyond census-type

data to the historical, cultural, and social structural conditions that shape the aging process in modern industrial societies. That is the goal of the remainder of this book.

References

American Council of Life Insurance. 1982. *Data Track 9*, "Older Americans." Washington, D.C.: ACLI.

Cantor, Marjorie H. 1983 "Strain among Caregivers: A Study of Experience in the United States." *Gerontologist* 23: 597-604.

Hayflick, Leonard. n.d. "Perspectives on Human Longevity." In Bernice L. Neugarten and Robert J. Havingshurst (eds.), *Extending the Human Life Span: Social Policy and Social Ethics*. Washington, D.C.: National Science Foundation.

Heaton, Tim B. 1983. "Recent Trends in the Geographical Distribution of the Elderly Population." In Matilda White Riley, Beth B. Hess, and Kathleen Bond (eds.), *Aging in Society*. Hillsdale, N.J.: Lawrence Erlbaum Associates.

Hess, Beth B., and Beth J. Soldo. 1984. "The Old and the Very Old: A New Frontier of Age and Family Policy." Paper presented at the Annual Meeting of the American Sociological Association, San Antonio, Texas, August.

Manton, Kenneth G. 1982. "Differential Life Expectancy: Possible Explanations during the Later Years." In Ron C. Manuel (ed.), *Minority Aging: Sociological and Social Psychological Issues*. Westport, Conn.: Greenwood.

Markides, Kyriakos S. 1983. "Minority Aging." In Matilda White Riley, Beth B. Hess, and Kathleen Bond (eds.), *Aging in Society*. Hillsdale, N.J.: Lawrence Erlbaum Associates.

Mazess, Richard B., and Sylvia H. Forman. 1979. "Longevity and Age Exaggeration in Vilcamba, Ecuador." *Journal of Gerontology* 34:94-98.

Medvedev, Zhores A. 1974. "Caucasus and Altay Longevity: A Biological or Social Problem?" *Gerontologist* 14:381-87.

Neugarten, Bernice L. (ed.). 1982. *Age or Need? Public Policies for Older People*. Beverly Hills, Calif.: Sage.

Rabushka, Alvin, and Bert Jacobs. 1980. *Old Folks at Home*. New York: Free Press.

Rosen, Sumner M. 1983. "The Social Security Crisis: Poor Economics, Dangerous Politics." *Social Policy* (Summer):39-40.

Siegel, Jacob S., and Maria Davidson. In press. "Demographic and Socioeconomic Aspects of Aging in the United States." U.S. Bureau of the Census, Special Studies, series P-23.

Soldo, Beth J., and Jaana Myllylouma. 1983. "Caregivers Who Live with Dependent Elderly." *Gerontologist* 23:605-11.

U.S. Bureau of the Census. 1983a. *Geographical Mobility, March 1981 to March 1982*. Current Population Reports, series P-20, no. 377. Washington, D.C.: U.S. Government Printing Office.

―――. 1983b. *Marital Status and Living Arrangements, March 1982*. Current Population Reports, series P-20, no. 380. Washington, D.C.: U.S. Government Printing Office.

―――. 1983c. *Household and Family Characteristics, March 1982*. Current Population Reports, series P-20, no. 381. Washington D.C.: U.S. Government Printing Office.

_____.1983d. *Households, Families, Marital Status, and Living Arrangements, March 1983 (Advance Report)*. Current Population Reports, series P-20, no. 382. Washington, D.C.: U.S. Government Printing Office.

_____. 1983e. *Money Income and Poverty Status of Families and Persons in the United States, 1982 (Advance Data from the March 1983 Current Population Survey*. Current Population Reports, series P-60, no. 140. Washington, D.C.: U.S. Government Printing Office.

_____. 1983f. *Characteristics of Households Receiving Selected Noncash Benefits, 1982*. Current Population Reports, series P-60, no. 141. Washington, D.C.: U.S. Government Printing Office.

_____. 1983g. *America in Transition: An Aging Society*. Current Population Reports, series P-23, no. 128. Washington, D.C.: U.S. Government Printing Office.

_____. 1984a. *Marital Status and Living Arrangements, March 1983*. Current Population Reports, series P-20, no. 389. Washington, D.C.: U.S. Government Printing Office.

_____. 1984b. *Characteristics of the Population below the Poverty Level, 1982*. Current Population Reports, series P-60, no. 144. Washington, D.C.: U.S. Government Printing Office.

_____. 1984c. *Money Income and Poverty Status of Families and Persons in the United States, 1983 (Advance Data from the March 1984 Current Population Survey*), series P-60, no. 145. Washington, D.C.: U.S. Government Printing Office.

U.S. Department of Health and Human Services, National Center for Health Statistics. 1983a. "Annual Summary of Births, Deaths, Marriages, and Divorces: United States, 1982." *Monthly Vital Statistics Report* 31 (no. 13, October 5).

_____.1983b. "Advance Report of Final Marriage Statistics, 1980." *Monthly Vital Statistics Report* 32 (no. 5, August 10), supplement.

U.S. House of Representatives, Select Committee on Aging. 1981. *The Early Retirement Myth: Why Men Retire before Age 62*. Comm. Publ. 97-298. Washington, D.C.: U.S. Government Printing Office.

U.S. Senate, Special Committee on Aging. 1982. *Developments in Aging, 1981*. Rept. 97-314, vol. 1. Washington, D.C.: U.S. Government Printing Office.

_____. 1983. *The Proposed Fiscal Year 1984 Budget: What It Means for Older Americans*. S.Prt. 98-19. Washington, D.C.: U.S. Government Printing Office.

PART I

AGING ACROSS TIME AND SPACE

Introduction

The first two sets of chapters in this section display the most recent work of gero-anthropologists and historians. As Corinne N. Nydegger puts it, there are two myths to be examined: that of a "Golden Age" and that of the "Golden Isles." The former refers to the belief that the status of the aged in the historical past was more favorable and secure than in the present. In this view, modernization—the forces of industrialism, urbanism, and secularism—automatically and universally diminishes the role of old people. While such a conclusion may be broadly accurate, it is greatly oversimplified. The reality is far more complex and variable than commonly assumed.

Historian Brian Gratton and sociologists Jill Quadagno and John B. Williamson all represent a new breed of social historian whose use of public documents and private letters has recreated the past in its own words and deeds. Gratton's chapter is a broad-based critique of simplistic modernization theories of both the structural and cultural variety. In addition, Gratton provides new insights into the political history of our Social Security policies. Quadagno's goals are more limited: to trace the effects of early industrialization on the work and family relationships of English elderly, showing how families adapted to the structural changes taking place outside the home. As also shown in the work of Tamara Hareven (1982), the family system is not a passive victim of economic development, but a flexible set of relationships by which individuals cope with their world.

John Williamson's focus is the origin and development of social welfare policies in colonial and nineteenth-century America. In contrast to England, with whom the colonists shared a language and culture, the course of welfare reform took different directions over time. Williamson locates the source of such variations in the peculiar character of frontier America and its unique interpretation of the "work ethic." The historical view detailed by Gratton and Williamson will aid our understanding of the current controversy over social welfare covered in the last section of this book.

If the search for a "Golden Age" is full of unexpected pitfalls, that for the "Golden Isles" is equally hazardous. The idea that old people are more esteemed and valued in simple societies is as compelling as the belief in an innocent preindustrial past. Yet Nydegger's review of the anthropological literature demonstrates how misleading are most blanket statements about the status of old people in less complex societies, a point that will be echoed in Nancy Foner's study of family care for the frail elderly in Part IV of this book. Although the details of different societies are fascinating, anthropological analysis teaches us a larger lesson: the meaning of a culture trait can only be found within that society. The dangers of describing other cultures through our own way of thinking (ethnocentrism) is neatly illustrated in the manuscript discovered by Paul M. Baker that describes the uneasy relationship between the Nacirema tribe and its Dega minority.

Until recently, moreover, little was written about the ways in which aging might be experienced differently by women and men in different societies. Either it was assumed that aging had universal psychosocial effects or that the status of women would be encompassed by that of their male relatives. Linda Cool and Justine McCabe examine the stereotypes and reality of women's aging across modern and premodern societies. Their findings offer a healthy corrective not only to our ethnocentrism but to our belief in biological or psychological determinism.

When considering America's elderly, we must also be aware of *subcultural* differences, that is, the extent to which race and ethnicity affect aging and the family supports available to the aged. And here, too, myths have often dominated our thinking: romanticization of the ethnic family coupled with a too-easily accepted assumption of "double jeopardy" in the case of Black (and often Hispanic) elderly. Kyriakos S. Markides looks at the condition of older Blacks and Hispanics along such dimensions as income, physical and mental health, and mortality, in an attempt to test some of these taken-for-granted beliefs. There is no question that Blacks and Hispanics of all ages suffer many disadvantages in our society; aging does not necessarily worsen their condition (which says more about inequality than aging).

What of other minority groups? Charlotte Ikels, in her research on Chinese and Irish families in Boston, goes a long way toward de-mystifying these family systems. By focusing on the crucial question of which adult child becomes the caretaker of an aged parent, Ikels is able to find underlying rules at work in both types of family, and also to illuminate the links between immigrant history and family functioning.

The final set of readings in this section deals with cultural stereotypes as these are used to shape our perception of old people. Arnold Arluke and Jack Levin present a rather chilling picture of the infantilization of the elderly through the popular media. How easily we slip into treating old people as if they were simply big children! People who are either too young or too old to be productive members of the labor force, it appears, are non-persons who must be gently patronized.

Lastly, Andrea S. Walsh shows how the various liberating currents of the 1960s and 1970s have influenced the "experts'" views of parent-child relationships in later life. As seen in recent advice books to middle-aged children of older parents, the message is acceptance not sacrifice, honest attempts to find comfortable ways of staying in touch and helping out.

The new direction, therefore, in all these areas, is away from dogmatic and idealized visions of aging and of intergenerational relations, and toward more subtle, conditional, and conflicted understandings of the status of the elderly.

Reference

Hareven,Tamara K. *Family Time and Industrial Time.* Cambridge: Cambridge University Press, 1982.

2

Factories, Attitudes, and the New Deal: The History of Old Age

Brian Gratton

Until the last decade, little empirical research was available on the history of old age in America. Most scholars applied the basic tenets of modernization theory to the aged, arguing that industrialization and urbanization had reduced the status of older men and women and impoverished them. But recent historical work has shaken confidence in modernization theory; the central argument in recent histories is that attitudinal rather than structural forces have been most important in change in the status of older people. Whereas modernization theory explained the history of the aged in terms of structural differences between traditional and modern societies, the new historians view "ageism" as an independent force and see a culture's attitudes toward old age as the crucial influence in changing status.

The Critique of Modernization Theory

The application of modernization theory to the American elderly stemmed from early twentieth-century concern over old age poverty and dependency: it was presumed that the shift from an agricultural to an industrial nation was the source of older Americans' plight. This interpretation of the decline of the aged was an intuitive construct: it appealed to common sense, nostalgia, and fear of industrialization and urbanization. The first advocates of old age pensions seized upon modernization—though they did not call it that—as a ready explanation for the pitiful state of the elderly in industrial America and as a justification for government relief (e.g., Epstein, 1928, pp. 1-13).

In the 1950s modernization flowered as a general scholarly theory when

American intellectuals, faced with an emerging Third World, sought a Western model to explain the process of economic development (Grew, 1977; Lerner, 1958). Reference to modernization theory among social gerontologists soon reached the level of dogma (Cowgill and Holmes, 1972). The application of modernization theory to the aged stressed the following points.[1]

In stable agricultural societies, the aged enjoy relatively good economic circumstances and high status. This good fortune follows from five conditions. First, landed property is power in agricultural economies; the old tend to control such property, hence they maintain authority over a needy younger generation. Second, the family is the unit of economic organization and the property rights of the older members result in a very direct and forceful influence over the lives of the younger members. Since the family is extended, patriarchal authority is quite broad and security in old age is guaranteed. Third, as farmers who control their own employment, old people continue to perform a work role which is useful and valued. Fourth, high fertility and high mortality result in a very small proportion of the aged in the population, a circumstance said to enhance their status. Finally, in such societies illiteracy is the norm and the aged are repositories of wisdom born of long experience; it is they who pass on to the younger generation skills, knowledge, and traditions (including the veneration of age).

In modern societies the economic circumstances and status of the aged are relatively low. Landed property is no longer the major source of wealth and power in an industrial economy and the family is no longer the unit of economic organization. Under these conditions, the aged lose control over younger family members. According to the theory, the extended family disintegrates into nuclear units which are more suitable for the geographic and economic mobility needed in industrial societies. As workers who sell their labor power, old people are not superior to other workers, and, since they are often judged to be inferior, they suffer high unemployment (i.e., retirement). The aged lose both income and the work role necessary to high status. In a literate population, knowledge is greater among the young than the aged (who have received less and inferior schooling) and communication of information, skills, and tradition does not depend on the old–timers. Finally, as a result of these changes and a demographic transition large numbers of the elderly become impoverished and dependent.

Criticism of modernization theory grew first out of a general distaste for the abrupt break between traditional and modern societies (Laslett, 1976, 1977). Historians were sensitive to the great differences among traditional societies and some social gerontologists argued that, even in modern nations, culture might be more important than economic conditions (Palmore, 1975). But the most striking criticism sprang from the startling discovery that the nuclear household was the dominant family form in preindustrial Western societies (Laslett, 1976, 1977). Thus the aged could not have exercised power through an extended family. Since social gerontologists had begun to find that the aged in modern societies maintained close contact with their kin, a sharp break between past and present seemed unlikely. Historians also found evidence of strong hostility toward the aged in traditional societies (e.g., Achenbaum, 1978a; Thomas, 1976). American historians threw even more suspicion on structural interpretations by locating a shift from veneration toward vilification of the aged which was independent of industrialization and urbanization (Achenbaum, 1978a; Fischer, 1978).

These criticisms expose the weaknesses in the broad and vague generalizations characteristic of modernization theory, attack the structural dynamic at its heart, and focus our attention on the force of ageism in the history of the elderly. Nonetheless, a review of the new historical literature suggests that its conclusions are also at best incomplete. It provides no sustained analysis of the control exercised by the aged over land, business, skills, and wealth in agricultural societies. Yet the anthropology of old age, and the new history itself, reveal that a diversity of cultures exhibit a universal pattern: where older people control resources necessary to satisfy the needs of younger persons, the elders' status will generally be high (Amoss and Harrell, 1981; see also Gutmann, 1980; Keith, 1979; Maxwell and Silverman, 1982; Sheehan, 1976).

Such control is, however, most likely in societies where property may be privately held. Family tensions and intergenerational conflicts—often cited as proof that the elderly were not well regarded in the past (e.g., Nydegger, 1983; Stearns, 1982)—are actually symptoms of the power of older persons in the economic inheritance system. Historical study of peasant Europe and colonial America provides similar evidence of the authority available to elders in landowning economies (e.g., Berkner, 1972; Demos, 1979). Property-based status relied only indirectly on age, but its significance in age relations is obvious. In these societies, the natural consequence of growing older was to come into possession of the means of production and thereby to exercise some control over one's environment and over younger generations.

One would fully expect that an economic transition of the magnitude of industrialization, which undermined the previous economic system and its age relations, would have a direct effect on the place of the aged in society. But the new histories of aging in America explicity reject this logic: they see the structural change from farm to factory as of little consequence. Rather, the decline in the elderly's status is connected to an independent force, ageism. Cultural attitude is seen as more important than structure.

The New History of the American Elderly

David Hackett Fischer first argued that American history demonstrated the failure of modernization theory because the decline in the status of the aged occurred before "industrialization, urbanization, and the growth of mass education . . . [before] 'modernization' in the ordinary meaning of the term." Fischer proposed that a period of exaltation of the aged (1607-1770) was shattered by a "new set of ideas," resulting in a "revolution in age relations" (1770-1820). American society was from this point set on a "straight and stable" course toward the triumph of gerontophobia (fear of old age) (Fischer, 1978, pp. 76-78, 101-2, 109-13, 231).

After initial enthusiasm, most scholars have come to doubt Fischer's analysis (Dahlin, 1978; Achenbaum, 1978b). Fischer's reliance on urban sources provides little evidence for transformation in the lives of the mass of men and women in America, who, as farmers, were part of a local, familial, and traditional network. This distinction is perfectly expressed in a remark made by Reverend William Bentley of Salem, Massachusetts, when visiting rural Andover, Massachusetts, in 1793. Bentley noted that the country people gathered to dance "in classes due to their ages, not with regard to their condition as in the Seaport Towns" (Henretta, 1978, p. 7).

In fact, Fischer unintentionally supports the theory he criticizes. In a penetrating account of seventeenth and eighteenth–century New England, he finds that this society's literature cautioned the young to venerate their elders as wise and as specially favored by God (1978, pp. 26-76). The aged often served in high office; as owners of property, they exercised great authority over their sons and daughters, such that "land was an instrument of generational politics" and "youth was the hostage of age" (p. 52). Indeed, the high status of the elderly led many people to report themselves older than they were: in two large censuses taken in 1776 and 1787 (Maryland and Connecticut) the observable biases in the reporting of age run in the opposite direction of all known modern censuses, showing a clear preference for greater age (pp. 82-6). Instead of excess number of persons stating that they are 39, or 49, excess numbers report themselves 41 or 51. This is a most exciting finding! The bias toward youth is so pronounced in our time that we must conclude that the view Americans took toward age was utterly different in the late eighteenth century. No more telling evidence exists in the social history of the aged.

When we combine this evidence with other studies of the power and security enjoyed by property-owning elderly in America's agricultural, family-based economy,[2] the picture of a "traditional" world is remarkably like that proposed in modernization theory. A father in colonial Virginia directs in his will: "Sons Michael, Rupert, and Matthew are to obey their mother and follow her orders or they are not to get their land" (Dean, 1972, p. 170). This pattern can be found in other studies of old age which find that respect for the aged in early New England reveals a "gerontocratic society founded . . . by patriarchs, which gave office to its elders, not its youth, and believed in hierarchy" (Smith, 1978a, pp. 290, 296, citing Waters, 1968).

Fischer's very convincing case for the exaltation of the aged in early America is not succeeded by a persuasive one for a sudden social revolution in age relations in the period 1770-1820. Loss of status in the heavily populated northeastern area occurred in the eighteenth century because farm holdings were too small for distribution among children: "During most of the eighteenth century scarcity increased and the older matrix of values sustaining respect for the aged withered" (Smith, 1978a, p. 296). However, this was a long process which began anew in each area of frontier settlement (Henretta, 1978). The census data Fischer reports show strikingly high esteem during the period when degradation is supposed to be occurring, and no general census data are presented for subsequent years, when industrialization takes hold. It remains a more reasonable hypothesis to view decline in the status of the aged as a fairly steady trend across the nineteenth century, a consequence of the relative decline of agriculture in the American economy.

Nonetheless, this is but hypothesis, for we remain quite in the dark for solid evidence about the crucial transition period of the nineteenth century. Fischer relies on an impressionistic reading of literature. His use of Whitman's poetry is selective and inaccurate and his review of a number of literary works proves only that one can find negative references to the elderly in a survey of American literature and popular culture between 1800 and 1970.

Rather more light has been shed on the nineteenth century by W. Andrew Achenbaum, whose major history of old age in America also stressed attitudinal change over structural forces (1978a). Again, industrialization and urbanization are seen as insufficient in explaining declines in status; because, in this case, they occur both before and after the onset of the degradation of old age (pp. 57-86). Achenbaum commands a great range of evidence and he uses his sources with care and sensitivity. In an exhaustive survey of middle-class literature since 1790, he found ambiguity toward the aged at all times, but a relatively favorable climate before the Civil War. In the late nineteenth century, a decisive break occurred—a broad denial of the aged and the emergence of a cult of youth—with hostility to age seen in medical texts and in perceptions of the aged worker (pp. 3, 9-37, 39-54).

Achenbaum was the first to identify this as a critical period (1974) and most scholars now accept his dating. His argument that the attitudinal shift at this time occurred independently of structural change (the aged's occupational and demographic status) depends on an analysis of labor force participation rates, to which we will return.

Carole Haber agrees with Achenbaum that the late nineteenth century brought forth a new order which oppressed the aged, but she emphasizes physicians' equation of old age with sickness (1977, 1978, 1983). In her critical history of geriatrics (the medical treatment of old age), Haber notes its simultaneous reliance on advances in scientific medicine and on cultural prejudices. By the late nineteenth century the result was the segregation of the aged in a medical category which labelled old age as sickness but offered no cure. Haber finds the same emphasis on classification and segregation of the aged as dependents in studies of the labor market, institutionalization, and charity work. She connects new discriminatory practices directly to structural change in economic and familial relations, and her recognition of the reciprocal relationship between structural poverty among older people and the bureaucratic response to it among the "helping professionals" greatly enhances our understanding of the origins of ageism. Haber argues that a new concept of the work cycle, terminated by the novel status of retirement, was a result first of an excessive labor supply and second of the tendency of various elites to emphasize the incapacity of the aged. However, her labor supply argument does not fit well with employers' favorable attitudes toward immigration at the turn of the century, and her treatment of retirement, while sensitive to the negative effects of pensions as a substitute for work, fails to address the most obvious question: what proportion of workers was actually affected by these ideas? Pension plans and mandatory retirement applied to a very few workers as late as 1930. It is debatable whether mandatory retirement has ever affected a large proportion of American workers, yet most of the new historians use any instance of it as proof of the general downgrading of the aged (Cole, 1980; Fischer, 1978; Graebner, 1980). Nonetheless, Haber joins Graebner in rightly emphasizing the issue of retirement. The eventual broad implementation of this idea in the Social Security Act was to rewrite age relations.

Some historians have examined religion as an index to the nineteenth-century history of the aged, arguing that changes in religious expression have important repercussions for the elderly (Cole, 1980; Farrell, 1980). For example, in exhorting self-discipline and self-control, a "rigid form of moral self-government," evangelical ministers connected age with decay and dependency; "old age emerged as the most poignant—and loathsome—symbol of the decline of the bourgeois self-reliance" (Cole, 1980, p.

12). Thomas Cole agrees with Achenbaum that "values, ideas, feelings, perceptions, and attitudes toward aging, old age, and the aged clearly changed prior to changes in longevity, age-composition of the population, employment, and living arrangements (1980, pp. 9-10).

However, little concrete evidence is provided to prove this contention; most of Cole's sources are men from a middle-class stratum most likely to reflect the impact of industrialization. Cole actually relies quite consistently on the links between the religious forces he studies and the capitalistic social order which they supported, and his most stimulating observation is that the Protestant view of aging was linked to an emerging capitalist economy.

Historians of the family have focused on the composition of households and the timing of life events. Tamara Hareven and her colleagues have examined the life course, or stages of the life cycle, for various cohorts, calculating the timing of transitions such as marriage (Chudacoff & Hareven, 1978, 1979; Hareven, 1976, 1977). This research has given us a new understanding of the typical experience of the aged, has stressed the absence of sharp discontinuities from life at younger ages and has shown that such life events as a long "empty nest" period for older couples is a phenomenon which has become prevalent only in our time.

Potentially the most important undertaking in the field of family history is the work of Daniel Scott Smith and his colleagues who have taken national samples of the aged American population from the 1880 and 1900 manuscript censuses (Dahlin, 1980; Smith, 1978b, 1979a,b). The samples record the somewhat limited information provided for individuals, as well as data regarding the family and neighborhood of aged persons. This material will permit much more sensitive analysis of kinship, occupation, and ethnicity. Although the decision to take every aged person found on a systematically chosen page may bias the sample toward aged persons who live in proximity, that is, married couples, the device does allow the investigators to gather interesting data on kinship, occupation, and ethnicity in the neighborhoods of the aged.

Smith's design precludes analysis of change over time, but he argues that "change in the family status of the older population has been *slow* historically, with most of the change occurring only in recent decades" (emphasis mine; 1978b, p. 67). This assumption will come as a surprise to some of his colleagues. Its consequence is that we do not have two points in the period of rapid industrialization and urbanization for measurement. In essence Smith's assumption is a rejection of modernization theory's contention that industrialization and urbanization undermined the status of the aged. Yet Smith oversamples urban places in 1900 in part because, "Most of the social problems of old people . . . were concentrated in the urban-industrial states" (1978b, p. 67).

Although confined on measurement of change, these studies have given us an informative description of old age at the turn of the century: older people were relatively independent, they tended to head or be spouses of head of households, and the men among them had high labor force participation rates. Smith's findings support the continuity of life which Hareven has emphasized. The sampling procedure allowed analysis of the aged's neighborhood and kinship ties: 15 percent of the 1900 elderly sample had same-surname kin within 5 census households (Dahlin, 1980). Preliminary analysis of household composition shows little instability by reason of age; thus marital status is a much better predictor than age of an older man's chances of heading his household (Smith, 1979a). Moreover, the three-generation household was a rare experience for the turn-of-the-century American, because of the aged's household independence and because the three-generation family was relatively uncommon. Nonetheless, in 1880, 35 to 40 percent of those over 65 lived in extended households (Dahlin, 1980; Smith, 1978b). When an older person was not the head or spouse of the head, he, or more often, she, lived with a child. Thus the family was "the welfare institution for old people." Smith does not believe that this was a product of "economic necessity," despite the fact that the co-residents were generally aged women (Smith, 1979a, pp. 296-7).

In his most recent examination of these data (1983), Smith concludes that the era of change in the family history of the elderly is the twentieth century and especially the period since 1940. But he is skeptical of interpretations that view such change as a product of the welfare state or of shifts in the composition of the aged population. Smith's most striking assertion is that rising income cannot explain recent declines in co-residence of children and aged parents, since he found the lowest level of co-residence in poorer families and high levels in the middle classes at the turn of the century. Smith concludes that some change of values must have occurred. While the income effect is not really tested, since even the middle classes in 1900 have low incomes by present standards, correlation between income and co-residence is counter to the expected pattern and should prompt further inquiry.

Other quantitative studies suggest reassessment of contemporary gerontological theory. For example, although some social gerontologists perceive residential segregation of the ages as a rather recent phenomenon (Clark, 1971), Kleinberg found evidence of residential segregation in nineteenth–century Pittsburgh (1971). Investigation of occupational distribution by age in Boston between 1890 and 1950 (Gratton, 1980) indicates that at any cross-sectional point, the aged seem to be excluded from certain jobs. However, these distributions are in large part a product of cohort effects. New occupations will at first be staffed by younger workers, but across time they begin to exhibit a broader distribution of age groups.

Until quite recently, twentieth–century histories of the elderly focussed on, and were influenced by, the early reform movements that addressed the poverty of old people (Holtzman, 1963; Lubove, 1968; Putnam, 1970). In an innovative piece, the social critic and historian Christopher Lasch (1978) recently linked the degradation of the elderly in contemporary America to the rise of a "narcissistic personality" which dreads age; since Lasch believes that the helping professions—from medical experts to social reformers—have encouraged this personality, he has little faith in their capacity to address the needs of older people. Lasch concedes that the objective conditions of the aged have declined in a society that finds the old useless and "forces them to retire," but he claims that it is an "irrational panic" which lies at the heart of negative views of aging (pp. 209-10). As in all Lasch's recent work, the nineteenth-century middle class is the exemplar of a better moral order; yet the work of Cole and Farrell suggests that it was the moral code of this social class which first devalued age.

Industrial Capitalism and the Older Worker

Achenbaum's (1978a) twentieth-century material is especially rewarding in summarizing Social Security policy, but is marred by a failure to address the negative effects of New Deal legislation on the labor force participation of the elderly. His optimistic view of the mid-nineteenth century aged worker leads to the judgement that decline in status came all in a rush in the twentieth century, propelled by "negative attitudes" toward the aged. Since "ideas . . . have a life of their own," the rise of ageism after the Civil War was not directly connected to "*actual* demographic, occupational, and economic" conditions. Instead, like Fischer's "deep change," but a hundred years later, an attitudinal shift sets in motion a general decline in the status of the elderly (Achenbaum, 1978, p. 57, 86).

The Social Security Act is thus interpreted as a legislative solution to the problems of the aged. In *Shades of Gray* (1983), Achenbaum argues that such legislation showed "an unprecedented concern for the elderly by the federal government" (p. 47). Again, he emphasizes the role of ideas and values in the evolution of national policy.

Achenbaum's ideational argument rests on a particular treatment of the aged labor force, one which has prompted agreement among a number of scholars (e.g., Graebner, 1980). Achenbaum maintains, contrary to conventional structural theory, that nineteenth-century industrialization did not undermine the status of the aged (1978a, pp. 66-75, 183-4). Instead, a late nineteenth-century attitudinal shift against the aged set in motion an inevitable decline, subsequently expressed by their declining activity in the labor force (1978a, pp. 95-106).

Testing the proposition is difficult, since reliable labor force participation data are not available for the nineteenth century. But Achenbaum's estimates of steady and high nineteenth-century participation rates are internally inconsistent (Gratton, 1980) and unlikely to be sustained in future research. In addition, the declines in participation in the twentieth century are certainly misread. Although participation rates fall before 1930, they do so at a slow pace. Using Achenbaum's data (1978a, p. 102), it can be seen that there are no relative declines for older agricultural workers and only slight ones for industrial workers. The source of the general fall in participation rates is the relationship between these sectors. As the economy industrializes, the relatively low participation of older men in industrial work begins to dominate general participation rates. This is exactly as structural theory would have it. But still more intriguing is the replacement of this continued but slow decline in participation with a precipitous drop after 1930. Whereas the general labor force participation rate declines 15 percentage points between 1890 and 1930, it drops 34 percentage points between 1930 and 1970. Given the establishment and expansion of Social Security during this period, it seems likely, as many economists presently maintain, that social security benefits acted as a magnet, drawing older workers out of the labor force. Thus, rather than seeing government legislation as a benevolent response to the inutility of the older worker, it appears to be creating useless workers.

It is likely that nineteenth-century labor force participation rates exhibited the same slowly declining pattern found in the early twentieth century, as the shift from an agricultural to a nonagricultural economy proceeded. Farms and the small-scale enterprises which evolved from skilled trades favored the aged, who often controlled access to skill and capital (Dawley, 1976; Soltow, 1975). But the development of large-scale industry undermined their status, diminishing older people's capacity to control their own employment as well as that of the sons and daughters on whom they then depended in old age. Industrialization reduced, although it did not eliminate, the value of their bequests (Thernstrom, 1964). Even for those elderly who farmed, industrial cities drew away the children whom they hoped would honor and work for them in the traditional way. The end of the nineteenth century witnessed a great transition in the industrial work force, the destruction of the capacity of senior workers to control production, and the spread of scientific management through which employers stripped away the advantages of older workers (Stone, 1974; Braverman, 1975).

Even so there is little proof that the aged's position within the industrial sector declined more dramatically during the early twentieth century than in the nineteenth. Scattered findings indicate a fairly consistent and stable pattern of high participation rates and some accumulation of wealth for the majority, and downward mobility, poverty, and dependency on children for a minority (Chudacoff & Hareven, 1978; Dahlin, 1980; Gratton, 1980; Katz, 1976; Smith, 1979a; Soltow, 1975). Since the debate among economists is not whether, but how much, social security reduces participation of older workers, historians would be well advised to consider carefully what kind of labor force was emerging before such welfare measures. Before 1935, most older men remained in the labor force and the proportion of aged men among workers steadily increased. Yet less than two decades after the Social Security Act, most older men were retired.

The origins and consequences of this momentous Act have been insightfully examined by William Graebner in *A History of Retirement* (1980). Graebner's revisionist view of the New Deal leads to a powerful critique of conventional interpretations of government legislation and of the periodization of the history of old age. Graebner's argument is in one sense attitudinal: like Haber and Achenbaum, he locates the rise of a retirement concept harmful to the aged in the late nineteenth century. But Graebner's original contribution lies in his analysis of a series of experiments in retirement which, stimulated first by concern for efficiency and subsequently by fear of unemployment, led directly to the Social Security Act. Exploring the history of railroad retirement in the early thirties and the inner workings on the Committee on Economic Security which drafted social security legislation, Graebner concludes that the 1935 Act was a "piece of unemployment legislation" (1978), "designed within a labor market context" to make room for young workers (1980, p. 189). This has been said before, but never with such penetrating effect.

Some reservations about this account are necessary. Social security and the state pensions which preceeded it were popular measures, opposed by powerful elites who receive little attention in this book. These pensions were not the product of efficiency experts or retirement experimenters, but of the working class, which underwrote the long and expensive campaigns (Anglim and Gratton, 1984). Yet it is clear that the architects of policy in Roosevelt's Committee on Economic Security were moved by the idea of using retirement as a way of making room for younger workers. In this strategy they were joined by powerful political allies, the Townsendites, a movement of older people and their allies who demanded government pensions for old people, asserted the positive consequences on unemployment rates, and threatened to remove opponents from office (Gratton, 1982). In his historical work, Graebner has provided historians and social gerontologists with a critical insight: the Social Security Act created dependency as much as it reduced it.

Such revision of conventional interpretations of the Social Security Act should lead us to reconsider the meaning of retirement in contemporary America. The welfare state has completely rewritten the experience of being old. However well structural forces explain the history of old age before 1935—and to that date they constitute the best model—they do little to illuminate the post New Deal world. The roots of the welfare state are the subject of lively debate among social scientists. James O'Connor (1973), Larry Griffin (1981), Theda Skocpol (1983), and John Myles (1983) have provided both theoretical and empirical studies of the origins, growth, and current crisis of the Western welfare state. Their insight that the capitalist state uses welfare systems to balance the demands of the monopoly business sector against the demands of political constituencies runs directly counter to modernization theory, in which welfare legislation is a simple, depoliticized response to need. Myles's stimulating discussion of the retirement wage is crucial to the history of old age, since his interpretation reveals the connections among the structural effects of industrialization, the deliberate building of the welfare state, and the satisfaction of working class demands for a wage not determined by market criteria.

Conclusion

Having exposed the weaknesses of modernization theory, most new historians have rejected structural factors in favor of culture: change in values, the rise of ageism. But their premise that industrialization did not undermine the advantages of the aged in an agricultural economy remains unproven and the first task facing future researchers is to assess the consequences for older men and women of the loss of control of the means of the production with the rise of a wage labor system.

The next task, a critical history of the origins of the welfare state, goes beyond the structural effects of industrialization. We need to consider the Social Security Act as both a democratic measure and one which served specific economic purposes, and we should hesitate to assign this Act any final meaning without considering the history and function of social security in other nations. That these questions are difficult goes without saying. They are the legacy of a decade of energetic and productive scholarship.

Notes

1. A critical scholar can find every conceivable excess in modernization literature; another scholar could reproduce a theory with no flaws. My purpose is to recapitulate its consistent theses about aging in history. The sources from which my summary is drawn are: Burgess, 1960a, 1960b, 1960c; Clark, 1967, 1972; Clark and Anderson, 1967; Holmes, 1976; Kalish, 1967; Maxwell and Silverman, 1970, 1982; Mead, 1968; Palmore, 1969; Palmore and Manton, 1974; Parsons, 1942, 1943; Parsons and Bales, 1956; Parsons and Platt, 1972; Philbert, 1965; Rosow, 1974; Simmons, 1960, 1970; Thomas, 1976; Tibbitts, 1960.
2. The power of property-owning elders in colonial America, a power which extended to the control of sexuality, can be reviewed in a rapidly growing literature: Dean, 1972; Greven, 1966, 1970; Gross, 1976; Keyssar, 1974; Levy, 1978; Smith, D.B., 1978; Smith, D.S., 1973, 1978a; Smith and Hindus, 1975; Souden, 1976.

References

Achenbaum, W. A. "The Obsolescence of Old Age in America, 1865-1914." *Journal of Social History* 8, 1974. pp. 48-62.

_____. *Old Age in the New Land: The American Experience Since 1790.* Baltimore: Johns Hopkins University Press, 1978a.

_____. "From Womb through Bloom to Tomb: The Birth of a New Area of Historical Research." (Review of *Growing Old in America,* by D. H. Fischer, and *The Damned and the Beautiful: American Youth in the 1920s,* by P. S. Fass). *Reviews in American History* 6, 1978b, 178-83.

_____. *Shades of Gray: Old Age, American Values, and Federal Policies since 1920.* Little, Brown, Boston, Mass. 1983.

Amoss, P. T., and Harrell, S. Introduction: "An Anthropological Perspective on Aging." In P. T. Amoss and S. Harrell, eds., *Other Ways of Growing Old.* Stanford University Press, Stanford, Calif.: 1981.

Anglim, C., and Gratton, B. "Old Age Pensions and State Federations of Labor: The Working Class and the Welfare State." Unpublished manuscript, 1984.

Berkner, L.K. "The Stem Family and the Developmental Cycle of the Peasant Household: An Eighteenth-Century Austrian Example." *American Historical Review* 77, 1972. pp. 398-418.

Braverman, H. *Labor and Monopoly Capital: The Degradation of Work in the Twentieth Century.* Monthly Review Press, New York, 1975.

Burgess, E. W. "Aging in Western Culture." In E. W. Burgess, ed., *Aging in Western Societies.* University of Chicago Press, Chicago, Ill. 1960a.

_____. "Family Structure and Relationships." In E. W. Burgess ed., *Aging in Western Societies.* University of Chicago Press, Chicago, Ill. 1960b.

_____. "Résumé and Implications." In E. W. Burgess, ed., *Aging in Western Societies.* University of Chicago Press, Chicago, Ill. 1960c.

Chudacoff, H., and Hareven, T.K. "Family Transitions into Old Age." In T.K. Hareven, ed., *Transitions: The Family and the Life Course in Historical Perspective.* Academic Press, New York, 1978.

_____. "From the Empty Nest to Family Dissolution: Life Course Transitions into Old Age." *Journal of Family History* 4, 1979. pp. 69-83.

Clark, M. "The Anthropology of Aging: A New Area for Studies of Culture and Personality." *Gerontologist* 7, 1967. pp. 55-64.

———. "Patterns of Aging Among the Elderly Poor of the Inner City." *Gerontologist* 11, 1971. pp. 58-66.

———. "Cultural Values and Dependency in Later Life." In D. Cowgill and L. D. Holmes, eds., *Aging and Modernization*. Appleton-Century-Crofts, New York, 1972.

Clark, M., and Anderson, B. G. *Culture and Aging: An Anthropological Study of Older Americans*. C. C. Thomas, Springfield, Ill., 1967.

Cole, T. *Past Meridian: Aging and the Northern Middle Class*. Ph.D. diss., University of Rochester, 1980.

Cottrell, F. "The Technological and Societal Basis of Aging." In C. Tibbitts, ed., *Handbook of Social Gerontology*. University of Chicago Press, Chicago, Ill. 1960.

Cowgill, D. "A Theory of Aging in Cross-Cultural Perspective." In D. Cowgill and L. D. Holmes, eds., *Aging and Modernization*. Appleton-Century-Crofts, New York, 1972.

———. "The Aging of Populations and Societies." In F.R. Eisele, ed., *Political Consequences of Aging: Annals of the American Academy of Political and Social Science* 415. 1974.

Cowgill, D., and Holmes, L.D., eds. *Aging and Modernization*. Appleton-Century-Crofts, New York, 1972.

Dahlin, M. "Review of *Growing Old in America*, by D.H. Fischer." *Journal of Social History* 11, 1978, pp. 449-52.

———. "Perspectives on the Family Life of the Elderly in 1900." *Gerontologist* 20, 1980, pp. 99-107.

Dawley, A. *Class and Community: The Industrial Revolution in Lynn*. Harvard University Press, Cambridge, Mass., 1976.

Dean J.W., Jr. "Patterns of Testation: Four Tidewater Counties in Colonial Virginia." *American Journal of Legal History* 16, 1972. pp. 154-76.

Demos, J. "Old Age in Early New England." In D.D. Van Tassel, ed. *Aging, Death and the Completion of Being*. University of Pennsylvania Press, Philadelphia, Penna. 1979.

Epstein, A. *The Challenge of the Aged*. Macy-Masius, Vanguard, New York, 1928.

Farrell, J.J. *Inventing the American Way of Death, 1830-1920*. Temple University Press, Philadelphia, Penna. 1980.

Fischer, D.H. *Growing Old in America,* exp. ed. Oxford University Press, New York, 1978.

Goody, J. "Aging in Nonindustrial Societies." In R.H. Binstock and E. Shanas, eds., *Handbook of Aging and the Social Sciences*. Van Nostrand Reinhold, New York, 1976.

Graebner, W. "Retirement and the Corporate State, 1885-1935: A New Context for Social Security." Paper presented at the annual meeting of the Organization of American Historians, New York, April 1978.

———. *A History of Retirement: The Meaning and Function of an American Institution, 1885-1978*. Yale University Press, New Haven, Conn., 1980.

Gratton, B. *Boston's Elderly, 1890-1950: Work, Family, and Dependency*. Ph.D. diss., Boston University, 1980.

———. "The Virtues of Insecurity." *Reviews in American History* 10, 1982, pp. 17-23.

Greven, P.J., Jr. "Family Structure in Seventeenth-Century Andover, Massachusetts." *William and Mary Quarterly* 23, 1966. pp. 234-56.

_____. *Four Generations: Population, Land and Family in Colonial Andover, Massachusetts.* Cornell University Press, Ithaca, N.Y., 1970.

Grew, R. "Modernization and its Discontents." *American Behavioral Scientist* 21, 1977, pp. 298-312.

Griffin, L.J., Devine, J.A., and Wallace, M. "Accumulation, Legitimation, and Politics: The Growth of Welfare Expenditures in the United States Since the Second World War." Paper presented at the annual meeting of the American Sociological Association, Toronto, August 1981.

Gross, R.A. *The Minutemen and Their World.* Hill & Wang, New York, 1976.

Gutmann, D. "Observations on Culture and Mental Health in Later Life." In J.E. Birren and R.B. Sloane, eds., *Handbook of Mental Health and Aging.* Prentice-Hall, Englewood Cliffs, N.J., 1980.

Haber, C. "The Old Folks at Home: The Development of Institutionalized Care for the Aged in Nineteenth-Century Philadelphia." *Pennsylvania Magazine of History and Biography* 51, 1977. pp. 240-57.

_____. "Mandatory Retirement in Nineteenth-Century America: The Conceptual Basis for a New Work Cycle." *Journal of Social History* 12, 1978, pp. 77-96.

_____. *Beyond Sixty-Five: The Dilemma of Old Age in America's Past.* Cambridge University Press, Cambridge: 1983.

Hareven, T. "The Last Stage: Historical Adulthood and Old Age." *Daedalus* 105, 1976. pp. 13-27.

_____. "Family Time and Historical Time." *Daedalus* 106, 1977. pp. 57-70.

Henretta, J.A. "Families and Farms: *Mentalite* in Pre-Industrial America." *William and Mary Quarterly* 35, 1978. pp. 3-32.

Holmes, L.D. "Trends in Anthropological Gerontology: From Simmons to the Seventies." *International Journal of Aging and Human Development* 7, 1976. pp. 211-20.

Holtzman, A. *The Townsend Movement: A Political Study.* Bookman Associates, N.Y., 1963.

Kalish, R.A. "Of Children and Grandfathers: A Speculative Essay on Dependency." *Gerontologist* 7, 1967, pp. 65-9.

Katz, M.B. *The People of Hamilton, Canada West.* Harvard University Press, Cambridge, Mass. 1976.

Keith, J. "The Ethnography of Old Age: Introduction." *Anthropological Quarterly* 52, 1979, pp. 1-6.

Keyssar, A. "Widowhood in Eighteenth-Century Massachussetts: A Problem in the History of Family." *Perspectives in American History* 8, 1974. pp. 83-122.

Kleinberg, S. "Aging and the Aged in Nineteenth-Century Pittsburgh." Unpublished manuscript, Western College, Miami University, Miami, Ohio 1977.

Lasch, C. *The Culture of Narcissism: American Life in an Age of Diminishing Expectations.* W.W. Norton, New York, 1978.

Laslett, P. "Societal Development and Aging." In R.H. Binstock and E. Shanas, eds., *Handbook of Aging and the Social Sciences.* Van Nostrand Reinhold, New York, 1976.

_____. "The History of Aging and the Aged." In *Family Life and Illicit Love in Earlier Generations: Essays in Historical Sociology.* Cambridge University Press, Cambridge, 1977.

Lerner, D. *The Passing of Traditional Society: Modernizing the Middle East.* Free Press, Glencoe, Ill., 1958.

Levy, B. "'Tender Plants': Quaker Farmers and Children in the Delaware Valley, 1681-1735." *Journal of Family History* 3, 1978, pp. 136-49.

Lubove, R. *The Struggle for Social Security, 1900-1935.* Harvard University Press, Cambridge, Mass. 1968.

Maxwell, R.J., and Silverman, P. "Information and Esteem: Cultural Considerations in the Treatment of the Aged." *Aging and Human Development* 1, 1970. pp. 361-92.

_____. "Cross-Cultural Variation in the Status of Old People." In P.N. Stearns, ed., *Old Age in Preindustrial Society,* Holmes & Meier, New York, 1982.

Mead, M. Review of *Culture of Aging* by M. Clark and B.G. Anderson. *Journal of Gerontology* 23, 1968, pp. 232-33.

Myles, J.F. *Old Age in the Welfare State: The Political Economy of Public Pensions.* Little, Brown, Boston, Mass. 1983.

Nydegger, C.N. "Family Ties of the Aged in Cross-Cultural Perspective." *Gerontologist,* 23, 1983, pp. 26-31.

O'Connor, J. *The Fiscal Crisis of the State.* St. Martin's Press, New York, 1973.

Palmore, E.B. "Sociological Aspects of Aging." In E.W. Busse and E. Pfeiffer, eds. *Behavior and Modification in Late Life.* Little Brown, Boston, Mass., 1969.

_____. *The Honorable Elders: A Cross-Cultural Analysis of Aging in Japan.* Duke University Press, Durham, No. Car., 1975.

Palmore, E., and Manton, K. "Modernization and the Status of the Aged: International Correlations." *Journal of Gerontology,* 29, 1974, pp. 205-10.

Parsons, T. "Age and Sex in the Social Structure of the United States." *American Sociological Review* 7, 1942. pp. 604-16.

_____. "The Kinship System of the Contemporary United States." *American Anthropologist* 45, 1943, pp. 22-38.

Parsons, T., and Bales, R.F. *Family, Socialization and Interaction Process.* Routledge and Kegan Paul, London, 1956.

Parsons, T., and Platt, G.M. "Higher Education and Changing Socialization." In M.W. Riley and A. Foner, eds., *Aging and Society* 3. *A Sociology of Age Stratification.* Russell Sage Foundation, New York, 1972.

Philibert, M.A. "The Emergence of Social Gerontology." *Journal of Social Issues* 21, 1965, pp. 4-12.

Putnam, J.K. *Old-Age Politics in California.* Stanford University Press, Stanford, Calif., 1970.

Rosow, I. *Socialization to Old Age.* University of California Press, Berkeley, Calif., 1974.

Sheehan, T. "Senior Esteem as a Factor of Socioeconomic Complexity." *Gerontologist* 16, 1976, pp. 33-40.

Simmons, L. "Aging in Preindustrial Societies." In C. Tibbitts, ed., *Handbook of Social Gerontology: Societal Aspects of Aging.* University of Chicago Press, Chicago, Ill., 1960.

_____. *The Role of the Aged in Primitive Society.* Archon, Hamden, Conn., 1970, (c. 1945).

Skocpol, T. "Explaining the Belated Origins of the U.S. Welfare State." Paper presented at the conference Researching the Welfare State, Indiana University, Bloomington, Ind., March 1983.

Smith, D.S. "Parental Power and Marriage Patterns: An Analysis of Historical Trends in Hingham, Massachusetts." *Journal of Marriage and the Family* 35, 1973, pp. 419-28.

———. "Old Age and the 'Great Transformation': A New England Case Study." In S.F. Spicker, K.M. Woodward, and D.D. Van Tassel, eds., *Aging and the Elderly: Humanistic Perspectives in Gerontology.* Humanities Press, Atlantic Highlands, N.J., 1978a.

———. "A Community-Based Sample of the Older Population from the 1880 and 1900 United States Manuscript Censuses." *Historical Methods* 11, 1978b. pp. 67-74.

———. "Life Course, Norms, and the Family System of Older Americans in 1900." *Journal of Family History* 4, 1979a. pp. 285-98.

———. "Historical Change in the Household Structure of the Elderly." Paper presented at Workshop on the Elderly of the Future, Committee on Aging, National Research Council, Annapolis, Md., May 1979b.

———. "Accounting for Change in the Families of the Elderly in the United States, 1900 to the Present." Paper presented at the conference The Elderly in a Bureaucratic World, Case Western Reserve University, Cleveland, Ohio, April 1983.

Smith, D.S., and Hindus, M.S. "Premarital Pregnancy in America, 1640-1971: An Overview and Interpretation." *Journal of Interdisciplinary History* 5, 1975. pp. 537-70.

Soltow, L. *Men and Wealth in the United States, 1850-1870.* Yale University Press, New Haven, Conn., 1975.

Souden, D.O. "The Elderly in Seventeenth-Century New England: Personal and Institutional Care in Old Age." Paper presented at the annual meeting of the Society for the Study of Social Problems, N.Y. August 1976.

Stearns, P.N., ed. *Old Age in Preindustrial Society.* Holmes & Meier, New York, 1982.

Stone, K. "The Origins of Job Structures in the Steel Industry." *The Review of Radical Political Economics* 6, 1974. pp. 61-97.

Thernstrom, S. *Poverty and Progress: Social Mobility in a Nineteenth-Century City.* Harvard University Press, Cambridge, Mass., 1964.

Thomas, K. "Age and Authority in Early Modern England." *Proceedings of the British Academy* 62, 1976. pp. 205-48.

Tibbitts, C. "Origin, Scope, and Fields of Social Gerontology." In C. Tibbitts, ed., *Handbook of Social Gerontology.* University of Chicago Press, Chicago, Ill., 1960.

Waters, J.J. "Hingham, Massachusetts, 1631-1661: An East Anglian Oligarchy in the New World." *Journal of Social History* 1, 1968. pp. 351-70.

3

Old Age in
Industrializing England

Jill Quadagno

Although the broad issue of status has been intriguing to many historians and sociologists, other researchers have turned to more specific issues and questions about work, retirement, family life, and old age dependency. Precise studies using historical data allow us to discard some myths about the past.

The Family and Old Age Dependency

According to modernization theory, industrialization destroyed the economic basis of the extended family by removing production from the home. Family members no longer worked together farming or in some household endeavor, and the nuclear family unit composed solely of parents and children replaced the extended family. Factory production accelerated the process of urbanization, and younger family members moved to cities, diminishing the likelihood that an aged parent would be taken into a child's home. The high proportion of older people living alone or solely with a spouse in modern society is often cited as evidence of the breakdown of extended family ties. The loss of support for the family forced the aged to rely increasingly upon the state.

This argument contains many misconceptions about family life in the past, for there is no single household type that characterizes traditional society (Shorter, 1975:29). Rather, research indicates tremendous diversity in typical patterns of household composition, ranging from simple, nuclear family types in England, the Low Countries, and northern France to complex stem households in Austria, Germany, and Japan (Wrigley, 1969:78).

The explanation for this diversity rests partly on different demographic conditions and partly on different cultural traditions. For example, Laslett

(1976:110) has shown that older people in preindustrial England were not much more likely than they are today to be living in the homes of married children. Under the demographic conditions that existed in preindustrial England, typical family size was larger, and offspring continued to be born late in the life span of their mothers. Child rearing was extended over a longer portion of the life cycle. This factor combined with lower life expectancy meant that the aged in the past were living in a family situation in greater proportions than they are today simply because they were still living with their own unmarried children.

This does not mean, however, that the ideal-typical extended family household, consisting of two married couples, is a myth. Rather, coresidence between parents and married children was likely to occur only during a limited phase of the family life cycle when the parents wished to retire or when one became widowed. From the Middle Ages to the nineteenth century, wills and retirement contracts between peasant farmers and their children indicate that property rights and ownership were exchanged for care and provisions in old age (Homans, 1940; Braun, 1966; Drake, 1969; Demos, 1970; Greven, 1970; Berkner, 1972; Howell, 1976; Sabean, 1976; Thomas, 1976; Stearns, 1977). Often these contracts were highly detailed, specifying the amount of food and other goods to be provided to the parents as well as what portion of the house they would occupy. For example, in one contract from Denmark in 1785 the retiring parents suggested that:

> Our son-in-law Peder will pay to us for the farm Gentofte once and for all 100 rigsdaler. We reserve the use of the old large house and Peder will build a new one for himself.
>
> In addition he will yearly pay us a pension of 20 rigsdaler, 3 barrels of good rye flour, 3 barrels of malt brewed into good quality beer, 1 barrel of unmilled rye, 1 barrel of barley, 1 barrel of oats. 4 geese with their goslings well fatted, 4 sheep with their lambs fed winter and summer, 2 fresh swine yearly and 1 barrel of good butter. 2 pots of milk daily when the cows are milking and 8 loads of peat-turf. Care and maintenance with woollens, linens and cleanliness [quoted in Gaunt, 1979].

Control of property gave the aged a good deal of power over their children. For example, among Austrian peasants a son could not marry until his father died or retired and gave him control of the farm. Then the son and his bride would live with his retired parents until their death. Although this custom provided security for the aged, the disadvantage was that is created tensions between generations. There are many folktales describing fighting and even murder between parents and children. An anonymous writer in the Westfalisches Anzieger in 1798 proposed the establishment of a Court for Morality to decide in conflicts between peasant parents and children (Gaunt, 1979:13). In Sweden and Germany and elsewhere in the Low Countries, there were recorded many cases of abuse of older people by their children after they retired and turned over their property. This conflict is expressed in an Austrian folk song from the early twentieth century.

> *Father, when ya gonna gimme the farm,*
> *Father, when ya gonna sign it away?*
> *My girl's been growin' every day,*
> *And Single no longer wants to stay.*
>
> *Father, when ya gonna gimme the farm,*
> *Father, when ya gonna gimme the house?*
> *When ya gonna retire to your room out of the way,*
> *And dig up your potatoes all day?*
> [quoted in Berkner, 1972:403]

The increase in wage labor has been associated with both the disappearance of retirement contracts and the rise of the nuclear family household. As children gained the freedom to take industrial employment, they were no longer dependent on their inheritance for the right to marry. Braun (1966:61) found that in late eighteenth-century Switzerland, landless cottage laborers no longer received allowances from children, whereas those with property still practiced *Rastgaben*. Similarly, in Austria the nuclear family predominated among the poor and landless (Berkner, 1972:408). Thus, extended family households were maintained in preindustrial Western societies not because parents and married children worked together as an economic unit, but rather because children had to care for retired parents in order to gain the right to marry and take over the farm. When other work opportunities became available, children chose other options.

In seventeenth-century New England, where land was abundant, sons also waited to marry until their fathers made them economically independent. Sometimes sons were deeded land outright; in other instances they were forced to wait for full ownership until the father died (Greven, 1970). Deeds of gift were often used like retirement contracts, specifying obligations owed to parents. Sometimes these obligations included money payments, and both deeds and wills carefully provided for widows, obligating children to give their mother lodging, as well as food and income.

In colonial New England, older couples enjoyed proximity to children but preferred to look after themselves (Demos, 1978:268). Under some circumstances they did require assistance, in widowhood or when in failing health, and then children were often a resource. However, older people were cautious about placing too much trust in the goodwill or natural affections of children. In many instances, a husband would spell out in his will with extraordinary precision arrangements for his widow. Often the widow herself was empowered to see that these duties were fulfilled, with a penalty to be extracted from the child if they were not. Widowed men, too, sometimes made formal arrangements for their own care following the death of their wives, promising bequests on their deaths in exchange for care and maintenance in old age. Although pure familial affection was also the basis of care for the old and infirm, sometimes children challenged probate proceedings, arguing for charges for food and care rendered parents earlier. Nonfamilial support was a last resort, and those with no kin to rely upon had to appeal to the public authorities for charity. Thus, in preindustrial times coresidence of married parents and children in much of Europe and the United States was predicated on retirement and widowhood.

How, then, did industrialization affect family life? Some of the misconceptions about old age and family life arising from a broad modernization schema have been corrected by more precise studies investigating how industrialization affected household composition. Anderson (1972:225) compared rural and urban regions of Lancashire, England, in 1851. Contrary to expectations, he found that few old people lived apart from a relative in either region but that more older people were living with married children in urban Preston than in the rural portions of the county.

Anderson's findings contradict the hypothesis that industrialization destroyed the economic basis of the extended family household—an hypothesis that would predict low rates of coresidence in urban areas. Several factors explain the lower rates of coresidence between older parents and married children in rural areas. First, in rural farm families the family plot of land was often small, incapable of supporting several generations. Thus, even though children might not go far from home, the household generally separated both residentially and economically as children became independent (Anderson, 1971:82). Second, in urban, industrial areas wives of factory workers often worked outside the home, and older parents were a helpful resource in caring for young children (Litchfield, 1978:192). Third, housing shortages in urban areas may have contributed to increased rates of coresidence.

Chudacoff and Hareven (1978:217) also studied the impact of urbanization and economic change on the household and family structure of the aged. They used data from four communities in Essex County, Massachusetts, in 1860 and 1880 to examine the functions of old people in the family. Confirming Anderson's research, they also found that aged men and women in urban areas were more likely to be living with children, in this instance as a result of housing shortages and economic strains caused by a recession. Chudacoff and Hareven (1978) concluded that "conditions of late nineteenth century urbanization moved aging parents closer to their progeny rather than isolating them. Further, the aged were not burdens on their children. Rather they entered into interdependent relationships with them, sharing housing in exchange for other resources [p.239]." Thus, it appears that urban, industrial life temporarily increased the likelihood of an aged parent being taken into the household. However, it should be emphasized that this was apparently a transitional phase, since rates of coresidence did decline in the twentieth century.

Demographic change has also affected household structure and partially explains why rates of coresidence declined in the twentieth century. Uhlenberg (1978:65) analyzed the life course patterns of successive birth cohorts in the nineteenth and twentieth centuries to explicate how societal trends in demographic behavior produce specific types of change in family structure. He found that declining mortality between 1830 and 1920 increased the proportion of women surviving to age 60, so that the likelihood of a female reaching the empty-nest phase of the life cycle increased over time. Mortality declines also increased the duration of the empty nest, as did decreases in the age at birth of the last child (Uhlenberg, 1978:90). In addition, expectancy of life for women at age 60 increased more than the expectation of the duration of marriage. The higher proportion of older people, and particularly older women, living alone in modern society is at least partially attributable to significant demographic changes.

Reliance on kin continued to be the primary source of assistance for the aged in the United States until at least 1914 (Achenbaum, 1978:75). In Massachusetts as late as 1895, for example, few older people lived alone or with strangers. As in earlier times, the local community assumed responsibility for relieving the needy only if family members did not live in the area or had defaulted on their obligations. In many places, this aid took the form of care in an almshouse, where unfortunate and feeble old people could go to die. Throughout the nineteenth century, the proportion of almshouse residents who were old increased sharply, and after 1860 the number and variety of private institutions for the aged increased rapidly as well.

As part of the golden age mythos, it has been argued that state support of the aged became necessary because of a decline in familial support. The increase in institutions and the increase in the proportion of older people living alone have been cited as evidence. For example, Paillat (1977) views the demographic increase in the proportion of the aged as problematic, in that "the family network, which offered help and assistance during many centuries, does not—or cannot—play its role as completely and efficiently as before [p. 64]." This he attributes to the fact that the solidarity between generations has passed from the family network to society, with traditional family support replaced by bureaucratic structures (Paillat, 1977:66,69). Halper (1978) ties this loss specifically to the pension system:

> The adoption of Social Security, for instance, was greeted as a great boon to the elderly, and yet it is obvious by now that its blessings have been very mixed. For the assertion of a governmental responsibility to provide for the aged would seem to have permitted the loosening of the bonds of family responsibility thereby making it easier for persons to neglect their debts to their elderly relatives. It is not quite so hard to shunt them aside, after all, when one believes that the government will take care of them [p. 324].

Finally, Stannard (1978) sees families as unable to absorb without trauma "the tedium of demographically unprecedented decades of isolated companionship with one or two others," which makes us "more and more dependent on large, impersonal, bureaucratic institutions for even minimal amounts of that needed support [p.12]." In all of these arguments, a common theme is that large-scale, bureaucratically organized support of the aged is the enemy, either necessarily taking over familial tasks due to the breakdown of the family or actually causing this breakdown to occur.

Anderson (1977) examined changes in governmental policies in income maintenance in Great Britain in the nineteenth century to determine their effect on family relationships. In the prepension period in Britain before 1908, the main source of financial aid for the destitute aged was the poor law. Poor law policy toward the aged was comparatively lenient until 1871, when new policies were implemented that reduced payments to the aged and forced children to maintain their aged parents. The threat of the workhouse loomed for those older people whose children refused to help maintain them. Anderson found that reductions in support to the aged coupled with the threat of the workhouse increased the number of institutionalized aged and that forcing kin to contribute to the support of an aged parent increased family tensions. When the Old Age Pensions Act was passed, it reduced interfamilial tension by allowing the generations to function on the basis of mutual interdependency rather than one-sided dependency. Anderson (1977:57) concluded that the view that state-provided income maintenance undermines family relationships is false and that defining strong family relationships in terms of financial assistance demonstrates a lack of understanding of the basis of harmonious interaction.

The belief that the aged are neglected or repudiated by their children in modern industrial society is no longer an issue. Study after study has shown that this view of modern society is inaccurate, that children perform a variety of personal and protective services for their aged parents and that these relationships tend to be reciprocal.

There is no doubt that there has been an increased reliance on governments for support in old age in many Western and non-Western nations. However, this does not mean that increased bureaucratization of support for the aged has intruded into family relationships in a negative way. Rather, it may be, as Kreps (1977:24) has suggested, that there is now a new role for children in modern-industrial society, as they provide a means of entry into the social order and act as a buffer against the pressures of bureaucracy.

Work in Old Age

The question of how industrialization affected work for the aged is perhaps the most complex. Modernization theory suggests that a variety of factors reduced work for the aged, leading to increased rates of retirement. One factor was the decline in domestic production that did away with the jobs that older workers typically performed. The shift from the home to the factory also eliminated autonomy in the workplace, so that older workers could no longer decide for themselves how long to continue working. Further, increases in life expectancy accompanying modernization led to increased intergenerational competition for jobs, with technological changes making the skills of the aged less valuable. Modernization theory also predicts that a decline in agriculture, which represents a predominant form of domestic production, should be accompanied by higher rates of retirement.

One of the difficulties in responding to these issues is that there is a paucity of information about the organization, nature, and quantity of work for the aged under preindustrial modes of production. One comparative study of 31 countries found a clear relationship between the percentage employed in agriculture and rate of retirement, "the less in agriculture, the more retirement and unemployment among the aged [Palmore and Manton, 1974:208]." Yet the evidence of the retirement contracts cited earlier certainly indicates that retirement is not a modern phenomenon and that peasants did retire in the past.

There is a sparse but intriguing literature describing patterns of work among older people who had no property to use in retirement. In England the gangs of migrant-type labor, the least desirable employment, that were commonly found in agricultural districts often included old men and women (Kitteringham, 1975:91). Old women also sometimes took care of young children and infants whose mothers had gone to work in the fields, reportedly caring for as many as 35 suckling infants in some districts

(Heath, 1893:119). Generally, the work of the aged was marginal and sporadic, as in the following account:

> An old lady still living in the village used to scare crows for the whole of the harvest holidays: she was paid six shillings. She was given a wooden clapper and had to keep making noise with it: if she once stopped and the clapper was silent, the man who hired her would look out of his house to see what she was doing [Evans, 1957:175].

Demos (1978:271) has described a pattern of partial or gradual retirement that appeared to predominate in preindustrial New England, as old people worked at a variety of jobs, mowing grass, hauling grist to the local mill, acting as midwives, and performing other assorted occupations. Demos (1978:273, 275) also notes that withdrawal from office because of age was not uncommon and that some people were dismissed from positions for the same reason. Data from late nineteenth-century Massachusetts indicates high levels of employment, over 90 percent, for males over 55.[1] Their patterns of work differed from younger men in that they were less likely to be employed in manufacturing and more likely to be involved in building, retailing, service, and general labor (Chudacoff and Hareven, 1978:228). It may be that they drifted into menial service and labor jobs as they grew older, or they may have had fewer opportunities to acquire industrial employment as young men because they entered the labor force before factory employment was widely available.

Women in the nineteenth century tended to work when their children were young, leaving the labor force when children were old enough to contribute to the support of the family. They would sometimes return to work in old age when they became widowed or when their husbands were ailing or unemployed, although their "low levels of skill and sporadic employment experience restricted them to unskilled, irregular, and low-paying jobs [Tilly and Scott, 1978:128]." In general, rates of employment for aged women were low, and when older women did work, they held jobs as domestics and washerwomen (Chudacoff and Hareven, 1978:230).

In summary, it appears that people in the past retired when they had the resources, either land or wealth, to do so. Those who continued to work did so out of financial necessity rather than out of desire. This does not mean that industrialization had no impact on retirement, for the modern form of retirement involving a formal system of income transfer administered through a large-scale bureaucracy appears to be historically unique.

In my research on old age in nineteenth-century England (Quadagno, 1982), I reached the following conclusions about family life and work for older people. Perhaps the most significant finding was that in neither preindustrial nor industrial settings were older people neglected by their kin. In the absence of formal government systems of income maintenance, most of the aged lived with a spouse, an adult child, or some other relative.

Under a preindustrial mode of production, when the economic environment was uncertain, family members pooled their resources in order to survive. In three-generation households, it was not just the old who were taken in by younger family members. Rather, many reciprocal arrangements existed. In some cases, older people gave a home to grandchildren, or, more frequently, allowed a daughter with an illegitimate child to return home, or took in a widowed son or daughter with offspring. Thus, the financial and familial management of the household was shared among several generations.

After industrialization changed the nature of the economic system from one based on producing crafts in the home to one based on factory production, new household arrangements developed to meet the different needs of various family members. For example, unmarried children lived longer with their parents, and the more successful relatives took in the widowed. Thus, most older people found themselves still living in a household with other kin. Although family relationships were often marked by tension, high levels of reciprocity also bound the generations together. Overall, therefore, it is not accurate to state that industrialization destroyed the extended family. Rather, families continued to operate as a unit, responding to social structural changes through flexible internal rearrangements.

In a variety of complex ways, however, industrialization did have a negative impact on work opportunities for older people in nineteenth-century England. Late in the century, social scientists began to notice that unemployment was associated with advanced age but could not clearly identify the cause. One factor was the rate of technological change which led to the phasing out of many older workers. But the issue is more complex than that. In the newest occupations that were truly creations of technological advance, it is more accurate to say that older workers entered at a lower rate than younger workers, rather than being pushed out. The role of technology, then, is less important than the fact that older workers were already established in other occupations and were unable or unwilling to change jobs.

Technology had its greatest negative impact on the elderly in traditional occupations such as weaving, in which hand looms were replaced by machines. Older workers already employed as wage laborers were unable to acquire the skills that would allow them to compete successfully against younger workers, and those who were self-employed could not manufacture products as cheaply as those using the new machines.

Another effect of industrialization was the creation of large numbers of unskilled and semiskilled workers in heavy industry. Rates of retirement were high among those whose only resource in old age was their ability to earn cash income. Few had alternative sources of income, as indicated in the high rates of poverty among the aged. Older workers who did not retire carried on at low-paying part-time jobs with little security. Thus, in this transitional period, retirement meant unemployment and was characterized by poverty and uncertainty.

Note

1. Chudacoff and Hareven (1978:228) assume that if an occupation was listed for an individual, it meant that that person was presently employed and that the reference was not to a previous occupation. This may not be true, in which case 90 percent employed would be an overestimation of the labor-force participation of the aged.

References

Achenbaum, W.A. *Old Age in the New Land.* Baltimore: Johns Hopkins University Press, 1978.

Anderson, M. *Family Structure in Nineteenth Century Lancashire.* London: Cambridge University Press, 1971.

――――. "Household Structure and the Industrial Revolution: Mid-Nineteenth Century Preston in Comparative Perspective," in P. Laslett, ed., *Household and Family in Past Time.* Cambridge: Cambridge University Press, 1972, pp. 215-35.

――――. "The Impact on the Family Relationships of the Elderly of Changes since Victorian Times in Governmental Income Maintenance," in E. Shanas and M.B. Sussman, eds., *Family, Bureaucracy and the Elderly.* Durham, N.C.: Duke University Press, 1977, pp. 36-59.

Berkner, L. "The Stem Family and the Developmental Cycle of the Peasant Household: An Eighteenth-Century Austrian Example," *American Historical Review* 77, 1972, pp. 398-418.

Braun, R. "The Impact of Cottage Industry," in D.S. Landes, ed., *The Rise of Capitalism.* New York: Macmillan, 1966, pp. 53-64.

Chudacoff, H., and T. Hareven. "Family Transitions into Old Age," in T. Hareven, ed., *Transitions, the Family and the Life Course in Historical Perspective.* New York: Academic Press, 1978, pp. 217-43.

Demos, J. *A Little Commonwealth: Family Life in Plymouth Colony.* New York: Oxford University Press, 1970.

――――. "Old Age in Early New England," *American Journal of Sociology* 84, 1978, pp. 248-87.

Drake, M. *Population and Society in Norway, 1735-1865.* Cambridge: Cambridge University Press, 1969.

Evans, G.E. *Ask the Fellows Who Cut the Hay.* London: Faber and Faber, 1957.

Gaunt, D. "The Retired Farmer: His Property and His Family Relations Since the Middle Ages, Northern and Central Europe." Paper presented to the Cambridge Group for the History of Population and Social Structure, 1979.

Greven, P.J. *Four Generations: Population, Land and Family in Colonial Andover, Massachusetts.* Ithaca, N.Y.: Cornell University Press, 1970.

Halper, T. "Paternalism and the Elderly," in S.F. Spicker, K.M. Woodward, and D.D. Van Tassel, eds., *Aging and the Elderly: Humanistic Perspectives in Gerontology.* Atlantic Highlands, N.J.: Humanities Press, 1978.

Heath, R. *The Peasant.* London, 1893.

Homans, G.C. *English Villagers of the Thirteenth Century.* Cambridge, Mass.: Harvard University Press, 1940.

Howell, C. "Peasant Inheritance Customs in the Midlands, 1280-1700," in J. Goody, J. Thirsk, and E.P. Thompson, eds., *Family and Inheritance.* Cambridge: Cambridge University Press, 1976.

Kitteringham, J. "Country Work Girls in Nineteenth-Century England," in R. Samuel, ed., *Village Life and Labor.* London: Routledge and Kegan Paul, 1975, pp. 75-138.

Kreps, J.M. "Intergenerational Transfers and the Bureaucracy," in E. Shanas and M.B. Sussman, eds., *Family, Bureaucracy and the Elderly.* Durham, N.C.: Duke University Press, 1977, pp. 21-35.

Laslett, P. "Societal Development and Aging," in R. Binstock and E. Shanas, eds., *Handbook of Aging and the Social Sciences.* New York: Van Nostrand Reinhold, 1976, pp. 87-116.

Litchfield, R.B. "The Family and the Mill: Cotton Mill Work, Family Work Patterns, and Fertility in Mid-Victorian Stockport," in A.S. Wohl, ed., *The Victorian Family.* London: Croon Helm, 1978, pp. 180-96.

Paillat, P. "Bureaucratization of Old Age: Determinants of the Process. Possible Safeguards and Reorientation," in E. Shanas and M.B. Sussman, eds., *Family, Bureaucracy and the Elderly.* Durham, N.C.: Duke University Press, 1977, pp. 60-74.

Palmore, E.B. and K. Manton. "Modernization and the Status of the Aged: International Correlations," *Journal of Gerontology* 29, 1974, pp. 205-10.

Quadagno, J. *Aging in Early Industrial Society: Work, Family, and Social Policy in Nineteenth-Century England.* New York: Academic Press, 1982.

Sabean, D. "Aspects of Kinship Behavior and Property in Rural Western Europe Before 1800," in J. Goody, J. Thirsk, and E.P. Thompson, eds., *Family and Inheritance.* Cambridge: Cambridge University Press, 1976, pp. 96-111.

Shorter, E. *The Making of the Modern Family.* New York: Basic Books, 1975.

Stannard, D.E. "Growing Up and Growing Old: Dilemmas of Aging in Bureaucratic America," in S.F. Spicker, K.M. Woodward, and D.D. Van Tassel, eds., *Aging and the Elderly: Humanistic Perspectives in Gerontology.* Atlantic Highlands, N.J.: Humanities Press, 1978, pp. 9-20.

Stearns, P. *Old Age in European Society.* London: Croon Helm, 1977.

Thomas, K. "Age and Authority in Early Modern England," *Proceedings of the British Academy* 62, 1976, pp. 205-48.

Tilly, L. and J. Scott. *Women, Work and Family.* New York: Holt, Rinehart and Winston, 1978.

Uhlenberg, P. "Changing Configurations of the Life Course," in T. Hareven, ed., *Transitions, the Family and the Life Course in Historical Perspective.* New York: Academic Press, 1978, pp. 65-98.

Wrigley, E.A. *Population and History.* New York: McGraw Hill, 1969.

4

Old-Age Relief Policies in the New Land, 1650-1900

John B. Williamson

In recent years a number of historical studies have described trends in the status of the elderly in colonial and nineteenth-century America.[1] During the past several decades there has also been much historical research on the origins of social welfare policy in the United States.[2] But to date there has been no systematic attempt to trace the historical development of old age relief policy. Such an analysis is necessary as a foundation for understanding the development of twentieth-century public policy toward the aged.

We are currently witnessing a major shift in attitudes toward poor relief, including policy toward the dependent elderly. The trend had been for the government to assume an ever increasing role in providing economic security for the elderly, but many of the assumptions of the welfare state are now under attack. For many years friends of the elderly have told us that the aged are poor, frail, socially dependent, objects of discrimination, and above all deserving. During the four decades between the mid 1930s and the mid 1970s the elderly benefitted from these compassionate stereotypes, as a vast array of federal aging programs were enacted. But recently, the American public has come to view the elderly as relatively well-off, as a powerful political force that votes its self-interest, and more importantly as a burden on the economy that will become overwhelming in the years ahead. In short, the elderly have become a scapegoat for America's economic ills.[3] However, this is not the first time the elderly have been scapegoated; it happened at several points during the nineteenth century in response to the economic ills of that era. If we do not pay attention to this history of public policy toward the dependent elderly, we may be condemned to repeat mistakes of the past.

During the seventeenth and particularly the early eighteenth century, old age relief policy was more restrictive (confining) in England than in the American colonies; but by the middle of the nineteenth century this situation was reversed. Why did relief policy in the United States become increasingly restrictive over this 200-year period? And why did relief policy become more restrictive in the United States than in England by the middle of the nineteenth century?

The answer to the first question, we believe, lies in an analysis of the impact of an emerging market economy. The second question will be more difficult to deal with. An analysis that emphasizes the role of an emerging market economy and capitalist economic structures cannot by itself account for the observed differences between England and the United States, since both nations followed similar economic paths. Thus, we must take into account such social and environmental differences as the abundance of land, the isolation of frontier communities, and the influx of immigrants that affect social structures and ultimately norms and values. Such social and environmental differences had a profound influence on the ways in which English ideas about poor relief were adapted and evolved in the American colonies.

Poor Relief in Colonial America

During the early part of the seventeenth century, the colonial population was made up of new arrivals who tended to be young adults; but by the end of the century the proportion who were elderly was starting to increase. From the limited data available, it is estimated that by 1700 approximately 6 percent of the colonial population was over age sixty and approximately 2 percent was over age sixty-five,[4] considerably smaller percentages than for seventeenth-century England.[5]

It might seem that poor relief for old people would rarely have been necessary in colonial America. Not only was the population young, it was rural with more than 90 percent living on farms.[6] Many of the elderly had a farm to pass on to their children, and it was common for an aged parent to be cared for in old age by one of their children (often the youngest) who in return was given the homestead and some land.[7] Those who owned substantial farm land had at least some economic protection in old age. But many, particularly laborers in the towns, did not have significant economic assets to pass along to their children.[8]

As most early American colonists came from England, they brought with them English ideas about how to deal with the elderly poor; but the policies which evolved in the New World were shaped by an environment very different from that of England. In the colonies there was a different age structure, a less rigid class system, and a much more equal distribution of wealth.[9]

While the abundance of land provided economic protection for some of the elderly, it created problems for others. In 1703 at least 40 percent of the aged were not living in three generational households.[10] Young people were continually moving west to seek their fortunes and settle lands. They were often disappointed in these efforts and typically had little or no extra funds with which to help out their aging parents back east.

Many of the colonists found themselves in small isolated frontier communities, where neighborly mutual aid was the only help for those in need.[11] This geographic isolation and insecurity led to a lessening of Protestant individualism and the development of community solidarity and a sense of social responsibility,[12] including a willingness to provide for needy persons who were members of the local community.[13]

The early colonial settlements were willing to provide for their own elderly poor in a way that was generally adequate, but they were often unwilling to care for poor outsiders.[14] This reluctance was particularly difficult for old people who were displaced by natural disasters or by frontier hostilities with the French and native Americans.[15] It was thought that an older person, particularly one who was in some way disabled or showing signs of the infirmities of old age, was not a good risk and might end up dependent on the community without having first made a sufficient contribution to justify such support.[16] As early as 1636 an ordinance was passed in Boston requiring anyone housing an outsider for more than two weeks to secure official permission which could be denied if it seemed likely that the guest would become dependent on public support.[17]

During the seventeenth century the colonies all passed statutes for dealing with the poor,[18] which were modified versions of the Elizabethan Poor Law of 1601 in England.[19] These rules specified that poor relief was to be organized at the level of the local community and to be paid for by a local poor tax. Such laws established the right of the local poor to support but also permitted residency requirements that could be used to deny support to people who had not lived in the community for a specified length of time.[20]

Most communities were also quick to adopt rules based on the English Law of Settlement and Removal of 1662, allowing such procedures as "warning out" and "passing on" for handling the problems of indigents (poor people) from outside the community.[21] If newcomers seemed likely to become dependent on the community, they were told to leave (warned away) by local officials,[22] and sometimes "passed on" by being officially escorted from one town to the next town. This process continued until indigents were delivered to their town of legal residence.[23]

A variety of arrangements for caring for the elderly poor evolved during the colonial period. As in England, the elderly poor tended to get lumped together with other categories of the powerless and penniless, the disabled, and those with mental disorders.[24] The laws often stated only that the community was responsible for providing for its poor, without any effort to define the term "poor."[25]

The colonists differed from their seventeenth and eighteenth-century English counterparts in minimizing the value of institutionalization[26] or other disruptions in the lives of recipients.[27] If an elderly widow had her own home or a place in the home of one of her children, her relief would often take the form of a small pension.[28] In many communities this was the most common form of relief, along with paying a neighbor or some other member of the community to provide care when the widow without close relatives was unable to take care of herself.[29]

There were also other, less common approaches, including the controversial policy of auctioning off the poor to the lowest bidder.[30] This solution minimized the costs to local taxpayers, but rarely improved the living conditions of relief recipients. Another form of relief was an abatement (reduction or elimination) of taxes[31] for people with serious economic problems. In some communities, particularly the larger seaport towns, almshouses[32] (institutions for the poor) were constructed as the relief alternative of last resort.[33] If the relief recipient required more care than could be given by a neighbor or had serious physical (or mental) health problems, then the almshouse alternative was more likely.

Not only were colonists unwilling to provide relief for indigent non-residents, they were also reluctant to provide for residents of questionable moral character. Those who led a corrupt life were held responsible for their poverty and could be refused assistance.[34] People of low social standing in the community were most likely to be considered morally undeserving of any relief.[35]

In many New England towns, laws were passed making those who brought servants into the community economically responsible for them in their old age.[36] There seems to have been considerable variability in the treatment of elderly slaves. Some, particularly those who had been domestic servants, were well treated; but many more were poorly treated. Common practices included selling off slaves before they became a burden, freeing them to fend for themselves, or sending old slaves off to live in huts in the woods. If the slaves were fortunate enough to have relatives in the area willing to help with the provision of food, it was possible to survive for a time in the woods. With few exceptions, slaves were not well provided for, particularly when they were no longer capable of work.[37]

There was a gemeinschaft character to these small pre-industrial communities due in part to ethnic homogeneity (similarity). During the colonial years a great deal of local aid was given and the aged were provided for, with the understanding that both those giving and receiving the aid shared a common ethnic background: White, Protestant, and English-American.[38] People from other ethnic groups tended to avoid public relief and the hostility directed toward relief seekers of non-English background.

These other ethnic groups began to establish their own relief institutions. As early as the 1650s there were alternative charitable societies among the Scots, French, and Jews; and by the 1760s, one Jewish group, Shearith Israel, had developed an old age pension system.[39] The needy of non-English background were given support from their mutual aid societies in much the same fashion as English-Americans were given support from public relief.

By the end of the eighteenth century some towns, particularly port towns, had substantial indigent populations. With the growth in the size of towns there was a subtle but important shift in the attitude toward the poor, who had originally been viewed as neighbors or peers fallen on hard times, and who deserved support from the community. The poor were increasingly viewed as a lower class made up of sinners, vagabonds, and other disreputable types who were in large measure personally responsible for their poverty and who, therefore, did not deserve public assistance.

Nineteenth-Century Relief Policy

In the early part of the nineteenth century, particularly during the severe depression of 1815-21, there was a sharp increase in the number of people on relief, which led to a corresponding increase in the poor tax.[40] As was the case in England this increase in the poor tax burden led to studies of the poverty problem. The English Poor Law Reform of 1834 also had a significant impact on thinking and policy in the United States,[41] where it was mistakenly thought that the English had decided to eliminate all relief to persons outside of institutions.[42] The English "reform" was used to support the decision in the United States to put a much heavier emphasis on the institutional alternative. But policy in the United States was most heavily influenced by a number of studies of poverty that were carried out by individual states, particularly the Yates Report (1824) on poor relief policy throughout New York State.[43]

One conclusion of the Yates Report was that an overly generous relief system was contributing to idleness, crime, and other forms of deviance.

One recommendation of the report was to forbid public assistance to any able-bodied person between the ages of 18 and 50. Another was that relief to the elderly, the blind, and other such needy groups should be given only in an institution, not in their own homes.[44] A third recommendation was that the administrative unit for poor relief should be the county, not the town.[45] In response to this report the State of New York enacted the County Poorhouse Act (1824) which called for the construction of at least one almshouse in each county in the state.[46] Each state took a somewhat different approach to dealing with the sharp increase in the cost of relief, but the trend during the first half of the nineteenth century was toward the institutional alternative.[47]

This movement toward the almshouse solution was not confined to poor relief but must be seen as part of a more general movement at that time toward institutionalization of all deviant populations, including criminals and the mentally ill.[48] The extent of the shift from outdoor relief (relief to persons living in their own homes) to indoor relief (relief in an institution) did vary from state to state and from one community to another, but the general trend was clear.[49] During the colonial period almshouses were, for the most part, confined to the large port towns; but by the middle of the nineteenth century almost every town had one.[50] By the end of the Civil War, 80 percent of those receiving long-term relief in Massachusetts were in institutions.[51] This proportion was lower in some states and higher in others.[52]

Between 1825 and 1860, in Boston, from one-fourth to one-third of relief expenditures went to outdoor relief; the rest went to indoor relief.[53] From this evidence it is clear that most public money was being spent on relief in institutions, although a substantial portion still went to people living in their own homes.[54] In New York State during this same period, outdoor relief accounted for between a third and a half of relief expenditures, a figure that rose steeply during periods of financial panic and depression.[55] While a significant proportion of the population, including many elderly persons, continued to receive outdoor relief, the tendency to emphasize indoor relief continued for the rest of the century.[56] As early as 1848, 30 percent of those in the Blockley Almshouse in Philadelphia were elderly; and by 1900, most almshouses had become heavily populated with the elderly.[57]

Where History Meets Sociology

It should not be assumed, however, that the only sources of relief during the nineteenth century were those controlled by the state or county and financed with public taxes. The ethnic mutual aid societies established during the colonial period still flourished. There were, as well, several utopian and other communal societies established in response to the isolation of the frontier. These communities had their own means of caring for the elderly and needy. The Shakers, well established by 1742, had very carefully planned rules governing family life: all private property was given to the community for care and use; in return, the family received food, lodging, clothing, and assurance that each member would be cared for in old age.[58] Among the Amish a small home for the elderly parents was often built on the farm of one of the children. Elderly unable to care for themselves were taken into the home of an adult child; or, if relatives were not available, the church would assist them.[59] There was a great deal of security in joining these utopian communities[60] as they assured members of having food, shelter, a job, education for their children, and care in old age.[61]

By the middle of the nineteenth century indoor relief predominated in the United States while outdoor relief predominated in England.[62] This reflected a significant difference in relief policy between the two nations. Policy in England was now more restrictive than it had been during the sixteenth century, but it was less restrictive than in the United States. This difference is particularly noteworthy in light of the generally more liberal policies in America during the early colonial era.

With the evidence that we have considered to this point we are now in a position to address the two central questions of this article: Why did the institutional response to relief come to be so much more extensively used in this country? Why did relief policies in the United States become so much more restrictive between the early colonial era and the Jacksonian era? We will address the latter question first.

Various theories have been offered to account for the dramatic shift toward institutionalization during the Jacksonian era. Andrew Scull, for example, suggests the change was a response to the demands of a developing capitalist market economy.[63] A market economy produces structural pressures to get as much work from labor at as low a wage as possible. If certain categories of deviants and dependents are isolated in institutions, this frees a greater proportion of the labor force to participate fully in the work force and allows them to support their families on lower wages.[64] At the time, it was assumed that a greater emphasis on the almshouse alternative would also make the administration of poor relief more efficient and economical. The harshness of this approach would discourage all but the most needy from seeking assistance.[65] Institutions served as a means of disciplining the labor force, grim reminders of the fate of those who would refuse to work at the going rate.

This argument helps explain the trend toward institutional care in both England and the United States; but it does not adequately account for the fact that by the mid nineteenth century the practice was more common in the United States than in England, which had a much more fully developed capitalist economy.

To account for this difference it may be useful to look at ideological/ cultural as well as material/economic factors, by considering the influence of the Protestant ethic that the early colonists brought to the New World.[66] The individualism and work ethic of the Protestant ideology was present in both England and the New World, but the social and environmental contexts were very different. In England there was less opportunity for the poor significantly to improve their lot through individual effort and initiative. In colonial America there was an abundance of land, a high demand for labor, and a more fluid social structure.[67] This difference in opportunities for social mobility made it more likely that the poor would be held responsible for their poverty. To remain poor in America where so many opportunities existed suggested that the person must be very lazy or unusually inept.[68]

Shifts in land policies and holdings in the nineteenth century, however, made it increasingly more difficult for outsiders to settle and set up traditional subsistance farms. The panic of 1837 found landowners unable to resell their lands at a profit as they had intended, and money lenders could not collect on their mortgages.[69] Land renting, which began as early as 1823 became quite customary by 1836.[70] The rising value of land made it difficult for settlers to move from being a laborer or tenant to becoming part owner, and eventually full owner, which had been a common means of upward mobility during the eighteenth century.[71] By 1850 new American settlers without capital were virtually denied the option of ownership. Thus the myth of the land of opportunity, where anyone could settle and prosper was maintained, while that opportunity in actuality was rapidly decreasing. It is estimated that by 1860, approximately 20 percent of those engaged in agriculture were farm laborers, a proportion that grew to 33 percent by 1870.[72] Although warned not to emigrate from Europe or the East without capital, many found themselves on the edge of the frontier impoverished and unable to start their own farms.[73]

The impact of this change in land availability on the aging American population was significant. Unlike the traditional family organization, wherein the family homestead provided security for the aged, many family heads who had hoped to own their farms found themselves unable to meet mortgage payments, while others had their rented land sold out from under them. As a result many elderly settlers became drifters without any source of economic security in their old age.[74] There were large wealth differences between laborers, tenants, and estate owners which tended to break down the unity and homogeneity of the frontier society. The mutual support and community identification of the colonial era gave way to more individualistic alternatives for self-preservation. Privilege, individualism, and opportunism became the dominant principles of social life on the frontier as in the East.[75]

During the early nineteenth century, attitudes towards the poor also shifted with the changing ethnic composition of this segment of the population. New immigrant groups were not only culturally different, but they were also failing to conform to the American norm of caring for their own.[76] The dramatic influx of immigrants during the nineteenth century had a profound impact on both the size and ethnic composition of American cities;[77] and with these changes, public assistance for the first time became relief primarily for those with non-English backgrounds.

American attitudes concerning the community's responsibility for adequate and compassionate care of the less fortunate also began to change: the poor and the aged were no longer perceived as "deserving." This reaction among the English-Americans who dominated government and public policy was a major factor in the rapid growth of almshouses and the trend towards indoor relief.[78] The changing ethnic composition of the poor must be emphasized in any effort to explain why relief policies became more restrictive in America than in ethnically more homogeneous England.

Moreover, statistics on employment by industry for the years 1800 to 1900 show a rapid growth of jobs in manufacturing and trade, with a corresponding drop in agricultural employment.[79] An increasing number of immigrants were staying in the large cities to work in the textile industry as well as such heavy industries as iron and steel. With industrialization and the growth of large cities, the gap between the wealthy and the poor increased. Without property of their own, elderly workers were often left without any means of support when they became too old for the available jobs.

During the period between the Civil War and the end of the century, public policy toward the elderly poor did not become more generous. It was an era of unsympathetic attitudes towards the "less fit" in general.[80] A crude individualism, based on the belief that economic life was a jungle in which only the fittest survived, dominated American culture.[81] Believers in this doctrine (called "social Darwinism")[82] not only opposed all forms of public relief but went so far as to oppose private charity as well, though less strongly:[83] any form of assistance, even to the elderly poor, would undermine the motivation for the younger people to work hard and to be thrifty.[84]

The scientific charity movement was another important English influence on relief policy in the United States. The first American Charity Organization Society (COS) was established in 1877.[85] The ideology of the

COS movement was clearly influenced by social Darwinism.[86] The stated goal was to organize charity in a scientific manner. The COS leaders made it a point to assert that they would not be giving out any relief funds. Instead the COS would serve as a clearing house for persons seeking relief. They would screen applicants and where appropriate refer them to other relief granting agencies. Relief was viewed as at best a necessary evil.[87] The mission of the scientific charity movement was to encourage people to be self-sufficient and to make do with as little outside assistance as possible. They sought to substitute counseling and moral uplift for the direct distribution of relief funds.[88] The destitute elderly who decided to forgo relief so as to avoid the stigma of becoming public dependents were praised for their choice.[89]

Chapters of the COS spread through the country. By the turn of the century there were 138 COS organizations around the nation.[90] While the movement does not seem to have changed what was already a very restrictive attitude toward relief, it was one factor that reinforced a continuation of restrictive relief policies. Thus, by 1900, the antipoor strain in American culture and social structure was paramount. In the reality of the Great Depression of the 1930s the concept of societal responsibility for the poor was revived and guided public policy up to the late 1970s. Today, once more, we are witnessing the ascendency of social Darwinism, an echo of our not so distant past.

Notes

Revised version of paper presented at the annual meeting of the Society for the Study of Social Problems, Detroit, Michigan, August 1984. This research was supported in part by a grant from the Mellon Foundation to Boston College. The author wishes to thank Janet Boguslaw for her able research assistance.

1. See W. Andrew Achenbaum, *Old Age in the New Land* (Baltimore: Johns Hopkins University Press, 1978); David H. Fischer, *Growing Old in America,* expanded edition (New York: Oxford University Press, 1978); John Demos, "Old Age in Early New England," in Michael Gordon, ed., *The American Family in Social-Historical Perspective,* Second edition (New York: St. Martin's Press, 1978).
2. See David M. Schneider, *The History of Public Welfare in New York State 1609-1866* (Chicago: University of Chicago Press, 1938); Robert W. Kelso, *The History of Public Poor Relief in Massachusetts, 1620-1920* (Boston: Houghton Mifflin, 1922); Marcus W. Jernegan, *Laboring and Dependent Classes in Colonial America, 1607-1783* (Chicago: University of Chicago Press, 1931); Blanche D. Coll, *Perspectives in Public Welfare* (Washington, D.C.: U.S. Government Printing Office, 1969); Robert H. Bremner, *From the Depths* (New York: New York University Press, 1956).
3. Robert H. Binstock, "The Aged as Scapegoat," *Gerontologist* 23 (April 1983): 136-43.

4. These estimates are based on evidence from New Rochelle, New York for 1698, see Fischer, p. 272.
5. Peter Laslett, "Societal Development and Aging," in Robert H. Binstock and Ethel Shanas, eds., *Handbook of Aging and the Social Sciences* (New York: Van Nostrand Reinhold, 1976), p. 99.
6. Fischer, p. 102
7. Ibid., pp. 53-54.
8. One estimate is that a fifth of Whites were laborers without significant property holdings. The same authority estimates that in the late eighteenth century this "permanent proletariat" may have been as high as 30 percent of the population if Blacks are also considered; see Jackson T. Main, *The Social Structure of Revolutionary America* (Princeton: Princeton University Press, 1965), pp. 271-72.
9. Ibid., pp. 8-11.
10. Michael Zimmerman, "Old Age Poverty in Pre-Industrial New York City," in Beth B. Hess, ed., *Growing Old in America*, 2nd ed. (New Brunswick, N.J.: Transaction, 1980), p. 67.
11. William Bradford, *Of Plymouth Plantation* (New York: Capricorn, 1962).
12. Fischer, pp. 109-10.
13. Walter I. Trattner, *From Poor Law to Welfare State* (New York: Free Press, 1974), p. 17.
14. See David J. Rothman, *The Discovery of the Asylum* (Boston: Little, Brown, 1971), p. 5; Trattner, pp. 19-26; Fischer, p. 61. In 1720, for example, a law was enacted in New Jersey that instructed justices of the peace to search arriving ships for "old persons" as well as "maimed, lunatic, or any vagabond and vagrant persons," and to send such persons away so as to reduce pauperism in the colony; see James Leiby, *Charity and Corrections in New Jersey* (New Brunswick, New Jersey: Rutgers University Press, 1967), p. 7.
15. During King Philip's War (1675-1677) there was an influx of "impoverished refugees" from frontier settlements to towns such as Boston, New York, and Newport. More than 500 of these refugees arrived in Newport in 1675 alone; see Trattner, pp. 21-22.
16. In Plymouth Colony the two major reasons people were refused inhabitance were: (1) incompatibility in religious beliefs and (2) likelihood of early public dependency, a factor that was particularly problematic for the aged; see Robert W. Kelso, *The History of Poor Relief in Massachusetts, 1620-1920* (Boston: Houghton Mifflin, 1922), pp. 35-36.
17. Trattner, p. 19 Three years later an ordinance was passed which required that a townsman provide security (post bond) for any such persons; see Neil B. Betten, "American Attitudes toward the Poor: A Historical Overview," *Current History* 65 (1973): 2-5.
18. Stefan A. Riensenfeld, "The Formative Era of American Assistance Law," *California Law Review* 43 (1955), pp. 175-223.
19. Coll, p. 19.
20. In 1642 Plymouth Colony established the first residency requirement for relief eligibility; see Trattner, p. 20.
21. Marcus W. Jernegan, *Laboring and Dependent Classes in Colonial America, 1607-1783* (Chicago: University of Chicago Press, 1931), p. 193; Eleanor Parkhurst, "Poor Relief in a Massachusetts Village in the Eighteenth Century," *Social Service Review* 11 (September, 1937), p. 446.

22. Trattner, pp. 19-20.
23. In New York State some 1,800 people were subject to the process of "passing on" in 1822 alone; see Coll, p. 20.
24. Raymond A. Mohl, *Poverty in New York, 1783-1825* (New York: Oxford University Press, 1971), p. 7.
25. Rothman, p. 4.
26. The workhouse was far more common in eighteenth-century England than in the United States; see ibid., p. 31.
27. Ibid., p. 30.
28. Mohl, p. 7.
29. Parkhurst, p. 446.
30. Coll, pp. 21-22.
31. Trattner, p. 19.
32. Rothman, p. 30. In 1696 the town of New York rented a house for sick paupers and in 1736 the town's almshouse was constructed. By 1772 there were some 425 paupers in the facility; see Mohl, pp. 43-5.
33. Zimmerman, p. 70.
34. Rothman, p. 5.
35. Fischer argues that "old age seems actually to have intensified the contempt visiting upon a poor man." He also points out that in some cases poor widows were driven out of the community by neighbors who feared increases in the poor taxes; pp. 60-63.
36. Trattner, p. 21.
37. Fischer, pp. 64-66.
38. Alfred J. Kutzik, "American Social Provision for the Aged: An Historical Perspective," in Donald E. Gelfand and Alfred J. Kutzik, eds., *Ethnicity and Aging* (New York: Springer Publishing Company, 1979), p. 34.
39. Ibid., p. 72.
40. Coll, p. 21.
41. Rothman, p. 157.
42. Coll, p. 29.
43. For a thorough analysis of the Yates report see Schneider, Chapters 12 and 13.
44. Ibid., p. 228.
45. This shift turned out to be important because it tended to make the poor more distant from the middle class. Due in part to this shift they were more likely to be viewed as members of a lower class than as neighbors who had fallen on hard times.
46. Schneider, pp. 235-46.
47. Rothman, pp. 180-205.
48. Ibid.
49. Mohl, pp. 8-9.
50. Rothman, pp. 30-31, 184; Coll, p. 22.
51. Rothman, p. 183
52. Coll, pp. 30-32.
53. Ibid., p. 31.
54. By the end of the Civil War the number of long-term relief recipients in the almshouse was much greater than the number on outdoor relief, but if we take into consideration those persons receiving casual relief on a very short-term basis, then the total number of outdoor relief recipients was greater; see Rothman, p. 183.

55. Coll, pp. 29-30.
56. Rothman, p. 205.
57. Benjamin J. Klebaner, *Public Poor Relief in America, 1790-1860* (New York: Arno Press, 1976), p. 211.
58. Henri Desroche, *The American Shakers from Neo-Christianity to Presocialism* (New York: Oxford University Press, 1979), p. 190. The Shakers came to live long lives. The average age for the elders increased from 42 to 71 between 1790 and 1889 in one community and increased from 35 to 82 during the same time period in another community; see Edward D. Andrews, *The People Called Shakers* (New York: Dover, 1953), p. 198.
59. Elmer Schwieder and Dorothy Schwieder, *A Peculiar People: Iowa's Old Order Amish* (Ames, Iowa: Iowa State University Press, 1975), p. 67.
60. See Desroche, p. 193, for a discussion of the Amana.
61. Robert V. Hine, *California's Utopian Colonies* (New Haven: Yale University Press, 1966), p. 167.
62. In England in 1850 approximately 11 percent of those receiving relief were in institutions; see Michael E. Rose, "The Allowance System Under the New Poor Law," *Economic History Review* 19 (1966), pp. 607-20. But in the United States a majority, 80 percent by the end of the Civil War, were in institutions; see Coll, p. 29; Rothman, p. 183.
63. Andrew T. Scull, *Decarceration* (Englewood Cliffs, N.J.: Prentice-Hall, 1977), pp. 15-40.
64. Scull argues that in the nineteenth century the working and lower classes found the care of the aged and incapacitated relatives an intolerable burden, given the problems they were having providing for their own subsistence; see Ibid., pp. 128-29.
65. Edgar S. Furniss, *The Position of the Laborer in a System of Nationalism* (New York: Kelly, 1965), p. 107; Scull, p. 26.
66. By the early nineteenth century the laissez-faire ideology of classical economists such as Adam Smith and David Ricardo was reinforcing the earlier Protestant Ethnic ideology described by Max Weber, *The Protestant Ethic and the Spirit of Capitalism*, translated by Talcott Parsons (New York: Charles Scribner's Sons, 1958). Poor relief was viewed by those classical economists as a violation of a person's "natural right" to accumulate wealth.
67. Rothman, pp. 156-59.
68. This view can also be linked to the Enlightenment. The Enlightenment resulted from the growth of science as reflected in the work of Newton and the thinking of philosophers such as John Locke. Persons in this tradition argued that everyone possesses reason and can use this reason to understand the universe. The perspective also put an emphasis on equality among people and the belief that it was possible to solve social problems such as poverty. But, as Trattner (p. 50) points out, it led many to the conclusion that the poor themselves were responsible for their poverty.
69. Paul Wallace Gates, *Landlords and Tenants on the Prairie Frontier: Studies in American Land Policy* (Ithaca, New York: Cornell University Press, 1969), p. 5.
70. Ibid., p. 131
71. Ibid., pp. 3, 139-41.
72. Ibid., p. 304. In Iowa townships for example, the 1870 census indicates that of the agricultural population 53 percent owned farms and 47 percent owned no land.

73. Ibid., p. 324. By the end of the nineteenth century agricultural laborers and tenants outnumbered full owner operated farms in several states and all of the Upper Mississippi Valley.
74. David Ellis, ed., *The Frontier in American Development. Essays in Honor of Paul Wallace Gates* (Ithaca, N.Y.: Cornell University Press, 1969), pp. xxii-xxiv. In Kentucky, Vermont, and Tennessee from 1797 to 1830 the state legislatures provided reimbursements to evicted settlers for improvements they made on lands which had been previously claimed. In California occupancy laws were established temporarily in 1856. In other states occupancy laws had been in effect as early as 1797 to protect absentee landowners and settlers from false claims.
75. Gates, pp. 323-25.
76. Kutzik, p. 39.
77. Zimmerman, p. 71. For example, in New York City the population grew from 124,000 in 1820 to 313,000 in 1840.
78. Kutzik. Settlers on the frontier until about 1840 were primarily from New England and the Middle States with the foreign born comprising only 10 to 15 percent of the population. These were mostly from the British Isles. By 1860 the numbers had changed dramatically.
79. The labor force in agriculture decreased from 74 percent in 1800 to 55 percent in 1850 and to 40 percent in 1900. Between 1850 and 1900 the percent in manufacturing increased from 15 to 20 percent and the number in trades from 6 to 14 percent. See Series D 167-181 "Labor Force and Employment, by Industry: 1800 to 1960" in U.S. Bureau of the Census, *Historical Statistics of the United States, Colonial Times to 1970* (Washington, D.C.: U.S. Government Printing Office, 1975), p. 139.
80. Achenbaum, pp. 51-54; Joe R. Feagin, *Subordinating the Poor* (Englewood Cliffs, N.J.: Prentice-Hall, 1975), pp. 34-37.
81. David Duncan, *The Life and Letters of Herbert Spencer* (New York: Appleton and Company, 1908), p. 128.
82. Richard Hofstadter, *Social Darwinism in American Thought 1860-1915* (London: Oxford University Press, 1944), pp. 18-19. Social Darwinism provided a "scientific" basis for many tenets of laissez-faire ideology including the view that the only remedy for poverty is individual self-help; see Bremner, p. 19.
83. Trattner, p. 81.
84. While Darwin briefly discusses the application of his ideas to the poor, it was Herbert Spencer who coined the phrase "survival of the fittest." Social Darwinism combined laissez-faire economics with the doctrine of survival of the fittest; see Charles Darwin, *The Origin of the Species and the Descent of Man* (New York: Modern Library, 1936), p. 501.
85. The COS movement originated in London in 1869; see Coll, p. 44.
86. Feagin, p. 34.
87. Josephine S. Lowell, *Public Relief and Private Charity* (New York: G.P. Putnam's Sons, 1884), p. 89.
88. The motto of the COS was "not alms but a friend." The reference here is to the corps of middle class volunteers or "friendly visitors" who provided sympathy, hope, encouragement, and supposedly help with such problems as indolence, intemperance, and improvidence; see Trattner, p. 87.

89. The COS considered its approach scientific in part because of the thorough investigation of the applicant's financial situation. Relief, if given, was to take into consideration need. Also it was to be more efficient by avoiding fraud and duplication of benefits from different agencies; see Ibid., pp. 84-85.
90. Ibid., p. 84.

5

Family Ties of the Aged in Cross-Cultural Perspective

Corinne N. Nydegger

Anthropologists in multidisciplinary settings are likely to be "difficult." They offer dissenting evidence to comfortable generalizations through what has come to be known as the anthropological veto ("but not in New Guinea"), they debunk cherished myths about human nature and social systems, and they insist upon turning things upside down by questioning those very things we all take for granted. This paper follows that tradition. The value of bringing a cross-cultural perspective to bear on family ties of the elderly is not simply in the cataloguing of *other* societies' practices but in placing *our own* practices into the larger context which is generated by such studies. In so doing, we are forced to look at our institutions in a different light and may recognize aspects of family ties that we have neglected or preferred not to see.

True to still another anthropological tradition, this discussion focuses on myths—but not the intriguing totemic or creation tales of exotic cultures. Instead, it examines some of our own myths—ours as Americans and as gerontologists. Mythological systems are not mere assemblages of charming folk tales and cautionary morality plays; they are powerful unconscious shapers. By crystallizing ideology, they channel our thinking, often along unrealistic paths, which seriously hampers the effort to understand the world we live in. First, then, it is necessary to emphasize that most of our cherished beliefs about the treatment of the aged at other times and in other places are proving to be illusions. Second, our tendency to idealize late family ties should be balanced by admitting the reverse side of the coin—*unpleasant* aspects of familial relations.

Three Myths

A particular set of beliefs colors our view of aging worldwide. One common romance is that of a past Golden Age from which modern man has fallen, most often as a consequence of his own sinful acts. The historian Laslett (1965) has called this the "world we have lost" syndrome. A similar notion—the Golden Isles—displaces this paradise in space rather than time. It is to be found across the ocean, over the mountains, somewhere just out of reach. Here, as in the Golden Age of the past, are people without stain, a society without strain, and all who dwell therein are content. Interwoven through the fabric of these myths is the tenacious thread of the "natural" Rosy Family, a nuclear family with intergenerational extension, that provides strength, love, and sustenance to all its members.

It is reasonable to regard such tales as embodiments of cultural ideals, as visions of the perfect society, or as cautionary tales which foretell the pernicious consequences of moral lapses. But we all realize that it is not reasonable to regard such myths as history or as anthropology. At one level, these myths are on a par with the fabulous beasts found on old maps or those peculiar medieval hominids—one-footed or three-headed—reputed to dwell in distant lands.

However, Golden Ages or Golden Isles and their Rosy Families are more than merely fabulous constructs of the unknown: they embody many of our deepest desires and fears, and they are pointers to the way we believe things ought to be. They are crystallizations of our cultural concept of the good life. These images, in turn, are important forces shaping our attitude toward the world as it is. Although we are seldom fully aware of it, we often use these fables as ideal standards against which we judge reality. Not surprisingly, reality consistently fails to measure up.

Our society has elaborated subsets of these myths about the aged. They are identical to the generic Golden Age and Golden Isles fables, but these idyllic states are specific to the elderly. Because they are widely accepted as fact, these myths warrant an unsentimental scrutiny.

The Golden Age

In a skillful exegesis, Laslett (1976) identified the following content of the Golden Age myth: (1) "there has been a *before* and an *after*" in the social consequences of aging and the transition has been uniform and is associated with moderization; (2) in the past, the aged "were both entitled to respect and were universally accorded it"; (3) "the aged had specified and valued economic and emotional roles"; and (4) aged persons normally resided in multigenerational households and were cared for by their kinsmen (pp. 89-90). In recent decades, a number of important contributions have been made to gerontology by historians who have developed techniques to make ingenious use of archival data. The evidence they have marshaled demolishes these mythic postulates for the dominant American ethnic streams.

Take the linchpin concept of the "typical" multigenerational household. Actuarial statistics long ago indicated that, because of high mortality throughout the life cycle, fewer parents attained old age and fewer children survived to adulthood. Therefore, the multigenerational household should have been the unusual case. Now a number of historians have confirmed that, in the English and American past, the multigenerational family is the least frequent form recorded (Anderson, 1971; Demos, 1965, 1968, 1978; Greven, 1966; Kobrin, 1976; Laslett, 1969, 1976; Lockridge, 1966; Pryor, 1972; Stearns, 1977). Brody (1979), is the latest in a line of researchers to stress the fact that only in modernized nations with increased longevity can the multigenerational family occur with any real frequency.

Further, such data as are available indicate that, at least in colonial and nineteenth-century America and nineteenth-century England, the preferred residence for older persons was not with their children (Demos, 1978; Laslett, 1976; Seward, 1978). Coresidence, although more common, apparently was determined, as it still is, by economic conditions (Chudacoff and Hareven, 1978; Dahlin, 1980; Fischer, 1978). There is little question that the elderly and their children in our historic past valued the independence of separate residence as much as we do and that many elderly persons were not cared for by their families if other alternatives, such as institutions or hired help, were available (Laslett, 1976). When support was required, then—as now—the primary burden fell on the children, who received little help from the community. Certainly the total social burden in the past was lighter than that assumed now by our society. But for the individual families then involved in caretaking, the burden must have been even heavier than is presently the case, although we must keep in mind that they were spared catastrophic medical bills, for the acutely ill died more quickly in those days.

Evidence concerning respect for specific old age roles and for age itself is very scanty, but the few indices available suggest little community respect in the absence of wealth or prestige. Rather, historical studies agree that the pervasive view in Western Europe disvalued old age and was not tolerant of old people (Hendricks and Hendricks, 1977-78; Kastenbaum and Ross, 1975; Stearns, 1981). Stearns points out that "we can grant immense problems for the elderly at the present time, but we do not have to assume that their lot has ever been strikingly good in Western society" (1979, p.40). So what remains of this Golden Age for the aged in our past? Only the possibility of valued roles reserved for the aged, based on wishful thinking and a dearth of hard evidence to the contrary—although this is slowly being rectified.

In passing, we should look at another much-touted indictment of modernization: that geographic mobility on its current scale results in more widely dispersed and, hence, less effectively supportive families. In terms of actual mileage, this may be true enough. But in terms of dependable, rapid communication and transportation, quite the opposite is true (Litwak, 1960). We forget that children in the past did leave their homes in very large numbers and that a sailor on a clipper ship out of Boston might not be heard of for two years, that what was then considered the West was a month or more away, that just getting a message to a child in the next county was no simple matter of direct dialing.

Rapid mobilization of all family members is much likelier today than has ever been the case. Thus, although the bulk of daily care must still rest on the proximate child, distant children and other family members can be more actively involved in decisions and support than was possible in the past. If the extensive work of Shanas and her associates (e.g., Shanas and Streib, 1965; Shanas and Sussman, 1976; Shanas et al., 1968) has documented anything in modern Western societies, it is precisely this kind of involvement of children in the support of their aged kin.

The Golden Isles

If the lot of the aged has been overrated in our own past, is it not different some other place? Can we find the Golden Isles of the aged in ancestor-worshipping China or in small-scale, integrated societies? Now that we are accumulating a body of ethnographic material specifically focused on aging, our picture of such societies is no longer as simple as it once was. Two issues are involved that are often confounded: the first is the questions of relative power of the aged; the second is that of respect for age *qua* age. As to power, there is plenty of evidence that the control of resources or knowledge by elders compels respect, as specified by Rosow (1962). However, such control is seldom concentrated in the hands of the elderly in the rapidly changing societies of today (Cowgill, 1974; Cowgill and Holmes, 1972; Palmore and Manton, 1974). The critical question, then, is the degree to which such control by elders was *generally* high prior to modernization.

This issue is not yet settled and for many societies the necessary data are irretrievable, but critical inspection of the least modernized societies suggests that many claims are indigenous versions of the Golden Age. For example, true gerontocracy is the exception and, where it occurs, is associated with spectacular displays of intergenerational and intrafamilial competition and conflict (Baker, 1979; Forner and Kertzer, 1978; Levine, 1965; Shelton, 1972; Spencer, 1965). For these groups, modernization does indeed mean a rapid loss of power for the elderly, but we lack sufficient data and accurate indices to compare age distributions of power across a broad range of non-modernized societies. We do know it varies enormously; thus, under some conditions, modernization may have little effect (Holmes, 1972) and may even increase the resource base of the elderly (Amoss, 1981). At present, sweeping generalizations about the relative power of the aged in premodernized societies must be regarded as suspect.

With respect to general esteem for age *qua* age, claims based on selective readings of scriptural or moralistic literature (particularly popular in regard to the Orient) can be rejected out of hand: *all* societies provide quotable homilies about filial piety and respect for one's elders. Unfortunately, despite patient effort, the incidental data in archival collections are generally inadequate, and studies based on them may be misleading (Maxwell and Silverman, 1970; Sheehan, 1976). They cannot avoid confounding (1) professed attitudes with actual treatment of the aged (Glascock and Feinman, 1980) and "ritual deference" with "realistic appraisal" (Lipman, 1970), (2) respect for the aged per se with respect for the few powerful old, and (3) esteem of the aged in general with esteem for one's own aged kin (Nydegger, 1981). Simmons (1945), in the first cross-cultural study of aging, demonstrated a sensitivity to these issues wanting in many of his successors.

As early as 1964, Harlan drew attention to discrepancies between idealized reports of respect for old age and observed behavior, and Lipman (1970) pointed out that ritualistic deference was devoid of meaning. As anthropologists became more involved in gerontology, increasingly sophisticated ethnographies substantiated these warnings and lead us to conclude that the claim of other societies' general respect for the aged is yet another example of the "world we have lost" syndrome. They document again and again a point made by Simmons (1945): in no society do the aged constitute a homogeneous group. In all societies we must specify precisely which aged we are speaking of: the ill or the healthy, the chronologically ancient or only the generationally elder, male heads of households or family-less widows, wise leaders or village failures. The research by anthropological gerontologists proves that generalizations about "esteem of the aged" are generally as superficial and just plain wrong in other societies as in our own.

Sources of Variability

We can hazard a few suggestions concerning sources of variability in the status of elderly persons within and among societies:

(1) In most cases, control of resources is incorrectly attributed to the aged as a group or age grade; rather, it is differentially exercised by various older

individuals. All groups have members who are not respected and have little status or power at any age. Even in true age-grade societies, wherein entire age sets advance through hierarchical stages, not all age-peers are equal, and individuals compete for position at each stage (Baxter and Almagor, 1978).

(2) Where the elderly accumulate power, they do command respect, but it is due to their power, not their age (Press and McKool, 1972). The sole exception is the special case wherein increasing age augments supernatural power simply because one moves closer to its source (Lee and DeVore, 1968).

(3) We must draw a sharp distinction between reports of old individuals in relatively low-percentage elderly populations where only the sturdy survive and reports of age-grades in high-percentage elderly populations where many frail elderly survive (Isaacs et al., 1972). They involve significantly different conditions of aging.

(4) At the individual level, in all societies, including our own, the ability to function is critical for the position of the elderly (Glascock and Feinman, 1980). Nowhere is decrepitude valued.

(5) The elderly sometimes contribute substantially to the economic well-being of the group, but the only generic role assigned to the aged is that of old women's babysitting and kitchen help. Although male ethnographers have assumed that this is a fulfilling role, nowhere does it have high social status.

(6) Cultural values about aging vary, and they make a difference in people's acceptance of and accommodation to aging processes in themselves and their kin (e.g., Clark and Anderson, 1967; Holmes, 1972; Osako, 1979).

(7) The final responsibility for the aged and for decisions about their fate invariably rests with their closest kin, typically children. Usually this does mean support, but even in societies where the aged are killed when they can no longer function, the sons must make the judgment and carry it out—it is one of their filial duties (Glascock and Feinman, 1980). However, sizable percentages of elderly individuals have no surviving children and have only marginal and unenforceable claims on more distant relatives. Without personal resources and in the absence of institutionalized aid, their position is generally wretched even in societies professing reverence for the aged (Delaney, 1981). With few exceptions, charity really does begin at home—and ends there.

The "Natural" Nuclear Family

Integrated with the myths of golden time and place is a persistent set of beliefs about families that warrant detailed attention. The first is the conviction that the nuclear family is strong "naturally" (which seems to mean in a "state of nature"—a myth in its own right) but that modernization has stripped this natural unit of its inherent functions.

For most of us, the term "family" conjures up our type, the separate nuclear family of a married couple with their children, which may be extended to include the parents of the couple; but this is by no means a universal arrangement. For cross-cultural use, "family" is an ambiguous term with hazy boundaries because it refers to the intersection of the two basic principles of social organization: kinship and residence. Despite their apparent simplicity, humankind has elaborated each of these principles with ingenuity; combining the two yields still more diversity. Although anthropologists take care to keep these principles analytically distinct, any discussion of families necessarily involves both.

Because the term "family" is altogether too imprecise for cross-cultural use, Fortes (1949) and Goody (1958) have encouraged the use of "domestic group," thus focusing specifically on the residential unit. At any given time, several types of family (e.g., extended matrilocal, nuclear, etc.) can be identified in most communities. In longitudinal perspective, these different "types" often represent different residential phases of a few family forms as they evolve over the life course. From this perspective, "residence patterns are the crystallizations, at a given time, of the developmental process" (Fortes, 1958, p. 3).

Parenthetically, this approach could be used to advantage in studies of our own society, for taking the nuclear family as the "natural" unit presses us to treat any other pattern as an aberration. The result is a Ptolemaic complexity of forms. If we begin instead with the distribution of domestic groups, we then can determine which types represent developmental phases and which are genuinely divergent. Thus, the co-residence of a widow and her sibling need not be startlingly misrepresented as a "multi-generational family" (Mindel, 1979); rather, it is one of a number of domestic groups which is now being documented as a common form in late life. This approach also may clarify those situations where domestic groups do not fit our dominant nuclear family pattern, as in many ethnic minorities and in the complex kin-groupings now being produced by multiple remarriages (Furstenberg, 1980).

The nuclear family is the most widespread unit in marital terms, although it does not universally function as such (Fortes, 1949; Mair, 1965; Minturn and Hitchcock, 1966). Generally it is too small to be maximally efficient in other respects. Thus, the basic unit of social organization in most societies is the localized kin group, made up of a number of closely related, extended families. The basic residential unit generally includes a number of these kin groups, plus other more distantly related families.

In these settings, the typical nuclear family is not the independent unit we think of. Often such nuclear units are firmly embedded in the local kin group and their autonomy is quite limited. Autonomy varies, of course, with a host of factors such as type of economy, control of resources, residential arrangements, and marriage patterns, but it is far less than we generally take for granted. For example, major decisions are generally in the hands of kin group heads. They include not only questions of subsistence activities and social control but issues we regard as personal. For example, decisions about children's futures or transition events such as puberty rituals and marriage are undertaken only with their approval. But there are few truly personal matters because the individual is too interwoven into the social fabric of the group. The nuclear unit can be so completely submerged in the larger group that even its survival as a unit is of no great moment, and divorce is commonplace.

In short, the kin group guarantees its members continuity, security, and support throughout life and often beyond. The price is individual subordination to the group and limited autonomy of the nuclear family. The goal of socialization practices in such societies is to achieve the closest possible identification of self with the group (Benedict, 1946; Dyk, 1938; Levine, 1969, 1973; Nydegger and Nydegger, 1966; B. Whiting, 1963; J. Whiting, 1941). The nuclear family, then, cannot be said to be "naturally" strong.

As to its presumed loss of functions due to modernization, a better argument can be made that the once-strong kin group, not the dependent nuclear family, has lost the most. Indeed, in those situations wherein government can be depended upon to perform many of the kin group's functions, modernization is likely to increase the nuclear family's autonomy and its control over its own members. For example, among the Navajo of the American Southwest, the first consequence of urbanization was to strengthen nuclear family bonds—at the expense of the larger kin group (Nydegger, 1970; Sasaki, 1960). Newly independent nuclear families cherish their fresh autonomy. Those who romanticize the larger kin group do so because they never experienced the heavy hand of its authority.

Where kin groups dominate, the aged are favored since control traditionally is exercised by those who are mature and often old. This is one source of the Golden Isles notion, but it remains largely mythic, for such predominance is by no means universal. Even where the aged predominate, degree of control varies widely. Most importantly, as pointed out earlier, not all leaders are old and not all old men are leaders. *De jure* authority rests in the hands of the old as a group only in a small number of age-grade societies (Coult and Habenstein, 1965; Eisenstadt, 1956; Stewart, 1977) but de facto authority is *always* limited to a few regardless of age

(Baxter and Almagor, 1978). Control by an elite of elderly men cannot be equated with high status for the elderly.

Do historical and anthropological studies, and the promise of more in the future, signal the end of the widespread myths of golden times and places for the aged? No, not for some time to come. These myths express what we feel ought to have been; because they crystallize our desires and anxieties, we want to believe them. We are not alone in this. Everywhere, in all periods, the claim is made that the old days were better, that the world is going to hell. This complaint is easy to understand: social change is often unsettling, and in nostalgic retrospect the past is simplified and regularized and its ambiguities are resolved. Past miseries cannot pierce us as do immediate misfortunes, and personal recollections tend to be gently washed in a rosy tint (Brim and Ryff, 1980; Field, 1979; Gigy, 1978; Yarrow et al., 1970). Thus, it is all too easy to project current wishes onto the past. Dull facts cannot effectively compete, so such myths have a remarkable lease on life.

The Nature of Family Ties

Americans also have established a set of Norman Rockwell idealizations about family ties, including some specific to the aged. Although they are not altogether fabulous, they are part-truths—the "good" part—and they share the golden glow of the myths just discussed. They portray the Rosy or Pollyanna family, but even a cursory glance at the ethnographic literature reveals the less photogenic side of family ties.

First, Americans have a culturally unique view of kinship as a set of personal relationships rather than formal relations (Schneider, 1968). In line with this perspective, and impelled by the best of motives, gerontologists have solidly documented supportive kin behavior and positive bonds, speaking most often of meeting needs and providing emotional support—the spectrum of tender, loving care. Acrimony is seldom mentioned; rather, they speak more blandly of children's lack of support, of not understanding, and occasionally of an older person being "difficult." The older parent, generally a mother, tends to be portrayed as a colorless, passive victim of her failing health and social disregard, whose only resource is, in Dowd's chilling phrase, "the humble capacity to comply" (1975, p. 587) with her children's wishes.

Anthropologists, on the other hand, tend to focus on the interlocking and competing sets of rights and obligations which make up adult kingroup life. They have been less concerned with qualities of relationships as such unless they reflect significant features of the kinship structure. In anthropological discussions, controls and strategies figure prominently, along with competition and hostility: a kind of kin cold war. Strife and antagonism are given their due.

It would be beneficial if we looked at each other's questions more often. Anthropological accounts undoubtedly have been guilty of overemphasizing the problems of formal family structures and of neglecting affectional ties and qualitative variation in relations among kin. Gerontologists have made the opposite error of treating conflicts induced by kin structures as individual psychological problems and of neglecting the way kin structures shape family ties and are used by the aged.

For example, family statuses impose obligations and confer rights on their members everywhere. These family systems can be maintained in two ways: (1) developing mechanisms of control which will ensure that obligations generally will be met, or (2) relying on the affection, goodwill, and enlightened self-interest of their members. No society, including our own, relies solely on the latter, although we come close to this. It is particularly dangerous for the aged to do so because their contribution to family welfare is likely to be declining and they may constitute a very real burden on resources or caretaking capacity. Structurally, they become dependent charity cases, as exchange theorists have pointed out. Consequently, they have a vested interest in the social control of obligations (Lozier and Althouse, 1974).

Mechanisms used by the aged to ensure support vary widely in number and effectiveness from society to society. They include threat by witchcraft or appeal to supernatural agencies, by rousing public opinion through gossip and public complaint, or through legal action where that is possible. At the other extreme, guilt is a common lever to pry a little extra from kin, and women favor this technique with children, especially sons. It is often the only tool they have at their disposal but, if initiated early in the child's life, it can be powerful when needed in old age. The new gerontological ethnographies are particularly rich in accounts of complex manipulative programs undertaken by women to ensure strong positions in old age (e.g., Cool and McCabe, 1981; Kerns, 1980; Wolf, 1972).

The major institutionalized mechanism, and the surest, is inheritance. Much of the strength of kinship lies in the fact that, everywhere, kinship is the predominant conduit of inheritance. It may amount to only a small cash bequest or a few personal belongings, but in most groups it includes permanent status advantages and often the very resources for survival. The consequences of inheritance patterns, for both the individual and the group, cannot be overestimated. As they play themselves out in the short and long term, they can produce fragmentation of land holdings or consolidation of property; they can create dramatic status differentials among siblings; they may determine when one is considered adult and if and when one marries. They are the primary social determinant of the economics of old age.

Individuals vary as to how strongly they cling to active control in old age. In pre-modernized societies, most remain active, dying well before physical disability is pronounced. Where the aged do reliquish authority or ownership of property, inheritance is their primary means of control over future resources and care (Nason, 1981; Streib, 1972). For example, although inheritance is essentially asymmetrical, promises of future support commonly are built explicitly into the conditions of property transfer, converting the transaction into an exchange. Threats of future disinheritance can be manipulated, often with a skill that amounts to tyranny.

The uncritical presumption has been that the use of this mechanism is limited for most Americans and that modern inheritance typically provides only an education and a small cash start in life. Parents, as good consumers, are expected to use up their savings so that estates after death will be small. (The impact of disinheritance, however, as Rosenfeld [1979]points out, even when largely symbolic, should not be underestimated.) This picture is exaggerated. For many Americans, inheritance remains a viable method of control; among some farmers, land is still "the whip" (Salamon and Lockhart, 1980). And why have we failed to study our wealthy aged, who have sizable estates to distribute? Their families are likely to have little in common with the customary gerontological picture. At the very least, we could judge to what extent the wealthy old curmudgeon, aware of his power and using it to control his family, is a literary invention or a fact of American family life.

The possibilities of control inherent in different kinship structures and the ways in which they are used at various stages of life are among the major determinants of the complex, evolving nature of lifelong family ties. Mutual recrimination, tyranny and manipulation, rejection and hate are certainly not unknown in family life, as attested to by reams of clinical literature. Nor does this picture change simply because the family members grow older; indeed, it is often exacerbated (Calkins, 1972; Cath, 1972; Isaacs et al.,1972; Robinson and Thurnher, 1979; Sainsbury and DeAlarcon, 1970; Savitsky and Sharkey, 1972; Stein, 1978). But negative relations are not necessarily expressions of individual pathology or personality characteristics; some kin-residence structures virtually guarantee difficult relations among family members.

This paper has deliberately emphasized the reverse side of our idealizations. In simple justice it must be pointed out that loving, supportive families can be found in all societies. So can their opposites. We must accept these negative aspects as natural outcomes and attempt to pinpoint those structural features that encourage conflict before we can fully understand the aged and their family ties. Especially in light of the current movement to push our aged into the bosom of the family, we should be able to assess realistically the cost to parents and to children of trying to live out a myth.

References

Amoss, P. "Religious participation as a route to prestige for the elderly." In C. Fry, ed., *Dimensions: Aging, culture, and health.* Bergin, Brooklyn, 1981.

Anderson, M. *Family structure in nineteenth-century Lancashire.* Cambridge University Press, New York, 1971.

Baker, H. *Chinese family and kinship.* Columbia University Press, New York, 1979.

Baxter, P., and Almagor, U., eds. *Age, generation and time: Some features of East African age organizations.* Hurst, London, 1978.

Benedict, R. *The chrysanthemum and the sword.* Houghton Mifflin, Boston, 1946.

Brim, O., and Ryff, C. "On the properties of life events." In P. Baltes & O. Brim, eds., *Life-span development and behavior,* Vol. 3. Academic Press, New York, 1980.

Brody, E. "Message from the president." *The Gerontologist,* 1979, *19*, 514-515.

Calkins, K. "Shouldering a burden." *Omega,* 1972, *3*, 23-36.

Cath, S. "The institutionalization of a parent—a nadir of life." *Journal of Geriatric Psychiatry,* 1972, *5*, 25-46.

Chudacoff, H., and Hareven, T. "Family transitions into old age." In T. Hareven, ed., *Transitions: The family and the life course in historical perspective.* Academic Press, New York, 1978.

Clark, M., and Anderson, B. *Culture and aging.* Charles C. Thomas, Springfield, IL., 1967.

Cool, L., and McCabe, J. "The 'Scheming Hag' and the 'Dear Old Thing.'" In J. Sokolovsky, ed., *Growing older in different societies.* Wadsworth Press, New York, 1981.

Coult, A.D., and Habenstein, R. *Cross-tabulations of Murdock's world ethnographic sample.* University of Missouri Press, Columbia, MO, 1965.

Cowgill, D. "Aging and modernization: a revision of the theory." In J. Gubrium, ed., *Late life: Communities and environmental policy.* Charles C. Thomas, Springfield, IL, 1974.

Cowgill, D., and Holmes, L., eds. *Aging and modernization.* Appleton-Century-Crofts, New York, 1972.

Dahlin, M. "Perspectives on the family life of the elderly in 1900." *The Gerontologist,* 1980, *20*, 99-107.

Delaney, B. "Is Uncle Sam insane? Pride, humor, and clique formation in a northern Thai home for the elderly." *International Journal of Aging and Human Development,* 1981, *13*, 137-150.

Demos, J. "Notes on life in Plymouth Colony." *William and Mary Quarterly,* 1965, *22*, 264-286.

Demos, J. "Families in colonial Bristol, Rhode Island: An exercise in historical demography." *William and Mary Quarterly,* 1968, *25*, 40-57.

Demos, J. "Old age in early New England." In J. Demos & S. Boocock, eds., *Turning points: Historical and sociological essays on the family. American Journal of Sociology,* supplement to Vol. 84. University of Chicago Press, Chicago, 1978.

Dowd, J. "Aging as exchange: A preface to theory." *Journal of Gerontology,* 1975, *30,* 584-594.

Dyk, W., ed. *Son of Old Man Hat: A Navaho autobiography.* Harcourt Brace, New York, 1938.

Eisenstadt, S.N. *From generation to generation.* Free Press, New York, 1956.

Field, D. "Retrospective reports of personal events in the lives of elderly people." Unpublished paper presented at the meeting of the International Society for the Study of Behavioral Development, Stockholm, 1979.

Fischer, D. H. *Growing old in America.* Oxford University Press, New York, 1978.

Foner, A., and Kertzer, D. "Transitions over the life course: Lessons from age-set societies." *American Journal of Sociology,* 1978, *83,* 1081-1104.

Fortes, M. "Time and social structure." In M. Fortes, ed., *Social structure.* Oxford University Press, Oxford, England, 1949.

Fortes, M. "Introduction." In J. Goody, ed., *The developmental cycle in domestic groups.* Cambridge University Press, Cambridge, England, 1958.

Furstenberg, F., Jr. "Reflections on remarriage." *Journal of Family Issues,* 1980, *1,* 443-453.

Gigy, L. "Reconstruction of the personal past: differences in older women." Unpublished paper presented at the 31st Annual Scientific Meeting of the Gerontological Society, Dallas, 1978.

Glascock, T., and Feinman, S. "A holocultural analysis of old age." *Comparative Social Research,* 1980, *3.*

Goody, J., ed. *The developmental cycle in domestic groups.* Cambridge University Press, Cambridge, England, 1958.

Greven, P. J. "Family structure in seventeenth-century Andover, Massachusetts." *William and Mary Quarterly,* 1966, *23,* 234-356.

Harlan, W. "Social status of the aged in three Indian villages." *Vita Humana,* 1964, *7,* 239-252.

Hendricks, J., and Hendricks, C. "The age-old question of old age: Was it really so much better back when?" *International Journal of Aging and Human Development,* 1977-78, *8,* 139-154.

Holmes, L. "The role and status of the aged in changing Samoa." In D. Cowgill and L. Holmes eds., *Aging and modernization.* Appleton-Century-Crofts, New York, 1972.

Isaacs, B., Livingstone, T., and Neville, Y. *Survival of the unfittest.* Routledge & Kegan Paul, London, 1972.

Kastenbaum, R., and Ross, B. "Historical perspectives on care." In J. Howells, ed., *Modern perspectives in the psychiatry of old age.* Brunner/Mazel, New York, 1975.

Kerns, V. "Aging and mutual support relations among the black Carib." In C. Fry, ed., *Aging in culture and society.* Bergin, Brooklyn, 1980.

Kobrin, F. "The fall in household size and the rise of the primary individual in the United States." *Demography,* 1976, *13,* 127-138.

Laslett, P. *The world we have lost.* Methuen, London, 1965.

Laslett, P. "Size and structure of the household in England over three centuries." *Population Studies,* 1969, 23, 199-224.

Laslett, P. "Societal development and aging." In R. Binstock and E. Shanas, eds., *Handbook of aging and the social sciences.* Van Nostrand, New York, 1976.

Lee, R., and DeVore, I. *Man the hunter.* Aldine, Chicago, 1968.

Levine, R. "Intergenerational tensions and extended family structures in Africa." In E. Shanas and G. Streib, eds., *Social structure and the family: Generational relations*. Prentice-Hall, Englewood Cliffs, NJ, 1965.

Levine, R. "Culture, personality, and socialization: An evolutionary view." In D. Goslin, ed., *Handbook of socialization theory and research*. Rand McNally, Chicago, 1969.

Levine, R. *Culture, behavior and personality*. Aldine, Chicago, 1973.

Lipman, A. "Prestige of the aged in Portugal." *International Journal of Aging and Human Development*, 1970, *1*, 127-136.

Litwak, E. "Geographic mobility and extended family cohesion." *American Sociological Review*, 1960, *25*, 385-394.

Lockridge, K. A. "The population of Dedham, Massachusetts, 1636-1736." *Economic History Review*, 1966, *19*, 318-344.

Lozier, J., and Althouse, R. "Social enforcement of behavior toward elders in an Appalachian mountain settlement." *The Gerontologist*, 1974, *14*, 69-80.

Mair, L. *An introduction to social anthropology*. Oxford University Press, Oxford, England, 1965.

Maxwell, R., and Silverman, P. "Information and esteem: Cultural considerations in the treatment of the aged." *International Journal of Aging and Human Development*, 1970, *1*, 361-392.

Mindel, C. "Multigenerational family households: Recent trends and implications for the future." *The Gerontologist*, 1979, *19*, 456-463.

Minturn, L., and Hitchcock, J. *The Rajputs of Khalapur, India*. Wiley, New York, 1966.

Nason, J. "Respected elder or old person: Aging in a Micronesian community." In P. Amoss and S. Harrell, eds., *Other ways of growing old*. Stanford University Press, Stanford, CA, 1981.

Nydegger, C. "Effects of structural changes on Navajo familial roles." Unpublished master's thesis, Cornell University, Ithaca, NY, 1970.

Nydegger, C. "Gerontology and anthropology: Challenge and opportunity." In C. Fry, ed., *Dimensions: aging, culture, and health*. Bergin, Brooklyn, 1981.

Nydegger, W., and Nydegger, C. *Tarong, an Ilocos barrio in the Philippines*. Wiley, New York, 1966.

Osako, M. "Aging and the family among Japanese Americans." *The Gerontologist*, 1979, *19*, 448-455.

Palmore, E., and Manton, K. "Modernization and status of the aged: International correlations." *Journal of Gerontology*, 1974, *29*, 205-210.

Press, I., and McKool. M., Jr. "Social structure and status of the aged." *International Journal of Aging and Human Development*, 1972, *3*, 297-306.

Pryor, E.T., Jr. "Rhode Island family structure: 1815 and 1960." In P. Laslett and R. Wall, eds., *Household and family in past time*. Cambridge University Press, Cambridge, England, 1972.

Robinson, B., and Thurnher, M. Taking care of aged parents: A family cycle transition." *The Gerontologist*, 1979, *19*, 586-593.

Rosenfeld, J.P. *The legacy of aging: Inheritance and disinheritance in social perspective*. Ablex Publishers, Norwood, NJ, 1979.

Rosow, I. "Old age: One moral dilemma of an affluent society." *The Gerontologist*, 1962, *2*, 182-191.

Sainsbury, P., and DeAlarcon, J. "The effects of community care on the family of the geriatric patient." *Journal of Geriatric Psychiatry*, 1970, *4*, 23-41.

Salamon, S., and Lockhart, V. "Land ownership and the position of elderly in farm families." *Human Organization*, 1980, *39*, 324-331.

Sasaki, T. *Fruitland, New Mexico: A Navaho community in transition.* Cornell University Press, Ithaca, NY, 1960.

Savitsky, E., and Sharkey, H. "Study of family interaction in the aged." *Journal of Geriatric Psychiatry*, 1972, *5*, 3-19.

Schneider, D. *American kinship: A cultural account.* Prentice-Hall, Englewood Cliffs, NJ, 1968.

Seward, R. *The American family: A demographic history.* Sage Library of Social Research, Vol. 70. Sage, Beverly Hills, CA, 1978.

Shanas, E., and Streib, G., eds. *Social structure of the family: Generational relations.* Prentice-Hall, Englewood Cliffs, NJ, 1965.

Shanas, E., and Sussman, M., eds. *Older people, family, and bureaucracy.* Duke University Press, Durham, NC, 1976.

Shanas, E., Townsend, P., Wedderburn, D., Friis, H., Mihoj, P., and Stehouwer, J. *Old people in three industrial societies.* Atherton, New York, 1968.

Sheehan, T. "Senior esteem as a factor of socioeconomic complexity." *The Gerontologist*, 1976, *16*, 433-440.

Shelton, A. "The aged and eldership among the Igbo." In D. Cowgill and L. Holmes, eds., *Aging and modernization.* Appleton-Century-Crofts, New York, 1972.

Simmons, L. *The role of the aged in primitive society.* Yale University Press, New Haven, CT, 1945.

Spencer, P. *The Samburu: A study of gerontocracy in a nomadic tribe.* University of California Press, Berkeley, 1965.

Stearns, P. *Old age in European society.* Holmes & Meier, New York, 1977.

Stearns, P. "The evolution of traditional culture toward aging." In J. Hendricks and C. Hendricks, ed., *Dimensions of aging.* Winthrop, Cambridge, MA, 1979.

Stearns, P. "The modernization of old age in France: Approaches through history." *International Journal of Aging and Human Development*, 1981, *13*, 297-315.

Stein, H. "Aging and death among Slovak-Americans." *Journal of Psychological Anthropology*, 1978, *1*, 297-320.

Stewart, F.H. *Fundamentals of age-group systems.* Academic Press, New York, 1977.

Streib, G. "Old age in Ireland." In D. Cowgill and L. Holmes, eds., *Aging and modernization.* Appleton-Century-Crofts, New York, 1972.

Whiting, B. ed. *Six cultures: Studies of child rearing.* Wiley, New York, 1963.

Whiting, J.W.M. *Becoming a Kwoma.* Yale University Press, New Haven, CT, 1941.

Wolf, M. *Women and family in rural Taiwan.* Stanford University Press, Stanford, CA, 1972.

Yarrow, M., Campbell, J., and Burton, R. "Recollections of childhood: A study of the retrospective method." Society for Research in Child Development, Washington, DC, Monograph No. 35, 1970.

6

The Dega and the Nacirema:
Then and Now

Paul M. Baker

About 30 years ago, an anthropologist named Horace Miner described some of the peculiar body rituals among a tribe called the Nacirema. Most of his writing concerned the repressive sexual attitudes and primitive medical practices of that culture. Very little was said about the position of older people among the Nacirema. However, an unpublished manuscript was recently discovered which describes the relationship between the Nacirema and another tribe called the Dega. This manuscript was written in 1958 by Dr. L.N. Rekab of Adanac University, and portions of it are presented for the first time below.

I believe this material is vitally important because it gives us an eyewitness account of the abuses inflicted upon the Dega by the Nacirema culture, and because it offers a historical baseline by which we can judge the progress which has been made since that time.

"For some time now, members of the Dega tribe have been migrating into the village occupied by the Nacirema. Relations between the two cultures are far from cordial. Perhaps the best way to describe the situation is that the Nacirema treat the Dega like visiting relatives who have overstayed their welcome. The Nacirema prohibit the Dega from taking any active part in the economy, except for some child-care work, or tending the sick and the lame among their own group. This work is called *gnireet-nulov* and is never rewarded with pay or goods. The Nacirema explain that the Dega refuse to accept compensation because that would take away the honor of *gnireet-nulov* and turn it into mere labor. The Dega told me they had never been offered any pay."

"The Dega appear to be slaves to the Nacirema, although neither group seems aware of the relationship. The Dega are not subjected to long days of

86

hard labor, but are kept in a state of enforced idleness. They are given a meager allowance for food and clothing, called a *noisnep*, which gives them a standard of living not much better than the poorest Nacirema. Some of them are permitted to live in their own individual huts, but many of the Dega are forced to live in group quarters called *gnisrun* homes. They are confined to small rooms, usually shared with another Dega, all their personal possessions are taken away from them, and they are tended by apprentices of the village witch doctor."

"The daily life of the Dega is occupied mainly by sedentary activities. The Nacirema encourage them to play children's games and to do some weaving, but the articles they produce are given away, not sold in the market. A favorite pastime of the Dega is a sport called *flog*. Small white rocks are hit with a stick, over a large area of long grass, sand pits, and ponds. The aim of the game is to find the rock after you hit it. Each player has to buy a dozen special rocks from the Nacirema who makes them, who is called the *orp*. The player who returns at the end of the day with the most rocks is given free drinks by the other players. Sometimes the wealthy Nacirema also play *flog*, but never on the same day as the Dega. The Nacirema complain that the Dega take too long to finish the game. One of the Dega told me that the reason they played so slowly was that they had nothing else to do anyway, so enjoyed the company and the fresh air."

"Recently, television has come to the village. This modern technology was supplied by charitable organizations of the Western world to promote educational development, but it seems to be used almost entirely as a hypnotic device to amuse children and placate the Dega. During the day, while the children are at school and the Nacirema are working, the Dega spend a great deal of time watching game shows and soap operas. They are encouraged to take mood-altering drugs so that they do not notice the poor quality and the repetitious nature of the shows. At night, when the Nacirema come back to their huts to rest and relax, the Dega are prohibited from watching television and are sent to bed. In the *gnisrun* homes, only a single television set is provided; and the Dega there often argue loudly about what show should be watched. Many of them are deaf or blind, however, and so the choice of programs is often made by the witch doctor's apprentices, who are paid so little that they consider this television time as one of the fringe benefits of their jobs."

"Other activities of the Dega include frequent visits to the witch doctor and to the village temple. The witch doctor does not consider most of the illnesses of the Degas to be real ones, perhaps because of their low status in the village. Usually, various drugs are given out, including the same kind of hallucinogenic substances that are given to the young warriors before battles or ceremonies. Among the Dega, however, these drugs seem to have little effect, although it is difficult to tell, because they sit in a daze most of the time anyway."

"The temple is the major gathering place for the Dega. They attend the religious ceremonies regularly, but conversations with the priest and the Dega revealed a curious discrepancy. While the priest was sure that they believed fervently in the religious teachings, most of the Dega said that they did not really believe, but liked to see their friends and listen to the music."

"The temple is also used for activities which are a major source of excitement for the Dega. The most popular activity is a game of chance called *ognib* which consists of chanting by the priest and the creation of magic geometric shapes by the Dega. At the end of each chant, one of the players shouts the name of the game and jumps up and down with great excitement. The priest inspects the magic shape to see if it has been done correctly, and if it was, presents a clay pot to the winner. These games last far into the night, and seem to serve several functions for the village. First, because they are kept busy creating the magic shapes, the Dega improve their hand-eye coordination. Second, the games help to support the temple coffers, since each player has to pay a tithe to the priest before each game. A great scandal occurred while I was visiting the village, when the priest secretly rigged the games so there would be few winners. One of the Dega discovered this, bit him on the leg, and took all the clay pots. It took the priest 2 months to recover. The third, and perhaps most important function of these games appears to be population control. The games are so full of tension and excitement that almost every night one of the Degas collapses and dies of a heart attack."

"In fact, the death rate among the Dega is very high. This is due to their poor diet, inactivity, and abuse by the Nacirema. They eat very little, and most of their food lacks nutritive value. Some of them have been observed stealing the fodder given to cattle, because it is more nutritious than their prescribed diet. The inactivity of the Dega makes them weak, and susceptible to arteriosclerotic disease. The males commonly die from heart attacks or strokes, while both sexes have very brittle bones which break easily when they are "accidently" pushed down hills by the Nacirema. Many of the Dega die under mysterious circumstances, and it is difficult to determine whether a death was due to accident, suicide, or abuse."

"The sexual practices of the Dega are either nonexistent, or are very well-hidden. No births have ever been observed among the Dega, so it may be inferred that they are beyond their reproductive years. However, there seems to be no sexual activity at all. I asked one Nacirema warrior if he had ever heard of such activity among the Dega, but he just laughed loudly, saying "that would be like two rocks trying to lay an egg!" When I asked if any Nacirema had sexual relations with the Dega, he turned pale, spat on the ground, and told me he would rather sleep with a wild pig. Even though some of the Dega are very good-looking, the Nacirema consider them all as sterile, sexless individuals."

"What will become of the Dega? Their future looks bleak, but I observed that new members arrive almost daily from the forest outside the village. Because of this immigration, there seems to be an increase in their numbers each month. When food was scarce, there was some talk among the young Nacirema warriors of attacking the Dega, but this was discouraged by the older warriors, who seemed more sympathetic to them."

"The total population in the village seems to be kept in check by the disappearance of the Nacirema warriors after the ceremony of the gold sundial. This ceremony occurs only among the oldest of the Nacirema, who are given a small sundial and sent off into the forest to rest before they battle with the great spirits. Only one warrior ever returned while I was in the village, and he had gone crazy. He came back and began embracing the Dega, crying out 'Brother! Sister!' He was put out of his deluded misery by a young warrior."

What has happened in the quarter century since Dr. Rekab wrote this account? Well, the Dega have not died out. In fact, their numbers have increased dramatically since then, and most of the abuses put upon them by the Nacirema have disappeared. The *gnisrun* homes have been improved, the *noisnep* plans are providing a better standard of living for the Dega, and the Dega themselves are taking on a more active role in Nacirema society. To be sure, there are still some problems that need solving. However, it is a sure bet that the Dega will never again be second-class citizens.

Note

7

The "Scheming Hag" and The "Dear Old Thing": The Anthropology of Aging Women

Linda Evans Cool and Justine McCabe

One of the most salient features in the research now available on human aging is that there is no *one* entity that can be termed the "aged." Yet, in spite of a call for its recognition (Maddox, 1969b: 7-8), the issue of the heterogeneity of experiences and interests among older people has been largely preempted by an apparent desire to focus on homogeneity in the aging process. As a case in point, although there are obvious and universally recognized differences in the biological endowment and in the social, cultural, and psychological experiences of men and women, surprisingly little attention has been devoted to the question of whether and/or how women and men differ in the aging process. In fact, the attention that has been focused on the condition of older women has tended to center on two stereotypes that appear at opposite ends of a power/weakness continuum. On the one hand, many societies (and the anthropologists who study them) represent older women as scheming manipulators of personal and magical powers—powers over which they may not have full control. At the opposite extreme lie the representations of older women as smiling, kindly grandmothers whose main interest in life is amusing and spoiling grandchildren. In actuality, the experiences of older women may lie somewhere between these extremes, and, as for most people, the differences that do appear among them are the result of psychological, social, and cultural variables. Often the particular representation of a society's older women is as much a cultural myth and even a creation of the anthropologist's expectations as it is a depiction of a "social reality."

The implicit challenge to anthropology in the area of gerontology is to question existing theories of aging by putting them to the cross-cultural test and to formulate cross-cultural models of aging as a universal phenomenon which transcends the immediate sociopolitical situations of industrialized nations. As Shanas et al. have observed, we must seek both to ask and answer " . . . the basic question: can a hypothesis about social behavior be considered proved by a study carried out within a single culture?" (1968:7). This present work attempts to review, integrate, and evaluate the theories and data that do exist concerning female and male responses to aging. More importantly, this chapter provides, by means of detailed examples, a useful method of analyzing the aging process of men and women in the hope that new interest and dialogues may be kindled in this area.

Women and Aging: The Comparative Approach

Prior to the 1960s, Leo Simmons's (1945) monograph was the only anthropological work devoted to the subject of aging (Clark, 1973:79). As one facet of his study, Simmons compared sex-role related differences in the aging experience. He concluded by denying the existence of any "feminine patriarchy" in later life, at least in terms of *formal* office holding. In fact, only two of the societies which Simmons examined yielded examples of women (young or old) who held office. Based on such findings concerning formal office holding by women, Simmons dismisses women's ability to exercise control functions in society. However, in pursuing this argument, he overlooks very important areas of potential control and dominance for women, namely informal networks and *de facto* power: gossip groups which control others' actions by their negative and public commentary, self-help groups, communications networks for the sharing of information, and private dominance in the households.

In a later attempt to estimate the extent of possible matriarchy among older women, Gold (1960) questioned 24 anthropologists about their observations of age variations in the sex-role patterns of the various cultures they had studied: 13 reported a matriarchal shift; 11 reported no change; no one reported an increase in dominance among older men. Gold only partly concurs with Simmon's earlier generalizations:

> Like him, I find that matrilineality coincides with old women being dominant over old men. There is also some support of his finding that women tend to be dominant over old men in hunting-gathering societies, since two of the three examples in my sample [of 24] manifest the pattern (Blackfoot and Mohave versus the Pilaga). . . . The peasant communities (and urban middle class America), with their strong emphasis on ideal male supremacy but actual pattern of old women dominating old men, conflict with his observa-

tion that where there is settled agriculture, old men tend to be dominant; if the people are peasants, the old women get the upper hand [1960:II].

In a more recent attempt to study sex-role differences in aging by means of a large-scale, cross-cultural comparison, Bart (1969) selected 30 societies representing the eight culture areas of the world from data contained in the Human Relations Area Files. From these societies, she gathered information on the presence of "six post-child-rearing roles available to women" (1962:2): grandmother, mother or mother-in-law, economic producer, participator in government, performer of religious or magical rites, and daughter of aged parents. Working from the belief that in American society women lose one of their most important identity-giving roles (namely mother) which results in a "mutilated self" (Rose, 1962), Bart sought to document the relationship between changes in status and the availability of important roles. In general, she found that when society has a multiplicity of roles available for older women their status "not only does not drop necessarily at this stage of the life cycle, but in most cases also rises" (1969:15). According to Bart, only two of the six roles she examined are *not* associated with higher status for women, namely economic producer ("it cannot be concluded that the mere presence of an economic role will keep women's status from declining" [Bart, 1969:4]) and daughter of aged parents (a role found only rarely).

One obvious problem with studies of this kind involves definitions. For example, Bart says that she did not include housekeeping and food preparation as economic producer roles for they are so common. But, might not a woman's *control* and leadership in these activities in the context of her household or family be considered such a producer role, or at least provide the woman with a positive self-image? In a similar vein, Simmons, Gold, and Bart all include consideration of some formal aspect of control (Bart talks of "participator in government" and Simmons of "formal office holding") and conclude that women (of any age) rarely are allowed to fill such roles. Rather than focusing on *public* control through formalized offices, it seems that studies ought to deal with areas where women in a variety of cultures do seem to have some power: informal networks, the domestic situation, and personal attributes. These, of course, are difficult to recognize and code in nomothetic (based on public roles and laws) studies.

Finally, like so much of this nomothetic research, Bart's work has illuminated certain structural features of society which seem to be associated with a particular aspect of life. But she is unable to prove a casual relationship or deal effectively with individual manipulations of these structural features. For example, Bart has suggested that a woman's status does not remain static throughout the life cycle. However, she cannot illustrate *how* a woman undergoes such status variations. Is the change abrupt or gradual, is the woman able to control the timing of the status change or is she at the mercy of external forces? Even though Bart does examine six societies in more detail, the reader is not particularly enlightened in the dynamics of *how* and *why* the status changes come about. The remainder of this article will attempt to resolve these questions by examining structural and cultural factors which influence the female response to aging in a variety of cultures.

The Paradox of the Aging American Woman

Studies carried out in the United States have not only failed to provide clear-cut answers to questions concerning gender differences in the aging process, but have produced confusing and often contradictory results. This becomes evident in the kinds of portraits painted of older women by a variety of researchers.

The Ignored Older Women

Some studies characterize older American women as members of a minority group who see themselves as a social problem: a group of people who have been excluded from full participation in society, accorded an inferior position within it, and denied access to power and authority (Bell, 1970; Lopata, 1971; Palmore, 1971; Sommers, 1974; Sontag, 1972). In this perspective, women seem particularly disadvantaged as they age since the roles that are allowed them in American society either are never accorded real power or are rendered obsolete by time, for example childbearer or sex object. Older women's lack of power and status is reflected in their invisibility in American society and their absence as subjects in research endeavors. Lewis and Butler (1972) have pointed out that even the women's liberation movement has largely ignored the problems of older women by focusing on issues of special concern to younger women such as abortion and day care facilities. In all fairness, however, it must be stated that the social sciences are not the only area to render women invisible. Nancy Sheehan (1976:59), for example, notes that most historical studies of women are written by men who seem to be bent on preserving the status quo and that ". . . while histories of men are written concerning their relationship to the environment, histories of women are written concerning their relationship to men."

The Depressed Older Woman

An indication of the difficulties that American women face in growing older is reflected in the incidence of middle-age depression among women.

Although American folk wisdom (and often science) attributes such depression to biological changes occurring during "the change of life," Bart found no cross-cultural correlation between the biological fact of the menopause and depression: "Depressions in middle-aged women are due to their lack of important roles and subsequent loss of self-esteem rather than hormonal changes of menopause" (1972:139). The roles that women are allowed to play in America (wife and mother) are such that a woman's sense of worth comes not from her own accomplishments but from the lives of others, namely her husband and children. As these people change or depart, a woman must be able to change her self-concept or face debilitating psychological stress.

Other social scientists (e.g., Davis, 1979; Dowty, 1971; Flint, 1975; Neugarten and Kraines, 1965; Neugarten et al., 1963; Silverman, 1967; Vatuk, 1975) have also attempted to distinguish culturally determined responses to menopause from those biological imperatives shared by women in all societies. Like Bart, Flint (1975, 1976) links a woman's status from midlife on to the attitudes and symptoms that characterize menopause. In contrast to the experiences of American postmenopausal women, Flint describes the situation of Indian Rajput women for whom menopause marks the end of *purdah* and the beginning of a freedom and power previously unknown to them:

> When these women were asked if they had any problems associated with the menopause, a most ususual response was forthcoming. Few women were found who had other than menstrual cycle changes—there were no depression migraines, no incapacitations, nor any of the classical symptoms associated with what we call the "menopausal syndrome." Furthermore, these women informed the author that they were eagerly looking forward to achieving this event in their lives, if they had not yet achieved it, and if they had already reached the menopause, they were also most positive about this fact [Flint, 1976: 48].

In general, the aforementioned studies have all suggested that high or unchanging female status in middle age will be related to a positive attitude toward and/or the absence of difficulty with menopause. In contrast, Davis (1979) emphasizes the emic perceptions of menopause and the *total* biosocial self of the Anglican women she interviewed in a Newfoundland fishing village. These women were found to have a very high status and positive self-image *throughout* adulthood. Furthermore, this high status persisted in the face of the negative physical symptoms and attitudes that the *majority* of women experienced in menopause. Davis (1979:7) explains this by three factors: (1) that bodily, psychological, and sociocultural processes are not compartmentalized, (2) that menopause is viewed as a normal process, and (3) that the major symptoms of menopause are not considered unique to midlife or cessation of the menses. Within the anthropological literature on the menopause, Davis's study is unique in its treatment of the menopause as one more biosocial phenomenon—no more or less signifi-cant—within the context of *all* biosocial events of the culture in question:

> Newfoundland women do not distinguish among biological, psychological, and social realms of experience. The folk notions of nerves and blood act in the conceptual integration of these realms throughout adult life. They have a folk system which explains what is happening to their minds and bodies at menopause and provides a female support system for those who experience difficulty. This effective support system reflects the continual high status of Newfoundland women which is characterized by extensive social networks, open communication channels, and a varied range of meaningful activities [Davis, 1979:13-14].

What about the Men?

While Bart and Davis have approached the study of menopause dif-ferently, both researchers' data suggest a similar theory to explain some depression among middle-aged men. Typically, those older American men who suffer depression, according to Bart (1972:142), have immersed them-selves in their jobs just as the "feminine" women have immersed them-selves in their children and husbands. And, like the women whose children leave home, these men face depression upon retirement when all the public "props" to their self-esteem are removed. The severity (and disastrous con-sequences) of such depression is evidenced by the fact that in the urban American setting men die earlier than their female counterparts and also are more likely to commit suicide (Gutmann, 1980:442). Similarly, Davis (1979:5) indicates that because of the relentlessly strenuous physical life endured by the Newfoundland fishermen she observed, many of these men at middle age must relinquish the high status role of fisherman for the alien one of a land-based worker, supported by disability or unemployment insurance or work at the local fish plant. Thus it appears that in this case too, without the "props" to his self-esteem, and threatened by a loss of status, the middle-aged Newfoundland man—not the woman—is apt to become depressed.

The Older Woman as a Success Story

One general attitude fostered by some gerontological literature (see es-pecially Cumming, 1964) in comparing female and male reactions to the aging process is that personal adjustment to later stages of the life cycle is somehow easier for women than for men because of the women's "smoother life cycle." The argument here is that from girlhood to death, a woman's key roles (wife and mother) remain essentially unchanged, while men suffer the sudden and complete loss of their core roles (worker and provider) when they reach retirement age. Although this situation is particularly dramatic in industrialized nations like the United States which have artificially created mandatory retirement ages, Cumming's implication is that women universally face fewer age-related social and personal adjustment problems than do their male counterparts because of this "smooth," continuous social development.

While apparently agreeing with Cumming that women are more successful at adjusting to age changes, Kline (1975) suggests that this success may be due *not* to social role continuity (the "smooth" life cycle), but rather to women's socialization to repeated role loss and to their ensuing adaptability to role change. Thus, according to this argument, women experience fewer adjustment problems as they grow older because they are more accustomed to dealing with status and role variations, of which aging is merely one more example.

Age, the Great Leveler of Sex-Role Differences

The research of Lipman (1961) and Cameron (1967,1968) among aging populations in the United States generally provides a different outlook on the experience of aging. Their studies suggest that old age is in fact a greater leveler of sex-role differences, for men and women become increasingly more alike as they grow older. Specifically, Lipman (1961:271) finds that the retirement of the husband contributes to the apparent egalitarian character of the observed marriages, and that, consequently, such marriages appear to be happier. According to Lipman, this egalitarian state is fostered by the sharing of household tasks, which are no longer defined as the wife's duties, and by the emphasis on the expressive aspects of marriage, such as love, companionship, and affection. These trends lead Lipman to conclude that in such happy, older marriages, ". . . apparently role differentiation by sex is reduced with increased age and retirement" (1961:271).

In a similar vein, Cameron's data indicate that the *interests* of the aged may be typed as feminine, while their basic personality is more typically masculine than that of a comparison group of young people (1968:64). Although his data actually seem to support the concept that older men and women have convergent interests, Cameron interprets this tendency as a reflection of socioeconomic status rather than old age per se:

> Accessibility to and success in various kinds of endeavors also determine interests. The lower SES and general physical weakening of the aged often preclude participation in the relatively expensive and vigorous masculine activities. One often has to be content with what one can do, and what one does is generally what one professes to desire [1968:65].

Unfortunately, Cameron provides no examples of these "expensive and vigorous" interests.

Sex Role Reversal in Old Age: The Dominant Older Woman

The research of Cumming and Henry (1961), Kerckhoff (1966), Lowenthal et al. (1975), Neugarten (1968), and Neugarten and Gutmann (1968) contrasts with the position of Lipman. For example, Lowenthal et al. find that middle-aged and older women become more dominant in the family, and Kerckhoff (1966:179-80) believes that he has found data indicating

> a greater sensitivity to interpersonal relationships in the conjugal unit on the part of the husband and a greater concern with the practical activities of daily living on the part of the wife. If such an interpretation is acceptable, it would indicate a kind of role reversal from the presumed model of husband-wife relationship in our society which calls for the husband to emphasize an instrumental orientation and the wife to have more of an expressive orientation.

In attempting to make a comparison with non-American populations, one finds a relative dearth of cross-cultural gerontological literature with regard to gender differences in aging. For example, this possible "role reversal" among aging American men and women has been only alluded to in studies of other cultures.[1] In one of the more detailed comparisons, Kardiner et al. (1945:65) describe the older Comanche women:

> Women, with few exceptions, had no power before the menopause. After the menopause a woman could acquire power as readily as a man. It was common for a medicine man to have his wife assist him, teaching her everything that was required for curing, except rituals for the actual transfer of power. Immediately after the menopause, the husband gave power to her. . . .After the menopause, the distinction between the sexes, as far as medicine power went, was largely disregarded. . . .As she grows older her security becomes greater. . . .In comparison with the male, therefore, the woman starts with initial disadvantage, but she has greater mobility as she gets older.

Similarly, Borgese (1964) and Gutmann (1974,1977) note that over the life cycle women who had earlier been subordinate to men with regard to authority (Rosaldo, 1974), become quite dominant and powerful vis-à-vis men. In Gutmann's terms, men begin with active mastery of their biosocial environment and move toward passive mastery (characterized by dependence and passivity) with increasing age and lessening physical capabilities. Women, on the other hand, move from passive mastery (cultural deference to and resulting personal dependence on fathers and husbands) to active mastery of their social environments in later life. Gutmann argues that such inner subjective shifts together with their overt behavioral indicators are universal for men and women.

The Older Woman as Witch

A traditional context in which older women are seen as dominant and aggressive within the anthropological literature is the recurrent theme of the older woman as witch or sorcerer (for example, Evans-Pritchard, 1937; Fortes, 1962; Fuller, 1961; Harper, 1969; Kluckhohn, 1967; LeVine, 1963; and Nadel, 1952). In these cases, even implicit recognition by men of the power of senescent women can often be made only by ascribing evil motivations to their hegemony. Fuller (1961:51) confirms this in her description of the Lebanese villagers she studied: "Men sense this invisible power of woman. To older women, in particular, is attributed the power of witchcraft or of the evil eye, both signs of an uncanny force."

One possible explanation for this malevolent characterization of older women is a correlation suggested by Douglas (1966:120):

> Where the social system recognizes positions of authority, those holding such positions are endowed with explicit spiritual power, controlled, conscious, external, and approved—powers to bless or curse. Where the social system requires people to hold dangerously ambiguous roles, these persons are credited with uncontrolled, unconscious, dangerous, disapproved powers—such as witchcraft and evil eye.

Nadel's work among the Nupe of Northern Nigeria appears to support this viewpoint: older Nupe women occupy an ambiguous position in their society. They are female and therefore normatively inferior to men; yet, they resemble the male cultural ideal by possessing power (albeit *de facto* power). In other words, in these situations, because women are, in men's eyes, usurping what is "rightfully" male (i.e, the exercise of power), men "punish" older women by accusing them of witchcraft and other acts of malevolence.

> The general picture is that of a sharp sex-antagonism, which assigns the evil intentions to the female, and to the male, a benevolent and ideally decisive—if somewhat utopian role. . . . Men are never blamed or accused of witchcraft, and the main collective weapon against witchcraft lies in the activities of a male secret society which, by threats and torture, "cleanses" the villages of witchcraft. . . . In the majority of cases the alleged witch is a woman, usually an older and domineering female, who would attack a younger man who somehow fell under her dominance. . . . The men, though on the utopian or fantasy plane the masters of the female witchcraft, are, on the plane of "real" incidents and fears, its main victims.

A second possible explanation is that this pervasive ascription of evil motivation to older women is related to their actual powerlessness and low status position. This reasoning is pursued by Harper (1969) in his study of the belief system of the Havik Brahmins of South India. In this situation, Harper (1969:81) proposes that the dangerous nature attributed to Havik widows may be the result of guilt on the part of those who occupy high status positions (men) toward those who formally lack power and prestige and occupy the lowest positions (widows) in this social system.

Despite their explicitly inferior and powerless status, Havik women are, in fact, rather powerful, at least in a negative sense: They influence and affect the lives and behavior of others—especially men. In keeping with Havik men's attitudes toward all women, it is possible that widows, who are mainly older females, are feared simply because they are believed to possess the ultimately powerful weapon—death through witchcraft. However, Harper's explanation of guilt on the part of high status Havik men could be made even more compelling. At present, it merely emphasizes projections of *recent* resentment of Havik widows, and their *currently* intolerable status; instead, this explanation could be extended to attribute males' fears to projections of *long-hidden,* accumulated anger which men could expect these mainly older women to feel and express in response to a lifelong inferior position.

Culture and Women's Status

An increasingly significant source of data with regard to women's power in society is found in anthropological studies of women's status. This growing body of literature (e.g., Collier, 1974; Friedl, 1975; Lamphere, 1974; Murphy and Murphy, 1974; Quinn, 1977; Wolf, 1972) indicates that female solidarity, flexibility, and a keen perception of male-female relationships characterize women with age, and enable them to adapt with increasing success to situations normally controlled by men. One emphasis of this literature is that, although the power of women—old and young—increases most dramatically in informal, domestic settings, its expression is felt throughout the societies in question.

For example, Wolf (1972:40) describes the influence that older Taiwanese women have on men's behavior in a family of which they are never a member but to which they are essential:

> Taiwanese women can and do make use of their collective power to lose face for their menfolk in order to influence decisions that ostensibly are not theirs to make. Although young women may have little or no influence over their husbands and would not dare express an unsolicited opinion . . . to their

fathers-in-law, older women who have raised their sons properly retain considerable influence over their sons' actions, even in activities exclusive to
men. . . . When a man behaves in a way that they consider wrong, they talk
about it—not only among themselves, but to their sons and husbands.

By banding together in informal gossip and work groups, these Taiwanese
women have gained a great deal of power to effect changes and maintain
some independence in their lives—an ability unavailable to a lone woman
living in the "foreign" territory of her husband's patriclan. Without such an
informal control mechanism, the Taiwanese woman would be as powerless
and unsupported as the stereotyped image predicts.

We could continue to cite references to the increasing power to senescent
women in many dissimilar societies. However, it becomes increasingly
clear that two themes regarding gender differences in adaptation to aging
that have been reported in research carried out in the United States are not
apparent in the literature concerning the aging experience in other
cultures. The first is the theme of the older woman becoming depressed
with increasing age, and the second concerns age as the great leveler of sex-
role differences. This latter theme emphasizes the male loss of power to
bring him down to the level of women, while much of the cross-cultural
literature emphasizes the increased status of older women. This is not to
say that these themes are "wrong." These situations may hold in the United
States because of specific social and cultural features which must be determined. Whatever their cultural sources, these adaptations to the aging
process are not a universal or biological fact of life to be faced by all older
men and women.

Two conclusions appear from the cross-cultural evidence cited so far: (1)
Women in many disparate societies becomes increasingly dominant and
powerful as they age, and (2) with such a transition in female power and
status, there may be a concomitant decline in the power and dominance of
the older men in these societies. The remainder of this article will focus on
a detailed analysis of two distinct cultures in an effort to determine the
bases of self-perceived success in adjustment to growing older among men
and women. In particular, we will focus on two of the adaptive strategies
employed by women which were delineated earlier: (1) the self-assessed
success of older women as based on the continuity of the core role
throughout life *or* on their socialization throughout the life cycle to role
changes, and (2) the question of the increasing dominance (both in terms
of personality and social roles) of older women.

Aging Women in Mediterranean Society

Following the anthropological principle that researchers can best discover the operation of a variable when its functions are observed in

extreme cases, the ethnographic foci in the following analyses are two locales within the Mediterranean culture area: (1) the Niolo, a mountainous region composed of five autonomous villages in the center of the island of Corsica, and (2) Bayt al-'asir, a modernizing peasant community of about 600 people in southern Lebanon. These are "extreme" environments compared to the urban United States in several ways. First, the informants presented in the following analyses live in small towns where the traditional economy is based on pastoralism (the Niolo) or wage laboring with small-scale agriculture (Bayt al-'asir). In addition, both these locales are firmly entrenched in the Mediterranean culture area where one of the defining cultural characteristics is a seemingly obsessive (at least to Western eyes) concern with female modesty and submission, for male and familial honor is embodied in the chastity of kinswomen, especially wives. In this manner, it appears that these societies offer valuable cross-cultural checks on the general validity of some of the findings concerning the adaptive success and growing domination of women as they age.

In both societies, women perceive themselves (and are also considered by the men) to be aging successfully and to be better off than their male counterparts in old age. For example, aged Niolan men say that women adapt better to old age "because they have less desire to get out" and "because they are less independent." Older women are of the same opinion, but for different reasons: "Men find it harder to grow old well because they are not accustomed to resignation." The anthropologists' data agree with their informants' perception of the women's relative success in aging. However, in analyzing the perception of greater life satisfaction on the part of their female informants, Cool and McCabe tend to focus on different factors. Cool emphasizes the *individual* manipulations of a Niolan woman as she undergoes socialization to role change and personal adaptability in her move from timid bride to domineering older mother-in-law. McCabe stresses that this life-satisfying situation for older Lebanese women is the result of an accumulation of several cultural factors which are differentially emphasized at various points in the life cycle. With increasing age, Lebanese women become relatively more competent and confident in their roles than do men. There is a sense of *control* in their lives, which is absent in those of men.

The Niolo

Successful aging depends on the developmental cycle of the traditional Niolan household. It demands that a woman learn to adapt to changing roles and statuses.[2] Such socialization begins early for Niolan girls, for they learn the basic skills while helping their mother and sisters. The ideal was for all daughters to marry; but financial limitations of all but the wealthiest families sometimes prevented this realization. In the past, even the unmarried daughter who remained at home had important roles to perform: she first helped her parents and later her brother (the heir) and his wife. As a "blood" relative of the patricentric family, she had an important standing even though she would never be a "housewife," and often she developed a close, confidante relationship with her sister-in-law as the two women worked to increase the reputation of the household.

In the Niolo, a bride is expected to be fully capable of running a household upon marriage. This is the case even if the new couple is to live patrilocally. For upon arriving in her new home, the first person the young bride meets is her mother-in-law, the woman under whose authority she will live and work for the next several years. In this sort of patricentric household, the young bride's most important roles become those of wife and daughter-in-law, both of subservient status in traditional Niolan society. The young woman must work hard to establish herself in her new household and to win even grudging approval from the mother-in-law who is convinced that no one can care for her beloved son as well as his own mother.

A period of expansion in the developmental cycle of the household arrives with the pregnancy and birth of the young wife's first child. Although she continues in her submission to her mother-in-law's authority, the young mother finally is recognized as having personal value other than that of "another worker." In the role of mother, the young woman creates emotional bonds and achieves positive status in her husband's household. From her, the infant receives the emotional ties and support of which the young wife must herself feel deprived, especially when her husband is away with the animals. In this regard, some old women mentioned that the most important part of their lives was giving birth to a son and then raising him so that they would be assured of affection and care in their old age.

The peak stage (arriving eight to ten years after the marriage) for the Niolan household begins when the young wife has several children, for she begins to prove her own ability as a housewife and domestic decision maker. Her husband begins to appreciate her more as a partner, and the complementarity of the roles of wife and husband become clearer in the young couple's intense activity to support a nuclear family and a household. When she has reached 35 and has had five, six, or more children, her family may continue to expand but the older children have reached an age and a developmental stage where they can make useful contributions to the group. And in spite of the fact that this is the busiest period of her life, the housewife might have attained some peace. For by now, the mother-in-law, although still the privileged head housewife, begins to entrust her younger counterpart with more responsibilities in the household's management.

When the wife is aged 45 to 50 years, her first child usually leaves the home to emigrate or prepares to marry. Although the household still includes children, the wife's childbearing years are over and the remaining children are her youngest and last. Gerontologists predict that this shrinking circle stage is the most difficult for urban women: The urban housewife loses prestige as she ceases to perform the housewife role at its peak. The Niolan housewife, however, does not seem to experience this letdown as she herself acquires a new status and role, that of mother-in-law, as she welcomes her own son's wife into *her* household.

Finally, when most of the children are either married or away from home, the Niolan wife faces the likely prospect of widowhood. In spite of the loss of her role as wife, she continues as mother, grandmother, and organizer of the home. Child care which was once just another burden among other tasks becomes a pleasure since grandchildren need only be loved, not trained. Although her knowledge of house and children may be common to younger women, her advice in an emergency can be vital. Such advice includes the ability to diagnose illness as to whether it was caused by the evil eye and to effect cures. Although younger women may also perform this role (*signadore*), older women are more sought after since they have more experience and, probably, more successful cures about which they can boast. An older woman's knowledge of the community and its inhabitants is unique, and she often is skilled in problem solving. In this manner, the elder female in the Niolo is in a position not only to maintain her prestige, but to actually improve her status as well.

Thus we have traced the developmental cycle of the housewife from the timid, subservient bride to the respected and confident head of the domestic unit. The basic role concept remained the same. However, the woman constantly underwent modifications in the characteristics of each assigned role. These variations occurred as the woman entered different stages of the life cycle and correspondingly changed her definitions of her roles. Having reached old age, the housewife can look at her children and her home with a sense of pride in accomplishment. Women are not the submissive, powerless creatures which are often portrayed in the Mediterranean. Rather they are manipulators of people, events, and the rules themselves.

What about the life cycle of Niolan men? The young man selected as his father's heir is under the older man's domination. The young man acquires the role of father upon the birth of his first child, but his relationship to his children is remote due to his frequent and prolonged absences from the home while caring for the animals. In fact, the most commonly given description of a traditional Niolan father emphasizes his rigidity and distance:

> The mother is the person the child loves. The father has little significance. He commands the children, but he is less important to them than the mother [62-year-old man].

In time, a man's failing health requires him to delegate more and more responsibility to his son, and the old man must watch his role as the household's chief provider disappear. Some old men are able to assume the respected roles of advisor, arbitrator, or adjudicator in their later years. But, for the most part, the old men seem to be left with ephemeral authority as they tell their sons how best to manage the household's affairs. In changing from the aggressor to the negotiator, the aging Niolan male begins to show behavior that is less stereotypically masculine while his wife assumes more and more control within her own domain.

In analyzing such age-based changes in roles, Cottrell (1942) suggested that an individual will make an easy adjustment to a role change to the extent that he has undergone anticipatory preparation for the role. Kline attempted to pursue this viewpoint with regard to aging American women:

> Women have had considerable experience in adjusting to age-linked changes (children leaving home, menopause) and have therefore become accustomed to change and impermanence. Thus, women are not as devastated as men are likely to be when old age, another impermanence, separates them from the productive, involved . . . world of middle age [Kline, 1975:490].

From the analysis of the life cycle of a Niolan housewife, it appears that Niolan women do undergo role changes throughout the life cycle to a greater extent than do their male counterparts. It is suggested that this one reason for the apparent privileges of women in successful aging.

Bayt al-'asir, Lebanon

By the time a woman in Bayt al-'asir has reached her sixth decade of life, her ever increasing air of confidence has emerged with a rather bold and assertive countenance. Earlier, as a middle-aged woman, for instance, it is likely that she had already become a controller of her household budget and appropriator of its funds; these responsibilities were earned through deference paid, services rendered, and the manipulation of her various cultural assets (e.g., her sexuality, kinsmen, and children). However, as an even older woman, she fills her influential position with increasingly less dependence upon and consultation with her husband.

Thus, it is this older woman—not her husband—whom grown and dependent children and kin approach with requests for new clothing or other material (and emotional) needs. Indeed, where a younger, middle-aged woman would still *ask* her husband for money when the local peddler came around, the (healthy) woman approaching old age would often *tell* her husband to give her the money or use funds which she herself has put aside.[3]

The manifestation of the power of female sexuality changes as a woman ages: Before menopause, she influences male honor largely by her own sexual behavior; after menopause, she influences younger women's status and reputations (and male honor) by what she chooses to say about them in the community. Older village women have the credibility in the eyes of both men and women and can effectively pass judgment on another woman's virtue; moreover, their advice, and especially their approval, are sought by their sons and other young men who are contemplating marriage. To vital older women, respect and a kind of homage accrue: from younger women, an empathetic recognition for their having weathered a hard life, raised children, and contended (usually successfully) with a normatively second-class, powerless status; from men (especially sons) there is a gratitude and emotional dependency, and some recognition of the wise, prophetic, and mediating qualities of older women who are at the center of the community's daily social, cultural, economic, and political activities.

The first half of the life cycle of these Lebanese women is largely characterized by nurturance and attendance to the needs of others—husbands and children—rather than to personal needs and wants. As young wives and mothers, these women are so occupied with raising their children and maintaining their households that they virtually have no free time to devote to "frivolities" such as their own pleasure or interests. Although women of all ages extolled the virtues of "country" living, they wistfully spoke of the easier life of urban women or those depicted in Western television. By contrast, young husbands spent little time around their homes, coming and going with their male friends during nonworking hours.

With increasing age, village women realize that their strength, satisfaction, security, and influence ultimately derive from the very source of their hardships and struggle: marriage and motherhood. Nonetheless, some women express resentment and frustration at having to remain at home with so much work while their menfolk are able to move about—like children—unfettered by the demands of housework, children, etc. However, as the children mature and become independent and helpful, village women, too, have more time for themselves. Young and older women espouse the prevalent attitude of "better late than never" found among women in late middle age.

Accordingly, the psychological aging of the women of Bayt al-'asir is characterized by the Arab "masculine" qualities of self-assertiveness and confidence, at least partially replacing the "feminine" traits of self-denial and passivity. They not only approach equality with men, but appear also to surpass them at least with regard to the personal satisfaction of life task achievement (i.e., as mothers and homemakers).

Able older women in this community begin to be conspicuously more mobile, even going visiting or on errands out of the village. For example, some of the numerous visits by older women to the doctor in another community are regarded as "legitimate" desires for personal attention and/or simply for going on an outing. A village woman at this stage of life is even more candid in telling others that she does or does not like something that affects her personally, whether it is a kind of food, her child's spouse, or visitors. One 62-year-old matron rather eloquently expressed her perceptions of growing old:

> As I grow older, I have more confidence in myself, more faith in only *my* ability to make myself happy. I find that there is a greater sensitivity and listening to my feelings, thoughts, and even to my body.

Also, societal norms (i.e., with regard to modesty) have a decidedly lesser influence on old women's behavior, although they may still pay them lip service where *other* women are concerned. Moreover, because an old woman is no longer able to bear children or menstruate, she is perceived as having moved from the realm of women and nature (to which "femaleness" is likened) toward that of men and culture, an analogy which Ortner (1974) has duly elaborated. It is the perception of this symbolic shift that at least partly permits the often audaciously bawdy and otherwise inappropriate behavior of older women to occur without societal sanctions.

This bawdy, sometimes brash behavior of old women was amply illustrated during the research period. For example, one summer day, McCabe was standing near her village home speaking with an elderly neighbor, Zayna, a very vivacious grandmother of 72 years, in the presence of a few young, unmarried women and men. The conversation touched on several topics, including her opinions on the scandalous type of clothing young women were wearing (a subject she raised). In so speaking, Zayna unabashedly hoisted her skirt a considerable distance above her knees to expose her bloomerlike underpants, all the while disapproving the skimpy panties she knew the young girls were wearing. The onlookers' obvious embarrassment did not seem to disturb her in the slightest; she eventually pulled her skirt down and acted as if nothing extraordinary had happened. McCabe later asked the young people whether such behavior was considered shameful. They stammered a bit and said yes, it was, but that it really did not matter because " . . . she is an old woman."

In sum, an older woman's public behavior and attitude acquires the stereotypically Arab masculine dimensions of self-indulgence and assertiveness. According to McCabe's observations, an older woman spends more time visiting her cronies for the sake of socialization and not just under the guise of doing work with them or going on an errand. She is more likely to get around to preparing her husband's meals or fulfilling his requests when or if she feels like it, rather than automatically kowtowing to him as before.

Simultaneously, a man of the same age acquires the stereotypically Arab feminine dimensions of passivity and patience. As his job retirement approaches, he begins to gravitate toward home more and more, sitting there alone or with a few friends. According to older village women, these men just seem to get tired of cavorting and always trying to have fun. In his home—his wife's domain—an older man's feminine side is most evident. McCabe observed older women telling their husbands to do this or that. The old men complied and obviously did not care enough about the issue to disagree, preferring instead to avoid any potentially hostile situation. In the face of his often vivacious, but sometimes irascible wife, an older man stays out of her way or tries to mollify her in an argument—just as she often did as a younger women.

Therefore, over the lifetime of these Lebanese women, there occurs a transition from a feminine influence that is implicit, covert, and marked by subterfuge, to one that is increasingly overt, and recognized by at least those in an older woman's immediate environment. Essentially this transition involves a change from *de facto* to *de jure* control; that is, feminine power in older women acquires an aspect of authority. By contrast, the power enjoyed by men in this society is *de jure;* they have authority over women. However, due to certain psychosocioeconomic components, this masculine power is tenuous. As men age, the fragile nature of the foundations of their authority is increasingly exposed and eroded.

In conclusion, among the several ways by which these life cycle changes in the hegemony and concomitant life satisfaction of women and men occur in this society are the following:

There is little incongruity between the ideal and real life task of a Lebanese village woman. In one form or another, *mothering* (of children and even husbands) is still the role not only idealized by society and a woman herself, but also the one actually attained by her. By contrast, for a Lebanese man there is considerably less consonance between what his society expects him to be, and what it actually allows him to be. Generally, the men of this community are not wealthy, important, or powerful in the public marketplace—the sphere to which they have been assigned by society. Consequently, by middle age, men perceive themselves as unsuccessful, women perceive them as unsuccessful, and men perceive women's perceptions of them as unsuccessful. Hence, they become increasingly impotent vis-à-vis the successful and confident older women.

Female solidarity and support are great sources of comfort and power for women individually and as a group. By contrast, the divisiveness of men and their perception of one another as competitors and exploiters of one another's kinswomen allow them to become increasingly isolated as individuals in their later years.

Finally, the locus and source of female power and satisfaction over time are a woman's home and her children. With increasing age, she becomes the focal point of the lives of her husband, her children, and their own young families. The support of children for their mother, even in opposition to their father, cannot be overemphasized. Moreover, this locus of power (the home) for a village woman in the first half of her life continues to be such in the latter half. Her expertise and confidence in the performance of her life tasks are manifest in the same place over time. By contrast, the working life of a man in this wage-laboring community is characterized by absence from village, family, and other men. When he retires, a village man retires to his wife's domain of influence and expertise. Also, he is without benefit of the equality-enhancing symbols of the skills and seniority he may have acquired in his own work place—one which is still separate from where he will live out his old age.

Conclusion

Based on the cross-cultural evidence presented here, it does appear that women, especially in the later life cycle stages, are not the powerless, submissive creatures that have often been portrayed in the literature. Rather, some sources of power are available to women in all societies, and women's ability to manipulate their own lives and the lives of others around them increases with the passage of years. This emphasis on women as capable, energetic members (and sometimes the recognized leaders) of society has typically been overlooked. Most studies focus on *de jure* power (or authority, the publicly recognized right to exercise control) which is typically a male domain. Therefore, most cultural descriptions fail to examine the full range of social interactions in a society, focusing mainly on the more active, public, and dominant relationships. As Hammond and Jablow point out, ". . . descriptions of curing concentrate on the medicine man, not the patient; accounts of government focus on rulers, not the ruled; we are told a great deal about parental behavior to children and little of children's responses" (1976:132). When anthropologists turn their attention to *de facto* power and control that is exercised in the private rather than the public sphere, the strengths of women begin to appear. Thus, we find today that cross-cultural analyses of sex roles as Rosaldo and Lamphere's *Woman, Culture, and Society* (1974) and Schlegel's *Sexual Stratification* (1977), to name but two, are pointing to the relative power of women.

This article has focused on a cross-cultural analysis of women's greater adaptability and success in growing old and has indicated the sources of this success: women's socialization to continued changes in their roles and self-concept, their increasing expertise and confidence in their domain (the home), their move from covert use of power (in their manipulations of their children's affection) to overt and recognized control in the eyes of the larger community, and the strength and comfort they draw from female solidarity. Such an emphasis seems particularly compelling because the detailed ethnographic examples are drawn from the Mediterranean, an area of the world commonly thought to represent one of the extreme cases of the domination of men and the subordination of women. The message is clear. There is no biological imperative for a submissive (or powerful) female role. Women, like men, are products (and producers) of the particular culture in which they are socialized and live out their lives.

Notes

1. As just a few examples from the anthropological literature, see Fortes (1962, Tallensi of Kenya); LeVine (1963, Gusii of Kenya); Nadel (1952, Nupe); Spencer (1965, Samburu); Leonard (1967, Mexican-Americans); and Yap (1962, Chinese).
2. The stages of the life cycle of the Niolan housewife are adapted from the stages developed for an American housewife by Lopata (1966:5-22).
3. With regard to the latter, McCabe discovered that from a younger age, some village women in the constant struggle for economic security and independence had found one way to put money aside. Having paid for the article or service, they would then tell their husbands that it cost twice as much as it actually did, and they then would pocket half of the amount for themselves.

References

Bart, P. 1969. "Why Women's Status Changes in Middle Age: The Turn of the Social Ferris Wheel." *Sociological Symposium* 3:1-18.

————. 1972. "Depression in Middle Aged Women." In J. Bardwick, ed., *Readings on the Psychology of Women.* New York: Harper & Row.

Bell, I.P. 1970. "The Double Standard: Age." *TransAction* (November-December): 75-80.

Borgese, E. 1964. *The Ascent of Women.* New York: George Braziller.

Cameron, P. 1967. "Ego Strength and Happiness of the Aged," *Journal of Gerontology* 22:199-202.

_____. 1968. "Masculinity-Femininity in the Aged." *Journal of Gerontology* 25:63-65.

Clark, M. 1967. "The Anthropology of Aging: A New Era for Studies of Culture and Personality." *The Gerontologist* 7:55-64.

_____. 1973. "Contributions of Cultural Anthropology to the Study of the Aged," pp. 77-88 in L. Nader and T. Maretzki, eds., *Cultural Illness and Health.* Washington, D.C.: The American Anthropological Association.

Collier, J. 1974. "Women in Politics," pp. 89-96 in M. Rosaldo and L. Lamphere, eds., *Women, Culture, and Society.* Stanford, Calif.: Stanford University Press.

Cool, L.E. 1976. "Outsiders in their Own Land: Ethnicity and the Dilemma of Aging Corsicans." Unpublished doctoral dissertation, Duke University.

Cottrell, L. 1942. "The Adjustment of the Individual to His Age and Sex Roles." *American Sociological Review* 7:617-20.

Cumming, E. 1964. "New Thoughts on the Theory of Disengagement." In Robert Kastenbaum, ed., *New Thoughts on Old Age.* New York: Springer.

Cumming, E, and W. Henry. 1961. *Growing Old: The Process of Disengagement.* New York: Basic Books.

Davis, D.L. 1979. "Women's Status and Experience of Menopause in a Newfoundland Fishing Village." Paper presented at the Annual Meeting of the American Anthropological Association, November, Cincinnatti, Ohio.

Douglas, M. 1966. *Purity and Danger.* London: Routledge & Kegan Paul.

Dowty, N. 1971. "Women's Attitudes Towards the Climacterium in Five Israeli Subcultures." Doctoral dissertation, University of Chicago.

Evans-Pritchard, E.E. 1936. *Witchcraft, Oracles and Magic Among the Azande.* Oxford: Oxford University Press.

Flint, M. 1975. "The Menopause: Reward or Punishment?" *Psychosomatics* 16:161-3.

Fortes, M. 1962. *The Web of Kinship among the Tallensi.* London: Oxford University Press.

Friedl, E. 1975. *Women and Men: An Anthropologist's View.* New York: Holt, Rinehart and Winston.

Fuller, A.H. 1961. *Buraji: Portrait of a Lebanese Moslem Village.* Cambridge, Mass.: Harvard University Press.

Gold, S.S. 1960. "A Cross-Cultural Comparison of Changes with Aging in Husband-Wife Roles." *Student Journal of Human Development* (University of Chicago) 1:11-15.

Gutmann, D. 1974. "Alternatives to Disengagement: The Old Men of Highland Druze," pp. 232-45 in R. Levine, ed., *Culture and Personality: Contemporary Readings:* Chicago, Ill.: Aldine.

_____. 1980. "Observations on Culture and Mental Health in Later Life," pp. 429-44 in J. Birren and W. Sloan, eds., *Handbook of Mental Health.* New York: Van Nostrand Reinhold.

Hammond, D., and A. Jablow. 1976. *Women in Cultures of the World.* Menlo Park, Calif.: Benjamin/Cummings.

Harper, E.B. 1969. "Fear and the Status of Women." *Southwestern Journal of Anthropology* 25:81-95.

Kardiner, A. et al. 1945. *The Psychological Frontiers of Society.* New York: Columbia University Press.

Kerckhoff, A. 1966. "Family Patterns and Morale in Retirement," pp. 173-92 in I. Simpson and J. McKinney, eds., *Social Aspects of Aging.* Durham, No. Car.: Duke University Press.

Kline, C. 1975. "The Socialization Process of Women," *The Gerontologist* 15: 486-92.

Kluckhohn, C. 1967. *Navaho Witchcraft.* Boston, Mass.: Beacon Press.

Lamphere, L. 1974. "Strategies, Cooperation, and Conflict among Women in Domestic Groups," pp. 97-112 in M. Rosaldo and L. Lamphere, eds., *Women, Culture, and Society.* Stanford, Calif.: Stanford University Press.

Leonard, O.E. 1967. "The Older Rural Spanish-Speaking People of the Southwest," pp. 239-61 in E.G. Youmans, ed., *Older Rural Americans.* Lexington: University of Kentucky Press.

Levine, R. 1963. "Witchcraft and Sorcery in a Gusii Community," pp. 221-55 in J. Middleton and E. Winter, eds., *Witchcraft and Sorcery in East Africa.* New York: Praeger.

Lewis, M., and R. Butler, 1972. "Why Is Women's Lib Ignoring the Older Women?" *International Journal of Aging and Human Development* 3(3):223-31.

Lipman, A. 1961. "Role Conceptions and Morale of Couples in Retirement," *Journal of Gerontology* 16:267-71.

Lopata, H. 1966. "The Life Cycle of the Role of Housewife." *Sociology and Social Research* 51:5-22.

————. 1971. "The Living Arrangements of American Urban Widows." Department of H.E.W., Administration on Aging, Mimeo No. 34. Washington, D.C.: U.S. Government Printing Office.

Lowenthal, M.F., M. Thurner and D. Chiriboga. 1975. *Four Stages of Life.* San Francisco: Jossey-Bass.

Maddox, G.L. 1969. "Growing Old: Getting beyond the Stereotypes," pp. 5-16 in R. Boyd and C. Oakes, eds., *Foundations of Practical Gerontology.* Columbia: University of South Carolina Press.

McCabe, J. 1979. "The Status of Aging Women in the Middle East: The Process of Change in the Life Cycle of Rural Lebanese Women." Unpublished doctoral dissertation: Duke University.

Murphy, Y., and R.F. Murphy. 1974. *Women of the Forest.* New York: Columbia University Press.

Nadel, S.F. 1952. "Witchcraft in Four African Societies." *American Anthropologist* 54:18-29.

Neugarten, B. 1968. "Adult Personality: Toward a Psychology of the Life Cycle," pp. 137-47 in B. Neugarten, ed., *Middle Age and Aging.* Chicago, Ill.: University of Chicago Press.

Neugarten, B., and D. Guttmann. 1968. "Age-Sex Roles and Personality in Middle Age," pp. 58-71 in B. Neugarten, ed., *Middle Age and Aging.* Chicago, Ill.: University of Chicago Press.

Neugarten, B., and R. Kraines. 1965. "Menopausal Symptoms in Women of Various Ages." *Psychosomatics* 16:161-63.

Ortner, S. 1974. "Is Female to Male as Nature Is to Culture?" pp. 67-87 in M. Rosaldo and L. Lamphere, eds., *Toward an Anthropology of Women.* Stanford, Calif.: Stanford University Press.

Palmore, E. 1971. "Attitudes towards Aging as Shown by Humor." *The Gerontologist* 11:181-86.

Quinn, N. 1977. "Anthropological Studies on Women's Status." *Annual Review of Anthropology* 6:181-225.

Rosaldo, M.Z. 1974. "Woman, Culture and Society: A Theoretical Overview," pp. 17-42 in M. Rosaldo and L. Lamphere, eds., *Woman, Culture and Society.* Stanford, Calif.: Stanford University Press.

Rosaldo, M.Z., and L. Lamphere, eds., 1974. *Woman, Culture and Society.* Stanford, Calif.: Stanford University Press.

Rose, A. 1962. "The Subculture of Aging: A Topic for Sociological Research." *The Gerontologist* 2:123-27.

Schlegel, A. 1977. *Sexual Stratification.* New York: Columbia University Press.

Shanas, E., P. Townsend, D. Wedderburn, H. Friis, P. Milhoj, and J. Stehouwer. 1968. *Older People in Three Industrial Societies.* New York: Atherton Press.

Sheehan, N. 1976. "Planned Obsolescence: Historical Perspectives on Aging Women." pp. 59-68 in K. Riegel and J. Meacham, eds., *The Developing Individual in a Changing World.* Volume I. Chicago, Ill.: Aldine.

Silverman, S. "The Life Crisis as a Clue to Social Function." *Anthropological Quarterly* 40:127-38.

Sommers, T. 1974. "The Compounding Impact of Age on Sex: Another Dimension of Double Standard." *Civil Rights Digest* 7(1):3-9.

Sontag, S. 1972. "The Double Standard of Aging." *Saturday Review of the Society* 95 (September 23):29-38.

Spencer, P. 1965. *The Samburu: A Study of Gerontocracy in a Nomadic Tribe.* Berkeley: University of California Press.

Vatuk, S. 1975. "The Aging Woman in India," pp. 142-63 in A. de Souza, ed., *Women in Contemporary India.* Delhi: Manohar.

Wolf, M. 1972. *Women and the Family in Rural Taiwan.* Stanford, Calif.: Stanford University Press.

Yap, M. 1962. "Aging in Underdeveloped Asian Countries." In C. Tibbitts and W. Donahue, eds., *Sociological and Psychological Aspects of Aging.* New York: Columbia University Press.

8

Minority Aging

Kyriakos S. Markides

The area of ethnic minority aging is one of the most underdeveloped in social gerontology. Only recently have researchers probed beyond cross-group comparisons of sociodemographic variables such as income, education, sex, or life expectancy to explore the crucial questions of whether and how ethnicity and minority status affect the process of aging in the United States. Much of this research has concentrated on aging among Blacks and more recently Hispanics (mainly Mexican Americans), with other ethnic groups receiving less attention. To date, this research has largely failed to establish the knowledge base and theoretical sophistication necessary for generating testable hypotheses. As Bengtson (1979:14) notes: "Although we may be convinced—indeed take it as a basic premise—that ethnicity is an important dimension in aging . . . we who are converted have not been particularly convincing to our colleagues, or to policymakers . . . possibly because (we) too often focus on ethnicity per se, rather than ethnic strata within the context of other social stratification dimensions." Careful examination of the literature discloses that many conclusions regarding the existence of ethnic or cultural differences are not based on scientific evidence because many studies either lack appropriate data or perform inappropriate data analyses for establishing the existence of ethnic differences.

This review focuses principally on America's two largest ethnic-minority groups—Blacks and Hispanics. Most of the limited knowledge in the area is about these two groups. While the broader concept of ethnicity is not ignored, special emphasis is given to how ethnic *minority status* affects the process of aging, a theme of much current theory. Thus, the undertaking here, though set within limits, is nevertheless challenging: to outline the literature on Blacks and Hispanics that shows how membership in these ethnic minority groups makes aging any different from the majority experience. Although these two groups have distinct cultural backgrounds and social biographies, they also have some characteristics in common by virtue of their disadvantaged minority status. It is these similarities rather than differences that are emphasized here. To the extent that Blacks and Hispanics share certain experiences with other minority groups—such as Asians or Native Americans—much of what is discussed will also be relevant to those groups.

New fields of inquiry typically suffer from lack of theoretical integration—perhaps the most critical problem with the field of minority aging. Theoretical developments in the area of minority aging have largely concentrated on a multiple-hierarchy model of stratification in which ethnic-minority group membership is viewed as an aspect of social inequality along with age, sex, and social class (Bengtson, 1979; Foner, 1979). While some speak of triple and even quadruple jeopardies, as in the case of older minority women, most discussion has centered on the hypothesis of "double jeopardy," or the double disadvantage experienced by aged members of minority groups. A diametrically opposed hypothesis commonly referred to as the "age as leveler" hypothesis predicts a decline with age in the relative disadvantage of minority persons since all older people experience similar deprivations regardless of ethnicity. After these two hypotheses are outlined in the next section, empirical findings of research on Blacks and Hispanics are evaluated in terms of whether they lend support to either of the hypotheses. The areas of the literature reviewed are income, health, primary group relations, and psychological well-being.

Theoretical Development

Theoretical developments in social gerontology in recent decades have taken place with little, if any, attention to minority aging. One theoretical perspective relevant to minority aging theory is the sociology of age stratification (Riley et al., 1972; Riley, 1976) in which age is treated as a dimension of social stratification. While not directly an outgrowth of this model, current conceptualizations of minority aging are an extension of the stratification perspective in that race or minority status is viewed as an added dimension of inequality along with age, class, and in some formulations, sex. When several of these factors are considered together, we hear of triple, quadruple, or multiple jeopardies characterizing the aged in ethnic minority groups. Since low class, old age, female sex, and minority status are on the lower side of the stratification system, the bottom of the hierarchy is occupied by low class, older, minority women, and the top is occupied by middle or upper class middle-aged or younger White men. Most discussions, however, limit themselves to describing the situation of minority group elderly as one of "double jeopardy," emphasizing the double disadvantage of old age and minority status.

The double jeopardy hypothesis has its origins in the attempts of certain advocacy groups (National Urban League, 1964; National Council on the Aging, 1972) to highlight the relative disadvantage of aged Blacks in such important areas as health, income, housing, and life satisfaction. While the concept of double jeopardy was not intended to be a theoretical postulate around which knowledge on minority aging would be organized, it has become the dominant model in the area of research. And although it has not been adequately formulated, double jeopardy is now commonly used to describe the situation of the aged in other minority groups in addition to Blacks (Cantor, 1979; Dowd and Bengtson, 1978; Fujii, 1976) as well as in theoretical discussions on the effect of minority status and ethnicity on the process of aging (Bengtson, 1979; Dowd and Bengtson, 1978; Markson, 1979; Varghese and Medinger, 1979). The concept also figures prominently in discussions of minority aging in the rapidly multiplying textbooks in introductory gerontology (Crandall, 1980; Decker, 1980; Hendricks and Hendricks, 1977; Hess and Markson, 1980; Seltzer et al., 1978).

A serious attempt at formalizing a testable double jeopardy hypothesis was made by Dowd and Bengtson (1978) in their study of middle-aged and older Blacks, Mexican Americans, and Anglos (or Whites) in Los Angeles. The minority aged are said to bear a double burden:

> Like other older people in industrial societies, they experience the devaluation of old age found in most modern societies. . . . Unlike other older people, however, the minority aged must bear the additional economic, social, and psychological burdens of living in a society in which racial equality remains more myth than social policy [Dowd and Bengtson, 1978:427].

Dowd and Bengtson go on to suggest that a situation of double jeopardy could be demonstrated if the disadvantages observed at earlier ages were found to widen in old age[1] for minority persons compared to Whites.

The double jeopardy hypothesis thus suggests an interaction effect between two stratification systems—age and minority status. It predicts that aging has greater negative consequences for minority persons than for members of the dominant majority (Ward, 1980). While this hypothesis does not have its roots in a scholarly tradition, it has its intellectual counterpart in the mental health and psychological distress literature: the social stress hypothesis as applied to minority groups (Antunes et al., 1974). Here it is suggested that members of minority groups, in addition to bearing the deprivations associated with low social class, must face the added stresses of discrimination and oppression associated with minority status and are thus expected to exhibit higher levels of psychological distress than members of the dominant majority at the same level of social class. This, too, is a double jeopardy hypothesis in that it predicts an interaction effect between two stratification systems: minority status and social class. Both double jeopardy hypotheses may be subsumed under a larger, multiple-hierarchy stratification model which, in addition to minority status, age, and class, includes sex as another dimension of inequality.

The social stress hypothesis is an extension of the social stress interpretation commonly evoked to explain the greater levels of psychological distress in lower classes reported in community surveys and studies of psychiatric epidemiology (Dohrenwend, 1970, 1973; Dohrenwend and Dohrenwend, 1969; Fried, 1975; Kessler, 1979; Kessler and Cleary, 1980). More recent literature in this area is emphasizing that lower class people experience more psychological distress not only because of greater exposure to stressful events, but also, and more important, because they have fewer psychological and social resources for coping with stress (Kessler and Cleary, 1980). Presumably, the same can be said about the suggested relationship between minority status and psychological distress: Members of minority groups experience more distress than members of the dominant majority of similar social class not only because they are exposed to more stresses, but also because they have fewer resources for dealing with these stresses. Moreover, it may be argued that stress can have an even greater effect on the aged and the minority aged in particular since they have even fewer resources for coping with stress. This resource deficit experienced by the aged is even more acute among minority aged: "Not only are the minority aged exposed to greater numbers of stressors, they also have fewer coping resources after a lifetime of financial deprivation, subordination to other groups, and systematic exclusion from access to social and economic opportunity" (Varghese and Medinger, 1979:97).

These propositions rest on the assumption that old age itself constitutes a situation of jeopardy. To what extent this assumption is established by empirical data is not as clear as it might at first appear since the assumption depends on the choice of dependent variable indicating a situation of jeopardy. This brings us to another question: What are the critical variables to be used in evaluating the jeopardy of the minority aged? Four areas are chosen here primarily because they were used as the primary dependent variables in two important recent attempts to test empirically the viability of the double jeopardy hypothesis (Dowd and Bengtson, 1978; Ward, 1980): income, health, primary group relations, and psychological well-being. These indicators of well-being or quality of life are areas of great interest to gerontologists. In addition, they provide a useful framework for organizing this discussion of the literature on minority aging.

The literature review that follows is selective rather than exhaustive. It focuses primarily on studies that intentionally or unintentionally, directly or indirectly, provide evidence in support of or opposed to the notion that aging or the onset of old age is more disadvantageous for Black Americans or for Hispanic Americans than for the dominant Whites. That is, to what extent does the so-called double jeopardy hypothesis accurately depict the interaction between minority status and age? Do the disadvantages of minority persons observed in middle age actually increase with aging or is aging a great leveler of social and racial differences (Kent and Hirsh, 1969; Kent, 1971). After the literature on these questions is reviewed, some discussion of observed discrepancies is offered, along with suggestions for future research.

Empirical Evidence

As noted above, income, health, primary group relationships (family and friends), and psychological well-being (e.g., morale, life satisfaction, happiness) are important areas of gerontological concern. The last has been especially important since, in their attempts to offer theoretical formulas for "successful aging," gerontologists have used various measures of psychological well-being as primary indicators of adaptation or adjustment to old age. The other three variables, in addition to being important dependent variables in their own right, have been used as the key independent variables in the successful aging equation: Numerous studies have shown that health, income, and relations with family and friends are consistent predictors of life satisfaction or morale among the aged (Larson, 1978; Markides and Martin, 1979a).

The gerontological literature in these four areas is vast and growing rapidly. Attempts are increasingly being made to sort it out, to synthesize it and generalize about what growing older is like. In much of the empirical literature, however, minority groups have not been included, or inadequate analyses have been made. The following selective review of some of the literature on Black and Hispanic aging aims to stimulate further interest, both empirical and theoretical, among researchers in the future.

Income

There is little disagreement in the literature that the income of older people in the United States and other industrial societies is considerably lower than that of middle-aged people. What the literature does not always make clear is the source of this inequality: Is it aging or old age per se, or is it primarily a cohort or generation phenomenon since many of today's elderly worked at unskilled or semiskilled low-wage jobs that did not provide for adequate pensions, if any at all. Future cohorts of older people are likely to fare better, thus cutting the age differential in income. Given marked increases in real wages in the last three decades or so and a shift to more skilled and white-collar occupations, it is difficult to use cross-sectional data to evaluate the effect of aging on income. Longitudinal analyses are few, despite the fact that income data by age have historically been available in a form amenable to longitudinal analysis.

There is also widespread agreement in the literature that elderly members of ethnic minority groups are socioeconomically disadvantaged compared to elderly members of the majority group. The double jeopardy hypothesis, however, predicts that the disadvantage of the minority persons is greater in old age than in middle age. In their Los Angeles study of Anglos, Blacks, and Mexican Americans (aged 45 to 74), Dowd and Bengtson (1978) found empirical support for this prediction: The relative decline in income associated with age was significantly greater for Blacks and Mexican Americans than for Anglos even when controls for socioeconomic status, sex, and health were introduced.

Because the findings of Dowd and Bengtson (1978) are based on one city and on cross-sectional data, it is difficult to draw conclusions about the effect of aging on income. A study using a large national sample of Blacks and Whites (Ward, 1980) found that, with educational and occupational differences controlled, there is some leveling of income differences between the races in old age. Ward feels that this may "reflect the effects of income maintenance policies which benefit older Blacks because of their disproportionately low income." Ward's findings are consistent with those of an earlier study using Census data from 1950, 1960, and 1970 (Whittington, 1975), which found that the financial position of Blacks compared to Whites improved with age. Whittington's study, however, did not include persons 65 years old and over. Whittington's rationale for not including older people in his study is instructive because the results run counter to Dowd's and Bengtson's findings of increasing racial and ethnic disparities in income in old age:

> There are good reasons to expect that beyond age 65 years, the income of Blacks is much closer to that of Whites, although both are substantially reduced. This artificial increase in relative status . . . would be very misleading if included in the analysis. Not only would it portray improvement where none existed but would give more weight to the age variable than it actually deserved [Whittington, 1975:7].

Other available cross-sectional data support Ward's findings of narrowing racial differentials in income with age. Data from a 1978 Current Population Survey, for example, show that families headed by Blacks 65 years old and over had an income of $6,066 compared with $9,458 for families headed by Whites in the same age group (Administration on Aging, 1980:Table 8). Although this income gap is considerable, it is smaller than that observed in younger age groups, both in absolute dollars and in relative terms: Families headed by Blacks aged 25 to 64 had a median income of $10,880 compared to $18,697 for families headed by Whites. The Black-to-White ratio, which is 0.58 at this age group, increases somewhat to 0.64 at age 65 and over. The picture is about the same for unrelated individuals: The racial gap declines somewhat in old age with the Black-to-White ratio increasing from 0.66 to 0.71. Earlier Current Population Surveys show that a small narrowing of the racial income gap from middle to old age has been consistent over many years (Bureau of the Census, 1979:Table 24). For families headed by persons 65 years old and over, the Black-to-White income ratio in 1974 was 0.65 compared to 0.58 for families aged 55 to 64. The corresponding ratios were 0.61 and 0.57 in 1969, 0.65 and 0.55 in 1967, and 0.68 and 0.51 in 1964. If there is any trend in these figures over time, it is one of a small improvement in the position of middle-aged Blacks compared to Anglos, and little change in the relative position of older Blacks compared to older Whites. The net effect is a slight decline over the years in the narrowing of the racial income gap with age, indicating that the relative position of older Blacks compared to middle-aged Blacks is getting somewhat worse, not better. Yet the data still show a relative decline in the racial income gap in old age, a finding consistent with Ward's (1980) data, but not consistent with Dowd's and Bengtson's (1978) findings.

Data on Hispanics are not as readily available as data on Blacks. One recent survey (National Center for Health Statistics, 1978) provides added support for a decline in old age of the income gap between both Blacks and Hispanics, on the one hand, and Anglos, on the other (see Markides, forthcoming).

Health

There is little disagreement that aging is accompanied by a progressive though highly variable deterioration of health. Health differences by age observed in cross-sectional analyses are partially due to cohort membership, given the continued improvements in the health of successive cohorts (Fries, 1980). Yet a major share of the differences is undeniably due to aging. That different groups have variant patterns of aging and health decrements is an established premise in gerontology. There is considerable evidence, for example, that aging in the United States is more rapid among Blacks than among Whites (Morgan, 1968; Jackson, 1980). Measuring health status, however, among the aged or any age group is not a simple matter. According to Shanas et al. (1968:25), "A person's health may be evaluated by a physician in a physical examination, it may be evaluated by how a person says he feels, and it may be evaluated by how the person behaves." While the conflict between the "medical" and "functional" models of health in old age is not irreconcilable (Shanas and Maddox, 1976), much research on the health of older people is limited to self-ratings of health by the elderly subjects. Research has repeatedly shown that self-ratings correlate moderately with physicians' ratings (Maddox and Douglass, 1973) and to other more or less objective health indexes (Markides and Martin, 1979b), suggesting that older people are fairly realistic about their health. There is good reason to believe that self-ratings are also crude indicators of optimism, morale, or life satisfaction (Friedsam and Martin, 1963; Markides and Martin, 1979a, 1979b). The ambiguous meaning of self-ratings makes them somewhat problematic as indicators of health status; yet both major studies testing the double jeopardy hypothesis (Dowd and Bengtson, 1978; Ward, 1980) used self-ratings as their measures of health.

Dowd and Bengtson found that even with socioeconomic status, sex, and income held constant, older Blacks and Mexican Americans in Los Angeles were more likely to report poorer health than were older Anglos.[2] Since the racial and ethnic differences in self-ratings were greater among older persons than among middle-aged respondents, the authors concluded that, as it applies to health, the double jeopardy hypothesis was supported (Dowd and Bengtson, 1978:432).

The data analyzed by Ward (1980) showed that at all ages, Blacks gave consistently poorer health evaluations than did Whites. However, these differences did not increase nor did they decline with age, supporting neither the double jeopardy hypothesis nor the age-as-leveler hypothesis. (For a review of findings on self-ratings of health by older Mexican Americans, see Newton, 1980.)

Looking at more objective national data on health, a somewhat different picture emerges. For example, data from the 1976 Health Interview Survey (National Center for Health Statistics, 1978) show that middle-aged and older Blacks report considerably poorer health than Whites as measured by percent with limitation of activity, days of restricted activity, and bed disability days (see National Center for Health Statistics, 1977, for exact definitions of these terms). However, the increase in the prevalence of poor health from middle age to old age is higher among Whites than among Blacks. For example, the number of bed disability days per person per year increases from 16.9 among Blacks aged 45 to 64 to 18.5 among those aged 65 and over; among Whites, on the other hand, the figure increases from

8.0 to 14.6. Thus, although Blacks report considerably more disability days than Whites at both ages, the gap decreases with age.

The 1976 Health Interview Survey also reported data on persons of Spanish origin. Based on the indicators noted above, Hispanics are much closer in health to the Anglo population than are Blacks. For example, similar proportions of Hispanics and Anglos report limitation of activity at both middle age and old age. The number of days of restricted activity and the number of days of bed disability are a little higher among Hispanic persons than among Anglos in middle age, a gap that increases somewhat in old age. While these changes may not be statistically significant, they are in the direction predicted by the double jeopardy hypothesis in contrast to the leveling found in Black-White comparisons.

Data on specific health problems provide further evidence that while both middle-aged and older Blacks are considerably disadvantaged compared to Whites, the disadvantage is greater in middle age than in old age. Data from 1974 on hypertension, for example, a special health problem of Blacks (Jackson, 1978), show that the percentage of Blacks who have hypertension rises from 39.1 at ages 45 to 64 to 47.2 at ages 65 and over; the figure for Whites goes from 22.7 to 35.3, a substantially larger increase (National Center for Health Statistics, 1980:Table J). Similarly, the incidence of cerebrovascular disease among Blacks in 1972 is 2.5 times that for Whites at ages 45 to 64, while at ages 65 and over it is less than 1.3 times as great.

Recent National Center for Health Statistics data from 1976 and 1977 show that almost twice as many Blacks as Whites assess their health as poor at ages 45 to 64 (38.4 vs. 19.3 percent). This ratio declines to 1.53 (44.1 vs. 28.3 percent) at ages 65 and over, again suggesting some leveling of differences, not widening, as found by Dowd and Bengtson (1978). Some leveling is also observed between Hispanics and Whites since the Hispanic-to-White ratio declines from 1.47 to 1.29 (National Center for Health Statistics, 1980: Table 1).

In summary, substantial evidence suggests that the health disadvantage of Blacks compared to Whites is greater in middle than in old age, with some leveling of differences with age. The few data on Hispanics provide no conclusive evidence in support of either leveling or widening of differences with age.

Primary Group Relations

Although it is understandable why the double jeopardy hypothesis would predict negative effects of both race and age on income and health, it is not as clear why this should also take place in the area of primary group relations. Yet both major studies (Dowd and Bengtson, 1978; Ward, 1980) included frequency of interaction with relatives and friends as factors for examining the viability of the double jeopardy thesis. Dowd and Bengtson (1978:433) provide the following brief rationale: "While primary group interaction may not be as critical an indicator of relative status as income or health, it does indicate a source of reward available to the individual in the course of their daily lives that contributes significantly to overall 'quality of life.'"

Dowd's and Bengtson's (1978) findings provide no support for the predictions of the double jeopardy thesis. Mexican Americans and Blacks reported higher contact with relatives in middle age than did Anglos, a difference which declined somewhat in old age, though this decline was not statistically significant. On contact with friends and neighbors, Anglos appear to be advantaged compared to the minority, an advantage increasing somewhat with age. However, since there was no noticeable variation by age among the minority respondents on this variable, the situation was not characterized as one of double jeopardy (Dowd and Bengtson, 1978).

Ward's (1980) study found little evidence supporting the notion of double jeopardy in primary group relations among older Blacks. Racial differences in interaction with family and friends as well as differences in satisfaction derived from family and friends were generally small and showed no changing patterns with age that supported either double jeopardy or leveling.

The area of family relations of older people is of great importance in social gerontology. There is considerable disagreement and controversy over how supportive the family is of the individual, particularly the older person, among minority groups. In contrast to earlier writings, most writings in the 1970s emphasized the strengths of Black families, including the provision of support and meaningful roles for older people (Davis, 1971; Hill, 1978; Jackson, 1970; Wylie, 1971). Yet, as with other minority groups, the supportive role of the family toward the Black aged may have been overemphasized by some (see the discussion by Jackson, 1980:137).

The literature on the Mexican American family has had a somewhat different history than that on the Black family. In the 1950s and 1960s, it was customary, for example, to describe the Mexican American family as extremely warm and supportive of the individual. Findings of lower incidence of psychiatric treatment were explained in terms of the supportive qualities of the Mexican American family (Jaco, 1957, 1959, 1960). Based on his ethnographic observations in south Texas, Madsen (1969) argued that stress has a more negative effect on the Anglo who experiences it alone, rather than on the Mexican American whose family shares and relieves outside stress. Studies of elderly Mexican Americans in San Antonio (Carp,

1968; Reich et al., 1966) also described the family as entremely warm and supportive of older people. In the late 1960s and early 1970s, a clear shift in the literature is observed. Writers began criticizing earlier studies for presenting a romanticized picture of the Chicano family. Specifically dealing with the place of the elderly in the family, critical reports on the literature were provided by Moore (1971) and by Maldonado (1975). Whereas Moore criticizes the inability of writers to interpret data without stereotypical preconceptions, Maldonado emphasizes the impact of urbanization and modernization in weakening the strength of the extended family.[3] Maldonado (1975) feels that the romanticized stereotype of the place of the elderly in the family may deprive them of needed services. Yet much of the literature continues to report that older Mexican Americans enjoy an advantageous position in the family as compared to older Anglos (Cuellar, 1978; Newton and Ruiz, forthcoming).

If, as much of the literature suggests, older Blacks and Hispanics or other elderly members of minority groups enjoy an advantaged position in the family, then the notion of double jeopardy of minority elderly may not apply to the area of family relations. But what is critical from this theoretical perspective is how the differences, racial or ethnic, change from middle age to old age. Neither literature on family relations nor on relations with friends and neighbors has produced sufficient data for evaluating the double jeopardy versus leveling alternatives. Perhaps what is more important is determining what constitutes an advantage or disadvantage in primary group relations. Greater interaction with kin, for example, may not necessarily imply more satisfying or meaningful family life (Hess and Waring, 1978).

Psychological Well-Being

No other area of research in social gerontology has received as much attention as the area of life satisfaction, morale, or psychological well-being in general. While numerous studies have examined the relationship between age and psychological well-being, the results have been mixed and inconclusive. Some show a small decline in well-being with age (Bradburn, 1969; Edwards and Klemmack, 1973; Neugarten et al., 1961); but when controls for health, socioeconomic status, or other important variables are introduced, the relationship disappears (Edwards and Klemmack, 1973; Kivett, 1976). Still other research has found a positive relationship between age and psychological well-being (e.g., Alston et al., 1974; Bortner and Hultsch, 1970; Clemente and Sauer, 1976; Czaja, 1975; Orchowsky and Parham, 1979; Witt et al., 1980).

The findings on the relationship between race or ethnicity and psychological well-being are as inconclusive as those relating to age. Most studies show that while older Blacks and Mexican Americans may score lower than Anglos on various measures of psychological well-being, these differences disappear when such variables as socioeconomic status and health are controlled (Clemente and Sauer, 1974; Markides et al., 1980; Markides, forthcoming; Spreitzer and Snyder, 1974).

The lack of clear evidence that race or ethnicity or age negatively affects psychological well-being, at least when socioeconomic status and health are held constant, does not provide much support for applying the double jeopardy thesis to this variable. The findings of the two major studies testing the double jeopardy hypothesis corroborate this notion. Dowd and Bengtson (1978) found greater decline with age in "optimism" among Mexican Americans than Anglos, but no significant change in "tranquility" with age. The situation with Blacks provided no support for double jeopardy on either component of life satisfaction. Ward (1980) used data from several national surveys to compare Blacks with Whites in different age groups, and found that seven measures of subjective well-being yielded no patterns either in the direction of double jeopardy or in the direction of leveling. Four measures—Affect Balance Scale, Life Satisfaction Index, an index measuring satisfaction with several domains of life, and a measure of rating life as exciting—showed no changes with age that would support either double jeopardy or leveling. Black disadvantages in global happiness and anomia observed in the younger age group (18 to 39) decline with age. Ward (1980) does not interpret these findings as supporting leveling in old age, however, since they "may . . . reflect the characteristics and experiences of this younger cohort." The only measure of well-being that was in the direction of double jeopardy was a measure of self-esteem, which changed from a small advantage for younger Blacks to a small disadvantage in old age. Ward (1980) again warns that "this pattern could be interpreted as a reflection of cohort differences in Black pride or system blame, rather than being due to aging effects. Ward's statements underscore the difficulties encountered in evaluating the double jeopardy hypothesis with cross-sectional data.

A somewhat different variable which has been used as an indicator of psychological well-being, though not directly a measure of it, is an older persons' perception of aging. Minority group members have repeatedly been found to perceive themselves as reaching old age earlier than Anglos, or to have older age identities (Bengtson, Kasschau, and Ragan, 1977). These differences are, to a large extent, a reflection of socioeconomic disadvantages over a lifetime (Jackson, 1970; Moore, 1971). Yet there is some evidence suggesting that significant ethnic or racial differences in age identifications persist even when the effect of socioeconomic status is held constant (Busse et al., 1970; Markides, 1980). Since there is good reason to believe that youthful age identities on the part of older people indicate a certain degree of denial of old age, it is possible that the older age identities of minority elderly after socioeconomic status is controlled reflect their relative insulation "from the values of the greater society that, by and large, define old age as an undesirable stage in the life cycle" (Markides, 1980:665).

When subjective age is defined from the perspective of "awareness of finitude" (Munnichs, 1968), or estimating the time one expects to live, different and quite interesting results have been found. Two independent studies conducted in Los Angeles (Reynolds and Kalish, 1974; Kalish and Reynolds, 1976; and Bengtson, Cuellar, and Ragan, 1977) found that Blacks in both middle age and in old age expected to and desired to live longer than Whites and Mexican Americans. This is paradoxical given the lower life expectancy of Blacks. Reynolds and Kalish (1974:23) suggested that these findings may indicate that Blacks may be reluctant to give life up because they worked so hard to "gain a foothold on it." Yet they found this answer unsatisfactory in light of the low expectations and wishes for longevity expressed by Mexican Americans. In addition, there was no evidence that the high expectations and wishes for longevity of Blacks reflected greater fear of death or anxiety about the outcome of death (Reynolds and Kalish, 1974: 230; Bengtson, Cuellar, and Ragan, 1977). In a more recent discussion of the matter, Kalish and Reynolds (1976:99-100) suggested the following:

> Given the pressures and the prejudices, the stresses and the discrimination that Black Americans face, their desire to attain a relatively long life, especially in the face of their actuarial life expectancies, is remarkable. While one might patronize these views as unrealistic, to expect to live longer than your allocated time and to wish to live still longer would appear to reflect optimism and hope, particularly when the surrounding world works toward destruction of the hopes. In these data, we find both resilience and an appreciation of life, undoubtedly supported by religious faith.

Despite their inability to suggest a satisfactory explanation of the phenomenon, Kalish and Reynolds (1976:100) felt that the greater desires and expectations for longevity by Blacks are consistent with their low suicide rates in middle and old age (Davis, 1979). They are, however, inconsistent with findings on Mexican Americans, as well as other findings using other measures of subjective or psychological well-being.

Discussion

The double jeopardy hypothesis predicting widening differentials with age between the minority and majority group persons finds mixed support in the empirical literature on Blacks and Hispanics. Why do national data on both income and health contradict Dowd's and Bengtson's (1978) Los Angeles findings? One reason may be differences in measurement, sampling, and age—the Los Angeles study only included people up to age 74. In the case of income as noted above, there are good reasons why the income of older members of minorities should be closer to the income of Whites at old age than at middle age. Since there is a drop in income with retirement—though not as large as cross-sectional data might suggest (Henretta and Campbell, 1976; Riley and Foner, 1968:82)—we may expect that the relative reduction is lower among minority groups because of their lower incomes in middle age. Although the incomes of the two groups are closer in old age, this does not necessarily mean that the relative economic disadvantage—particularly of Blacks—declines. Income figures say little about the other sources of financial security—property, insurance policies, savings—more common among White elderly. One study, for example, showed that older Blacks are more dependent on money income than older Whites, the latter having greater access to savings and credit (Goldstein, 1971). In addition, greater home ownership by older Whites leaves more income for other uses. Although the racial gap in home ownership has declined somewhat in recent years (Hoover, forthcoming; Jackson, 1980), the disadvantage of older Blacks is still large.

While we may accept the above interpretations of why the minority-majority income gap declines in old age for the moment, explaining a decline in the health differentials between Blacks and Whites (no such pattern is observed with Hispanics) shown in national data presents a greater challenge, unless we use the same logic applied earlier to income. Thus it is possible that the *increase* in old age in the incidence of poor health is lower among Blacks because their health is so much poorer in middle age to begin with. There is also another factor here which, while receiving some attention from a methodological standpoint, is receiving virtually no attention regarding its possible effect on racial differences in health: the well-established racial mortality crossover which takes place at about age 75 (Manton and Poss, 1977; Manton et al., 1979; Manton, 1980). That is, the mortality rates of Blacks and Whites converge gradually in old age and "cross over" at about age 75 so that life expectancy at these advanced ages is higher among Blacks than among Whites. Attempts to explain this phenomenon in terms of errors in the data have failed to eliminate the crossover (Kitagawa and Hauser, 1973; Manton, 1980; Rives, 1977). Manton (1980:481) discusses the probable reason for the existence of a racial mortality crossover or a crossover between any disadvantaged group with a more advantaged one, as follows:

The probable basis of such population mechanisms is the effect of differential mortality selection on a heterogeneous population. Specifically it can be shown that, if the individuals in populations are heterogeneous with respect to their endowment for longevity, then a crossover or convergence of the age specific mortality rates of two populations can occur if one population has markedly higher early mortality. The crossover is a result of the differential early mortality which selects the least robust persons from the disadvantaged population at relatively earlier ages so that, at advanced ages, the disadvantaged population has proportionately more robust persons.

Manton's (1980:492) examination of racial crossover by major causes of death led him to conclude that:

a larger proportion of Whites survive to advanced age because of better medical treatment and management of the chronic effects of disease. Blacks, on the other hand, would be less likely to survive a disease event at earlier ages so that they would have a proportionately lower prevalence of chronic conditions at advanced ages.

Note that in this last statement, Manton is speaking about chronic conditions at *advanced* ages, after the racial crossover takes place—usually after age 75. The prevalence of chronic conditions among persons 65 years old and over is higher among Blacks than Whites. Since a sizable proportion of older people are over the age of 75, however, the mortality crossover at this age would lead to fewer overall health problems among Blacks 65 years old and over as a group than would be expected in the absence of a crossover. Put another way, the existence of a crossover means a lower increase in health problems among Blacks from middle age to old age (65+) than would be observed in the absence of the crossover or than is observed in the White population, as national data show.

This smaller relative increase in health problems from middle to old age among Blacks should not be interpreted as indicating an advantage of Blacks over Whites. On the contrary, it is an indicator of the great disadvantage of Blacks relative to Whites. The irony in this interpretation is that, other things being equal, any improvements in the relative status of Blacks to Whites which might reduce higher early mortality (before old age) can be expected to lead to a later mortality crossover, or to the elimination of it altogether. This may also mean an increase in the health disadvantage of older Blacks compared to older Whites in the future, since more of the less "robust" Blacks will be surviving to advanced ages due to better medical care. This increase in the Black disadvantage is likely to be greatest after age 75.

A related point should be raised here. Since, as Manton (1980) shows, the mechanism that leads to a racial mortality crossover is greater early mortality that selects the least biologically robust members of the disadvantaged group, it may be presumed that these people are also less likely than the survivors to be robust in an economic sense. If this assumption is correct, the racial mortality crossover may be contributing to the leveling of income differences observed in national statistics. Again, using the logic applied in the previous paragraph, it may be argued that, other things being equal, any reductions in the socioeconomic (and health) disadvantage of Blacks compared to Whites in middle age will ultimately lead to greater socioeconomic inequality between Blacks and Whites in old age, especially after age 75.

The existence of a racial mortality crossover is an indication of racial differences in physiological aging under social and environmental conditions in the United States (Morgan, 1968; Jackson, 1980). Thus, following convention, if we arbitrarily assume that old age begins at 65 for Whites, Blacks and other disadvantaged minority groups are biologically old a few years before 65. That they also become old earlier socially and psychologically is suggested by evidence of their older age identification. If these assumptions are correct, studying racial or ethnic differences in the transition to old age with only chronological age marking such transitions may be inappropriate or, at a minimum, insufficient.

Turning now to the empirical evidence on primary group relations and psychological well-being and how this evidence relates to the predictions of the double jeopardy hypothesis, some brief comments are in order. First, if minority group members are advantaged in terms of family-based supports and roles as much of the literature suggests, speaking of double jeopardy of minority elderly in this area is inappropriate.[4] But as pointed out earlier, the literature has not clarified the extent to which greater involvement with kin on the part of minority aged constitutes an advantage in family relations.

The general lack of support for the predictions of widening differentials with age in psychological well-being reflects the absence of any firm and consistent evidence that age and race (minority status) are, by themselves, significant predictors of psychological well-being. Since subjective evaluations of life satisfaction, happiness, or morale are made with important reference groups in mind (e.g., other elderly, other elderly they come in contact with, and earlier ages), it may be unrealistic to expect large differences in such subjective evaluations regardless of how large the differences might be in the objective conditions between age groups or between racial or ethnic groups. This is also why socioeconomic status is such a poor (though usually significant) predictor of life satisfaction or morale (Larson, 1978). Since subjective well-being is so dependent on expectations which are molded, to a great extent, by reference group orientations,[5] it may be inappropriate to use them to indicate the disadvantage of members of ethnic minority groups or older age groups. Otherwise, we run the risk—as most data would suggest—of indicating a lack of disadvantage when one exists, as vast differences in objective conditions resulting from poverty and discrimination would indicate.

To summarize the discussion thus far, the predictions of the double jeopardy hypothesis as currently formulated have not received strong empirical support. While some leveling influences of age might be at work, it is also the case that inappropriate variables (e.g., contact with family or life satisfaction) have been used to measure the disadvantage of older minority members. In addition, conceptualizations of old age in groups with considerably different mortality experiences have been inadequate. Finally, and related, to the extent that early mortality differentially selects the least robust members of minority groups, widening health (and possibly income) differentials in old age (conventionally defined) would be unlikely. This general lack of empirical support for the double jeopardy thesis should not be interpreted to mean that older Blacks and older Hispanics are not victims of double jeopardy in the sense that they are subject to discrimination related to both age and minority status.

It is tempting to suggest that race or ethnic stratification is much less important than class stratification as some writers have suggested (Jackson and Walls, 1978; Wilson, 1978).[6] It is also tempting to suggest that age stratification is far less important than social class stratification, as has also been proposed (Henretta and Campbell, 1976; Ward, 1980). Both suggestions may be appropriate. Yet the double jeopardy hypothesis is so poorly conceptualized and articulated—as is the general multiple-hierarchy statification model—that such conclusions may be somewhat premature. Much theoretical work as well as more appropriate empirical investigations are necessary in this important area of inquiry. Finally, if anything should be clear from the above discussion, it is the dynamic nature of the interactive relationship between race or ethnic stratification and age stratification (Ward, 1980:16).

Notes

In addition to John Santos, the author is grateful to Dianne Fairbank for her critical reading of an earlier version of this paper and for her important suggestions.
1. Dowd and Bengtson recognized that the double jeopardy hypothesis should ideally be tested with longitudinal data so that the effects of aging may be separated from cohort effects. Longitudinal data on minority aging, however, are almost nonexistent. In their study, Dowd and Bengtson relied on cross-sectional

data while acknowledging their limitations. Additional studies reviewed here for evidence supporting the double jeopardy hypothesis are based on cross-sectional data. Caution thus will be necessary in attributing differences to the effects of aging.

2. A study conducted in San Antonio found that, with these variables held constant, older Mexican Americans and Anglos did not differ in their self-ratings (Markides and Martin, 1979b).

3. For discussion of a modernization perspective on older Mexican Americans, see Korte (forthcoming). For a fairly comprehensive and up-to-date review of the literature on the Mexican American family, see Ramirez and Arce (forthcoming).

4. There is some evidence suggesting that the greater involvement of older Blacks with their kin has an economic rather than a racial basis (Jackson and Walls, 1978; Ward, 1980).

5. It may be pointed out here that reference group explanations have been drawn upon to account for the inability of recent research to show racial or ethnic differences in self-esteem. See Rosenberg (1979), Simmons (1978), and Taylor and Walsh (1979).

6. Race or ethnic stratification is, of course, important in that it is the major determinant of class stratification, at least as it applies to the disadvantaged ethnic groups. Thus, separating the two stratification systems may be somewhat artificial.

References

Administration on Aging. 1980. *Characteristics of the Black Elderly.* Statistical Report on Older Americans, No. 5. Washington, D.C.: U.S. Government Printing Office.

Alston, Jon P., George D. Lowe, and Alice Wrigley. 1974. "Socioeconomic correlates of four dimensions of self-perceived satisfaction." *Human Organization* 33:99-102.

Antunes, George, C. Gordon, Charles M. Gaitz, and Judith Scott. 1974. "Ethnicity, socioeconomic status and the etiology of psychological distress." *Sociology and Social Research* 58:361-68.

Bengtson, Vern L. 1979. "Ethnicity and aging: problems and issues in current social science inquiry." Pp. 9-31 in Donald E. Gelfand and Alfred J. Kutzik (eds.), *Ethnicity and Aging.* New York: Springer.

Bengtson, Vern L., Jose B. Cuellar, and Pauline K. Ragan. 1977. "Stratum contrasts and similarities in attitudes toward death." *Journal of Gerontology* 32:76-88.

Bengtson, Vern L., Patricia L. Kasschau, and Pauline K. Ragan. 1977. "The impact of social structure on aging individuals." Pp. 327-54 in James E. Birren and K. Warner Schaie (eds.), *Handbook of the Psychology of Aging.* New York: Van Nostrand Reinhold.

Bianchi, Suzanne M. 1980. "Racial difference in per capita income, 1960-1976: the importance of household size, headship, and labor force participation." *Demography* 17:129-43.

Bortner, Raymond W., and David F. Hultsch. 1970. "A multivariate analysis of correlates of life satisfaction in adulthood." *Journal of Gerontology* 32:593-99.

Bradburn, Norman. 1969. *The Structure of Psychological Well-Being.* Chicago: Aldine.

Bureau of the Census. 1979. *The Social and Economic Status of the Black Population in the United States: An Historical View, 1790-1978.* Current Population Reports, Special Studies, Series P-23, No. 80. Washington, D.C: U.S. Government Printing Office.

Busse, Ewald W., Frances C. Jeffers, and Walter D. Orbist. 1970. "Factors in age awareness." Pp. 381-89 in Erdman Palmore (ed.), *Normal Aging: Reports from the Duke Longitudinal Study, 1955-1969.* Durham, N.C. Duke University Press.

Cantor, Majorie H. 1979. "The informal support system of New York's inner city elderly: is ethnicity a factor?" Pp. 153-174 in Donald E. Gelfand and Alfred J. Kutzik (eds.), *Ethnicity and Aging.* New York: Springer.

Carp, Frances. 1968. *Factors in Utilization of Services by the Mexican American Elderly.* Palo Alto: American Institutes for Research.

Clemente, Frank, and William J. Sauer. 1974. "Race and morale of the urban aged." *Gerontologist* 13:106-10.

Clemente, Frank, and William J. Sauer. 1976. "Life satisfaction in the United States." *Social Forces* 54:621-31.

Crandall, Richard C. 1980. *Gerontology: A Behavioral Science Approach.* Reading, Mass.: Addison-Wesley.

Cuellar, Jose B. 1978. "El Senior Citizens' Club: the older Mexican American in the voluntary association." Pp. 207-30 in Barbara G. Myerhoff and Andrei Simic (eds.), *Life's Career-Aging: Subcultural Variations on Growing Old.* Beverly Hills: Sage Publications.

Czaja, Sara J. 1975. "Age differences in life satisfaction as a function of discrepancy between real and ideal self concepts." *Experimental Aging Research* 1:81-89.

Davis, Donald L. 1971. "Growing old black." In *U.S. Senate Special Committee on Aging, The Multiple Hazards of Age and Race: The Situation of Aged Blacks in the United States.* Washington, D.C.: U.S. Government Printing Office.

Davis, Robert. 1979. "Black suicide in the seventies: current trends." *Suicide and Life Threatening Behavior* 9:131-40.

Decker, David L. 1980. *Social Gerontology: An Introduction to the Dynamics of Aging.* Boston: Little, Brown.

Dohrenwend, Barbara S. 1970. "Social class and stressful events." Pp. 313-19 in Evan H. Hare and J.K. Wings (eds.), *Psychiatric Epidemiology.* New York: Oxford.

Dohrenwend, Barbara S. 1973. "Social status and stressful life events." *Journal of Personality and Social Psychology* 9:203-14.

Dowd, James J. 1980. *Stratification among the Aged.* Monterey, Calif.: Brooks/Cole.

Dohrenwend, Bruce P., and Barbara S. Dohrenwend. 1969. *Social Status and Psychological Disorders.* New York: Wiley.

Dowd, James J., and Vern L. Bengtson. 1978. "Aging in minority populations: an examination of the double jeopardy hypothesis." *Journal of Gerontology* 33:427-36.

Edwards, John N., and David L. Klemmack. 1973. "Correlates of life satisfaction: a reexamination." *Journal of Gerontology* 28: 497-502.

Featherman, David L., and Robert M. Hauser. 1976. "Changes in the socioeconomic stratification of the races, 1962-1973." *American Journal of Sociology* 82:621-51.

Foner, Anne. 1979. "Ascribed and achieved bases of stratification." Pp. 219-242 in Alex Inkeles (ed.), *Annual Review of Sociology.* Palo Alto, Calif.: Annual Review.

Fried, Marc. 1975. "Social differences in mental health." In John Kosa and Irving Zola (eds.), *Poverty and Health: A Sociological Analysis.* Cambridge: Harvard University Press.

Friedsam, Hiram, and Harry W. Martin. 1963. "A comparison of self and physi-cians' health ratings in an older population." *Journal of Health and Social Be-havior* 4:179-83.

Fries, James F. 1980. "Aging, natural death and the compression of morbidity." *New England Journal of Medicine* 303:130-35.

Fujii, Sharon. 1976. "Older Asian Americans: victims of multiple jeopardy." *Civil Rights Digest,* Fall:22-29.

Goldstein, Sidney. 1971. "Negro-white differentials in consumer patterns of the aged, 1960-1961." *Gerontologist* 11:242-49.

Hendricks, Jon, and C. Davis Hendricks. 1977. *Aging in Mass Society.* Cambridge, Mass.: Winthrop.

Henretta, John C., and Richard T. Campbell. 1976. "Status attainment and status maintenance: a study of stratification in old age." *American Sociological Review* 41:981-92.

Henretta, John C., and Richard T. Campbell. 1978. "Net worth as an aspect of status." *American Journal of Sociology* 83:1204-23.

Hess, Beth B., and Elizabeth W. Markson. 1980. *Aging and Old Age: An Introduc-tion to Social Gerontology.* New York: Macmillan.

Hess, Beth B., and Joan M. Waring. 1978. "Parent and child in later life: rethinking the relationship." Pp. 241-73 in Richard M. Lerner and Graham B. Spanier (eds.), *Child Influences on Marital and Family Interaction.* New York: Academic Press.

Hill, Robert. 1978. "A demographic profile of the black elderly." *Aging* 287-88: 2-9.

Hoffman, Saul. 1978. "Black-white earnings differentials over the life cycle." In Greg J. Duncan and James N. Morgan (eds.), *Five Thousand American Fam-ilies—Patterns of Economic Progress,* vol. 6. Ann Arbor: Survey Research Cen-ter, University of Michigan.

Hoover, Sally L. Forthcoming. "Black and Hispanic elderly: their housing charac-teristics and quality." In M. Powell Lawton and Sally L. Hoover (eds.), *Com-munity Housing Choices for Older Americans.* New York: Springer.

Jackson, Jacqueline J. 1970. "Aged Negroes: their cultural departures from statis-tical stereotypes and selected rural-urban differences." *Gerontologist* 10:140-45.

Jackson, Jacqueline J. 1978. "Special health problems of aged blacks." *Aging* 287-88:15-20.

Jackson, Jacqueline J. 1980. *Minorities and Aging.* Belmont, Calif.: Wadsworth.

Jackson, Jacqueline J., and Bertram F. Walls. 1978. "Myths and realities about aged blacks." In Mollie Brown (ed.), *Readings in Gerontology.* St. Louis: C.V. Mosby.

Jaco, E. Gartley. 1957. "Social factors in mental disorders in Texas." *Social Prob-lems* 4:322-28.

Jaco, E. Gartley. 1959. "Mental health of the Spanish Americans in Texas." Pp. 467-88 in Marvin K. Opler (ed.), *Culture and Mental Health.* New York: Macmillan.

Jaco, E. Gartley. 1960. *The Social Epidemiology of Mental Disorders.* New York: Russell Sage.

Jeffries, Vincent, and H. Edward Ransford. 1980. *Social Stratification: A Multiple Hierarchy Approach.* Boston: Allyn & Bacon.

Jiobu, Robert M. 1976. "Earnings differentials between whites and ethnic minor-ities: the cases of Asian Americans, blacks and Chicanos." *Sociology and Social Research* 61:24-38.

Kalish, Richard A., and David K. Reynolds. 1976. *Death and Ethnicity: A Psycho-cultural Study.* Los Angeles: University of Southern California Press.

Kent, Donald P. 1971. "The Negro aged." *Gerontologist* 11:48-51.

Kent, Donald P., and Carl Hirsch. 1969. "Differentials in need and problem solving techniques among low-income Negro and white elderly." Presented at the 8th International Congress of Gerontology, Washington, D.C.

Kessler, Ronald C. 1979. "Stress, social status and psychological distress." *Journal of Health and Social Behavior* 20:100-108.

Kessler, Ronald C., and Paul D. Cleary. 1980. "Social class and psychological distress." *American Sociological Review* 45:463-78.

Kitagawa, Evelyn M., and Phillip M. Hauser. 1973. *Differential Mortality in the United States: A Study in Socio-economic Epidemiology.* Cambridge, Mass.: Harvard University Press.

Kivett, Vira. 1976. *The Aged in North Carolina: Physical, Social and Environmental Characteristics and Sources of Assistance.* North Carolina Agricultural Experiment Station, Technical Bulletin no. 237.

Korte, Alvin O. Forthcoming. "Theoretical perspectives in mental health and the Mexicano elders." In Manuel R. Miranda and Rene A. Ruiz (eds.), *Chicano Aging and Mental Health.* San Francisco: Human Resources Corp.

Larson, Reed. 1978. "Thirty years of research on subjective well-being of older Americans." *Journal of Gerontology* 33:109-25.

Long, Larry H., and Kristen A. Hansen. 1975. "Trends in return migration to the South." *Demography* 12:601-14.

Maddox, George L., and Elizabeth B. Douglass. 1973. "Self-assessment of health: a longitudinal study of elderly subjects." *Journal of Health and Social Behavior* 14:87-93.

Madsen, William. 1969. "Mexican Americans and Anglo Americans: a comparative study of mental health in Texas." In Stanley Plog and Robert Edgerton (eds.), *Changing Perspectives in Mental Illness.* New York: Holt, Reinhart & Winston.

Maldonado, David. 1975. "The Chicano aged." *Social Work* 20:213-16.

Manton, Kenneth G. 1980. "Sex and race specific mortality differentials in multiple cause of death data." *Gerontologist* 20:480-93.

Manton, Kenneth G., and Sharon S. Poss. 1977. "The black/white mortality crossover: possible racial differences." *Black Aging* 3:43-53.

Manton, Kenneth G., Sharon S. Poss, and Steven Wing. 1979. "The black/white mortality crossover: investigation from the perspective of the components of aging." *Gerontologist* 19:291-300.

Markides, Kyriakos S. 1980. "Ethnic differences in age identification: a study of older Mexican Americans and Anglos." *Social Science Quarterly* 60:659-66.

Markides, Kyriakos S. Forthcoming. "Correlates of life satisfaction among older Mexican Americans and Anglos." *Journal of Minority Aging.*

Markides, Kyriakos S. Forthcoming. "Health, income and the minority aged: a reexamination of the double jeopardy hypothesis." *Journal of Gerontology.*

Markides, Kyriakos S., and Harry W. Martin. 1979a. "A causal model of life satisfaction among the elderly." *Journal of Gerontology* 34:86-93.

Markides, Kyriakos S. and Harry W. Martin. 1979b. "Predicting self-rated health among the aged." *Research on Aging* 1:97-112.

Markides, Kyriakos S., Harry W. Martin, and Mark Sizemore. 1980. "Psychological distress among elderly Mexican Americans and Anglos." *Ethnicity* 7:298-309.

Markson, Elizabeth W. 1979. "Ethnicity as a factor in the institutionalization of the ethnic elderly." Pp. 341-56 in Donald E. Gelfand and Alfred J. Kutzik (eds.), *Ethnicity and Aging.* New York: Springer.

Morgan, Robert F. 1968. "The adult growth examination: preliminary comparisons of aging in adults by sex and race." *Perceptual and Motor Skills* 27:595-99.

Moore, Joan W. 1971. "Mexican Americans." *Gerontologist* 11:30-35.

Munnichs, J.M. 1968. *Old Age and Finitude: A Contribution to Psycho-gerontology.* New York: Karger.

Nam, Charles B., Norman L. Weatherby, and Kathleen A. Ockay. 1978. "Causes of death which contribute to the mortality crossover effects." *Social Biology* 25:306-34.

National Center for Health Statistics. 1977. *Current Estimates from the Health Interview Survey: United States—1976.* Public Health Service, Vital and Health Statistics, Series 10, No. 119. Washington, D.C.: U.S. Government Printing Office.

——. 1978 *Health Characteristics of Minority Groups, United States, 1976.* Public Health Service, Vital and Health Statistics, Advance Data, No. 27. Washington, D.C.: U.S. Government Printing Office.

——. 1980. *Health United States—1979.* Public Health Service. Washington, D.C.: U.S. Government Printing Office.

National Council on Aging. 1972. *Triple Jeopardy: Myth or Reality.* Washington, D.C.: National Council on Aging.

National Urban League. 1964. *Double Jeopardy: The Older Negro in America Today.* New York: National Urban League.

Neugarten, Bernice L., Robert Havighurst, and Sheldon S. Tobin. 1961. "The measurement of life satisfaction." *Journal of Gerontology* 16:134-43.

Newton, Frank. 1980. "Issues in research and service delivery among Mexican American elderly." *Gerontologist* 20:208-13.

Newton, Frank, and Rene A. Ruiz. Forthcoming. "Chicano culture and mental health among the elderly." In Manuel R. Miranda and Rene A. Ruiz (eds.), *Chicano Aging and Mental Health.* San Francisco: Human Resources Corp.

Orchowsky, Stan J., and Iris A. Parham. 1979. "Life satisfaction of blacks and whites: a lifespan approach." Paper presented at the Annual Meeting of the Gerontological Society, Washington, D.C.

Poston, Dudley L., Jr., and David Alvirez. 1973. "On the cost of being a Mexican American worker." *Social Science Quarterly* 53:697-709.

Ramirez, Oscar, and Carlos H. Arce. Forthcoming. "The contemporary Chicano family: an empirically based review." In Augustine Baron, Jr. (ed.), *Explorations in Chicano Psychology.* New York: Praeger.

Reich, Julie M., Michael A. Stegman, and Nancy W. Stegman. 1966. *Relocating the Dispossessed Elderly: A Study of Mexican Americans.* Philadelphia: Institute of Environmental Studies, University of Pennsylvania.

Reynolds, David K., and Richard A. Kalish. 1974. "Anticipation of futurity as a function of ethnicity and age." *Journal of Gerontology* 29:224-31.

Riley, Matilda W. 1976. "Age strata in social systems." Pp. 189-217 in Robert H. Binstock and Ethel Shanas (eds.), *Handbook of Aging and the Social Sciences.* New York: Van Nostrand Reinhold.

Riley, Matilda W., and Anne Foner. 1968. *Aging and Society, Vol. 1: An Inventory of Research Findings.* New York: Russell Sage.

Riley, Matilda W., Marilyn Johnson, and Anne Foner (eds.). 1972. *Aging and Society, vol. 3: A Sociology of Age Stratification.* New York: Russell Sage.

Rives, Norfleet W. 1977. "The effects of census errors on life table estimates of black mortality." *Public Health Briefs* 67:867-68.

Rosenberg, Morris. 1979. *Conceiving the Self.* New York: Basic Books.

Rosenfeld, Rachael A. 1980. "Race and sex differences in career dynamics." *American Sociological Review* 45:583-609.

Sauer, William J. 1977. "Morale of the urban aged: a regression analysis by race." *Journal of Gerontology* 32:600-608.

Seltzer, Mildred M., Sherry L. Corbett, and Robert C. Atchley (eds.). 1978. *Social Problems of the Aging.* Belmont, Calif.: Wadsworth.

Shanas, Ethel, et al. 1968. *Older People in Three Industrial Societies.* New York: Atherton.

Shanas, Ethel, and George L. Maddox. 1976. "Aging, health and the organization of health resources." Pp. 592-618 in Robert H. Binstock and Ethel Shanas (eds.), *Handbook of Aging and the Social Sciences.* New York: Van Nostrand Reinhold.

Simmons, Roberta G. 1978. "Blacks and high self-esteem: a puzzle." *Social Psychology Quarterly* 41:54-57.

Spreitzer, Elmer, and Elden E. Snyder. 1974. "Correlates of life satisfaction among the aged." *Journal of Gerontology* 29:454-58.

Staples, Robert. 1976. "The Black American family." In Charles H. Mindel and Robert W. Habenstein (eds.), *Ethnic Families in America.* New York: Elsevier.

Stern, Michael P. 1979. "The recent decline in ischemic heart disease mortality." *Annals of Internal Medicine* 91:630-40.

Taylor, Marylee C., and Edward J. Walsh. 1979. "Explanations of black self-esteem: some empirical tests." *Social Psychology Quarterly* 42:242-53.

Varghese, Rahu, and Fred Medinger. 1979. "Fatalism in response to stress among the minority aged." Pp. 96-116 in Donald E. Gelfand and Alfred J. Kutzik (eds.), *Ethnicity and Aging.* New York: Springer.

Ward, Russell A. 1980. "The stability of racial differences across age strata." Revision of a Paper Presented at the Annual Meeting of the Gerontological Society, Washington, D.C., 1979.

Whittington, Frank. 1975. "Aging and the relative income status of blacks." *Black Aging* 1:6-13.

Wilson, William J. 1978. *The Declining Significance of Race.* Chicago: University of Chicago Press.

Witt, David D., et al. 1980. "The changing association between age and happiness: emerging trend or methodological artifact?" *Social Forces* 58:1302-1307.

Wylie, Floyd. 1971. "Attitudes toward aging and the aged among black Americans: some historical perspectives." *Aging and Human Development* 2:66-70.

9

The Process of
Caretaker Selection

Charlotte Ikels

From 1978 to 1981 the Laboratory of Human Development at the Harvard Graduate School of Education conducted research[1] among families of Chinese and Irish ancestry in selected locations within the greater Boston area. A major aim of the research was to assess the relative value of certain factors in predicting patterns of family support for the elderly. These factors included values and attitudes of parents and of adult children relevant to caretaking; the presence, absence, and degree of proximity of persons in these kin relationships to an older person; neighborhood characteristics; and the history of the ethnic population in the greater Boston area.

Because of our special concern with family support networks, we necessarily concentrated on determining whether, how, and why someone in a family assumes responsibility for the well-being of a particular older member. Such a focus tends to obscure the fact that many older people, far from requiring help, are themselves providing it to other family members such as spouses, siblings, or grandchildren. Indeed, the majority of the elderly whom we encountered were capable of meeting most of their own needs. Therefore, in order to gain a more comprehensive picture of caretaking preferences and practices we drew on family histories, genealogies, and on informants' knowledge of other older people in the community. We worked directly with 37 families of Irish ancestry and 53 families of Chinese ancestry. Through these families we learned about caretaking arrangements in their countries of origin as well as about modifications to these arrangements occurring in the United States. In an effort to establish some boundaries to our sample, this analysis is limited to the 123 elderly (60 and over) of Irish ancestry and the 119 elderly of Chinese ancestry who were known to our informants and who had lived in the United States between 1960 and 1980.

Furthermore, since our work as well as that of others (e.g., Fengler and Goodrich, 1979; Crossman et al., 1981) indicated that spouses provide the bulk of care to the elderly, this article concentrates on cases where spouses are absent. Thus the major goal of this article is to offer explanations for the emergence of particular children from among their siblings who are prepared to assume the caretaking role.

The Process of Caretaker Selection

The process of caretaker selection appears to follow rules that transcend cultural differences. Regardless of whether we were examining the circumstances of an Irish elder or a Chinese elder, we could relatively easily predict their probable caretaking arrangement on the basis of a very few background variables: their marital status and the sex and location of their children at a time of parental crisis. Cultural values mediate this process primarily with reference to the sex of the child expected to assume the caretaking role. In both groups actual physical care is usually provided by women—either daughters or daughters-in-law, but Irish parents will look first to their daughters while Chinese parents will look first to their sons.

In the case of the Chinese this pattern is consistent with both historical and current practices in Hong Kong and in China although in the United States, Chinese parents are now more willing to consider turning to daughters than in the past (Lang, 1946; Freedman, 1970; Hsu, 1971; Mitchell, 1972; Davis-Friedmann, 1977; Parish and Whyte, 1978; Ikels, 1983).

In rural Ireland in the nineteenth century the wife of the son who inherited the parental farm was expected to look after her parents-in-law, but in urban America women of Irish ancestry are expected to look after their own parents (Arensberg, 1959; Shannon, 1966; Arensberg and Kimball, 1968; Kane, 1968; Biddle, 1976; Lees, 1977). Our data on nearly 200 adult children reveal that except in high income areas, daughters are *twice* as likely as sons to remain in the parental district. In high income areas daughters and sons move out at approximately the same rates.

In the case of the Chinese the sex pattern is reversed although the variability by income is essentially the same. A major reason why elderly Chinese continue to follow the traditional pattern is their greater recency of immigration. A combination of historical factors including discriminatory immigration policies which favored Irish immigration while restricting Chinese immigration has meant that the Chinese elderly are much more likely than the Irish to be foreign-born. In our study four-fifths of the Chinese elderly are foreign-born compared to only one-third of the Irish elderly.

Despite differences in patterns of family organization and in immigration history, caretaking outcomes in the two groups nevertheless can be predicted with considerable regularity. The composition and location of a person's descendants, family history, and contingencies at the time a caretaking decision has to be made all have an impact on the selection of the child. Several factors may, of course, be intertwined and it is often difficult to establish a primary one. Proximity of a particular child, for example, renders this child a likely candidate for the role of caretaker, but the prior question of why this child is more proximate than others still remains. The factors involved in the selection of caretakers are listed below in approximate order of their explanatory power:

> *Demographic Imperatives*—The caretaker is the
>> only child
>> only child of preferred sex
>> only proximate child
>> only single child (relevant primarily for the Irish)
> *Antecedent Events*
>> gradual emergence
>> special obligations of reciprocity
> *Situational Factors*
>> least inconvenience
>> greatest motivation

Demographic Imperatives

As the above list suggests, we could most confidently predict the caretaker when the parent had only one child or when there was only one child of the preferred sex. Similarly predictable situations were those in which the parent had only one child in the vicinity or (in the case of the Irish) only one unmarried child. Children, even including only children, could escape these culturally predetermined roles, but only if they acted decisively and early in adulthood before conditions beyond their control such as parental widowhood made it impossible for them to reject the role.

Leaving town is one of the most acceptable ways of avoiding a caretaking future, but there are approved and disapproved reasons for leaving and these vary by the sex of the child and the socioeconomic status of the family. In many parts of the country going away from home is a necessary part of obtaining a college education. In the greater Boston area this is certainly not the case as there is a multitude of postsecondary institutions to meet almost any need for specialized or advanced education. We took care to record the location of the colleges or universities attended by the children of our focal elders and found that very few of the college-educated

Irish in our study were educated outside of the Boston area whereas substantial numbers of the Chinese were (this fact is partially accounted for by historical circumstances). Most of those educated outside of the Boston area remained outside following graduation. They took jobs elsewhere or married people from other parts of the country, thus decreasing the likelihood of being proximate at the time of need.

Another major difference between the Chinese and the Irish families in our study was the degree to which they felt bound to the greater Boston area. Chinese parents were much less placebound, and the relocation of an adult child was not so threatening. Instead of requiring a child to remain in the parental vicinity, Chinese parents were more willing to relocate to a place convenient to the children. A common parental strategy appears to be to wait until the children appear settled, and then, following their own retirement but prior to the development of any special needs, to move near the children. Such moves are usually preceded by lengthy visits to each child in an effort to determine the extent of compatibility. To the contrary, almost none of the Irish elderly considered moving in old age except to elderly housing or a small apartment within the same general area. The greater willingness of the Chinese parents to make long-distance moves is partly attributable to historical circumstances: many of them have already made at least one long-distance move in the course of coming to the United States, and many have personal friends living in or around Chinatowns in other states.

Our own observations suggest that a child's freedom of action is greatest while the parental unit is still intact and/or before dependence becomes an issue. Leaving a widowed parent alone—that is, with no other children in the area—appears unacceptable in both groups. Thus parental age and household composition at widowhood are antecedent events that have a strong influence on subsequent emergence of the caretaker. Two cases below illustrate this point.

The O'Rourke Family. Mrs. O'Rourke was born in England of Irish ancestry, but at a very early age immigrated to the United States with her parents and maternal grandparents. (Her mother was an only child, and probably for that reason her parents followed her to Boston. Most young adults who immigrated left their parents in Ireland where other youngsters could look after them.) Shortly after their arrival in the United States, Mrs. O'Rourke's father died. Within the next year her mother died, and Mrs. O'Rourke was brought up by her maternal grandparents and in turn cared for her grandmother until the latter's death. In 1972, Mrs. O'Rourke, then only 42 years old, suddenly lost her husband. This was a devastating blow, and she became heavily dependent on her high-school-aged daughter, sometimes pleading with the girl to stay home from school. Mrs.

FIGURE 9.1
The O'Rourke Family

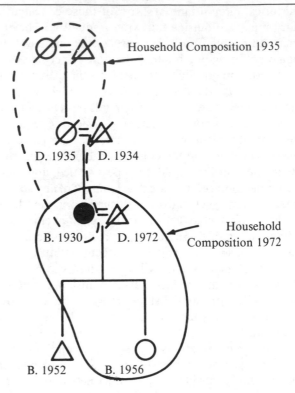

Household Composition 1935

D. 1935   D. 1934

B. 1930   D. 1972

Household Composition 1972

B. 1952   B. 1956

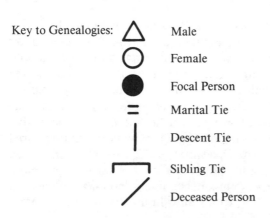

Key to Genealogies:

△ Male

○ Female

● Focal Person

= Marital Tie

| Descent Tie

⌐ Sibling Tie

╱ Deceased Person

O'Rourke's son was already attending a university out of state, and he has never returned to live in the Boston area. Miss O'Rourke acceded to maternal pressure to obtain her college education locally. She lived at home and since her college graduation has worked only a few blocks away. She is fully aware of her mother's hopes for an intense life-long relationship but is not yet prepared to commit herself.

In 1980 the young man with whom she had a serious relationship was transferred out of state by his company. After considerable soul-searching, Miss O'Rourke determined to accompany him. This decision was made difficult not only by her mother's situation, but also by the fact that she was not even formally engaged—a fact well known to the neighbors.

Following Miss O'Rourke's departure, Mrs. O'Rourke's son returned to help his mother adjust to her daughter's absence, but he was able to stay for only a few days. Mrs. O'Rourke became disorganized and desperate. Her deterioration was visible to everyone in the community including her daughter's friends who called Miss O'Rourke to inform her of her mother's condition. Miss O'Rourke managed to stay with her boyfriend for six months, but in the end returned to her mother because she "could not take the guilt." Miss O'Rourke's predicament is compounded by her sex, her mother's age at widowhood, her brother's absence from home, and the fact that her own mother had remained with a dependent senior family member as a caretaker.

The Chin Family. Mrs. Chin's father-in-law worked in the South Pacific and sent money back to his wife and son's family in China. Around the time of the Communist victory, the Chin family fled to Hong Kong where they set up a successful laundry business. Two of Mrs. Chin's children settled in New Zealand; her third child, a son, studied and subsequently found a job there; her fourth child, a daughter, married a man from New Zealand through her grandfather's introduction. In 1963 Mr. Chin became ill and realized that he did not have long to live. He recalled his New Zealand son to Hong Kong to discuss the family future. In view of educational and immigration considerations, the family decided that the second child, a daughter who had married and moved to the United States, would sponsor their immigration to the Boston area. The oldest child, a son, remained behind in Hong Kong for three years working out business and property arrangements.

Eventually all of the children with the exception of the two who had settled in New Zealand were living within a few doors of each other in Boston. Mrs. Chin lived with her youngest son while actually performing housekeeping and babysitting functions for both her eldest son and her by-then-married youngest daughter. By 1975 the number of grandchildren had multiplied, the neighborhood was deteriorating, and a family business ven-

FIGURE 9.2
The Chin Family

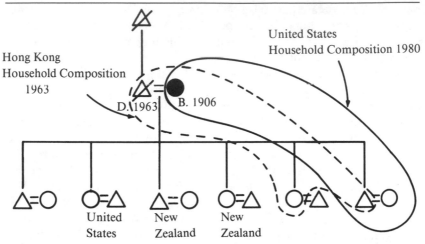

ture had gone sour. All these problems stimulated the various children to relocate. When her youngest son (now married) indicated his interest in purchasing a house in a more desirable area of Boston, Mrs. Chin moved along with him. In fact, she contributed a substantial amount of money to the down payment and justified it as his due since he had been too young at the time his father died to be considered in the division of property. Mr. Chin is the only child who has never lived apart from his mother and, as in Miss O'Rourke's case, this is largely due to the fact that he was the only child of the appropriate sex at home when his mother was widowed.

Antecedent Events

As we saw above, early age at widowhood usually means that dependent children are still at home. These children are slated early on for the caretaking role and gradually assume it. In many families, however, children reach middle-age with healthy parents and with no one of them overtly slated to assume caretaking responsibilities. When a parent becomes vulnerable in these circumstances, children have to make quick decisions about filial obligations. Proximity exerts tremendous influence on these decisions. If there is only one child in the area at the time of the crisis, that child has no choice but to step foward—another example of the force of the "demographic imperative." When several children of the appropriate sex are more or less equally proximate, other practical considerations arise. The child who owes the parent a special debt is a likely candidate. Such debts may be incurred as the result of special favors or assistance rendered by the parent when the child was undergoing a job change or emotional turmoil, or by the parent raising grandchildren after a child's divorce.

All other things being equal, a child with the fewest competing obligations is also a likely candidate for caretaking. A child with a disabled spouse, dependent children, or responsibility for parents-in-law enjoys exemption. If two candidates are employed, the one with the least well-paying job or the most marginal participation in the labor force becomes the caretaker. When someone other than the most proximate child or a child of the "wrong" sex (culturally speaking) becomes the caretaker, family history can usually provide an explanation for the unusual outcome, as the two following cases illustrate.

The Foley Family. In this family, sex and proximity as determiners of the caretaker are over-ridden by earlier events. The mother in this Irish-American family who gave birth to four sons and two daughters expects to be looked after by a son rather than a daughter and by a son who lives in the suburbs rather than the son who lives around the corner. The choice of this son as caretaker stems from considerations of alienation from other children and of his having incurred a special debt.

At the time of Mr. Foley's death, all of the children had already married and/or moved out. Following the death of her husband, Mrs. Foley made the culturally acceptable move to her younger daughter's home on the shore south of Boston. Unfortunately, after a few months Mrs. Foley realized that her daughter and son-in-law were exploiting her financially, and she returned to her own home. Her daughter's marriage has since dissolved, but Mrs. Foley has no plans to try again as she disapproves of her newly divorced daughter's moral standards. Her older daughter is married to a

FIGURE 9.3
The Foley Family

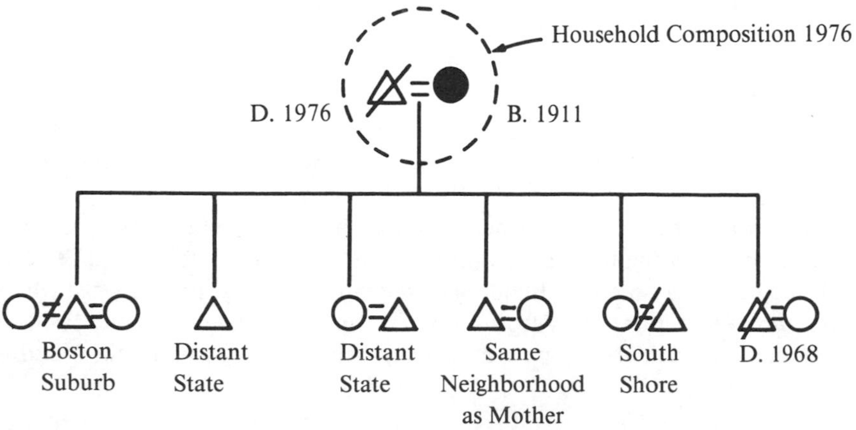

serviceman who has been stationed in a distant state and whose return to the Boston area is unpredictable.

Mrs. Foley's second son originally chose the religious life, but later withdrew and long ago settled in California. Her youngest son was killed in the Vietnam War. Thus only her first and third sons can be considered realistic prospects. Her third son married a girl from the neighborhood but only after overcoming extreme opposition from the girl's mother who refused to allow her daughter to marry him even though she was already pregnant. The precise reasons for the opposition were not spelled out, but it appears that the young woman's family had great aspirations for upward mobility and did not view the Foley family, whose men tended to have serious problems with alcohol, as likely to be helpful in reaching that objective. In order to marry this girl, Mrs. Foley's son appears to have agreed to integrate himself and his children into his mother-in-law's household. Although living only a short distance away, he sees his mother only once or twice a year—when accidentally encountering her on the street.

The oldest son is willing to become the caretaker not simply by default but because he is aware of a substantial debt owed to his parents. When his oldest child was only two years old, his (first) wife ran off with their infant daughter. He had no place to turn except to his parents, and Mrs. Foley raised her grandson for six years until her son remarried. Futhermore, when on his deathbed, the senior Mr. Foley admonished the oldest son to look after the mother.

The Ng Family. This immigrant family has not yet settled the issue of who will become the caretaker, but Mrs. Ng is clearly dissatisfied with the current situation which places her two daughters in the same block and her two sons thousands of miles away. Mrs. Ng had envisioned living with her older son in part because this was the one child of her four with whom she had lived the longest. Shortly after the Ng family fled to Taiwan, Mrs. Ng had been abandoned by her husband. Stranded with four young children, she was forced to break up the family temporarily. She and her older son were brought to Mexico where her father had been living for many years with his second family. The second child remained in Taiwan with a close family friend while the two youngest were sent to Hong Kong to live with Mrs. Ng's own mother. Mrs. Ng and her son eventually made their way to California where she met and remarried a widower who had no children of his own.

Following their return to her new husband's area (Boston), Mrs. Ng succeeded in bringing the remaining three children to the United States. While her older son was attending college in western Massachusetts, Mrs. Ng arranged a home-away-from-home for him with the family of a friend. An unexpected result of this arrangement was that her son and her friend's

FIGURE 9.4
The Ng Family

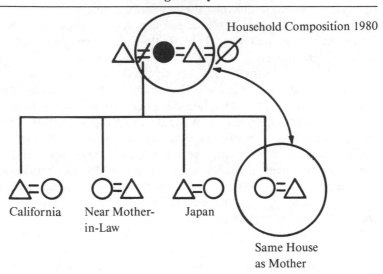

Household Composition 1980

California   Near Mother-   Japan
              in-Law

Same House
as Mother

daughter decided to get married. Mrs. Ng did not approve of this choice but did not say so directly. Instead she limited herself to remarking that she hoped he would think this over. The new daughter-in-law did not want to live with her mother-in-law, but the young couple did at first settle in the same block. Nevertheless it soon became clear that the two couples had no future together, and the younger couple soon moved to California.

Mrs. Ng's next child, a daughter, is married and living in the same neighborhood as her mother-in-law. The next child, a son, is married and is working in another country. The youngest child, a daughter, recently married, is living in her mother's dwelling and paying rent to the senior generation. The Ngs generally accept that this is a temporary situation. Mrs. Ng is trying to encourage her younger son and his wife to return to the United States, and as a special enticement has offered to finance a house purchase for him in California where she would like to return. Whether these efforts will succeed is unclear, but should a family catastrophe occur at this point Mrs. Ng will have to turn to her daughters.

Situational Factors

Siblings themselves may have to cooperate in determining and/or justifying their relative involvement in the caretaking role. Sometimes these decisions can be arrived at logically by careful evaluation of each child's

circumstances and previous contributions. At other times, for reasons of
his or her own a particular child will volunteer to assume the caretaking
role. The cases below illustrate these two situations.

The Lee Family. Mrs. Lee is one of very few elderly Chinese women to
have been born in the United States. Following an arranged marriage at the
age of 15, she moved to Boston's Chinatown with her husband and lived
there until 1979. At the time of her husband's death in 1975 only her 39-
year-old youngest son was still at home although he was scheduled to be
married two weeks later. Despite traditional prohibitions against the marriage of a child within a year of the death of a parent, Mrs. Lee herself
encouraged her son to hold the wedding as scheduled and she herself as
well as her children attended. Her son and his bride set up an independent
household in a nearby district of Boston while Mrs. Lee remained in her
own home. She was comfortable in Chinatown, able to manage most of her
own needs, and had as long-time neighbors in the same building a family
from her husband's village in China.

Mrs. Lee would probably have remained there until no longer capable of
independent living except for the fact that the building changed ownership
and the new owner required the tenants to vacate as he planned to do
extensive renovation. Mrs. Lee did not want a new apartment of her own,
nor did she want to move into elderly housing. Largely by rejecting all

FIGURE 9.5
The Lee Family

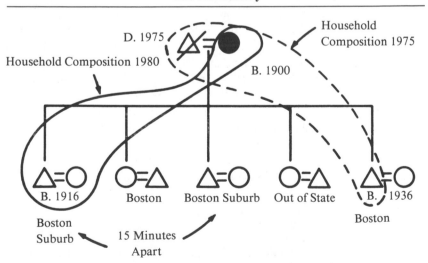

alternative propositions, she made it clear that she wanted to move into a child's home. At that time two children lived relatively close to Mrs. Lee, but one was a daughter who could be exempted on cultural grounds and the other was the youngest son who could claim to have fulfilled his obligations at an earlier stage—he had remained with his parents until he was 39 years old. Thus the choice narrowed down to the first or the third child, both sons living within a fifteen-minute walk of each other in a northern suburb.

The choice of the oldest son may have been partly based on cultural prescriptions, but family members themselves cited situational factors of convenience. The oldest son's wife worked nearby and could easily return home daily to share lunch with her mother-in-law. Furthermore, two of the three grandchildren were no longer living at home so there was enough space to easily include the old woman. On the other hand, one child was still at home so that there was somewhat more company than would have been the case at the third son's home where all the children had already left.

The Collins Family. Mrs. Collins's family situation reflects elements of both gradual emergence and greatest motivation. Mrs. Collins, a 72-year-old, third-generation Irish-American, had moved into her husband's community from a neighboring district. Shortly after the birth of her first child, her widowed mother and single sister moved in with her. (Mrs. Collins had only the one sister and had lost her father when she was eight years old. Her younger sister had never lived apart from their mother.) Her mother helped look after the children while her sister contributed to the household income. Mrs. Collins was widowed in 1948, and over the next 20 years her children gradually married and moved out of the community. Their ability to marry was facilitated by the fact that their marriages did not constitute abandonment of their mother. After all, their grandmother and aunt were still members of the household.

The two sisters remained together following the death of their mother and until the late 1970s were reasonably certain of which child would eventually fill the caretaking role. Of her four surviving children, two daughters and two sons, Mrs. Collins expected the third child to become the caretaker. Indeed, this daughter had explicitly stated that she would do so. We cannot be certain, but it appears that this daughter may have delayed her marriage as she was the only one of the four married children to have no children of her own. Childless marriages in our sample were usually linked to delayed marriage; this in turn was usually linked with caretaking responsibilities.

These expectations were altered, however, when the intended caretaker died at the age of 50 in 1979. The role did not devolve upon the remaining daughter as she already had responsibility for her mother-in-law. Instead

FIGURE 9.6
The Collins Family

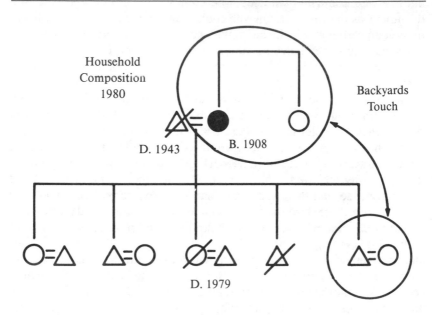

the role had to be assumed by one of the sons, both of whom lived in the same south shore community as their surviving sister. At this point the special motivations of the younger son played an important role in the final decision, for he—quite independent of his mother and aunt's situation—had reasons of his own for wanting to leave the community. He and his wife had been very active in their church and in some ways served as a model family in their parish. Unfortunately their eldest son destroyed the family's position by his irresponsible behavior which reached a crescendo shortly after his aunt's death. Embarrassed to remain in their old home, the younger Collinses turned the house over to their eldest son and his family and returned to their natal community, taking up residence in the same block as Mrs. Collins and her sister. As of 1980 Mrs. Collins was managing well, but she and her sister know that should there come a time when they need assistance it is always available just across the yard.

References to sentiment were strikingly absent from conversations with both parents and adult children. Affectional bonds were seldom cited as causal factors in caretaker selection although they were occasionally mentioned as an effect. A parent-child pair with a long history of coresidence frequently manifested intense solidarity, but there were also cases of care-takers hostile to their roles. Hostility was usually not expressed directly to the parent or even about the parent. Rather it took the form of resentment of the role itself for the way it constrained other aspects of the caretaker's life or resentment of siblings who, as one caretaker put it, "left me holding the bag." Similarly, parents who felt neglected could seldom bring them-selves to blame their children directly for an unhappy situation. Instead they blamed their children-in-law.

The Case of the Widower

In all of the cases mentioned so far, loss of a spouse has been an event of concern to women, but it was also a concern of some of the men in our study. In the case of Irish men, the consequences of losing a spouse de-pended largely on the age at which this occurred. A man who was widowed in his early years with dependent children frequently expected his mother or unmarried sisters to take on the roles of homemaker and mother to his children and perhaps later remarried. A man widowed with adult children still at home became the responsibility of a daughter if there was one. A man widowed with all children out of the home considered remarriage, moving in with a single or widowed sister, or persuading a nonresident child to return to the home. Almost no men moved in with a married child.

Historically, Chinese men were denied most of these options because of the acute shortage of women [Chinese railroad workers having been forbid-den to bring wives to the United States, and general immigration being limited up to the late 1940s — ed.] and the nature of the patrilineal kinship system which dispersed sisters at marriage and kept brothers in the same area. While immigration to the United States necessarily resulted in the dispersion of brothers, those men who did have a sibling nearby usually had a male sibling. Also the long years spent as de facto bachelors in the United States meant that the men were accustomed to relying on each other and not on women for meeting most of their needs. Old workmates sometimes became roommates or lived in semidormitories provided by district organizations in the days before elderly housing became available.

Conclusions

Through the cases presented above we hope to have demonstrated the value of the micro-level approach to the study of the circumstances of the elderly. By examining closely the life histories and the genealogies of our informants we were able to detect the underlying dynamic which leads to caretaker selection. While this process is mediated by cultural values and historical circumstances, it nevertheless appears to be guided by transcultural principles. Keeping in mind these principles, gerontologists can begin to interpret the impact of shifts in the age at marriage, birth of last child, or occurrence of widowhood on the process of caretaker selection. For example, women are now likely to encounter widowhood at later ages than before. In terms of household composition they are more likely to be widowed after the children have already left the home. This means that situational factors and motivations will have to be faced directly by siblings who in the past could avoid caretaking issues by letting the youngest get left "holding the bag." Or will mid-life divorce assume the dimensions formerly associated with widowhood? Detailed micro-level analysis will be helpful in answering these questions.

Note

1. This research was supported by a grant from the National Institute on Aging, R01 AG 01095, codirectors Robert Levine and Charlotte Ikels.

References

Arensberg, C. 1959. *The Irish Countryman.* New York: Macmillan.

Arensberg, C., and S. Kimball. 1968. *Family and Community in Ireland.* Cambridge, Mass.: Harvard University Press.

Biddle, E. H. 1976. "The American Catholic Irish family," in C. Mindel and R. Habenstein (eds.), *Ethnic Families in America: Patterns and Variations.* New York: Elsevier.

Crossman, L., C. London, and C. Barry. 1981. "Older Women Caring for Disabled Spouses: A Model for Supportive Services." *Gerontologist* 21(5): 464-80.

Davis-Friedman, D. 1977. "Strategies for Aging: Interdependence between Generations in the Transition to Socialism." *Contemporary China* 1(6):34-42.

Fengler, A. P., and N. Goodrich. 1979. "Wives of Elderly Disabled Men: The Hidden Patients." *Gerontologist* 19(2):175-83.

Freedman, M. 1970. *Lineage Organization in Southeastern China.* London: Athlone.

Hsu, F. L. K. 1971. *Under the Ancestors' Shadow* (1948). Stanford: Stanford University Press.

Ikels, C. 1983. *Aging and Adaptation: Chinese in Hong Kong and the United States.* Hamden, Colo.: Archon.

Kane, E. 1968. "Man and Kin in Donegal." *Ethnology* 17:245-58.

Lang, O. 1946. *Chinese Family and Society.* New Haven, Conn.: Yale University Press.

Lees, L., and R. Modell. 1977. "The Irish Countryman Urbanized: A Comparative Perspective on the Famine Migration." *Journal of Urban History* 3:391-408.

Mitchell, R. E. 1972. *Family Life in Urban Hong Kong.* Taipai: Orient Cultural Service.

Parish, W. L., and M. K. Whyte. 1978. *Village and Family in Contemporary China.* Chicago: University of Chicago Press.

Shannon, W. V. 1966. *The American Irish.* New York: Macmillan.

10

"Second Childhood": Old Age in Popular Culture

Arnold Arluke and Jack Levin

There is an extreme and unremitting bias against older adults in America, a bias so prevalent that it has been given the name "ageism" (Butler, 1968). Psychologically, ageism can be regarded as an attitude—a negative evaluation that serves to orient individuals toward old people as a group. In particular, it frequently predisposes individuals to discriminate, that is, to avoid contact, victimize, or otherwise do injury to old people based on their age status alone. Ageism is also a tendency to stereotype old people— which is, of course, another form of injury. We picture them as rigid, meddlesome, sexless, conservative, unhealthy, inactive, lonely, forgetful, and not very bright (Levin and Levin, 1980).

Many stereotypes portray old age as a time of second childhood. This dim view of the elderly suggests that they are losing, or have lost, the very things a growing child gains. It implies a backward movement to earlier developmental stages, with no recognition of the lifetime of experience that unquestionably separates the elderly from children (Gresham, 1973).

The image of old people as childlike has been with us for a long time. Tuckman and Lorge (1953) asked graduate students in psychology to indicate their agreement or disagreement with a number of statements about old people. Despite the fact that their subjects were well acquainted with psychology and enrolled in a course involving the aging process, there was a high level of agreement that old people like to collect many useless things, are poorly coordinated, cannot taste differences in foods, have to go to bed early, need a nap every day, are in the "happiest" period of their lives, cannot manage their own affairs, and are in their second childhood.

More recent research indicates that stereotyping continues to be an integral part of public images of the aged, and that a major thrust of this stereotyping still perpetuates the second childhood image. McTavish (1971) found considerable acceptance of an image of old people that is distinctly reminiscent of the toddler image known as "the terrible twos." Many of his subjects felt that old people are likely to be annoying, complaining, and inconsiderate. In 1975, the National Council on the Aging reported the results of a survey of 4,254 adult Americans (Harris, 1975). Old people were generally thought of as useless and inactive by participants in the survey. Subjects agreed that the elderly spend most of their time watching television or "doing nothing" in the true spirit of directionless adolescence.

Our society has not always mistreated or stereotyped its old people. In colonial America it was youth who encountered ageism. According to Fischer (1977), aged Americans living 200 years ago commanded inordinate respect, power, and privilege. Under Puritanism, old age was regarded as a sign of election and a special gift from God. In their dress and hairstyles, early Americans frequently tried to make themselves out to be older than they really were. Men would hide their natural hair beneath a wig, or they would powder their own hair to give it a white color associated with advanced age. Until the nineteenth century, the census taker frequently found that citizens represented themselves as older than they were. Today's census taker finds misrepresentations of age too, but in the opposite direction.

During the nineteenth century the privileged status of old age began to deteriorate as America modernized. First, as levels of literacy and education increased, there was less reliance on the older generation as a source of knowledge. Since the young became better educated, they began to hold a competitive edge with respect to jobs, status, and power. This led, second, to a retirement that reduced the standard of living and social status of the aged. Third, the nuclear family became more prevalent, so that older members of society were expected to live apart in independent households or to seek care. And finally, in the shift from agriculture to industry, older members of society lost control over land and were forced instead to compete with younger persons for nonagricultural positions.

By the twentieth century, ageism had become a cultural phenomenon—part of the normative order of our society. As such it was passed from generation to generation through the process of socialization much like other cultural phenomena—love of country and church, motherhood, the success ethic, and so forth. The result is that there is now widespread acceptance of ageism crosscutting differences in age, region, social class, and occupation. Studies have recorded agreement with age stereotypes not only among groups of physicians, nurses, ministers, and middle-aged children of aged parents, but also among institutionalized older persons and gerontologists.

Since ageism is so prevalent in society at large, it is hardly surprising to find ageism in popular culture which expresses, and in turn transmits, age prejudice. Television, in particular, has consistently assigned negatively stereotyped roles to the aged when it has not ignored the aged altogether. As revealed in his study of characters appearing in prime-time network TV drama, Aronoff (1974) reports that the aged comprised less than 5 percent of all characters, about half of the proportion that they actually occupied in the population of the United States at the time of his study. When they did appear, the aged tended to be depicted as evil, unsuccessful, and unhappy. TV commercials have similarly ignored or stereotyped the aged. One study found that only two out of 100 television commercials contained older characters (Francher, 1973). The focus of attention was on the "Pepsi Generation"—young and attractive characters who promise youthful appearance or behavior.

Newspapers are little better than television in their treatment of the elderly. According to MacDonald's (1973) analysis of 265 articles on the subject of aging, all appearing in a large midwestern newspaper, old people who are still active in their communities are ignored. The newspaper focus is largely on the problems of old age or the mere "human interest" side, which features retirees graduating from college at seventy-five or reminiscing about the "good old days."

Age stereotypes characterize the portrayal of old people in prescription drug advertisments as well. Smith (1976) found aged models in drug ads frequently described solely on the basis of old age as disruptive, apathetic, temperamental, and out of control.

Even birthday cards perpetuate age stereotypes. A study by Demos and Jache (1981) found contemporary birthday cards often depicting old age as a time of physical, sexual, and intellectual decline.

Infantilizing Elders

Most pernicious, perhaps, of all age stereotypes is that of "second childhood." It is certainly the most widely represented in popular culture. There are at least six ways in which second childhood is portrayed:

Old people and children are paired with each other. A TV commercial for "Country-Time Lemonade" shows an elderly man with children gathered round him as he claims that this tastes as good to him as lemonade did when he was young. A DuPont commercial shows an old man and young boy floating along in a small boat enjoying their idle time. A magazine ad for Yashica cameras has an old man snapping pictures of a small girl holding a stuffed dog, while an ad for the prescription drug Isuprel features an old man blowing bubbles as a young girl sits on his lap and watches him intently.

One seemingly favorable interpretation of these juxtapositions of age and youth is that children and the elderly share a special bond and that such pairing need not suggest that old people are childlike. Yet the equally plausible interpretation—and the tone of the ads heavily leans this way—is that they both have a lot of personality characteristics in common.

Some pairings of children and elders are not subtle. They clearly suggest the second childhood image of old age. Note the 1979 movie *Just You and Me, Kid* costarring teenager Brooke Shields and elder George Burns. Newspaper ads showed the two stars playing stickup and described the film as "the story of two juvenile delinquents." In an article called "The Fun Life for Young and Old," the *Boston Globe* provided "a guide to August activities for senior citizens and children." Pictures were shown of a puppet show and a magic act. Even the "Kiddies' Menu" of a popular Massachusetts ice cream parlor portrays an older man walking hand-in-hand with a young boy. As clearly stated on the face of the menu, "for all kids under 10 and over 65," the bill of fare consists of a "hot doggie," "kiddie burger," and "peanut butter and jelly sandwich."

Old people are given the personality and moods of children. It is common in prescription drug ads to describe the symptoms of senility in terms normally associated with the personality and behavior of children. A Mellaril ad "for the agitated geriatric" shows an elderly man angrily waving his fist. "Tantrums" is printed large across the page. Other drug ads for senility use terms such as "nuisance," "torment," "disruptive," "obstreperous," and "disorderly behavior" to describe elderly behavior. The recent children's book, *How Does It Feel to Be Old?* also implies a delinquent side of the aged personality. At one point, the elderly woman who is explaining to a young girl what it is like to be old compares herself to a "demon" who is "cranky." TV shows and movies characterize the personality of older people as childlike whether it is "Mother Jefferson's" cantankerousness, the silliness of Johnny Carson's "Aunt Blabby," or the impulsiveness and recklessness of Ruth Gordon in *Harold and Maude.*

Old people are given the dress and appearance of children. On the cover of one birthday card is a blackboard with "You're only young once!" chalked on it along with various doodles. Inside, an overweight, unshaven elderly man smoking a cigar is wearing a summer camp tee shirt, shorts, sneakers, and cap and is playing with a yo-yo and baseball bat. Above his grinning face the card says "Happy Birthday, Playboy." Clearly, the card suggests that you can be young twice—so young that "playboy" literally refers to the old man playing in his summer camp outfit. Equally child-like is an ad in *Esquire* showing an elderly woman dressed in a football helmet and varsity sweater playing an electronic football game.

Old people are given the physical problems of children. One ad for catheters, which appears in a geriatric nursing journal, shows the forearms and hands of a baby as its model instead of an elder. The caption below notes that at "Delmed, we don't want to hurt anyone's feelings." A prescription drug ad for the stool softener Doxidan features a smiling bifocaled older woman. The text reads: "Minnie moved her bowels today. The day started right for Minnie. That young doctor feller gave her Doxidan to take last night. And it worked! Minnie figures she's got the smartest doctor in town." It is not too farfetched to imagine that Minnie's smile not only expresses her physical relief but also her pride at being told she moved her bowels. Then again, on the cover of one birthday card is a large bottle of milk of magnesia wrapped in a bright red bow. Above the bottle the card says "Aging." On opening the card, the message reads: " . . . age is nature's way of telling us to wear looser underwear. May your birthday be anything but regular." One image suggested by this card is that of an elder in diapers.

Old people are given the activities and playthings of children. Parties for old people are characterized as children's parties. In a suburban small-town newspaper, a recent article reported that the patients at a local nursing home "held their very own Christmas party." The article went on to indicate that patients "planned the party, made the invitations, decorated the cookies made by the chef, and took part in the entertainment, which included group singing of Christmas Carols." The article thanked a local drugstore for supplying "Santa's gifts." The intentions were admirable, but the message rang loud and clear: Old people are like big children. Posters in a popular chain of fast-food restaurants urge customers to "have a senior birthday party at McDonald's." For the "birthday kid" who is "young at heart," McDonald's offers to provide the cake, hats, and party favors. Also consider Bell Telephone's ad for its custom phones which can be given as gifts to "celebrate any occasion." One such occasion is "Gertrude's" retirement party, complete with colorful ribbons and balloons. In honor of her retirement, Gertrude is shown receiving her own Snoopy phone from her coworkers. A similar Bell Telephone ad shows an elder receiving a Mickey Mouse phone at a party.

Even the "play" of elders is depicted to imply that they are children. A department store ad in *TV Guide* shows an elderly man riding a child's three-wheeler. The caption reads: "Wish they had Hot Cycles when I was a kid. . . . Yep, kids sure are lucky today. Hey, maybe when no one's around. . . ." Haldol, a prescription drug used to treat symptoms associated with organic brain syndrome, claims in an ad that it "usually leaves the

disturbed elderly patient in the nursing home more alert, more responsive." The photograph of an elderly woman shows her smiling limply and
holding a large red and white checked cloth flower. Above her is the caption: "I made a flower today." A similar arts-and-crafts portrayal of the aged
appears in a Roniacol ad, a drug used to improve circulation. Three elders
who are "deficient in peripheral circulation" but "proficient in the 'home'"
are shown hard at work making clay pots.

   The role of old people is reversed. Popular culture frequently portrays old
people as the children of middle-aged parents. The *Boston Globe* recently
ran an article on "Foster Care for the Elderly" which included a photograph of a "foster elder" standing in his room. What particularly stresses
the role reversal is the caption under the photograph. It notes that "Joe
Dionne lives with a family in Charlton. He helps with their chores and
joins their trips." On one TV program, a comedian told the following story:
"A small boy was sitting at a curb crying. An old man passed by and kindly
asked, 'Why are you crying, Sonny?' 'Because I can't do what the big boys
do.' So the old man sat down and cried too." On TV's popular series "The
Rockford Files," star James Garner frequently gets his aging father Rocky
out of trouble.

   We can also observe role reversal in prescription drug ads. In an ad for
Hydergine, an older woman is shown suffering "gray area" symptoms such
as confusion, lack of self-care, dizziness, moodiness, and unsociability.
Large print superimposed over her face reads: "I got lost—lost in my own
neighborhood . . . . Yesterday I was going to the grocery store . . . and
suddenly didn't know the way. I was all mixed up . . . I thought it was the
old neighborhood. It frightened me—and it's not the first time. My children say it's my second childhood. It's not fair, I took care of them as kids.
Please, doctor . . . what's happening to me?" Similarly, an ad for Pneu-
movax, an antipneumonia vaccine, shows an elderly man at his birthday
party. Noticeably taller are a middle-aged man and woman who are throw-
ing the party for their aged father just as they would for their children who
are also in the picture. Like the baby held by the elderly man, the caption
reads "Grandpa's a year older."

Implications

   Casting old people as children has detrimental effects on old and young
alike. The "second childhood" stereotype tends to make young people feel
distant from their elders. Having just graduated from childhood, what
adolescent wants to endure it again by associating with the old? The stereotype may well also encourage gerontophobia, the neurotic fear of old age.
How many adults want to be thought of one day as a 6-year-old who has

nothing to do but play with yo-yos, or as a cranky 2-year-old who is not toilet trained?

For old people, the second-childhood stereotype creates a self-fulfilling prophecy: After being socialized from an early age, many elderly people come to accept the second-childhood stereotype and play the infantilized role with enthusiasm. But is that because they fail to see any alternative? Our society has traditionally offered certain rewards to those elderly citizens who are willing to "stay in their place." Riding on a special bus for senior citizens, or dancing with other seniors to the tune of "Yankee Doodle" may isolate elderly people. But it may be preferable to watching reruns of "Marcus Welby."

Acting like children has three negative consequences for old people. First, such behavior lowers their social status because their individual responsibility has been diminished, while their dependency has increased. Second, the perception of infantile behavior in the elderly may allow certain things to be done to them that would otherwise not be considered: the prescription of psychoactive medications, institutionalization, and declaration of legal incompetency. Third, infantilization robs the "gray power" movement of adults who might otherwise work for political change and social betterment.

But not all old people buy the second-childhood stereotype. A large number of elderly Americans are thoroughly offended by infantilization and seek to avoid the consequences of the stereotype. For many, this means making efforts to "pass" for middle-age by dying hair, lying about their age, and using youth-oriented cosmetics. A positive form of avoidance is re-engagement, whereby old people seek to become either reemployed or remarried after the loss of a job or spouse. On the damaging side, an unknown number of cases of apparent senility (organic brain dysfunction) may actually represent a refusal to accept the second-childhood syndrome. Rather than comply, some elders may retreat into a more comfortable, more secure psychological state which ironically has the appearance of infantile behavior. For example, we might see lack of sexual interest, giddiness, forgetfulness, inability to maintain a stable relationship, and lack of control over bodily functions.

In contrast to mere avoidance, a growing number of elderly people have become aggressive in their response to attempts to infantilize them. This aggressive reaction seeks not to deny the second-childhood stereotype but to eliminate it. When the readers of *Retirement Living* magazine were asked to choose from a list of twelve words those that most accurately describe the way Americans over sixty are portrayed on television, their top three choices were "ridiculous," "decrepit," and "childish" (Hemming and Ellis, 1976). The Gray Panther's Media Watch Task Force is an important example of an organized effort to improve media images of the elderly in general and to eliminate the second-childhood stereotype in particular.

Clearly, efforts ought to be made to end the media's infantilization of the aged. Yet it must be remembered that the problem does not lie just with the media. Take for example the Kellogg's Rice Krispies ad which shows an elderly man and woman posed in a romantic embrace. The caption reads: "It's a perfect night for sparkin' on the front swing. For love that's still young." Aside from the ageist reference to young love, the Rice Krispies ad seems to go thoughtfully out of its way to avoid depicting older people as stereotypes. Indeed, they are portrayed in an activity—lovemaking—which although commonly associated with young adults is nonetheless not to be denied their elders as well.

Yet frustratingly, the problem is not thereby solved. The media in this case, via the Rice Krispies ad, has treated the aged with dignity. But readers' responses to the ad— "Aren't they cute! Aren't they sweet!"—are exactly those with which those same readers would greet the inappropriate behavior of children attempting to act like adults. Ageism is so deeply ingrained in our culture that an audience may interpret even the noblest ad to conform to its ageist predispositions.

References

Aronoff, C. "Old Age in Prime-Time." *Journal of Communications* 24 (1974): 86-87.

Butler, R. "Age-ism: Another Form of Bigotry." *Gerontologist* 9 (1969): 243-46.

Demos, V., and Jache, A. "When You Care Enough: An Analysis of Attitudes toward Aging in Humorous Birthday Cards." *Gerontologist* 21 (1981): 209-15.

Francher, J.S. "It's the Pepsi Generation: Accelerated Aging and the Television Commercial." *International Journal of Aging and Human Development* 4 (1973): 245-55.

Gresham, M. "The Infantilization of the Elderly." *Nursing Forum* 15 (1976): 196-209.

Harris, L., and Associates. *The Myth and Reality of Aging in America.* New York: National Council on Aging, 1975.

Hemming, R., and Ellis, K. "How Fair is T.V.'s Image of Older Americans?" *Retirement Living* (April 1976): 21-24.

Levin, J., and Levin, W. *Ageism: Prejudice and Discrimination against the Elderly.* Belmont, Calif: Wadsworth, 1980.

MacDonald, R. "Content Analysis of Perceptions of Aging as Represented by the News Media." Presented at the 26th Annual Meeting of the Gerontological Society, 1973.

McTavish, D.G. "Perceptions of Old People: A Review of Research, Methodologies, and Findings." *Gerontologist* 11 (1971): 90-101.

Smith, M.C. "Portrayal of the Elderly in Prescription Drug Advertising." *Gerontologist* 16 (1976): 329-34.

Tuckman, J., and Lorge, I. "Attitudes toward Old People." *Journal of Social Psychology* 37 (1953): 249-60.

11

Waiting for Dr. Spock:
Advice Literature for
the Children of Aging Parents

Andrea S. Walsh

Dr. Spock
helped you understand your children
Passages
helped you understand yourself

Now you need help with
The Other Generation Gap
—Back cover ad, Steven Z. Cohen and
Bruce Michael Gans, *The Other Generation Gap*

An old saying goes, "A mother can take care of ten children, but ten children can't take care of one mother." The dilemmas of adult children confronting the disabilities and dependencies of aging parents are hardly new. What is new, however, is the spate of recent popular advice manuals for mid-life children with such titles as *The Other Generation Gap* or *You and Your Aging Parent.* Together with a rash of popular magazine articles, seminars, workshops, and TV shows, these advice books constitute a commentary on both the rights and responsibilities of adult children toward aged parents as well as the nature of contemporary American families. This chapter analyzes the dominant ideology of these manuals and traces their sociohistorical roots.

Advice literature has always presented problems as well as opportunities for sociologists and social historians. The realm of popular American professional and religious prescription, for example, offers rich insight into the world of predominantly White, male, middle-class advice givers and their power and appeal for women and men of varied socioeconomic and racial groups. While one cannot immediately conclude that popular advice was

159

always accepted or followed, the world of prescriptive literature leads one to trace the linkages between advice and behavior. Advice literature also reflects the sensibility of middle-class America, whose values and beliefs are widely disseminated through the mass media, religious institutions, and educational system to a much broader population. Unless one lives in a subculture cut off from the mainstream, these are the standards against which most Americans define their own ideals and values—whether they lead to acceptance, modification, or reformulation of the dominant ideology.

The new advice literature for mid-life men and women coping with elderly parents is no different. It, too, expresses an emerging sensibility about aging, family, and personal life, forged in the 1970s and 1980s. This new sensibility contrasts sharply with the traditionalism of American family advice literature popular through the mid-1960s.

One of the first chapters of *You and Your Aging Parent* (Silverstone and Hyman, 1981) is entitled "Facing Up to Feelings." Avoiding the preachy professional-knows-all quality of previous generations of advice literature, these authors begin "from the bottom up," first exploring the conflicting and confusing emotions of "children in the middle": guilt, anger, love, hostility, respect, compassion, indifference, fear, and sadness. Reflecting a growing American acceptance of psychotherapy, Silverstone and Hyman conclude that this tangled ball of emotions is quite natural, perhaps desirable. There is no "right way to feel." Ambivalence is the essence of family relations—from birth to death—and we had better accept that fact before we are destroyed by guilt. The tone of the introductory chapters is comforting and tolerant; the ideal is always to love one's parents, but that is not always realistically possible. The "best solution" is only "best" in the circumstances.

The physical losses of aging are presented as a psychological crisis not only for the elderly but also for their mid-life offspring. In. *The Other Generation Gap,* Steven Cohen and Bruce Michael Gans (1978) note that coping with the disabilities of an aging parent confronts middle-aged children simultaneously with both enormous responsibilities and the inevitability of their own mortality. Ironically, men and women in their forties and fifties are in a life stage in which they are often seeking new avenues of public achievement and freedom from family obligations.

Reflecting a cultural pluralism with regard to family and lifestyle, these manuals examine a variety of scenarios: the "woman in the middle" caught between the demands of an aged arthritic father and her own family and career; the "black sheep" son who wants to show his love for his elderly mother, but cannot; the disabled forgetful mother whose pride will not allow her to ask the assistance of her daughters and sons; the adult child or grandchild who cannot accept the divorce and remarriage of an elderly parent or grandparent.

Family discord is explored with greater depth and openness than in many traditional family-advice manuals. *The Other Generation Gap* describes the variety of "old wounds" that continue to plague relationships between elders and their children: the anger of a daughter at a lifetime of emotional distance from her father; the resentment of a son who could never fulfill his mother's expectations. *You and Your Aging Parent* also asserts that sibling rivalries never die; they only lie submerged until an aged parent's infirmities create a situation which will rekindle them. The conformist will always envy the rebel, the "martyr" will resist the help of other family members, and siblings will compete forever in the eternal quest for parental approval and love. Family communication—through what Silverstone and Hyman term the "family task force model"—is key to resolving conflicts between and among mid-life siblings and their aged parents. However, the authors contend that the elderly parent, unless mentally incompetent, should have the final say in determining whatever options are acceptable in a situation in which an elder can no longer function independently.

This type of advice literature shows the influence of both the feminist and elder rights movements. Although women may be depicted in domestic roles, they are not assumed to be the "natural" caretakers of the aged, eager to put their own lives "on hold." Many of the cases presented in both *The Other Generation Gap* and *You and Your Aging Parent* concern middle-aged sons who are struggling both to be sensitive to the needs of their aged parents as well as to their own families. Nor are elders assumed to be incapable or disinterested in changing their own social and familial roles. Silverstone and Hyman counsel their readers, "It may well happen that your parents develop a lifestyle in their seventies or eighties that satisfies them perfectly well but that you find terrifying, unsatisfactory or embarassing. What if your father still pursues an active sex life and your mother talks about her dates and going dancing?"(p. 136). The authors advise adult children to respect, even if they do not approve, their parents' lifestyles.

Although nuclear family examples proliferate in this literature, single-parent and reconstituted families are presented in as "normal" terms as the traditional nuclear family. Hence, there are no "natural" caretakers or dependents; solutions to the many potential crises of aging parents and their mid-life children must be worked out with many individual variations and permutations.

Social services—in these advice manuals—are presented as a substitute or adjunct to family care and involvement. The necessity and legitimacy of supportive services for elders is a taken-for-granted assumption. Families are encouraged, however, to become knowledgeable about both the aging process and the options provided by the network of social services and entitlement programs from Social Security, to homemaking assistance, to nursing home placement.

Aging itself is presented as a very individual, complex, and often unpredictable process. One person's 80-year-old parent is radically different from another's. Thus, as Cohen and Gans assert in *The Other Generation Gap,* peer advice may not always prove helpful. The biological realities of aging necessitate a more open-ended approach than that found in child-rearing manuals. There can be no Dr. Spock to predict confidently the normal developmental crises of a 75-year old person. The aging clock is infinitely and perhaps eternally varied.

The moral universe of these manuals, deriving their tone in part from the current values-clarification literature, is one of "compassionate coping": the concerned adult child must weigh his/her feelings, needs, resources, and available options (psychic, social, and economic) in dealing with the aging and disability of a parent. The tone of these works is that of a counselor rather than a preacher.

Books such as *You and Your Aging Parent* and *The Other Generation Gap* were unknown 20, 30, or 40 years ago. What factors account for their popularity in the late 1970s and early 1980s? The answer lies in the interaction of a variety of sociohistorical cross-currents. One factor is simple demographics—the number of elder Americans and their mid-life children is rising and promises to climb for some time to come. Between 1976 (the first edition of *You and Your Aging Parent*) and 1981 (the second), the percentage of elders in the United States has risen 20 percent—from 10 to almost 12 percent of the population. The largest increase in the aged population is to be found among those over 75, who are most likely to be infirm and in need of medical and economic assistance. By the twenty-first century, when the current mid-life generation will be "seniors," the elderly may constitute over 20 percent of the population. As their numbers have increased, so has their political power and visibility.

In response to these demographic shifts and political pressures as well as other changes in family and lifestyle, the 1960s and 1970s marked the passage of key pieces of legislation for elders, most notably the Medicare/Medicaid Amendments to the Social Security Act (1965) and the Older Americans Act (1965, amended in the 1970s). These laws, born in the era of the Great Society and the War on Poverty, legitimatized the public social concerns of the elderly, and further weakened the already declining ideology that adult children are primarily responsible for their aged parents. The trends begun in the passage of the Social Security Act of 1935 were becoming solidified and consolidated, at least until the early 1980s.

Gerontological research has challenged the myth that families were abandoning their elders en masse. However, a variety of family changes have made the dynamics of mid-life children and aging parents more complex. Increased geographic mobility, especially among the middle class, has weakened extended family bonds. And sex roles and family patterns are in flux. Feminism, the rising divorce rate, and inflation have led to a reexamination of the "natural nurturer" role of women. More mid-life women are employed and unwilling or unable to assume the primary burden of caring for an aged, disabled parent. Single-parent and reconstituted families have become more common, creating a complex network of roles and responsibilities among the generations. In addition, Americans are having fewer children, making the dilemmas of aging parents more acute for the next generations. Many professional couples are deferring childbearing until their thirties; their offspring will cope with their parents' aging at younger and more economically vulnerable ages. And they will have fewer siblings to call upon for support. Moreover, advances in medical technology permit the prolongation of life, but create complex ethical and psychological dilemmas for elderly patients and their families.

Simultaneously, the social climate of the 1960s and 1970s prompted a new view of mid-life: as a time to reassess and renew commitments, explore untapped avenues of creativity, and reconstitute the self. Gail Sheehy's *Passages* popularized the notion of adulthood as a time of continuous crisis, as well as growth and development. The traditional assumption that one should "care for those who have cared for me" could hardly go unquestioned in this social milieu. New therapies proliferated and more open-ended models of family communication became popular, especially among the middle class. The tabooed subject of death and dying, prompted by the work of Elisabeth Kübler-Ross, emerged from the proverbial closet to become one of the most pressing topics in the contemporary mass media.

At the same time, the dark side of the domestic dream—family violence—became a focus of national concern, beginning with concern about child abuse in the 1960s, followed by exposés of wife battering in the 1970s, and most recently, reports of elder abuse in the family. Although far from a widespread phenomenon, the specter of beaten, neglected, and terrorized elders dramatized the fact that some families desperately needed help in coping with the multiple stresses of caring for frail and demented elders.

These advice manuals for mid-life children of aging parents reflect the multiple and sometimes contradictory influence of all these currents. Like other personal and family advice literature of the 1970s and 1980s such as *Our Bodies/Ourselves* and *Ourselves and Our Children* by the Boston Women's Health Book Collective, *Growing Up Free* by Letty Cottin

Pogrebin, and even the revised, nonsexist Dr. Spock, these works are a legacy of the social movements and cultural climate of the 1960s and early 1970s: consumer-oriented and reflecting a cultural and sexual pluralism. Unlike earlier twentieth-century American prescriptive literature, these manuals do not promote narrowly defined age, gender, and familial roles. If one were to categorize these works in a brief phrase, it would be "progressive family relations" — a quiet victory for critics of previous generations of advice literature and a serious challenge to both the vocal radical conservatism that seeks to reverse the social and cultural changes of the last twenty years and to the atomistic individualism that values the self above all.

PART II
AGING BODIES AND MINDS

Introduction

Although until relatively recently only a very small proportion of people could expect to live long enough to become elderly, descriptions of physical and psychological changes associated with the aging process are as old as recorded history. Many views of aging bodies and minds have been negative: Aristophanes described old age as a second childhood, Shakespeare as "mere oblivion, sans teeth, sans eyes, sans everything." Legends about ways in which aging might be averted, too, are deeply rooted in history. Long before Ponce de León sought the ancient fount, Greek and Hindu mythology referred to magical fountains of youth whose waters would bring eternal vigor. Contemporary searches include jacuzzi baths, yogurt, wheat germ, and vitamins.

Yet, although *life expectancy* at birth has increased by 26 years since 1900, the *life span* (maximum biologic limits to which we are able to survive) has not changed since ancient times. Tales of extraordinarily long lives, such as the Biblical Methuselah, who allegedly died at the age of 969, or of the long-living horsemen of the Caucasus in the Soviet Union, are modern counterparts of myths of the fountain of youth: in some far distant time or place remarkably long and healthy life is possible. If only one could learn the secret! The secret is, however, that different methods of counting years, wishful thinking, lack of documentation, and sometimes deliberate falsification of records (Medvedev, 1974) have been used to create an illusion. It is precisely in those times and places where birth registration has been nonexistent or faulty that unusually long life spans have been reported. Inasmuch as accurate birth registration is relatively recent, it is impossible to determine maximum life span accurately. However, the oldest living American with documented age credentials was a woman, Fanny Thomas, who lived to be 113 years old and incidentally attributed her long her life to eating applesauce three times a day and never getting involved with men (Walford, 1983).

Although biologic life spans for all living organisms appear to be both fixed and finite, the rate at which organisms age is not. Aging is not a single event but a dynamic process that begins at birth, ends at death, and occurs at different rates among various groups, depending on a variety of environmental and biologic factors. Socioeconomic factors, nutrition, exercise, exposure to chemical pollutants, and lifestyle all affect the aging process. Even within the same person, aging does not occur at the same rate. At twenty, for example, a college student may have the kidney function of a 30-year old, the muscles of a 40-year old, the memory retention of an 18-year old, and so forth. Although some slowing down of the body occurs with aging, in no way is aging synonymous with decay. Rather, aging is an inevitable part of the process of life.

The first set of readings covers many aspects of physical health and sexuality. Barbara F. Turner presents a broad-based introduction to male/female differences in health in later life, variations in behavior linked to these sex-linked disparities, and their impact upon psychological functioning. Since 1900, the proportion of Americans 65 plus has almost tripled and the number increased more than eight times: from 3 to over 25 million. The gain in life expectancy accounting for rapid growth of those 65 plus has been particularly dramatic for women. That females are the hardier sex has, as Turner points out, both behavioral and social consequences in old age. Although women have higher rates of acute illness and injuries and higher rates of prevalence of chronic conditions in later life than men, paradoxically it is men who have more life-threatening conditions, higher rates of disability, and higher death rates at all ages. Lois Verbrugge details variations in male/female patterns of illness and death and explores both sex-linked behaviors and attitudes and cohort differences contributing to present patterns of health, illness, and death.

Each age cohort ages in a different way, undergoes a particular history, and ages in a society which they have both been formed by and have formed. Yet attitudes toward aging may lag behind the experiences of an age cohort. For example, little is known about the sexuality of the elderly in past generations in the United States; sex in old age has been considered suspect and made the butt of jokes about "dirty" old men or women. Within the past eighty years or so, sexual beliefs in general and about women in particular have changed dramatically: from a necessary duty to a sport in which one's prowess is measured by orgasms. As Ruth Weg demonstrates, cultural views about sexuality in later life continue to overshadow the dreams, hopes, and realities of gratification among the elderly. Unlike the Stuldbrugs, described in *Gulliver's Travels*, who aged but did not die only to find themselves cut off from all pleasure, there are many sources of satisfaction, including sexuality, in old age.

Key to successful aging has been the notion of life satisfaction. Given that the aging process is ongoing and inevitable, what are the hallmarks of successful aging? The current search for ways to measure satisfaction at lease rivals earlier explorations for the fountain of youth. The ways in which gerontologists frame questions about life satisfaction shape responses and impose an implicit view of both time and social reality that may bear little resemblance to either as they are experienced. All of us participate in three types of time: objective time, internal time, and social time. *Objective time* is "clock time," a measurable, homogeneous, and infinitely divisible continuum with one dimension—duration—and one irreversible direction, past-future. *Internal time* encompasses thoughts, dreams, fantasies, and one's inner sense of self. Unlike objective time, internal time is multidirectional; one can go backward and forward in an instant but still experience oneself as the same "me" at seventy that one was at twenty. It is the realm in which one reflects upon past, present, and future experiences. *Social time* is still another span in which one performs various roles, occupies certain statuses, and acts and relates to others. Jaber F. Gubrium and Robert J. Lynott argue that the majority of measures of life satisfaction have used linear notions of clock time or internal time. Life satisfaction in old age has thus been treated as a cut-and-dried fact rather than as a social byproduct of constant interplay of various types of lived and anticipated time.

If life satisfaction is a state devoutly to be wished but still imperfectly measured, what of life dissatisfaction in old age? A growing body of literature has suggested that old age is frequently associated with depression. Marjorie Chary Feinson, in a careful analysis of survey data, challenges the conventional wisdom about old age and its discontents. Mental health or illness among the elderly, as throughout life, is not a constant but a variable, reflecting one's current and past state and life events. Even memory loss, as Elizabeth W. Markson suggests, may have social correlates, closely related to available past, present, and future social roles and life options. More negative myths survive about the aging mind than about all other aspects of old age. Yet, old age is not inevitably associated with either depression or senility. Throughout one's life, the self remains relatively plastic and can move in a variety of directions if economic and social opportunities permit.

The final set of articles explores ways of adapting to major life experiences from a lifecourse perspective. Among the major events occurring in later life, retirement has received much attention and often is described as a benchmark for the beginning of old age. David A. Karp and William C. Yoels examine the ways in which our involvement with work influences the ways in which we think about both past and future. Entering, progressing, and leaving the work force are significant transitions linked not only to job gratification, health, and economic situation, but to self-definition of age itself.

That work shapes one's sense of self, from first stage of preparation and exploration to exit through retirement, emphasizes the importance of lifelong development with patterns of stability and change in personality, behavior, and motivations of people. Each period of life has its own opportunities for stress, potential, and growth. Leonard I. Pearlin and Clarice Radabaugh emphasize life as a developmental process but challenge the assumption that there are given, sequential, "normal" steps up which one must climb to move on to the next. Rather, aging is a transaction between each individual and the larger society, and personality factors must be viewed within their historical and social context. Each birth cohort is distinct from another; each has been both shaper of and shaped by social change. To study old age thus involves both the change of individuals and social change, a theme elaborated upon by Matilda White Riley. The old of today illustrate but one pattern of aging in an ever-changing kaleidoscope of history.

For example, the increased labor force participation among women has challenged earlier views about what paid employment and retirement mean in the lives of women. Maximiliane E. Szinovacz depicts both what we have erroneously assumed and are beginning to learn about women and retirement today.

The directions in all these readings is away from visions of old age as a period of inevitable mental and physical decline or as a fixed state. Aging is a subtle, unfolding interaction between biological processes, gender roles, personality, and social and historical context. The sum of these factors provide the touchstones by which aging may be understood.

References

Medvedev, A.A. "Caucasus and Altay Longevity: A Biological or Social Porblem?" *The Gerontologist* 14 (1974): 381.
Walford, Roy A. *Maximum Life Span*. New York: Avon Books, 1983.

12

Health Is the Main Thing:
Sex Differences, Health, and
Psychological Variables in Later Life

Barbara F. Turner

Sex-related differences in health in later life are of compelling interest to psychologists because of the important influence of health upon psychological measures such as cognitive performance, self-concepts, morale, and general adaptation. There is also a lively, if not violent, controversy regarding the causes of these sex-related differences in health, that is, the influence of behavior upon health. This paper addresses two topics: (1) what are the sex-related differences in behavior that cause sex-linked health differences? and (2) how do sex-related differences in health affect psychological functioning? I will begin with a summary of sex-related differences in mortality, since mortality necessarily forms the context for examining sex-related differences in health.

Mortality

Expectation of life at birth in the United States in 1976 was 76.7 years for women and 69 years for men, a difference of nearly 8 years (U.S. Statistical Abstract, 1978). A large part of this difference is accounted for by differential death rates for women and men over age 65. In 1975, White women at 65 could expect to live for another 18.1 years and non-White women for 17.5 years, but men, regardless of race, could expect only 13.7 more years (Kovar, 1978). The mortality differential between women and men over 65 has widened since 1900. Heart disease is responsible for 44 percent of the deaths of people 65 years and over. Together, heart disease, cancer, and cerebrovascular disease (primarily stroke) account for 75 percent of all deaths of people over 65. Males die more frequently and also more readily of these leading causes of death. There is only one leading cause of death to which women are more likely to succumb than men—diabetes mellitus. At any older age, men are more likely to suffer from lethal conditions while women are prone to more chronic conditions that are rarely lethal.

What are the causes of these sex-related differences in mortality? Most writers suggest that behavioral factors underlie much, if not all, of the female/male mortality differential (Enterline, 1961; Palmore, 1971; Retherford, 1972; Waldron, 1976; Waldron and Johnston, 1976). (Genetic factors account for part of the differential, but these will not be discussed in this paper.) Cigarette smoking appears to account for the greatest portion of the mortality differential, almost entirely through the relationship of smoking to heart disease, lung cancer, and emphysema. Cigarette smoking is estimated to account for one-third (Waldron, 1976) to nearly one-half (Retherford, 1972) of the sex mortality differential. The higher fatalities of men from accidents, suicide, and cirrhosis of the liver—each a leading cause of death—have been attributed to behavior culturally encouraged in males more than in females: risk taking, aggressiveness, and heavy use of alcohol (Waldron, 1976).

But the behavioral factors related to disease that have been of most interest to psychologists are the behaviors that typify the Type A or Coronary Prone Behavior Pattern (Siegler, Nowlin, and Blumenthal, 1980). These include a chronic, driving sense of time pressure and *excessive* competitiveness and aggressiveness (Friedman and Rosenman, 1974). Friedman and Rosenman (1974) suggest that a looming sense of time urgency, or "hurry sickness," is the most significant lethal trait of the Type A individual. Huyck (personal communication) has noted, however, that secondary sources often erroneously describe the Type A individual as merely "aggressive and competitive." Aggressive and competitive behavior, however, is frequently displayed by Type B individuals—whose incidence of coronary disease is quite low (Friedman and Rosenman, 1974). Unaccompanied by time pressures, aggressiveness may *improve* survival chances in later life. In a study of adaptation to the stress of entering an institution for the aged, for example, an aggressive, even combative stance predicted survival and adaptation within the institutional setting among both women and men (Turner, 1969; Turner, Tobin, and Lieberman, 1972). Pugnaciousness—and rejection of passivity—are central characteristics of long-lived men in preliterate societies (Gutmann, 1977). Gutmann suggests that longevity may require the capacity to externalize aggression. The resulting stance of active vigilance may tune up the cardiovascular system, thereby avoiding death (Gutmann, 1977). To be sure, aggressive and competitive behavior may limit smooth interpersonal relations. The social disapproval meted out in

White America to assertive women of any age, furthermore, surely inhibits the expression of aggressive tendencies in White women more than in men. It is apparent, in any case, that further research should focus upon disentangling the relationships of each of the traits that comprise Type A behavior to coronary heart disease (CHD).

In research done in the United States, the pattern of several psychosocial traits that comprise Type A behavior makes a substantial contribution to the higher rate of CHD among men, and Type A behavior is more prevalent among men than women (Friedman and Rosenman, 1974). Most research on Type A behavior has sampled only men, but at least one study (cited in Friedman and Rosenman, 1974) found that Type A women suffered as much coronary heart disease as their male counterparts. Friedman and Rosenman (1974) suggest that the lethal essence of the American work ethic comprises deadlines, excessive competition, and hostility. They argue, therefore, that as women enter the labor force, they too will suffer a greater incidence of coronary heart disease, presumably mediated by the increased Type A behavior that the work ethic encourages. The labor force participation of American women has increased rapidly since 1940, from 27 percent in 1940 to 48 percent in 1977 (U.S. Statistical Abstract, 1978). Over this period, however, women's death rates for coronary heart disease have fallen more rapidly than men's (Siegal, 1978). It is possible that there have not been large enough numbers of women in the labor force for a sufficient number of years to show up in the death rates. In the Soviet Union, however, where rates of female labor force participation have been high for many decades, there is an even greater gap in life expectancy at birth (9.2 years in 1970) than here (Siegel, 1978). In the Framingham Heart Study, Type A women between 45 and 74 who had worked for pay for more than half their adult lives were not more likely to have developed heart disease than Type A homemakers (Haynes, Feinleib, Levine, Scotch, and Kennel, 1979). Haynes (cited in Ehrenreich, 1979) also found a higher incidence of coronary heart disease among female clerical and sales workers than among women in professional and business or blue-collar positions. But the Coronary Prone Behavior Pattern was *not* associated with heart disease among these "pink-collar" women. Instead, the psychosocial factors related to heart disease among the clerical and sales workers were having a nonsupportive boss and having suppressed hostility.

The Framingham findings indicate that Type A behavior is not the only cluster of psychosocial factors mediating work-related stress and coronary heart disease. The psychosocial factors mediating work-related stress and heart disease may differ for women and men. The multiple responsibilities of employed women who are wives and mothers, for example, may also increase stress (and stress-related diseases). Haynes (cited in Ehrenreich, 1979) found that among employed women, marriage and child rearing increased the incidence of heart disease.

Health

Paradoxically, though males have higher death rates, females appear to have worse health. Women aged 65 and over report more days of restricted activity and more days in bed for an illness than males (U.S. Bureau of the Census, 1979). Further, a higher percentage of older women than men report one or more chronic conditions (Kovar, 1978). Males, however, are more likely to have more serious and incapacitating chronic conditions (Nathanson, 1975, 1977; Verbrugge, 1977). Common experience corroborates Health Information Survey reports that older men are considerably more likely than older women to report limitation of major work and maintenance activities due to chronic health problems (U.S. Bureau of Census, 1979). Men with chronic conditions also report more mobility limitation than similarly afflicted women, suggesting that males' chronic conditions are more severe than females' (Verbrugge, 1977). In almost any group of older people, the women display more vitality than the men, even when the women are as old as the men.

The apparent contradiction between the sex differences in morbidity and mortality largely disappears when data on specific disorders are examined. As Verbrugge (1977: 285) reports,

> when we consider chronic ailments that force a person to restrict activity, a pronounced male excess appears for the majority of conditions. Among them are several leading causes of death. Females have excess morbidity for one major killer (diabetes mellitus) and for less fatal conditions such as mental/nervous conditions, varicose veins, arthritis/rheumatism, and genitourinary conditions—causes of much greater morbidity than mortality.

Diabetes mellitus is the only major cause of death for which women have a higher mortality rate than men, consistent with women's higher morbidity rate. In general, males have both greater mortality *and* morbidity for most leading causes of death. Thus, the apparent poorer health of women is based primarily on higher rates of mild acute disorders (such as the common cold) as well as nonlethal chronic conditions (such as arthritis and hypertension without heart disease).

The causes of *these* differences in health between the sexes are highly controversial. There are three competing hypotheses regarding the causes of higher female morbidity. The first is that the sex differences reflect real differences in physical vulnerability to particular diseases; the second is that women are simply more likely than men to *report* certain illnesses; and the third is that women are more able than men to adopt the sick role (Gove and Hughes, 1979). Unfortunately, age differences have not been examined in the studies that have focused on one or more of these hypotheses. Methodological and conceptual problems, furthermore, are acutely prominent in this recently developed area of research (cf. the exchange of Verbrugge [1980], Mechanic [1980], and Gove and Hughes [1980] on sex-related differences in physical health).

Consequences of Sex-Related Differences in Health and Longevity

These sex-related differences in health and longevity have many behavioral and interpersonal consequences. Female superiority in longevity, for example, is a mixed blessing. As Huyck (1977) has commented, it increases a woman's chances of living to be very old, alone, and ill. In 1975, there were 69 men aged 65 and over for every 100 women of that age group in the United States (Siegel, 1979). (This ratio is expected to fall further by the year 2000, to 65 males per 100 females.) Due to the female/male difference in life expectancy and the social expectation that women will marry men older than themselves, the ratio of married women increases sharply in later years. Over the age of 65, 75 percent of men but only 37 percent of women are married (U.S. Bureau of Census, 1979). "Singled" women thus find fewer men available for remarriage, while singled men have many women from whom to choose. In 1970, there were fewer than 3 brides per 1,000 single women 65 and over, compared to 17 grooms per 1,000 single men in this age group (NCHS, 1974).

Sex-related differences in health in the later years are exaggerated by the differential interpretation of good and poor health for the two sexes. If a woman experiences a reduction in vigor associated with health decrements, she is not perceived as defeminized. The physical image of masculinity for adult males, however, requires an active, vigorous presentation of the total body. The self-esteem of older men is especially vulnerable to health-related decrements in activity level (Nowak, 1976), which represent a blow to the image of masculinity. Huyck (1977) notes that middle-aged men may be especially likely to find illness threatening. "Some undoubtedly respond with denial of the symptoms, because illness is equated with passivity and the femininity they wish to deny in themselves; they may threaten their health of later years by postponing care and sabotaging medical treatment" (Huyck, 1977:3). Elderly men are also more likely than women to deny ill health. In the Duke University longitudinal studies of Durham residents aged 60 and over, men were more likely than women to deny clear signs of poor health (Maddox, 1964; Maddox and Douglas, 1973). Men predominated among the one-fourth of the sample whose self-rated health was more favorable than physician ratings despite painstaking feedback to respondents regarding their objective health status.

On the other hand, authorities (Busse and Blazer, 1980; Pfeiffer, 1977) have concluded that hypochondriasis is more common among older women than men. Hypochondriasis is defined as excessive and unwarranted preoccupation with the body (Busse and Blazer, 1980; Pfeiffer, 1977) in conjuction with a pattern of prolonged and frequent medical contacts (Busse, Dovenmuehle, and Brown, 1960). In studies that have compared self-rated health with physician ratings, between 8 to 12 percent of elderly rate their physical health as poorer than their objective health status (Blazer and Houpt, 1979; La Rue, Bank, Jarvik, and Hetland, 1979; Maddox, 1964; Maddox and Douglas, 1973). Women in the Duke University longitudinal studies (Maddox, 1964; Maddox and Douglas, 1973) were more likely than men to rate their health as poorer than it actually was. In a community survey of nearly 1,000 Durham County residents conducted in 1972, however, no sex-related differences in "health pessimism" appeared (Blazer and Houpt, 1979). Similarly, La Rue, Bank, Jarvik, and Hetland (1979) also failed to report a sex-related difference in "health pessimism" in their sample of aged twins. Hypochondriasis, in short, may *not* be more common among older women than men.

There are many psychological consequences of the sex-related health differential. Health has an important influence on psychological measures such as cognitive performance (Birren, Butler, Greenhouse, Sokoloff, and Yarrow, 1963; Botwinick and Birren, 1963; Eisdorfer and Wilkie, 1977; Palmore and Jeffers, 1971; Siegler, 1980; Speith, 1964), morale (Campbell, Converse, and Rodgers, 1976; Larson, 1978; Palmore and Luikart, 1972), and general adaptation (Maas and Kuypers, 1974).

Poor health—especially cardiovascular disease (CVD)—produces cognitive decrement (Botwinick and Birren, 1963; Eisdorfer and Wilkie, 1977; Obrist, 1972; Speith, 1964, 1965). Men are more likely than women to die of CVD, which appears to take a more benign course in women (USDHEW, 1971), producing less behavioral and psychological decrement than in men. In Hertzog, Schaie, and Gribbin's (1978) cross-sequential study of CVD and changes in intellectual functioning from middle to old age, men with CVD were significantly more likely than men free of disease to drop out of the study. Proportions of women dropouts and participants with CVD did not differ significantly. Thus, considerably more women than men participants had CVD. Participants with CVD, as anticipated, showed poorer performance on several cognitive subtests; nevertheless, the intellectual functioning of the women studied was substantially similar to that of the men. Since it is the less able who tend to drop out of longitudinal studies, subjects with CVD who dropped out of this study very likely showed even more intellectual decrement, on the average, than those with CVD who continued. Thus, the poorer health of older men also implies greater cognitive deficit among men than among women in the elderly population at large. (The findings of Hertzog et al. [1978] do not necessarily imply that women are better able than men to withstand the negative effects of equivalently severe CVD. The women in this study may well have had less severe forms of CVD, on the average, than the men.)

Good health in later years is both directly (Edwards and Klemmack, 1973; Medley, 1976; Palmore and Luikart, 1972; Spreitzer and Snyder, 1974; Tornstam, 1975) and indirectly (Markides and Martin, 1979) related to life satisfaction. We have seen that really poor health is less common among older women than men. Thus, older women, being less likely to suffer from poor health, should enjoy a happier, more vigorous outlook on life than older men. Further, older women are less likely than men to report limitation in major activity (Kovar, 1978), and such limitation is a potent predictor of morale at older ages.

Given the many sex-related differences in health and the interrelationships of health and psychological functioning reviewed in this paper, investigators are well advised to attend to the measurement of health. As Siegler et al. (1980) point out, the methodological and assessment problems in this area are well understood; unfortunately, adequate solutions have not yet been found.

Bibliography

Birren, J.E., Butler, R.N., Greenhouse, S.W., Sokoloff, L., and Yarrow, M.R. (eds.). *Human Aging.* Washington, D.C.: Public Health Service (Publication no. 986), 1963.

Blazer, D.G., and Houpt, J. "Perception of Poor Health in the Healthy Elderly." *Journal of the American Geriatric Society* 27 (1979): 330-34.

Botwinick, J., and Birren, J.E. "Mental Abilities and Psychomotor Responses in Healthy Aged Men." In J.E. Birren, R.N. Butler, S.W. Greenhouse, L. Sokoloff, and M.R. Yarrow (eds.), *Human Aging.* Washington, D.C.: Public Health Service (Publication No. 986), 1963.

Busse, E.W., and Blazer, D.G. "Disorders Related to Biological Functioning." In E.W. Busse and D.G. Blazer (eds.), *Handbook of Geriatric Psychiatry.* New York: Van Nostrand, 1980.

Busse, E.W., Dovenmuehle, R.H., and Brown, R.G. "Psychoneurotic Reactions of the Aged." *Geriatrics* 15 (1960): 97-105.

Campbell, A., Converse, P.E., and Rodgers, W.L. *The Quality of American Life.* New York: Russell Sage, 1976.

Edwards, J.N., and Klemmack, D.L. "Correlates of Life Satisfaction: A Re-Examination." *Journal of Gerontology* 28 (1973): 497-502.

Ehrenreich, B. "Is Success Dangerous to Your Health? The Myths and Facts about Women and Stress." *Ms.* (May 1979): 51-54.

Eisdorfer, C., and Wilkie, F. "Stress, Disease, Aging, and Behavior." In J.E. Birren and K.W. Schaie (eds.), *Handbook of the Psychology of Aging.* New York: Van Nostrand, 1977.

Enterline, P.E. "Cause of Death Responsible for Recent Increases in Sex Mortality Differentials in the United States." *Milbank Memorial Fund Quarterly* 39 (1961): 312-28.

Friedman, M., and Rosenman, R.H. *Type A Behavior and Your Heart.* New York: Fawcett Crest, 1974.

Gove, W.R., and Hughes, M. "Possible Causes of the Apparent Sex Differences in Physical Health." *American Sociological Review* 44 (1979): 126-46.

Gove, W.R., and Hughes, M. "Sex Differences in Physical Health and How Medical Sociologists View Illness (A Reply to Mechanic and Verbrugge)." *American Sociological Review* 45 (1980): 514-22.

Gutmann, D.L. "The Cross-Cultural Perspective: Notes toward a Comparative Psychology of Aging." In J. Birren and K.W. Schaie (eds.), *Handbook of the Psychology of Aging.* New York: Van Nostrand, 1977.

Haynes, S.G., Feinleib, M., Levine, S., Scotch, N., and Kennel, W.B. "The Relationship of Psychosocial Factors to Coronary Heart Disease in the Framingham Study: II. Prevalence of Coronary Heart Disease." *American Journal of Epidemiology* 107 (1978): 384-402.

Hertzog, C., Schaie, K.W., and Gribbin, K. "Cardiovascular Disease and Changes in Intellectual Functioning from Middle to Old Age." *Journal of Gerontology* 33 (1978): 872-83.

Huyck, M.H. "Sex, Gender, and Aging." *Humanitas* 13 (1977).

Huyck, M.H. Personal communication, 1980.

Kovar, M.G. "Elderly People: The Population 65 Years and Over." In U.S. Department of Health, Education, and Welfare, *Health: United States, 1976-1977* (DHEW Publication no. 77-1232). Washington, D.C.: U.S. Government Printing Office, 1978.

Larson, R. "Thirty Years of Research on Subjective Well-Being of Older Americans." *Journal of Gerontology* 33 (1978): 109-25.

LaRue, A., Bank, L., Jarvik, L., and Hetland, M. "Health in Old Age: How Do Physicians' Ratings and Self-Ratings Compare?" *Journal of Gerontology* 34 (1979): 687-91.

Maas, H.S., and Kuypers, J.A. *From Thirty to Seventy.* San Francisco: Jossey-Bass, 1974.

Maddox, G. "Self-Assessment of Health Status." *Journal of Chronic Diseases* 17 (1964): 449-60.

Maddox, G.L., and Douglas, E.B. "Self-Assessments of Health." *Journal of Health and Social Behavior* 14 (1973): 87-93.

Markides, K.S., and Martin, H.W. "A Causal Model of Life Satisfaction among the Elderly." *Journal of Gerontology* 34 (1979): 86-93.

Mechanic, D. "Comment on Gove and Hughes, *ASR,* February, 1979." *American Sociological Review* 45 (1980): 513-14.

Medley, M.S. "Satisfaction with Life among Persons 65 Years and Older." *Journal of Gerontology 31* (1976): 448-55.

Nathanson, C. "Illness and the Feminine Role: A Theoretical Review." *Social Science and Medicine* 9 (1975): 57-62.

Nathanson, C. "Sex, Illness, and Medical Care: A Review of Data, Theory, and Method." *Social Science and Medicine* 11 (1977): 13-25.

National Center for Health Statistics. *Vital Statistics of the United States, 1970.* Vol. 3, *Marriage and Divorce.* Washington, D.C.: U.S. Government Printing Office, 1974.

Nowak, C.A. "Age and Sex Differences in the Perception of Personal Age and Self-Esteem." In B.F. Turner (chair), *The Double Standard of Aging: A Question of Sex Differences.* Symposium presented at the 29th Annual Scientific Meeting of the Gerontological Society, New York City, 1976.

Obrist, W.D. "Cerebral Physiology of the Aged: Influence of Circulatory Disorders." In C.M. Gaitz (ed.), *Aging and the Brain.* New York: Plenum, 1972.

Palmore, E. "Summary and the Future." In E. Palmore and F.C. Jeffers (eds.), *Prediction of Life Span.* Lexington, Mass: D.C. Heath, 1971.

Palmore, E., and Jeffers, F. (eds.). *Prediction of Lifespan.* Lexington, Mass.: D.C. Heath, 1971.

Palmore, E., and Luikart, C. "Health and Social Factors Related to Life Satisfaction." *Journal of Health and Social Behavior* 13 (1972): 68-80.

Pfeiffer, E. "Psychopathology and Social Pathology." In J.E. Birren and K.W. Schaie (eds.), *Handbook of the Psychology of Aging.* New York: Van Nostrand, 1977.

Retherford, R.D. "Tobacco Smoking and the Sex Mortality Differential." *Demography* 9 (1972): 203-16.

Siegel, J.S. *Demographic Aspects of Aging and the Older Population in the United States.* (Bureau of the Census, Current Population Reports, Special Studies Series P-23, no. 59, 2d printing, rev.) Washington, D.C.: U.S. Government Printing Office, 1978.

Seigel, J.S. *Prospective Trends in the Size and Structure of the Elderly Population, Impact of Mortality Trends, and Some Implications.* (Bureau of the Census, Current Population Reports, Special Studies Series P-23, no. 78.) Washington D.C.: U.S. Government Printing Office, 1979.

Seigler, I.C. "The Psychology of Adult Development and Aging." In E.W. Busse and D.G. Blazer (eds.), *Handbook of Geriatric Psychiatry.* New York: Van Nostrand, 1980.

Siegler, I., Nowlin, J.B., and Blumenthal, J.A. "Health and Behavior: Methodological Considerations for Adult Development and Aging." In L.W. Poon (ed.), *Aging in the 1980's: Psychological Issues.* Washington, D.C.: American Psychological Association, 1980.

Speith, W. "Cardiovascular Health Status, Age, and Psychological Performance." *Journal of Gerontology* 19 (1964): 277-84.

Speith, W. "Slowness of Task Performance and Cardiovascular Disease." In A.T. Welford and J.E. Birren (eds.), *Behavior, Aging, and the Nervous System.* Springfield, Ill.: Thomas, 1965.

Spreitzer, E., and Snyder, E.E. "Correlates of Life Satisfaction Among the Aged." *Journal of Gerontology* 29 (1974): 454-58.

Tornstam, L. "Health and Self-Perception: A Systems Theoretical Approach." *Gerontologist* 15 (1975): 264-70.

Turner, B.F. "Psychological Predictors of Adaptation to the Stress of Institutionalization in the Aged." Doctoral diss., University of Chicago, 1969.

Turner, B.F., Tobin, S.S., and Lieberman, M.A. "Personality Traits as Predictors of Institutional Adaptation among the Aged." *Journal of Gerontology* 27 (1972): 61-68.

U.S. Bureau of the Census. *Social and Economic Characteristics of the Older Population, 1978.* (Current Population Reports, Special Studies Series P-23, no. 85.) Washington, D.C.: U.S. Government Printing Office, 1979.

U.S. Bureau of the Census. *Statistical Abstract of the United States, 1978.* 99th ed. Washington, D.C.: U.S. Government Printing Office, 1978.

U.S. Department of Health, Education, and Welfare. *Health in the Later Years of Life.* (Public Health Service, National Center for Health Statistics no. 1722-0178.) Washington, D.C.: U.S. Government Printing Office, 1971.

Verbrugge, L.M. "Comment on Walter R. Gove and Michael Hughes, *ASR,* February, 1979: Possible Causes of the Apparent Sex Differences in Physical Health." *American Sociological Review* 45 (1980): 507-13.

Verbrugge, L.M. "Sex Differences in Morbidity and Mortality in the United States." *Social Biology* 23 (1977): 275-96.

Waldron, I. "Why Do Women Live Longer Than Men? *Social Science and Medicine* 10 (1976): 349-62.

Waldron, I., and Johnston, S. "Why Do Women Live Longer Than Men?" *Journal of Human Stress* 2 (1976): 19-29.

Note

From F.B. Livson (organizer) and L.E. Troll (chair), Sex Differences in Health in Later Life: Physical, Mental, Developmental. Symposium presented at the 88th Annual Convention of the American Psychological Association, Montreal, Canada, September 1980. Portions of this paper are drawn from Barbara F. Turner, "Sex-Related Differences in Aging," in B.B. Wolman and G. Stricker (eds.), *Handbook of Developmental Psychology* (Englewood Cliffs, N.J.: Prentice-Hall, 1981).

13

Women and Men: Mortality and Health of Older People

Lois M. Verbrugge

To soothe the feelings of her children when they lost a sibling battle, my mother would say, "Everything will even out by the time you're 80." While this may be true for minor matters like candy bars and checkers games, it is certainly not true for the important matters of health and mortality. Individuals in different demographic and social groupings differ sharply in their chances of reaching older ages (65+) and in their health during later years. The differences are greatest by sex: Men have notably higher death rates at all ages; thus, fewer of them ever reach age 65. And among older men and women, the men appear to have more serious health problems. In contrast, the women have more numerous but apparently milder problems.

Although large sex differences in health and mortality have existed throughout this century, we scarcely know the reasons for them. They emerge from some combination of genetic risks for each sex, from risks acquired during life, and from attitudes that influence symptom perception and curative behavior. Men's overall risks are higher than women's, but we do not know which risks are most important in causing their disadvantage. Will women's favored status continue in coming decades? It is popularly believed that as women participate more in the labor force and adopt lifestyles similar to those of men, their health and longevity will suffer. It is true that if women and men have more similar roles and activities in the future, their health profiles and death rates will be somewhat more similar throughout life, including the older ages. But the future may be one of lower mortality for both sexes rather than of increased rates for women.

This chapter reviews data on health and mortality of older men and women, and it suggests some reasons for these sex differences. We will focus on physical health and the psychosocial factors that explain sex

181

differences—that is, how people's social and psychological characteristics influence their health status, health behavior, and mortality.

A few definitions are in order:

"Health status" refers to measures of illness, injury, and symptoms, including people's own evaluations of their health, interview reports of health problems, and data from medical examinations.

"Health behaviors"[1] refers to all curative and preventive actions, relating to short-term disability ("restricted activity"), long-term disability ("functional limitations"), use of health services, and use of medications.

The Population of Older Men and Women

As detailed in the opening chapter, the rapid growth of the older population of the United States in this century has been characterized by a growing imbalance in the ratio of men to women, particularly at the very oldest ages.

By the end of this century, the sex ratio will be a bit lower than it is now (about 67 men per 100 women) and remarkably low for the very elderly (39 men per 100 women). By 2050, there will be 33.4 million women and 22.1 million men aged 65 and over, with a sex ratio of 66 men per 100 women.

Sex composition of the older population is influenced by several factors during the life span of birth cohorts: the sex ratio at birth, mortality rates across life, and net immigration. Major events that a cohort experiences can have lasting impact on its sex composition. For example, heavy immigration of young males early in the century has resulted the relatively large number of men now aged 75 and over. Because of World War II deaths, they will be followed in the next two decades by cohorts with relatively few men. This historical sequence of cohorts will cause some fluctuations in sex ratios and growth rates for the older population in coming years, but the general trend will be for sex ratios to drift downward because women's death rates have dropped faster than men's throughout this century and will probably continue to do so for some decades.

Increasingly, the older population will be dominated by women, especially among the very elderly.

Population aging will not continue forever. Projections indicate that if fertility and mortality remain at their current low levels, the population age structure and sex ratios will have become constant by 2050.

Even allowing for some fluctuations in fertility and mortality (due to family size preferences, medical breakthroughs, wars, etc.), the population structure will be more stable than it is now. Most population aging will be over, and the older age category will grow at about the same slow rate as the total population.

Mortality of Older Men and Women

Mortality rates for older men are higher than for older women (Table 13.1). This is true for all age categories after 65 and for all leading causes of death.[2] Men's disadvantage is largest at the earlier ages (65-69), then decreases with advancing age.[3] Older men's death rates are strikingly higher than women's for bronchitis, emphysema, and asthma and for suicide.

Life expectancy figures as described in Chapter 1 reflect older men's disadvantage. Using current mortality rates, we can determine how many years a person reaching age 65 can expect to live. Men who are 65 now

TABLE 13.1
Sex Differentials in Mortality for the Older U.S. Population, 1978

	Older ages			All ages[1]
	65-74	75-84	85+	
Death rates (per 100,000)				
All causes of death				
Males	4185	9385	17259	803
Females	2138	5863	13541	447
Sex ratios (M/F)[2]				
All causes of death	1.96	1.71	1.54	1.80
Diseases of heart[3]	2.14	1.52	1.20	2.04
Malignant neoplasms	1.83	1.93	1.88	1.50
Cerebrovascular				
diseases	1.39	1.14	0.98	1.19
Influenza and				
pneumonia	2.29	1.89	1.52	1.83
Arteriosclerosis	1.63	1.22	1.03	1.28
Diabetes mellitus	1.00	0.92	0.91	1.02
Accidents	2.12	1.74	1.48	2.85
Motor vehicle	2.21	2.50	4.25	2.85
All other	2.15	1.56	1.34	2.85
Bronchitis, emphysema,				
and asthma	3.63	4.71	3.77	2.92
Cirrhosis of liver	2.59	2.30	2.34	2.17
Nephritis and nephrosis	1.65	2.02	1.97	1.59
Suicide	4.19	6.43	9.47	2.98

1. Age-adjusted. Rates are standardized to the age distribution of the 1940 total U.S. population.
2. Ratio is male rate divided by female rate.
3. The 10 leading causes of death for people 65 + are listed in rank order.
    Suicide (rank 11) is also included because of its notable sex differentials.
Sources: National Center for Health Statistics, Monthly Vital Statistics Report, Vol. 29, No. 6, Supplement 2, 17 September 1980; and unpublished tabulations from the National Center for Health Statistics.

expect about 14 more years of life, compared to 18 for women. The female advantage appears in every age category after 65. Even at age 85, women can anticipate living 1.4 years more than men who reach that age.

Males suffer a mortality disadvantage at all ages. Across the entire age span, sex differences are greatest at ages 15-24 and 25-34, when men's mortality rates are more than twice those of women. From age 35, the gap closes substantially and remains relatively constant throughout ages 65-74. After about age 75, sex differences become smaller for "all causes" of death and for most leading causes (Table 13.1). Apparently, as men and women approach biological limits of human life, their risks of dying become more similar than before. But we must not forget that even near those limits, a man still has less chance of surviving from one year to the next than a woman of the same age.

In this century, mortality rates dropped for both sexes until about 1950. From 1950 to 1970, death rates were relatively stable. Around 1970, they began a sudden and remarkable turn downward. These historical trends have appeared in virtually all age groups of males and females, but during the periods when rates declined, females benefited more than males. Their death rates have dropped faster, resulting in an everwidening gap in life expectancy between the sexes.

The 1970s merit special attention as a clue to the future. Among the older population, rates dropped for virtually all leading causes; the drop was especially large for heart diseases and cerebrovascular diseases. Only malignant neoplasms (cancers) registered an increase during this period. The percentage declines for "all causes" and for leading ones were generally greater for older women than older men. Other age groups showed similar trends in the 1970s. Thus, both sexes now have greater longevity than a decade ago, with women having gained slightly more than men.[4]

If the decline in mortality continues, men and women will enjoy longer lives in 2050 than now. Current projections are that life expectancy at birth in 2050 will be 81.0 years for females and 71.8 years for males. The gap between women and men is projected to increase, but at a declining rate. In other words, the biggest gains for women compared with men have already occurred, and future gains will be smaller.

These projections for 2050 indicate what will happen if current mortality trends continue. "Real life" may be quite different. Some demographers think that as women participate more in the labor force and the community, their risks of death will become increasingly similar to men's. If so, the special advantage enjoyed by women in the 20th century will end, and the gap between men's and women's mortality will narrow. Although this scenario is fundamentally different from current projections, it is certainly plausible and possible.

What are the implications of changing social behavior of older men and women? People who live long have endured many insults to their health and survived them. If women do behave "more like men" in their young and middle adult years, their health profiles and mortality risks in old age are likely to resemble those of men, and mortality differentials for the older population should narrow. Yet, as I will discuss later, it is unlikely the sexes will ever have equal rates.

Health Status and Disability of Older Men and Women[5]

With increasing age, resistance to new diseases declines, while chronic conditions developed earlier in life tend to deteriorate; and although acute conditions are less frequent, the recovery period for them is longer. Heart disease, cancer, and hypertension are common companions of old age; three-fourths of older people ultimately die from heart disease, cancer, or stroke. Less life-threatening but prevalent and bothersome are arthritis, digestive disorders, foot and skin problems, and chronic respiratory symptoms. Sensory (vision, hearing, balance) and mental faculties often decline; bones and muscles weaken.

For most chronic diseases a period of poor health usually precedes death. Given this sequence, we expect older men to be less healthy than older women, especially from conditions that are leading causes of death. Health data confirm that older men are more seriously ill than older women, but the data also indicate that older women are more *frequently* ill than men. This is an intriguing difference. Data on subjective perceptions of health status, acute and chronic conditions, and disability for acute and chronic conditions support this conclusion.

Self-Rated Health Status

The majority (78 percent) of noninstitutionalized older people consider their health "excellent" or "good" (Assistant Secretary for Health, 1978). Older people probably compare themselves to age peers, including friends who have died. Thus, their evaluation is more positive than if they compared their health to younger adults or to their own health when younger. Only slightly more older men (32 percent) than women (30 percent) consider their health "fair" or "poor."[6]

If institutional residents were included, reports of poor health would undoubtedly increase. Only about 5 percent of the population 65 and over are in institutions, but these people have poorer health than people outside of institutions (Fillenbaum, 1979). Older women's self-ratings especially would worsen, since a larger percentage of them are institutionalized than older men.

Acute Conditions and Resulting Disability

Older women have higher incidence rates of acute illnesses and of injuries (Table 13.2). Most injuries for both sexes occur at home, especially for women. It is therefore no surprise that older women have more days of restricted activity and bed disability for acute conditions in a year. However, an intriguing fact is that older women have more short-term disability *per condition;* that is, they cut down more on usual activities for an acute problem (especially injuries) than men do.

TABLE 13.2
Acute Conditions and Resulting Disability for Older Men and Women, United States, 1977-78
(Rates for 100 persons per year)

	Men 65 +	Women 65 +
Acute conditions (rate)[1]	97.3	120.6
Injured persons (rate)[2]	16.1	26.0
Percent of injured persons whose injuries occurred at home	50%	63%
Restricted activity days for acute conditions (rate)	988.0	1361.0
Average days per condition	10.2	11.3
Bed disability days for acute conditions (rate)	435.0	559.0
Average days per condition	4.5	4.6
Restricted activity days for injuries (rate)	412.0	827.0
Average days per injured person	25.6	31.8
Bed disability days for injuries (rate)	117.0	193.0
Average days per injured person	7.3	7.4

1. Acute conditions are counted if they caused restricted activity or required medical attention.
2. Age-sex specific rates for other types of acute conditions than injuries (infective and parasitic diseases, respiratory conditions, digestive system conditions, all other acute conditions) are available for 1957-58 in Vital Statistics, Series B, No. 6, but not since then.
Sources: National Center for Health Statistics, Vital and Health Statistics Series 10, No. 132 (for July 1977-June 1978), and Series 10, No. 130 (for 1978). See also Series 10, No. 126, for 1977 calendar year.

Chronic Conditions and Resulting Disability

Heart disease, hypertension, arthritis, and diabetes are much more prevalent among older people than younger adults. Data from health examinations of the U.S. population show that older women have higher rates than older men for all of these, particularly for hypertension, arthritis, and diabetes. In addition, more older women have high serum cholesterol levels (viewed as a risk factor for cardiovascular diseases). However, two important qualifications stand out. First, there are various kinds of heart disease (coronary, hypertensive, rheumatic, etc.). Coronary heart disease is especially life-threatening, and for this, older men have higher prevalence rates. Second, although more women have moderate or severe arthritis, more men suffer from mild arthritis.

National health examination data also show that women have lower blood hematocrit levels (a sign of anemia). Older men have more serious skin conditions.

Information about chronic conditions is also available from interview surveys and hospital records. These show that older women have higher prevalence rates than men for many more kinds of chronic problems.

For example, rates of hypertension, arthritis, diabetes, anemia, migraine, sciatica, hypertensive heart disease, varicose veins, digestive and urinary problems, allergies, and orthopedic impairments are higher for women. Most of these are bothersome problems, but seldom causes of death. Also, older women are more likely than men to have several (multiple) chronic conditions. In contrast, the list of diseases for which men have higher rates is shorter, but it contains most of the leading causes of death for older people: heart conditions (especially coronary heart disease), cerebrovascular disease, arteriosclerosis, pneumonia, and emphysema/asthma.[7] (Men also have higher rates for some problems that seldom cause death, for example, gout, peptic ulcer, hernia, psoriasis and sebaceous gland diseases, paralysis, and absence of extremities.) The sex difference for orthopedic problems (higher for women) merits comment: Up to age 65, men have more orthopedic problems; after that age, women do. This is largely due to increased vulnerability of women to injury and impairment from osteoporosis (decrease in bone tissue), which increases sharply after menopause (Gordon and Vaughan, 1977).

What do men and women suffer from most? If we rank the chronic conditions that cause limitations, women are troubled most by arthritis/rheumatism, heart conditions, hypertension, and back/spine impairments. For men, the top problems are heart conditions, arthritis/rheumatism, back/spine impairments, and lower extremity/hip impairments (Bureau of the Census, 1980). The impression that older men have more serious chronic problems is borne out in data on limitations (Table 13.3). A much larger percentage of older men say they are limited in their major activity. Women, however, report more problems in their secondary activities (clubs, church, etc.), mobility, and personal care activities (bathing, eating, etc.). They have more restricted activity and bed disability days for chronic

TABLE 13.3
Chronic Conditions and Resulting Disability among Older Men and Women, United States

	Men 65 +	Women 65 +
Limitation of activity due to chronic condition (1978)		
Limited in major activity (percent)	43.2%	34.9%
Limited but not in major activity	5.0	7.8
Limitation of mobility due to chronic condition (1972)		
Has trouble getting around alone (percent)	5.4%	6.1%
Needs help in getting around	6.0	7.2
Confined to house	4.9	5.4
Disability days for chronic conditions (1977)[1]		
Restricted activity days (per person/year)	22.8 days	27.6 days
Bed disability days	8.2	11.2
Percent with difficulty in common tasks (1962)		
Walking stairs (percent)	24.0%	35.0%
Getting around the house	4.0	8.0
Washing/bathing	7.0	13.0
Dressing/putting on shoes	7.0	9.0
Cutting toenails	15.0	22.0

1. Estimated from total disability days (1977) minus disability days for acute conditions (July 1977-June 1978).

Sources: National Center for Health Statistics, Vital and Health Statistics, Series 10, Nos. 96, 126, 130; and Shanas et al. (1968) for common tasks items.

conditions. And more of them use special aids such as a cane, walker, wheelchair, or special shoes, typically reflecting the result of accidents at an earlier age rather than of chronic illness in old age (Black, 1980).

The data seem contradictory at first glance, but they are not. For the question about major activity, most older men are asked about problems in having a paid job; most women, about keeping house. For older people, a paid job is probably more physically demanding than housework. (At the very least, a job is less flexible in permitting rests and private time.) Therefore, even if men and women were equally sick, older men would report more limitation in "major activity." Also, regardless of their roles during life, older women may reduce their activities when chronic conditions are at an earlier, milder stage. This would boost women's reports of functional limitations and short-term disability for chronic ailments. That older men report more problems in a major social role while women report more trouble in common daily activities reflects their roles and reactions to chronic problems, as well as their levels of real morbidity (illness).

Sensory, Dental, and Nutritional Status

Older women have more vision problems than men, with poorer visual acuity both for uncorrected vision ("glasses off") and corrected vision ("glasses on"). Although women visit ophthalmologists and optometrists more than men do, they still see things less well in daily life.

On the other hand, older men have poorer hearing and dental status. Examinations reveal they have more imparied hearing at all decibel levels and more limitations in daily life from hearing impairments. More older men have periodontal disease and are considered to need prompt dental care. Interestingly, more older women are edentulous (have no natural teeth), and more of their natural teeth have had decay or fillings. It appears that women receive more dental care at earlier ages, whereas older men's current troubles reflect the accumulation of untreated problems which have worsened over time. The data cannot tell us whether men or women are intrinsically more pronc to dental problems. They do show that most older women have had problems treated already, but many older men have not.

Older women have poorer nutritional status. They consume less protein, calcium, and iron than recommended, whereas men consume the recommended levels or more (Abraham et al., 1977:53). All three of the nutrients are critical to physical well-being, especially at older ages. In addition, more older women than men are obese (Assistant Secretary for Health, 1978).

Comparisons with Other Age Groups

As people age, acute conditions become less frequent for both sexes, and chronic conditions predominate. Generally, older men and women are more similar in their acute conditions and disability than at earlier ages, but they are less similar in chronic conditions and limitations. In middle age, women have notably higher rates of acute conditions than men, partly because of reproductive events. Chronic conditions begin to emerge for both sexes in middle age, with men already showing higher rates for "killer" conditions and more major activity limitations than women.

Discussion

In summary, older women have more acute conditions and more chronic ones; they are bothered more by their chronic conditions, but these diseases are seldom life-threatening. Older men have higher rates of life-threatening conditions, which leads to employment restrictions and earlier death. In one sense, older women are "sicker," because their daily lives are more troubled by symptoms; but in another sense, older men are "sicker," because their chronic ailments are more severe and more likely to result in early death. When asked to summarize their health status, older men and women give a similar array of answers—but based on very different health experiences. It is possible that by cutting down activities and accepting limitations for health problems, older women may actually increase their longevity.

The data suggest that older women accommodate to health problems earlier and better than do older men. Although women have more symptoms and chronic problems, their health behavior may reduce the pace of deterioration and enhance life expectancy. Men's relative lack of response to health problems in middle age may ultimately exact a large toll. If older men delay getting medical care when symptoms appear, the chances are reduced of controlling the problem by medication or by changes of habit. And even after diagnosis, older men may be more reluctant than women to respond by changing their behavior; this, too, increases their chances of early death.

Thus, attitudes and behavior towards illness could be very important in explaining sex differentials in short-term disability, limitations, and death among older people. We know little about how older people cope with acute and chronic problems, and how these reactions ultimately affect their longevity.

We should not forget that the majority of older men and women rate their health "good" or "excellent." Health perceptions are critical to how they feel about life and how they behave. People who perceive their health favorably tend to be happier, more satisfied, more involved in social activities, less tense, and less lonely (Pollock et al., 1980; Tissue, 1972; Wan, 1976). The causal ties among these variables are not fully understood, but even so, it is clear that life is much more pleasant for older people who feel healthy than for those who feel unhealthy. This is true for both sexes.

Health Services and Drug Use by Older Men and Women

Older men and women need more health care than do younger adults. For acute problems and chronic flare-ups, older people can get medical treatment in familiar ways, often from a physician who has cared for them for years. The same is true for dental problems. However, discontinuities and difficult decisions loom when physical problems become severe and cause limitations. Then older people and their kin must think about institutionalization versus home care.

Because older men are more seriously ill, we might expect them to use more health services and drugs. Indeed, their hospitalization rates are higher. Nevertheless, older women exceed men in utilizing other types of short-term care (visits to physicians and dentists and drug use) and long-term care (institutions and community-based services).

Short-Term Care

Older women tend to make more physician visits per year than do older men (Table 13.4). Also, the time interval between visits is shorter for women. Visits to other health specialists mirror the sex differences for chronic conditions; older women see orthopedists, ophthalmologists, optometrists, and podiatrists more often, whereas men see dermatologists more (Carpenter et al., 1974:152). Visits to chiropractors are similar for older men and women. Women appear to have slightly higher use of dental care. For both physician and dental visits, sex differences for older people become smaller with advancing age; by age 75, visit rates are much closer for men and women than before. Most medical and dental care for older people is curative. Although preventive care is important for this age group, little is known about the preventive health services used by older men and women.

Hospitalization rates are higher for older men, but women tend to stay longer for an episode.

How do these patterns of short-term care compare with earlier ages? At all ages, women have more physician visits than men, especially during the childbearing years. Sex differences are much narrower for children and older people. Women also see dentists more often at all ages, though the frequency of visits declines with age for both sexes and becomes more similar.

From ages 17 through 44, women have much higher hospital discharge rates than men; but when childbirth and other sex-specific conditions are excluded, the sex difference in hospital rates almost disappears. At about age 45, hospitalization rates begin to rise steeply for men; women's rates drop for a number of years but then also rise, though less rapidly than men's. Before age 65, men tend to have longer hospital stays (even when childbirth stays are excluded). This pattern reverses at older ages (65 and older). I shall offer a possible reason in the discussion section of this paper.

Long-Term Care

Long-term care refers to "professional or personal services required on a recurring or continuous basis by an individual because of chronic or permanent physical or mental impairment" (National Center for Health Statistics, 1980). The clientele for long-term care are people with functional

TABLE 13.4
Health Services Use by Older Men and Women, United States
(Ages 65 + unless otherwise stated)

	Men 65 +	Women 65 +
Number of physician visits in past year (per person) (1978)		
Age 65-74	5.5	6.8
75 +	6.4	6.4
Number of visits to office-based physicians (1977)	3.8	4.4
Time interval since last physician visit (1978)		
Less than 6 months	65%	72%
6-11 months	12	10
1 year	7	6
2-4 years	10	7
5 or more years	6	4
Never	0	0
Don't know/NA	1	1
Number of dental visits in past year (per person) (1978)	1.0	1.4
Time interval since last dental visit (1978)		
Less than 6 months	23%	25%
6-11 months	8	8
1 year	8	8
2-4 years	15	13
5 or more years	45	44
Never	1	1
Don't know/NA	1	1
Discharges from short-stay hospitals (per 100 persons/year) (1978)		
(Health Interview Survey)	29.7	24.7
(Hospital Discharge Survey— non-Federal hospitals)		
Age 65-74	34.0	27.9
75 +	56.1	49.2
Average length of hospital stay (days per episode) (1978)		
(Health Interview Survey)	10.9	11.3
(Hospital Discharge Survey)		
Age 65-74	10.1	10.7
75 +	11.0	11.9

Sources: National Center for Health Statistics, Vital and Health Statistics, Series 10, No. 130, and Series 13, Nos. 43, 44, 46.

limitations—those who have trouble in mobility or transportation, personal care, basic housekeeping activities, and self-management (taking medication, using the telephone). Until recently, long-term care was viewed as synonymous with institutional residence (in nursing or personal care homes, chronic disease hospitals, or mental hospitals). Increasingly, however, home care and other community-based services are available, and data are being gathered about their use by older men and women (Kane and Kane, 1980; Office of Management and Budget, 1980; Weissert, 1978).

Institutionalization

Most older people who are institutionalized live in nursing and personal care homes, where women constitute the majority of residents. This becomes increasingly true with advancing age. For chronic disease hospitals and mental hospitals, older men happen to have higher residence rates, but the proportions of older people in such institutions are low and the sex differences narrow at advanced ages (75+) (Bureau of the Census, 1973).[8]

Older women in nursing and personal care homes are "sicker" than older men residents. They are less able to take care of their personal needs (e.g., bathing, dressing, toilet, eating); they need more assistance in walking, have poorer vision, and have poorer mental status; they have more chronic conditions and need more nursing care (NCHS, Series 12). (Only for hearing status are men residents more disabled than women residents.) One reason for the women's poorer functional status is their older average age (83 for women, 81 for men in 1969), but that is not the only reason, as I will suggest in the discussion section.

In contrast, for younger ages, the men in nursing and personal care homes are likely to be more numerous and sicker than the women residents. The reversal for older people suggests that social factors are important in determining whether to institutionalize a man or woman. Under age 65, disabled men may be difficult for relatives to accept (they are "supposed to be working"), and their wives may have to seek outside employment, leaving no one at home to care for them. At older ages, these job-related factors disappear. Disabled older men are more likely to have a living spouse to care for them than disabled older women, who must find help from other kin or in institutions.

Community-Based Care

Most older people with health problems are able to live in the community, given some assistance from kin or social service agencies. Little is known about how many older people obtain long-term care from community-based sources (e.g., day care away from home, foster homes, hospice care).

We know somewhat more about home health care needs as a result of National Health Interview Surveys in 1979 and 1980. Approximately 13 percent of persons 65+ required some type of home care assistance, and three-fourths of these received all such care from relatives and friends (Soldo, 1983).

Self-Care

In the past two decades, some older people have developed organizations to promote their well-being and social status through local social activities and political lobbying. At the same time, the women's movement and "self-care movement" have grown. Not surprisingly, some organizations have emerged which are devoted solely to older women and to self-care for older people (Butler et al., 1979; Women and Health Roundtable, 1979). The former have questioned the medical establishment's and the drug industry's care of older women, but they have not actively promoted self-care. Older people are strongly attached to the modern health care system, and surveys indicate that they are very satisfied with the care they receive. This minimizes the viability of self-care programs (at least for current cohorts). Organizations for older women and elderly self-care are politically valuable, but they probably influence relatively few older men and women.

Drug Use (Medications)

There are limited data on older people's use of drugs for curative and preventive health care, but the sparse data consistently show that older women use more prescribed and nonprescribed medicines per year than older men. They also use more psychotropic drugs. Higher drug use by women occurs at all ages, not just among older people (Bush and Rabin, 1976; Mallinger et al., 1974; Parry et al., 1973; Rabin and Bush, 1976; NCHS, Series 10, No. 108).

Discussion

In summary, older women use more ambulatory health services than men for both medical and dental care. Older men are hospitalized more often, but they stay fewer days for an episode than hospitalized women. Older women are more likely to receive home care services and to reside in a health institution (especially nursing and personal care homes). They also use more prescription and nonprescription drugs.

How can we explain these differences? Certainly, morbidity is an important factor prompting use of health services and drugs; it represents "need" for care. But many other factors come into play, such as attitudes about health care ("predisposing factors") and access to services and drugs ("enabling factors"). The evidence on attitudes and access factors for older people shows that older people are very satisfied with their medical care (more so than younger people). Few feel that they have unmet health care needs. Older people are eager to comply with physician recommendations about drug therapy and referral to other physicians. They tend to accept medical authority without challenge (Aday et al., 1980; Haug, 1979; Kovar and Drury, 1978; Verbrugge, 1978).

Attitudes about the efficacy of medical care and drugs are important determinants of health behavior. Physician visits, dental visits, and drug use are highly discretionary; people can choose whether or not to utilize them. If older women have more faith in doctors, are more concerned about their health, or perceive symptoms more readily than men, this will encourage their use of health services and drugs. Hospitalization is often another matter, motivated more by the presence and seriousness of a health problem ("need") than by attitudes about benefits of hospital care.

Compared to other age groups, older people tend to have a regular source of medical care, extensive coverage of medical costs through Medicare and Medicaid, and relatively few time constraints. Nevertheless, there are some impediments to seeking care: Older people have fewer financial resources to pay for services not covered by Medicare/Medicaid, travel time to a physician's or dentist's office is longer and often arduous, and office waiting times tend to be longer than at other ages.

Research shows that having a regular source of care (a personal physician) is an important determinant of health care visits (Aday, 1975; Aday and Anderson, 1975; Freeburg et al., 1979: vol. 3:814-816). Older women are more likely than older men to have a regular source of care, but they have lower household incomes and wait much longer in offices and clinics. Overall, whether their "access" is better or worse than men's is not clear.

What about access to institutions? Here the critical factors concern availability of home care. An older man is much more likely to have a living spouse, who can provide home care if he is disabled (Shanas, 1979). In contrast, older women are often widowed and have no one willing or able to give long-term care. Institutional residence may be the only solution.

I can suggest three possible reasons for the sex differentials in health services and drug use among older people. These are postulates which are plausible but not yet·demonstrated by research.

First, women's higher use of discretionary health services and drugs is related to need, attitudes, and access. Older women are symptomatic more often with acute conditions and chronic flare-ups, and therefore they need more primary care. Also, they are likely to have more positive attitudes about the efficacy of medical care, dental care, and medicine. This comes from health socialization and experiences during childhood and adult years: greater sensitivity to body discomforts, attentiveness to their family's health, and familiarity with the medical care system (e.g., through re-productive care and pediatric care for their children). When they become old, women hold fast to these attitudes and are much more likely than older men to take some action for symptoms; men may try to ignore symptoms and carry on as usual. Having a more regular source of care also boosts women's rates of health care visits.

Women's attitudes can help explain their longer hospital stays. They may be less insistent about going home or may actually ask to stay additional days. Access factors also enter the picture: Women without a spouse have sparser services waiting for them at home, and this prolongs their hospital stays.

Second, in contrast to physician visits, hospitalization rates should re-flect need more than health attitudes or access to care. Thus, men's higher rates are compatible with their more serious morbidity. Their chronic con-ditions lead to more "surprise attacks" (e.g., heart attack and stroke) which necessitate immediate hospital care. In addition, men's conditions may generally be more advanced, which boosts their need for hospital care.

Third, decisions to institutionalize people are largely based on need and access factors. If only needs were operative, we might expect men to have higher rates since they are more seriously ill. But women's needs actually seem to fit better: Living longer, older women accumulate more health problems. Even when not life-threatening, multiple problems take a grad-ual toll and lead to functional limitations. Thus, an 85-year-old woman will typically have more symptoms and more problems in daily living than an 85-year-old man, but he is more likely to die because his problem is medically serious. The importance of functional limitations is reflected in the health status of institutional residents: Women residents have more limitations than men. Access factors are also critical. Having fewer social and financial resources than men, older women in poor health find it more difficult to stay in the community. Many women become institutional residents in order to secure needed social and health services.

Thus sex differences in health services and drug use by older men and women match their health profiles. Short-term problems (acute conditions or chronic flare-ups) generate short-term care—more for women. (Recall also their higher rates of restricted activity and bed days.) Serious problems generate hospital care—more for men. Accumulated problems ultimately urge institutional care—more for women. But health attitudes and access also act to increase women's use of out-patient and institutional services and their use of drugs.

Explaining Sex Differences in Health and Mortality

There are five basic reasons older men and women differ in health status, health behavior, and death rates: inherited risks of illness, acquired risks of illness and injury, illness attitudes and enabling factors, illness behavior, and reporting behavior. Because people often bring health problems into older age from younger ages, we need to consider these factors across the entire life span.

Inherited risks refer here to biological vulnerability to illness because of one's sex. It is believed that males have less resistance to "killer" chronic conditions, so these conditions develop more readily and deteriorate more rapidly for them (Waldron, 1976). Women apparently have some protection from degenerative disease before menopause because of high estrogen levels; but the protection then disappears, and women's rates for "killer" conditions (especially cardiovascular) increase rapidly. Inherited risks probably exert a larger toll on males throughout their lives, even on the hardy ones who survive to very old age.

Men and women tend to differ in their work and leisure activities, lifestyles, and (possibly) levels of stress and reactions to stress. Thus, they are exposed to different *acquired risks* of illness and injury. The largest differences in roles and activities are at young and middle adult ages. Generally, men have more risks because of their job activities, job-related travel, sports and leisure activities, smoking and drinking behavior, and coping behaviors for stress (often smoking and drinking). In particular, men's smoking behavior is believed to be a key factor in their higher mortality rates (Preston, 1970a, 1970b; Retherford, 1975). Higher alcohol consumption by men is also certainly detrimental. Behaviors in young and middle ages set the stage for chronic conditions that will persist in older ages (65 and over) or cause death before then.

Even at older ages, men may still engage in social activities and lifestyles that elevate their disease risks compared with women. This would increase their chances of developing a new chronic condition and also their chances of having an "old" condition deteriorate. Men's activities may also expose them to more injury risks, but women's more fragile bone structure at older ages makes them actually incur more injuries.

Illness attitudes refer to people's symptom perceptions, assessments of symptom severity, and readiness to take curative and preventive health actions. It is widely believed that women are more sensitive than men to body discomforts, interpret them as illness more often, and are more willing and able to restrict activities, seek medical and dental help, and use drugs. These attitudes predispose women to use more health services and take more time off for illness than men do. In addition, *enabling factors,* such as access to services and knowledge of services, are important determinants of health behavior. Sex differences in illness attitudes and enabling factors are probably strongest in middle age when women are less likely to be employed and more likely to be attuned to health due to reproductive events and family health care. At older ages, the sex differences in symptom perception, symptom evaluation, and attitudes about health care and health knowledge may persist. Some access factors change: Older women experience more financial and transportation problems in seeking medical care than do older men.

Slowing down for illness and obtaining preventive and curative health care may promote a person's health. These *illness behaviors* not only help a person recuperate from a current problem, but also enhance resistance to later ones. In addition, frequent medical and dental care increases the chances of early diagnosis and treatment of health problems. Women's greater short-term disability and ambulatory medical care (which imply poorer health at the time they occur) may actually provide long-term health benefits.

Health data are usually collected through personal interviews. If women are more interested in health or have better recall of their health experiences, these *reporting behaviors* can boost their rates of morbidity and illness behavior compared to men's.

All five factors are important in explaining sex differences in health status and health behavior, and all but the last help explain the timing and cause of death (see also Mechanic, 1976; Nathanson, 1977; Verbrugge, 1979, 1981a). The presence of multiple causes (some medical, some psychosocial) helps us see why sex differentials are complex and sometimes seemingly contradictory. Inherited and acquired risks are generally higher for males, but illness attitudes and reporting behavior raise morbidity rates for females. Some access factors encourage health actions for women; others do so for men. In the long run, the illness behavior of females enhances their health and reduces their mortality at older ages.

These conclusions also suggest that public policies designed to lengthen life and reduce the functional limitations of older persons must be tailored more efficiently and sensitively to the differing situations of males and females at all ages.

The Future: Cohorts to Come

The health of older people is dynamic in two respects. First, individuals experience health changes during their lives. Chronic problems that appear in young and middle-aged adults often persist in older ages. Gradually, chronic illnesses and impairments accumulate for older people and cause functional limitations or death. This is an individual level or life-course perspective. We have considered it at length in this chapter.

Second, the older population changes its membership over time. New cohorts of elderly may differ sharply in economic status, family and marital life, health habits, roles and role attitudes, and health experiences

(Riley et al., 1972). For example, people now 75-84 were born around 1900. As children, they had high risks of death from acute conditions. They suffered the Depression in their thirties, which diminished their childbearing and hindered their career development. They had traditional sex roles, with men responsible for family income and women responsible for child-rearing and housework. In the year 2000, people of ages 75-84 will be quite different. They fought in World War II and they produced the Baby Boom and economic prosperity after the war. This group too had traditional sex roles during their childbearing years. In 2020, men and women now age 35 will reach the 75-84 age group. They are bearing few children, and they are modifying roles so that job and domestic tasks are more alike for men and women. (This is not a uniform trend for all couples, of course, but the cohort overall is making remarkable changes in sex roles.) Over 60 percent of the women are employed, and many are establishing long-term work careers. This cohort has lived in a generally healthy physical environment, and it is aware of the harmful effects of smoking and heavy drinking.

These three cohorts have experienced a wide variety of health risks, health attitudes, and health behaviors during their lives which should result in different health profiles when they become old. For example, men now 65 and over smoked heavily in middle age; this is reflected in their health problems and diminished longevity compared to older women who smoked little. But coming cohorts of older women will have more smoking experience; they will undoubtedly suffer more respiratory and cardiovascular problems during (and before) old age.

What will contemporary young adults be like when they become the older population? Compared to the current older cohorts, will they have different health problems, make different decisions about health care, and have different mortality rates when elderly? Probably so, but we cannot describe their health profiles for certain. Their behavior in the next few decades is critical. Will young men and women reduce their smoking and drinking, eat moderately, and have sufficient exercise throughout middle age? Will women's increasing participation in the labor force make them happier and healthier, or will it increase stress and exposure to harmful materials, thereby causing poorer health? Current evidence suggests that both men and women are adopting more healthful lifestyles and that women's employment has a beneficial impact on their health (Verbrugge, 1981c). Also, the future may see medical advances for the control of cardiovascular diseases and cancer. All these factors suggest that death rates will continue their current decline for both sexes,[9] thus a higher proportion of men and women will reach older ages. However, it is possible that functional limitations will increase in the older population. More people may have illnesses which are controlled but which impede mobility, physical activity, or social activities. (This can occur even if incidence rates for "killer" conditions decrease.)

What will happen to sex differentials in health and mortality? The roles of young men and women are becoming more similar; more women are combining family and job activities, and more men are sharing in domestic responsibilities. This trend toward more similar roles will probably continue for cohorts who are now children. The more similar men's and women's roles are, the more similar their health risks, attitudes, and behaviors are likely to be. Ultimately, this may lead to more similar death rates. I do not think that equal mortality rates will ever occur because women probably do have an intrinsic durability which gives them a longevity advantage even if roles were absolutely identical. But sex differences in health and death should narrow as morbidity and mortality rates fall for both sexes.

In summary, I think the following is very plausible scenario for the future: As women engage in more social roles, they will be less frequently ill in middle and older ages. Their rates of acute conditions and short-term disability will decrease. As working environments and lifestyles improve and as people learn to cope better with the stresses of multiple roles, chronic problems should decrease for middle-aged men and women. Men especially will gain from these changes. Both sexes will enter older ages with fewer life-threatening conditions, or milder cases of them. But by living longer, older men and women will tend to accumulate more chronic troubles, and they may have more functional limitations during their final years. All of these trends lead to more similar health and mortality profiles for older men and women.

These are sweeping forecasts, and we will have to wait many years to see if they are right. Before, then, there is plenty to learn about health, mortality, and their determinants for the current older population and for younger cohorts. Data collection and analysis should take both a short-term and a long-term perspective so that we can document current health status and problems of age groups, and also have cumulative information to understand the cohorts' whole experiences when they finally become the older population.

Notes

In addition to Helena Z. Lopata and George C. Myers, the author is grateful to Berit Ingersoll, Tom Hickey, Edith Gromberg, and Tom Wan for their critical reading of an earlier version of this paper and for their important suggestions. Jean Kracke provided competent research assistance.

1. As used here, "health behavior" encompasses Kasl and Cobb's (1966a, 1966b) three terms: health behavior, illness behavior, and sick-role behavior.

2. The one exception is diabetes, for which rates are virtually the same for older men and women. This is a recent phenomenon; for many years, women had higher rates than men.
3. This statement is based on sex ratios (M/F). If we consider sex differences (M-F) instead, we find that the gap widens with advancing age. There is no contradiction: Death rates rise so sharply with advancing age that the absolute differences (M-F) can expand while the relative differences (M/F) shrink.
4. For further discussion of recent trends in sex mortality differentials, see Metropolitan Life Insurance Company (1980) and Verbrugge (1980). Recent trends in mortality for elderly people (85+) are examined by Rosenwaike et al. (1980). The remarkable drop in heart disease mortality in the 1970s is examined in Havlik and Feinleib (1979), Keys (1980), Kleinman et al. (1979), and Stallones (1980). Other good references are Siegel (1979), for long-term trends in mortality of older people, and Myers (1978), for cross-national comparisons of mortality for older people.
5. This section and the next summarize health data for older men and women. Previous reviews are available in Atchley (1977), Carpenter et al. (1974), Kovar (1977, 1979), National Center for Health Statistics (1971), Riley and Foner (1968), and Shanas and Maddox (1976).
6. Other studies find similar results (Larson, 1978; Maddox, 1962). How subjective health is related to a number of health problems for older men and women is studied by Ferraro (1980) and Fillenbaum (1979).
7. What about the other leading causes of death? (1) Women have higher morbidity rates for diabetes, but men now have slightly higher mortality rates. (2) Women report more malignant neoplasms but they are hospitalized less often and have lower cancer death rates than men. This discrepancy can reflect two things: (a) Women have their cancers diagnosed and treated earlier, so they know about their problems when interviewed. Also, more of women's cancers can be controlled, leaving a female population with cancer experience but lower risk of cancer mortality. (b) Women may be more willing to report cancer than men. (3) No prevalence rates are available for cirrhosis of the liver and nephritis/ nephrosis. (4) Accident deaths result from injuries. Injury rates are higher for older women, but accident mortality rates and hospitalization rates are higher for men. Apparently, women's injuries are less severe and therefore less likely to cause impairment or death. (The data on disability days for injuries—higher for women—are not necessarily contradictory. Women may take better care of themselves for an injury than men do. This would readily account for their higher restricted activity and bed disability per injury.)
8. These statements are based on the 1970 Census of Population. Rates for earlier years are reported in Carpenter et al. (1974:141), and some of the sex differences there do not match the 1970 Census. This may have more to do with rapid changes in types and numbers of institutions available to older people than to changes in decisions about sending men and women to nursing homes versus other institutions. For the same reason, data for the 1980 Census of Population may show marked changes compared with 1970.
9. Further declines in overall mortality will be small. This is because most decendents are elderly, and if their chances of surviving one disease improve, they become more vulnerable than before to death from another cause. The topic of "competing risks" has been analyzed by demographers (Keyfitz, 1978; Tsai et al.,

1978; see also comments in the *American Journal of Public Health*, 70(11), 1980).

References

Abraham, Sidney, Margaret D. Carroll, Connie M. Dresser, and Clifford L. Johnson. 1977. *Dietary Intake Findings, United States, 1971-74.* Vital and Health Statistics, Series 11, no. 202. Hyattsville, Md.: National Center for Health Statistics.

Aday, LuAnn. 1975. "Economic and Non-Economic Barriers to Use of Needed Medical Services." *Medical Care* 13:447-56.

Aday, LuAnn, and Ronald Andersen. 1975. *Development of Indices of Access to Medical Care.* Ann Arbor: Health Administration Press.

Aday, LuAnn, Ronald Andersen, and Gretchen V. Fleming. 1980. *Health Care in the United States: Equitable for Whom?* Beverly Hills: Sage.

Assistant Secretary for Health. 1978. *Health, United States, 1978.* DHEW Publication no. (PHS) 78-1232. Hyattsville, Md.: National Center for Health Statistics.

Atchley, Robert C. 1977. *The Social Forces in Later Life.* Belmont: Wadsworth.

Black, Ethel R. 1980. *Use of Special Aids, United States, 1977.* Vital and Health Statistics. Series 10, no. 135. Hyattsville, Md.: National Center for Health Statistics.

Bureau of the Census. 1973. *1970 Census of Population: Persons in Institutions and Other Group Quarters.* Subject Report PC (2)-4E.

———. 1980. *A Statistical Portrait of Women in the United States, 1978.* Current Population Reports, Series P-23, no. 100.

Bush, Patricia J., and David Rabin. 1976. "Who's Using Nonprescribed Medicines?" *Medical Care* 14:1014-23.

Butler, Robert N. 1969. "Ageism: Another Form of Bigotry." *Gerontologist* 9:243-46.

Butler, Robert N., Jessie S. Gertman, Dewayne L. Oberlander, and Lydia Schindler. 1979. "Self-Care, Self-Help; and the Elderly." *International Journal of Aging and Human Development* 10(1):95-117.

Carpenter, James O., Ray F. McArthur, and Ian T. Higgins. 1974. "The Aged: Health, Illness, Disability, and Use of Medical Services." In Carl L. Erhardt and Joyce E. Berlin (eds), *Mortality and Morbidity in the United States.* Cambridge: Harvard University Press.

DiFederico, Elaine. 1978. "Health Planning and the Elderly." Working Paper 5904-13. Washington, D.C.: Urban Institute.

Ferraro, Kenneth F. 1980. "Self-Ratings of Health among the Old and the Old-Old." *Journal of Health and Social Behavior* 21:377-83.

Fillenbaum, Gerda G. 1979. "Social Context and Self-Assessment of Health among the Elderly." *Journal of Health and Social Behavior* 20:45-51.

Ford, Charles V., and Robert J. Sbordone. 1980. "Attitudes of Psychiatrists toward Elderly Patients." *American Journal of Psychiatry* 137(5):571-75.

Freeburg, Linnea C., Judith R. Lave, Lester B. Lave, and Samuel Leinhardt. 1979. *Health Status, Medical Care Utilization, and Outcome: An Annotated Bibliography of Empirical Studies* (4 vols.). DHEW Publication no. (PHS) 80-3263. Hyattsville, Md.: National Center for Health Services Research.

Gelfant, Seymour, and J. Graham Smith, Jr. 1972. "Aging: Noncycling Cells—An explanation." *Science* 178 (27 October):357-61.

Gordon, Gilbert S., and Cynthia Vaughan. 1977. "The Role of Estrogens in Osteoporosis." *Geriatrics* 32(9):42-48.

Grove, Robert D., and Alice M. Hetzel. 1968. *Vital Statistics Rates in the United States, 1940-1960.* PHS Publication no. 1677. Washington, D.C.: National Center for Health Statistics.

Haug, Marie. 1979. "Doctor-Patient Relationships and the Older Patient." *Journal of Gerontology* 34(6):852-60.

Havlik, Richard J., and Manning Feinleib (eds.). 1979. *Proceedings of the Conference on the Decline in Coronary Heart Disease Mortality.* NIH Publication no. 1610. Washington D.C.: U.S. Government Printing Office.

Hayflick, Leonard. 1980. "The Cell Biology of Human Aging." *Scientific American* 242(1):58-65.

Holahan, John, Judith Feder, Judith Wagner, Robert Lee, Karen Lennox, and Jane Weeks. 1978. "Health and the Elderly: A Policy Research Agenda for the Administration on Aging." Working Paper 5904-5. Washington, D.C.: Urban Institute.

Jarvis, George K., Roberta G. Ferrence, F. Gordon Johnson, and Paul C. Whitehead. 1976. "Sex and Age Patterns in Self-Injury." *Journal of Health and Social Behavior* 17:146-55.

Kane, Robert L., and Rosalie A. Kane. 1980. "Long-Term Care: Can Our Society Meet the Needs of Its Elderly?" In Lester Breslow (Ed.), *Annual Review of Public Health,* vol. 1. Palo Alto: Annual Reviews.

Kasl, Stanley V., and Sidney Cobb. 1966. "Health Behavior, Illness Behavior, and Sick-Role Behavior: I. Health and Illness Behavior. *Archives of Environmental Health* 12:246-66.

———. 1966b. "Health Behavior, Illness Behavior, and Sick-Role Behavior: II. Sick-Role Behavior." *Archives of Enviromental Health* 12:531-41.

Keyfitz, Nathan. 1978. "Improving Life Expectancy: An Uphill Road Ahead." *American Journal of Public Health* 68:954-56.

Keys, Ancel. 1980. *Seven Countries: A Multivariate Analysis of Death and Coronary Heart Disease.* Cambridge: Harvard University Press.

Kleinman, Joel C., Jacob J. Feldman, and Mary A. Monk. 1979. "The Effects of Changes in Smoking Habits on Coronary Heart Disease Mortality." *American Journal of Public Health* 69:795-802.

Kovar, Mary Grace. 1977. "Elderly People: The Population 65 Years and Over." In *Health, United States, 1976-1977.* DHEW/HRA 77-1232. Hyattsville, Md.: National Center for Health Statistics.

———. 1979. "Health of the Elderly and Use of Health Services." *Public Health Reports* 92(1):9-19.

Kovar, Mary Grace, and Thomas F. Drury. 1978. "Use of Medical Care Services by Men and Women in Their Middle and Later Years." Paper presented at the Gerontological Society meetings, Dallas, November.

Larson, Reed. 1978. "Thirty Years of Research on the Subjective Well-Being of Older Americans." *Journal of Gerontology* 33:109-25.

Maddox, George L. 1962. "Some Correlates of the Difference in in Self-Assessment of Health Status among the Elderly." *Journal of Gerontology* 17:180-85.

Marx, Jean L. 1974. "Aging Research (I): Cellular Theories of Senescence." *Science* 186 (20 December): 1105-07.

Mechanic, David. 1976. "Sex, Illness Behavior, and the Use of Health Services." *Journal of Human Stress* 2(4):29-40.

Mellinger, Glen D., Mitchell B. Balter, Hugh J. Perry, Dean I. Manheimer, and Ira
H. Cisin. 1974. "An Overview of Psychotherapeutic Drug Use in the United
States." In Eric Josephson and Eleanor A. Carroll (eds.), *Drug Use: Epi-
demiological and Social Issues.* Washington, D.C. : Hemisphere.
Metropolitan Life Insurance Company.1980. "Mortality Differentials Favor
Women." *Statistical Bulletin* 61(2):2-7.
Milliren, John W. 1977. "Some Contingencies Affecting the Utilization of Tran-
quilizers in Long-Term Care of the Elderly." *Journal of Health and Social Be-
havior* 18:206-11.
Myers, George C. 1978. "Cross-National Trends in Mortality Rates among the
Elderly." *Gerontologist* 18 (5, pt. 1): 441-48.
Nathanson, Constance. 1977. "Sex, Illness, and Medical Care: A Review of Data,
Theory, and Method." *Social Science and Medicine* 11:13-25.
National Center for Health Statistics. 1971. *Health in the Later Years of Life.* GPO
Stock no. 1722-0178. Rockville, Md.
———. 1980. *Long-Term Health Care Minimum Data Set.* DHHS Publication no.
(PHS) 80-1158. Hyattsville, Md.
National Institutes of Health. 1979. *The Older Woman: Continuities and Discon-
tinuities.* NIH Publication no. 79-1897. Bethesda, Md.: National Institute on
Aging.
Office of Management and Budget. 1980. *Data Coverage on the Functionally Lim-
ited Elderly.* Report of the Interagency Statistical Committee on Long-Term
Care for the Elderly. Washington, D.C.
Parry, Hugh J., Mitchell B. Balter, Glen D. Mellinger, Ira H. Cisin, and Dean I.
Manheimer. 1973. "National Patterns of Psychotherapeutic Drug Use." *Archives
of General Psychiatry* 28: 769-83.
Pollock, John C., Andrew J. Kelley, Kathy Bloomgarden, Peter Finn, and Adam
Snyder. 1980. *Aging in America: Trials and Triumphs.* Monticello, Ill.: Amer-
icana Healthcare.
Preston, Samuel H. 1970a. *Older Male Mortality and Cigarette Smoking: A Demo-
graphic Analysis.* Population Monograph Series no. 7. Berkeley: Institute of
International Studies, University of California.
———. 1970b. "An International Comparison of Excessive Adult Mortality." *Popu-
lation Studies* 24 (1).
Rabin, David L., and Patricia J. Bush. 1976. "Who's Using Prescribed Medicines?"
Drugs in Health Care 3:89-100.
Retherford, Robert. 1975. *The Changing Sex Differential in Mortality.* Westport:
Greenwood.
Riley, Matilda W., and Anne Foner. 1968. *Aging and Society.* Vol. 1: *An Inventory of
Research Findings.* New York: Russell Sage.
Riley, Matilda W., Marilyn Johnson, and Anne Foner. 1972. *Aging and Society.* Vol.
3: *A Sociology of Age Stratification.* New York: Russell Sage.
Rosenwaike, Ira, Nurit Yaffe, and Phillip C. Sagi. 1980. "The Recent Decline in
Mortality of the Extreme Aged: An Analysis of Statistical Data." *American
Journal of Public Health* 70(10):1074-80.
Shanas, Ethel. 1962. *The Health of Older People.* Cambridge: Harvard University
Press.
———. 1979. "The Family as a Social Support System in Old Age." *Gerontologist*
19(2):169-74.

Shanas, Ethel, and George L. Maddox. 1976. "Aging, Health, and the Organization of Health Resources." In Robert H. Binstock and Ethel Shanas (eds.), *Handbook of Aging and the Social Sciences.* New York: Van Nostrand Reinhold.

Shanas, Ethel, Peter Townsend, Dorothy Wedderburn, Henning Friis, Paul Milhoj, and Jan Stehouwer. 1968. *Old People in Three Industrial Societies.* New York: Atherton.

Siegel, Jacob S. 1976. *Demographic Aspects of Aging and the Older Population in the United States.* Current Population Reports, series p-23, no. 59. Washington, D.C.: Bureau of the Census.

Soldo, Beth J. 1983. "In-Home Services for the Dependent Elderly: Determinants of Current Use and Implications for Future Demand." Center for Population Research, Georgetown University, Washington, D.C.

Stallones, Reuel A. 1980. "The Rise and Fall of Ischemic Heart Disease." *Scientific American* 243(5):53-59.

Surgeon General and Office of the Assistant Secretary for Health. 1979. *Healthy People: The Surgeon General's Report on Health Promotion and Disease Prevention.* DHEW/PHS 79-55071. Washington, D.C.: Public Health Service.

Tissue, Thomas. 1972. "Another Look at Self-Rated Health among the Elderly." *Journal of Gerontology* 27:91-94.

Tsai, Shen P., Eun S. Lee, and Robert J. Hardy. 1978. "The Effect of a Reduction in Leading Causes of Death: Potential Gains in Life Expectancy." *American Journal of Public Health* 68:966-71.

Verbrugge, Lois M. 1978. *Differentials in Medical Care for Acute Conditions, United States.* Biostatistics Technical Reports Series, no. 17. Ann Arbor: Department of Biostatistics, School of Public Health, University of Michigan. (Accompanies Vital and Health Statistics, series 10, no. 129.)

————. 1979. "Female Illness Rates and Illness behavior: Testing Hypotheses about Sex Differences in Health." *Women and Health* 4(1):61-79.

————. 1980. "Recent Trends in Sex Mortality Differentials in the United States." *Women and Health* 5(3):17-37.

————. 1981a. "Women and Men's Health: Research Issues for the 1980's." Ms. available from author.

————. 1981b. "Women's Social Roles and Health." In Proceedings of the Conference on Women, a Developmental Perspective: Conference on Research, Bethesda, November 1980. Bethesda: National Institute of Child Health and Human Development.

————. 1982. "Sex Differentials in Health." *Public Health Reports* 97:417-37.

Verbrugge, Lois M., and Richard P. Steiner. 1981. "Physician Treatment of Men and Women Patients: Sex Bias or Appropriate Care? *Medical Care* 19:609-32.

Waldron, Ingrid. 1976. "Why Do Women Live Longer Than Men?" *Social Science and Medicine* 10:349-62.

Wan, Thomas T.H. 1976. "Predicting Self-Assessed Health Status: A Multivariate Approach." *Health Services Research* 11:464-77.

Weissert, William G. 1978. "Long-Term Care: An Overview." In *Office of the Assistant Secretary for Health, United States, 1978.* DHEW Publication no. (PHS) 78-1232. Hyattsville, Md.: National Center for Health Statistics.

Women and Health Roundtable. 1979. *Roundtable Report* 4(4, April). Washington, D.C.

14

Beyond Babies and Orgasm

Ruth B. Weg

It is as absurd to pretend that one cannot love the same woman always, as to pretend that a good artist needs several violins to execute a piece of music.
—Honoré de Balzac (1799-1850)

In the lives of women, measurable progress has occurred in areas of self esteem, income, and career opportunities. However, to be female in this society is still to be *less than*—less than healthy, less than normal, less than competent, less than worthy, less than sexual.

Physiologically, to be born female is advantageous. Females are sturdier and demonstrate a lower mortality rate from in utero existence forward; females live longer than males. Nevertheless, to grow up female continues to be a psychosocial challenge. Despite the positive changes occurring today in the lives of women, to be female, old, and fulfilled is a test of emotional and physical survival skills. To be female, old, and express one's sexuality can be the ultimate frustration. Before we discuss these changes further, let's look at our history—how have women accumulated diminished categories?

And They Stood Up

A glance back to our primate beginnings finds the female of the species presenting her back to the male for quick and rough intercourse. With the advent of bipedal movement and the adoption of the upright position, the face to face mating stance evolved.[1] Some conjecture that the experience of female orgasm became possible with this new position, a response missing from the nonhuman primate sexual repertoire.[2]

On the basis of archeological findings, we can make some assumptions about the personal lives, thinking, and behavior of early homo sapiens. For example, there must have been some religious and humanitarian beliefs that included instructions for burying the dead, caring for the sick and elderly. But the sexuality in the lives of contemporary primitive peoples left no particular clues. We must assume that, like all other human behavior, sexuality was also the product of the millions of years that went before.

There appears to be no identifiable evidence that either monogamy or polygamy prevailed in paleolithic times. Unlike most nonhuman primates, the early human female had no estrous cycle. It is logical, then, that the menstrual cycle and ongoing female readiness for intercourse could have led to monogamy. However, in an examination of the 5000 years of written human history, polygamy has appeared more widespread than monogamy. Also, it is likely that environment may have governed the state of the union between male and female. When living was harsh, near monogamy might have been essential to ensure survival of offspring and the genetic pool, and when living was easier, polygamy was more probably.[3] Moreover, "it may have been the women, not the men who were promiscuous—for it was they who were in the minority."[4] Based on skeletal remains of humans of a million years ago, archeologists have found that males outnumbered females three to two. Further, they suggest that early males may have outlived females by about eight years—exactly the number of years by which today's average older female outlives the male.

She Becomes Mother—He Is Finally Father

From neolithic times to 700 years later when recorded history began, she worked hard. Formerly a nomadic food gatherer with other men, women, and children, she became a farmer, housekeeper, found the fuel, bore and reared the children, and prepared the grain that she grew.

In both agricultural and pastoral societies that developed, women began increasingly to take on a *chattel* assignation. In the former, the land and its fruits were still major; animal herding was relatively minor, and the work of man and woman was comparable in importance. Instead of hunters, men became shepherds, domesticators of animals. They had time and energy to think, question, create, and invent new products for the growing civilization. He bred the stock, created the draft animal, tilled the soil. Still warrior, he also was the guardian of family and home. The pastoralists continued the mobility of paleolithic hunters, moving with their herds to the fertile grazing areas of the world. Men were clearly dominant; women were herded along with the animals.

The power ascent of man had begun. Clearly, women's freedom and position became increasingly limited, tied to one group, to home and hearth and to the dictates of a master.

The Woman's Sexual Heritage

Although sexual traditions of the societies of the Near East grew increasingly restrictive and repressive, especially in relation to all forms of sexual expression outside of procreation, sex was a fact of life. Women were the child bearers—and were married for procreation not companionship. So primary was that role that sterility was a legal basis for divorce. Adultery was not a moral sin, but a violation of a husband's property. A wife could be put to death for fornication, which a husband was free to practice.

Egyptians, though generally monogamous, permitted their noble and powerful males to have more than one wife and many concubines. Sexual activity began early since girls were married by age 12 or 13, and boys at age 15 or 16. Among the wealthy, slave girls were available to satisfy the sexual urges of young men in the household. Circumcision may have been used first by the Egyptians and was performed on girls as well as boys. In some areas of modern Egypt excision of females is still practiced and involves removing part or all of the clitoris and labia minora. This surgery prevents orgasm and effectively eliminates erotic stimulation in the external genitalia. The connection between sexual morality and religious salvation did influence the West, as it filtered through the traditions of the Jews and Greeks to the early Christians.[5]

The sexual attitudes and practices of the ancient Hebrews fluctuated in keeping with the various lifestyles of defeat, exile, near-elimination and independence. But all through Jewish history, there has been emphasis on social control of sexual expression, and the primary objective of sexual activity was procreation. During the Talmudic period (also the early centuries of the Christian Era) the rigid rules of sexual behavior appeared to relax. Rabbis acknowledged, even emphasized, the appropriate pleasure of sex within marriage. The Friday night marital act was often alluded to as a religious duty.[6] Masturbation was disapproved, and some Talmudic writers suggested the practice was a crime with death as a suitable punishment.

In Jewish writings women are described as having more consistent, aggressive, sexual appetites. For example, Eve led Adam to fall from grace, Rachel and Leah negotiated for the sexual rights of their husband, and Delilah weakened Samson. The Talmud writes of woman's orgasm and advises men that they could ensure a male offspring by stimulating their wives to orgasm before the men reach their own. Although the loss of semen via coitus interruptus or masturbation was punishable, women were permitted to practice contraception by placing a spongy substance in the vagina. It would appear that the male semen was finally thought to be central to conception while the female only supplied a protected environment for development. Even then, it was clear that not all sexual encounters resulted in pregnancy and that there must be more to sexual relationships than procreation. It was a post-menopausal Sarah, wife of Abraham, who was blessed with a pregnancy after agonizing over the relationship between her servant and husband. Talmudic writings also depicted a fear of woman's sexuality and needs and prohibited a widow from keeping a pet dog or acquiring a slave. The third book of the Bible, Leviticus, calls homosexuality an abomination. Adultery was addressed in Jewish law but was punishable by death only when a married woman had intercourse with a man who was not her husband. In summary, the ancient Jews acknowledged sexuality as pleasurable, not an evil, nor for procreation only. There were certain norms and expectations, and sexual intercourse between men and women in marriage was encouraged. Withal, Judaism was a male-oriented religion, and women clearly existed to serve men.

The Greeks focused on the beautiful body, prohibited very little of sexual activity, and encouraged sensuous pleasures. Homosexuality was regarded as appropriate between an adult male and an adolescent boy but was regarded negatively between two adult males or an adult male and prepubertal boy. Masturbation was accepted only when a partner was unavailable for intercourse. Though references to masturbation for women are few, the Greeks did have *self-satisfiers,* instruments that helped women in masturbation and possibly during intercourse as well. Men were encouraged to seek concubines, courtesans for pleasures and daily needs, and wives who would provide legitimate offspring and be trusted caretakers of home and children.

The Greeks also perceived women as oversexed, and gave them permission to use a variety of contraceptive procedures. Menstruation required no purification ceremony. The Greeks still believed that the male was primary in reproduction, that semen provided the form, and the female contained the substance that could be shaped. In Athens, women had the same legal or political rights as slaves and were controlled by their male next-of-kin. Positive attitudes and encouragement for marriage and family existed, but women remained secondary. Whatever the age or marital state, woman was the bearer of children. During the Hellenistic era, there also existed a denial of worldly pleasures and an emphasis on the spiritual, which was contrary to the pleasure-seeking philosophy and marked the beginning of the later religious celibate fervor.

Changing Morality

The early Christians borrowed and elaborated on the Greek and Judaic sexual pronouncements. In general, sexual activity was considered evil though procreative marital sex less evil. Christianity held celibacy as the ideal. St. Augustine believed that the sinfulness of sexual lust was visited as well upon the children by the "inherent lust that separated humanity from God."[7]

Co-existing and contrasting with the early Christian era (by the end of fourth century B.C.) were the Islamic, Hindu, and Oriental sexual philosophies, which were more open, accepting and affirming. Chinese Taoism emphasized the immortality potential of a highly disciplined ritual sexual life. Sex manuals of ancient India, China, and Japan provided graphic instructions in the joys of sexual activities.[8]

The Middle Ages and Renaissance saw a firming up of the early Christian sexual traditions, generally oppressive and hypocritical.[9] So called high-ranking women were bequeathed a new behavior code that included romanticism, secrecy, and a semi-immaculate state. The pure love/courtly love of famous poetry and literature looked down on satisfaction of bodily drives. Husbands required wives to wear metal chastity belts to insure their faithfulness.[10]

During the sixteenth and seventeenth centuries, sexual restrictions became fewer, courtly love diminished, and celibacy and chastity were no longer virtues unto themselves. In America, the Puritan ethic prevailed and extra-marital sex was condemned; adultery and premarital sex were publicly punished.

The Woman Repressed

Contradictions between pronounced sexual mores and widespread practices were significant in the Victorian era. On the one hand, there was repressive antisexuality. Prudery and modesty were the norm and supposedly were necessary to preserve the virtue and innocence of women and children. Pornography was banned. On the other hand, prostitution was legalized and regulated by the English Parliament in the 1860s.

Medical practice mirrored and exacerbated the antisexual ambiance. Women, considered physically and intellectually inferior to men, were also considered incapable of sexual response. This is not surprising, since the Victorian ideal women was untouched and untouchable, devoid of desire, and therefore considered superior and worthy of respect because of her comfort with near-celibacy. Only the needs of the future—children—assured the *good* woman of periodic sexual activity.[11]

Sexuality: Scientific Objectivity

Victorian attitudes and sexual behavior continued to prevail. Remnants still exist today. In the early 1900s, however, came the first steps in the legitimization of the scientific study of human sexuality. At the end of World War I, women were in a period of economic and social growth and also found themselves part of a developing sexual revolution. The birth control movement was under way. Marriage manuals made their appearance with explicit and technique-oriented texts.[12]

Two students of sexuality led the path out of ignorance and silence— Sigmund Freud (1856-1939) and Havelock Ellis (1859-1939). Freud, a Viennese physician, was the dominant figure in theoretical and practical psychiatry. For the first time, libido was identified as a prime motivating force for all human activity, and some sexual repression was considered as a part of normal sexual development.[13] Freud's statements regarding female sexuality as incompletely male, and clitoral orgasm as immature have had long-term negative consequences for woman's sensual and sexual life.

Ellis, an English physician, was considered the father of the scientific study of human sexuality. He contributed significantly to the dissemination of scientific knowledge and the erosion of the ignorant sexual beliefs and practices of his time. His views contrasted with those of Freud. Sexual expression was a natural, instinctively human quality unnecessary to curb; masturbation did not promote insanity; and homosexuality was not degenerate. He recognized female sexuality as appropriate and sexual activity as enjoyable.[14]

However, it was not until Kinsey and colleagues' extensive survey of American sexual behavior was published that the existing variation and range of behavior was recognized.[15] Because Kinsey considered objectivity and the scientific method basic to the acceptance of human sexuality, he surveyed the *number* of orgasms from all sexual behavior including intercourse (homosexual/heterosexual), fellatio/cunnilingus, and self stimulation. Among those interviewed were women, some middle-aged and older. Postmenopausal women were described as maintaining sexual interest, capacity, and satisfaction; and some experienced even greater pleasure as the fear of impregnation diminished. The nature and quality of human relationships were not investigated or discussed, an omission that kept sexuality confined to genital encounters.

A laboratory study into the physiology of sexual arousal and response among adult volunteers was undertaken and reported by Masters and Johnson.[16] This investigation continued the clinical, scientific emphasis and dispelled the major myth that there were two kinds of female orgasm.[17] Masters and Johnson reported little or no difference in the anatomical and physiological responses to effective stimulation in coition, breast, or clitoris. Thus, women have been increasingly freed from the burden of inadequacy and confusion that came from the belief that the vaginal orgasm is the only appropriate response of the mature woman. Although only 4.5% of the total population studied (694 subjects) were older (data supported Kinsey's findings concerning the older woman), "there is no time limit drawn by the advancing years of female sexuality."[18]

One of the major longitudinal studies of aging, begun in 1954 by the Duke Center for the Study of Aging and Human Development, found that among older persons between age 60 and 94 an active sex life in the earlier years is an accurate predictor of sexual activity in the later years.[19] Although there is a decline in sexual interest and behavior with age, one-half of the seniors reported interest at age eighty and ninety. Interest exceeded activity which diminished due to a variety of reasons such as illness, lack of partner, living situation, boredom, etc. This is in contrast to the sexless stereotype that presumes sexual feelings and interests of older persons are deviant.[20] Married women reported a higher level of activity than single females. Older females appeared to decrease activity at a faster rate than males but attributed this change to their male mates (illness, boredom, or impotence) who later confirmed the fact. Women showed a higher interest than men after age 78. For both men and women, interest, frequency, and enjoyment of sexuality in the younger years determined later activity. Two additional factors modified sexual expression: for the older male, poor health represented a major barrier (affecting capacity, engendering fear); for the older female a sanctioned (marriage) partner was important.

Sexuality: A Youth Prerogative?

Through all the changing images and meanings of sexuality in human history—pleasurable, procreative; natural, bestial; powerful, weak—no period in time has lacked the drive to create and enhance sexual capacities. Magic, sorcery, and alchemy all have been used to fulfill the promise of everlasting youth, potency, and possible immortality.[21] Sexual activity and potency have ensured vigor and long life, yet the poetry and passion for such pleasures were relegated only to the young. The search continued. The vitality and fire of earlier years are the goals for those who seek to restore lost youth with today's magic—ginseng, gerovital, exercise, and diet. Aging and old are perceived as defeat and must be denied; if acknowledged, they vanquish libido and potency.

It is as if only genitalia and the physical acts of intercourse and orgasm constitute sexuality. The whole person knows, remembers, and desires the joys and pains of a relationship in which orgasm and intercourse may or may not be significant. Human sensuality/sexuality is more than the physiology of genital systems, more than procreation, intercourse, hormones, or orgasm; it is part of the entirety of man or woman at any age. Intimacy, love, friendship and play, caring and touching are other human needs and attributes that are being recognized as part of human affectional relationships.[22] Further, the accumulated data on sexual interest and capacities of older persons cannot be ignored. Human sexuality begins shortly after birth and is lifelong, changing in character, form, and expression. Elders themselves increasingly reject the sexless stereotype, and older women in particular are awakening to their own sexuality and accepting these needs in others.[23] Moreover, it is the older woman, widowed, divorced, or never married, who knows the frustrations, and hungers for affection and loving.

Society bestows the meaning and power of sexual expression. Such expression is for people of any age. It is a learned, dynamic lifeline to the vitality of life, to other persons, and it is a symbol of reaffirmation of self.[24] The exclamation, "Not at your age!" surely violates the human right to mental and physical health, and is another reflection of the increasing narcissism of the last 50 years. In addition to the mythology of aging is a double standard that promotes women as the old bag or dumpy matron and he the attractive, mature man graying at the temples. Her positive self image, so necessary for self-caring and for loving and being loved, is endangered if not destroyed under such conditions.

Woman as Decoration

Is there a woman who has not been socialized to believe that one of her major societal functions is to be decorative? The media promote cosmetic, surgical, fashion, and magical techniques to achieve the glorious fantasy of young, unlined, curvaceous, unblemished bodies—and the older woman is beyond the pale. When do the laugh lines become crow's feet? Why do the first wrinkles send countless middle-aged and older women to the plastic surgeon (if they can afford it) or to Oil of Olay? What reasoning can defend a beauty product slogan "A man is a man—it doesn't matter if he's ugly. But a woman must look as beautiful as she can, because both are happier that way."[25] Only history can explain though not excuse. As the years add up, hormonal and other systemic changes do signal more than altered physiology for the woman.

Leaving Youth Behind

When potential procreation is over, by choice, hormonal changes, or surgery, how do women fare in the post-menopausal time of their lives? What interests, capacities, and opportunities remain for sexual expression?

The climacteric for the woman is a time generally beginning between age 40 to 50 and includes a sequence of phases over a number of years: reduced or absence of fertility, irregular menses, final cessation of menses and menopause, blood vessel instability, some atrophy in genital and other systemic tissues, and measurable hormonal changes. She begins to look different. Body contours gradually become more angular; muscle tone and skin elasticity diminish so that arms, legs, and abdomen can wrinkle and sag. The tissue alterations, fat and hair distribution on face, breast, vulval and vaginal tissues remain fairly intact, often for as long as eight to ten years after menopause. Stories of madness and depression or disease as the inevitable consequences of menopause belong with the 1850s revelations in "Dr. Chase's Last Receipt Book Household Physician."[26] Unfortunately, gynecological texts still contain such outdated, erroneous adjectives to describe the menopausal woman—complaining, depressed, defeminized, unstable, and asexual.[27]

A number of uncomfortable, inconvenient, subjective symptoms are generally attributed to all women. Yet studies indicate that the climacteric (and particularly menopausal) experience is an individual one. Some women report few or no changes; others have noted one or more of the following: hot flash, sweating, headache, anxiety, dizziness, high blood pressure, palpitation, nervousness, appetite loss, and insomnia.[28] Many of these symptoms easily could have other bases unrelated to menopause, especially since they also have been identified in younger women.[29]

There is considerable support for the proposition that these essentially emotional and psychological complaints are a reasonable response to a destructive psychosocial situation for many women in contemporary societies.[30] In some societies, women are rewarded when they reach the end of their fertility—such women show few symptoms.[31] In those societies that punish women who outlive their youth and productivity, women experience more symptoms.[32] The importance of the psychosocial components is again invoked in the comparison of women who have given most of their energies and affection to husband, children, and home with those women who have functioned in additional roles such as work. The latter group report minimal or no symptoms.[33]

Sexual interest and activity of the middle-aged woman is at a peak and often remains so into the sixties and seventies and later if opportunities exist and societal attitudinal barriers can be overcome. In contrast to the stereotype, today's menopausal and postmenopausal woman reports heightened libido and interest.[34] Since this climacteric period for the male is frequently a low in sexual interest and activity, with increasing concerns about sexual responsiveness and performance, men and women are out of phase. Unmet expectations and apparent lack of affection and emotional support leave many women feeling unloved and unlovable, which tends to confirm the societal stereotype of asexuality. Happily, evidence suggests other initiatives and responses in the contemporary woman. The trend finds women more comfortable with feelings and expressions of their sexuality—with seeking a more active rather than traditionally passive sexual role, and increasingly taking the first step in the sexual dimension of different kinds of relationships.[35]

Older woman: lover and loved capacities. The gradual anatomical and functional changes leave the older woman sexually advantaged as compared to the older man—she remains responsive, as multiorgasmic as she was. Hormonal depletion (estrogen, progesterone) and the decreased circulatory efficiency contribute to the eventual decrease in vulval tissue, a reduction in the cervix, ovaries, and uterus. The uterus, in and under a state of hormonal deprivation, may contract spasmodically with cramping and pain rather than earlier rhythmic contractions. There may be a minimal decrease in the size of the clitoris, no significant loss in sensate focus, and little if any consequence for responsiveness.[36]

Age-related changes in the vaginal canal and related soft tissues are most germane to any potential discomfort or dysfunction. The mucosa thins, the length and circumference are reduced, elasticity diminishes and the rugal pattern gradually smooths out. Two common complaints include estrogen deficient vaginitis, and a reduction in lubrication. Dry, thin vaginal walls can make intromission problematic and painful (dyspareunia), and bleeding possible. Urinary tissues (bladder and urethra) also show moderate atrophy and may intensify the genital symptoms. Intercourse may cause burning and frequent urination, which irritates already inflamed areas. None of these relatively normal, age-related changes are significant enough to interfere with effective sexual expression. Most of them can be slowed and diminished in extent with hormone replacement therapy.[37]

As a sexual partner. For some older women, the vaginal changes and uterine arrythmia may lead to withdrawal since coitus may be less satisfying. But other older females, who have rejected the Victorian mores of their younger years, have explored stimulation by other means such as self or partner masturbation, cunnilingus, breasts.

The normal, age-related changes in the neuroendocrine system do affect responsivity patterns and alter the timing and extent of phases in sexual stimulation and response. The time for lubrication increases from 15-40 seconds to five minutes, vasocongestion is diminished and skin coloration is less. Clitoral response to effective stimulation is intact, but time to excite and elevate the tissue is prolonged. Uterine contractions may become spastic and reduced to one or two rather than three to five. Orgasmic duration is gradually decreased between the ages 50 to 70, and a more rapid resolution follows, comparable to similar behavior in older men. A range of anatomical, physiological, and behavioral variations in the older woman still leave her sexually competent and vigorous. Major deficiencies relate to the negative societal feedback and the lack of an appropriate, interested and interesting partner.[38]

A new meaning of sexuality. As people grow older, the youthful goal of the passionate orgasm loses its primacy, and the nature of the sexual encounter is different. Lovemaking gradually becomes more caring, gentle, and prolonged in the important search for person-oriented intimacy. "For many women that most compelling complaint is the inability to achieve a sense of intimacy in the sex act."[39]

The usual respected human attributes of age and experience are ignored in the choice of a sexual partner as tradition continues to place a premium on the young and uninitiated. Butler and Lewis discuss a "second language of sex," practiced more by the old rather than the young, in which sexual expression is "emotional, communicative and physical."[40] The older woman has learned the sensitivity and giving, the caressing and gentle play, the whispers and the humor, the holding, the sensuous joys of body warmth that make up the second language. The sex act may or may not be part of the conversation at any one time. But the significance of the energizing commitment that is sensual, sexual activity renews the self, drives motivation, and releases emotional and physical tensions. Dare the society continue to deprive older women and men of such basic needs and wants?

Singledom. Life as a single person covers a majority of older women over age 75 who are never-married, divorced, or widowed. Single, older women may have long since adapted to being without a permanent partner or any partner. They may have learned to enjoy their sexuality in any number of alternative ways—alone, with others. Levels and kinds of activity in the single woman are similar to that of older, married women.[41]

Masturbation. With the growth of the women's movement, self-pleasuring has become more acceptable. It starts early and continues into age. The learned taboo from childhood about touching themselves is a barrier that is being overcome by women in general, and older women in particular. Kinsey found that masturbation was the highest percentage of the total sexual outlet for single women;[42] for married women, only 10%.[43] It has been necessary for the older woman to shed the guilt and condemnation of religious morality and Victorian ethos. Masturbation may serve as an assist in the maintenance of responsivity of aging genitalia. "For the person, masturbation can release tensions, stimulate sexual appetite and contribute to well-being."[44] Yet, loneliness remains and the need for a loving, caring relationship is not eliminated.

Homosexuality. It is clear that homosexuality and bisexuality are part of the range of human sexual behavior. Careful studies of the homosexual are still relatively few, but recent investigations may help to eliminate the ignorance and stereotypes that surround the gay and lesbian communities.[45] Bell perceives aging for the lesbian as less problematic than for the gay male.[46] Lesbians appear to have longer commitments to a relationship. Laner suggests that the older lesbian may even have an advantage over older nonlesbians, since the number of eligible partners may be larger than for the heterosexual woman who may be seeking the traditional older male.[47] The sex ratio (68 men to 100 women) suggests that the lesbian studies may have implications for the present and future aging population.

Pathology: Implications for Sensual and Sexual Behavior

Aging is not disease. Pathology is not inevitable with age, but the diminishing systemic efficiency does increase vulnerability to disease. Some older persons do become seriously ill; most do not.[48] The myth of the invalid elder has imposed the *sick role* classification of older persons, permitting them to be removed from those activities, such as sexual expression, that are usually reserved for the well young. Keep in mind that depression, overeating, overdrinking, drug abuse, and systemic disorders all can affect sexuality at any age. Fatigue, malnutrition, anemia, and diabetes ignored and untreated, can inhibit desire, abort arousal and sexual climax.

Perhaps the most frequent health status barrier for the older woman derives from pelvic surgery, which unnecessarily has signaled an end to sexual activity. There is no supportable evidence that hysterectomies inevitably lead to depressed desire and orgasmic response.[49] Neither is libido nor orgasmic response dependent upon the intact uterus. A retrospective study of women who have undergone surgical menopause concluded that psychosocial factors, such as loss of feminity play the major role in changed sexual desire and activity rather than the altered physiology.

The mastectomy represents another assault on the integrity of the female and is a threat to self-image as a woman. Fear of loss of a love relationship is added to the already existing fears of cancer and death. With both hysterectomy and mastectomy patients it has been demonstrated that pre- and post-surgical counseling with health professionals and peers serves to defuse the fears and extend an important knowledge base.

Illness does not eliminate the human need for caring, loving, and sexual activity; it may even be heightened. In fact, the pleasure, satisfaction, and emotional support enhances coping capacities. Even institutionalization does not close down desire or need. Sexual expression of elder residents is too frequently suppressed or distorted by rules of behavior that dehumanize and serve the needs of nursing home staff and their image of appropriate elder behavior.[50] Studies have found that a significant number of such residents consider sexual desire and physical love important in their lives.[51]

Summary

The historical perspective illuminates a basic reality concerning sexuality. Peoples through the centuries have held same and different conceptions of the place and purpose of human sexuality in the life span. A spectrum ranging from the marriage bed to prostitution, from celibacy to hedonism, reflects the essentially learned, culturally dependent sexual behavior of civilizations.

Emotionally charged and ego-centered physiology of the sexual response changes and diminishes with age. The societally endowed power of sexuality has been identified with the vitality and desirability of youth. Middle-aged and older persons can accept, however grudgingly, the slipping efficiency of the organ systems, but the first signs of natural aging in the reproductive system are a threat to identity and an awesome reminder of the rolelessness and sexlessness ahead—so society has predicted. This has led to the inevitable, often frantic search for the impossible fountain of youth to enhance life-long potency and youthful sex appeal. An active sex life was thought by some to promote longevity. Early in human societies, aging and old were largely missing from sexual considerations because few people attained great age. It was assumed that, with procreation coming to an end, interest and capacity were equally drained.

Throughout history, more than half of humanity—women—have been alternately debased as adultress, evil and oversexed, or glorified as innocent, exalted, pure, and incapable of sexual needs and passionate response. In most instances her sexuality was meant to serve procreative and male requirements—only the bad woman enjoyed sexual pleasures. No longer full bodied and decorative, the older woman became a sexual discard earlier than the older man.

The facts about elders are otherwise, but mythology dies slowly. Early in this century, investigations into human sexual behavior established sexuality as an appropriate area of scientific inquiry. Primarily quantitative and objective measures were made to establish acceptance by the scientific community. Recent and contemporary studies have provided increased information about sexuality and aging. The data considered worthwhile and reportable emphasize the genital function: incidence of masturbation, intercourse, heterosexual/homosexual patterns, oral/genital sex, physiology of the sexual response and other alternative sexual behaviors. Older persons surprised and reinforced the researchers' views. Large numbers of the study groups maintained interest in sexual stimulation and satisfaction and some remained sexually active into the ninth decade. The retention of their multiorgasmic capacities in addition to expressed needs, interests, and complaints of many older women, who had unwillingly become relatively inactive, were most contrary to the long-held stereotype.

A relatively small number of elders do put aside the physical act of intercourse; some do become impotent. The majority retain interests and capacities, their activity limited by opportunity and a partner. The most damaging barrier for older women and men is not the real and gradual diminution in capacities and behavior but the negative societal attitudes. As the social world of the old grows smaller, there is even a greater need for loving, caring relationships. The hostile, societal feedback shakes an already at risk self-esteem, threatens yet another role loss of lover. For the middle-aged and older woman this *not applicable* in sexuality has been one more notch in the belt of constraints she has worn for centuries.

The important human dimension of the quality of caring, affectional relationships has been minimized in the studies. Emphasis on technique and orgasm effectively remove the person—a heavy price for the altar to genital pleasures. Little has been reported concerning the lifegiving energy of the caressing, touching and holding, the continuing sexual dreams and fantasies of older men and women. The significance of intimacy and affection in different-sex, same-sex liaisons is finally being addressed. Sex therapy and enhancement programs only recently have included the old as suitable for help. Health professionals have begun to think in terms of the whole person and sexuality as part of that whole. This means that concerns must move beyond orgasm and intercourse to those qualities of affection, sensuality, and relationships that give meaning to human sexual expression beyond physical release.

Conclusion

Little is worthwhile unless there is some eye to kindle in common with our own, some brief word uttered now and then to imply that what is precious to us is precious alike to another mind.

—George Eliot (1819-1880)

Sexuality is indeed not the same for the older woman or man as it is in youth. What human attribute is? The culture is in turmoil in many areas. Changing sex roles appear to provide support for changing sexual perspectives and behavior. Furthermore, since sexual behavior, like so much of human behavior, is a learned, complex product of lifelong socialization, nonfunctional attitudes and behavior can be changed and new learning is possible.

What she doesn't need or deserve is a new mythology—the old woman as the multiorgasmic machine. Society must recognize that sexuality cannot be conferred by societal forbearance only on the young. Sexual expression is each person's prerogative. What is needed is society's admission that the *neuter* label applied to the older women has been cruel, ignorant, and mindless—and that it will be no more. The mythology that has condemned the older woman to years of emotional and physical starvation must be eliminated and replaced by an ambiance that encourages living in her own way with freedom to explore and expand her sensual, sexual self into the later decades. As she grows into roles beyond mother, wife, and house-keeper and adds worker, community activist, and lover, she will be increasingly herself with age, a continuum of behavior that is instrumental and affective, gentle and assertive, accepting and initiating. She, young and older, is more confident and flexible and will not be less than or more than, but she will be whole.

Notes

1. C.E. Darlington, *The Evolution of Man and Society* (London: Allen and Unwin, 1969).
2. C.W. Ford and F.A. Beach, *Patterns of Sexual Behavior* (New York: Harper & Row, 1951).
3. E.O. Wilson, *Sociobiology: The New Synthesis* (Cambridge, Mass.: Harvard University Press, 1975).
4. R. Tannahill, *Sex in History* (New York: Stein & Day, 1980).
5. V.L. Bullough, *Sexual Variance in Society and History* (New York: Wiley, 1976); Tannahill, *Sex in History.*
6. Bullough, *Sexual Variance.*
7. W.H. Masters, V.E. Johnson, and R.C. Kolodny, *Human Sexuality* (Boston: Little, Brown, 1978.)
8. Tannahill, *Sex in History.*
9. G.R. Taylor, *Sex in History* (New York: Vanguard, 1954).
10. Masters, Johnson, and Kolodny, *Human Sexuality.*
11. Tannahill, *Sex in History;* Bullough, *Sexual Variance;* Masters, Johnson, and Kolodny, *Human Sexuality.*
12. Tannahill, *Sex in History;* Masters, Johnson, and Kolodny, *Human Sexuality.*
13. J.H. Gagnon and B. Henderson, *Human Sexuality: An Age of Ambiguity,* Social Issues Series, no. 1 (Boston: Educational Associates, Division of Little, Brown, 1975).
14. S.R. Leiblum and L. Pervin, *Principles and Practice of Sex Therapy* (New York: Guilford, 1980).
15. A.C. Kinsey, W.B. Pomeroy, and C.I. Martin, *Sexual Behavior in the Human Male* (Philadelphia: W.B. Saunders, 1948); A.C. Kinsey, W.B. Pomeroy, C.I. Martin, and P.H. Gebhard, *Sexual Behavior in the Human Female* (Philadelphia: W.B. Saunders, 1953).

16. W.H. Masters and V. Johnson, *Human Sexual Response* (Boston: Little, Brown, 1966); W.H. Masters and V. Johnson, *Human Sexual Inadequacy* (Boston: Little, Brown, 1970).
17. S. Freud, *The Letters of Sigmund Freud,* ed. E.L. Freud (New York: Basic Books, 1960).
18. Masters and Johnson, *Human Sexual Response.*
19. A. Verwoerdt, E. Pfeiffer, and H.S. Wang, "Sexual Behavior in Senescence," in *Normal Aging: Reports from Duke Longitudinal Study, 1955-1969,* ed. E. Palmore (Duke, N.C.,: Duke University Press, 1970).
20. H. Berlin, "Effect of Human Sexuality on Well-Being from Birth to Aging," *Medical Aspects of Human Sexuality* 10 (1976): 10-31.
21. E.J. Trimmer, *Rejuvenation: The History of an Idea* (Cranberry, N.J.: Barnes, 1970).
22. J. Gagnon and W. Simon, *Sexual Conduct: The Social Sources of Human Sexuality* (Chicago: Aldine, 1973); Gagnon and Henderson, *Human Sexuality;* R.B. Weg, "The Physiological Perspective," in *Sexuality in Later Years: Roles and Behavior,* ed. R.B. Weg (New York: Academic Press, forthcoming).
23. M. Kirkpatrick, "Women's Sexual Complaints," *Medical Aspects of Human Sexuality* 10 (1976): 118-25.
24. R.B. Weg, "The Physiology of Sexuality in Aging," in *Sexuality and Aging,* 2nd ed. rev., R.L. Solnick (Los Angeles: University of Southern California Press, 1980); R.B. Weg, "Sexuality in Aging," in *Textbook of Geriatric Medicine,* ed. J. Pathy (New York: Wiley, forthcoming).
25. R.B. Weg, "More Than Wrinkles," in *Looking Ahead: A Women's Guide to the Problems and Joys of Growing Older,* ed. L. Troll, J. Israel, and K. Israel (Englewood Cliffs, N.J.: Prentice-Hall, 1977).
26. R.B. Weg, "Young/Beautiful or Banished," (Paper delivered at the Women: Midstream Decision Conference, Miami Univ., Oxford, Ohio, June 20-22, 1976).
27. D. Scully and P. Bart, "A Funny Thing Happened on the Way to the Orifice: Women in Gynecology Textbooks," in *Changing Women in a Changing Society,* ed. J. Huber (Chicago: University of Chicago Press, 1973).
28. G. Bates, "On the Nature of the Hot Flash," *Clinical Obstetrics Gynecology* 24(1981): 231-41: Weg, "Sexuality in Aging."
29. S. McKinlay and J. McKinlay, "Selected Studies on the Menopause," *Journal of Biosocial Science* 5 (1973): 533-55.
30. D. Alington-Mackinnon and L.E. Troll, "The Adaptive Function of the Menopause: A Devil's Advocate Position," *Journal of American Geriatrics Society* 29 (1981): 349-53; T. Detre, T. Hayashi, and D.F. Archer, "Management of the Menopause," *Annals of Internal Medicine* 88 (1978): 373; B. Neugarten and N. Datan, "The Middle Years," *Journal of Geriatric Psychiatry* 9 (1976): 45; W.H. Utian, "Definitive Symptoms of Post-Menopause Incorporating Use of Vaginal Parabasal Cell Index," *Frontiers Hormone Research* 3 (1975): 74; R.B. Weg, "Drug Interaction with Changing Physiology of the Aged: Practice and Potential," in *Drugs and the Elderly,* ed R.C. Kayne (Los Angeles: University of California Press, 1978).
31. M. Flint, "Cross-Cultural Factors That Affect Age of Menopause," in *Consensus on Menopause Research,* ed. P.A. Van Keep, R.B. Greenblatt, and M. Albeaux-Fernet (Baltimore: University Park Press, 1976).
32. P.A. Van Keep, "Psychosocial Aspects of Climacteric," in *Consensus on Menopause Research,* ed. P.A. Van Keep, R.B. Greenblatt, and M. Albeaux-Fernet (Baltimore: University Park Press, 1976).

33. Neugarten and Datan, "Middle Years."
34. H.S. Kaplan, *The New Sex Therapy* (New York: Brunner-Mazel, 1974.)
35. R.R. Bell, "Sexuality and Sex Roles." Paper delivered at the Working Conference to Develop Teaching Materials on Family and Sex Roles, Detroit, Mich., November 10-12, 1975.
36. W.H. Masters and V.E. Johnson, "Sex and the Aging Process," *Medical Aspects of Human Sexuality* 16 (1982): 40-57.
37. W.H. Masters and V.E. Johnson, "Sex and the Aging Process," *Journal of American Geriatrics Society* 29 (1981): 385-90; Weg, "The Physiological Perspective."
38. Masters and Johnson, *Human Sexuality Inadequacy;* Masters and Johnson, "Sex and the Aging Process," 1981, 1982.
39. Kirkpatrick, "Women's Sexual Complaints."
40. R.N. Butler and M.I. Lewis, *Sex After Sixty* (New York: Harper & Row, 1976).
41. N. Corby, "Old and Alone: The Unmarried in Later Life," in *Sexuality in the Later Years,* ed. R.B. Weg (New York: Academic Press, forthcoming).
42. Kinsey, Pomeroy, Martin, and Gebhard, *Sexual Behavior.*
43. A.J. Silny, "Sexuality and Aging," in *Handbook of Human Sexuality,* ed. B.B. Wolman and J. Money (Englewood Cliffs, N.J.: Prentice-Hall, 1980).
44. R.B. Weg, "Sexual Inadequacy in the Elderly," in *The Physiology and Pathology of Human Aging,* ed. R. Goldman and M. Rockstein (New York: Academic Press, 1975).
45. A.P. Bell and M.S. Weinberg, *Homosexualities: A Study of Diversity among Men and Women* (New York: Simon & Schuster, 1978).
46. R.R. Bell, *Social Deviance* (Homewood, Ill.: Dorsey, 1971).
47. M.R. Laner, "Growing Older Female: Heterosexual and Homosexual," *Journal of Homosexuality* 4 (1979): 267.
48. R.B. Weg, "Changing Physiology of Aging: Normal and Pathological Changes with Time," in *Aging: Scientific Perspectives and Social Issues,* ed. D. Woodruff and J. Birren (Monterey, Calif.: Brooks/Cole, forthcoming).
49. Weg, "Changing Physiology of Aging."
50. V. Kassel, "Long-Term Care Institutions," in *Sexuality in the Later Years: Roles and Behavior,* ed. R.B. Weg (New York: Academic Press, forthcoming).
51. N.D. West, "Sex in Geriatrics: Myth or Miracle?" *Journal of American Geriatrics Society* 23 (1975): 551.

15

Rethinking Life Satisfaction

Jaber F. Gubrium and Robert J. Lynott

The life satisfaction of old people has been a perennial concern of researchers in the field of aging. Beginning with the work of Cavan et al.
(1949) on the meaning and measurement of personal adjustment to aging,
researchers have explored and delineated its causes, correlates, and consequences. In the course of this activity, the meaning of life satisfaction has
been reviewed and criticized. The ongoing attempt to measure it has generated diverse scales and indices, some of which have been refined (Kutner et
al. 1956; Cumming and Henry 1961; Neugarten et al. 1961; Wood et al.
1969; Lawton 1972, 1975).

It is clear that the concept and condition of life satisfaction have been
troublesome (George 1979; George and Bearon 1980; Nydegger 1977).
While few have questioned its existence, terms used to describe it have
varied: life satisfaction, morale, adjustment, well-being, happiness, successful aging. Its dimensionality has been debated, some claiming it to be
unidimensional (e.g., Kutner et al. 1956) and others conceiving of it as
multidimensional (e.g., Lawton 1972). Its behavioral status has been variously defined, some choosing to see it as an internal, psychological state
(e.g., Neugarten et al. 1961) and others emphasizing its overt behavioral
features (e.g., Cavan et al. 1949). Furthermore, the cross-validation of varied measures has been calibrated and improved, yet not convincingly (Lawton 1972; Neugarten et al. 1961).

By and large, both the concern and the trouble have been treated as
technical challenges, leading to attempts at refinement, revision, and delin-
eation, rather than to reconceptualization. The validity of the measures
largely has been technically resolved by comparing results with trained
observer ratings, each being informed by common and accepted conceptualizations of the subject matter. While validity allegedly raises the
issue of what behavioral reality is at hand, it typically is circumvented by

means of technical comparisons with the results of other devices whose own validity goes unquestioned or is assumed to be apparent, or is based on yet other devices whose own validity has been similarly addressed. Presumably, the more the results of separate measurement devices confirm each other, the greater the validity of any one device, a strategy that glosses over the possibility that all devices may be generated out of some taken-for-granted orthodoxy, namely, that it is more or less commonly known what the concept and condition of life satisfaction are in reality. Cumming et al. (1958:6) poignantly, but perhaps inadvertently, reveal the glossing of the validity problem when they state: "We assumed, in other words, that *whatever* morale is, it is possible to recognize it through the myriad complicated symbolic communications of the interview and to gauge its extent, or level."

This paper is not as concerned with the technical troubles of life satisfaction measurement as it is with its conceptualization. The aim is to consider the behavioral reality being referenced when old people and their researchers address the topic of life satisfaction, not whether some measurement device truthfully represents a reality that is intuitively, yet imprecisely, known. Three questions are addressed. First, what is the image of life and satisfaction presented to subjects by the five most commonly used scales and indices? Second, how might the image enter into the process of measurement? And third, how does the image compare with experiences of life and its satisfactions among elders revealed by studies of daily living?

The Image of Life and Satisfaction

To ask a question of anyone is not simply to obtain a response. Questions are not just elicitors of information; they direct attention to something. Questions are active features of interrogation, intended to be answered in particular ways (Schutz 1967, 1970). Whether we casually ask someone "How're you doing?" or more formally request people to consider, evaluate, and record their satisfactions with life, we intend particular responses by the sense of our questions. Something about the questions, in part, produces the responses given.

In this regard, suppose one were interested in the developmental quality of adult lives, as Kimmel (1974) is in his book *Adulthood and Aging.* Kimmel asks his subjects a variety of routine questions about life in terms of time, which he illustrates in several vignettes. Subjects are asked about life changes, particular stages, and what Kimmel refers to as "milestones." The vignettes reveal that it is not always clear to the subjects what Kimmel intends to ask about by his questions. Some ask Kimmel what *he* means by what is being asked, which the author attempts to clarify. When the author's intended sense of some aspect of life is accepted by a subject, the subject then formulates a response. A few declare that they have not, or do not think of their lives in a certain way, yet go on trying to do so at Kimmel's behest. It is evident that Kimmel's subjects are not simply reporting the developmental facts of their lives, but are doing so within the substantive purview of what they take to be the author's requests. The author's questions seem to be as much a part of his data as is the content of his subjects' lives (Gubrium and Buckholdt 1977). Every question contains a sense of things asked about—an image of them—which serves to frame or interpret them. The varied items of existing life satisfaction measures are a kind of question, many resembling those that Kimmel put to his subjects.

The five most commonly used life satisfaction measures are the Chicago Attitude Inventory (Cavan et al. 1949); Kutner's morale scale (Kutner et al. 1956); Cumming's morale index (Cumming and Henry 1961); Life Satisfaction Indexes A and B, or LSI-A/LSI-B (Neugarten et al. 1961); and the Philadelphia Geriatric Center, or PGC, morale scale (Lawton 1972). There is considerable homogeneity across the measures as a result of the common usage of select items. To some extent each newly developed measure was expressly compiled out of items selected from existing measures. For example, items that were originally part of Kutner's morale scale were used to derive the LSI-A and LSI-B (Neugarten et al. 1961:140). The PGC morale scale was constructed, in part, from items taken from existing scales (Lawton 1972:146). Indeed, it might be said that the Chicago Attitude Inventory set the tone for all subsequent scales and indexes. At least three of the measures (Chicago Attitude Inventory, Cumming's morale index, LSI-A/ LSI-B) grew out of the continuing research of members of the Committee on Human Development at the University of Chicago. It is evident in the literature that while the measures are spoken of as five in number, they are tightly bound organizationally. The image of life satisfaction they contain is one they share.

The image articulated by the items of the measures has at least three themes. One theme is a sense of life as being wholly conceivable and universally relevant to each of its considerations. When elderly subjects are asked about their satisfaction with changes in their lives, they are to think of life as a transcendent object, as if its whole continuity were being evaluated, not that particular occasion's sense of the continuity. The questions request them to think of life as continuous, yet changeable, not as a collection of discrete moments joined together by retrospective interpretation (Garfinkel 1967).

Take the following typical items. It is not the particular choice of answers that is relevant here, but the sense of life articulated by the items:

"As I look back on life, I am fairly well satisfied." (agree, disagree, not sure)
"As I get older, things are (better, worse, same) than/as I thought they would be."
"I am just as happy as when I was younger." (agree, disagree, not sure)
"What age would you most like to be?"
"Things just keep getting worse and worse for me as I get older." (agree, disagree)

Such questions assume that what life was at some earlier point in time is not wholly discrete and qualitatively distinct from what it wholly is currently. Life is not experienced as a different thing each time the subject encounters questions about it. Upon being asked, say, if things are better, worse, or the same as he thought they would be, the subject considers some time past in his life, compares it with the present, and makes his judgment accordingly. The possibility that life is circumstantially constructed for consideration, understood within the context of the relevancies at hand, or made over for the purpose of examination each time one encounters a question about it, is not entertained.

Not only is the elderly person who completes the various measures treated as if he had a whole, universally relevant life to inspect for its satisfaction, but that life is presented as having a beginning or middle, and an end or, at the very least, an earlier portion and a later part. This is a second theme of the image, one that carries a distinct temporal quality. The sense of time presented is mechanical and linear, like clock time, as distinguished from the stream of experienced time (Hendricks and Hendricks 1976).

Clock time flows forward. This feature is apparent in various items of the life satisfaction measures. For example, subjects are asked to think about whether things have gotten better, worse, or remained the same "as [they] get older." It is clear that the current point in time is older, not younger. What they look back upon is a younger life, as suggested by the item, "I am just as happy as when I was younger." Indeed, there is something implicitly pathological about an elderly person who expresses a desire to make time flow backward (or forward in the opposite direction). The pathology is revealed in Cumming's (1961:262) codes for the item "What age would you most like to be?" A score of one is given for the answer, "The age I am," which enhances one's overall morale index. Needless to say, an expressed desire to be younger serves to lower one's measured morale.

There is an overall sense that the present, relative to the past, is life gone by. Subjects are not asked to think about life but to "think back over" it. A current endpoint is implied by a clause (emphasized) in one of Kutner's items: "How much do you regret the chances you *missed during your life* to do a better job of living?" The item places the subject, as a current respondent, outside of his life and asks him to retrospectively evaluate it. The present is, ironically, not substantively during the subject's life. That life has gone by; it is a thing to be perused for how adequately it *was* lived, now that it has been lived. The words (emphasized) of one of Lawton's items rather straightforwardly locate the subject toward the end of time: "I am as happy *now* as I was when I *was younger.*" It informs those who respond to it that now is older and some time past, or then, was younger, not the reverse. "Then" is certainly not an earlier time or place when one might have felt "older," or the many times past when one felt older and then, strangely, younger at the same time. The various measures do not present such complex times to subjects. Not being asked to evaluate them, subjects produce no corresponding data.

The substance of this unitary, progressive lifetime is a third theme of the image. As Rosow (1963) has pointed out, there is a special style of living presumed to be normal in the various measures. While the response codes, of course, provide for alternative answers—routinely from "agree" to "disagree"—the contents of the items themselves are parochial. They present a fixed lifestyle to subjects, who then are free to evaluate it.

Though they are not all concrete about it, several items imply that past life, youthful life, not old age, is the time one does, or one should have made the most of life, when life's important events occurred. The LSI-A, for example, contains the following items:

"I would not change my past life even if I could." (point awarded for "agree")
"When I think back over my life, I didn't get most of the important things I wanted." (point awarded for a "disagree")
"I've gotten pretty much what I expected out of life." (point awarded for an "agree")

A premium is given to those subjects who respond that they would not change their past life, as one item states, "even if I could."

Compare this with a selection of items that refer only to the present, presumably to old age. As always, subjects are free to agree, disagree, or respond in some alternate fashion.

"I feel just miserable most of the time." (agree, disagree, not sure)
"I am perfectly satisfied with my health." (agree, disagree, not sure)
"I have so few friends that I am lonely much of the time." (agree, disagree, not sure)

"I sometimes feel that life isn't worth living." (no, yes)
"I get upset easily." (no, yes)
"I have a lot to be sad about." (no, yes)
"I feel my age, but it does not bother me." (agree, disagree, not sure)
"How much unhappiness would you say you find in your life today? (almost none, some, a great deal)
"I can't help feeling now that my life is not very useful." (agree, disagree, not sure)

As presented to respondents, the vision of old age in the items is one nearly empty of concrete human affairs, the practical events that people encounter in doing the business of daily living. With a few general exceptions such as health and finances, being old has no concrete objects. One is asked if he gets upset easily, but over what? One is asked if she is miserable most of the time, but with what or whom? One is asked if he feels life is worth living, but no particular aspect of it is specified.

The items that pertain to the present suggest that old age is made of feelings. When an object is specified, is may be a nebulous reference to self, as in "I feel miserable most of the time," or an equally vague reference to life, as in "I sometimes feel life isn't worth living." Other exceptions emphasize an emotional orientation to their objects, not a practical one. For example, items about one's relations with friends and family deal primarily with the subject's satifactions with his frequency of contact with them, as in this typical item from the Chicago Attitude Inventory: "I would be happier if I could see my friends more often." Some dwell on the presumed felt isolation of a lack of contact, as in the item: "I have so few friends that I am lonely much of the time." The unidimensionality of the exceptions, in their portrayal of the subject's relations to objects such as friends, glosses over the many practical contingencies and conceptual transformations of friendship. Is friendship, at any age, a relationship that one just has more or less of, that ideally one has more of? What of the mutual economic obligations of friendship (Siegel 1978; Stephens 1976; Teski 1979; Wiseman 1970)? The interpretation of friendship as an everyday economic contingency—as a negative factor in personal solvency—is not within the technical capability of unidimensional conceptions of it.

As a theme, the relatively empty substance of late life reflects what Burgess (1960) once called the "roleless role" of the aged. In early life, one possesses a number of socially recognizable roles, such as work and parental roles. Upon becoming old, however, such roles disappear for the most part, and it becomes unclear what one is or should be. What is left, presumably, is a history of roles, roles typical of earlier life. Together with this residue one has feelings about how much the present reflects what one possessed at an earlier point in time.

The Image in Measurement

The second question raised at the beginning of the paper concerns how the image might enter into the process of measurement. Contrast what is assumed to be the measurement behavior of the subject with what some recent social research suggests about the individual and collective cognitive organization of responses to similar demands (Garfinkel 1967; Cicourel 1974; Perrucci 1974; Pfohl 1978; Buckholdt and Gubrium 1979).

What the life satisfaction literature tells us directly about subjects' measurement behavior, concerns the technical problems that arise in the administration of scales and indices, problems such as item clarity and the fatigue of respondents, and researchers' attempts to deal with them, such as methods of increasing reliability and test validity. Little is said about working subjects other than that some respond slowly or inappropriately, their background characteristics are such and such, and the like. Yet we can reconstruct what the working behavior of the subject must be assumed to resemble if the methodology of life satisfaction measurement is accepted.

The logic of life satisfaction measures assumes, in principle, that when subjects respond to items concerning their lives and satisfactions, they respond in terms of what the items ask about, not for the sake of the items themselves. That is, the items of the measures do not, upon the *occasion* of their presentation, serve to generate life satisfaction or dissatisfaction in whatever degree they do so. It is not at the behest of measurement that life and its satisfactions appear as they do. It is taken for granted, after all, that there is a thing called "life" that is perusable as a whole, that can be addressed by subjects for evaluation, and that would be recognizable as such on any evaluative occasion. Moreover, it is assumed that each item independently taps this same reality. Should a subject raise questions about the clarity or legitimacy of select items, he is taken to be technically dissatisfied with them, not essentially so. Whether in constructing a new scale or in administering an established one, subjects who have or cause trouble in responding to items are treated as if they would not have done so had the items been clear and to the point. This means that items can be constructed that precisely elicit information about life and its satisfactions. The logic of measures like morale scales cannot entertain essential dissatisfaction. For example, in regard to existing measures, a respondent who saw his life as disconnected and thereby as appreciable in a multiplicity of ways, and who chose to make his thoughts and evaluations known on measurement protocols, would be uncodeable. His "completed" protocol would be discarded.

Validation procedures for the various measures, of course, are used to justify the presumed behavioral realities being tapped. The measures are not asserted to be valid at face value. For example, responses to items of the PGC morale scale were compared with the independent evaluation of staff members of institutions where subjects were residents. And the performance of subjects on the LSI-A and LSI-B was checked against ratings of life satisfaction made by a clinical psychologist. In the case of the PGC morale scale, even the elimination of items not contributing to validity did not appreciably change the .47 correlation of the 22-item scale with the judgments of the criterion staff (Lawton 1972:151). As for the LSI-A and LSI-B, coefficients of correlation with judges' ratings were no better, being .39 and .47, respectively (Neugarten et al. 1961:142).

While the developers of both measures agree that the coefficients serving as the basis for validity claims are rather low, surprisingly they then justify them on various grounds, from the special (superior) psychological make-up of respondents used to validate the items to the following curious conclusion (Neugarten et al. 1961:142):

> Nevertheless, the more important point is undoubtedly that direct self-reports, even though carefully measured, can be expected to agree only partially with the evaluations of life satisfaction made by an outside observer [in this case, the judges who made the LSR ratings].

Why this should be expected is not explained. But what is even more peculiar is that these authors seem to be attempting both to establish the validity of the LSI-A and LSI-B and to dismiss the very basis on which an undesirably low index of validation has been obtained.

Whether or not one is justified in being satisfied with the validity assertions made in the literature does not deny that the measures have been treated as valid. With various cautions, each of the measures is reported to be usable by their respective developers. Moreover, each has been used successfully in numerous studies of life satisfaction/morale, constituting a very large area of research activity in the field of aging. If not on empirical grounds, then by the sheer force of usage the various measures have earned a certain validity. This brings us again to the question of the measurement behavior of the working subject. The ground for making claims about it seems not to be as much empirical as it is conventional. The widespread use of measures takes for granted that the subject who is administered, say, the PGC morale scale or the Chicago Attitude Inventory behaves in accordance with the vision of life satisfaction articulated by their items.

To ask an elderly person whether "things have gotten worse and worse as [he's] gotten older" and to treat his response as a general one is to assume that, barring inconsistency in measurement and granting test validity, the person who responds with disagreement, for example, would judge his life likewise on any other current occasion. The assumed stability of judgment takes for granted that the subject tacitly and principally organizes his responses within the framework of established test reliability and validity. But does the subject naively do so? Is it not possible that when the subject does satisfactorily complete a life satisfaction questionnaire or interview, he does so against a background of known and unknown, connected and unconnected events in his life, which, perhaps for the sake of the test, he treats as known and connected and, somehow, thereby comparable? Is it not possible that when responses are obtained, they are produced by a different means than assumed?

The behavior of the working subject assumed in life satisfaction measurement is the behavior of a "cultural dope" (Garfinkel 1967). In principle, the validity of such measurement rests on the expectation that the subject accepts the measures' realities as the essential concrete features of life and that the acceptance is a general feature of his attention to such matters. The assumption is that the measures and the situations in which they are administered are not themselves critical (epistemological) features of subjects' responses, that subjects simply respond to the items, not to "What this here is all about, anyway?" or to "What these people [researchers] mean by these questions?" or even to "What these [same] people want from me?" Such fleeting thoughts or casual expressions raise laypersons' brands of ontological, epistemological, and procedural questions, respectively. Taken seriously, they abrogate the cultural dope who participates in life satisfaction measures.

Investigations of what subjects talk of, and do, in practice, in response to demands on their knowledge about their own and others' lives suggest that what is tapped in life satisfaction measures is not satisfaction in general with life in general, but life satisfaction as understood by subjects on the occasion of their acceptance of the task of responding to questions about life and its satisfactions in terms of the image presented to them. In one widely cited experiment, Garfinkel (1967) solicited undergraduate students to participate in what was said to be an alternative means of psychotherapy. Each student was asked to describe what he considered to be a serious problem in need of advice and to address a (confederate) counselor with questions that permitted yes or no answers. Students and counselor were located in separate rooms and communicated by means of intercom. After each answer, students were instructed to unplug their end of the intercom and to tape record their reactions to the exchange. Unknown to subjects, counselors' yeses and noes were predecided by random number.

Recorded reactions showed that subjects actively participated in their counseling, not only posing questions but interpreting the answers given by the counselors. Each question became a partial document of the developing and attributed sense of the answers given by the counselors. The tacit contribution that subjects made to their own counseling (in the main, believed to be the professional counselors' activity) suggests that they were, in practice, anything but "cultural dopes," as, in a different setting, Kimmel's vignettes also suggest.

The subject who participates in life satisfaction measurement faces a task similar to that encountered by Garfinkel's student subjects. Each is asked to address and evaluate what the meaning is of life experiences. Can we be sure that the subjects of life satisfaction measurement treat its items discretely? As an elderly person proceeds through a scale or index, might he perhaps not, as did Garfinkel's students, get a sense of what each particular item means from what he, upon consideration, *now* understands to have been the meaning of items already completed, from what he now, and later then, takes to be the sense of the measurement exercise? Each retrospective interpretation might serve to completely transform the ongoing sense of earlier items and answers as subjects proceed through the protocols, yet perhaps leave unaltered their already recorded responses.

Not only might the behavior of the working subject cast doubt on the independence of life satisfaction items, and responses to them (which would make coding, indexing, scaling, and statistical analysis dubious), but the subject's well-intentioned attempt to answer the items reasonably might, in its own right, serve to display his life in a particular way for measurement purposes. Life satisfaction items, after all, ask subjects certain things, not just anything. To the extent that subjects attempt to respond reasonably to what is asked of them, they interpret their lives accordingly. This brings us full circle to the place of image in measurement. The working subject is not a cultural dope on two counts. First, as Garfinkel reminds us, he virtually consititutes whatever he confronts. Second, the things he is confronted by, such as life satisfaction items or questions, are not innocent choices or interrogations but are ontologically suggestive in their own right. In responding to what he is presented, the acquiescent subject reproduces and confirms its image of life.

There is a growing body of empirical research that lends credence to the reality-constructing quality of images in everyday life, especially in formal decision-making situations. The research suggests that, in their use, images serve to frame experience, to organize it (Goffman 1974). Pfohl (1978), for example, has shown in considerable detail how panels of human service experts (social workers, psychologists, and psychiatrists) articulate the formal demand to think of incarcerated mental patients as either dangerous or not for the eventual purpose of reducing the patient census in a maximum security hospital for the criminally insane. His documentation of the working communication between panel members shows that a legal image of insanity constantly confronts medical, behavioral, and less formal images of it, and that to complete their assignment, members attempt to arrive at a legal decision based on their nonlegal expertise. Similar or related findings are reported by Tuchman (1978) and Altheide (1976) for the mass media, Wiseman (1970) for the treatment of alcoholics, Perrucci (1974) in describing how patients "go to staff" in a mental hospital, Gubrium and Buckholdt (1982) for reporting practices in rehabilition, and Edelman (1977) in the helping professions, among others.

What, then, might all of this tell us about the data produced by the elderly subjects who complete life satisfaction measures? It suggests that while such measurement is completable, what gets done is not simply a more or less reliable and valid report of life satisfaction. There is reason to believe that what life satisfaction scales and indices measure is old people's interpretations of their lives and related satisfactions within the framework of the particular image presented to them on measurement occasions. While interpretation is a pervasive feature of everyday life, images do vary, which is the measurement issue of the next section.

Unmeasured Satisfactions

The third question raised at the beginning of the paper asks how the image of life and its satisfaction presented in measurement compares with experiences of life and its satisfactions on other occasions. Relevant data are reported by a number of ethnographic accounts of the daily life of old people, from accounts of life in a nursing home (Gubrium 1975) to apart- ment buildings (Hochschild 1973; Jacobs 1975; Ross 1977), a retirement hotel (Teski 1979), single-room occupancy (SRO) dwellings (Stephens 1976; Siegel 1978; Eckert 1980), urban neighborhoods (Frankfather 1977; Wiseman 1970), retirement communities (Jacobs 1974; Johnson 1971), and activity centers (Hazan 1980; Myerhoff 1978). Though the specific topics of the accounts differ, they do describe the ongoing issues and sentiments of daily living among the elderly when the latter are not being formally measured.

Take the theme that life is a unitary entity and, as such, relevant to all its considered occasions. The ethnographic data show that for old people (though not implying only old people) the quality of life is articulated through the ongoing experiences of those who live it. This is not to suggest that its quality is determined by particular living conditions such as health or finances. Rather, the data indicate that the meaning of life is understood in relation to its now current, later current, and still later current consid- erations. Life seems to be many things: the whole thing it was then, the whole thing it is now, and the whole thing it may come to be.

Ross (1977) describes the daily lives of the elderly French men and women of Les Floralies, a retirement residence for Parisian construction workers and their wives or widows. People of their age in France are referred to as the '14 generation because they were young during World War I. Most experienced that war either as active combatants or by having lost relatives to it. World War II claimed sons from some of the residents. Such was part of what life was like for these elderly. Ross writes (p. 86): "For all of them [the residents], it provided a pair of symbols, Vichy and the Resistance, in terms of which they still orient their lives." But Ross then notes (p. 86): "Although few people fought in the Resistance, and few people gave active support to Petain, almost everyone who lived through the occupation now feels that he or she made a choice between the two." The meaning of having been a collaborator or active in the Resistance is not something that simply grew out of past life and which one now looks back upon in satisfaction or dissatisfaction. For those residents who now speak of having had a part in the Resistance, the experience is, if not actual, then at least a symbol of claims to the worth of one's life. It is not so much the facts of past life in their own right that determine one's current evaluation of life as a whole as it is current social considerations that retrospectively serve to articulate both what life was and how satisfying it is said to have been. Consequently, as residents of Les Floralies in the company and culture of other members of the '14 generation, the facts of life take on a certain meaning. For all practical purposes, they become new facts and their lives new lives. As residents, to report that one fought in the Resistance means that one's life has been meritorious or undistinguished, which one depending on one's political orientation, on whether one's sympathies are Communist or not, on which of Les Floralies' social and/or political factions enter into one's daily affairs in the residence.

The elderly community residents described by Frankfather (1977), who "loop" various urban scenes and agencies in managing their ostensible senility or deviance, present a multiplicity of lives. Frankfather shows that as an elder loops from, say, a community residence to encounters with the police, medical hospitalization, mental hospitalization, nursing home residence, and deinstitutionalization, his life fluctuates among many senses of what it is and has been. Life comes to be a set of "multiple and contradicting interpretations of the same 'facts'" (p. 15).

By Frankfather's account, there are at least two views of the etiology of senility operating in the daily encounters of the community residents. The one taken by most professionals is that senility is a pathological condition that is irreversible. Its "symptoms" are a routine expectation of aging. Another view, Frankfather maintains, holds that senile "characteristics" (note the change in language) are products of current living conditions and encounters. This view is not typical of professionals but is variously maintained by community members like neighbors and the personnel of local commercial establishments. One is likely to be "routinely and obviously" senile should he encounter a professional agent who sees elderly dependency and fragility in those terms. To encounter someone who sees dependency and fragility differently is not to have to deal with one's senility. Thus, to loop various urban scenes is now to experience senility and now to not. It is not just that one tends to become senile as one ages but that, if it must be described in terms of becoming, one risks becoming senile in circumstances where this ostensible fact to life exists and does not when it is absent.

In their own fashion, elderly persons understand this. It is a kind of tacit knowledge that serves to inform their management of daily affairs. To be satisfied with life may then mean that one has, for the time being, managed to avoid undesirable senses of it (which, perhaps, might be one of the unforeseen benefits of being a nonrespondent in life satisfaction measurement).

The temporal theme of the image of life satisfaction makes it reasonable to ask questions about satisfactions with what life has or has not become. The ethnographic data, however, show that time is complicated by a variety of practical conditions, such that in certain situations, for example, the present has no past.

Hazan's (1980) fieldwork was conducted in a day center for elderly Jews in Marlsden, a London borough. His aim was to show how the elders' pre-Center lives in Marlsden were transformed in quality upon their becoming Center participants, especially how the elders experienced changes in the way they reckoned the course of their lives in time. Hazan interprets his data to reveal that lifetime reckoning is not purely developmental, that one's sense of the past, future, and present does not just grow, regress, or cycle in an orderly or sequential fashion. Rather, it is shown that people—old people—may experience a multiplicity of time worlds and that changes in lifetime reckoning are experienced within the ongoing course of their everyday affairs. Upon becoming full Center participants, the elders' time world flattened. Where in the pre-Center period the present was reckoned in terms of an alienated past and future, life became mainly present-specific in the Center. Important elements of their past, such as growing up in the East End of London, were renounced by participants, not to be spoken of nor to be used as a background against which to evaluate present matters. In the Center, the future was a period that became, at best, something fatalistically vague, not seriously entertained nor estimated. Those few participants who dared to dwell on the past or to prognosticate on the future were summarily called to task. As Hazan writes, it is "almost as though time does not exist in the Center itself, but is capable of being a nuisance outside" (p. 89).

When time enters into their conversation, Center members are fatalistic: whatever was, was; whatever will be, will be. To them, as Hazan (p. 98) states, "nothing is really in a process of change and progression." This is the normal Center sense of lifetime reckoning. To evaluate members against the standard of time presented by the measurement image of life satisfaction would be to produce related morale scores that have no meaning for participants' Center lives. Health, for example, is not something that can be evaluated for whether or not it has been stable or has deteriorated.

> Participants usually refer to their medical condition as if it was static. No cure is to be expected, but deterioration is unlikely. Thus people with terminal disease speak freely of their present hardships, but rarely contemplate a possible worsening in their condition. The implicit feeling is that the Center is a sanctuary, impervious to the ordinary processes of change dominating the "normal" course of events in the outside world [p. 99].

Yet there are select occasions when time is expanded. For example, participation in the East End demonstrations against Fascism in the 1930s is recalled with pride. Depending on the occasion, the past bursts forth for these elders, or is carefully edited, or most commonly, is completely missing. The working version of time at the Center is a sharp contrast to the theme of linear, progressive time. It is, moreover, believed by participants to be the normal view, one that Hazan expressly notes, integrates elders into the Center. Organizing one's Center life in accordance with the measurement theme of time results in demoralization. Indeed, given Center participants' low tolerance for time supposition and linear reckoning, it is doubtful if any of the life satisfaction indexes and scales could be successfully, if not validly, administered to them.

As practiced and lived by elders, time has other dimensions that make its measurement theme a particular, not general, reflection of it. Gubrium (1975) describes how daily time and daily life satisfactions in a nursing home are worked through the contingencies of staff/patient interaction. For example, the widely used technique of behavior rehabilitation called "reality orientation" or "RO" is informed by a clock time chronology. Yet, in application, it continually confronts the multiple senses of timing held by patients and working therapists (Gubrium and Ksander 1975). Hochschild's (1973) discussion of what she called "altruistic surrender" is a form of nested time, in which a community of 43 grandmothers, who live in a small apartment building near San Francisco Bay, conduct a good share of their daily lives. The 43 women keep track of each other's daily lives and satisfactions, in part in terms of the ongoing daily lives and satisfactions of their children. And Myerhoff's (1978) Venice, California, Jewish elders do not "number their days" as isolated individuals. Their daily, past, and future satisfactions are intertwined with each other: Olga's happiness is tied to Gita's, Basha's feeling of loneliness sympathetically reflects Rachel's, Heschel's depression is really Jake's, and so on.

The third theme of the measurement image of life satisfaction suggests that life's major events, whatever they are, occur at an earlier time, not in old age. Old age primarily is a time of feelings. The ethnographic data show, on the contrary, that old people do play definite concrete roles. They are not only more or less satisfied with their past, but present events impinge critically on their satisfactions. Moreover, the routine substantive concerns of old age presented to elders in measurement—such as social contact, solvency, and health—are complicated in meaning by a variety of contextual considerations. The substance and complications of elders' lives and satisfactions cannot be understood only in terms of an ostensible past life but must be interpreted against a background of continually lived experiences.

In her ethnography of Mayfair, a Chicago retirement hotel, Teski (1979) describes various territories in the public areas of the ground floor: the Card Room, the gift shop, the Theatre Room, and the Greenhill Lounge.

> Through time, the different public areas in the hotel have become associated with different groups of people, and there is shared consensus about the type of activities which take place in these different locations. The feeling that certain areas "belong" to certain groups is very strong and many residents say firmly that they "never go into" certain rooms [p. 48].

The various areas are routinely used to define their frequenters as types of persons. Those who spend most of their time in one of the rooms come to be identified as "one of them." The informal territorial identities generate a set of roles or behavioral rules that, together with other identities, both articulate and enter into the management of everyday interactions in the hotel.

The Card Room contrasts dramatically with the Greenhill Lounge. The Card Room has a clublike atmosphere, is considered to be particular men's territory, is smoke filled, and resounds of hearty laughter and men's talk. Its occupants consider themselves to be rational people, albeit some have admittedly unusual opinions. On occasion, a resident believed to be senile walks into the room and falls asleep. Such a person is treated with repugnance, his or her territorial invasion generating disgust and grumbling. The Card Room, after all, is not believed to be for "that kind," but rather, as might be heard there, for "our kind of people."

The Greenhill Lounge, on the other hand, is viewed by regular occupants of the Card Room as a "repository for senile-seeming and sometimes repulsive old women." The lounge has chairs along the walls and a few others scattered in open space. There is a television area located within the Lounge. In contrast to the atmosphere of the Card Room, the lounge is very quiet. Many of its occupants sit in easy chairs and sleep. Conversation is hushed; new arrivals are stared at by those who are not sleeping. Card Room devotees believe the lounge to be a kind of "nursing home area," an opinion shared by some of the other residents. The lounge is also known to be gossip-ridden, a place where people "sit and spend their time inventing and spreading vicious stories about their fellow residents."

Whether or not occupants of the Card Room and Greenhill Lounge would differ in their rationality and self-control on objective behavioral grounds does not deny the fact that hotel residents organize their talk about, and orientation to, room regulars in accordance with such a belief. For whatever personal or interpersonal reason an occupant takes a place in either room, his behavior is considered to reveal the type of individual he is, which in turn serves to interpret his actions. To be, say, a Card Room regular is to imply publicly who one is, to play a kind of role in the daily life of the hotel. Such a role, like others that enter into daily hotel life, articulates life's satisfactions and dissatisfactions.

Other lifestyles claiming elderly adherents present them with additional concrete roles. Stephen's (1976) and Eckert's (1980) SRO hotels confront their permanent aged residents with younger, weekend transients who are, like Teski's Greenhill Loungers, "not like us." Hochschild's (1973) Merrill Court organizes a hierarchical system of roles around an informal rule of "poor dear" references. A woman who routinely refers to another as a "poor dear" commands the satisfaction that she is in greater luck than the latter, which, as Hochschild cautiously suggests, serves "to buttress a sense of her own achieved or ascribed superiority" (p. 59). And Gubrium's (1975) Murray Manor, a nursing home, not only is a place for what some gerontologists call "abnormal aging" but, like other places, also serves as a setting for the use and abuse of a wide range of roles—from the good resident to the seemingly well-recognized combative types, sweet patients, isolates, know-it-alls, mentals, and those who have "all their marbles."

Life in each of these places is full of roles taken and roles abandoned, roles claimed and roles assigned. None are places from which the aged only look back on a life that was lived, feeling one way or another about how it was compared to how it is now. In each instance, it is evident that, as Ross (1974) puts it, "life goes on." As life concretely flows, so do its satisfactions.

The routine substantive concerns of old age do not, in some straightforward degree, influence satisfaction with life. In the life satisfaction literature, it commonly is argued that a modicum of social contact, especially with relatives and friends, has a positive effect on life satisfaction. However, the social settings in which elders organize their lives complicate this. For example, Stephens (1976) and Eckert (1980) show how being socially unattached in the down-and-out world of the SRO is a desirable lifestyle, one that breaks down under the economic burdens and interpersonal obligations of attachment. The satisfactions of SRO marginality hinge on being a "loner," the familiarities of social contacts posing the constant threat of trouble. Even the meaning of health is interpreted against varying background understandings. To talk about one's aches and pains in vivid detail, for instance, is not to be morbid nor is it necessarily a sign of low morale. It may, indeed, be a conversational resource that commands the attention, recognition, and respect that others, who merely listen, do not share (Gubrium 1975; Teski 1979).

Rethinking Life Satisfaction

The preceding questions, analytic problems, and body of data suggest that it is time to rethink life satisfaction in old age. First, what has been and continues to be troublesome both conceptually and empirically is the extent that varying measures of life satisfaction dwell on past life, on one's younger years. The ongoing lives of the elderly are evaluated in a past-oriented time frame, something that tends to shortchange the current practicalities of lived experience. It is evident that the aged, like other people, do seriously live in their practical presents, and that they do produce and reproduce their acknowledged pasts, presents, and futures in relation to current considerations. To ignore this is to cheat their lives of its persistent richness.

Second, some conceptual and technical provision might best be made for revealing the multiplicity of life. This, it seems, is not within the technical capacity of life satisfaction measurement as currently conceived. Current measures do not allow for co-equal dialogue between subject and researcher about the content of items and responses. Rather, subjects are allowed to make moves in a preset game, as it were. Dialogical data, on the other hand, at least would not conceptually foreclose the entertainment of other games. Such data, of course, would be largely narrative, and furthermore, would be emergently revealing of life satisfaction. The aim of a dialogical strategy would not as much be to be precise about life satisfaction measurement, as to be adequate to it. Linking a dialogical strategy to a concrete concern with the context of dialogue would approximate ethnographic method.

Third, measures of life satisfaction are unjustifiably individualistic in two ways. It is assumed that index or scale scores represent the life satisfaction of each of their respective subjects. Should a woman's LSI-A score be, for example, 18 out of a possible 20, it would be concluded that *she* was quite satisfied with life. The score of 18 is taken to belong to her, not to anything else, not to the measurement occasion, not to the themes presented in measurement items, not to the logic of score computation. The assumption permits arithmetic calculations, such that, for example, out of a sample of 100 subjects, it is possible to conclude (given one has calculated correctly) that one quarter or 25% scored 16 or higher. The logic of arithmetic requires each score to be independent of every other one. Responses to individual measurement items are also assumed to be independent, which originally allowed the arithmetic calculation of each subject's score: responses to any one item do not depend on the subject's analytic assessment of his response to other items.

The individualistic character of life satisfaction measurement displaces the social features of daily living. The measurement vision is of a collection of independent individuals who each in his own right confronts and evaluates life. The measures do not reveal the social ties and social flux of life confrontations and assessments. Even the practical activity of being a subject in life satisfaction measurement is social, for it is, like all human action, dialectically an activity-in-relation-to something, whether measurement items or something else (Giddens 1979). Merely to assume that subjects can think about and assess themselves is simultaneously to assume action (thoughts and evaluations of self), which at once is dual and social (what one thinks and feels about oneself). One is social even in technical isolation. Life satisfaction measurement glosses over this. But, curiously, it is what must be assumed in order to achieve measured life satisfaction responses in the first place. As currently conceived, life satisfaction measurement floats on an unacceptable, yet preferably unanalyzed, foundation.

References

Altheide, David. 1976. *Creating Reality.* Beverly Hills, Calif.: Sage.
Buckholdt, David R., and Jaber F. Gubrium. 1979. *Caretakers.* Beverly Hills, Calif.: Sage.
Burgess, Ernest W. 1960. "Aging in Western Culture." In *Aging in Western Societies,* ed. Ernest W. Burgess. Chicago: University of Chicago Press.
Cavan, Ruth Shonle, Ernest W. Burgess, Robert J. Havighurst, and Herbert Goldhamer. 1949. *Personal Adjustment in Old Age.* Chicago: Science Research Associates.
Cicourel, Aaron. 1974. *Cognitive Sociology.* New York: Free Press.

Cumming, Elaine, Lois R. Dean, and David S. Newell. 1958. "What Is 'Morale'? A Case History of a Validity Problem." *Human Organization* 17:3-8.
Cumming, Elaine, and William E. Henry. 1961. *Growing Old.* New York: Basic Books.
Eckert, J. Kevin. 1980. *The Unseen Elderly.* San Diego: Campanile.
Edelman, Murray. 1977. *Political Language.* New York: Academic Press.
Frankfather, Dwight. 1977. *The Aged in the Community.* New York: Praeger.
Garfinkel, Harold. 1967. *Studies in Ethnomethodology.* Englewood Cliffs, N.J.: Prentice-Hall.
George, Linda K. 1979. "The Happiness Syndrome: Methodological and Substantive Issues in the Study of Social-Psychological Well-Being in Adulthood." *Gerontologist* 191:210-16.
George, Linda K., and Lucille B. Bearon. 1980. *Quality of Life in Older Persons.* New York: Human Sciences.
Giddens, Anthony. 1979. *Central Problems in Social Theory.* Berkeley: University of California Press.
Goffman, Erving. 1974. *Frame Analysis.* New York: Harper & Row.
Gubrium, Jaber F. 1975. *Living and Dying at Murray Manor.* New York: St. Martin's.
Gubrium, Jaber F., and David R. Buckholdt. 1977. *Toward Maturity: The Social Processing of Human Development.* San Francisco: Jossey-Bass.
_____. 1982. *Describing Care: Image and Practice in Rehabilitation.* Cambridge,Mass.: Oelgeschlager, Gunn, & Hain.
Gubrium, Jaber F., and Margaret Ksander. 1975. "On Multiple Realities and Reality Orientation." *Gerontologist* 15:142-45.
Hazan, Haim. 1980. *The Limbo People: A Study of the Constitution of Time among the Aged.* London: Routledge.
Hendricks, Jon, and C. Davis Hendricks. 1976. "Concepts of Time and Temporal Construction among the Aged, with Implications for Research." In *Time, Roles, and Self in Old Age,* ed. Jaber F. Gubrium. New York: Human Sciences.
Hochschild, Arlie. 1973. *The Unexpected Community.* Englewood Cliffs, N.J.: Prentice-Hall.
Jacobs, Jerry. 1974. *Fun City.* New York: Holt, Rinehart.
_____. 1975. *Older Persons and Retirement Communities.* Springfield, Ill.: Thomas.
Johnson, Sheila K. 1971. *Idlehaven.* Berkeley: University of California Press.
Kimmel, Douglas. 1974. *Adulthood and Aging.* New York: Wiley.
Kutner, Bernard, David Fanshel, Alice M. Togo, and Thomas S. Langner. 1956. *Five Hundred over Sixty.* New York: Russell Sage.
Lawton, M. Powell. 1972. "The Dimensions of Morale." In *Research, Planning, and Action for the Elderly,* ed. Donald P. Kent, Robert Kastenbaum, and Sylvia Sherwood. New York: Behavioral Publications.
_____. 1975. "The Philadelphia Geriatric Center Morale Scale: A Revision." *Journal of Gerontology* 30:85-89.
Myerhoff, Barbara. 1978. *Number Our Days.* New York: Simon & Schuster.
Neugarten, Bernice L., Robert J. Havighurst, and Sheldon S. Tobin. 1961. "The Measurement of Life Satisfaction." *Journal of Gerontology* 16:134-43.
Nydegger, Corinne, ed. 1977. *Measuring Morale: A Guide to Effective Assessment.* Washington, D.C.: Gerontological Society.
Perrucci, Robert. 1974. *Circle of Madness.* Englewood Cliffs, N.J.: Prentice-Hall.

Pfohl, Stephen J. 1978. *Predicting Dangerousness.* Lexington, Mass.: Lexington.

Rosow, Irving. 1963. "Adjustment of the Normal Aged." In *Processes of Aging,* vol. 2, Richard H. Williams, Clark Tibbitts, and Wilma Donahue. New York: Atherton.

Ross, Jennie Keith. 1974. "Life Goes On: Social Organization in a French Retirement Residence." In *Late Life,* ed. Jaber F. Gubrium. Springfield, Ill.: Thomas.

———. 1977. *Old People, New Lives.* Chicago: University of Chicago Press.

Schutz, Alfred. 1967. *The Phenomenology of the Social World.* Introduction by George Walsh. Evanston, Ill.: Northwestern University Press.

———. 1970. *On Phenomenology and Social Relations,* ed. Helmut R. Wagner. Chicago: University of Chicago Press.

Siegal, Harvey Alan. 1978. *Outposts of the Forgotten.* New Brunswick, N.J.: Transaction.

Stephens, Joyce. 1976. *Loners, Losers, and Lovers.* Seattle: University of Washington Press.

Teski, Marea. 1979. *Living Together.* Washington, D.C.: University Press of America.

Tuchman, Gaye. 1978. *Making News.* New York: Free Press.

Wiseman, Jacqueline P. 1970. *Stations of the Lost.* Chicago: University of Chicago Press.

Wood, Vivian, Mary L. Wylie, and Bradford Sheafor. 1969. "An Analysis of a Short Self-Report Measure of Life Satisfaction: Correlation with Rater Judgments." *Journal of Gerontology* 24:465-69.

16

Aging and Mental Health: Challenging Scientific Myths

Marjorie Chary Feinson

A quiz on aging and mental health issues taken by 392 undergraduates included the following "true or false" statement "Depression occurs more frequently among older people than among the young."

Not surprisingly, the number of incorrect answers was very high.[1] Almost 85 percent thought depression was more frequent among older than younger adults (Pruchno and Smyer, 1983). The undergraduates were undoubtedly influenced by commonly held perceptions of older adults and mental health problems. Those perceptions have received support and reinforcement from many quarters. For example, the President's Commission on Mental Health, Task Panel on the Elderly, stated that depression increases with each decade of life (*Mental Health and the Elderly*, 1978:3). Similarly, a former director of the Center for the Study of Mental Health and Aging at the National Institute of Mental Health, wrote that "mental illness is more prevalent with the elderly than with younger adults; 18 to 25% of older persons have significant mental health symptoms" (Cohen, 1980:972). Gerontologists Ethel Shanas and George Maddox concluded that 20 percent of older adults "appear to be at least moderately impaired in psychological functioning" (1976:606). Finally, from psychiatrist Gerald L. Klerman: "Mental illnesses, in general appear to be more prevalent among the elderly than among younger adults" (1983).

These professional statements have helped to shape the perceptions influencing the undergraduates' answers. The students accepted the current view in much the same way as an official at the National Center for Health Statistics: "I have been told that depression is very prevalent among the elderly. I do not know how to evaluate that statement but I am prepared to accept it" (Kovar 1980:322-23).

This assumption of widespread psychological distress among older adults persists despite the lack of consistent and convincing evidence. As Dr. Adrian Ostfeld notes: "Again and again we hear the comment that depression is a very serious problem in the elderly although none of us have data on its prevalence" (1980:355). And mental health demographers Redick and Taube observe: "Up to the present time, there have been no studies or surveys which could be used as a reliable and valid basis for estimating the prevalence of mental disorders" in older adults (1980:60).

There is a need for data to document or discredit the prevailing perceptions. The focus of this chapter is to review existing studies and present new data from a recent mental health survey of older adults. The discussion is structured by the following questions: (1) How much distress exists among older adults? Are the estimates of up to 25 percent accurate or inflated? (2) Are mental disorders more prevalent among older or younger adults? (3) In addition to age, is distress associated with other demographic characteristics such as gender, race, marital status, income, and education?

Relevance of the Questions

These three questions are important for several reasons. One is demographic: the increase in the older population described in chapter 1 makes it imperative to have accurate data on elders' mental health, especially if they are presumed to have more mental disorders than other age groups.

A second reason concerns prevention and control of mental disorders. To prevent disorders, baseline information concerning their frequency and distribution in the population is required. That is, how often do they occur and who is affected by them? This type of information is provided by epidemiological studies which are also designed to shed light on the causes of disorders. Epidemiology differs from clinical medical studies in that the former focuses on populations while the latter examines the health of individuals (Dohrenwend, 1983).

There are various types of epidemiological studies.[2] One type measures *how often* the disease occurs, that is, its prevalence and incidence rate. Prevalence refers to the number of persons (or cases) with active symptoms or diagnoses at any one time, while incidence includes the number of new cases that develop within a specific period.

Another type of study focuses on *trends* (increases and decreases) in rates over time. As an example, the authors of the Midtown Manhattan Study measured prevalence rates of mental disorders in both 1954 and 1974 and concluded, to the surprise of many, that there had been a *decrease* in distress over the 20-year period (Srole et al., 1962; Srole and Fischer, 1980).

A related type of epidemiological study examines the *distribution* of disorders in the population associated with characteristics such as gender, age, race, income, education, and marital status. A goal of these studies is to provide a basis for establishing causal relationships. For example, if it can be documented that depression occurs more frequently in women over sixty-five, this group would be studied to search for clues regarding its cause. In addition to demographics, mental health research examines other factors as possible causes of particular disorders. These include the role of stressful life events, social support networks, and community environments.

A fourth study looks at *utilization patterns*—who seeks help, for what kinds of disorders, at what types of facilities, and under what conditions. Such studies have shown that older adults do not utilize out-patient mental health facilities, particularly community mental health centers. The low utilization rates prevail despite a presumed high level of needs. These studies document such patterns and attempt to highlight both the individual and social factors which contribute to them.

A similar kind of study documents *unmet needs* for services. Here, research is undertaken to measure the gap between need for services and their availability. For example, how large is the gap between the presumed high level of needs of older adults and their low utilization of out-patient facilities? Do older adults not use community mental health centers because of transportation, financial, or stigma considerations? Or, is it that they do not know that such services exist or that they have a need which can be met by existing services?

This brief summary of several types of epidemiological studies suggests another compelling reason for pursuing the questions posed in this chapter, namely, planning and policy considerations. The design and implementation of effective policies and programs require data concerning prevalence and incidence rates, utilization patterns, and unmet needs. Moreover, it is crucial to know which population groups are at greatest risk. For example, federal legislation has mandated that older adults be targeted for community mental services based on their presumed high level of mental disorders. Yet, who among the 25 million people over 65 should be singled out for services and for what kinds of mental disorders? With limited resources, epidemiological data are necessary to establish priorities relevant to the mental health needs of the population.

Concept of Mental Disorders

The term *mental disorders* is used interchangeably in the literature with psychological distress, psychiatric impairment, psychiatric disorders, emotional problems, and mental illness. Regardless of which term is used, the concept remains vague and includes a wide variety of conditions which have little in common. "Although this term [mental illness] is frequently used by psychiatrists as well as laymen, it is basically a social label describing deviation of specified types rather than a clear medical phenomenon (Mechanic, 1978:99).[3]

Despite confusion over its precise meaning, mental disorders are commonly divided into two broad categories: organic and functional. Organic disorders are those with a physiological basis such as organic brain syndrome. Functional disorders have no known organic basis and are related to personality and life experiences. They include affective psychoses, neuroses, and personality disorders. Functional disorders are characterized by disordered thought processes, patterns of atypical behavior, and a general state of unpleasant arousal or emotion. Psychological distress, a functional disorder, is a general state of unpleasant emotions usually accompanied by physiological symptoms such as nervousness, dizziness, and sleep and appetite disturbances. These emotional states, if intense, may limit the daily functioning of the individual (Thoits and Hannan, 1979). The following discussion concerns psychological distress and its prevalence in the older adult population.

Prevalence of Distress

Prevalence rates of distress for older adults are derived from two available sources: findings from studies conducted during the past 30 years, and data collected in a recent mental health survey (directed by the author) of 313 older adults living in the community.

At the outset, several observations about the findings from other studies are warranted. First, very few studies, exactly four, focus solely on older adults, especially those 65+. Second, those studies which include older respondents tend to treat them as a single age cohort for comparison with younger groups. For example, respondents aged 20 to 65 are often subdivided into three, four, or even five age groups, while the oldest respondents are combined into a single category (60+ or 65+) or, in some instances, two groups (usually 65-74 and 75+). This differential treatment suggests that age distinctions are viewed as important for young and middle-aged adults, but not for a group whose age ranges from 60 to 100.

To determine accurate prevalence rates for older adults, a brief review of both types of studies follows. Only studies which utilize random probability samples of elders living in the community are included. By design, this excludes surveys conducted in nursing homes, senior centers, nutrition sites, and out-patient clinics because the self-selection process involved in these samples introduces a bias which does not permit generalizations to the total population over 65.

Studies of Older Adults

Four studies conducted over a 20-year period focus primarily on older adults (Lowenthal and Berkman, 1967; Blazer and Williams, 1980; Gurland et al., 1983; Murrell, Himmelfarb, and Wright, 1983).[4] In each, a different measure of psychological distress and different lower age limits were used (see Table 16.1). The earliest study, by Lowenthal and Berkman (1967), was conducted in San Francisco with a stratified random sample of 600 respondents age 60 and over. Out of 272 respondents who reported one or more of seven symptoms, professionals rated 33 "severely" disabled and 60 "moderately" or "mildly" disabled. These 93 respondents represented a prevalence rate of 15.5 percent, of whom 5 percent were judged to be severely disabled. The balance of the sample or 84.5 percent were considered "'unimpaired' or 'normal' or 'mentally healthy'" (1967:33).

Approximately 12 years later, a study of 997 older adults (65+) was conducted in Durham County, North Carolina, to determine true prevalence rates of a particular type of distress, namely, depression (Blazer and Williams, 1980). The researchers, using the OARS Depressive Scale, determined that 14.7 percent of their stratified random community sample displayed substantial depressive symptoms.

In the mid-1970s, Gurland et al. (1983) conducted a community survey with 445 residents of New York City who were 65 and over. They measured depression with 30 symptoms from a scale called CARE (Comprehensive Assessment and Referral Evaluation). Based on ratings by a psychiatrist, 13 percent of the sample was found to have "pervasive depression" or a level comparable to clinical depression.

The fourth study of older adults, also focused on depression, was conducted in Kentucky in 1981 (Murrell, Himmelfarb, and Wright, 1983). These researchers interviewed 2,517 respondents with a different instrument, the CES-D, and reported prevalence rates by gender and age. As shown in Table 16.1, depression rates for women aged 65-74 were 14.5 percent and at age 75+, 26.0 percent. For men, the comparable rates were 12.9 percent and 17.5 percent.

These four studies cannot be directly compared because different symptoms were measured (distress or depression), with different instruments, for different age groups. To establish age-related prevalence rates it is essential to examine epidemiological surveys in which older adults are included as part of a larger sample. The second part of Table 16.1 includes studies

TABLE 16.1
Community Studies of Prevalence of Distress in Older Adults

Author & Pub. Date	Year of Study	Measure of Impairment	Sample Size	Age	Percent	Impaired %
A. Studies of Older Adults						
Lowenthal and Berkman (1967)	1960	7 items of distress rated by psychiatrists	600	60 +		15.5
Blazer and Williams (1980)	1972	OARS Depressive Scale	997	65 +		14.7
Gurland et al. (1983)	1970s	38 depressive symptoms; rated by psychiatrists	445	65 +		13
Murrell, Himmelfarb, and Wright (1983)	1981	CES-D (depression)	2517	55 +	*Men* 65-74 / 75 + / *Women* 65-74 / 75 +	12.9 / 17.5 / 14.5 / 26.0
B. Studies Including Older Adults						
Gurin, Veroff, and Feld (1960)	1957	5 items of anxiety	678	55 +		22
Phillips (1966)	not given	Langner (distress)	150	60 +	4 + symptoms / 7 + symptoms	26 / 6
Haberman (1970)	1960-61 1963	Langner (distress)	N/A N/A	60 + 60 +	4 + symptoms / 4 + symptoms	24.8 / 24.8
Weissman and Myers (1978)	1967 and 1969	8 depressive symptoms	N/A	65 + *1967* 65 75 *1969* 65 75	*Females*[1] 11 / 21 11 / 13	*Males* 22 / 20 18 / 16

Study	Year of Data	Measure	N	Age	Subgroup	%
Warheit, Holzer, and Schwab (1973)	1968-73	18 items of depression	317	60+	60-69 / 70-79	22.3 / 28.3
Schwab, Fennell, Warheit (1974)	1968-73	11 psycho-physiologic symptoms	N/A	60+		22.2
Gaitz and Scott (1972)	1969	Langner (distress)	427	65+	4 + symptoms / 7 + symptoms	36.7 / 16.8
Comstock and Helsing (1976)	1971-74	CES-D (depression)	657	65+	Whites / / Blacks	12.3 / 18.1 / 25.6
Srole and Fischer (1980)	1974	83 items of mental disturbance	333	60+	60-69 / 70-79	12 / 18
Weissman and Myers (1980)	1975-76	SADS (psychiatric disorders)	111	66+	Depression / Any Diagnosis	8.1 / 11.7
Veroff, Douvan, Kulka (1981)	1976	5 items of anxiety	729	66+		17
Frerichs, Aneshensel, Clark (1981)	1979	CES-D (depression)	126	65+		16.7
Uhlenhuth et al. (1983)	1979	Hopkins Symptom Checklist	N/A	65-79	Depression / Anxiety / Other High Distress	5.1 / 7.1 / 6.4
George, Landerman, and Melville (1983)	1980s	DIS (psychiatric disorders)	1159	65+	Any Psych. Disorder / Affective Disorders / Anxiety Disorders	10 / 2.2 / 7.9

1. These figures are approximate as they are taken from a graph.
Source: Compiled by the author.

conducted over a 25-year period with a variety of measures and slightly different age groups.

Studies of Younger and Older Adults

In 1957, Gurin, Veroff, and Feld (1960) included 678 persons aged 55 and over in a sample of 2,411 respondents. A 5-item psychological anxiety measure produced a 22 percent distress rate for those 55 and over. Twenty years later, Veroff, Douvan, and Kulka (1981) repeated the original study and included 729 respondents aged 55 and over. They determined a distress rate of 17 percent for this age group. In other words, mental distress rates among older respondents *declined* over the 20 years.

In the early 1960s, Phillips (1966) examined the mental health status of 600 New Hampshire residents, 150 of whom were age 60 and over. A scale of 22 distress items (the Langner scale) produced a definite impairment rate of 6 percent and a probable impairment rate of 26 percent.[5]

Also, in the early 1960s, Haberman (1970) conducted two studies, one in the Washington Heights section of New York and the second in New York City. Using the same scale as Phillips (1966), he reported a probable distress rate of 24.8 percent for older adults in both studies.

In 1967 and 1969, Weissman and Myers (1978) measured distress with eight depressive symptoms in a sample which included respondents aged 65 and over. As shown in Table 16.1, depression rates in 1967 for women aged 65 were 11 percent and 21 percent at age 75. For men, the comparable rates were 22 and 20 percent. In 1969, the rates for women aged 65 were again 11 percent, but quite a bit lower for women aged 75, 13 percent. For men, the comparable rates were lower in both age groups: age 65, 17 percent, and age 75, 15 percent.

In a large-scale epidemiological survey in northern Florida spanning five years (1968-73), Warheit, Holzer, and Schwab (1973) included a subsample of 317 respondents aged 60 and over. Based on responses to 18 depressive symptoms, they reported a 22.3 percent rate for the 60-69 age group and a 28.3 percent rate for those aged 70 and over. Using the same sample Schwab, Fennell, and Warheit (1974) also measured distress with 11 psychophysiologic symptoms. They found that 22.2 percent of the sample age 60+ reported having two or more symptoms.

In 1969, Gaitz and Scott (1972) measured distress for 427 respondents aged 65+ out of a total sample of 1,441 respondents. These researchers, using the same 22 items as Phillips (1966) and Haberman (1970), reported a probable impairment rate of 36.7 percent and a definite impairment rate of 16.8 percent.

Another large population survey in the early 1970s focused on depression symptoms and included 657 adults aged 65+ in Missouri and Maryland (Comstock and Helsing, 1976). Using 20 depressive symptoms (the CES-D scale), the researchers reported prevalence rates of 12.3 percent and 18.1 percent for older Whites and a prevalence rate of 25.6 percent for older Blacks.

Although the original Midtown Manhattan sample (Srole et al., 1962) did not include anyone over age 59, the restudy conducted with the same subjects in 1974 had respondents aged 60-69 and 70-79—the same people who were 20 years younger in the initial study. Using psychiatric ratings of 83 symptoms of mental disturbance, Srole and Fischer (1980) reported a 12 percent prevalence rate for the 60-69 age cohort and an 18 percent rate for those aged 70-79. These rates were lower than when the subjects had been younger.

In 1975 and 1976, Weissman and Myers (1980) conducted a follow-up study in New Haven, Connecticut. Their sample of 511 respondents included 111 aged 66 and over. Instead of a screening scale used in the previous studies, they used a diagnostic instrument, the Schedule for Affective Disorders and Schizophrenia (SADS) to measure psychiatric disorders. They found that 11.7 percent of the oldest respondents had some psychiatric diagnosis while 8.1 percent had major or minor depressions.

A Los Angeles study conducted in 1979 included 126 respondents aged 65 and older in a total sample of 1,000 (Frerichs, Aneshensel, and Clark, 1981). These researchers, using the same measure and same cut-off as the earlier study in Missouri and Maryland, reported a prevalence rate of 16.7 percent, compared to the 12.3 percent and 18.1 percent recorded by Comstock and Helsing (1976) for their older White respondents.

Also in 1979, Uhlenhuth et al. (1983) used 43 items from the Hopkins Symptom Checklist to measure specific disorders with a national sample. These researchers reported the following rates for respondents aged 65-79: 5.1 percent for depression; 7.1 percent for anxiety; and 6.4 percent for any other form of high distress.

The final study including older adults was conducted in Durham County, North Carolina, in the early 1980s (George, Landerman, and Melville, 1983). This sample, designed to have an overrepresentation of elders, included 1,159 respondents aged 65+ out of a total sample of 3,796. Using a new instrument created for this survey with specific diagnostic categories (Diagnostic Interview Schedule or DIS), the researchers reported a 10.01 percent prevalence rate for any psychiatric disorder among older respondents. The prevalence rate for affective disorders was 2.2 percent and for anxiety disorders, 7.9 percent.

These epidemiological studies represent the preponderance of data on the prevalence of distress among older adults. Yet, even with 18 studies, it is exceedingly difficult to compare prevalence rates because of variations in what type of distress is measured, how it is measured (with a screening scale or a diagnostic instrument), differing age ranges, and different ways of reporting the rates. However, if only those studies which measure similar disorders are considered, it is possible to generate rates for some categories. Beginning with studies measuring *depressive symptoms* with screening scales, prevalence rates range from 11 percent (Weissman and Myers, 1978) to 28.3 percent (Warheit et al., 1973). The median rate for depressive symptoms across these studies is 16.9 percent. Concerning *general distress* also measured with screening scales, the rates range from 6 percent (Phillips, 1966) to 36.7 percent (Gaitz and Scott, 1972). The median rate across all distress studies is 20 percent.

In contrast to these studies which used screening scales are three studies which used measures based on diagnostic categories to provide psychiatric diagnoses (Weissman and Myers, 1980; George et al., 1983; Uhlenhuth et al., 1983). The rates for *depression* (as contrasted with depressive symptoms) from these studies are 5.1 percent and 8.1 percent while the rates for *any psychiatric disorder* are 10.01 percent and 11 percent. Thus, median rates using diagnostic instruments are approximately 6.6 percent for depression and 10.9 percent for any psychiatric disorder.

In sum, median rates provided by studies using screening scales are 16.9 percent for depressive symptoms and 20 percent for general distress. These are substantially higher than the rates from studies using diagnostic instruments—6.6 percent for depression and 10.9 percent for any psychiatric disorder. Clearly, these rates, especially those provided by diagnostic instruments, are substantially lower than the professional estimates of up to 25 percent quoted earlier.

Data from a Mental Health Survey of Older Adults

The rates derived from these 18 studies can be further refined by examining data from a random probability sample of 313 older adults living in the community. This epidemiological survey was conducted in conjuction with staff and faculty of the Community Mental Health Center of Rutgers Medical School, University of Medicine and Dentistry of New Jersey. The data were collected in face-to-face interviews during 1980 and 1981 from residents aged 65 and over living in Middlesex County, New Jersey. The county consists of several large urban centers, many suburban towns, and a large rural area. Approximately 10 percent of the total county's population (594,984) is over age 65, a proportion similar to the national average.

An advantage of this study over some of the previous ones is the measurement of psychological distress. The latter was measured with two instruments, one which is specific and related to diagnostic categories and one which taps general feeling states. The first measure of distress is a self-report symptom scale (the Hopkins Symptoms Checklist or the SCL-90-R, Derogatis et al., 1973) developed during the past 10 to 15 years, tested for internal consistency, and scaled to represent meaningful dimensions of psychological disorder (Dohrenwend and Dohrenwend, 1982). It measures psychological distress by asking respondents how much they were bothered by each of 90 symptoms in the past week: not at all (0); a little bit (1); moderately (2); quite a bit (3); and extremely (4). The 90 symptoms form nine subscales and three measures of overall distress. From these, three of the most reliable subscales were used: depression, anxiety, and somatization (physical problems associated with mental disorders). Also used was one measure of overall distress (GSI).[6]

The second instrument used to assess distress was a modified General Well-Being Scale (Rand, 1979) that included 15 items representing general mental health status or emotional feeling states during the past month (e.g. How much of the time have you felt cheerful? How often did you get rattled or flustered?) Six response choices are offered for each item ranging from extremely positive to extremely negative evalutions. The reliability of this scale is quite high.[7] On all five measures of psychological distress, higher scores reflect more distress. Thus, the General Well-Being scale is more aptly termed General Malaise (lack of well-being).

Sociodemographic variables included year of birth, education, income, and employment status. The interviewers recorded both the gender and race of the respondent.

Table 16.2 presents the prevalence of moderate and severe distress for the five measures. Beginning with *depression,* the rate from this study of 11.5 percent for moderate depression is higher than rates provided by other diagnostic studies, while the 5.1 percent rate for severe depression is comparable to the 5.1 percent reported by Uhlenhuth et al. (1983) and the 8.1 percent reported by Weissman and Myers (1980). Because these three studies are similar in what they are measuring (depression rather than depressive symptoms) and the diagnostic instruments utilized, they can be used to establish a median rate for depression of 6.6 percent. This 6.6 percent rate for diagnosed depression is considerably lower then the previously established rate of 16.9 percent for depressive symptoms derived from screening scales.

Also reflected in Table 16.2 is the finding that depression is *not* the most prevalent emotional disorder reported by older adults. Moderate anxiety and somatization are apparently more widespread, as is severe somatiza-

TABLE 16.2
Percentage of Older Adults[1] Reporting Distress

Measure of Distress	Moderate[2]		Severe[3]	
	%	N	%	N
Depression	11.5	(36)[4]	5.1	(16)[4]
Anxiety	12.5	(39)	3.8	(12)
Somatization	14.7	(46)	5.4	(17)
General distress (GSI)	11.2	(35)	4.5	(14)
General malaise[5]	16.6	(52)	3.8	(12)

1. Number of Respondents = 313; age 65 and over.
2. Moderate symptoms defined as 1 or more standard deviations above the group mean.
3. Severe defined as 2 or more standard deviations above the group mean.
4. Number of respondents in parentheses.
5. General Malaise is the Rand HIS General Well-Being Scale reversed.

tion. This is consistent with findings reported by others (Uhlenhuth et al., 1983; George et al., 1983). Clearly, these data do not support the statement, frequently found in the gerontological literature, that depression is the most widespread mental disorder of later life.

The rates shown in Table 16.2 for moderate *overall distress* are not similar: 11.2 percent for GSI and 16.6 percent for General Malaise. As in the previous discussion, this may be due to the measurement of different phenomena (specific symptoms versus general feeling states) with different types of instruments (a diagnostic instrument versus a general screening scale). To begin with General Malaise, it is similar to other screening scales measuring overall distress. The General Malaise rate of 16.6 percent is lower than the median distress rate of 20 percent established with previous studies. Thus, it is reasonable to establish an *overall distress* rate of 17 to 20 percent for older adults.

In contrast to General Malaise, the GSI is derived from a diagnostically related instrument, similar to ones used by Weissman and Myers (1980), George et al. (1983), and Uhlenhuth et al. (1983). The GSI rate of 11.2 percent for moderate distress supports the rates of 11.7 percent and 10.01 percent from two of these studies. The 4.5 percent rate for severe GSI distress is lower than rates from the other studies. The rates derived from these studies can by used to establish a median rate for diagnostic distress of 9.4 percent which is comparable to the rate of 10.9 percent established previously for *any psychiatric disorder.*

With the establishment of these median rates, 6.6 percent for depression, 16.9 percent for depressive symptoms, 17 to 20 percent for overall distress, and 9 to 11 percent for any psychiatric disorder, it becomes clear that professional estimates of up to 25 percent are not accurate reflections of mental disorders among older adults. The data from the New Jersey survey, along with findings reported by others, support considerably lower rates. Moreover, this analysis demonstrates the importance of specifying what is being discussed—depressive symptoms or overall distress as measured by screening scales in contrast to depression or psychiatric disorders as measured by diagnostic instruments.

Having established these prevalence rates, it is appropriate to consider the second major question, namely, how do these rates compare to those for younger age groups? Stated another way, is it accurate to claim that older adults experience more mental disorders than younger adults?

Age Comparisons for Mental Disorders

Comparative rates of distress for older and younger adults are considered first by reviewing other studies and then with data from the mental health survey of New Jersey elders. Again, the variations in the studies outweigh the similarities in terms of number of respondents, measurement of distress, age groupings, and the method of reporting rates (by age, by age and gender, and by age, gender, and type of distress). However, the findings from the studies, as summarized in Table 16.3, provide essential information concerning the age-distress relationship.[8] (A detailed description of these studies is available from the author.) The first compelling finding is that the largest number of studies, 11 in all, *report evidence of no age differences.*

The next largest group of studies, numbering seven, provides data showing that *younger adults are more distressed than older adults.* Combined, these 18 studies present evidence of either no age differences or more disorders among younger adults. Moreover, three studies show mixed results with the highest rates in both the youngest and oldest age groups.

In contrast to these 21 studies, there are three studies which show significantly more distress among older adults (Warheit et al., 1975; Schwab et al., 1974; Murrell et al., 1983—re: depression among men). Of these three studies, the one by Schwab et al. reports on measures of psychophysiological or physical symptoms. These types of symptoms may reflect either psychiatric or physical conditions. As Gurland noted: "In view of the high prevalence of chronic diseases among the elderly, the distinction between physical and psychiatric symptoms is crucial for making comparisons of the rates of psychiatric symptoms with those for other age groups." In one study, according to Gurland (1976 :285) when psychiatrists eliminated symptoms seemingly related to physical illness, 24 percent of the high-scoring respondents were reduced to low-scoring status. Thus, the study by Schwab et al. (1974) showing higher psychophysiological rates for

TABLE 16.3
Summary of Studies Showing Relationship between Age and Distress

No Age Differences	Younger Adults Significantly Higher	Older Adults Significantly Higher
Phillips (1966) re: distress	Hogarty and Katz (1971) re: general psychopathology	Schwab, Fennell, and Warheit (1974) re: psychophysiologic symptoms
Haberman (1970) re: distress in NYC sample	Warheit, Holzer and Arey (1975) re: general psychopathology	Warheit, Holzer, and Arey (1975) re: anxiety
Hogarty and Katz (1971) re: anxiety, nervousness	Comstock and Helsing (1976) re: depression	Murrell, Himmelfarb, and Wright (1983) re: depression in oldest men
Gaitz and Scott (1972) re: distress, affect	Weissman and Myers (1980) re: depressive personality	
Warheit, Holzer and Arey (1975) re: phobia, anxiety function	Frerichs, Aneshensel, and Clark (1981) re: depressive symptoms	
Weissman and Myers (1978) re: depression	George, Landerman, and Melville (1983) re: affective disorder, substance abuse disorder, any psychiatric disorder	
Sayetta and Johnson (1980) re: depression	Uhlenhuth, et al. (1983) re: phobias, all other distress	
Weissman and Myers (1980) re: any diagnosis, 2 or more diagnoses, major depression		
Veroff, Douvan, and Kulka (1981) re: psychological anxiety		
George, Landerman, and Melville (1983) re: anxiety disorder		
Uhlenhuth, et al. (1983) re: major depression, anxiety, agoraphobia		

Mixed Results (older and younger higher)	Older Adults Higher (significance not reported)
Berkman (1971) re: psychological well being	Gurin, Veroff, and Feld (1960) re: psychological anxiety
Warheit, Holzer and Arey (1975) re: depression	Haberman (1970) re: distress in Washington Heights sample
Murrell, Himmelfarb and Wright (1983) re: depression in oldest and youngest women	Srole and Fischer (1980) re: distress

Source: Compiled by the author.

older adults may actually describe increased rates of physical illness in old age rather than psychological disorders.

There are an additional three studies listed in Table 16.3 which indicate a *trend* toward more distress among older adults (Gurin et al., 1960; Haberman, 1970; Srole and Fischer, 1980). However, because statistical tests have not been reported, it is not clear if these trends are significant or may have occurred by chance alone. However, including these three studies but excluding the one which confounds psychological and physical symptoms leaves *five studies* showing that older adults are more distressed than younger adults. This is hardly convincing evidence when contrasted with the *21 studies* that show no age differences, higher rates among younger people, or mixed results.

In addition to the meager data supporting the perception of more distress among older adults, *none* of the studies of depression, with one exception (older men in Murrell et al., 1983) documents that older adults experience more *depressive symptoms* than younger adults. This lack of data has hardly begun to undermine prevailing perceptions about aging and depression such as the following: "While no age group in American society is immune to depression, the elderly, those 65 and over, are more likely than some younger cohorts to be subject to the condition" (Haug and Breslau, 1983:xi).

Age Differences and Distress among Older Adults

Discussion of the relationship between age and distress should also consider age differences which may exist among those over 65. Data from the survey of New Jersey elders are presented in Table 16.4. The percentage of respondents reporting moderate to severe symptoms for the five distress measures are shown according to three age groups: under 75; 75 to 84; and 85 and over. On four of the five measures (depression, anxiety, somatization, and GSI), the oldest respondents report significantly more symptoms. Only for General Malaise is the trend of more distress with increasing age not a significant one (i.e., could be due to chance). These data provide initial evidence that for those age 65 and over, some types of distress increase significantly with age.

One additional important finding from Table 16.4 concerns the prevalence rates for those under 75. On four of the five measures, the reported rate of distress is below 10 percent, a rate comparable to the overall prevalence rate of 10 percent for the total U.S. population (Redick and Taube, 1980:60). This finding implies that those between 65 and 75 years may be more similar to those under age 65 than to those over 75. Again, the fallacy of treating all older adults as one age cohort is demonstrated.

TABLE 16.4
Percentage of Older Adults[1] Reporting Distress

	Depression		Anxiety		Somatization		GSI[2]		General Malaise[3]	
	%	N	%	N	%	N	%	N	%	N
Under 75 (213)[4]	7.0	(15)	8.5	(18)	9.9	(21)	8.5	(18)	14.1	(30)
75-84 (79)	19.0	(15)	17.7	(14)	24.1	(19)	15.2	(12)	21.5	(17)
85 and over (21)	28.6	(6)	33.3	(7)	28.6	(6)	23.8	(5)	23.8	(5)
Significance (Chi²)	14.522 p=.0007		13.532 p=.0012		12.714 p=.0017		6.249 p=.04		NS	

1. Number of respondents = 313; age 65 and over.
2. GSI reflects the mean score for all 90 symptoms (number and frequency) reported on the SCL-90-R.
3. General Malaise is the Rand HIS General Well-Being Scale reversed.
4. Number of respondents indicated in parentheses.

TABLE 16.5
Zero-Order Correlations between Distress and Demographics in a Random Community Sample of Older Adults[1]

CHARACTERISTICS

	Age	Gender[2]	Race[3]	Marital Status[4]	Income	Education
Distress Measures						
General distress (GSI)	.15***	.001	.07	−.09	−.11*	−.04
Depression	.20***	.06	.07	−.16**	−.16**	−.07
Anxiety	.19***	−.01	.06	−.12*	−.17**	−.02
Somatization	.12*	−.07	.07	−.05	−.10	−.14*
General malaise[5]	.13*	.02	−.08	−.04	−.01	−.06

*p < = .05
**p < = .01
***p < = .001

1. Number of respondents = 313; age 65 and over.
2. Gender coded 1 for male, 2 for female.
3. Race coded 1 for Black/Hispanic, 2 for White.
4. Marital status coded 1 for not married, 2 for married.
5. General Malaise is the Rand HIS General Well-Being Scale reversed.

Another method for examining the age-distress relationship utilizes correlational analysis (the one-to-one relationship between the variables). Table 16.5 presents zero-order correlations between five demographic characteristics and five distress measures. The coefficients (with asterisks) listed under column 1, "Age," indicate that age is significantly related to all five measures. That is, more distress is reported by older respondents. However, the size of the correlations reveals that the age-distress relationship is weak. (An impressive correlation would be at least .50 or higher.) In regard to the other variables, the data show that gender and race are not significantly related to any of the distress measures. Marital status and income are slightly related to anxiety and depression; education is weakly related to somatization. Again, even though significant, these relationships are quite weak.

In addition to examining the relationship between age and mental disorders, it is important to control for the effects of other key sociodemographic variables. The danger of drawing conclusions using only a 2-variable relationship was persuasively demonstrated by Warheit et al. (1975) in their analysis of race and mental illness. They found that without controlling other variables, Blacks had significantly higher scores than Whites on all five measures of distress. Twice as many Blacks as Whites were "high" on general psychopathology and three times as many were "high" on the phobia measure. However, when the effects of other variables were controlled, the results were quite different. The effect of race was minimal when income, education, and marital status were taken into account. That is, for individuals in similar income, educational, and marital statuses, there was little difference between Blacks and Whites in distress rates.[9] Thus, Warheit et al. (1975:254) concluded that race, as an independent variable, was not an important predictor of mental illness.[10]

Table 16.6 presents multiple regression coefficients for each demographic variable and the five distress measures. These coefficients reflect the relationship between the demographic variable and the distress variable while controlling for the effects of all other demographic factors. For example, the relationship between age and depression is examined controlling for the effects of gender, race, marital status, education, and income. While age and depression were significantly correlated when just these two variables were considered (.20 on Table 16.5), age was not significant (.12) when all other variables were controlled. In fact, age remained a significant variable only for anxiety and GSI. In addition, the amount of variation in distress rates that is explained by age plus the other demographic variables was very small (5 percent for anxiety and 9 percent for GSI), indicating that neither age nor other sociodemographic characteristics help to predict distress rates.

TABLE 16.6
Regressions of Five Distress Measures upon Demographic Characteristics[1] for a Random Community Sample of Older Adults[2]

	General Distress[3]	Depression	Anxiety	Somatization	General Malaise[4]
Female (0,1)	23.16	.21	8.06	1.15	−13.23
White (0,1)	8.27	1.88	.97	1.89	−4.29
Age (in years)	.75*	.12	−.17***	.09	.16
Age X gender	−.43	−.01	−.13*	−.05	.14
Married (0,1)	−8.35	−1.17	−.92	−1.67	−2.97
Married X gender	10.05	.58	1.06	1.93	4.67
Education (in years)	.18	−.001	.07	−.16	−.15
Income[5]	−.84	−.19	−.22*	−.08	.26
Intercept	−31.61	−4.90	−10.00**	.01	29.42*
R^2	.05	.07	.09	.05	.04
F value	2.08*	2.76**	3.66***	2.11*	1.42
N	311	310	309	311	312

*$p <= .05$
**$p <= .01$
***$p <= .001$

1. Unstandardized regression coefficients are presented. N's vary due to missing values on some variables.
2. N = 313 respondents age 65 and over.
3. General Distress or GSI reflects the mean score for all 90 symptoms (number and frequency) reported on the SCL-90-R.
4. General Malaise is the Rand HIS General Well-Being Scale reversed.
5. Income coded as follows:

1-under 3,000;	6-11,000 to < 13,000;	11-21,000 to < 23,000;
2-3,000 to < 5,000;	7-13,000 to < 15,000;	12-23,000 to < 25,000;
3-5,000 to < 7,000;	8-15,000 to < 17,000;	13-25,000 to < 30,000;
4-7,000 to < 9,000;	9-17,000 to < 19,000;	14-30,000 to < 35,000;
5-9,000 to < 11,000;	10-19,000 to < 21,000;	15-35,000 and over.

In sum, these data provide strong evidence that among older adults, neither age nor other background variables are important factors in accounting for distress rates. Clearly, there are many factors yet to be examined which may explain distress. Among them are physical health, social support, organizational activities, and mobility, all of which may decline with advanced age and thus contribute to the significant increase in distress among those age 75 and over.

Conclusion

The preceding discussion should not be the basis for dismissing or even minimizing the mental health problems of late life. It is hardly appropriate to trivialize a 9 to 11 percent rate for psychiatric disorders in any age group. Indeed, a problem that affects 2.5 million people is a major social problem. On the other hand, the preceding analysis clearly demonstrates the need to put matters into perspective. For too long, the idea that mental health problems are more prevalent among older then younger adults or the idea that these problems are an integral part of the aging process have been accepted as valid. These findings expose those perceptions as "scientific myths." Like other myths that have been socially constructed, it is time to replace them with reality. One reality is based on the preponderance of studies that show either no age differences or more distress among younger adults. Another reality is that age and other sociodemographic characteristics are not powerful predictors of distress. As with other stereotypes of older adults, the myth of increasing mental disorders needs to be exposed. These findings provide the basis for undermining perceptions that have permeated the society, passed for gerontological truth, and had major implications for both older and younger adults.

Notes

Funding for this research was provided by the National Institute of Mental Health, MH16242; Department of Health and Human Services, Administration on Aging, OHD90AT2006/1; NIMH Technical Assistance Grant, Region II, 3/1/80-2/28/81; Community Mental Health Center of Rutgers Medical School, UMDNJ; Middlesex County Mental Health Administration and Comprehensive Training and Employment Act.

1. The authors correctly distinguish between depressive symptoms and depression which is based on a diagnosis. However, they state that depressive symptoms are more frequent after age 65. That statement is not supported by the studies presented in this chapter.
2. Epidemiological information has been gathered and summarized from a number of sources including Blazer (1980) and Dohrenwend (1983).

3. For a full discussion see Mechanic (1980, esp. Chs. 2, 6).
4. An earlier study by Bellin and Hardt (1958) has not been included because respondents were assigned mental impairment status according to whether they were certifiable for mental hospital admissions.
5. Definite impairment rate determined as seven or more symptoms while probable impairment rate reflects four or more symptoms.
6. The alpha coefficients reflecting internal consistency were .83 for depression, .80 for anxiety and somatization, and .95 for overall distress, GSI.
7. Coefficient alpha for this scale was .90, comparable to the .93 reported by the developer.
8. Only the rates for Comstock and Helsing's (1976) White samples are used in this comparison, since Whites comprise the majority of respondents in other studies.
9. The implication of the original finding is that Blacks showed up as more distressed than Whites because they are more likely to have lower incomes, lower educational levels, and be unmarried — all variables associated with psychological distress.
10. In addition, race, in combination with other demographic variables, explained a relatively small amount of variation in the five distress measures (Warheit et al., 1975:254).

References

Bellin, S.S., and R.H. Hardt. 1958. "Marital Status and Mental Disorders among the Aged." *American Sociological Review* 23(1):155-62.
Berkman, P.L. 1971. "Measurement of Mental Health in a General Population Survey." *American Journal of Epidemiology* 94:105-11.
Blazer, D. 1980. "The Epidemiology of Mental Illness in Late Life." In *Handbook of Geriatric Psychiatry,* ed. E.W. Busse and D.G. Blazer. New York: Reinhold.
Blazer, D., and C.D. Williams. 1980. "Epidemiology of Dysphoria and Depression in an Elderly Population." *American Journal of Psychiatry* 137(4):439-44.
Cohen, G.D. 1980. "Prospects for Mental Health and Aging." In *Handbook of Mental Health and Aging,* ed., J.E. Birren and R.B. Sloane. Englewood Cliffs, N.J.: Prentice-Hall.
Comstock, G.W., and K.J. Helsing. 1976. "Symptoms of Depression in Two Communities." *Psychological Medicine* 6(4):551-63.
Derogatis, L.R., R.S. Lipman, K. Rickels, E.H. Uhlenhuth, and L. Covi. 1973. "The Hopkins Symptom Checklist (HSCL): A Self-Report Symptom Inventory." *Behavioral Science* 19:1-15.
Dohrenwend, B.P. 1983. "The Epidemiology of Disorders." In *Handbook of Health, Health Care, and the Health Professions,* ed. D. Mechanic. New York: Free Press.
Dohrenwend, B.P., and B.S. Dohrenwend. 1982. "Perspectives on the Past and Future of Psychiatric Epidemiology." *American Journal of Public Health* 72(11):1271-79.
Frerichs, R.R., C.S. Aneshensel, and V.A. Clark. 1981. "Prevalence of Depression in Los Angeles County." *American Journal of Epidemiology* 113(6):691-99.
Gaitz, C.M., and J. Scott. 1972. "Age and the Measurement of Mental Health." *Journal of Health and Social Behavior* 13(1):55-67.

George. L.K., R. Landerman, and M.L. Melville. 1983. "Age Differences in the Relationships between Physical Illness and Psychiatric Disorder." Paper presented at the 36th Annual Meeting of the Gerontological Society of America, San Francisco, California.

Gurin, G., F. Veroff, and S.C. Feld. 1960. *Americans View Their Mental Health.* New York: Basic Books.

Gurland, B.J. 1976. "The Comparative Frequency of Depression in Various Adult Age Groups." *Journal of Gerontology.* 31(3):283-92.

Gurland, B.J., J. Copeland, J. Kuriansky, M. Kelleher, L. Sharpe, and L.L. Dean. 1983. *The Mind and Mood of Aging.* New York: Haworth.

Haberman, P.W. 1970. "Ethnic Differences in Psychiatric Symptoms Reported in Community Surveys." *Public Health Reports* 85(6):495-502.

Haug, M.R., and L.D. Breslau. 1983. "Preface." In *Depression and Aging: Causes, Care, and Consequences,* ed. L.D. Breslau and M.R. Haug. New York: Springer.

Hogarty, G.E., and M.M. Katz. 1971. "Norms of Adjustment and Social Behavior." *Archives of General Psychiatry.* 25(5):470-80.

Klerman, G.L. 1983. "Problems in the Definition and Diagnosis of Depression in the Elderly." In *Depression and Aging: Causes, Care, and Consequences,* ed. L.D. Breslau and M.R. Haug. New York: Springer.

Kovar, M.G. 1980. "Morbidity and Health Care Utilization." In Second Conference on the Epidemiology of Aging, ed. S.G. Haynes and M. Feinleib. U.S. Department of Health and Human Services, Public Health Service, NIH Publ. no. 80-969.

Lowenthal, M.F., P.L. Berkman, and Associates. 1967. *Aging and Mental Disorder in San Francisco: A Social Psychiatric Study.* San Francisco: Jossey-Bass.

Mechanic, D. 1980. *Mental Health and Social Policy,* 2nd ed. Englewood Cliffs, N.J.: Prentice-Hall.

———. 1978. *Medical Sociology,* 2nd ed. New York: Free Press.

Mental Health and the Elderly: Recommendations for Action. 1978. The Reports of the President's Commission on Mental Health: Task Panel on the Elderly and the Secretary's Committee on Mental Health and Illness of the Elderly. (OHDS)80-20960. Washington, D.C.: U.S. Government Printing Office.

Murrell, S.A., S. Himmelfarb, and K. Wright. 1983. " Prevalence of Depression and Its Correlates in Older Adults." *American Journal of Epidemiology.* 117(2):173-85.

Ostfeld, A.M. 1980. " Five Year Perspective on the Elkridge Conference." In Second Conference on the Epidemiology of Aging, ed. S.G. Haynes and M. Feinleib. U.S. Department of Health and Human Services, Public Health Service, NIH Publ. no.80-969.

Phillips. D.L. 1966. "The 'True Prevalence' of Mental Illness in a New England State." *Community Mental Health Journal* 2(1):35-40.

Pruchno, R., and M.A. Smyer. 1983. "Mental Health Problems and Aging: A Short Quiz." *International Journal of Aging and Human Development* 17(2):123-40.

Rand Health Insurance Study. R.H. Brooks, J.E. Ware, Jr., A. Davies-Avery, A.L. Steward, DC.A. Donald, W.H. Rogers, K.N. Williams, and S.A. Johnston. 1979. "Overview of Adult Health Status Measures Fields in Rand's Health Insurance Study." *Medical Care* 17 (7, July).

Redick, R.W., and C.A. Taube. 1980. "Demography and Mental Health Care of the Aged." In *Handbook of Mental Health and Aging,* ed. J.E. Birren and R.B. Sloane. Englewood Cliffs, N.J.: Prentice-Hall.

Sayetta, R.B., and D.P. Johnson. 1980. "Basic Data on Depressive Symptomatology: U.S. 1974-75." *Vital and Health Statistics,* series 11, no. 216. DHEW Publication no. PHS 80-1666.

Schwab, J.J., E.B. Fennell, and G.J. Warheit. 1974. "The Epidemiology of Psychosomatic Disorders." *Psychosomatics* 15(2):88-93.

Shanas, E., and G.L. Maddox. 1976. "Aging, Health, and the Organization of Health Resources." In *Handbook of Aging and the Social Sciences,* ed. R.H. Binstock and E. Shanas. New York: D. Van Nostrand.

Srole, L., and A.K. Fischer. 1980. "The Midtown Manhattan Longitudinal Study vs. 'The Mental Paradise Lost Doctrine.'" *Archives of General Psychiatry* 37 (2, February): 209-21.

Srole, L., T. Langner, S. Michael, M. Opler, and T. Rennie. 1962. *Mental Health in the Metropolis: The Midtown Manhattan Study,* vol. 1. New York: McGraw Hill.

Thoits, P.A., and M. Hannan. 1979. "Income and Psychological Distress: The Impact of an Income Maintenance Experiment." *Journal of Health and Social Behavior* 20:120-38.

Uhlenhuth, E.H., M.B. Balter, G.D. Mellinger, I.H. Cisin, and J. Clinthorne. 1983. "Symptom Checklist Syndromes in the General Population." *Archives of General Psychiatry* 40:1167-73.

Veroff, J., E. Douvan, and R.A. Kulka. 1981. *The Inner American: A Self-Portrait from 1957 to 1976.* New York: Basic Books.

Warheit, G.J., C.E. Holzer, and S.A. Arey. 1975. "Race and Mental Illness: An Epidemiologic Update." *Journal of Health and Social Behavior* 16 (3, September): 243-56.

Warheit, G.L., C.E. Holzer, and J.J. Schwab. 1973. "An Analysis of Social Class and Racial Differences in Depressive Symptomatology: A Community Study." *Journal of Health and Social Behavior* 14 (4, December): 291-99.

Weissman, M.M., and J.K. Myers. 1980. "Psychiatric Disorders in a U.S. Community." *Acta Psychiatrica Scandinavica* 62:99-111.

———. 1978. "Rates and Risks of Depressive Symptoms in a U.S. Urban Community." *Acta Psychiatrica Scandinavica* 57:219-31.

17

Gender Roles and Memory Loss in Old Age: An Exploration of Linkages

Elizabeth W. Markson

At birth and throughout the life span, women in the United States have a greater life expectancy than men and in old age far outnumber them. This is a relatively recent phenomenon. In 1930, for example, the proportion of older men and women in the U.S. population was almost equal. By 1980, however, there were 100 women for every 69 men aged 65 and over, and by the year 2000, this sex differential is expected to widen. Despite the growing number of older women, only recently have social scientists begun to address differences between the sexes in aging and gender-linked patterns of growing old.

That there are gender-linked differences in the experiential quality of aging is evident (DeBeauvoir, 1972; Markson and Grevert, 1972; Neugarten, 1975; Hess, 1980; Markson, 1983). In American society, traditionally there have been fewer events external to the family that cut short old women's social activities so that the role losses associated with growing old have been more gradual for women than for men (Cumming, 1963; 1970). The interplay between gender-linked roles, memory, and construction of the self seems intriguing. The gradual dropping away of social roles as children leave home, parents and husband die, and so forth texture the fabric of many now-old women's lives. Is this normative feminine pattern of role loss associated with the ways in which older women relate to others and recollect or forget the past? This was the guiding question behind the present inquiry which uses a case study approach to examine speech patterns, specifically pronoun use, by three elderly working-class women, all of whom had been labeled as mentally ill.

The Self, Memory, and Social Roles

The Self

Relatively little attention has been paid to the linguistic patterns of older people in general and to gender-linked and class-linked arrangements of speech in old age in particular. Yet language behavior is critical to all aspects of human functioning and, if G.H. Mead is correct, is key to formation and maintenance of the self. The self, according to Mead, is developed through social interaction. Through the process of role taking, each of us projects himself or herself into the role of another, learns to view one's self from the perspective of others, and to develop an "I" and "me." The "I" is the creative, acting aspect of the self that reflects upon and responds to the "me," that is, the internalized attitudes of others. The self thus is a constant process, in which the "I" interacts with the "me" in a constant mental dialogue, creating the perceptions which form the self-concept. As a result of this ongoing mental conversation, meaningful social interaction is possible.

Memory

Memory in old age, as throughout our lives, is a vital connecting link in developing and maintaining the self as it joins together past events with present and future actions. Some psychologists have distinguished between *episodic* memory, that is, isolated events or happenings, and *generic* memory, or recollection of general rules (Schonfield and Stones, 1979). Each episodic memory is a potential candidate for generic memory; that is, generic memories are selected from a large number of episodic memories. To form generic memories, each of us abstracts from an immense variety of daily events to develop more general "rules" to be stored for recollection.

Episodic memory, however, seems to be susceptible to decay unless the particular episodes or happenings are personally meaningful. What we remember or forget is thus a psychosocial product, for generic memory is not a candid photo of what actually happened but an imaginative portrait: a recreation of past events and interactions (Ornstein, 1970).

While there is a vast literature on memory loss (for example, see Schonfield, 1980 for a review), relatively little attention has been paid to sex differences in its occurrence. Yet women are twice as likely as men to be diagnosed as having severe memory loss related to organic changes in old age (Gruenberg, 1977). Is this greater rate of organicity among women in old age an artifact of their longer life expectancy, a reflection of the inevitable wear and tear of brain cells that would affect both sexes equally if men survived into old-old age as often as women? Or, is it a reflection of diagnostic practices or of imperfect tests that do not differentiate between different psychiatric problems in old age? The answers to these questions remain fragmentary and provocative. The difference between "normal" and "pathological" memory loss are as difficult to tease out as the reasons that they occur.

For example, there is apparently little or no *inevitable* deterioration in ability to recall material still at the level of conscious attention or in memory span until relatively late in life and that tends to be negligible (Craik, 1977). Logical abilities also remain intact (Blackburn, 1984). These findings are reinforced by experimental work (Diamond, 1978), suggesting that the nervous system has the potential to oppose marked deterioration with age. Organic changes associated with the aging process may be neither always necessary nor sufficient causes for recollecting the past and experiencing the present. Even among people with organic brain disease such as Alzheimer's disease, the process by which memory becomes impaired remains poorly understood. Nor is very old age in itself a reliable indicator of either memory loss or lack of sense of a personal future. Rather, a sense of the future coupled with a review of one's past life (Butler, 1963) seem necessary for optimum aging for either sex. For example, centenarians who have successfully dealt with their own pasts tend to have plans for the future while those without command over their pasts are unlikely to have a concept of themselves beyond the present (Costa and Kastenbaum, 1967).

Social Roles

It is by now a tired truism to note that gender roles in the United States (as elsewhere) have been segregated. Despite gains made by the women's movement, recent research has shown that adult females today have been socialized to be more nurturant, obedient, and dependent on others for feelings of self-worth and identity than are men (Weitzman, 1980; Foxley, 1981). The identity of adult women has generally been defined by their domestic and familial rather than occupational or other roles (Oakley, 1974). For the now-old working-class woman, her career pattern may indeed have been employment-wife/ mother-employment (Harris, 1983), but her major, culturally approved sources of gratification and indeed sense of self were familial. Other sources of selfhood were considered less socially legitimated (Rubin, 1976).

In old age, when key family roles diminish, many women who have relied heavily on their families as sources of indentity are placed in an *anomic* or normless situation where they lack the touchstones to maintain their identity. Bart (1970) has described one such situation: the depression of the "empty nest" middle-aged supermom who has no one left to mother. The role loss that such women experience in midlife also colors their old age, for, among now-old women at any rate, their self-esteem still appears heavily dependent upon their life events (Turner, 1980). Put another way, social role loss in old age may lead to anomie, especially for those women with limited social roles upon which to draw. For both sexes, social roles are the mechanism for integration of life events. When few meaningful social roles or experiences exist in the present, memory becomes increasingly important as a source of selfhood. Yet this is a double-edged sword, for without meaningful present roles to frame one's past experiences, or to anticipate the future, memory is likely to be constructed of past, uninte-grated, relatively meaningless relationships, which in turn lead to a nar-rowing of horizons and inability to take the role of the other. In sum, the self-reflexive process described by Mead slows down; episodic memories may decay since present events have no interest, and the touchstones of recollection become impaired. Memory loss, regardless of its origin, may be viewed as a type of anomie: the loosening of social constraints and norms on rationality (Delay, 1970).

In social terms, regardless of its etiology, memory loss may be a way of coping with harsh reality. For those without meaningful social roles in old age, few resources outside one's self remain as a basis to assess the social world. Formal mechanisms for defining social reality have fallen away; life is now exactly as one constructs it. In this sense, much of what we term "senility" may be a social interaction and the reappearance of more primi-tive, unsocialized, emotional, or cognitive states.

Focus on elderly working-class women who have been labeled as men-tally ill (sometimes only because they were old) seems particularly relevant. Martin Roth (1971) commented that symptoms of obvious memory loss are much more common among those of lower socioeconomic back-grounds. There are no truly senile dowager duchesses, he suggested, for women of upper-class background seem better able to compensate for organic changes. They have extensive past role repetoires upon which to draw. A history of processing various social cues can be called upon, and a wide range of responses to various social situations has become habit. Women in the lower classes, however, have less resources upon which to draw; they have in general more years of widowhood, harder, often unre-warding work, lower incomes, and more constricted life spaces. Since expe-riencing of the present relies heavily upon both memory and anticipation of the future, loss of either contextual aid makes past and present events more difficult to organize.

In viewing memory loss, two elements seem particularly relevant: rela-tionships with others and self-preoccupation. In the following analysis of three case studies, the degree of self-preoccupation, group affiliation, and object relations was assessed through an analysis of the type of pronouns (first and third person) used (see Gottschalk, et al., 1957). When older women withdraw more and more from obligatory social roles, they become more free to follow their own interests (or lack thereof) at their own speed. If a person is focused primarily upon herself, it seems reasonable to expect that her speech will show a high usage of first-person-singular pronouns. Feelings of affiliation with others (or "we-ness") will be characterized by first-person-plural pronouns; object relationships may be identified by third-person (singular or plural) pronouns. Erik Erikson (1959) has suggested that old age is the final stage of personal development, involving the crisis of identity versus despair. Identity encompasses a sense of comradeship with "mankind" and "my kind" (sic—Erikson's theory was developed primarily on men) while self-absorption and despair go hand and hand. Comparison of the types of pronouns used to all pronouns used in conversational speech were analyzed in the following three case studies to provide a measure of self and group affiliation.

Three Case Studies of Memory and Self/Other Relatedness

As part of a larger study, three elderly, white, working-class women who had been admitted in old age for the first time to a mental hospital were asked: "tell me about your friends." "Friends" was chosen as a topic for discussion while allowing each woman to provide as much or as little detail as she chose. In addition, the subject of "friends" was expected to provide potentially high levels of group affiliation and object relations inasmuch as women are more likely than men to have an intimate friend who complements and supplements kinship networks in old age (Hess and Markson, 1980). Friendship relations are also conducive to high morale and life satisfaction in old age (Hess, 1977). Each interview was tape-recorded and transcribed. The number of words used to describe friends was counted, as were the number and types of pronouns (first person singular, first person plural, and third person singular and plural) for each of the three respondents.

In addition to information on friends, the interview covered a variety of topics and past social roles. Factual data were also compiled, including information from clinical case records, to provide a basis for assessing significant life events and their social context. The following cases are presented to illustrate the way in which an analysis of pronouns may be used to shed light on self/other preoccupations of elderly women and how these relate to memory loss.

Case 1: Gertrude

Gertrude was a 76-year-old Jewish woman at the time of interview. Born in Poland where she never attended school, she came to the United States in her teens and began to work as a seamstress. Widowed at 50, she then took in work, making wigs, to support herself and her children. She has had several physical illnesses within the past few years, including a stroke four years ago, high blood pressure, an umbilical hernia, cataracts, and a dislocated shoulder. She was admitted to a state mental hospital four years prior to the interview after attempting suicide following her first and only stroke. At the time of her interview, she resided in a board-and-care home, where both mental patients and "normal" elderly lived.

Gertrude described herself: "I am a terrible jealous person . . . so what can I do?" She recalled that prior to her hospitalization, "everything was mine. Jealousy eats up my whole existence. I was always like this. Now it's more because I'm disabled."

She commented about her roommate: "You know, the roommate is sick. She cries and she yells; she don't want to eat, and she don't come down for meals. She makes me also unhappy. I'm out of luck, what can I do? I would choose a roommate she could help me a little, not crying. She says it's her health, it's her eye, it's her heart; she only wants to die—She can't sleep, she cries, she moans; she makes me unhappy. I can't help her! I want they [the management] should give me another but I can't ask."

Despite her unhappiness and sense of powerlessness with her current life, Gertrude is a keen observer of the world around her and sharp social commentator on life in the home. She is oriented to time, place, and person and lives in the present. She is fully ambulatory and has no obvious impairment from her stroke four years ago.

Case 2: Kathleen

Kathleen, born in Ireland, was 84 when interviewed. She received a fifth-grade education, was sporadically employed as a domestic, and is widowed. She was admitted to a state mental hospital because her family could not cope with her; she allegedly turned on the gas jets, talked with her dead mother, and threatened her grandchildren with a cane. No major physical illnesses have been noted since her admission. At the time of interview, she was living on a geriatric ward at a state hospital where she was ambulatory and a potential candidate for placement in the board-and-care home where Gertrude lived.

Kathleen describes herself: "We are very happy, darling; we worked well, and we're very much loved for our good work. . . . They loved my way of working, darling. We do everything we think is right." Kathleen made no clear specific references to identifiable persons throughout the interview. She mentioned that she came from a large family but was confused about the names of brothers, sisters, and children and does not recall their exact number. There were hints of many unhappy past events, such as an alcoholic husband who died and left her with a family to support, and a forced marriage. As she observed: "If I don't start thinking about my home and my mother, I'm all right because we love the people and are happy, but when I start thinking about my dear mother, I don't feel so . . . "

Kathleen appears to live in an atemporal past where she is unaware of time, place, and person. It is almost impossible to tell who the "we"s in her conversation are. There seem to be few positive experiences in her past or present.

Case 3: Mary

Admitted to a state hospital three years before, Mary was a 75-year-old widow at time of the interview. She was born in Ireland, attended Catholic elementary school, and worked as a housewife. She was brought to the hospital by her daughter with whom she lived; the daughter complained that Mary suffered from insomnia and "hysterical fits." While not suffering from any diagnosed physical illness or disease, she is in what her medical record described as "fading physical condition" and seemed very frail. She was living in the same board-and-care home as Gertrude at the time of the interview.

Mary, like Kathleen, lives in the past but is fixed in time to her sixties, the age to which she most frequently refers. Although it is difficult to determine from her interview (which was characterized by "I forget"), her husband in fact died when she was in her sixties: "I miss my husband. But God wanted him and took him." Since his death, she has screened out most events and persons around her. She believes she is still in the mental hospital rather than the board-and-care home although the two physical settings are very different. About her inseparable friend, a woman with whom she spends all her day every day, she said: "Yeah, she's a good friend. I forget her name." Life seems nearly over: "Sometimes I worry about things, and sometimes I just don't want to think about anything. Think I'm going to die soon . . . I don't want to die. I want to live a little while longer. I can't do anything about it."

Comparing the number of words and usage of pronouns in each woman's discussion of her friends (see Table 17.1), several points emerge. The first is the relative talkativeness of the three. By far, Gertrude, who used 488 words in her description, was the most talkative; Mary, with 174 words, was the least.

Talkativeness was also inversely related to self-preoccupation: as the distribution of pronouns shows, Mary, who said the least, was the most self-preoccupied. About 73 percent of her pronouns were first-person singular, self-references. Kathleen also had a high level of self-preoccupation with 70 percent of her pronouns self-reference. Despite Gertrude's description of

TABLE 17.1
First Person Singular, First Person Plural, and Third Person of all Pronoun References in Discussion of "Friends"

Respondent	First Person Singular	First Person Plural	Third Person	Talkativeness (Total Number of Words)
	%	%	%	%
Gertrude	52	8	40	488
Kathleen	70	25	5	244
Mary	73	0	27	174

herself as a jealous, self-centered person, only about half (52 percent) of her pronouns referred to herself, perhaps because she complained so much about everyone in her present social world.

Examining first-person-plural references, Mary has no apparent sense of group affiliation or "we-ness"; she had zero "we" references. Gertrude, with 8 percent, had a very weak degree of group affiliation. Kathleen's references included a surprisingly high 25 percent of "we" references, a finding that should be interpreted with caution inasmuch as it is unlikely that she knows who comprise the "we."

Discussion

What may be concluded from this analysis? It appears that as self-references increase, indicators of group affiliation ("we-ness") and object relationships (he, she, they) are altered although not in a straightforward way. Mary and Kathleen demonstrate very strong self-preoccupation and little concrete sense of connection with others. Kathleen's relatively large proportion of references to the first-person-plural may reflect self-preoccupation as well for she has incorporated a vague notion of group affiliation into her self-concern.

In sharp contrast, Gertrude, who showed the least memory loss and the greatest awareness of her environment, used both first-person-singular (52 percent) and third-person pronouns (40 percent) but had relatively few "we" references, suggesting that her relationships to others are colored more by feelings of how other people impinge upon her than any sense of "my kind" in Erikson's terms.

Earlier, I suggested: (1) women are socialized to be more dependent upon others for a sense of self and for gratification which may be especially problematic for working-class women when their usual social roles fall away; and (2) high self-preoccupation may be associated with memory loss in old age. These three case studies tend to support these two premises. All three women, although in different ways, emerge as primarily self-concerned, and their references to other people decrease as memory loss increases. The relatively weak relationships with others in old age that Mary and Kathleen had suggest a narrowing and constricting of experiences: a paradoxical lack of identity despite strong self-preoccupation. Gertrude has maintained involvement with others if only as a source of annoyance but lacks any real sense of group affiliation. These findings hint at a sense of despair as proposed in Erikson's model of personality development.

Women who have had relatively limited life opportunities in the past and have few, if any, meaningful social roles available to them in old age, such as the three working-class women I have described, may be particularly likely to find old age a period of despair. Their language may, as was Kathleen's, be dominated by seemingly irrelevant references or by few utterances, as in the case of Mary. In contrast, persons with rich repertoires of real or vicarious experience upon which to draw may show patterns of enriched speech in old age. For example, older master story-tellers use greater elaboration of speech in rendering tales than do younger story-tellers (Obler, 1980).

Women such as Kathleen, Mary, and Gertrude were socialized in an era and as members of a social class where rich experiences—even as listeners to master story-tellers—were not readily available to them within the confines of feminine behavior. In one sense, they are "deviant cases"; that is, they differ from their age peers because they have been labeled as mentally ill in old age. Yet they represent a number of women who have experienced anomie associated with the limited options provided by their gender-linked roles. They have shared the same slice of history.

References

Bart, P.B. "Portnoy's Mother's Complaint." *Transaction* (November-December 1970).

Beauvoir, S. de. *The Coming of Age.* New York: Putnam, 1972.

Blackburn, J.A. "The Influence of Personality, Curriculum, and Memory Correlates on Formal Reasoning in Young Adults and Elderly Persons." *Journal of Gerontology* 39 (1984):207-9.

Butler, R.N. "The Life Review: An Interpretation of Reminiscence in the Aged." *Psychiatry* 26 (1963).

Costa, P., and Kastenbaum, R. "Some Aspects of Memories and Ambitions in Centenarians." *Journal of Genetic Psychology* 110 (1967):3-16.

Craik, F.I.M. "Age Differences in Human Memory." In J.E. Birren and K.W. Schaie (eds.), *Handbook of Psychology of Aging.* New York: Van Nostrand, 1977.

Cumming, E. "Freedom and Constraint in Old Age." Third annual Hugh C. Arrell memorial lecture, Hamilton, Ontario, October 19, 1970 (manuscript).

Cumming, E. "Further Thoughts on the Theory of Disengagement." *International Social Science Journal* 15 (1963):377-93.

Delay, J. *Les Maladies de la Mémoire.* Paris: Presses Universitaires de France, 1970.

Diamond, M.D. "The Aging Brain: Some Enlightening and Optimistic Results." *American Scientist* 66 (1978):66-71.

Erikson, E. "Identity and the Life Cycle." *Psychological Issues* 1, New York: International Universities Press, 1959, pp. 1-165.

Foxley, C.H. *Nonsexist Counseling: Helping Women and Men Redefine Their Roles.* Dubuque, Iowa: Kendel-Hunt, 1979.

Gottschalk, L., et al. "Verbal Behavior Analysis." *Archives of Neurology and Psychiatry* 77 (1957).

Gruenberg, E.M. "The Failures of Success." *Milbank Memorial Quarterly* (Health and Society) 55 (1977):3-24.

Hess, B.B. "Sex Roles, Life Course, and Friendship." Paper presented at Miami University, Oxford, Ohio, June 20, 1977.

Hess, B.B. "Old Women: Problems, Potentials, and Policy Implications." In E.W. Markson and G.R. Batra (eds.), *Public Policies for an Aging Population.* Lexington, Mass: Lexington Books of D.C. Heath, 1980.

Markson, E.W. (ed.). *Older Women: Issues and Prospects.* Lexington, Mass.: Lexington Books of D.C. Heath, 1983.

Markson, E.W., and Grevert, P. "Circe's Terrible Island." *Journal of Aging and Human Development* 3 (1972).

Neugarten, B.L. (ed.). *Middle Age and Aging.* Chicago: University of Chicago Press, 1975.

Oakley, A. *Women's Work: The Housewife—Past, Present, Future.* New York: Vintage, 1974.

Obler, L.K. "Narrative Discourse Styles in the Elderly." In L.K. Obler and M.K. Albert (eds.), *Language and Communication in the Elderly.* Lexington, Mass.: Lexington Books of D.C. Heath, 1980.

Ornstein, P. *The Perception of Time.* New York: Penguin, 1970.

Roth, M. Notes from a lecture to the NYS Dept. of Mental Hygiene, Albany, N.Y., 1971.

Rubin, L. *Worlds of Pain.* New York: Basic Books, 1976.

Schonfield, D. "Learning, Memory, and Aging" In J.E. Birren and R.B. Sloane (eds.), *Handbook of Mental Health and Aging..* Englewood Cliffs, N.J.: Prentice-Hall, 1980.

Schonfield, D., and Stones, M.J. "Remembering and Aging." In J.F. Kuhlstrom and F.J. Evans (eds.), *Functional Disorders of Memory.* Hillside, N.J.: Erlbaum, 1979.

Turner, B. "The Self Concepts of Older Women." *Research on Aging* 1 (1980).

Weitzman, L. "Sex Role Socialization." In J. Freeman (ed.),*Women: Feminist Perspective.* Palo Alto, Calif: Mayfield, 1980.

18

Work, Careers, and Aging

David A. Karp and William C. Yoels

A tradition of sociological research illustrates the centrality of work to personal identity. Occupation is a status that often supercedes other personal attributes in forming our self-definitions and others' views of us. In recent years, gerontologists have developed a wide-ranging literature on the place of work, and non-work, in the later years of life (see especially, Sheppard, 1976). To date, however, there have been few efforts to link up the literature on work and professions with the study of aging as a *life-long process*. By focusing solely on the aged, gerontologists have directed their attention to a specific group of persons at one point in their lives. In so doing, they have deflected attention from the ongoing processes by which persons occupying different locations in social space interpret and respond to varying messages about the meaning of age.

The central thesis of this paper is that our work involvement "frames" the ways we experience the passage of time. Work influences how we think about the present, anticipate the future, and thus is a significant cue for our "sense of aging" (Sarason, 1977). The meanings attached to chronological age are, in large measure, derived from or arise out of the interaction one has with his or her fellows at work. Those who pursue quite different work lives or work careers will hear different messages about the meaning of age. One's viability as a worker is in some instances vitally affected by age, and in others it is not. In most societies the work career and the aging career overlap. Different career patterns involve varying conceptions of what it means to be "on time," "ahead of time," or "late." The way individuals measure and evaluate their own life progress, and so their experiences of growing older, is significantly a function of where they are "supposed to be" occupationally at any given time. Since different work career curves exist, we postulate a variety of aging patterns.

In this article we will explore the implications of research on work and professions for our view of aging as a continual process. More specifically, we will examine the connection between career patterns and aging. As an important aid in examining these issues we also propose a generic, or underlying sequence of career "stages" that clarifies our understanding of how persons subjectively experience aging.

Career Patterns and Aging

The notion of career is central to our analysis since it is the nature of careers that, by definition, they are *age-graded*. Career is a most useful concept for helping us to understand the linkage between the varieties of work in any society and the age meanings that emerge in those work situations. Individuals whose adult lives from age twenty or so to retirement are built around particular career contingencies will experience aging significantly in terms of the age-related expectations of those careers.

In his voluminous and influential writings on work, Everett Hughes (1958) has shown the value of conceptualizing career as "the moving perspective in which the person sees his life as a whole and interprets the meanings of his various attitudes, actions, and the things which happen to him." Hughes certainly recognizes that there is an objective aspect to occupational careers; that there are formally prescribed stages to careers, often established within particular work organizations. Should one pursue a medical career, for example, he or she will inevitably pass through a predictable series of stages (Hall, 1948).

Hughes' definition directs attention to a second aspect of the career process. Based on communication with others in their work situation, persons attach subjective and evaluative responses to the typical sequence of movement constituting the objective career patterns they pursue. The notion of career is, then, not just a conceptual tool employed by social scientists to look at the nature of work. Career is a notion used by all of us to interpret where we are in the life course and how the things happening to us at any point in our lives make sense.

Whatever the specific occupational path we embark upon, the regularized career pattern associated with it helps us to evaluate our life performance to that point and also helps us to preview our likely futures. Persons feel uneasy if there is a discrepancy between where they stand in their careers and where persons their age are generally expected to be. In other words, success in a career, as judged by the individuals themselves and their colleagues, is closely connected with age. "One's career is 'working out' if one has 'made the grade' at the appropriate age. Getting there earlier gives grounds for special pleasure and a reputation as a 'comer' or 'flier.' Getting there late brings first anxiety then relief" (Sofer, 1970:53).

A number of factors may account for irregular career routes. Some may find themselves in organizational settings where their mobility is blocked because there are fewer places above them than persons seeking those spots. In such cases, individuals will feel stifled by the feeling that there is nowhere to go and that their future is limited. Alternatively, older members of the organization may die suddenly, opening up spaces and making possible mobility at a faster rate than might otherwise be expected. Some persons will be sponsored by someone above them and singled out for quick advancement. Others may deem it reasonable to transfer to units within an organization where they believe their chances for movement will be increased. At some point during their careers workers may come to recognize that they have achieved the highest position they will. As Howard Becker (1970:253) points out: "Even when paths in a career are regular and smooth, there always arise problems of pacing and timing. While, ideally, successors and predecessors should move in and out of offices at equal speeds, they do not and cannot."

In an interesting article on the subject, Robert Faulkner (1974) argues that *age* may be the fundamental variable along which career lines are established. Age defines the roles available and unavailable to persons within certain work organizations, and consequently affects the construction and meaning of their work commitments. In his piece, Faulkner is concerned with how individuals acquire career outlooks as part of the process of "coming to terms" with organizational structures that are "youth-intensive" and which produce very rigid career lines. To illustrate the interconnection between the career demands within certain occupations and our personal sense of aging, Faulkner draws data from two occupations: from the worlds of professional hockey players and orchestra musicians. Careers within these occupations raise special contingencies for those involved and force onto their participants an especially direct age consciousness. Listen to the words of a hockey player who recognizes the decreased probability of making it to the "majors" beyond a certain age.

> This is a business and they go with youth. I'd say that after 28, the odds are against you. . . . You take a look at what others are doing and you see where you are and with guys who have had as much experience as you've had, the guys in the same position as you are. My wife and I say we'll give it till 26 or 27 maybe, then I'll know if I'll be in the NHL. After that they give up on you (Faulkner, 1974:156).

In the second occupation studied by Faulkner, there are also concerns about making it to the "majors." In the case of orchestra musicians, making it to the majors means getting a job with one of only a select few city orchestras. As in any occupation, many who reach a certain age and take stock of their occupational position must adapt to the fact that they will not make it to the big leagues:

> Look, let's not kid ourselves. I'm nearly forty years old. I make a good living here, I do some recording work on the side, I'm not going to be first in the New York Philharmonic anyway, not at my age . . . [but] things could be worse, like being stuck in some bush league place with little money and no musical satisfaction.

As symbolic interactionists maintain, our selves are formed and transformed through interaction with others. Using symbols one learns to take on the attitudes, values, and moods appropriate to particular social circles. Through the reflected appraisals of others, we come to define ourselves as certain kinds of persons. This point is nicely demonstrated in an article by Bernice Neugarten (1968:96) on the acquisition of a middle-aged consciousness. She maintains that persons' awareness of middle age comes about through their recognition of others' definition of them as middle aged:

> Men . . . perceive the onset of middle age . . . often from the deferential behavior accorded them in the work setting. One man described the first time a younger associate held open a door for him; another, being called by his official title by a newcomer in the company; another, the first time he was ceremoniously asked for advice by a younger man.

Such examples lead us to amend the old saying "you are as young as you feel." Equally, and perhaps more precisely, "you are as young or old as *others* make you feel."

The data above also suggest that every occupation generates its distinctive career paths and consequently its own set of symbols and meanings of age. Those in any occupation are required to engage in a continual process of interpretation and reinterpretation about their current occupational position and its meaning. Periodically persons must assess the degree of their success, whether they are currently "making it" and their future chances for making it. These questions about career success and failure constantly call attention to age. Age consciousness, then, is "an aspect of occupational and organizational life whose centrality . . . has a paramount reality in experience" (Faulkner, 1974:167).

There is one further and related point to make here. Although our focus has been on the *variable* of career, we should stress that careers do not simply exist in the world as "thing-like" entities, mechanistically "causing" particular aging conceptions. A more accurate description of the connection between careers and aging requires a dialectical view of things. By causing us to focus on the aging process, careers become part of that process. Once occupation enters into our consciousness as a cue for interpreting our movement through the life course, it alters our conception and experience of the life course itself.

While we can name objective, structural arrangements associated with particular careers, we best conceptualize career as a process that is constantly "negotiated" (Strauss, 1978) by persons in their day-to-day working lives. Through the commonplace daily events and work-situated conversations that often pass as trivial by those involved in them (Gubrium and Buckholdt, 1977), career structures may be either sustained or modified. Each time that workers in an organization talk about how one or another event affects their careers, they produce a new, plausible conception of those careers. A number of such dialogues over time can create wholly new career "typifications" (Schutz, 1964) which workers then use to make sense of their day-to-day work lives. Following Gubrium and Buckholdt (1977), a phenomenological approach to the study of aging will attend to how career structures give rise to work-situated, age-related dialogues that consequently change the very structures which stimulated such talk. Among the objective aspects of career that constitute the "frame" for individuals' discussions and interpretations of chronological age are the following.

1. The length of the career ladder.
2. The extent to which the capacity to do the work is intrinsically related to physical attributes which decline with age.
3. The relationship between age and earning in the career.
4. The degree of personal autonomy in the occupation generally and at each career point.
5. The relationship between age and career mobility.
6. The nature and degree of intersection between work life and family life.
7. The age distribution of colleagues.
8. Whether the career requires the continual acquisition of new talents, skills, or information.
9. The extent to which one's career movement is influenced by changes (e.g., technological changes) in the larger society.

Although the factors named probably cluster together in predictable ways, they allow for many different combinations in different work settings. These variables would be central as the basis for more detailed empirical research into the work/aging relationship. Plainly the number of permutations and combinations of occupational, cultural milieus that define aging expectations and contribute to individuals' sense of age is staggeringly large. There are as many specific senses of age as there are specific career positions in specific organizations.[1]

Careers: A Generic View

To say, as we just have, that the number of subjective responses to work settings can be enormously large, need not paralyze our analysis of the connection between work, careers, and aging. We need not resort to a kind of individual reductionism that requires the description of each individual's special case. Social life would be impossible were there not general agreement concerning the meanings we give to objects, events, and situations (career situation being a major one) in our lives. There are collective definitions and shared meanings given to occupational careers which derive from the general expectations of the society. In the following pages we will analyze broad stages of working life that cut across occupational levels. Most workers go through a process that involves at least these "stages": (1) preparation and exploration, (2) learning the ropes, (3) coming to grips, (4) settling in, and (5) exiting.

In naming these stages we recognize that they simplify the nature of work lives. We also recognize that each of the stages we have named might be further subdivided into additional stages. We consider the stages named as a tool for guiding and organizing our thinking about the relationship between work and aging over the course of the life cycle. These stages will also provide a useful framework for ordering, pulling together, and showing the plausible connections between what are now two discrete bodies of literature—that on work and that on aging. To our knowledge, ours is the first effort in this direction.[2]

Preparation and Exploration

Our society, like other modern industrial societies, expects persons to seek work as a full-time activity only after they have completed a very long period of schooling. Although many leave school before graduating from high school, such "dropping out" is defined as a "problem." Americans consider it desirable to achieve at least a high school education, and in many quarters a college degree. The ante, however, keeps increasing and many occupational positions previously filled by college graduates now require graduate degrees.

The long period of education requisite for many occupational positions creates a situation where a large proportion of the population does not enter the work world in a full-time fashion until their middle twenties and sometimes later. In the case of certain professional careers which demand expecially long training processes, persons may not enter the occupational world on a full-time basis until their early to mid-thirties. On average, then, a considerable number of contemporary Americans spend about a third of their life *preparing* for the remaining two-thirds.

The long period of training prior to entering an occupation has significant implications for persons' developing sense of self, including their subjective view of their own age status (White, 1966). Until we have entered an occupation we are not considered as fully occupying an adult status. We might say that the long period of schooling in American society keeps persons in a kind of protracted adolescent "holding pattern." After all, it is through occupational involvement that we acquire the things normally associated with being an adult. Adults have control over their personal lives and this control is accomplished chiefly by having the economic resources that only a job provides. Those without work do not have the money to shape a life style and acquire the goods (an automobile, one's own apartment) that symbolize one's adultness to the world.

> A set of generalized attitudinal expectations about the relations of an adult male to the work world operates in our society. . . . At a given age (which varies in different parts of the society) a man is expected to have assumed a particular occupational role. Such adult responsibilities as marriage require him to have made arrangements guaranteeing the financial independence necessary for adulthood by making such an occupational commitment. With increasing age he is expected to behave "sensibly" and stick with such a choice once made, thus demonstrating his maturity [Becker, 1970:207].

Social scientists have constructed several models that attempt to describe the process through which individuals come to occupy a particular occupational niche. For example, in an early study based on biographical data from a group of middle-income children, Eli Ginzberg describes a progressive narrowing of their aspirations from a fantasy stage extending between ages six to eleven, to a tentative stage of adolescent vacillation to a stage of realistic choice beyond this point (Ginzberg, 1951). Other sociologists have examined the influence of such specific factors as social class (Blau and Duncan, 1967), peer group influence (Coleman, 1961), and the college experience itself (Jencks and Riesman, 1977) on occupational choice. Whatever the specific processes described in this literature or the variables stressed, the studies describe or imply a process through which the individual achieves adult status. Socially confirmed adulthood, we might say, is the end product of the lengthy process leading up to full entrance into the occupational world.

Learning the Ropes

The process of socialization does not stop in childhood. We are continually learning how to perform correctly the variety of roles that are part of being an adult. Especially in complex and changing societies, ". . . One cannot be socialized in childhood to handle successfully all of the roles he will confront in the future" (Brim and Wheeler, 1966:19). Socialization continues on throughout the life cycle. However, it seems apparent that the socialization we undergo in adulthood is more intense at certain junctures; one of these periods being the early years within the occupation we choose. Whatever work organization persons enter as fresh recruits, they must learn the ropes of that organization.

The period of learning the ropes is especially intense for new workers since they are being evaluated by superiors who may have a significant say regarding the course that their careers will take within the organization. One's whole career fate can be influenced by the relationships that one builds or fails to build with superiors. Plainly the question of power comes to the forefront when discussing the early career-building years of workers. New entrants are the least powerful members in the work setting and they must learn how to manage their subordinate status. As Daniel Levinson (1978) points out, the early career years are likely to be the time during which young workers, particularly in professional occupations, look to older workers as their role models. As Levinson describes it, these older workers, who already know the ropes and are in positions of power often become "mentors" who take an interest in, sponsor, and provide advice to the young worker.

> In the usual course, a young man initially experiences himself as a novice or apprentice to a more advanced, expert and authoritative adult. As the relationship evolves, he gains a fuller sense of his own authority and his capability for autonomous, responsible action. The balance of giving/receiving becomes more equal. The younger man increasingly has the experience of "I am" as an adult, and their relationship becomes more mutual. This shift serves a crucial developmental function for the young man: it is part of the process by which he transcends the father-son, man-boy division of his childhood. Although he is officially defined as an adult at 18 or 21, and desperately wants to be one, it may take years to overcome the sense of being a son or a boy in relation to "real" adults [Levinson, 1978:100].

Much is going on for the individual during these early years of his or her work life. Most primarily, the effect of the socialization at this career point is to increase the young worker's *identification* with and *commitment* to the occupational choice made. Gradually, the "junior" member of the work organization identifies more strongly with his or her work. This increased identification results from growing pride in the acquisition of new occupational skills, the progressive development of an occupational ideology, the sponsorship of older members of the occupation and, through interaction with others on the job, the internalization of specific motives for engaging in the occupation's work (Becker and Carper, 1956).

The complexities of the socialization process occurring during the early years of the career process is a substantial topic by itself. Suffice it to say that early career years constitute a period of intense involvement during which the young worker is actively building a life structure. In terms of our interest, it is a period during which one is made to feel "youthful." Having acquired an occupational identity, the person is accorded the deference associated with adult status in the larger society. Still, within the work context, being only on the first rungs of the career ladder, one is "the young man or woman" from the point of view of the older workers in the organization. During the years in which workers are learning the ropes, establishing a work identity and becoming committed, they are considered by others and by themselves as novices, apprentices, junior members of the organization, and so on. Such definitions contribute to an age consciousness of oneself as "young."

In a social psychological sense, age consciousness is significantly related to one's image of both the past and the future. The consciousness of the young worker we are describing at this point in the career route is exclusively on the *future*. These people are busy building their lives. They sense themselves at the beginning of a journey, the work journey, and are in the process of making and exercising their opportunities. They are still very much creating themselves, still "becoming" something. Theirs is a life trajectory that seems very much at its beginning and which they view as extending far into the future. The sense of change, movement, vitality, growth, and the emphasis on building for the future contributes to a sense of just "starting out," to a youthful self perception.

A turning point or transition in one's aging consciousness, the point at which one begins to "feel older," corresponds to that juncture in the work career when the basic structure of one's life has been established. It is the point when one has an occupational past to look back upon and when the general parameters of one's future work growth have been determined. Toward the middle of their career, persons develop a clearer sense of what they have, in fact, become. Now they are no longer the youngest members of their respective work organizations. They are no longer learning the ropes. Instead, they are probably teaching the ropes to the new recruits. They are no longer advice-seekers, but advice-givers. At this point workers must assess, interpret, and evaluate their career successes and failures. We are not suggesting here that persons stop experiencing work growth and change in their middle years (although some do), but that in their mid-life years workers acquire a clearer vision of the occupational identity they have created and must come to grips with that vision.

Coming to Grips

By the age of forty or so, workers have reached an occupational plateau. Whatever might have been their private dreams, aspirations, or fantasies, they must now acknowledge the realities of their occupational positions. By mid-life the lawyers who are partners in a small law firm know that they will never sit on the bench as judges; doctors in private practice know that they will not be renowned medical innovators; academics with a few publications know that their names will not be recognized by the great majority of colleagues in their field; factory workers on the line know that they will not become supervisors; supervisors of several years know that they will never wear a business suit to work. However far persons have advanced in their occupations, they pretty well know, by mid-life, how much change they can realistically expect throughout the remainder of their work careers. Certainly some new opportunities will arise, some alterations in work tasks can be anticipated, and there will still be regular increments in salary and status. However, the central parameters and basic forms of one's occupational life will have been established. As a result, many are, for the first time, sharply awakened to their own aging.

> When I hit 40, it was really a traumatic experience. As long as I was in my thirties, I visualized myself as a kid. When I hit 40, I really felt that I'd always viewed myself as a young guy who is doing pretty well, a young guy on his way up, and all of a sudden, I am not a young guy anymore. I cannot do things I once did. It's kind of scary [Levinson, 1978:170].

In much of the developmental literature on aging it is currently fashionable to describe the so-called "mid-life crisis." In fact, the idea of a mid-life crisis, as popularized in books such as Gail Sheehy's *Passages* (1977), has now become part of the public's everyday image of the mid-life period. It is hard to attend a gathering composed of persons approaching or experiencing their mid-life years without hearing some reference, often in a joking fashion, to the mid-life crisis. We suspect that the existence of the mid-life crisis idea, newly minted in the psychological literature, provides those in their early forties a way of interpreting any bad feelings they may be having. Of course, many persons in their mid-years do experience severe psychological crisis in their lives. However, we are wary of any view of human behavior postulating rigidly uniform human experiences. While we question the *inevitability* of crisis in mid-life, we would imagine that, at mid-life, all but the most unreflective persons must think about the congruence between what they hoped their lives would be like and the reality of their lives.

Data from other occupational contexts indicate that workers at all occupational levels redefine their goals during the mid-life period. A classic sociological study describing how blue collar workers create and are forced to redefine their occupational ambitions is Ely Chinoy's (1955) *The Automobile Worker and the American Dream.* The automobile workers studied by Chinoy deeply believed in the American dream of occupational advancement and success. For them, success was defined as eventually leaving the factory and becoming independent entrepreneurs. However, Chinoy's story is one describing how the workers come eventually to abandon hope in the dream. Over and over, he heard the words of those who, by age thirty-five, had relinquished plans for leaving the auto plant and had surrendered the dream. Their psychology is summed up by the worker who told Chinoy: "I've got a family and I can't take chances."

As they get older and pass into their forties, most of the men accept the fact that they will remain in the plant for the rest of their working lives. At this point, the focus of the workers turns to the steady pay that the job provides and their growing seniority. Ambitions to leave the plant are replaced by security goals. The central life satisfactions of the worker now come from outside the factory. Their families, their homes, their vacations, and their hopes for their children become the locus of their emotional investments.

Certainly it is not our intention to picture all mid-life workers as unhappily grappling with the questions of work meaning and satisfaction. Available data, however, do indicate that workers at all levels of the occupational structure must come to grips with the life structure they have built by mid-life.

> Mid-life is a confrontation between myth and reality. It is more like a war in which many battles or skirmishes are being fought. Death starts to take away parents, colleagues, friends, and loved ones. Marriage may become imprisonment. Children may not "turn out well" or they will leave for distant places, leaving emotional vacuums. And, of course, one begins to reevaluate whether one wants the future of one's career to be a continuation of its past, and in that battle is the question: What are my alternatives? [Sarason, 1977:105].

Settling In

Most of the available literature on work describes career experiences through the mid-life period. There is, however, a paucity of research on the experience of work during the decade or so following the mid-life period. We know very little about the way workers aged forty-five to fifty-five define themselves and their occupational lives up to the point when they begin to think of retirement. For some these might be the "glory years" when they are at the height of their personal power and influence. Following Levinson (1978), this may be a period during which workers become "mentors" for younger workers. For still others, these years may vary little from the experience of work in preceding years. Therefore, we are forced, in the absence of reliable data, to speculate on the meaning of this time period in workers' lives. Data exist, however, making certain lines of argument plausible. We suggest that during the forty-five to fifty-five year decade, many workers reevaluate how they will distribute their energies among work and other spheres of their lives.

Consider the type of data that persuades us that workers rearrange their commitments to work and other life spheres during "middle to late adulthood." While we must be wary of variations that remain hidden in any aggregated data (such as social class, ethnic, and occupational level differences), there is evidence that work satisfaction regularly decreases with age. In a recent article, Richard Cohn (1979) demonstrates a decline in "intrinsic" work satisfaction during the later stages of work force participation. As part of his own analysis, Cohn presents data on work satisfaction from two earlier studies, one done in 1953 and the other in 1971. The comparison provided in Table 18.1 shows: (1) a general decline in work satisfaction between 1953 and 1971, and (2) a systematic decline in each successive age group.

At the same time that work satisfaction decreases, as shown above, there is a corresponding increase in rates of participation in social and political activities (Smith, 1980). Persons in the middle age range have higher rates of voluntary action participation than younger or older persons (Verba and

TABLE 18.1

Percent Who Would Continue to Work if There Were No Financial Necessity, by Age of Worker (currently employed males)

	Study	
	Morse & Weiss[1] 1953 (N = 354)	Campbell, Converse, & Rodgers[2] 1971 (N = 652)
Age Group	%	%
21-34	90	82
35-44	83	81
45-54	72	68
55-64	61	57
Total	80	75

1. "If by some chance you inherited enough money to live comfortably without working, do you think you would work anyway or not?"
2. "If you were to get enough money to live as comfortably as you'd like for the rest of your life, would you continue to work?"

Nie, 1972; Curtis, 1971; Hallenstveldt, 1974). In his book *Participation in Social and Political Activity* David Smith (1980) also shows that with age there is a gradual increase in virtually all spheres of leisure activity. Even when researchers control for gender and social class, there is a regular and uninterrupted increase in such leisure time activities as participation in cultural activities, movie going and reading. Not surprisingly, the only leisure activities which decrease with age are those involving rigorous physical activity. Most important for us is the finding that the increased leisure activity *peaks* during the forty-five to fifty-five year decade.

We should repeat the caveat that the argument we are presently offering needs refinement. We should like to know more about the relative degree to which members of different occupational groups rearrange their priorities during the forty-five to fifty-five life cycle period. It should follow from the general perspective outlined above that the greatest redistribution of activity from work to non-work settings will occur in those sectors of the occupational world where dissatisfaction is highest. In other words, it would be instructive to see precisely the associations between work level, work satisfaction, and the nature of changed commitments to different life sectors.

In recent years a number of observers (for example, Oppenheimer, 1974; Estes and Wilensky, 1978) have described the effects of what they term the "life cycle squeeze." The "squeeze" arises from the situation where a man's resources are inadequate to meet the needs engendered by the number and ages of his children. Studies of how economic needs vary by family life-cycle indicate that an exceptionally high point of need occurs when men are in their forties and early fifties. Further, the squeeze, as you might expect, is greatest for blue collar and lower level white collar jobs. At these occupational levels, median earnings are highest for younger men. Their income during the later years when their children may be entering college, for instance, does not correspond to their needs. Alternatively, those with relatively high paying professional, managerial, or sales occupations are more insulated from this live cycle squeeze. Thus, there is a decline in personal morale that begins in the late forties and typically reaches its low point in the mid-fifties (Estes and Wilensky, 1978).

In the last few pages we have pieced together existing data reflecting the character of the work/family/leisure experience of workers during the 10 to 15 years after they have come to grips with their occupational position. Although we report that curiously little is known about this period in the life cycle, the data persuade us that much is happening; that it is a period posing its own unique problems and struggles for individuals. Perhaps the notion of the life cycle squeeze is an important connecting link between family life, work satisfaction at different occupational levels, and the way persons redistribute interests and energies during the middle forties to late fifties.

Exiting

When the work world has been discussed in the gerontology literature, the focus has been most primarily on the nature and consequences of retirement. Social scientists have compiled an enormous amount of data on such topics as the relationship between demographic changes and mandatory retirement policies (Cowgill, 1974; Riley, Johnson, and Foner, 1972), the extent to which persons view retirement favorably or unfavorably (Katona, 1965; Riley and Foner, 1968; Atchley, 1977), how retirement decisions are made (Barfield and Morgan, 1969; Palmore, 1964), the nature of the retirement process itself (Atchley, 1976), whether or not a retirement role exists (Rosow, 1974), and the effects of retirement on personal adaptation (Thompson, Streib, and Kosa, 1960; Streib and Schneider, 1971). As you might expect by now, the literature shows substantial variability in the meanings persons attach to leaving the work world.

We should not be dismayed by differences in the way that individuals approach the end of their work lives. Some workers, apparently increasing in numbers, look forward to early retirement, while others wish to maintain their occupational positions as long as possible. Despite the wide range of studies dealing with numerous features of the retirement process, we still "know very little about the complexity of the retirement transition *as it is experienced by individuals*" (Ward, 1979:203; italics added). We wish to know how leaving the work force makes one *feel* about his or her aging. Although this is a matter for empirical research, we speculate that, like becoming a grandparent, leaving the work force constitutes a significant transition to old age.

Whether workers have enjoyed their jobs or found them alienating, they mutually face a range of cultural definitions associating work, retirement, and age. First, since persons are often required to retire at a particular age (usually sixty-five years old) their attention is dramatically called to age by that concrete fact alone. Probably more critical to older persons' sense of age, however, is the recognition that, regardless of their physical and mental conditions, they must leave their jobs to make room for *younger* workers. In short, during the years immediately preceding retirement, workers hear a chorus of associates defining them as approaching too old an age to continue working. In addition, older workers face the stereotyped images of many younger workers that they suffer from declining performance because of poor health and intellectual failings. Although evidence does not at all support such stereotypes (Meier and Kerr, 1976), their existence nevertheless constitutes a social fact that influences interactions between older and younger workers, and so the aging conception of both.

In his frequently cited model of the retirement process, Robert Atchley describes a *pre-retirement period* that includes "a *remote* phase, in which retirement is seen by the individual as a vaguely positive something that will happen someday, and a *near* phase, in which individuals orient themselves toward a specific retirement date" (Atchley, 1977:154). As he describes it, the far phase may begin at the outset of the work career since even then there is the realization that one will someday leave the work force. We would, however, be most interested in learning just when the "near" phase begins for persons in different occupations and at different occupational levels. Many workers probably develop an "exiting consciousness" several years prior to actual retirement. It is, we presume, a consciousness forged by subtle changes in the way they are viewed by younger workers as they enter the later years of their working lives. The specific manner in which an exiting consciousness is constructed and impacts on workers' subjective aging conceptions should be a concern of future inquiry.

Conclusion

This paper began with the somewhat obvious assertion that the work we do is central to our developing identities, including our aging identities. From that base, our effort has been to elaborate more precisely on the way work shapes our sense of age. Central to our analysis has been the concept of career. Because careers are typically age-graded, they serve as constant reminders of where we stand in the life course more broadly. Career frames our expectations about what we should be doing at different points in our lives and becomes, for that reason, a yardstick against which we measure our life progress, interpret the past, and anticipate the future. Aside from showing the overall significance of work to the way we experience the passage of time, our analysis points to the mutually transformative character of persons' work and non-work lives.

Since we claim the importance of an ongoing, processual view of aging that relates our age perceptions at any given point to earlier constructed meanings, we examined the work-aging relationship over the whole life cycle. Thus, we proposed five generic career "stages" that help us to understand regularities across occupational levels in the way individuals subjectively respond to the work experience. We have tried to demonstrate how each of the work-life periods named corresponds to and fashions distinctive aging consciousnesses.

Our entrance into the occupational world makes us feel like adults. During the early years of our work lives we are made to feel youthful in comparison to older workers from whom we learn the ropes of our respective jobs. During the middle years of our lives we must come to grips with the discrepancies between our earlier dreams, aspirations, and fantasies and the reality of what we have "become" occupationally. Many of the problems and "crises" of middle age relate to confrontations between myth and reality. We proposed that the decade roughly following mid-life is a period during which workers reevaluate how they will distribute their energies between work and non-work aspects of their lives. Last, we reviewed literature suggesting how the anticipation and experience of retirement may constitute an important transition to old age.

Notes

1. The general line of analysis in the last few pages carries special interest for analyzing the career paths of women. Many women have delayed entry into the labor market until after their children have become school age. This had meant entering an occupation anywhere from their mid-thirties to their early forties or beyond. Given the rigidity of both age and sex role expectations, the women who violate both career/age and related gender role expectations may, in fact, be defined as deviant. Troll and Turner (1978:16) comment that "mid-life women are limited to what is perceived to be appropriate behavior for their age and sex; they are expected to be in step with the social clocks. To be off time is to be 'age deviant.' For a fifty-five year old woman to start work on a graduate degree or a forty-two year old woman to have a first child is considered to be 'age deviant.'" There are many unanswered questions about the increasing numbers of women in the age-career position we have been describing. What kinds of age-graded career expectations can these women have? How do they talk about and "typify" their careers? Do they experience status inconsistencies when they relate to much younger male colleagues higher in the status hierarchy? Do women think about careers and evaluate job success differently than men? These are among the questions for which we have little current data. Social scientists are only now beginning to understand how women are reshaping the work world and how they will themselves be reshaped in turn.
2. While we claim that the stages named above constitute a useful heuristic device for analyzing work at a variety of occupational levels, our discussion is skewed in the direction of white collar and professional workers. This is so because the available literature, on which our analysis is based, has attended most primarily to these groups. We also recognize that the following discussion glosses over the temporal experiences of those who do not conceptualize their work in career terms. Future investigation might profitably consider whether work is a more or less salient aging cue at different occupational levels.

References

Atchley, R. 1976. *The Sociology of Retirement,* New York: Wiley.

_____. 1977. *The Social Forces in Later Life*. California: Wadsworth.

Barfield, R., and J. Morgan. 1969. *Early Retirement: The Decision and the Experience*. Michigan: University of Michigan, Institute of Social Research.

Becker, H. 1970. *Sociological Work: Method and Substance*. Chicago: Aldine.

Becker, H., and J. Carper. 1956. "The Development of Identification with an Occupation." *American Journal of Sociology* 61:289-98.

Becker, H., and A. Strauss. 1956. "Careers, Personality, and Adult Socialization." *American Journal of Sociology* 62:253-63

_____. 1957. "Adjusting of Conflicting Expectations in the Development of Identification with an Occupation." *Social Forces* 36:51-56.

Blau, P., and O. Duncan. 1967. *The American Occupational Structure*. New York: Wiley.

Brim, O., and S. Wheeler. 1966. *Socialization after Childhood*. New York: Wiley.

Chinoy, E. 1955. *The Automobile Worker and the American Dream*. New York: Random House.

Cohn, R. 1979. "The Effect of Employment Status Change on Self-Attitudes." *Social Psychology.* 41:81-93.

Coleman, J. 1961. *The Adolescent Society.* New York: Free Press.

Cowgill, D. 1974. "Aging and Modernization: A Revision of the Theory." In J. Gubrium (ed.), *Late Life: Communities and Environmental Policies.* Illinois: Thomas.

Curtis, J. 1971. "Voluntary Association Joining: A Cross-National Comparative Note." *American Sociological Review* 36:872-80.

Estes, R., and H. Wilensky. 1978. "Life Cycle Squeeze and the Morale Curve." *Social Problems* 25:278-92.

Faulkner, R. 1974. "Coming of Age in Organizations." *Sociology of Work and Occupations* 1:131-74.

Ginzberg, E., et al. 1951. *Occupational Choice: An Approach to a General Theory.* New York: Columbia University Press.

Gubrium, J., and D. Buckholdt, 1977. *Toward Maturity.* San Francisco: Jossey Bass.

Hall, O. 1948. "The Stages of a Medical Career." *American Journal of Sociology.* 53:327-36.

Hallenstveldt, A. 1974. "Formal Voluntary Associations in Norway." In D. Smith (ed.), *Voluntary Action Research.* Mass: Lexington.

Hughes, E. 1958. *Men and Their Work.* New York: Free Press.

Jencks, C., and D. Riesman. 1977. *The Academic Revolution.* Chicago: University of Chicago Press.

Katona, G. 1965. *Private Pensions and Individual Savings.* Michigan: University of Michigan, Survey Research Center.

Levinson, D. 1978. *The Seasons of a Man's Life.* New York: Ballantine.

Meier, E., and E. Kerr, 1976. "Capabilities of Middle-Aged and Older Workers: A Survey of the Literature." *Industrial Gerontology* 3:147-56.

Neugarten, B. 1968. "The Awareness of Middle Age." In B. Neugarten (ed.), *Middle Age and Aging.* Chicago: University of Chicago Press.

Oppenheimer, V. 1974. "The Life-Cycle Squeeze: The Interaction of Men's Occupational and Family Life Cycles." *Demography* 11:227-45.

Palmore, E. 1964. "Retirement Patterns among Aged Men." *Social Security Bulletin* 27:3-10.

Riley, M., and A. Foner. 1968. *Aging and Society,* vol.1: *An Inventory of Research Findings.* New York: Russell Sage.

Riley, M., M. Johnson, and A. Foner. 1972. *Aging and Society,* vol.3: *A Sociology of Age Stratification.* New York: Russell Sage.

Rosow, I. 1974. *Socialization to Old Age.* Berkeley: University of California Press.

Sarason, S. 1977. *Work, Aging, and Social Change.* New York: Free Press.

Schutz, A. 1964. *Collected Papers II: Studies in Social Theory.* The Hague: Martinus Nijhoff.

Sheehy, G. 1977. *Passages.* New York: Bantam.

Sheppard, H. 1976. "Work and Retirement." In R. Binstock and E. Shanas (ed.), *Handbook of Aging and the Social Sciences.* New York: Van Nostrand Reinhold.

Smith, D. 1980. *Participation in Social and Political Activity.* San Francisco: Jossey-Bass.

Sofer, C. 1970. *Men in Mid-Career: A Study of British Managers and Technical Specialists.* Cambridge: Cambridge University Press.

Strauss, A. 1978. *Negotiations.* San Francisco: Jossey-Bass.

Streib, G., and C. Schneider. 1971. *Retirement in American Society.* New York: Cornell University Press.

Thompson, W., G. Streib, and J. Kosa, 1960. "The Effect of Retirement on Personal Adjustment: A Panel Analysis." *Journal of Gerontology* 15:165-69.

Troll, L., and Turner. 1978. "Overcoming Age-Sex Discrimination." In *Women in Midlife: Security and Fulfillment.* Washington, D.C.: U.S. Government Printing Office.

Verba, S., and N. Nie. 1972. *Participation in American: Political Democracy and Social Equality.* New York: Harper & Row.

Ward, R. 1979. *The Aging Experience.* New York: Harper & Row.

White, R. 1966. *Lives in Progress.* New York: Holt, Rinehart, & Winston.

19

Age and Stress: Processes and Problems

Leonard I. Pearlin and Clarice Radabaugh

The field of aging provides a rich vantage point for observing a number of fundamental concerns of social science. Social structure, social events, and social change all intersect in the aging process and underlie the psychological developments of people through the life course. But the very richness of the field of aging has contributed to the accumulation of substantive and methodological issues. In this chapter we shall attempt to develop a few broad critical perspectives on some of the more important aspects of research into the life course of adults and draw upon our own studies of the effects of potentially stressful tasks and challenges that people confront in their family and occupational roles.

Underlying our perspectives are a number of assumptions that need to be specified at the outset. One such assumption is that the developmental changes experienced by individuals across the life course are activated by changes in their social and economic conditions. This emphasis does not mean that early experiences or the individual personality have no part in adult development. It does mean, however, that personality factors by themselves do not provide a very useful explanation of how people develop unless such factors are viewed within the context of changing environmental circumstances. Conversely, it is difficult to predict developmental processes solely from knowledge of people's external circumstances. The coping repertoires and social networks of people and their personality resources all have a part in regulating the impact that life circumstances exert on adult change (Pearlin and Radabaugh, 1976; Pearlin and Schooler, 1978). In subtle ways, moreover, personality may direct people toward the very circumstances that will, in turn, come to affect them.

Essentially, then, the study of life span development must also be a study of what exists and what changes in the social and economic environments of people. Of course, there are many unexpected and unusual events having little or nothing to do with the more organized features of social life: one can be struck by an automobile while crossing the street, work for a firm whose funds were embezzled by its president, have a home destroyed by lightning, and so on. Thus, our second assumption is that, since there are so many circumstances that can alter people's lives, we must search for unified groups of important events and conditions. A principal research strategy we have used to identify these important life circumstances is to focus on *social roles.* It is around occupational roles, bread-winning, marriage, and parenting that people organize their perceptions of their lives. Furthermore, the losses and gains that people experience as they move through the life span are best understood in the framework of social roles. Indeed, it is through role gains and role losses across the life course that aging is linked to the larger social structure (Riley, 1976).

The boundaries of major social roles do not, of course, encompass all significant life experiences. But, if we are primarily interested in the developmental course of ordinary people engaged in a variety of ordinary life activities rather than in unusual individuals doing exotic things, the daily social roles in which people are engaged provide an excellent place to begin our inquiry. By looking longitudinally at the events and changing conditions that are organized around people's multiple roles, we are able to see the effects of historical time and personal time (aging).

A third assumption, evident from what has already been stated, needs only brief mention. Development is not limited to a particular age; the "formative years" are coextensive with life itself (Clausen, 1972). As Brim (1968) argues, "Socialization is continuous through life, for though individuals enter the adult world with some anticipatory socialization, the socialization experienced in childhood is not enough to meet the demands of later years."

However, despite our certainty that developmental processes extend through the entire life course, we are less certain about the very concept of "development" itself. It is not clear, for example, whether the concept implies progression; i.e., if it is a process leading to a better or more desirable state of being than that which preceded it. Such an implication may be found in some theories of ego development that confuse maturity with virtue (van den Daele, 1975). Our own use of the concept certainly does not imply the desirability of developmental changes, particularly as some changes involve psychological distress.

A second problem with the concept of development stems from its relationship to biological maturation in which the notion of adult development is confused with the assumption that changes involve a series of fixed stages, going from the simple and undifferentiated toward the more complex and highly differentiated, just as the biological organism matures

(Neugarten and Datan, 1973). There is nothing observable in social development that would permit us to accept this biological model. Among adults, certainly, there is little to support a view that development moves toward increased complexity—or that movement in one direction cannot later be reversed. The social and emotional development of adults is neither directly caused by nor patterned after biological development.

Our view of adult development, then, places a great deal of emphasis on external forces that affect individuals and especially on those experiences anchored in major social roles across the entire life span. Thus, we view developmental processes as emerging from the social transactions between individuals and the society at large. Within this perspective five specific issues are considered in this chapter: (1) the quality of the criteria used to measure development or change; (2) assumptions regarding the circumstances that contribute to change and development; (3) the need for comparisons between age groups; (4) the need for comparisons within age groups; and (5) the need for comparison through time. In discussing each of these issues, we shall use data from our own studies.

Background and Methods

Our data were collected in two waves of interviewing, the first conducted in 1972-73, the second in 1976-77. A sample of 2,300 people, representative of the urbanized area of Chicago, was originally interviewed. The initial inquiry had three major components: (1) an assessment of the daily, recurring problems and hardships experienced by people in their roles as workers and breadwinners, husbands and wives, and as parents; (2) the way people deal with such problems; and (3) a variety of psychological outcomes.

As part of the 1972 interview we asked people if they would be willing to be reinterviewed at a later date. Eighty-eight percent indicated such a willingness; in 1976, this time in collaboration with Morton A. Lieberman of the University of Chicago, we were able to reinterview 48 percent of the original sample. The social characteristics of the follow-up subsample, such as sex, race, age, education, occupational level and economic resources, differ only slightly from the original sample. The second interview focused on the same three topics as the first, but also included questions about crises and life-cycle transitions experienced by the respondents during the 4-year interval between interviews and, second, about their use of social resources in dealing with these events.

The two waves of interviewing, then, provide us with a rather large body of data, including accounts of role strains and their change over a 4-year period, reports of a number of disruptive life crises, and key life-cycle transitions experienced by respondents.

What Develops in Adult Development: Specific vs. General Change

The dimensions along which people are capable of changing are varied. They include, for example, the many aspects of mental functioning called "cognition" (the manner in which we shape and organize our thoughts and solve our problems). There is every reason to believe that cognition can be modified in adulthood, indeed, intellectual flexibility can change with the nature of one's job (Kohn and Schooler, 1978). Certainly, *values*—conceptions of what is good and desirable—probably undergo developmental changes, along with *ideologies* and attitudes (do people really become more conservative with age?).

There is evidence, too, that *self-attitudes* change during the transition from childhood to adulthood (Rosenberg and Pearlin, 1978); not only the broad aspects of self-image, but more focused concepts of one's self, such as those involved in masculinity or femininity, may be modified in the postparental portion of the life cycle (Guttmann, 1975). Elements of *lifestyle,* such as tastes and preferences in the use of material resources and time, are very changeable. Alterations in the amount (Cumming and Henry, 1961) and quality of *social interactions* (Lowenthal and Haven, 1968) and, of course, *adjustments to emergent health problems* also are among the observable changes in adult development. Our own research, finally, primarily deals with still another important variable, *emotional well-being,* an aspect of functioning that is quite sensitive to changes in life conditions.

This partial list of "dependent variables," potentially affected by changing conditions of life during the aging process, should suggest the difficulties of measuring how specific or how general any observed development may be. There are several ways to illuminate this issue, one of them by asking if the changes that people experience in one role produce changes in other roles, that is, whether a developmental alteration, such as psychological distress, is confined to the specific role in which it originated, or whether the development extends generally to other roles as well. For example, if an unfavorable occupational event produces anxiety, is the psychological effect confined to the job or does it generalize to other roles? If one were to adopt a strictly sociological view, one might reason that because roles are separated in time and space, the impact would be confined to a specific role. In contrast, personality theory would suggest a more general effect; people, after all, are whole organisms, they do not leave part of themselves behind as they move back and forth among their multiple roles.

In fact, the issue of the specificity or generality of effects may be more complex than either of these extreme positions. We know from our analysis of coping (Pearlin and Schooler, 1978), for example, that people often create a hierarchy of roles so that the roles that yield the most rewards are also most central in importance and those that are less satisfying are given less importance. One consequence of the hierarchical ordering of the different parts of our lives is that changes occurring in the more central roles are likely to affect those on the margins, but alterations in marginally important areas of life probably have little effect on those that are more important. Thus, for example, if we assume that family roles are of supreme importance to most people, they would be fairly resistant to changes occurring in other roles. But for the same reason, changes initiated in the family should have a strong effect on other areas of life. Therefore, the generality of developmental changes will vary according to the centrality of the role in which such changes originate.

Another aspect of the specificity or generality of adult development is concerned with the *multidimensionality* of change, that is, how widespread are the effects of change? For example, the effects of being fired or laid-off the job will probably be associated with a range of psychological outcomes. As one might predict threats to one's work life are highly related to anxiety and depression, both of which may be seen as representing overall states of psychological disturbance, as well as to a more limited measure of economic stress. Yet there are limits to the spread of effects. In this case, no relationship was found between losing one's job and measures of marital or parental stresses. What about self-attitudes? Here we have two measures, one of self-esteem and the other of mastery (the extent to which a person feels in control of the forces affecting his or her life). One might reasonably expect that involuntary job loss would have a negative effect on both self-attitudes. Although we find a limited sense of mastery, self esteem does not appear to be lessened.

These data provide a warning signal that conclusions about the generality of developmental changes must be carefully drawn. Research in this area that takes into account only a single role or a single dependent variable will fail to uncover the many dimensions along which important development might take place.

Sources of Change and Development

Contrary to much popular writing, the movement of people through the various levels of the age structure by itself does not predict processes of individual development. For example, knowing that someone has reached middle age is not enough to predict that the person will experience a "mid-life crisis." Merely being at the middle portion of the life span does not account for the inner upheavals that one may feel. We must combine knowledge of where people are located in the life span with knowledge of the events and conditions they are experiencing as a consequence of their locations. The problem with looking for such common circumstances is not that they are difficult to find, but that they are so plentiful they rather urgently need some theoretical clarification.

Several strategies have been used to identify the life circumstances that act as levers for change. One such strategy has been to focus on a single, key life event. The event may be the birth of a first child (Lemasters, 1957; Hobbs and Cole, 1976), retirement (Streib and Schneider, 1971), death of a spouse (Kastenbaum, 1969), or some other occasion that is automatically assumed to require a reordering of life priorities. The gaps left by studies focusing exclusively on single events have been partially filled by investigators using standardized instruments that score a large variety of life events (Holmes and Rahe, 1967). Efforts to assess life events in this manner have been criticized because of methodological flaws and because of their buck-shot approach to important experience (Brown, 1974; Rabkin and Struening, 1976). Despite the limitations of much of the life event research, it has succeeded in creating an awareness of a wide range of social experiences that shape our inner lives.

We still do not know how individuals actually organize their social experiences. In our own work (Pearlin and Lieberman, 1979), we have found it useful to distinguish three types of experience, based on the multiple roles that people play. One type is made up of events built into the life cycle itself; these are "normative transitions" in the sense that they are expected and scheduled ("on-time"). Examples include marriage in one's twenties, parenthood soon after, retirement around age 65, and widowhood for women in their eighties. A second type consists of unscheduled ("off-time") events. Some, such as divorce, may be quite widespread and commonly experienced, but one does not enter marriage with the firm expectation of becoming divorced at a later time. Job loss, early retirement, and young widowhood are also non-scheduled life events. The third and final type consists of relatively durable problems, frustrations, conflicts and other strains that are built into daily roles. Whereas important life events often involve movement in and out of roles, these strains are persistent; they do not have clear beginnings and endings in time, as do events.

Though these life situations are conceptually distinct, they often occur together in real life. For example, the retired population includes both former workers who are happy to leave endlessly frustrating job conditions, as well as people reluctant to lose employment. Some retirees will have the economic resources to enjoy an active social life, while others must struggle for economic survival in relative isolation. Our data indicate that the impact of the event—in this case retirement—is determined more by the *role contexts* than by the event itself. The same was found to be true of other events. There is every indication that the developmental outcomes of scheduled and unscheduled role losses or gains are affected by the durable characteristics of the roles, rather than the fact of transition itself.

The conceptual distinction among transitional events, unscheduled changes, and role strains has enabled us to identify which circumstances have the capacity to affect psychological functioning (Pearlin and Lieberman, 1979). First, with regard to *occupation,* we found unscheduled events—involuntary job disruptions in particular—to be most closely associated with a combined measure of anxiety and depression. *Marriage* has more complex outcomes: both the unscheduled events of divorce/separation and the transitional event of becoming widowed are associated with psychological distress. However, the most intense distress is found among people in intact marriages with persistent problems, suggesting that a disrupted marriage is not as psychologically damaging as a bad marriage that continues.

In the *parental* area, we found that normative events have virtually no psychological impact. Thus, the birth of a first child, the movement of children into school, and the advent of adolescence are experiences that parents seem to take in stride. Only the marriage of the last born has an impact, and this is to reduce distress. These findings indicate that theories that link the psychological development of adults to the life-course transitions of their children are missing the mark. Where their children are located in the life cycle is far less important to parent's well-being than what their children are doing with their lives, particularly failure to live up to parental expectations.

Thus, a wide variety of circumstances affects emotional functioning: life-cycle transitions, eruptive events, and the more durable structured experiences of life. Clearly, then, research into the emotional development of adults must take into account the number and range of potential influences and, second, must recognize that the forces underlying change in one role may be quite different from those that are most influential in another. These data also underline the danger of generalizing too widely from processes observed in a single role.

Inter-Age Comparisons of Developmental Circumstances

Some research issues are relevant only to particular age groups. To study the effects of entering the labor market or of retirement from it does not require a broad comparison of age groups. We know that the former experience is largely confined to young adults, the latter experience to old adults. In general, comparisons among age groups are not needed to understand the consequences of single events, such as these, that are closely bound to the life cycle.

But if, for example, we want to know whether the middle-aged are exposed to more profound changes than those in other age groups, or whether they are confronted with tasks that impose greater challenge to their adjustment capacities, or whether they undergo more self-redefinition than do other age cohorts, then we must have comparison groups. It makes perfectly good sense to conceptualize the life cycle as being made up of distinctive segments, but the distinctive character of any segment is visible only in the context of the entire age-differentiated society (Riley, 1971). When attention is focussed exclusively on a single portion of the life span, it is easy to assume that the life conditions and psychological problems we are observing are unique to the particular age under examination, which may not be accurate. In addition, the conditions experienced by members of one historical cohort may not be similarly experienced by other cohorts (people at the same stage of the life course but at different historical eras). Our data illustrate the value of interage comparisons. Table 19.1 lists life circumstances by the social role in which they are found and by whether they represent normative transitions, unscheduled life events, or relatively persistent role strains. For simplicity we have divided the sample into three age groups, the youngest composed of respondents less than 40 years old, the middle-aged being from 40 to 55, and the oldest being older than 55.

One would expect that age would be closely associated with transitional events since these are geared to the unfolding of the life cycle. Although it is important not to confuse chronological age with "social age" (Neugarten and Hagestad, 1976), the two are closely related. The life-cycle transitions in the various roles may not come at identical moments in the lives of people of the same age, but as Table 19.1 shows, there is a close fit between location in the age structure and location in the life cycle. This is reflected, for example, in the youngest group's being most involved in entrance into occupational, marital and parental roles. Conversely, older people are most likely to see their children depart from the home, while retirement and widowhood are primarily experienced by the oldest respondents. It is quite evident, therefore, that there are many linkages between chronological age and life-cycle transitions.

The age distribution of "off-time" life events is not quite as easy to predict as events anchored to the life cycle. It is not easy to predict the ages at which people are most at risk of being fired or laid off from work, yet we see in Table 19.1 that those under 40 years of age are typically *more* likely

TABLE 19.1
Life Circumstances in Different Social Roles by Age (% experiencing)

Life Circumstances	Age of Respondents		
	Under 40 N = 423	40-55 N = 390	55+ N = 290
Normative Transitions			
A. Occupation			
1. Entry, re-entry into job	15%	5%	1%
2. Retirement	—	3	15
3. Leave Work for homemaking	3	4	1
B. Marriage			
1. Marriage. remarriage	8	3	2
2. Loss of spouse from death	5	8	5
C. Parental			
1. First child born	9	—	—
2. Later child born	27	5	—
3. First child entered school	14	8	—
4. Last child entered school	14	13	1
5. First child became teen	16	9	—
6. Last child became teen	2	21	5
7. First child left home	2	17	3
8. Last child left home	—	5	9
Non-normative Transitions			
A. Occupation			
1. Being fired, laid-off	6	6	3
2. Demotion	2	3	1
3. Unemployed for health reasons	5	8	1
4. Change job or employer	14	7	3
5. Promotion	22	16	5
B. Marriage			
1. Loss of spouse through divorce or separation	7	3	1
2. Illness of spouse	6	7	11
C. Parental			
1. Illness of child	6	8	9
2. Death of child	1	1	2
Role Strains			
A. Occupation			
1. Job pressures, overloads	35	28	13
2. Inadequate rewards	27	29	19
3. Depersonalizing work relations	35	29	15
4. Stressful work environment	25	23	11

TABLE 19.1 (Continued)

Life Circumstances	Age of Respondents		
	Under 40 N = 423	40-55 N = 390	55+ N = 290
B. Marriage			
1. Non-fulfillment of expectations	41	37	27
2. Lack of reciprocity	45	48	48
3. Non-acceptance by spouse	38	35	31
C. Parental			
1. Unacceptable behavior	22	40	10
2. Failure to act toward parental goals	1	24	14
3. Disrespect for parent	21	41	12
D. Economic			
1. High degree of economic problems	37	32	27

than older people to experience this type of role disruption. So, also, do the unscheduled (but more desirable) events of promotion and job change typically occur early in life, declining markedly in older age groups.

In marriage, the youngest are again most likely to have the disruptive experience of either divorce or separation. On the other hand, serious illness of one's spouse is more likely to arise in the older groups. In the parental role there is little difference in the likelihood of parents of all ages having a very ill child. However, of the nine parents who had a child that died in the 4-year interval between interviews, a majority were over 55 years. The distribution of unscheduled experiences across the three role areas indicates that there is no single age group that has a monopoly on events of this type.

To examine the age distribution of the relatively persistent role strains, we compare the proportion of each group whose score is above the average for the sample as a whole. In the occupational area, we can see quite clearly that the oldest group is *least* likely to feel occupational strains, with the younger and middle groups more often experiencing work overload, low rewards, depersonalizing experiences with fellow workers and authorities, and working in a setting with too much noise, dirt or danger. In marriage, the freedom from strain of the oldest subjects is most evident with regard to the fulfillment of expectations. However, marital problems involving inequality in the give and take (low reciprocity), and an inability to realize one's "real" self in marriage are more equally distributed among people of different ages. In the parental area, finally, it is the groups in the middle years that most commonly have to cope with the kinds of strains under examination here. Problems concerning general behavior, the attainment of future goals, and a lack of respect for their parents do not yet surface among the children of young adults and may have lessened among the more mature children of the older parents. It would seem, however, that if there is a distinctly mid-life challenge, it is in the area of parenthood.

Overall, these age comparisons show younger people to be most caught up in transitional events involving role entry while older adults experience transitions involving role relinquishment. Key life-cycle transitions most often affect people at opposite ends of the adult age structure. By contrast, events that are more unexpected than the scheduled transitions are most apt to be experienced by younger people. And the most continuous problems and frustrations present in one's daily roles tend to decline at older ages.

These data illustrate how comparisons across different segments of the life cycle can clarify our views of any one portion of it. If we had looked only at the middle-aged group, for example, we would probably come away with the impression that the middle-aged are vulnerable to many conditions capable of arousing emotional distress. And, of course, this is somewhat accurate. What would *not* be known if we had observed the middle years apart from other years is that such experiences are found at each turn and twist of the life cycle; while there may be mid-life problems, the middle years do not represent the outstanding time of crises. In fact, the age group most vulnerable to the stresses of social and economic strains is young adults. It is they who are entering major institutional roles—work, marriage, and parenthood, all within a very short time span. As one gets older and more established in one's occupation, income usually becomes larger and more stable, one's children are less and less dependent, and marital conflicts have either been worked through or ended by divorce.

It should not be implied from these statements that the younger people in our sample will eventually resemble those who are currently middle-aged, and the middle-aged will come to experience the life conditions that now affect older people (Elder, 1974). Each age group lives through a set of historically unique circumstances that stamp each cohort with its own distinctive mark. The experiences of one age group cannot be taken as precise indicators of the future experiences of succeeding age groups. However, the historical differences that set cohorts apart should not obscure an important lesson to be learned from comparing different age groups: change and challenge occur throughout the entire life course and are not the exclusive experience of a particular age group.

Intra-Age Comparisons

As important as comparisons between age groups may be, those *within* age strata are often of greater urgency. Such comparisons, where they are systematically made, can reveal quite different developmental patterns among people of the same age. However, researchers emphasizing the life tasks that people confront at different stages of life or who are searching for what is uniquely characteristic of a life cycle segment, tend to overlook the differences that criss-cross the members of an age cohort (Erikson, 1963; Gould, 1972; Levinson, 1977). The recognition of such in-group variation requires that research be designed to sample from all major social and economic groups. We simply cannot learn about the developmental course of women of a particular age, for example, by studying only men of that age; nor can we learn about the poor by observing only the privileged.

Our data indicate that potentially stressful life-circumstances among age-mates are often experienced differently by people having different status characteristics. In terms of social class, for example, involuntary job loss is a highly distressful experience that does not occur equally among those having different locations in the class structure. The risk of being fired or laid off is highest for people in low status jobs. Moreover, this association increases with age, so that in the oldest group of workers the likelihood of job loss is related even more to lower levels of job skill than for younger workers. Thus, one highly stressful event is unequally distributed by social class, but the relationship between job loss and occupational status varies by age group.

There are other illustrations of how, within age groups, the occurrence of potentially stressful experiences largely depends on status characteristics. In each age group, for example, divorce and separation tend to vary with class position, being more frequent among those in the lower ranks of education and occupation. Certain parental strains, too, are linked to social class; thus, working-class parents are more apt than middle-class mothers and fathers to feel that their children fail to give them the consideration or respect that is due them as parents. In general, location in the stratification system has a crucial impact on both stressful conditions that people are likely to face and the coping resources available to them.

The same observations can be made with regard to sex; men and women who share the same ages may still live in worlds apart. We recognize, for example, that many elderly women are widows, while men of the same ages are likely to have spouses, but fail to explore all the developmental outcomes of this fact. Similarly, women move in and out of the labor force with greater frequency than do men. Thus, even when they are of the same age and in the same occupations men and women are likely to have had very different job histories and probably face very different job futures. Under these conditions it is very possible that the meaning and impact of current occupational life will not be the same for men and women. Research into the organization of the life course around occupational careers should consider not one or two career patterns, but a broad range.

Perhaps the greatest difference between the sexes lies in the ways each experiences marriage and marital problems. By way of illustration, women more than men feel that there is a disadvantageous imbalance in the give and take of their marriages, and this difference increases with age. There also is a greater tendency for women to feel unrecognized and unaccepted by their spouses, and this too increases with age. Thus, important life circumstances tend to be organized around people's statuses and background characteristics so that comparisons within age strata are necessary to an understanding of developmental change.

In fact, once such comparisons are made, the real challenge begins: to go beyond merely establishing relationships between a status characteristic and a dependent variable to explaining relationships. For example, although it has been known for some time that both women and people who were formerly married show more symptoms of depression than do men or people in intact marriages, it is only in recent years that research has begun to explain some of the social, economic, and experiential bases for these relationships (Radloff, 1975; Warheit, 1976; Pearlin and Johnson, 1977).

The important events faced by members of a particular age group are not so universal or so powerful as to override existing social and economic divisions within the cohort. People do not necessarily follow a uniform developmental path through the life-span and we cannot assume that the nature of the tasks that people confront at different ages nor their responses to challenges, will be similar. Although people at the same point in their lives will have much in common, such similarities often obscure our recognition that people who are differentially located in other social structures may be exposed to many dissimilar conditions of life. These conditions of life, in turn, help to regulate the kinds of experiences people have, the meaning they attribute to these experiences, and their efforts to cope with them. The net result is that there is likely to be at least as much variation as sameness among people of the same age. There are as many patterns of development and change within a cohort as there are important social and economic groups contained in the cohort.

Comparisons through Time

Ideally, research into developmental processes should avoid assuming that external events precede and influence psychological states. An appropriate research design would observe psychological functioning before and after the event under study. Only thus can *change* be measured, particularly when studying development—a concept that refers to a state that is not the same at a later time as it was at an earlier time. The very idea of development calls for longitudinal research.

There is a second aspect of research into development that calls for comparisons across time: the fact that age cohorts move through the unique historical conditions that may exist for a limited period of time. This means that one cohort cannot be used to derive universal "stages" or as the standard for judging the character of succeeding groups as they reach that age. We cannot look at people who are presently 60 in order to learn how 20-year-olds will behave 40 years from now. Age cannot be used as a substitute for the passage of history. Consequently, if we want to study developmental processes we must compare the same people over time. Moreover, these longitudinal studies should not be limited to the features of development we happen to be interested in, but should include also the external conditions that affect internal states. At the same time that we examine shifts in psychological functioning we need to search for prior changes in life conditions. A well-designed study should reveal as much about social organization as it does about personal development.

Conclusion

This paper identifies some of the desirable directions for future research into social aspects of aging. The freshness of the field, combined with the rising interest among researchers coming from diverse backgrounds, insures that for some time in the future more questions will be generated than answered. Under these conditions, it is doubtful that there will be—or should be—any widespread agreement concerning either the theoretical importance of substantive issues or the best research approaches to these issues.

Social research into aging and adult development faces formidable problems by virtue of having to consider very diverse forces longitudinally. Some of these are historical, some concern broad features of social organization, some have to do with the events that unexpectedly surface in the lives of people, some involve the changes built into the life cycle, and—very importantly—some concern the active efforts of people to reconcile and cope with the many circumstances they confront throughout adulthood. To sort out the multiple elements that affect behavior, cognition, and emotional well-being across space and through time is indeed a challenge. Yet, it is a challenge whose rewards are potentially great, for it joins two central concerns of social scientists: social change and change in individuals.

References

Brim, Orville G., Jr. 1968. "Adult Socialization." In John Clausen (ed.), *Socialization and Society*. Boston: Little, Brown, pp. 182-226.

Brown, B. Bradford. 1978. "Social and Psychological Correlates of Help-Seeking Behaviors among Urban Adults." *American Journal of Community Psychology* 6:425-39.

Brown, George W. 1974. "Meaning, Measurement and Stress of Life Events." In B.S. Dohrenwend and B.P. Dohrenwend (eds.), *Stressful Life Events*. New York: Wiley, pp. 217-43.

Clausen, John A. 1971. "The Life Course of Individuals." In Matilda White Riley, Marilyn E. Johnson, and Anne Foner (eds.), *Aging and Society*, vol. 3: *A Sociology of Age Stratification*. New York: Russell Sage, ch. 11.

Cumming, Elaine, and William E. Henry. 1961. *Growing Old*. New York: Basic Books.

Elder, Glen H, Jr. 1974. *Children of the Great Depression*. Chicago: University of Chicago Press.

Erikson, Erik H. 1963. *Childhood and Society*, 2nd ed. New York: Norton.

Gould, Roger. 1972."The Phases of Adult Life: A Study in Developmental Psychology." *American Journal of Psychiatry* 129:521-31.

Gutmann, David G. 1975. "Parenthood: A Key to the Comparative Study of the Life Cycle." In Nancy Datan and Leon Ginsberg (eds.), *Life-Span Developmental Psychology*. New York: Academic Press.

Hobbs, D.F., Jr. and P.P. Cole. 1976. "Transition to Parenthood: A Decade of Replication." *Journal of Marriage and the Family* 38:723-32.

Holmes, Thomas H., and Richard H. Rahe. 1967. "The Social Readjustment Rating Scale." *Journal of Psychosomatic Research* 11:213-18.

Kastenbaum, Robert. 1969. "Death and Bereavement in Later Life." In A.H. Kutscher (ed.), *Death and Bereavement*. Springfield, Ill.: Thomas.

Kohn, Melvin L., and Carmi Schooler. 1978. "The Reciprocal Effects of the Substantive Complexity of Work and Intellectual Flexibility: A Longitudinal Assessment." *American Journal of Sociology* 84:24-52.

LeMasters, E.E. 1957. "Parenthood as Crisis." *Journal of Marriage and the Family* 19:352-55.

Levinson, Daniel. 1977. "The Mid-Life Transition: A Period in Adult Psychosocial Development." *Psychiatry* 40:99-112.

Lowenthal, Marjorie Fiske, and Clayton Haven. 1968. "Interaction and Adaptation: Intimacy as a Critical Variable." *American Sociological Review* 33:20-30.

Lowenthal, Marjorie Fiske, Majda Thurnher, and David Chiriboga. 1976. *Four Stages of Life*. San Francisco: Jossey-Bass.

Menaghan, Elizabeth G. 1978. "Seeking Help for Parental Concerns in the Middle Years." *American Journal of Community Psychology* 6:477-88.

Mullan, Joseph T., and Morton A. Lieberman. 1978. "Does Help Help? The Adaptive Consequences of Obtaining Help from Professionals and Social Networks." *American Journal of Community Psychology* 6:499-517.

Neugarten, Bernice L., and Nancy Datan. 1973. "Sociological Perspectives on the Life-Cycle." In Paul B. Baltes and K. Warner Schaie (eds.), *Life Span Developmental Psychology: Personality and Socialization*. New York: Academic Press.

Neugarten, Bernice L., and Gunhild O. Hagestad. 1976. "Age and the Life Course." In Robert H. Binstock and Ethel Shamas (eds.), *Handbook of Aging and the Social Sciences*. New York: Van Nostrand Rheinhold

Pearlin, Leonard I. 1975. "Sex Roles and Depression." In Nancy Datan and Leon Ginsberg (eds.), *Life-Span Developmental Psychology.* New York: Academic Press.

Pearlin, Leonard I., and Joyce S. Johnson. 1977. "Marital Status, Life Strains, and Depression." *American Sociological Review* 42:704-15.

Pearlin, Leonard I., and Morton A. Lieberman. 1979. "Social Sources of Emotional Distress." In Roberta Simmons (ed.), *Research in Community and Mental Health.* Greenwich, Conn.: JAI.

Pearlin, Leonard I., and Clarice Radabaugh. 1976. "Economic Strains and the Coping Functions of Alcohol." *American Journal of Sociology* 87:652-63.

Pearlin, Leonard I., and Carmi Schooler. 1978. "The Structure of Coping." *Journal of Health and Social Behavior* 19:2-21.

Rabkin, Judith G. and Elmer L. Struening. 1976. "Life Events, Stress, and Illness." *Science* 194:1013-20.

Radloff, Lenore. 1975. "Sex Differences in Depression: The Effects of Occupation and Marital Status." *Sex Roles* 1:249-65.

Riley, Matilda White. 1971. "Social Gerontology and the Age Stratification of Society." *Gerontologist* 11:79-87.

———.1976. "Age Strata in Social Systems." In Robert H. Binstock and Ethel Shanas (eds.), *Handbook of Aging and the Social Sciences.* New York: Van Nostrand Rheinhold.

Rosenberg, Morris, and Leonard I. Pearlin. 1978. "Social Class and Self-Esteem among Children and Adults." *American Journal of Sociology* 84:53-77.

Streib, Gordon F., and C.J. Schneider. 1971. *Retirement in American Society.* Ithaca, N.Y.: Cornell University Press.

van den Daele, Leland D. 1975. "Ego Development and Preferential Judgment in Life-Span Perspective." In Nancy Datan and Leon Ginsberg (eds.), *Life-Span Developmental Psychology.* New York: Academic Press.

Warheit, George J., Charles E. Holzer, III, Roger A. Bell, and Sandra Arey. 1976. "Sex, Marital Status, and Mental Health: A Reappraisal." *Social Forces* 55:459-70.

20

Aging, Social Change, and the Power of Ideas

Matilda White Riley

Individuals who belong to the same generation, who share the same year of birth, are endowed, to that extent, with a common location in the historical dimension of the social process.
—Karl Mannheim, "The Problem of Generations"

We know that death is inevitable. And we are widely led to believe that aging over the life course is also inevitable, that the process of growing up and growing old must inexorably follow an immutable pattern. Yet a principle tenet of the sociology of age, a newly emerging scientific specialty,[1] is that aging is not inevitably prescribed, that there is no "pure" process of aging, that the ways in which children enter kindergarten, or adolescents move into adulthood, or older people retire are not preordained. In this view, the life course is not fixed, but widely flexible. It varies with social change—not only with the changing nature of the family, the school, the workplace, the community, but also with changing ideas, values, and beliefs. As each new generation (or cohort)[2] enters the stream of history, the lives of its members are marked by the imprint of social change and in turn leave their own imprint.

The theme of this essay concerns the relationship between the life course and social change. It concerns the dynamic process by which social change molds the course of our lives and by which the course of our collective lives creates social change. The essay touches first upon this theme in general and its intellectual background, then focuses on one aspect of the theme, on the meaning of our lives as we age from birth to death. The meanings we attach to the life course, the theories of aging we espouse, have power over individual lives. For human lives in the aggregate, too, these meanings have power to shape social norms and institutions, to guide social change. According to the well-known dictum of W.I. Thomas, if situations are defined as real, they are real in their consequences. A sociology of age points to the differing life situations that arise with social change, to the differing definitions of these situations by successive cohorts of human beings, and to the consequences of these differing cohort definitions for further social change.

Aging and Social Change: A Sociological Perspective

For the past fifteen years, a number of us have been at work in the sociology of age,[3] formulating and specifying the conceptual scheme that underlies this essay. The aim has been to integrate and to reinterpret two seemingly disparate strands of work on: first, the aging process as individuals move through the social structure; and second, changing social structures as they environ successive cohorts of human lives.

In recent decades, scholars in several social science fields have been concerned with selected aspects of the aging process. Many have focused on discrete stages of the life course, and there are substantial literatures on childhood, on adolescence, on social gerontology, and more recently on middle age. In psychology, the predominant emphasis on childhood "development" or on old age "decrements" has been countered by attention to the entire lifetime among "life-span psychologists" (including Warner Schaie, Paul Baltes, John Nesselroade, and others), whose intellectual roots can be traced back to Quetelet and other eighteenth- and nineteenth-century scholars.[4] Current attention is being turned to the interaction of social, biological, and psychological aspects of the aging process,[5] and sociologists like Brim[6] and Clausen are examining the connections between the full life course and the social structure. In an extended treatment, Clausen has described the sequence of roles within the changing society in which the individual makes continual adjustments during his lifetime, to which he brings his accumulated stores of past experience and future aspirations, and through which he seeks to preserve some sense of personal continuity and identity.[7]

A very different set of studies has dealt with aspects of the changing age structure of society. Focusing on age structure, sociologists (like Parsons[8] and Eisenstadt[9]) and anthropologists (like Linton)[10] have noted that every society is stratified by age; thus people at varying ages differ in their capacity to perform key social roles, while the social system depends upon the continuing performance of numerous age-specific roles and functions. Karl Mannheim, in his seminal essay "The Problem of Generations,"[11] pays greater heed to the dynamic than to the structural aspects of social change. Subsequently amplified in the writings of Ryder[12] and Cain,[13]

Mannheim's essay shows how each new cohort, starting its life course at a unique point in time, has unique characteristics because of the particular historical events undergone or the particular knowledge or attitudes acquired in childhood. Mannheim's concern with generations as contributing to "the dynamic of historical development"[14] has a close parallel in the current work of social historians and historical demographers who use reconstructed genealogies, biographies, or parish records to study changes in political ideology or in such age-stratified systems as the family or the school.[15]

Pondering over these diverse intellectual strands, each largely ignored in the other, we have devised a conceptual model[16] for continuing examination of their obvious, yet still unexplored, connectedness. In its most general form, this conceptual model comprises pivotal elements in the two types of interdependent changes I am discussing: changes in the society and its age-graded roles, and changes in people as they grow up and grow old. Two different dynamisms are involved, each with its own tempo. Society changes as it undergoes wars, famines, economic fluctuations; revolutions in beliefs and tastes; changes in the state of science and the arts; shifts in social norms, roles, and institutions; revisions in the age criteria for role entry and exit. Meanwhile, people change. They age over the life course from birth to death. And they are replaced by a succession of new cohorts, each composed of people who are aging.

It is useful to visualize this model schematically as a series of horizontal bars, staggered across the axis of historical time. Each bar represents a cohort of people all born during the same time period. Within each cohort, people are aging—socially as well as biologically and psychologically; moving through roles; accumulating knowledge, attitudes, experiences. In the meantime new cohorts are continually succeeding one another. This seemingly obvious schematic representation has the distinct use of forcing us to keep in mind that each cohort cuts off a unique segment of historical time—confronts its own particular sequence of social and environmental events. That is, because society changes, the modal life-course patterns of people in different cohorts cannot be precisely alike. This point, as initially formulated by Norman Ryder,[17] deserves the emphasis of repetition: because of social change, *different cohorts age in different ways.* Cohorts born recently in this country differ from earlier cohorts because of intervening social changes of many sorts: in education, in nutrition, in the occupational and income level at which people begin their careers, in the political zeitgeist surrounding their first voting experience. If for no other reason, then, the members of each new cohort *cannot follow precisely* in the footsteps of their predecessors. For example, as the Vietnam War has given way to such new critical issues as inflation and unemployment, today's cohorts of college students are more job-oriented, less dedicated to "causes," than the activist cohorts of the 1960s. Or, with reports of mounting crime and violence in the society, today's cohorts of young Americans are more likely to urge capital punishment than were their more humanitarian counterparts just a few years ago.

The scheme also illustrates societal elements in a sociology of age. It directs us to sequential cross-section views of all the coexisting cohorts. At any single moment of history, such as 1978 or 1928, a vertical slice through the staggered cohorts divides the population into age strata—the young, middle-aged, and old. These different strata are simultaneously acting out their respective age-assigned roles in society—as in an age-graded school. Comparison of several sequential cross-section slices (such as 1928 with 1948 with 1978) suggests how society is changing, just as longitudinal analysis of several sequential cohorts suggests how individuals age over their life course.[18]

The essence of this model centers in the continuing interplay between these two dynamisms: social change and the process of aging. Social change affects the situations in which people age. And the *way* in which people age—the process of aging itself—responds to these changing situations. Inherent in this interplay is the central problem of timing: the tension and strain produced by the difference between the tempo of mankind and the tempo of society. It is clear that cohorts of people follow one another in constant succession, even though particular races may eventually die out. And the biological lifetime of man has a definite rhythm from birth to death (albeit with secular variations in longevity within an apparently fixed total span). But the timing of societal process has no comparable rhythm or periodicity. The diverse ideas, beliefs, and artifacts of culture have varying lifetimes of their own, from the newspaper tossed away after one reading to the pyramids of Egypt. The wide range of social structures (from tribes or cities to nation-states) that concern us as sociologists also endure over varying periods of months, years, or centuries. Poets and philosophers, each in his own way, have attemped to define the course and the periods of societal time, from Heraclitus or Aristotle, through Ibn Khaldun or Herbert Spencer. And many early thinkers, including Hume and Comte, have made varying attempts to measure societal time in quantitative terms, seeking cyclical or "generational" or other rhythms—all such attempts dispatched as abortive by both Mannheim [19] and Sorokin.[20]

Whatever the nature of the processes of social change and stability—whether they are short-term or long-term, disintegrative or reconstitutive[21]—societal processes are certainly not synchronized with the lifetimes of the people progressing through the social structure in endless succession. As seen in the model, the society, itself moving through time, is the composite of the several unique cohorts—at varying stages of their journey, and often traveling divergent paths. Only by understanding this fact can we comprehend the sources of tension and pressure for change inherent in the differing rhythms of individual aging and societal change. Each individual must endure continual tension throughout his lifetime because, as he learns new roles and relinquishes others, he must adjust to shifting, often unpredictable and seemingly capricious, societal demands. And difficulties can beset the society because each new cohort that is born—characterized by its own size, sex composition, distribution of genetic traits and family backgrounds—requires continual allocation and socialization for the sequence of roles it must encounter within the prevailing social structure. Small wonder, then, that there can be no fixed process of aging!

As many of us continue to work with this conceptual model, to specify and adapt it, we find that a new window has been opened upon social reality. A fresh perspective is introduced—one that takes into account the human beings who are themselves changing as society changes.

Myths and Fallacies about Aging

The model has the further use of identifying many long-held and widespread myths, mistaken beliefs, and erroneous theories about age and aging. In an earlier reanalysis of the literature on older people,[22] we encountered numerous examples of myths that, on closer scrutiny, proved to be unfounded. We discovered the following to be true: (1) Most old people are not (as the myth has it) destitute, dependent, or residing in nursing homes; (2) most are not seriously disabled; (3) work productivity does not invariably decline in old age; and (4) most old people *do* feel adequate—most are satisfied with their roles.

How then do such myths arise? Several types of fallacies or misinterpretations have been identified[23] and are becoming widely recognized as resulting from lack of such a conceptual model or inappropriate application of it. I shall mention only three. First, there is the "life-course fallacy," which erroneously interprets cross-section data as if they referred to the aging process. In cross-section, for example, old people have lower educational attainment than young people. This obviously does not mean that a person's educational level declines *because* of growing older. The apparent decline occurs because the more recent cohorts are better educated than their predecessors. In cross-section, too, teenagers generally score higher on intelligence tests than members of older age strata. Again, this obviously does not mean that an individual's intelligence necessarily declines *because* of growing older—although many psychologists thought so until a few longitudinal studies pointed to the life-course fallacy.[24] What had been overlooked were the cohort differences in life-course patterns. Second, there is the "fallacy of age reification," in which chronological age itself is treated as if it were a casual factor. (One wants to "become one's own man" because he is age forty, according to Daniel Levinson,[25] or one "becomes resigned" because he is age fifty, according to Gail Sheehy.[26]) Yet particular years of age (like particular historical dates) have no meaning in themselves; they are mere indexes, useful only as they reflect socially or theoretically relevant components of personal or social change.[27] (Preferable, perhaps, is the folk wisdom that forty is the old age of youth, fifty is the youth of old age.) And third, there is the "fallacy of cohort-centrism," which I shall discuss in some detail—the fallacy of overgeneralizing from the experience of a single cohort (usually one's own).

Thus there are many ways of being lured into erroneous ideas and theories of aging and the sequence of life events. Yet ideas and theories, no matter how erroneous or ill-founded, have their own power both over a person's life course and over societal change. They can, in Robert Merton's term, become "self-fulfilling prophecies."

Cohort-Centrism: One's Own Theory of Aging

This brings me to the special focus of this essay, to definitions or theories of the life course and their consequences. Let us consider how such theories are formed, and to what extent they may be flawed by ill-founded myths and stereotypes and by the fallacy of cohort-centrism.

Each of us, moving along the trajectory from birth to death, constructs his own biography. We attach special meanings to past events. We look to the future with special hopes or anticipations, with special apprehensions or fears. Doubtless each of us also tends to generalize from this personal theory of one's own life—to treat it implicitly as *the* process of aging. Here lies the danger. For it can be stated as an axiom that each of us tends to define "*the* life course" as we have experienced it in our particular cohort. As William Graham Sumner suggested when he coined the term, we tend to be ethnocentric. I suggest that we tend also to be "cohort-centric." Yet, as the model reminds us, cohorts can age in different ways.

The absurdity of attempting to build a general theory of the life course from one's own experience seems clear enough. The meaning of life and of its sequence of life events is colored by the cohort to which a person belongs—and by the sex and class-segment of that cohort. In Mannheim's phrase, members of the same cohort share "a common location" in the social process. Those who reached the age of thirty in 1940, for example, had all experienced World War I and the Great Depression; they were currently exposed to World War II; and they confronted the future of the 1940s through the 1970s. At given stages in their lives, they were exposed to much the same zeitgeist; and they were finding their way into, and learning to play, roughly similar sets of roles. As Robert Merton puts it, "Structure constrains individuals variously situated within it to develop cultural emphases, social behavior patterns and psychological bents."[28] Thus any personal biography, or even the aggregate biographies of the members of a cohort, can only emphasize the constraints imposed by social structure and social change, by the social exigencies and prescriptions of the particular slice of history involved.

Obvious as the point seems, however, many definitions and theories on which we act—which are real in their consequences—are cohort-centric. As individuals, each of us is often guided by his own personal experience as he construes it. And when many of us in the same cohort are similarly affected by social change, we come to attribute similar meanings to our lives, to share similar assumptions about aging, to be beguiled or threatened by similar life events. Collectively, we develop "cohort definitions of the life course" that are implicit, unspoken. As each new cohort confronts a different set of social and environmental events, these cohort definitions subtly change. Thus one generation's folklore and "common-sense" about the life course may no longer make sense to a later generation.

Even sophisticated philosophies, and the basic assumptions underlying professional practice or public policy, are sometimes beset by this potential danger of cohort-centrism. Erikson, whose ideas of the eight stages of life are widely influential in social science and psychiatry, derives his views from the "evidential field" of his own contemporary clinical observations.[29] Thus one wonders how universal are his postulated stages, how closely tied to particular ages, how inexorable their sequence (as from autonomy versus doubt, to intimacy versus isolation, to integrity versus despair).[30] One wonders also about the presumed universality and sequencing of Kohlberg's stages of moral development (also derived from contemporary studies).[31] One can question how certainly a man must "get into the adult world" precisely in his midtwenties or "become one's own man" precisely in his late thirties, as Levinson contends in postulating the "species-specific periods" that "have governed human development for the past five or ten thousand years" (conjectures based on recent studies of forty middle-aged men).[32] One need only look back at Freud's views of the life course—at the submerged hatreds and fears, the sublimated sexuality—to appreciate some respects in which even his theories are less pertinent today than to the Viennese cohorts of his own time.

To be sure, the danger of cohort-centrism is peripheral to the centrally important aim of many such theories of stages, patterns, stability and change over the life course. Their search is for *universals* in the aging process—for the similarities among cohorts rather than for the differences I have been emphasizing. This search can provide cogent insights. (It can also afford guidelines for counseling and therapy. In its popular versions, such as Gail Sheehy's *Passages*, it can offer reassurance, if sometimes misleading reassurance, to millions of readers undergoing life transitions of their own.)

Though there is little proof, a number of universal principles have been postulated. For example, there are the biologically rooted principles of *aging* and *cohort flow*. Mankind as a species invariably grows up, becomes fertile, grows old, and dies; and cohort flow persists as long as the society survives. There are certain empirical principles of the *sequencing of events* over the life course. For example, unlike such a socially prescribed (hence flexible) sequence as completing school, beginning to work, marrying, producing a child, it seems universally probable that a child cannot walk before standing, cannot solve moral problems before understanding words, or solve complex mathematical problems before understanding numbers. Of interest to us also has been the principle of *accumulation*.[33] By definition, the longer a person lives, the greater his chances of having acquired irreversible characteristics, such characteristics as a higher level of educational attainment or a chronic disease (if "chronic" is defined as "incurable").

How can the universality of such principles be tested? Which personal characteristics are inevitable, regardless of sociotemporal context? Which life sequences persist across time and space, rather than being culturally variable? One can only begin to answer such questions through studying and comparing many cohorts, not just one (as the increasing use of cohort analysis by social scientists attests). No "pure" process of aging occurs in any single concrete cohort observable in reality. A theory of aging, of universals, must be an abstraction from the experiences of many cohorts at many times and places.

Consider this example. Cumming and Henry concluded from the cohort they were studying that old people "naturally" disengage (withdraw) from society. But when we examined[34] another cohort, the cohort of young men who were unemployed during the Great Depression, we found that these young men also tended to disengage. Thus the cohort comparison indicated that not necessarily age at all, but exclusion from the labor force was the major precursor of disengagement.

This and many other findings point less to a fixed pattern of aging than to the ranges and variabilities in the ways people age. Indeed, that life-course patterns of successive cohorts are continually subject to change may prove to be another universal principle. There is intrinsic strain toward adjustment in the life course, because each new cohort must contend with the older cohorts that precede it; though they live as contemporaries, they are not coevals in age or experience. And there is the strain engendered by the differences in timing between social change and the processes of aging and cohort flow. Even in simple societies, where social change is deemed to be comparatively slow, the collective lives of successive cohorts are continually being altered as the society undergoes famine, pestilence, or conquest.[35]

The evidence is overwhelming that a person's life is not inexorably fixed, but highly flexible. The ages for beginning to learn, becoming a responsible adult, retiring from work, even reaching the onset of menarche are not irrevocably ordained. Declines over the past century in the age of menarche from seventeen to twelve or thirteen (attributed to changes in the social environment in the Western countries observed)[36] merely illustrate the variability in even the biological life-course patterns. Similarly, life constraints imposed by disease can be relaxed through medical advance, or biological processes involved in the aging of cells or of the brain may become modifiable as scientific understanding increases. Yet, despite the evidences of flexibility, misleading stereotypes and fixed-stage theories still abound. Just consider the consequences if a mother must assume abnormality in a baby that does not discover its own hand by age six weeks, if a man must expect a midlife crisis between age forty and forty-five, if a mathematician must assume at age thirty that he or she is necessarily past the peak, or if a worker at age sixty-five must be regarded as necessarily unable to earn a living!

Cohort-centric theories can produce such stereotypes. They can give each individual the false sense that the aging process is immutable. And, as such theories of the life course come to be shared within a cohort, these cohort definitions subtly alter the meanings and norms that guide our collective lives. Becoming self-fulfilling prophecies, they have consequences for social change.

Cohort Norm Formation and Social Change

As new cohorts, reflecting social change, differ from their predecessors, these cohorts in turn press upon the society for further change. Cohort definitions, even when false, can become institutionalized as new norms and new role expectations, crystallized as new customs or laws. For, according to the conceptual model, there is a continuing interplay, as in a feedback system, between social change and the life course. One can think of many examples of this interplay as it affects the nature and meaning of the life course, but I want to conclude with just two. Each example, described in highly simplified form, has potentially profound implications for us today and in the future—the first, for the meaning of death; the second, for the meaning of life.

First, consider the long-term decline in mortality in industrialized nations (commonly associated with societal changes in standard of living, nutrition, sanitation, recent medical advances, and so forth). As Kingsley Davis argues,[37] this decline in mortality (coupled with urbanization and industrialization) ultimately had an historic impact on fertility, both on fertility rates and on the meaning, the social valuation, of fertility. Instead of bearing enough children so that at least a few might survive, succesive cohorts of young people increasingly utilized whatever means of fertility control they knew (withdrawal, abortion, postponement of marriage) in order to reduce the number of children they bore. One can well imagine the motivating factors as the progeny were no longer winnowed by death: rivalry with their numerous surviving siblings; concern for the responsibility of rearing, educating, and launching their own children. The desire for high fertility in earlier cohorts tended to give way to the desire for low fertility in more recent cohorts. And in its turn, the reduced fertility of these new cohorts had still further societal consequences: smaller families, children with fewer siblings, parents with reduced responsibility for child-rearing, more time for mothers to take on new roles, and perhaps fewer children to support or care for parents in *their* old age.

Before continuing with this illustration, let me underscore the process I am describing. A social change in one factor (mortality) evokes a cohort response, a change in the life-course patterns of the new cohorts (reduced fertility), which in turn contributes to further social changes (smaller families, enhanced social status). Of central theoretical importance, such cohort response was not imposed from above. There were no birth control clinics when fertility began to decline in the nineteenth century in this country, no moral imperatives toward zero population growth or the "replacement level" family. The cohort response consists, rather, of countless separate but similar *individual* decisions (private decisions by husbands and wives about whether to conceive another child). I shall call this the process of "cohort norm formation," wherein these many separate decisions by cohort members gradually crystallize into standards or norms that then govern decisions of future cohorts, or perhaps the whole society.

Returning to the example of declining mortality, I venture to suggest further that the current continuing decline in mortality may now, by a parallel process, be affecting the meaning of death. That is, just as the earlier decline in mortality may have gradually diminished the positive value of fertility, the continuation of this decline may be subtly diminishing the negative value of mortality. Mortality rates are now near a minimum among the young, where death seems most poignant; in recent cohorts, most deaths occur in old age, near the completion of a full life. Current deaths are both more protracted and require more decisions than in the past. More deaths today result from chronic and lingering ailments such as heart disease and cancer, and they typically occur in hospitals, where the patients are apart from family and friends. Ironically, advances in bio-medical science and technology, in saving life, are prolonging the process of dying. Many decisions about when and how to die must now be made deliberately by the human beings involved.[38]

How, then, are today's cohorts making these decisions? Is a process of new norm formation at work? Are we seeing culture being made? Is the meaning of death being reassessed? Here the answers are difficult to discern, for any drastic change in the valuation of death could contravene deeply held ethical and moral beliefs. Yet some evidence of cohort norm formation does exist. For example, there is a movement to use a "living will" for protection in case of terminal illness against heroic measures for life support. A major study of doctors shows a widespread practice to acquiesce in the desire expressed by terminally ill patients to die.[39] A recent United States survey finds a majority of the public believing that "when a person has a disease that cannot be cured, doctors should be allowed by law to end that patient's life by some painless means if the patient and family request it"—an astonishing finding in view of earlier studies.[40] There may even be an emerging acceptance of "social death," as observed in the an-thropological tradition, when old people, entirely bereft of meaningful roles or solidary human relationships, without religious faith or dedication to a cause, without the inner strength to live apart from social supports, lose the will to live.[41] Despite the public mores against suicide, private mores may condone the will to die.

If, under such conditions, death were to be more readily accepted, what might be the societal consequences? One can only speculate. But there might develop greater emphasis in the health professions on care of termi-nal patients rather than on hopeless cures, more open discussion of the good death and euthanasia, and the fact of death once again becoming a celebration of renewed solidarity in family and community. Indeed, greater acceptance of death might strengthen the links across generations, as gener-ations seek to talk with one another about this long-avoided topic. Most importantly, a change in the meaning of death might lead to changes in the meanings of life itself.

This brings me to my last example of the interplay between social change and the life course, an example of equal concern to us all, I believe, if not equally imponderable. Consider social change (past and future) as it relates to the modal patterning over the lifetime of education, work, and leisure.

In recent history, the case of women is more innovative than that of men, and may perhaps be instructive for the lives of men in the future. The rapid increases in female participation in the labor force over the past several decades is well known. What is less well known (revealed only by comparison of successive cohorts) is the complete reversal of women's work life: a shift from *declining* participation with age among cohorts coming into adulthood at the turn of the century, to *increasing* participation with age among those born more recently.[42] Here again one can look for concomitant social changes—rising educational attainment, expansion of demand for labor during World War II, emergence of the "empty nest" stage which produced leisure for middle-class women, and so on.[43] Here again, the *process* of change (in women's work life) consisted of millions of independent individual decisions by women in the affected cohorts, cohort norm formation that only now appears in its true light as a radical revision of the norms governing women's roles. Here the *consequences* for further social change are apparent in the drastic restructuring of both the family and the work force; in the diversity of the woman's combined work and family roles and the flexibility of accommodation required of her; and, significantly, in the pressure on the life course of men for complementary changes.

Contrast the situation of men. Unlike the varied options available to women, men's lives today (outside the family) are compressed into "three boxes:"[44] education in early life, work in midlife, leisure (more precisely, retirement) in later life. Historically, these sharp age divisions also arose from a gradual process of cohort norm formation. In those countries now classified as industrialized, there have been long-term tendencies for successive cohorts to stay in school longer, and to enter the labor force at increasingly *older* ages, but to leave the labor force at increasingly *younger* ages. In the United States, the proportion of men sixty-five and over in the work force has declined sharply from about two-thirds in 1900 to only one-fifth today. These striking changes in the age of retirement, and in the onset of long years of leisure, did not arise from any considered overall plan, but again because of millions of individual decisions, by employers to discharge, discourage, or fail to hire older men and by older workers to retire, to withdraw from the labor force. Only gradually did the norms crystallize, as ages of retirement became institutionalized in the United States through pension plans and (by 1935) through Social Security legislation (for which the choice of age sixty-five was made quite arbitrarily, and far above the average age of retirement today).[45]

What changes are now underway in the life-course patterning of work, education and leisure? One can imagine two scenarios for men and women alike. (Here one must keep in mind *all* the coexisting cohorts, each with its unique experience and its special normative claims, but all simultaneously pressing for differing changes in society.) In the first scenario, the cohorts starting out today might simply follow their predecessors, remain imprisoned in the "three boxes." With what future consequences? Predictably, there would be sustained age-based inequities in the burden of work and taxes placed on the middle-aged, in the exclusion from the labor force of both young and old (inequities exacerbated by the continuing increases in longevity). Predictably, too, age segregation in education and work would be accompanied by age segregation in the family, the community, and other social spheres; it would be accompanied by failures of empathy and communication across age line; by anomie and alienation in the excluded age strata. This is clearly a scenario of conflict, filled with intergenerational strains and tensions that could in their turn exert strong pressures for still further social change.

In the alternative scenario, new and more flexible life-course patterns might be introduced. (Here the implicit process of cohort norm formation might be given explicit direction through deliberate policy planning.) Many of us have been urging that education, work, and leisure be interspersed over the life course,[46] that social and economic structures be so modified that people of all ages might elect first, to work at one career, then to go back to school to learn another career; that leisure be apportioned more evenly from youth to old age, not concentrated at the very beginning and the end of life. And there are incipient changes that could be captured within such a scenario: older people going back to school for professional, vocational, or humanistic goals; legislation against a fixed age of retirement; pension plans for midcareer annuities; sabbatical leaves for all occupations; four-day work weeks; job sharing; flexible work hours; and models that have been set by women of combining many roles, as wives, mothers, homemakers, students, workers, all in one.[47]

What would be the future consequences if such a flexible integrative scenario were played out? At work, substitution of performance criteria for age ascription? Redistribution over the life course of challenge, responsibility, and usefulness? More options at every age? More equal sharing of child-rearing and bread-winning tasks? Greater solidarity in the kin network (in this era when there have never been so many generations of a family alive at the same time)? A closer integration of leisure into other life pursuits, with renewed evaluation of its seriousness and its purpose? Such questions currently press for answers. Cohort norm formation is underway.

Aging, the Power of Ideas, and Everyday Life

Thus a sociology of age makes clear that the meanings we attach to age have power. They become age stereotypes, shaping our personal plans,

hopes, and fears. They become age constraints, built into the social structure, molding the course of our lives, directing social change. They are
continually affecting the way we grow up and grow old and (as in my
examples) modifying the values attached to life and death, pressing toward
societal conflict or integration. Because of this power, the sociology of age
contains within it both responsibilities and opportunities.

We face a heavy scientific responsibility to broaden the base of understanding and to disseminate the soundest available knowledge to planners,
professionals, and the public. Age and aging as a topic of scientific concern
is prematurely popular today, when there are best-selling books on how to
rear the young, negotiate life's turning points, adjust to dying—treatments
that too often pay little regard to potentially misleading stereotypes. Meanwhile much serious discourse, though burgeoning,[48] lies hidden in scholarly journals and arcane compendia. Yet serious students of the aging
process have special access to the topic because of the principle of cohort
flow itself: many different cohorts coexist at any given period of observation, and their past histories and future anticipations are available for
comparison. Thus we are in a position to look with some dispassion upon
the aging process, to help avoid the shibboleths of cohort-centrism, to
assess the range of variabilities, and to anticipate the consequences of
alternative policy decisions. And in looking toward the future, because of
our focus on cohort flow we have a special advantage: we can make use of
what has already happened, what is already knowable about the cohorts
alive today who will become, respectively, the young, middle-aged, and old
people of the future.[49]

We have an opportunity too to act upon the broadening knowledge base,
to exert control over life course definitions as they develop. The meanings
of age are not unchangeable. They respond to the pressures of each new
cohort through the everyday interactions of cohort members, the millions
of apparently unrelated individual decisions, the gradually emerging cohort definitions which then merge into new or altered norms, contracts,
laws, social institutions. Whether we like it or not, age and aging *are* being
defined. They will continue to be redefined and given new meanings. And
each of us as we age (every day, every minute!) is playing an active, if often
unwitting, part in this process of redefinition. As individuals, we can mod-
ify the remainder of our own life course by acting upon the best available
knowledge. In a "self-help" society, each of us can, for example, heed
current mandates from the medical profession to guard our health, or from
social scientists to maintain our intellectual flexibility.[50] As citizens and
policymakers, we can make explicit the potential personal and societal
consequences of legislation aimed, for example, to postpone the entrance

into adulthood, to alter the age of retirement, or to revise the pension level of the elderly.

In short, there is scope for us, personally and as members of the changing society, to benefit from the understanding that the process of aging is neither inexorable nor immutable, that to a considerable degree we ourselves are in control.

Notes

Portions of this article were delivered as a Presidential Address to the Eastern Sociological Society, Philadelphia, April 1978.

1. For many of the ideas here, the author is indebted to her long-time collaborators, Marilyn Johnson, Anne Forner, Beth Hess, and Joan Waring; and for continuing suggestion and criticism to John W. Riley, Jr., Robert K. Merton, Orville G. Brim, Jr., and others.
2. "Cohort" is used here to mean a set of people born at the same time. "Generation," reserved for the kinship context, indicates cohorts of relevance to particular individuals or families.
3. This work began with the preparation of the Russell Sage Foundation volumes entitled *Aging and Society*: Matilda White Riley and Anne Foner, *I. An Inventory of Research Findings* (1968); Matilda White Riley, John W. Riley, Jr., and Marilyn Johnson, *II. Aging and the Professions* (1969); and Matilda White Riley, Marilyn Johnson, and Anne Foner, *III. A Sociology of Age Stratification* (1972). A small core of sociologists at Rutgers has gradually expanded into an "invisible college," spanning several disciplines in many countries, dedicated to this emerging sociological field.
4. Paul B. Baltes, "Life-Span Developmental Psychology: Some Observations on History and Theory," address at annual meeting, American Psychological Association, San Francisco, 1977.
5. See the volume edited by Orville G. Brim, Jr., and Jerome Kagan, *Constancy and Change in Human Development: A Volume of Review Essays* (in preparation). A Committee on Life-Course Perspectives on Middle and Old Age has been established by the Social Science Research Council to address these and other neglected aspects of social research on aging.
6. Orville G. Brim, Jr., "Socialization through the Life Cycle," in Orville G. Brim, Jr., and Stanton Wheeler, *Socialization after Childhood: Two Essays* (New York: Wiley, 1966), pp. 1-49.
7. John A. Clausen, "The Life Courses of Individuals," in Riley, Johnson, and Foner, *A Sociology of Age Stratification*, ch. 11.
8. Talcott Parsons, "Age and Sex in the Social Structure of the United States," *American Sociological Review* (1942):604-16.
9. S.N. Eisenstadt, *From Generation to Generation: Age Groups and Social Structure* (Glencoe, Ill.: Free Press, 1956).
10. Ralph Linton, "Age and Sex Categories," *American Sociological Review* (1942):589-603.
11. First published in German in 1928, this essay appeared in English in Paul Kecskemeti, ed., *Essays on the Sociology of Knowledge* (London: Routledge & Kegan Paul, 1952).

12. Norman B. Ryder, "The Cohort as a Concept in the Study of Social Change," *American Sociological Review* (1965): 843-61.
13. Leonard D. Cain, Jr., "Life Course and Social Structure," in Robert E. L. Faris, ed., *Handbook of Modern Sociology* (Chicago: Rand McNally), pp. 272-309.
14. Mannheim, "The Problem of Generations," p. 320.
15. See for example John Demos and Sarane S. Boocock, *Turning Points: Historical and Sociological Essays in the Family* (Chicago: University of Chicago Press, 1978); also the Spring 1968 issue of *Daedalus*, "Historical Population Studies," and the Winter 1971 issue, "Historical Studies Today."
16. For further detail see Riley, Johnson, and Foner, *A Sociology of Age Stratification*, ch. 1; also Matilda White Riley, "Age Strata in Social Systems," in Robert H. Binstock and Ethel Shanas, eds., *Handbook of Aging and the Social Sciences* (New York: Van Nostrand Reinhold, 1976).
17. Norman B. Ryder, "Notes on the Concept of a Population," in Riley, Johnson, and Foner, *A Sociology of Age Stratification*, ch. 3.
18. See Matilda White Riley and Edward E. Nelson, "Research on Stability and Change in Social Systems," in Bernard Barber and Alex Inkeles, eds., *Stability and Social Change* (Boston: Little, Brown, 1971), pp. 438-42.
19. Mannheim, "The Problem of Generations."
20. Pitirim A. Sorokin, *Social and Cultural Dynamics*, vol. 4: *Basic Problems, Principles, and Methods* (New York: American Book), p. 505ff.
21. These are the dimensions used by Neil J. Smelser, "Toward a General Theory of Social Change," in Neil J. Smelser, *Essays in Sociological Explanation* (Englewood Cliffs, N.J.: Prentice-Hall), p. 195ff.
22. Riley and Foner, *Aging and Society, I.* as summarized on p. 7.
23. Matilda White Riley, "Aging and Cohort Succession: Interpretations and Misinterpretations," *Public Opinion Quarterly* (Spring 1973):35-49.
24. Riley and Foner, *Aging and Society, I*, p. 256.
25. Daniel J. Levinson et al., *The Seasons of a Man's Life* (New York: Knopf, 1978).
26. *Passages* (New York: Dutton, 1976).
27. The current dabate over "disentangling the effects of age, cohort, and period" verges upon reification unless the relevance of the concepts underlying these indexes is clearly defined. See Riley, Johnson, and Foner, *A Sociology of Age Stratification*, ch. 2; Karen Oppenheim Mason, William M. Mason, H.H. Winsborough, and W. Kenneth Poole, "Some Methodological Issues in Cohort Analysis of Archival Data," *American Sociological Review* (1973): 242-58.
28. Robert K. Merton, *Social Theory and Social Structure* (Glencoe, Ill.: Free Press, 1957).
29. Personal communication, 1976.
30. Erik H. Erikson, *Childhood and Society* (New York: Norton, 1950). Note references in Erikson's more recent work to connections among the individual life cycle, the "cycle of generations," and "evolving social structure"; cf. Erikson, "Dr. Borg's Life Cycle," *Daedalus* (Spring 1976), "Adulthood."
31. See for example Lawrence Kohlberg, "Stage and Sequence: The Cognitive-Developmental Approach to Socialization," in David Goslin, ed., *Handbook of Socialization Theory and Research* (Chicago: Rand McNally, 1969).
32. Daniel J. Levinson et al., *The Seasons of a Man's Life*, pp. 41, 322.
33. See Riley, "Age Strata in Social Systems."

34. Matilda White Riley, Anne Foner, Beth B. Hess, and Marcia L. Toby, "Socialization for the Middle and Later Years," in David A. Goslin, ed., *Handbook of Socialization Theory and Research* (Chicago: Rand McNally), pp. 951-82.
35. Anne Foner and David I. Kertzer, "Transitions over the Life Course: Lessons from Age-Set Societies," *American Journal of Sociology* (March 1978): 1081-1104. See also Riley, Johnson, and Foner, *A Sociology of Age Stratification*, ch. 12.
36. J.M. Tanner, "Growing Up," *Scientific American* (September 1973): 17-28.
37. Kingsley Davis, "The Theory of Change and Response in Modern Demographic History," *Population Index* (October 1963):345-65.
38. Among the relevant sources see John W. Riley, Jr., "What People Think about Death," in Orville G. Brim, Jr., et al., eds., *The Dying Patient* (New York: Russell Sage, 1970), pp. 30-41; Robert M. Veatch, *Death, Dying, and the Biological Revolution* (New Haven, Conn.: Yale University Press, 1976).
39. Diana Crane, *The Sanctity of Social Life: Physicians' Treatment of Critically Ill Patients* (New York: Russell Sage, 1975).
40. National Data Program for the Social Sciences, General Social Survey 1977 (Chicago: National Opinion Research Center), computerized data file.
41. Leo W. Simmons, *The Role of the Aged in Primitive Society* (New Haven, Conn.: Yale University Press, 1945), pp. 217-44.
42. See Riley, Johnson, and Foner, *A Sociology of Age Stratification*, p. 56.
43. Studying these phenomena in the 1930s, I expressed in an unpublished manuscript the hope that middle-class women would seize upon these changes as an opportunity to transform the definition of leisure, abjuring both its Romantic and its Utilitarian images as pure escape, and imbuing it with the more serious goals that men had been desperately seeking in work. But instead, those early—not yet "liberated"—cohorts of women merely followed men into the work force. Thus do the norms of particular cohorts have power over the trajectory of their lives!
44. The expression "three boxes" was the tag used in an April 1977 conference called by the Center for Policy Process, on the topic of Life Cycle Planning: New Strategies for Education, Work, and Retirement in America. That this conference drew several hundred participants (including many outstanding scholars, professionals, and public officials) is just one indication of the mounting popular concern.
45. Among the relevant sources, see Riley and Foner, *Aging and Society, I,* pp. 42-43, 105; Riley, Johnson, and Foner, *Sociology of Age Stratification*, pp. 372-73.
46. Matilda White Riley, "The Perspective of Age Stratification," *School Review* (1974): 85-91.
47. Perhaps another term need be coined here, if these remarks sound "sex-centric."
48. As one small example, a number of sociologists, psychologists, economists, physicians, and futurists participated in a January 1978 symposium sponsored by the American Association for the Advancement of Science, entitled Aging from Birth to Death. These papers are to be published as a volume by the AAAS.
49. For example see Peter Uhlenberg, "The Impact of Demographic Change upon Three Generations of Old People," in Matilda White Riley, ed., *Aging from*

Birth to Death: Interdisciplinary Perspectives (American Association for the Advancement of Science, forthcoming).

50. See Melvin L. Kohn and Carmi Schooler, "The Reciprocal Effects of the Substantive Complexity of Work and Intellectual Flexibility," in Riley, ed., *Aging from Birth to Death.*

21

Beyond the Hearth: Older Women and Retirement

Maximiliane E. Szinovacz

In their later years, men retire and women remain housewives—or so previous work on aging women would have us believe. Indeed, it was not before the early 1970s that researchers started to discover female retirement, and the number of studies on female retirement is still extremely limited. Why this neglect of women's retirement in the literature? An analysis of recent texts indicates that research on labor-force participation and retirement has been guided by the assumption that retirement constitutes a significant life transition only for men.

Implicitly, this assumption is evident in the conscious exclusion of women in retirement studies. Most investigations on retirement conducted in the United States as well as in other countries relied entirely on male subjects (Simpson, Back, and McKinney 1966; Havighurst et al. 1969). The inherent assumption that research on retirement is necessarily research on male retirement becomes even more obvious when some scholars altogether fail to mention the sex of their subjects in their sample descriptions (George and Maddox 1977; Walker and Price 1975) or do not include a question on sex in their questionnaires (Kimmel, Price, and Walker 1978). Friedman and Orbach (1974, p. 636) describe this trend well when they state: "[Women] have been used as a basis for comparisons with men, and almost no study has been devoted to women's attitudes and responses to retirement outside the context of their adjustment to aging per se."

In addition, many texts contain empirically unsustained statements indicating the primary importance of the retirement transition to men as compared to women. Work is believed to constitute a more-prevalent and salient role for men than for women. Since women have discontinuous work histories and are less committed to their work—if they work at all—it is argued, they are unlikely to experience loss of the work role as a significant life event with potential negative consequences to their self-concept, morale, or life satisfaction (Cumming and Henry 1961; Blau 1973). Women are also expected to experience less retirement stress than men because their major life interests are believed to center entirely around familial roles and household activities that continue beyond retirement and that offer women socially accepted roles in later life (Blau 1973). For men, retirement is viewed as a significant role loss leading to decreases in social prestige, self-esteem, and a lack of meaningful activities (see Beeson 1975; Lehr 1977; J.H. Fox 1977 for other critiques of this viewpoint).

Applying this perspective to the family literature, researchers also have emphasized retirement as the major family life-cycle transition for aging men but the launching of the children and widowhood as the salient and critical life-cycle transitions for middle-aged and aging women (Duvall 1977; Blau 1973; Troll 1971). The retirement of the husband is assumed to affect the couple and to require adjustments on the part of both spouses (Duvall 1977; Eshleman 1981).

Only within the last few years have some scholars come to question this one-sided view of retirement and started to investigate the incidence and significance of the retirement experience for women. Preliminary findings from these studies seriously question previous assumptions on women's retirement. This chapter reviews the meaning and importance of retirement for women. Given the small number of existing studies and the prevalence of small, exploratory investigations among them, many of our conclusions will have to remain tentative. It is evident, however, that results from the population of retired men cannot be generalized to female retirees. Therefore, investigations dealing exclusively with male retirement (which have resulted in a fair body of literature) are not considered in this chapter.

The Life Situation of Retiring Women

Retirement has been conceptualized as a process, an event, and a role (Atchley 1976a; 1980). As a process, retirement constitutes the transition from the status of worker to that of nonworker and/or recipient of retirement benefits, and it signifies withdrawal from the work role and entry into the rather vaguely defined role of retiree. Viewing retirement as a process implies that its meaning evolves from a person's preretirement experience and life situation. The significance and meaning of retirement thus are tied inherently to the significance and meaning of work within the total life context of retiring individuals. Indeed, it is precisely because researchers attributed little importance to work outside the home in the lives of women that they anticipated retirement to have few if any effects on aging women. In order to understand fully the impact of retirement on women's lives, it is thus necessary to consider major aspects of the life situation of women at the threshold of retirement.

Labor-Force Participation and Retirement

If retirement were a life transition that affected only a minority of women, it surely would be of little social significance. However, during the last decades increasing numbers of women have joined the labor force, and this trend has been particularly pronounced among middle-aged women. In 1950, 25.9 percent of all women aged 55-59 years and 20.6 percent of all women aged 60-64 years were in the labor force as compared to 47.6 percent and 36.2 percent, respectively, in 1970 and 47.7 percent and 31.7 percent, respectively, in 1978 (U.S. Bureau of the Census 1978a; 1978b). For the 54-59-year age group, labor-force-participation rates are even higher (52.4 percent in 1970 and 53.8 percent in 1978).

These increases in labor-force participation among middle-aged women are accounted for largely by changes in the work status of married women. In the period between 1948 and 1979, the proportion of nonmarried women aged 55-65 in the labor force remained relatively stable at about two-thirds of this group, whereas the proportion of married workers more than doubled (16.9 percent in 1948 and 37.4 percent in 1979; U.S. Department of Labor 1980; Schwab and Irelan 1981, p. 22).

These trends in labor-force participation have led to a pronounced increase of female retirees among women aged 57 years and over. Between 1952 and 1978, the proportion of retired women in this age group increased by 29 percentage points, whereas the proportion of homemakers decreased by 31 percentage points (Pampel 1981, p. 70). The exact proportion of retirees among the population of aging women has been difficult to estimate because official data sources often collapse housewives and retirees into the category of nonworkers. Data from the Harris report suggest that the overwhelming majority of women aged 65 and over consider themselves retirees (50 percent) rather than housewives (30 percent). An additional 17 percent of the women in this age group were still employed or looking for employment and can be expected to join the group of female retirees (Harris and Associates 1975).

Given these changes, there can be little doubt that female retirement has become a socially significant phenomenon. It is also clear that participation in the labor force and retirement are no longer restricted to a marginal group of single or divorced women but involve growing numbers of married women, many of whom re-enter the labor force in mid-life (Mallan 1974; Lopata and Norr 1980). Also, as more women combine work and family roles, the image of the aging housewife dreading the empty nest and her husband's retirement characterizes a decreasing proportion of the female population (Sweet 1973; Lopata and Norr 1980).

Work Patterns

Not only are increasing numbers of middle-aged women employed, but also they exhibit more-continuous work patterns than in the past. Certainly, many aging women discontinued employment during their childbearing years. These interruptions have a significant impact on women's social-security benefits and retirement incomes, but they are not necessarily a sign of lacking attachment to the labor force during the women's later life stages. Data from the Continous Work History Sample (Mallen, 1974) show that the majority of women (65 percent) newly entitled to retired-worker benefits in 1970 had spent over fifteen years of their lives in the labor force. Twenty-five percent worked continuously for fifteen or more years and 40 percent with some disruptions. Census data further indicate a sharp increase in the median number of years spent in their current jobs by women aged 55 to 65 years, from 4.5 years in 1951 to 8.8 years in 1973 (U.S. Bureau of the Census 1978). There is also some evidence that despite breaks in their careers, women remain within similar occupations throughout their working lives (Rosenfeld 1974).

In addition, greater diversity in women's life-styles caused by later entry into and a greater proportion of time spent altogether outside familial roles signifies a "decrystallization of female life patterns" (Lopata and Norr 1980). These trends suggest that more and more women will experience work outside the home as a significant part of their lives and, consequently, are likely to view retirement as an important, though not necessarily critical, life transition.

Work Commitment and Centrality of the Work Role

One reason why retirement has been thought to present fewer problems for women than for men concerns the centrality of work outside the home in women's lives. Increasing labor-force participation rates and length of gainful employment provide clear evidence that women now spend a greater part of their lives in occupational roles, but they may still attach little significance to their work. If this were the case, retirement may indeed be experienced as a relatively unimportant event or even as a relief.

Data concerning women's work commitment and the salience of work in their lives again contradict previous assumptions. For one thing, women are increasingly participating in the provider role. Single, divorced, and some widowed women often have to work to support themselves and their children. For these women, gainful employment constitutes their major source of income, and insufficient retirement benefits force some women to remain working beyond the usual retirement years. Also, many wives now obtain employment to help pay family expenses and significantly contribute to the family income (Hoffman and Nye 1974; Hesse 1979).

Career women, of course, are known to demonstrate considerable work commitment and to consider work outside the home as a major life interest (Epstein 1970; Fogarty, Rapoport, and Rapoport 1971; Holmstrom 1972; Pepitone-Rockwell 1980). However, even among women in less-specialized and nonprofessional occupations, work motives are not entirely economic. Rather, multidimensionality of work commitment prevails (Haller and Rosenmayr 1971; Lindenstein Walshok 1979; Szinovacz 1979). For instance, in her study of women in blue-collar and service occupations, Lindenstein Walshok indentified four major work motives in addition to financial work incentives—namely, the desire to get out and do something, desire for social contacts, desire for challenge and personal satisfaction, and the need for achievement and recognition (1979, pp. 73-74).

Furthermore, because of their interrupted work histories, women's work and career patterns differ from those of men. Middle-aged women who return to the work force after the childrearing years may not be able to accomplish occupational goals by the time of retirement. These women are particularly likely to view retirement as a disruptive experience (Atchley 1976b; 1976c).

Research dealing more directly with women in the preretirement years also supports the notion that work represents a salient role for women. For instance, Streib and Schneider (1971) found women to have less-positive feelings about retirement than men. Women more than men reported that they missed social contacts at work and the feeling of doing a good job. In his study of retired telephone-company employees and teachers, Atchley (1971; 1976b; 1976c) found particularly female teachers to be highly work oriented and to carry this orientation into retirement. Employed women of all age groups investigated by Prentis (1980) not only indicated relatively positive attitudes toward retirement but also mentioned missing work, social contacts at work, use of time, and finances as a potential problem at the time of retirement. These findings suggest that women obtain important rewards from their participation in the labor force. In addition to economic independence and security, work provides women with social contacts and a sense of usefulness and accomplishment, the loss of which could seriously hinder adjustment to retirement.

Finally, arguments concerning sex differences in the centrality of the work role fail to consider that individuals of both sexes may attach similar importance to more than one life role. Marital and kin relationships, social contacts, and diverse leisure activities have been shown to play an important role in the life satisfaction of both aging men and women (Campbell, Converse, and Rodgers 1976; Markides and Martin 1979; Palmore and Kivett 1977; Larson 1978). Some research also indicates that work is not necessarily the central life interest of men (Dubin 1956; Fogarty, Rapoport, and Rapoport 1971; Bailyn 1970; Friedman and Orbach 1974; Maddox 1966). Also, with increasing numbers of retirees and the trend toward earlier retirement (Pampel 1981), the retiree role has become more socially acceptable and less threatening in terms of the potential status loss previously associated with retirement (Sussman 1972; Friedman and Orbach 1974; Bell 1976; Maddox 1966; Taylor 1972; Sheppard 1976). We thus may speak of a plurality of life interests and diversity of needs among men and women at the preretirement and retirement stages (Neugarten 1977; Kahana and Kiyak 1977; Block et al. 1978). Some of these interests are facilitated by outside employment (for example, social contacts and income), but others are pursued parallel to and relatively independent of the individual's work role. Retirement adjustment is, therefore, not only contingent on the extrinsic and intrinsic rewards gained from work but also on the extent to which participation in the labor force facilitated other life interests.

Income

For most individuals, retirement involves a significant reduction in income (Fox 1979; Friedman and Sjogren 1981; Schwab and Irelan 1981). Even though the reduction in absolute income is highest for married men and lowest for nonmarried woman, this reduction means substantial economic loss, particularly to unattached women (Friedman and Sjogren 1981). Since aging women in general and unattached women in particular have lower incomes than other population groups, an income reduction upon retirement of over 40 percent often leads to postretirement incomes below the poverty level. In 1971, for example, the median income for all nonmarried women aged 65 and over was $1,720; for nonmarried men, $2,270; and for married couples, $3,970 (Thompson 1974). Sixty percent of the nonmarried women, 40 percent of the nonmarried men, and 20 percent of the couples in this age group had incomes below the poverty level. These income differentials by sex have been attributed to a variety of factors including women's discontinuous and part-time work patterns and their overrepresentation in lower-level jobs and in female occupations with lower wage levels (Pampel 1981; Rosenfeld 1974; Mallan 1974; Thompson 1974; Muller 1980; Parnes et al. 1976). Furthermore, women tend to retire earlier than men and are thus more likely to receive reduced social-security benefits (Foner and Schwab 1981). However, with the increasing trend among men to opt for earlier retirement, this difference has been decreasing as have income inequalities between the sexes among the higher age groups (Foner and Schwab 1981; Pampel 1981). Finally, women are less likely to be covered by private pensions, a factor that may also contribute to their lower retirement incomes (Beller 1980).

Not only are women's incomes considerably lower than men's, they also possess fewer assets than both married and nonmarried men. In 1975, the median net worth was $19,359 for married men as compared to $5,621 for nonmarried men and $4,908 for nonmarried women; and the assets owned by nonmarried women were more likely to be tied up in home equities than those of either married or nonmarried men (Friedman and Sjogren 1981).

Particularly, nonmarried women thus face retirement from an especially difficult economic position. While married women also have few independent economic resources, they may and often are better off relying on the higher retirement incomes of their husbands. Indeed, as Hess and Markson (1980, p. 200) point out: "It is a sad commentary on women's wages that many working wives do better to accept half of their husband's Social Security rather than their own entitlement."

Family Status and Family Roles

Women have also been assumed to experience few retirement difficulties because of the continuity of their familial and household roles. Several arguments can be brought forward against this claim. Women often return to the labor force in their middle or later years in order to escape the empty-nest household. These women gain satisfaction and self-confidence from the newly gained ability to employ their assertive skills and to obtain personal and economic independence (Livson 1976; 1977; Rubin 1979; Spence and Lonner 1971; Barnett and Baruch 1978). Such life changes also can lead to a shift in women's orientations—that is, from relation-centered values to an increased emphasis on their own abilities and feelings (Back 1974). The assumption that women can substitute former work activities easily with increased involvement in household and family roles thus disregards the fact that many women choose to work in order to escape a full-time household routine or because they are not fully occupied with household and family tasks once their children have reached school age or have left the parental home (Sobol 1974). In this case, household activities are unlikely to represent an adequate substitute for former employment status. Being forced to assume full responsibility for an unsatisfactory or at least unfulfilling role might prove as stressful to women as loss of status due to retirement may be to men (Szinovacz 1980). Also, it is quite doubtful that women who preferred to work rather than to remain full-time housewives in their middle years will develop strong interest and find fulfillment in these same activities once they retire. Keeping busy and involvement in meaningful activities thus may become important areas of concern for women at the threshold of retirement (Laurence 1961; Prentis 1980).

It is also often overseen that female retirees are bound to spend the majority of their working lives outside a marital relationship. In 1978, 52 percent of women aged 65 years and over were widowed, and this proportion increases to 69 percent among those aged 75 and over (*Older Women: The Economics of Aging* 1980). Additionally, 70 percent of all women aged 55 years and over were living alone as compared to only 36 percent of the men in this age group (*Older Women: The Economics of Aging* 1980). Many women thus may face retirement and widowhood within a relatively short time period, and such asynchronized and/or accumulated life changes have been shown to hinder adaptation processes (Seltzer 1976; Bengtson 1973; Morgan 1977). It is also conceivable that some wives retire early with their husbands, resume work after the husband's death, and then retire again after a relatively short time period in the labor force. However, data to confirm this speculation are currently not available.

The fact that many female retirees are or become widows also implies that their home-centered activities are no longer services for others. Both retirement and widowhood have been described as roles lacking relational content (Rosow 1974). While the young mother may derive a sense of accomplishment and fulfillment from providing services to her husband and children, the widowed retiree performs household activities primarily for herself. While some of her home-centered activities may be intrinsically satisfying, they surely lack the importance of doing things for others (Matthews 1979). Occasional help provided to adult children is unlikely to substitute fully for the daily exchange of services between spouses.

Social Contacts and Leisure Activities

Research on women's work motives as well as on their concerns in regard to retirement suggests that their participation in the labor force provides women with an important source of social contacts; and social contacts have been shown to affect women's psychological well-being greatly (Powers and Bultena 1976; Lowenthal and Haven 1968). One of the reasons why working women may find retirement a difficult transition is that they have developed a network of social contacts among work colleagues rather than or at least in addition to acquaintances made in nonwork activities. Loss of this network at retirement could result in a serious reduction in the women's social contacts and psychological well-being. These contacts cannot be replaced easily by increased attention on the part of the husband because the women's confidant and close contacts are usually same-sex friends and fulfill other social needs rather than those served by the husband (Powers and Bultena 1976; Candy 1977). Specifically, same-sex friends can increase women's sense of status and power (Candy 1977). Furthermore, retirees who become widows shortly after retirement will have to cope with a dual loss in social supports.

Unfortunately, current research provides little evidence as to the prevalence and importance of co-workers within women's social networks. A recent study by Stueve and Fischer (1978) shows that somewhat less than 10 percent of middle-aged women's social networks consist of co-workers (a mean number of 1.7 co-workers among a mean number of 18.4 network persons). Since these data comprise nonworking women, this proportion is probably considerably higher for middle-aged workers. Among women aged 65 years and over, co-workers practically disappear from the social network. Obviously, this decrease could be attributed to the fact that retirees may identify past co-workers as friends rather than co-workers. The authors' results indicate, however, that this is not the case: "[T]here is little evidence that older respondents continue relationships with former work colleagues. . . . This suggests that exit out of the work role tends to syphon off relationships with most of one's former co-workers" (p. 26).

In addition, social contacts at work not only serve as a source for developing new friendships but also provide routine social encounters with a variety of people. While these contacts may remain quite superficial, they still may contribute to a woman's self-concept, feelings of usefulness, and social accomplishment. For instance, in her pilot study of nonprofessional university employees, Szinovacz (1978, p. 7) found that retired women express regret over the loss of former work colleagues as well as the daily contacts with students. This attitude is very well expressed in the comments of one of the women in this sample: "And I just miss the people. And I knew everybody. After all, if you work in a place for 40 years you can't help but know them. I see them on the street, but it isn't like being in the office. If I'm lonely here, there are various meetings and we enjoy that, but I really enjoyed young people. This is where I miss working more than anything."

Another problem area mentioned by retirees or women at the threshold of retirement concerns their leisure-time activities, or more generally, their ability to keep busy after retirement. While men may face similar problems, married women or widows may be particularly disadvantaged in this regard. Women in general lack socialization for leisure-time activities, and working wives in particular are usually too restricted in the amount of leisure time available to them to develop outside interests and hobbies (Lehr 1978; Szalai et al. 1972; Walker and Woods 1976). This lack of leisure-time socialization may leave female retirees quite literally with a void of meaningful activities. Also, even if they engage in postretirement activities like volunteer work, these activities often cannot substitute fully for paid work (Sommers 1976).

Another reason why married and widowed retirees particularly may have difficulties developing independent leisure activities could be attributed to their socialization into dependence on their husbands as well as to social norms against the participation of unaccompanied women in public places (Rosenkaimer et al. 1976; G.L. Fox 1977). At least some of these suggestions are grounded in evidence. Data from a nationally representative sample of Austrian women ($N = 28,400$) show that female retirees engage more regularly in home-centered leisure activities (for example reading and watching TV) than employed women but are less likely than employed women to participate in outside activities such as going to the movies, eating out, taking walks, or playing sports (Szinovacz 1979). Since U.S. retirees have been noted to be more action oriented than Europeans (Havighurst et al. 1969), these observations may not hold for female retirees in this country. Indeed, some evidence indicates that older women may increase their involvement in socializing activities and organizations (Hendricks 1977), but further empirical research clearly is needed to clarify this issue.

The Retirement Transition

Given current societal norms, most individuals expect to retire. The retirement decision, therefore, centers primarily on the question when to retire rather than whether or not to retire at all (Atchley 1976a). This does not imply, however, that the retirement decision always reflects personal preference.

Individuals retire because they are forced out of the labor force (mandatory retirement), because they are unable to work, or because they feel that leaving the labor force would be appropriate and would offer them the opportunity to pursue other preferred activities. There is clear evidence that women retire earlier and more for voluntary reasons than men (Atchley 1976b; 1976c; Palmore 1965; Mallan 1974; Foner and Schwab 1981) In explaining this trend, Palmore (1965) referred primarily to women's lack of job commitment. Atchley (1976a) criticized Palmore's interpretation and argued that women's earlier retirement may be attributed to a variety of reasons, including societal pressure to retire and take care of retired or ill husbands, their economic support by the husband, lack of job satisfaction among women in lower-level jobs, and a trend toward joint retirement of spouses.

Some more recent studies on retirement tend to support Atchley's (1976a) statements. In her study of nonmarried women aged 58-63 years,

Sherman (1974) found labor-force participation negatively related to age, widowhood, education, and racial background (black). The racial and age differences were partially a function of the differing health status of women in these groups. These women also were shown to be less likely to work if they had health problems, received social-security benefits, or obtained support from their children (Sherman 1974). For married women, labor-force participation at a more-advanced age seems to be encouraged by economic responsibilities for others and for oneself (support for dependent children, lack of a pension coverage on the part of the husband), the economic resources of the wife (lack of coverage by retirement pensions), and by familial responsibilities (for example, taking care of an ill or disabled husband) (Henretta and O'Rand 1980).

Increasing evidence also shows that couples decide together about retirement and opt for joint retirement. Since wives are usually younger than their husbands, joint retirement may lead the wife to retire earlier at the husband's usual retirement age. However, other evidence suggests that joint retirement is more likely to delay retirement for both spouses (Anderson, Johnson and Clark, 1980); Clark, Johnson, and McGermed 1980). Overall, their economic security and familial considerations tend to discourage labor-force participation among aging married women. In 1976, only 7 percent of all married women aged 65 years and over were in the labor force as compared to 8.3 percent of the widowed, divorced, or separated women and 15.6 percent of the single women (Hess and Markson 1980, p. 186). The importance of economic considerations for the labor-force participation of aging women is also evident from the work motives of these women. In her report of Austrian women, Szinovacz (1979) found over one-third of currently working women over 60 years of age to mention retirement benefits as a work motive. Participation in a family enterprise, interest in the work, social contacts, and support for the family were also relatively common work motives for this group of women.

These and other findings (Barfield and Morgan 1978a) would suggest an overriding effect of health and economic reasons on retirement timing by women, a trend that corresponds with results on retirement timing by men (Clark and Spengler 1980; Foner and Schwab 1981). Women thus retire earlier than men either because they can afford to retire or because they are unable to continue working. In addition, they may feel retirement to be appropriate at a certain age or life-cycle stage (for example, when the husband retires) or obligatory in regard to new family responsibilities (for example, failing health of the husband). There is little evidence that would suggest, however, that women's decision to retire is prompted primarily (or more than men's) by the alternative attractions seen in postretirement activities and a reflection of low work commitment. Of course, some women may be pushed out of the labor force owing to negative job experiences and many do look forward to retirement, but these trends and orientations are expressions of a societal redefinition of retirement and apply to both sexes (Friedman and Orbach 1974; Atchley 1976a).

Recent studies have shown consistently that most people look forward to retirement and expect no major adjustment problems to retirement (Seldon, McEwen, and Ryser 1975; Harris et al. 1975). This trend applies to both sexes, but some studies did find women to express more-negative attitudes than men and to be more anxious about the future (Streib and Schneider 1971; Atchley 1976b; 1976c; Atchley and Corbett 1977; Anderson et al. 1978; Jacobson 1974; Laurence 1961). However, contradictory evidence that indicates more positive retirement attitudes on the part of women rather than men is reported by Prentis (1980) and Beuther and Cryns (1979).

Investigations of determinants of retirement attitudes suggest that high work commitment may increase women's reluctance to retire, whereas financial security and leisure plans for retirement increase positive retirement attitudes. Thus, women in high occupational positions proved to have relatively negative retirement attitudes (Prentis 1980; Streib and Schneider 1971). Low resistance to retirement was found to be furthered by women's financial resources and the number of activities planned for retirement (Johnson and Price-Bonham 1980).

Specific problems and advantages women anticipate for their retirement are reported by Prentis (1980). He found middle-aged women to look forward to leisure activities (travel, hobbies), more free time, as well as a more flexible time schedule. Loss of social contacts, financial problems, and lack of meaningful activities were among potential problems foreseen for the postretirement period. This author also reports that most of his middle-aged subjects had thought about retirement, although only 24 percent had made serious plans. Retirement plans were made more often by married women and women with higher incomes.

Overall, these findings suggest that women approach retirement with a relatively positive attitude even though they appear to be somewhat more reluctant to retire than men. Women who are strongly committed to their work, whose work provides them with many social contacts, and who have low incomes seem to express more negative feelings and thus could be expected to experience more adjustment problems than other groups.

Retirement Effects

In evaluating the effect retirement has on individuals, it is essential to differentiate between retirement adjustment and other individual or situational retirement effects that suggest changes in a person's life-style but that have little impact on adjustment or life satisfaction. Research on female retirement has focused primarily on retirement adjustment in general and, in a few cases, determinants of retirement adjustment. To what extent women's life pattern changes after retirement is virtually unknown. Indeed, an overview of the literature on the effects of retirement on women reveals one dominant and typically shared opinion—namely, that our knowledge of this phenomenon is too limited to draw definite conclusions (Beeson 1975; Atchley and Corbett 1977; Little 1981). The few studies that have been carried out, however, do provide some interesting insights into women's reactions to retirement and imply important questions for future research.

Adjustment to Retirement

In direct contradiction to previous assumptions that retirement would be a more-difficult transition for men than for women, current studies suggest that women are more likely than men to experience retirement as a stressful life event. While both sexes have been shown to adjust to retirement reasonably well, women were reported to be somewhat less satisfied with retirement than men and to take longer to adapt to the retirement transition (Streib and Schneider 1971; Atchley 1976b; 1976c). Furthermore, women, but not men, who approached retirement with a negative attitude seem unable to adjust to retirement even after a lengthy time period (Levy 1980). In comparison to men, female retirees were more likely to feel useless and lonely and to miss social contacts and the feeling of doing a good job. Perceptions of financial problems were also more pronounced among women than among men (Streib and Schneider 1971; Atchley 1976b; 1976c). Somewhat divergent results are reported by Sheldon, McEwan, and Ryser (1975). These researchers found women to be more anxious about retirement and to show less preference for the retirement status than men but to adjust better and more quickly to this life transition.

Studies comparing different groups of aging women (employed, retired, housewives) further support the notion that retirement may have negative effects on at least some women. For instance, retirees proved to have lower morale and affect balance than employed aging women (Jaslow 1976; J.H. Fox 1977). Comparisons of retirees and housewives resulted in somewhat contradictory evidence. Whereas Jaslow (1976) found housewives to have lower morale than either retirees or employed women, J.H. Fox's (1977) data indicated that retirees score lower on affect balance than housewives.

Even though the overall effect of retirement may be somewhat more negative for women than men, retirement always entails positive as well as negative consequences. In-depth analyses from a small sample of married female retirees show that positive effects of retirement are attributed primarily to the decrease in women's role obligations and the increased opportunity to engage in new and interesting activities. Some of the negative retirement experiences mentioned by these women included feelings of wasting their time, feeling cut off and useless, lack of stimulation and achievement, fear of becoming dull, being bored and lonesome, missing people at work, and difficulties in settling down to daily chores (Szinovacz 1978).

Determinants of Retirement Adjustment

Inquiry into the factors that affect retirement adjustment is important not only because it offers explanations of differential adaptation among divergent population groups but also because it provides an important basis for social intervention. Knowledge of the conditions that hinder retirement adaptation processes can help us to identify specific risk or target groups for intervention, and it can serve also as a guideline for program development. Given our extremely limited information on female retirement, current retirement programs must rely primarily on the evidence obtained for male retirement. However, the problems and needs of female retirees may differ substantially from those of men (Johnson and Price-Bonham 1980; Levy 1980).

In addressing the effects of retirement on individuals, one must consider both direct and indirect consequences. Retirees may miss their work, but also they may experience problems because retirement deprives them of means essential for the fulfillment of other life goals. For instance, the loss of income that often is associated with retirement could force retirees to forego some of the social or leisure activities they could afford while they were still working. Furthermore, retirees may be faced with problems that are age related and not a direct function of the retirement transition but that can affect adaptation process and adjustment to retirement.

Income. Research on male retirement provides clear evidence that income constitutes one of the most potent determinants of retirement adjustment and morale after retirement. Indeed, Atchley (1976a; 1980) suggests that most individuals will experience few negative retirement effects if they can afford meaningful leisure roles. As was indicated in the previous sections, women usually suffer a significant reduction in income after they retire from the labor force, and nonmarried women have lower postretirement incomes and assets than any other group of aged individuals. These differences in income at least partially account for the relatively low morale of retired women. For example, Jaslow (1976) reports that controlling for income greatly reduces the positive relationship between employment and morale found in his sample of aging women. Indeed, within the highest income group, retirees proved to have a higher morale than the employees. In her study of 115 female retirees, Szinovacz (1982a) also discovered a clear relationship between income and retirement satisfaction. Furthermore, women with a retirement income of less than $10,000 were somewhat more likely than women with higher incomes to state that they would have preferred to retire later than they did. Finally, women not only have lower incomes than men, but also they are less likely than men to perceive their retirement incomes as adequate (Atchley 1976b; 1976c).

Income provides retirees with the means to engage in diverse social and leisure activities. Thus, it may indirectly affect retirees' life satisfaction through its effect on their social and leisure participation (Markides and Martin 1979).

Because of their relatively low incomes, female retirees must be considered a potential risk group in regard to retirement adjustment. Women may require special preretirement information in regard to their postretirement income situation and will also need education in money management to deal effectively with loss of income after retirement. Also, programs developed for female retirees will have to be cheap in order to attract low-income women.

Health. Another factor that has been found consistently to affect retirement adjustment is individuals' physical well-being. Health problems often force a person to retire before she or he is prepared for this life transition, and they preclude participation in a variety of social and leisure activities. In the case of women, failing health of a family member, particularly the husband, also plays an important role in the decision to retire and may thus force a hasty and unplanned transition; and care for ill family members can seriously restrict a women's ability to engage in outside activities.

There is some evidence that health problems in fact hinder women's life satisfaction and morale (Jaslow 1976; J.H. Fox 1977). However, women may be more able than men to overcome the negative effects even of serious health problems. In her comparative study of healthy and chronically ill retirees, Levy (1980) found even chronically ill women to adjust relatively well to retirement provided their attitude toward this life transition was positive. This was not the case for chronically ill men. Based on these results, Levy (1980, p. 109) concludes: "[The woman's] needs are radically distinct from [the] aging male's. . . . The aging woman seems to be especially vulnerable to a social isolation which has come about as a consequence of differential social expectations and training. Her distinct need lies in the area of social construction."

Since health problems constitute perhaps the primary reasons for retirement among persons otherwise unwilling to leave the labor force, and since negative retirement attitudes seem to have profound and lasting effects on women, female retirees with health problems constitute another target group for social programs. These women may learn to deal with their physical handicaps, but they may never fully adjust to their forced retirement. Women who are known to retire because of illness may benefit particularly from preretirement programs designed to reduce negative retirement attitudes.

Attitude toward retirement. Levy's (1980) results already suggest a clear relationship between retirement attitudes and postretirement morale. Other studies also show that both men and women who approach retirement with a negative attitude experience problems in adjusting to retirement and score lower on diverse satisfaction and morale measures than individuals with positive attitudes (Sheldon, McEwan, and Ryser, 1975; Atchley 1976a). If, as Levy (1980) indicates, negative retirement attitudes have more-lasting effects on women than on men, then this could also explain why women tend to take longer to adjust to retirement than men (Atchley 1976b, 1976c; Streib and Schneider 1971).

In evaluating the relationship between retirement attitudes and adjustment, it is important to keep in mind that negative attitudes may be prompted by or reflect the anticipation of difficult and unsatisfactory life circumstances upon retirement. Negative retirement attitudes could thus represent a relatively valid, global indicator of future retirement problems and, in this capacity, provide another means to identify potential risk groups. This approach would be particularly appropriate for women if future research supports the existing evidence in regard to a stronger persistence of the relationship between retirement attitudes and adjustment for this population group.

Social and leisure activities. Meaningful social and leisure activities seem to represent a prerequisite for successful adaptation to retirement. While there is some indication that retirement results in a loss of social contacts with former work colleagues (see previous discussion), the effect of women's retirement on their social contacts with other persons remains unclear. Atchley (1976b; 1976c) reports differential effects for divergent occupational groups: A decline in social contacts occurred primarily among female teachers but not among the telephone-company employees. J.H. Fox (1977) found smaller social networks among retired than among the employed women, but retirees had more close friends than the employees and engaged in more interactions with neighbors.

That social contacts have an important effect on women's retirement adjustment was demonstrated in several studies. For instance, J.H. Fox (1977) found social contacts to be more-important predictors of the affect balance of retired than other groups of women, and lack of social contacts ranks among the most frequently mentioned concerns of female retirees (Sheldon, McEwan, and Ryser 1975; Szinovacz 1982a).

Obviously, retirement leads to an increase in free time. While some women view this change positively, allowing them more time for interesting activities and decreasing stress due to overload problems and the adherence to a rigid time schedule, others find it hard to develop a new routine, complain about wasting their time, and express feelings of boredom and uselessness (Szinovacz 1978; 1980). However, little is known about how retired women spend their leisure time. The Austrian data referred to earlier suggest a relatively high level of home-centered activities among female retirees (Szinovacz 1979); but this trend may not apply to other nations (Havighurst et al. 1969). Some U.S. studies indicate an increase in diverse leisure activities among middle-aged women (Hendricks 1977), and it also has been suggested that retirement leads primarily to an extension of those activities performed prior to the retirement transition. For instance, Atchley (1976a) found his sample of retired teachers to be quite busy with the management of financial and social affairs. Overinvolvement in social roles can be used as a means to reduce role strain. Thus, on the one hand, working women can legitimize underperformance in some roles by their work commitments. Retired women, on the other hand, will find it much harder to excuse themselves from diverse social and other obligations by referring to role stress. This could lead to a sudden increase in role obligations and could explain why some women claim to be extremely busy after retirement. Thus, those women who were not involved in a variety of leisure activities before retirement may find it difficult to develop new interests and hobbies.

Overall, most retired women seem able to occupy their time in a meaningful and satisfactory way unless health problems or low income prevent their participation in social and leisure activities (Sheldon, McEwan, and Ryser 1975; Barfield and Morgan 1978b). Indeed, among 115 recently retired women, retirement was perceived to lead to positive changes in the use of free time. Only one-fifth of these women indicated a decrease in satisfaction with the way they spend their time after retirement. For this sample, the most frequent leisure pursuits included church-related activities and volunteer work; but many women also indicated some interest in charity and educational programs, trips, and arts-and-craft groups (Szinovacz 1982a). The organization of such activities for retired women may constitute an important task for agencies serving the aging population. It is also obvious from these results that increased efforts to involve retired women in volunteer and charity programs may benefit both the women and the agencies.

Marital relations after retirement. Interest in the effects of male retirement led to a fair number of studies investigating reactions of wives to their husbands' retirement. Research on husbands' or couples' adjustment to the wife's retirement is, however, practically nonexistent (for some new evidence, see Szinovacz 1982b). Even critics of the neglect of female retirement in past research failed to propose an integrative approach that considers the employment status and retirement of both spouses (Beeson 1975; Kline 1975; Lehr 1977). It is likely that earlier studies on wives' reactions to their husbands' retirement are biased owing to this restricted perspective. For instance, frequent complaints about husband's interference with household tasks may be typical for housewives but not for retired wives (Darnley 1975; Fengler 1975).

While some studies indicate little involvement of wives in their husbands' retirement (Kerckhoff 1964; 1966), others do suggest concern with the husband's retirement on the part of the wife (Fengler 1975). The one consistent finding on aging couples is that companionship, mutual understanding, and expressive orientations are necessary conditions for marital satisfaction at this life stage (Cavan 1962; Roberts and Roberts 1980; Lipman 1960; 1961; Darnley 1975). After the husband's retirement, both spouses need to develop a more-expressive rather than instrumental orientation in order to adapt successfully as a couple to this life transition (Lipman 1960; 1961). If such support by the husband is lacking, women may find retirement particularly stressful.

Major problems experienced by couples with retired husbands center around his involvement in household tasks. Particularly, lower-class wives tend to view their husbands' increased participation in household activities as interference in their domain, are dissatisfied with his performance of household roles, and complain about having the husband underfoot. Among middle-class couples and couples with retired wives, conversely, the household participation of the husband is more accepted although spouses may disagree on how tasks are to be performed (Kerckhoff 1966; Heyman and Jeffers 1968; Maas and Kuypers 1974; Keating and Cole 1980; Szinovacz 1980).

The importance of retirement of either spouse for the marital relationship can be seen in the fact that during their working lives, spouses spend a good part of their time in activities outside the home. After retirement, they are reunited at home and may have to learn to adapt to each other's presence and previously unnoticed habits (Foote 1956). Data from a small study of female retirees and their spouses suggest that retirement adjustment of couples may be furthered by joint retirement. These couples planned not only for joint retirement timing but also for joint retirement activities that clearly reduced the stress of this life transition for both spouses. One of the most commonly noted positive consequences of the wife's retirement was the reduction in time stress experienced by many dual-work couples and the spouses' increased ability to engage in mutually satisfactory and joint activities. In contrast to previous findings, these wives did not object to their husbands' involvement in household tasks and only rarely perceived the husband's continuous presence at home in a negative way. Improvement in marital relations after the wife's retirement was also particularly pronounced among those couples in which the husband objected to his wife's working and/or held traditional attitudes regarding marital role-allocation patterns. However, if the wife experienced significant retirement-adjustment problems and attempted to rely solely on her husband for emotional support, serious problems in the marriage did occur (Szinovacz 1978; 1980).

One of the most common assumptions in regard to wives' retirement is that they will reassume their full-time household roles after retirement and that the division of tasks between spouses will become more sex segregated. Research evidence suggests, however, that this is only rarely the case. The assumption is contingent on the husband's remaining in the labor force after the wife's retirement or on traditional sex-role attitudes on the part of the husband. Also, the division of household tasks among aging couples seems to remain relatively sex segregated even if the wife works, thus necessitating little change after her retirement. Particularly if both spouses retire together, there is little reason for them to alter their previously established division of labor in the home. Both spouses may spend more time with these activities and may improve their performance of household roles (for example, the wife cooks fancier meals), but the overall distribution of tasks is not altered drastically. Indeed, some women complained that they find it particularly difficult to settle down to household tasks after their retirement (Szinovacz 1978; 1980).

Future research will have to consider both spouses' retirement patterns in order to arrive at a fuller understanding of retirement effects on married persons. Also, the marital-adjustment processes necessitated by retirement are seldom considered in retirement-preparation programs. Couples probably should be made aware of potential effects of retirement for the couple, and such programs ought to include both spouses.

Needs of female retirees. The limited literature on female retirement has not as yet provided us with sufficient information as to the specific needs of female retirees. Findings reported in this section suggest that an adequate income, meaningful social and leisure activities, and in the case of married women, mutual adaptation processes on the part of both spouses constitute important prerequisites for successful coping with this life event.

Compared to men, women seem somewhat disadvantaged in retirement because of their relatively low income and also because they often lack socialization for leisure activities and depend more on social contacts than men. Indeed, in her study of 115 retired women, Szinovacz (1982a) found "difficulties in meeting new people" among the most frequently mentioned problems. Another major area of concern indicated in this study was house maintenance and heavy household work. Even though these women had few health problems and were quite able to lead an independent life, they found it increasingly difficult to deal with heavy household work and home repairs. Given, particularly, nonmarried women's limited economic resources, they also cannot afford to hire outside help.

What seems evident is that women's retirement needs are distinct from those experienced by men because of their divergent socioeconomic position as well as their specific responsibilities and interests. These differences in the life situation of retired men and women may account for the sex differences in retirement adjustment shown in previous research. There can be little doubt that preretirement and other programs designed for retirees will have to take these differences into account.

Summary and Conclusion

Female retirement has received little attention from researchers because work was not considered a central or important role for women and because women were assumed to become full-time housewives again after they retire. The few studies that have been conducted so far lend little support to these assumptions. Indeed, women seemed to experience more retirement problems than men and to take somewhat longer in adapting to retirement.

Ironically, it may be precisely the factors referred to in these myths about women's retirement that render their adjustment to this life transition rather difficult. In their later years, women work outside the home either for financial reasons or because work offers them other rewards such as interesting activities, social contacts, and feelings of usefulness and accomplishments that are left unfulfilled by their household and familial responsibilities at home. Because they have chosen to work rather than to remain full-time housewives, retiring women may experience withdrawal symptoms when they retire and may find it particularly hard to adjust to the household routine they tried to escape in the first place (Atchley and Corbett 1977). Also, their interrupted work histories leave women quite frequently with low retirement incomes, and particularly late re-entry into the labor force after the launching of children can prevent many women from achieving their career goals (Atchley and Corbett 1977). Owing to their low incomes, retired women may be unable to engage in a variety of retirement activities, a condition that has been shown to render retirement adjustment difficult. Also, nonfulfillment of career goals can result in so-called goal frustration and negative retirement attitudes, particularly if retirement occurred for nonvoluntary reasons or was not planned (Atchley and Corbett 1977; Levy 1980). Finally, recent evidence also refutes the assumption that retirees happily return to the hearth and find fulfillment in the housewife role. Among married couples who retired together, the division of labor between the spouses seems not be changed drastically after retirement, and even those women who become more involved in household activities are not necessarily fulfilled by these responsibilities. Their preferred roles include volunteer work and other leisure or social activities.

The evidence presented in this chapter leaves us clearly with more questions than answers. Not only are many of the existing studies on female retirement based on unrepresentative and/or small samples, some of the results are also contradictory. However, these investigations demonstrate beyond doubt that retirement constitutes an important life event for women that deserves careful study. Existing evidence also suggests that women's retirement needs differ from those of men. Preretirement programs and agencies dealing with retirees will have to take these differences into consideration. Specifically, female retirees require financial information and would profit from programs offering social contacts and leisure activities. The development of adequate retirement programs for women depends upon our understanding of this increasingly widespread social phenomenon; to acquire such understanding we need additional longitudinal and large-scale research on women's retirement.

References

Anderson, K.; C. Higgins; E. Newman; and S.R. Sherman. "Differences in Attitudes toward Retirement among Male and Female Faculty Members and Other University Professionals." *Journal of Minority Aging,* 1978, pp. 5-13.

Anderson, K.; R.L. Clark; and T. Johnson. "Retirement in Dual-Career Families." In *Retirement Policy in an Aging Society,* edited by Clark, pp. 109-127. Durham, N.C.: Duke University Press, 1980.

Atchley, R.C. *The Social Forces in Later Life.* Belmont, Calif.: Wadsworth, 1980.

_____. *The Sociology of Retirement.* New York: Halsted, 1976a.

_____. "Orientation toward the Job and Retirement Adjustment among Women." In *Time, Roles, and Self in Old Age,* edited by J.F. Gubrium, pp. 199-208. New York: Behavioral Publications, 1976b.

_____. "Selected Social and Psychological Differences between Men and Women in Later Life." *Journal of Gerontology* 31 (1976c):204-211.

_____. "Retirement and Work Orientation." *The Gerontologist* 11 (1971): 29-32.

Atchley, R.C., and S.L. Corbett. "Older Women and Jobs." In *Looking Ahead. A Woman's Guide to the Problems and Joys of Growing Older,* edited by L.E. Troll, J. Israel, and K. Israel, pp. 121-125. Englewood Cliffs, N.J.: Prentice-Hall, 1977.

Back, K.W. "Transition to Aging and the Self-Image." In *Normal Aging II,* edited by E. Palmore, pp. 207-215. Durham, N.C.: Duke University Press, 1974.

Bailyn, L. "Career and Family Orientations of Husbands and Wives in Relation to Marital Happiness." *Human Relations* 23 (1970):97-113.

Barfield, R.E., and J.N. Morgan. "Trends in Planned Early Retirement." *The Gerontologist* 18 (1978a):13-18.

_____. "Trends in Satisfaction with Retirement." *The Gerontologist* 18 (1978b):19-23.

Barnett, R.C., and G.K. Baruch. *The Competent Woman.* New York: Halsted, 1978.

Beeson, D. "Women in Studies of Aging: A Critique and Suggestion." *Social Problems* 23 (1975):52-59.

Bell, B.D. "Role Set Orientations and Life Satisfaction: A New Look at an Old Theory." In *Time, Self, and Roles in Old Age,* edited by J.F. Gubrium, pp. 148-164. New York: Behavioral Publications, 1976.

Beller, D.J. "Coverage Patterns of Full-time Employees under Private Retirement Plans." *Social Security Bulletin* 44 (1980):3-10.

Bengtson, V.L. *The Social Psychology of Aging.* Indianapolis: Bobbs-Merrill, 1973.

Beuther, G., and A. Cryns. "Retirement: Differences in Attitudes, Preparatory Behavior, and Needs Perception among Male and Female University Employees." Paper presented at the Annual Meeting of the Gerontological Society, Washington, D.C., 1979.

Blau, Z.S. *Old Age in a Changing Society.* New York: Franklin Watts, 1973.

Block, M.R.; J.L. Davidson; J.D. Grambs; and K.E. Serock. *Unchartered Territory: Issues and Concerns of Women over 40.* College Park, Md.: Center on Aging, University of Maryland, 1978.

Campbell, A.; P.E. Converse; and W.L. Rodgers. *The Quality of American Life.* New York: Russell Sage, 1976.

Candy, S. "What Do Women Use Friends for?" In *Looking Ahead, A Woman's Guide to the Problems and Joys of Growing Older,* edited by L.E. Troll, J. Israel, and K. Israel, pp. 106-111. Englewood Cliffs, N.J.: Prentice-Hall, 1977.

Cavan, R.S. "Self and Role in Adjustment during Old Age." In *Human Behavior and Social Process,* edited by A.M. Rose, pp. 526-536. Boston: Houghton Mifflin, 1962.

Clark, R.L., and J.J. Spengler. *The Economics of Individual and Population Aging.* Cambridge: Cambridge University Press, 1980.

Clark, R.L.; T. Johnson; and A.A. McGermed. "Allocation of Time and Resources by Married Couples Approaching Retirement." *Social Security Bulletin* 43 (1980):3-17.

Cumming, E., and W.E. Henry. *Growing Old: The Process of Disengagement.* New York: Basic Books, 1961.

Darnley, F. "Adjustment to Retirement: Integrity or Despair." *Family Life Coordinator* 24 (1975):217-225.

Dubin, R. "Industrial Workers' World: A Study of the Central Life Interests of Industrial Workers." *Social Problems* 3 (1956):131-142.

Duvall, E.M. *Marriage and Family Development.* Philadelphia: Lippincott, 1977.

Epstein, C.F. *Woman's Place: Options and Limits in Professional Careers.* Berkeley: University of California Press, 1970.

Eshleman, J.R. *The Family: An Introduction.* Boston: Allyn & Bacon, 1981.

Fengler, A.P. "Attitudinal Orientations of Wives toward Their Husbands' Retirement." *International Journal of Aging and Human Development* 6 (1975):139-152.

Fogarty, M.P.; R.H. Rapoport; and R.N. Rapoport. *Sex, Career, and Family.* Beverly Hills: Sage, 1971.

Foner, A., and K. Schwab. *Aging and Retirement.* Monterey, Calif.: Brooks/Cole, 1981.

Foote, N.N. "Matching of Husband and Wife in Phases of Development," Repr. no. 7. Chicago: Family Study Center, University of Chicago, 1956.

Fox, A. "Findings from the Retirement History Study." *Social Security Bulletin* 42 (1979):17-40.

Fox, G.L. "Nice Girl: Social Control of Women Through a Value Construct." *Signs* 2 (1977):805-817.

Fox, J.H. "Effects of Retirement and Former Work Life on Women's Adaptation in Old Age." *Journal of Gerontology* 32 (1977):196-202.

Friedman, E.A., and H.L. Orbach. "Adjustment to Retirement." In *American Handbook of Psychiatry,* vol. 1, edited by S. Arieti. New York: Basic Books, 1974:609-645.

Friedman, J., and J. Sjogren. "Assets of the Elderly as They Retire." *Social Security Bulletin* 44 (1981):16-31.

George, L.K., and G.L. Maddox. "Subjective Adaptation to Loss of the Work Role: A Longitudinal Study." *Journal of Gerontology* 32 (1977): 456-462.

Haller, M., and L. Rosenmayr. "The Pluridimensionality of Work Commitment." *Human Relations* (1971).

Harris, L., and Associates. *The Myth and Reality of Aging in America.* Washington, D.C.: National Council on Aging, 1975.

Havighurst, R.J.; J.M.A. Munnichs; B.L. Neugarten; and H. Thomae. *Adjustment to Retirement: A Cross National Study.* Assen: Van Gorkum, 1969.

Hendricks, J.A. "Women and Leisure." In *Looking Ahead. A Woman's Guide to the Problems and Joys of Growing Older,* edited by L.E. Troll, J. Israel, and K. Israel, pp. 114-120. Englewood Cliffs, N.J.: Prentice-Hall, 1977.

Henretta, J.C., and A.M. O'Rand. "Labor-Force Participation of Older Married Women." *Social Security Bulletin* 43 (1980):10-15.

Hess, B.B., and E.W. Markson. *Aging and Old Age.* New York: Macmillan, 1980.

Hesse, S.J. "Women Working: Historical Trends." In *Working Women and Families,* edited by K.W. Feinstein, pp. 35-62. Beverly Hills: Sage, 1979.

Heyman, D.K. and F.C. Jeffers. "Wives and Retirement: A Pilot Study." *Journal of Gerontology* 23 (1968):488-496.

Hoffman, L.W., and F.I. Nye. *Working Mothers.* San Francisco: Jossey-Bass, 1974.

Holmstrom, L.L. *The Two-Career Family.* Cambridge, Mass.: Schenkman, 1972.

Huston-Stein, A., and A. Higgins-Trenk. "Development of Females from Childhood to Adulthood: Career and Feminine Role Orientations." In *Life-span Development and Behavior,* edited by P.B. Baltes, pp. 258-297. New York: Academic, 1978.

Jacobson, C.J. "Rejection of the Retiree Role: A Study of Female Industrial Workers in Their 50's." *Human Relations* 27 (1974):477-492.

Jaslow, P. "Employment, Retirement, and Morale among Older Women." *Journal of Gerontology* 31 (1976):212-218.

Kahana, E., and A. Kiyak. "The Nitty-Gritty of Survival." In *Looking Ahead: A Woman's Guide to the Problems and Joys of Growing Older,* edited by L.E. Troll, J. Israel, and K. Israel, pp. 172-177. Englewood Cliffs, N.J.: Prentice-Hall, 1977.

Keating, N.C., and P. Cole. "What Do I Do with Him 24 Hours a Day? Changes in the Housewife Role after Retirement." *The Gerontologist* 20 (February 1980):84-89.

Kerckhoff, A.C. "Husband-Wife Expectations and Reactions to Retirement." *Journal of Gerontology* 19 (1964):510-516.

———. 'Family Patterns and Morale in Retirement." In *Social Aspects of Aging,* edited by I.M. Simpson and J.C. McKinney, pp. 173-192. Durham, N.C.: Duke University Press, 1966.

Kimmel, D.C.; K.F. Price; and J.W. Walker. "Retirement Choice and Retirement Satisfaction." *Journal of Gerontology* 33 (1978): 575-585.

Kline, C. "The Socialization Process of Women." *The Gerontologist* 15 (1975):486-492.

Larson, R. "Thiry Years of Research on the Subjective Well-Being of Older Americans." *Journal of Gerontology* 33 (1978):109-125.

Laurence, M.W. "Sources of Satisfaction in the Lives of Working Women." *Journal of Gerontology* 16 (1961):163-167.

Lehr, U. *Psychologie des Alterns.* Heidelberg: Quelle & Meyer, 1977.

———. "Die Situation der Aelteren Frau: Psychologische und Soziale Aspekte." *Zeitschrift fuer Gerontologie* 11 (1978):6-26.

Levy, S.M. "The Adjustment of the Older Woman: Effects of Chronic Ill Health and Attitudes toward Retirement." *International Journal of Aging and Human Development* 12 (1980):93-110.

Lindenstein, Walshok M. "Occupational Values and Family Roles: Women in Blue-Collar and Service Occupations." In *Working Women and Families,* edited by K.W. Feinstein, pp. 63-84. Beverly Hills: Sage, 1979.

Lipman, A. "Marital Roles of the Retired Aged." *Merrill Palmer Quarterly* 6 (1960):192-195.

———. "Role Conceptions and Morale of Couples in Retirement." *Journal of Gerontology* 16 (1961):267-271.

Little, V.C. "Retirement Roles of Women: Use of Time and Self.": Paper presented at the International Congress of Sociology, Hamburg, 1981.

Livson, F.B. "Patterns of Personality Development in Middle-Aged Women: A Longitudinal Study." *International Journal of Aging and Human Development* 7 (1976):107-115.

———. "Coming Out of the Closet: Marriage and Other Crises of Middle Age." In *Looking Ahead: A Woman's Guide to the Problems and Joys of Growing Older,* edited by L.E. Troll, J. Israel, and K. Israel, pp. 81-92. Englewood Cliffs, N.J.: Prentice-Hall, 1977.

Lopata, H.Z., and K.F. Norr. "Changing Commitments of American Women to Work and Family Roles." *Social Security Bulletin* 43 (1980):3-13.

Lowenthal, M.F., and C. Haven. "Interaction and Adaptation: Intimacy as a Critical Variable." In *Middle Age and Aging,* edited by B.L. Neugarten, pp. 390-400. Chicago: University of Chicago Press, 1968.

Maas, S., and J. Kuypers. *From Thirty to Seventy: A Forty-Year Longitudinal Study of Adult Life Styles and Personality.* San Francisco: Jossey-Bass, 1974.

Maddox, G.L. "Persistence of Life Style among the Elderly: A Longitudinal Study of Patterns of Social Activity in Relation to Life Satisfaction." *Proceedings of the Seventh International Congress of Gerontology,* Vienna, 1966.

Mallan, L.B. "Women Born in the Early 1900's. Employment, Earning, and Benefit Levels." *Social Security Bulletin* 37 (1974):3-24.

Markides, K.S., and H.W. Martin. "A Causal Model of Life Satisfaction among the Elderly." *Journal of Gerontology* 34 (1979):86-93.

Matthews, S.H. *The Social World of Old Women.* Beverly Hills: Sage, 1979.

Morgan, L.A. "Toward a Formal Theory of Life Course Continuity and Change." Paper presented at the Annual Meeting of the Gerontological Society, San Francisco, 1977.

Muller, C.F. "Economic Roles and the Status of the Elderly." In *Aging and Society,* edited by E.F. Borgatta and N.G. McCluskey, pp. 17-41. Beverly Hills: Sage, 1980.

Neugarten, B.L. "Personality and Aging." In *Handbook of the Psychology of Aging,* edited by J.E. Birren and K.W. Schaie, pp. 626-649. New York: Van Nostrand Reinhold, 1977.

Older Women: The Economics of Aging. Washington, D.C.: Women's Studies Program and Policy Center, George Washington University, 1980.

Palmore, E.B. "Differences in the Retirement Patterns of Men and Women." *The Gerontologist* 5 (1965):4-8.

Palmore, E.B., and V.R. Kivett. "Change in Life-Satisfaction. A Longitudinal Study of Persons Aged 46-70." *Journal of Gerontology* 13 (1977):311-316.

Pampel, F.C. *Social Change and the Aged.* Lexington, Mass.: Lexington Books, D.C. Health, 1981.

Parnes, H.A., et al. *Dual Careers: A Longitudinal Analysis of the Labor Market Experience of Women.* Columbus: Ohio State University Press, 1976.

Pepitone-Rockwell, F. *Dual-Career Couples.* Beverly Hills: Sage, 1980.

Powers, E.A., and G.L. Bultena. "Sex Differences in Intimate Friendships in Old Age." *Journal of Marriage and the Family* 38 (1976):739-747.

Prentis, R.S. "White-Collar Working Women's Perception of Retirement." *The Gerontologist* 20 (February 1980):90-95.

Roberts, W.L., and A.E. Roberts. "Significant Elements in the Relationship of Long-Married Couples." *International Journal of Aging and Human Development* 10 (1980):265.

Rosenfeld, R.A. "Women's Occupational Careers." *Sociology of Work and Occupations* 6 (1974):283-311.

Rosenkaimer, D.; A. Saperstein; B. Ishizaki; and S.M. MacBride. "Coping with Old Age: Sex Differences." Paper presented at the Annual Meeting of the Gerontological Society, New York: 1976.

Rosow, I. *Socialization to Old Age.* Berkeley: University of California Press, 1974.

Rubin, L.B. *Women of a Certain Age: The Midlife Search for Self.* New York: Harper & Row, 1979.

Schwab, K., and L.M. Irelan. "The Social Security Administration's Retirement History Study." In *Aging and Retirement: Prospects, Planning, and Policy,* edited by N.G. McCluskey and E.F. Borgatta, pp. 15-30. Beverly Hills: Sage, 1981.

Seltzer, M.M. "Suggestions for the Examination of Time-Disordered Relationships." In *Time, Roles, and Self in Old Age,* edited by J.F. Gubrium, pp. 111-125. New York: Behavioral Publications, 1976.

Sheldon, A.; P.J.M. McEwan; and C.P. Ryser. "Retirement, Patterns and Predictions," DHEW Publication no. (ADM) 74-79. Washington, D.C.: NIMH, 1975.

Sheppard, H.L. "Work and Retirement." In *Handbook of Aging and the Social Sciences,* edited by R.H. Binstock and E. Shanas, pp. 286-309. New York: Van Nostrand Reinhold, 1976.

Sherman, S.R. "Labor-Force Status of Nonmarried Women on the Threshold of Retirement." *Social Security Bulletin* 37 (1974):3-13.

Simpson, I.H.; K.W. Back; and J.C. McKinney. "Orientations toward Work and Retirement, and Self-Evaluation in Retirement." In *Social Aspects of Aging,* edited by Simpson and McKinney, pp. 75-89. Durham, N.C.: Duke University Press, 1966.

Sobol, M.G. "Commitment to Work." In *Working Mothers,* edited by L.W. Hoffman and I.F. Nye, pp. 63-80. San Francisco: Jossey-Bass, 1974.

Sommers, T. *Aging in America: Implications for Women.* Oakland, Calif.: NCOA, 1976.

Spence, D., and T. Lonner, "The 'Empty Nest': A Transition within Motherhood." *Family Coordinator* 20 (1971):369-375.

Streib, G.F., and C.J. Schneider. *Retirement in American Society.* Ithaca, N.Y.: Cornell University Press, 1971.

Stueve, A., and C.S. Fisher, "Social Networks and Older Women." Working Paper no. 292. Berkeley: Institute of Urban and Regional Development, University of California, 1978.

Sussman, M.B. "An Analytical Model for the Sociological Study of Retirement." In *Retirement,* edited by F.M. Carp, pp. 29-74. New York: Behavioral Publications, 1972.

Sweet, J.A. *Women in the Labor Force.* New York: Seminar Press, 1973.

Szalai, A., et al. (eds.) *The Use of Time.* The Hague: Mouton, 1972.

Szinovacz, M. "Female Retirement: Personal and Marital Consequences. A Case Study." Paper presented at the Annual Meeting of the Gerontological Society, Dallas, 1978.

_____. *The Situation of Women in Austria. Economic and Family Issues.* Vienna: Federal Ministry of Social Affairs, 1979.

_____. Female Retirement: Effects on Spousal Roles and Marital Adjustment." *Journal of Family Issues* 1 (1980):423-440.

_____. "Women's Adjustment to Retirement. Preliminary Results." Report to the NRTA-AARP Andrus Foundation. Florida State University, 1982a.

_____. ed. *Women's Retirement. Policy Implications of Recent Research.* Beverly Hills: Sage, 1982b.

Taylor, C. "Developmental Conceptions and the Retirement Process." In *Retirement,* edited by F.M. Carp, pp. 75-116. New York: Behavioral Publications, 1972.

Thompson, G.B., "Work Experience and Income of the Population Aged 60 and Older, 1971." *Social Security Bulletin* 37 (1974):3-16.

Troll, L.E. "The Family of Later Life: A Decade Review." In *A Decade of Family Research and Action,* edited by C.B. Broderick. Minneapolis: National Council of Family Relations, 1971, pp. 187-214.

Troll, L.E.; J. Israel; and K. Israel. *Looking Ahead. A Woman's Guide to the Problems and Joys of Growing Older.* Englewood Cliffs, N.J.: Prentice-Hall, 1977.

Troll, L.E.; S.J. Miller; and R.C. Atchley. *Families in Later Life.* Belmont, Calif.: Wadsworth, 1979.

U.S. Bureau of the Census. *Census of the Population. 1970: General Social and Economic Characteristics.* Final Report PC(1)-C1, United States Summary. Washington, D.C.: U.S. Government Printing Office, 1978a.

_____. *Demographic Aspects of Aging and the Older Population in the United States.* Current Population Reports, series P-23, no. 59. Washington, D.C.: U.S. Government Printing Office, 1978b.

U.S. Department of Labor. *Employment and Training Report of the President.* Washington, D.C.: U.S. Government Printing Office, 1980.

Walker, J.W., and K.F. Price. "Retirement Choice and Retirement Satisfaction." Paper presented at the Annual Meeting of the Gerontological Society, 1975.

Walker, K.E., and M.E. Woods. *Time Use: A Measure of Household Production of Family Goods and Services.* Washington, D.C.: American Home Economics Association, 1976.

PART III
SOCIAL STRUCTURES AND AGING

Introduction

In this section we move to the level of social structure, to the family systems, the residential settings, and the economic and public policy variables that affect the well-being of America's elderly.

Family Settings and Intergenerational Relationships

The first set of readings covers many aspects of family life and intergenerational relations. Gary R. Lee examines the effects of contemporary trends in divorce, remarriage, and coresidence and finds that the prophets of doom have overlooked the more positive and adaptive features of our family system. This chapter is one more corrective to the romanticization of the "family of Western nostalgia."

If the weight of evidence has finally corrected our view of the American past, idealization of the ethnic family still persists. In part, the belief that Black, Hispanic, Asian-American, Jewish, and White ethnic families practice a purer form of intergenerational responsibility than do the fully assimilated may be seen as a protective device for minority group members. In part, this view does reflect reality, but more as a consequence of economic necessity than of enduring subcultural values. The data on Black and Hispanic families reported by Charles H. Mindel, along with the description of caretaking patterns among Chinese and Irish families in Boston by Charlotte Ikels in part 2, illustrate the degree to which economic considerations and generational shifts become paramount, often washing out cultural differences.

One, often hidden, assumption of the "golden age/golden isles" literature is the belief that relations among family members, particularly between parents and children, are naturally warm and close. Thus, where such bonds appear lacking, some outside cause must be found—geographic mobility, an ethic of selfishness, overreliance on government, flawed personalities, and the like. But it may be more accurate to treat intergenerational relationships as inherently problematic; that is, as likely to be characterized by envy and hostility as by love and cooperation. One need only look to the Bible or the great dramas of early Greece to find stories of sibling rivalry and parent/child conflict. Much will depend upon the norms of the culture and the ability of the group to support its members economically, as seen in Nancy Foner's cross-cultural review of caregiving to frail elderly. Nor are contemporary families spared the consequences of intrafamily tension, evidenced in the phenomenon of elder abuse. Nonetheless, as Claire Pedrick-Cornell and Richard J. Gelles demonstrate, the data on elder abuse must be carefully evaluated, lest we contribute to the manufacture of yet another social problem. In general, the elderly are the least likely to be victims of all types of crime, including family violence (U.S. Department of Justice, 1983).

In Western societies, intrafamily conflict is often reflected in the wills through which property is passed from one generation to another. These "last wills and testaments" provide fascinating data for the reconstruction of family relationships as these change over historical time (Engler-Bowles and Kart, 1983). Jeffrey P. Rosenfeld, who has published a number of studies of such wills, here traces age group differences in testamentory behavior, reflecting many contemporary social trends.

Residential Settings

In the community. As noted in Part I of this book, their home is the major asset of most elderly, but this is hardly a "liquid" asset, i.e. one that brings immediate income. Finding alternatives is not easy, particularly since government-sponsored housing programs have been drastically slashed by the current administration. A number of creative options are analyzed by Anne Woodward, although it must be kept in mind that the great majority of elders perfer to live fully independent of adult children.

To maintain this independence and also to enhance geographic mobility, increasing numbers of older people are choosing the mobile home option, becoming the "seasonal migrants to the sunbelt" described by Deborah A. Sullivan and Sylvia A. Stevens. Others age in place hoping that their neighborhoods will undergo positive changes as a byproduct of urban revitalization. But the needs of elderly community residents are often overlooked in the course of urban renewal. In Atlantic City, New Jersey, for example, the dramatic turnabout in the city's fortunes brought by casino gambling has thus far failed to upgrade the living conditions of the poor in general and the elderly in particular, as described by Marea Teski and her colleagues.

Many older people whose physical or financial status makes it impossible to maintain independent residence will join the household of an adult child, typically a daughter. While this arrangement can be burdensome for members of both adult generations, most families manage to cope quite well, particularly if there are supportive services in the community (Hess and Soldo, 1984). Yet, at some point, the health of the older person may deteriorate dramatically, or the caregiving family come under financial or emotional strains that limit its ability to provide adequate care. Under such circumstances, some older persons will be institutionalized. Others find their way to nursing homes and state hospitals because there is no one else able to care for them.

In institutions. The three readings on institutionalization touch upon a common theme: to understand the behavior of patients, one must examine the structure of institutional life. Nursing homes and similar facilities are "total institutions" (Goffman, 1961) with needs of their own: to run smoothly, to process large numbers of difficult individuals, to stay in business, and the like. These needs inevitably conflict with many basic goals of such institutions, such as rehabilitation or maximizing the personal autonomy of patients. The typical outcome is "goal displacement" in which the patient's lives are structured to preserve institutional order.

Ellen J. Langer and Jerry Avorn present an overview of experimental research on the processes whereby the environment of the institution affects patient health and behavior, often contrary to original intentions. The fallacy of diagnosing patients on the basis of a single observation is demonstrated in the research reported by John Cumming and his colleagues, but few institutions for the elderly have the professional staff to conduct constant obervation. Thus, the traffic in patients from one institutional setting to another is unnecessarily prolonged. As Martin Hochbaum and Florence Galkin note, few institutions even provide minimal discharge planning services; the assumption is that the move to the nursing home is the end of the line, which, indeed, it so often is.

Economic Status and Public Policy

The final set of chapters deals with topics of immediate concern to the quality of life of the elderly today and in the future. Economic security, along with good health, are essential preconditions of successful aging. Although ours is the last modern industrial society to have done so, we have, over the past 50 years, reached consensus over the principle that income maintenance and health care of the aged is a public rather than private responsibility. Hence, the continual broadening of Social Security coverage and the introduction of Medicare in the mid-1960s. Today, however, both programs are being challenged and trimmed, under attack from business interests and the ideological right (Hess, 1984).

Robert H. Binstock suggests that the aged have become modern "scapegoats" for major failures in public policy, as new myths replace old ones, and as intergenerational tensions are reinforced. Both the old image of the elderly as mired in poverty and political impotence and the new perception of old people as relatively well-off, possibly overcompensated, and politically powerful have obscured the great heterogeneity among the aged. Thus, programs to aid old people have generally benefited the least needy, while little is being done to help the "truly needy" aged.

As Binstock notes, these issues came to the fore with the recent perception of crisis in the Social Security system. Carrying this analysis one step further, John Myles sees the current attack on social welfare programs for the elderly as the cutting edge of an ideologically-based attempt to discredit the public sector altogether in favor of private enterprise. If a program as deeply entrenched as Social Security can be dismantled, what other public program is safe? Not surprisingly, similar doubts are now being raised about Medicare, in favor of private medical insurance accounts. These proposals would divert billions of dollars into the profit-making sector.

A more conservative, but also provocative, analysis of the Social Security "crisis" is presented by Nathan Keyfitz, who proposes a far more flexible system than the one currently in place. The possibility of drawing benefits at earlier ages in order to retrain for other occupations has great merit in a society characterized by rapid technological change. Both Keyfitz and Hochbaum and Galkin follow the convention of using the generic "he" for all persons, yet the majority of Social Security recipients are women as are the great majority of nursing home residents.

Indeed, so strong is the tendency to perceive problems of aging in terms of the male life course that the most recent revisions of the Social Security Act failed to address major gender inequities. Maxine Forman reviews the new amendments in terms of their implications for women, concluding on balance that much remains to be done before both employed women and those who work at homemaking are fairly treated in retirement. Income maintenace in old age is only one of many economic issues that negatively affect older women. Since the older population will increasingly be composed of women, it is fitting that this book closes with the essay by Carroll L. Estes, Lenore Gerard, and Adele Clarke on "Women and the Economics of Aging," for it is our treatment of older women that will determine the quality of life of most elderly in the decade ahead and into the twenty-first century.

References

Engler-Bowles, Carol A., and Cary S. Kart. "Intergenerational Relations and Testementary Patterns: An Exploration," *Gerontologist* 23 (1983): 167-73.

Goffman, Erving. *Asylums*. Garden City, N.Y.: Anchor, 1961.

Hess, Beth B. "Aging Policies and Old Women: The Hidden Agenda." In Alice S. Rossi (ed), *Gender and the Life Course*. New York: Aldine, 1984.

Hess, Beth B., and Beth J. Soldo. "The Old and the Very Old: A New Frontier of Age Policy." Paper presented at the annual meeting of the American Sociological Society, San Antonio, 1984.

U.S. Department of Justice. *Report to the Nation on Crime and Justice: The Data*. NCJ-87068, October 1983. Washington, D.C.: U.S. Government Printing Office.

22

Marriage and Aging

Gary R. Lee

Prediction of any sort is a hazardous business. Predictions of what the family may be like in the near future are especially hazardous. A primary reason is that change in social and cultural institutions such as the family is, unlike technological change, neither unidirectional nor cumulative. An equally important obstacle to accurate prediction is the emotional nature of the topic—virtually all of us have fairly strong feelings about what the family should be and how its reality differs from this ideal. We may thus predict that the family will move closer to our own ideal, not because it really is doing so, but because we may be in an optimistic frame of mind. The reverse error may be committed with equal ease in a pessimistic mood. Because prediction is difficult in any sphere of the social sciences, and because the family is a topic that has subjective importance to most people, it is easy to fall into the trap of basing predictions on personal values rather than empirical/theoretical premises.

The increasing divorce rate and the decreasing incidence of co-residence by aging parents and their adult offspring are two behavior changes which have implications for the future of the family. These two phenomena ostensibly have little or nothing to do with one another. However, they are both susceptible to a variety of emotional interpretations, and are both frequently used as grist for the doomsayers' mill. In these respects each trend is representative of many other family-related phenomena, and may thus be productively employed as examples of the hazards in emotional or "common-sense" interpretations of social behavior.

Divorce Rate

According to the Vital Statistics Reports provided by the Department of Health and Human Services, the 1979 divorce rate in the United States was

5.3 divorces per 1,000 population. This compares with a rate of 3.2 only ten years earlier and a rate of 2.2 as recently as 1962. The trend, as everyone knows, has been sharply upward since the mid-sixties. What we do not know is whether this trend will continue and, perhaps more importantly, what it means. The divorce rate has shown signs of stabilizing in the last year or two, but there is no denying its rapid increase in the preceding fifteen years, and there is certainly no sign of a decrease. In a very short span of time, a high divorce rate has become characteristic of the American family, and while it may not get much worse it is not likely to get better soon. There is no sense in arguing that divorce is not problematic. It is, to varying degrees, traumatic, painful, and disruptive in virtually every aspect of the lives of the people involved. Divorces, and the great variety of events and circumstances which lead to them, are not pleasant experiences. There is very little to be said in their favor. If one accepts the overwhelming probability that our society will continue to be characterized by a divorce rate as high or higher than its current level, one must question the implications of this trend. These implications must be considered on two levels: the individual and the societal.

On the individual level, there will be more of the emotional trauma which accompanies divorce. There will be more single-parent families, with the diminished financial resources and increased role burdens which almost inevitably follow. There will be more children with only one resident parent. There will be more litigations involving property settlement and child support. There will be more remarriages. Except for the last, this is an impressive list of what many might term social problems. As divorce itself is problematic for individuals, so, too, are the events which typically follow it. But despite its problematic nature, divorce is undertaken because it is perceived as a *solution* to other problems, as a way of minimizing or eliminating the apparently less desirable consequences of staying married. From this point of view, it makes better sense to think of marriage as the difficulty (or the possible source of difficulties) and the rising divorce rate in itself as neither cause for alarm nor social problem. But does this rising divorce rate indicate that marriage is becoming increasingly problematic, that the quality of marital relations is progressively deteriorating on a large scale, and that the institution of marriage is less capable than formerly of satisfying the needs of individuals? I think not. Divorce has become more common because it has gained credibility as a viable solution to marital problems. This is due in some part to legal changes, such as the development of "no-fault" divorce laws and the liberalizing of grounds for divorce to include incompatibility, mental cruelty, and the like. But much more critical here is cultural change: to a considerably greater extent than in the past, divorce is accepted as an extreme, but nonetheless legitimate, solution to marital problems.

The causes of this cultural change are diverse and impossible to determine precisely. An inquiry into them necessitates a shift to the societal level of analysis. Here the concern is not the causes of individual divorces, but rather the causes of the increasing *rate* of divorce. What is it about the institution of marriage that causes individual unions to be terminated with such frequency? Is there something wrong with the institution of marriage, or with the fabric of society itself, that causes or is caused by our high divorce rate? Is divorce symptomatic of social disorganization? Again, I think not. The concept of social disorganization is frequently employed by social scientists and others to refer to a form of social organization whose principles are not understood. Although the divorce rate in the United States is among the highest for modern industrial nations, there are many stable and highly organized nonindustrial societies with substantially higher divorce rates. Many such societies are typified by matrilineal kin groups. High divorce rates do not threaten societal stability because stability depends on the effective functioning of these kin groups, and the kin groups do not depend upon conjugal ties. Paternity is virtually irrelevant: kin-group membership is conferred by maternity, and property and authority pass from mother's brother to sister's son. Fragile marital bonds do not threaten the system; in fact, their very fragility keeps them from competing for the loyalties of kin-group members and thus threatening the system. The United States, of course, does not have a matrilineal kinship system. The point, however, is that a high divorce rate does not necessarily constitute a disruption in a social system, but may be an integral part of it. The divorce rate is neither causally nor epistemically related to social disorganization.

In general terms, there are probably two kinds of causes of our high divorce rate. One is historical. The proximate cause of the high divorce rate we will have in the eighties is the high divorce rate we had in the seventies. This generalization is not as trite as it first appears. Divorce, like other social customs, feeds on itself. As it becomes more common it becomes more visible, and this visibility means that more people will consider it to be a possible, if not entirely normative, solution to marital difficulties.

The second kind of cause has to do with the expectations we have of marriage. We now expect much more from our spouses than a division of labor and an opportunity to perpetuate the species. Our culture tells us that marriage is the primary source of all manner of emotional rewards: love, friendship, security, comfort, companionship—the list could go on indefinitely. We go through a very extended period of adolescence and young adulthood during which we search for a mate, investing enormous amounts of psychological energy in the process. The mythology tells us that after we finally marry, we will live happily ever after. A goal has been accomplished, thereby assuring continued success and happiness. Marriage is the means by which we are to achieve further goals, most of which involve emotional gratification. Our culture invests marriage with emotional and psychological significance to a degree unmatched in other times and places. We did not invent Cinderella, but we made her famous.

Probably no marriage fully satisfies all expectations. This has more to do with the expectations than the marriage. Our high divorce rate is, in this context, not particularly surprising. Much more surprising is our high remarriage rate: the substantial majority of people who divorce remarry, and do so fairly soon after the divorce. This, more than anything, indicates the continuing strength of the marital institution. The rising divorce rate does not mean that people are losing faith in marriage, but that they believe marriage can be better than it often is. When marriages fall far short of expectations, people have become more willing to try again. Giving up on *a* marriage is very different than giving up on *marriage*.

None of this, of course, eliminates or minimizes the problem of single-parent families or the other personal difficulties that often accompany divorce. But these are not new problems, even in degree. While more families are now broken by divorce, fewer are broken by death at points in the life cycle where children are likely to be present. Except for the very latest stages of life, increases in voluntary marital dissolution have been largely counterbalanced by decreases in involuntary marital dissolution.

Many people and philosophies oppose divorce on moral grounds. These arguments cannot be shaken by the position expressed here. However, arguments that divorce in itself is a major social problem, that it causes or results from or indicates social disorganization, or that it constitutes a new and unique threat to the previously "healthy" institution of marriage are not warranted by either logic or data. The eighties will, in all probability, be characterized by divorce rates as high as, or higher than, those of the seventies. We will continue to expect a great deal from marriage; we will therefore continue to be disappointed with some frequency; and we will continue to try again.

Intergenerational Co-Residence

Another cause of substantial concern among some observers of social trends is the rapid decrease, during the twentieth century at least, in rates of co-residence between aging parents and their grown children. The best estimates of residential arrangements, based on census data, show that at the turn of the century over sixty percent of the elderly (aged 65 and over) lived with at least one child; the comparable figure for 1970 was about eighteen percent. Furthermore, there have been substantial increases in the proportion of the elderly who live alone, and much of this increase has been quite recent. Living alone is more common for elderly females than males, largely because wives tend to outlive their husbands. The percentage of older women living alone rose from about thirteen percent as recently as 1940 to over thirty-three percent in 1970. There are no indications that this trend will not continue.

That fewer and fewer older people are living with family members, and increasing numbers are living alone, is cause for alarm in many quarters. One reason is that rates of solitary residence are highest in precisely that segment of the elderly population where poverty rates are the highest: widowed women. Older people who live alone may also be afflicted by personal problems, of which loneliness and social isolation are not the least. Advanced age may bring declining health, failing eyesight, and other chronic conditions which mean that people need physical help as well as social support.

Who cares for these people? The percentage of the elderly in nursing homes and similar institutions is not increasing dramatically, and these alternatives are generally regarded as undesirable by both the elderly themselves and their families. It is revealing nonetheless to note that persons without children or other kin are disproportionately likely to be admitted to such institutions. Still, elderly people who do have families are not likely to make their homes with them.

What does this tell us about the treatment we accord our elderly? The obvious, and quite common, answer to this question is that we are ignoring them. We do not share our homes with our aging parents; therefore we do not care for or about them, we fail to live up to our responsibilities toward them, and we allow old age to be a time of emotional as well as physical misery. This, along with the rising divorce rate, is often taken as another sign of the decay of our family system, and our society along with it.

The error inherent in the moralistic interpretation of this phenomenon is even more flagrant and obvious than in the case of the divorce rate. As a gerontologist, I have frequently noted that the authors (and students) who argue that the elderly are being ignored and left to fend for themselves are likely, in the next chapter or class session, to extol the virtues of independence for the elderly. It is often remarked, with good reason, that the American elderly value their independence above all else. Fears of sickness and poverty among older people are directly connected with fears of dependence: on children, on other kin, on the government. The value of independence was strongly ingrained in this generation of Americans, and there is no sign that this value decreases in old age.

Too many people have an image of the elderly drawn from journalistic human-interest stories: good copy, but not really representative. They are often seen as destitute, friendless, in poor health, dependent on a small government dole, begging to be taken in by their children but, more and more, being turned away. There are, of course, some who are destitute, some who are in poor health, and even some who are waiting for their kids to invite them in. But not many.

Old age simply is not like this for most people. Few are rich, but surprisingly few live in the sort of poverty often believed to be typical among the elderly. In 1977, 14.1 percent of all persons aged 65 and over fell below the federally established poverty level; the comparable figure for the total population was 11.6 percent. While this is hardly a source of pride, the difference between the older population and the general population is not nearly as large as is commonly believed. Furthermore, the improvement for older people during the 1970s was quite dramatic. The percentage of the total population in poverty dropped only 1 percent (from 12.6 percent to 11.6 percent) between 1970 and 1977, while for the elderly the decline was over 10 percent (from 24.5 percent to 14.1 percent). There are still many poor old people; but there are still many poor young people, too. And most of the people who are old and poor were poor before they were old; poverty is rarely directly attributable to old age.

We still have a long way to go to ensure an adequate standard of living for our elderly, but we have made remarkable strides in the twentieth century. This has a great deal to do with their living arrangements. While we have good evidence that the elderly *did* frequently live with their children around the turn of the century, we have no evidence that they *wanted* to do so, then or now. In our culture, unlike some others such as the Japanese, dependence on children in one's old age is no virtue, and most older people seem to prefer to avoid dependence and the appearance of dependence if they have the necessary resources. They have been increasingly likely to have these resources. Because of this, they have been increasingly able to stay in their own homes, or in homes of their own choosing, and have less often been forced to rely on the largesse of children. They are not being ignored, they are being independent.

Ethel Shanas, a national leader in research on the family relations of the elderly, has come up with some excellent documentation of the desire of the elderly for "intimacy at a distance" with respect to relations with their children. Her survey data, extending over a period of several decades, show that while rates of co-residence between aging parents and their adult children have been decreasing, rates of separate but *proximate* residence have been increasing. One consequence of this is that the proportion of elderly parents who live within any given distance of at least one child has remained virtually constant for at least a generation. The same is true for rates of interaction, the exchange of mutual aid and services between generations, and many other indicators of social relationships between the elderly and their relatives.

As a category, the American elderly are afflicted by many social and personal problems. Collective neglect by their families is not one of them, although it certainly occurs in some number of individual cases. Decreasing rates of intergenerational co-residence do not indicate societal failure to care for elderly; they indicate instead that the elderly have been somewhat successful in achieving independence. The former interpretation constitutes, even more clearly than in the case of the divorce rate, the perception of a problem where in fact we have a solution.

Future Nostalgia

Certain kinds of demographic predictions about the American family in the 1980s are relatively easy to make. Our divorce rate, if it does not increase further, will at least remain quite high, and the trend away from household sharing between aging parents and their middle-aged children will, in all probability, continue unabated. Predictions about age at marriage, premarital cohabitation, fertility, and many other rates and measures could also be made within varying margins of error.

In some ways, however, it is more important to ask what the changes mean than to ask what they will be. American culture is perhaps more conservative in its conception of the family than of any other social institution. Change in the family is rarely interpreted neutrally. When change occurs, it is typically viewed as negative. William Goode's concept of the "classical family of Western nostalgia" is instructive in this regard: the belief that families in the unspecified past were strong, stable, happy, and other good things, while current families are the opposite. It reflects our tendency to idealize the family of the past and results in negative and often moralistic interpretations of any kind of change in family patterns or behaviors.

This concept has little or no basis in empirical fact. The kind of family it describes never really existed on any large scale. The family of the past is probably idealized because most of us tend to idealize our childhoods and identify them with a simpler way of life. Life was not really simpler then, but we saw it from the perspective of children. Since most of us spent our childhoods in families, we idealize the family along with childhood. Our own children will, in all probability, do the same thing.

A few generations down the line someone will probably reinvent or rediscover the concept of the "classical family of Western nostalgia" and apply it to the 1980s, with a slightly different content. If the divorce rate were to drop unexpectedly in the next decade or two, many of us might long for the "good old days" when people were not forced to stay in unhappy marriages. If the practice of sharing homes between adult generations ever comes back into fashion, many of us, young and old, would bemoan the loss of independence such a practice entails and wish for the "intimacy at a distance" we now enjoy.

The greatest difficulty with a social-problems approach to family change is our tendency to idealize family life, particularly past family life. Consequently, whatever characteristics the family currently possesses come to be defined as problems, and the solution involves going back to the way it used to be. But it never was the way it "used to be." In spite of the changes in the divorce rate and residential arrangements, the American family system has been remarkably stable over time. But change has, paradoxically, been part of this stability. There is no good reason to expect this situation to change dramatically in the 1980s.

Bibliography

Lee, Gary R. *Family Structure and Interaction: A Comparative Analysis.* Philadelphia: Lippinocott, 1977.

Lee, Gary R. "Kinship in the Seventies: A Decade Review of Research and Theory." *Journal of Marriage and the Family* 42 (November 1980)

Shanas, Ethel. "Social Myth as Hypothesis: The Case of the Family Relations of Old People." *Gerontologist* 19 (February 1979): 3-9.

Winch, Robert F. *Familial Organization: A Quest for Determinants.* New York: Free Press, 1977.

Yoder, Jan D., and Nichols, Robert C. "A Life Perspective Comparison of Married and Divorced Persons." *Journal of Marriage and the Family* 42 (May 1980): 413-19.

23

The Elderly in Minority Families

Charles H. Mindel

Discussions of ethnicity and family life have often been the subject of numerous myths and mythologies. At times the myths are positive, at times they are negative, and often they are in contradiction. It is sometimes suggested that there is an "American family" that reflects the so-called melting pot theory of racial and ethnic assimilation. At other times there is a notion of American society as a conglomerate of "unmeltable ethnics" existing in a somewhat tenuous societal pluralism. Within these two polar extremes various descriptions of ethnic families are often made. Some ethnic groups are attributed to have more superior qualities than others. Thus we often hear about the "strong" families of some ethnic groups, and the disintegrating and "pathological" families of other ethnic groups. The truth, of course, lies somewhere within all of this, though it has been quite difficult at times to discover where the truth actually lies.

The family is an extremely important institution with respect to the continuation of ethnic identities in American society, and within this context the elderly are often important participants. It is within the family that primary socialization occurs, in which the ethnic culture is learned and in which future behavior is often channeled. The family is the institution that transmits the culture, the important beliefs, values, and norms both of the family and the ethnic group. Thus, it is within the family that a whole range of activities, which are often perceived by individuals as distinctively ethnic, are transmitted. Such matters as the size of the family, for example, or husband-wife role relationships, attitudes toward divorce, attitudes toward relatives and other kin, notions of filial responsibility and support for the elderly, and the larger issue of "familism" and the importance of family life in the social world of the individual, are all mediated and learned.

In the paragraphs to follow, the patterns and variations distinctive to ethnic minority families and their relationships with the elderly will be described. These variations can be categorized into three broad areas: (a) the structure and organization of the nuclear family; (b) the relationships between nuclear family units and the nature of their interdependence; (c) the relationship of the family unit, both nuclear and extended, with the wider society.

With regard to the structure of the family, matters that are relevant to the place of the elderly include authority relations, sex-role differences, generational differences, and the relative importance of lineal versus collateral kin. The interdependence of nuclear families is also of tremendous concern to the elderly, for it is in the exchange network and support network between and among nuclear families that much care and service is rendered to elderly members. It is in this area that much of the research on interchanges between nuclear families and their elderly kin has taken place (see Bengtson and Schrader, 1982; Mindel, 1982, for a review of these studies). A significant amount is known about the visiting patterns, mutual aid relationships, and relative proximity to kin that family members have. Last, the interaction of elderly within the family context and the wider society is another area of increasing importance. Families differ and are changing the extent to which they will relate to an external, nonfamily support system and to what extent they insist that care be provided entirely or mostly in their family. What appears to make sense in one cultural context—for example, the willingness of members to accept aid from strangers or agencies—is often seen as abhorent and a sign of failure and weakness in other cultural contexts.

Discussions of the ethnic family and kinship relations typically have not focused centrally on the elderly, inasmuch as they have been generally concerned with kinship activities and mutual aid arrangements. However, when the issue of extended family relationships is being discussed, it is clear on closer examination that, by and large, the relationships being discussed are parent-child relationships. Studies examining visitation with kin are more often than not examining visitation of adult children with their parents and to a much lesser extent visitation with other kin. Mutual aid between kin usually translates as aid between parents and adult children (or perhaps siblings). Numerous studies have made it clear (see Mindel, 1980; Adams, 1968b; Hill, Foote, Aldous, Carlson, and MacDonald, 1970; Sussman, 1953) that, for the most part, aid between more distant kin is minimal and idiosyncratic. Thus, the studies of kinship relations of ethnic and minority groups as well as majority groups tend to be discussions of older parent-adult child relations. It is in this context, then, that the research on elderly and their family relationships can be viewed.

In the discussion to follow, the distinctive family patterns of the two largest ethnic minority groups, American Blacks and Mexican Americans, will be presented. Generally speaking, ethnic groups that still maintain relatively strong ethnic identities among their members tend to have more closely knit and more highly structured extended kinship relationships. An important analytical point to bear in mind is the question of how much a particular family pattern is a culturally defined arrangement, and to what degree it is a functional adaptation to a particular position in the stratification system. For example, do members of a particular ethnic group maintain close ties to kin because of family tradition passed down through the years, or are close ties maintained as a survival mechanism in a poverty-level existence? Invariably, both of these factors are intertwined, but it is well to keep them analytically distinct.

Mexican Americans and Their Elderly

Structure of the Family

As numerous writers (Alvirez and Bean, 1981; Maldonado, 1975; Gallego, 1980) have noted in recent years, to speak of "the" Mexican American family can be misleading and potentially erroneous. Not only has the Mexican American family changed over time, but it also differs with respect to urban-rural setting, socioeconomic status, and extent of acculturation. Even though these differences exist, it is probably worthwhile to describe the traditional Mexican and Mexican American family as well as some of the changes that have happened to it. It is also useful to describe this family type in a discussion of the elderly, since for many of the elderly their perception of the family is tied to this image of the traditional family. Keep in mind, however, that this family description no longer exists in many cases.

Three structural characteristics or features of the traditional Mexican American family that have been widely described in the literature are familism, male dominance, and subordination of younger persons to older persons.

Familism

Grebler, Moore, and Guzman (1970:359) have stated that, with respect to the importance of familism,

> the major theme dominating the classic portrayal of the traditional Mexican family is the deep importance of the family to all its members. The needs of the family collectively supersede the needs of each individual member. . . . Mutual financial assistance, exchange of work and other skills, and advice and support in solving personal problems are ideally available in the extended kin group.

This statement is typical of many statements regarding the nature and importance of familism and extended familism in the Mexican American family. In recent years there have been a number of challenges to the continuing importance of this factor (see Gallego, 1980; Gilbert, 1978; Grebler et al., 1970). Gallego, for example, in studying Mexican American elderly in Utah, found that "Mexican American family solidarity and reciprocity and friendship support systems are a myth and this need for human interpersonal relationships is absent in the Mexican American elderly population." He suggests that such factors as urbanization, vertical mobility of offspring, and nuclearization of the family possibly have eroded the natural and familial support system of the Mexican American family for the Mexican American elderly. Gilbert (1978) also stresses that "extended family among Mexican Americans is not a unitary and constant configuration nor do norms of obligations unvaryingly extend over the entire universe of kin." Implied here is that distinctions are made among parents, siblings, children, and other, more extended kin, such as aunts, uncles, and cousins. Gallego (1980) concluded that there were no differences between the Mexican American elderly that he studied with regard to family and friendship network support systems, and Anglo elderly, in that "with regard to children there was no difference between the visitation of Anglo children and the Mexican American children to their elderly parents" and that "all of the recent studies suggest that the family and natural support systems that have always been associated with Mexican American families are no longer there."

It should be remembered that Mexican American scholars have for many years stressed the fact that the Mexican American family system and Mexican Americans are extremely heterogeneous with respect to class, status, and generational differences (see Hernandez, 1976; Melville, 1980; Miranda, 1975). Among these different strata, whether social, cultural, or regional, different attitudes toward the elderly and different expectations exist. It is not surprising, then, that we will find discrepancies between cultural values and actually existing behaviors.

Authority Relations

One of the most widely discussed characteristics of the Mexican American family and one that is most emphasized in popular literature is the issue of male dominance and male superiority. Embodied largely in the popularly misunderstood concept of *machismo,* the role of males and the role of females in the family is actually much broader and more important than the currently popular notions about sexual virility, masculine pride, and the like would suggest. In the traditional Mexican American family, the father is seen as the head of the family, with absolute authority over wife and children. His authority and power are delegated primarily through males; women and younger children are expected to carry out his orders. *Machismo* in a broader context implies manliness, but not just with regard to sexual prowess. Alvirez and Bean (1981) state that it "includes the elements of courage, honor, and respect for others, as well as the notion of providing fully for one's family; and maintaining close ties with the extended family." Murillo (1971) argued that one important aspect of *machismo* was the encouragement of the "use of authority within the family in a just and fair manner." Thus, while *machismo* and its meaning of masculinity and manliness might include to some degree extramarital sexual behavior, its important cultural meaning for the family is its requirement of being a good husband and man to the family in providing for its needs.

Along with the notion of male dominance in the traditional Mexican American family is the complementary notion of female submissiveness. As Grebler et al. (1970) note, "the bearing and rearing of children continue to be seen as perhaps the most important function of a woman, symbolizing her maturity." Traditionally her primary role is of a homemaker and mother occupying a place secondary to the husband and other family members. It has been argued that these traditional distinctions between males and females are breaking down. For example, Grebler et al. (1970) suggest that with increasing urbanization and length of stay in the United States, Mexican American family sex-role authority relationships are becoming increasingly egalitarian. With declining sex-role authority, the historical respect that the elderly mother and father had can also be expected to decline.

Generational Differences

One other very important characteristic of the traditional Mexican American family is the subordination of the younger to the older. Alvirez and Bean (1981) argue that "older people receive more respect from youth and children than is characteristic in Anglo homes." Respect is reflected in speech patterns and in manners and behavior. It is clearly part of the Mexican American culture that elderly are deserving of respect from youth. The pattern of subordination of the younger to the older has been traditionally widespread throughout the family. Not only are the elderly supposed to be more highly respected than younger family members but even older siblings have higher authority and greater power in the family than younger children.

The issue of the respect and authority of older versus younger has come under considerable analysis in recent years, and it is clear from numerous studies that this pattern is breaking down. For example, Gallego (1980) found that second- and third-generation Mexican American youth who are raised in primarily Anglo areas tend to devalue the worth of the family ties and the worth of the elderly. He suggests that "with the high fertility rates of the Mexican American population and the emphasis on youth, old age is devalued and ofttimes the elderly feel highly threatened and abused verbally and physically by the youth." Sotomayor (1973), in analyzing Chicano grandparents in an urban "barrio," found that grandparents still played an important role in child rearing, that they were often turned to in times of crisis, and that they still maintained a certain amount of influence over family decisions. However, Sotomayor found that there was less of a role for grandparents in the areas of religious upbringing and the transmission of family and ethnic cultural history and heritage. It would appear that a substantial amount of authority and respect still resides in the elderly, but that perhaps with time and increasing modernization these aspects of Mexican American culture are declining.

Marital Status and Living Arrangements

The Hispanic elderly, in terms of marriage patterns, generally follow the trend of the larger white population. However, as can be seen in Table 23.1, there are some noticeable differences.

Most Hispanic as well as Anglo elderly men are married, but slightly less than half of the elderly women are currently married. The major differences occur after age 75, when substantially fewer Hispanics are married. There appears to be a marked increase in the number of Hispanic widows and widowers.

TABLE 23.1
Marital Status of Hispanic and Anglo Elderly by Age, 1978

Marital Status	Hispanic		Anglo	
	65-74	75 +	65-74	75 +
Females				
Married	47.0	15.8	49.3	23.5
Widowed	37.1	76.3	40.4	68.3
Divorced	6.7	3.3	3.6	2.1
Never marrried	8.3	4.7	6.8	6.1
Males				
Married	82.8	66.2	82.7	72.2
Widowed	7.1	25.4	8.7	21.8
Divorced	5.6	1.4	3.2	1.4
Never married	4.5	7.0	5.5	4.6

Source: Data are from U.S. Bureau of the Census statistics, appearing in Jackson, 1980, pp. 129-31.

TABLE 23.2
Living Arrangements of Hispanics by Sex, 65-74 and 75 +, 1970

	Hispanic		Anglo	
	65-74	75 +	65-74	75 +
Males				
Primary individuals	13.9	16.2	13.0	20.3
Family heads	74.4	59.1	81.1	66.0
With other relatives	10.1	22.4	4.6	13.6
Secondary individuals	1.6	2.3	1.3	0.1
Females				
Primary individuals	21.4	25.0	33.2	41.1
Family heads	12.6	12.2	7.8	9.8
Wives of family heads	38.6	18.4	45.4	21.0
With other relatives	25.6	42.8	12.2	26.3
Secondary individuals	1.6	1.6	1.4	1.8

Source: Data are from U.S. Bureau of the Census statistics, appearing in Jackson, 1980, p. 134.

A better example of differences between Anglo and Hispanic family characteristics occurs when the living arrangements of the elderly are compared. Table 23.2 indicates clear differences between the two groups. Substantially more Hispanic elderly than Anglo elderly live with relatives, and many fewer Hispanic elderly live alone as primary individuals. Fewer Hispanic elders live as heads or wives of heads of their own households than do Anglo elderly.

In an attempt better to understand the phenomenon of shared households, Mindel (1979) examined census data on living arrangements of elderly. He found shared households (with relatives) rarely included the elderly couple; rather, when the living arrangement did occur it most often involved a "single" elderly person (that is, a widowed, divorced, or never-married elder). He found that 6.5 percent of all the male elderly and 16.1 percent of all the female elderly lived with relatives in 1970. However, when the single elderly were viewed separately, it was found that 34.6 percent of the single males and 37.4 percent of the single females were living with relatives. The rates for Hispanics based on the data in Table 23.2, which includes all elderly, married as well as single, suggest a shared household rate substantially higher than that of the Anglo group. If we could examine the rate for single elderly, a figure twice the national figure would probably not be an inaccurate assessment of the shared household rate. Certainly, a majority of the "old-old" single Hispanic elderly could be expected to share households with their relatives.

Sena-Rivera (1979) has argued that multigenerational households have "never been the norm for Mexico or Mexicans in the U.S. or for other Chicanos, except at times of individual extended family or conjugal family stress or periods of general societal disorganization." This assessment of the normative belief is consistent with other studies on attitudes toward multigenerational families and supporting elderly (see, for example, Dinkel, 1944; Wake and Sporakowski, 1972); nonetheless, the presence of this family type is more prevalent among Hispanics. Ramírez and Arce (1981) maintain that there is no consensus on whether the Chicano extended family is primarily a cultural holdover or primarily a functional adaptation. Analysis of data on the persistence of multigenerational households at different social class levels is not yet available.

Kinship Relations and Family Support

While elderly sharing residences with kin, either as the primary household heads or as dependents, represent an important component of the family status of Hispanic elderly, another important component concerns mutual aid and informal support implicit in the extended family system. A number of studies have found that Mexican Americans and other Hispanics have a highly integrated kin network providing emotional and financial support. Generally the exchange of aid and services was higher than among Anglos (Mindel, 1980; Wagner and Schaffer, 1980; Keefe, Padilla, and Carlos, 1978, 1979; Gilbert, 1978). Hispanics also tend to live in greater proximity to their kin; and Mindel (1980) found that location and presence of kin in a community was associated with migration to that community. Mindel (1980), in his study of Hispanics, Blacks, and Anglos in Kansas City, found that Mexican Americans have a more highly developed mutual aid network than the other two groups. Numerous other sources have shown that Mexicans prefer to rely on family for support than on friends or other, more formal sources (see Ramirez and Arce, 1981; Keefe et al., 1978, 1979; Saunders, 1954; Clark, 1959).

Recently, writers have been noting the decline of the extended family support system. Maldonado (1975), Penalosa (1968), Moore (1971), and Gallego (1980) have suggested that increasing urbanization, industrialization, and social mobility have caused a breakdown of the extended family, leaving many aged without support. Grebler et al. (1970), in their study of Mexican Americans, cite increased acculturation and assimilation as also contributing to decline of the functional aid system of the extended family. Other research has found that Hispanics as compared to whites feel that the government was more responsible than the family for meeting certain needs, such as living expenses, housing, medical costs, and transportation (Crouch, 1972; Bengtson, 1979a; Crawford, 1979).

The question of whether or not the extended family system of Hispanic elderly is breaking down is probably not answerable yet, since historical data on the subject are not available. What is clear is that there are discrepancies between what had been believed to be the cultural norms and the actual experience of Hispanic family members. There is no doubt that there has been a decline of extended family aid to the elderly, especially with the growth of institutional and entitlement programs. Whether this signifies a major cultural breakdown or merely a shift in structural arrangements in the society is difficult to tell. Recent research by Mindel and Wright (1982b) on use of government- and agency-provided services vis-a-vis family-provided services for the elderly found a division of labor emerging. The government and agencies were seen as the source of basic maintenance and survival services, financial aid, food, medical care, and the like, whereas the family provided personal care, transportation, and aid that did not have a direct monetary character. Thus, it may be that it is not that the mutual aid system is "breaking down," but rather that it is taking a different character in light of the role of government and other formalized systems of support.

Black Americans and Their Elderly

Structure of the Family

Discussions of the Black family over the last fifteen to twenty years have often been stormy and hotly debated. Though the "Moynihan Report" (Moynihan, 1965) was originally the focal point for discussions of the Black family, issues raised in this report go back at least thirty years earlier than its publication. Most discussions until the publication of the Moynihan Report concerned the problems of lower-class Black families and the so-called pathology of the lower-class Black family. The report acted as a lightning rod, and for a number of years research on Black families tended to be confined to either support (see Rainwater, 1966) or rebuttal (see Billingsley, 1968; Hill, 1971; Staples, 1981). However, out of these discussions challenging the arguments of the Moynihan Report—that the Black family was a "sick" version of the middle-class white family—came a larger understanding of the cultural uniquenesses and cultural validity of the Black family. The argument came to be made that the structure of the Black family is grounded in its own cultural heritage and is not merely an inadequate copy of the white family (see Ladner, 1971; Hill, 1971; Staples, 1981). With additional work by anthropologists such as Shimkin, Shimkin, and Frate (1978), who examined Black extended families in Mississippi and Chicago, a greater understanding of the extended family system and the structure of the Black family was reached. In general, it was found that the larger Black extended family system was highly integrated, was not based on female dominance, and provided important resources for the survival and social mobility of its members. In recent years considerable new work has been done examining the nature of the Black extended kin support system and its ability to care for its members. With respect to the elderly, this support system often becomes crucial, considering that in many cases formal governmental support systems are not always sufficient. A common theme which runs through much of the discussion of the Black family is the important function of the Black family as a social and psychological refuge, for individual members. For example, Stack (1974) found extensive networks of kin and friends supporting and reinforcing each other, devising schemes for self-help "strategies for survival in a Black community of severe economic deprivation."

The elderly tend to be an important element in the structure of this family system. In fact, Wylie (1971) argued that the elderly are more apt to be included in the Black family structure than in white families. Cantor, Rosenthal, and Wilker (1979) found that elderly Black women continued to carry out instrumental and effective familial roles far beyond the period customary among whites. Their argument was that the elderly Black women were more highly involved in a mutual assistance system among and between family members.

Marital and Living Arrangements

Before we begin a more detailed discussion of the family system into which the Black elderly are integrated, some statistical and demographical data on the Black elderly relevant to their family life should be examined. In Table 23.3 the marital status of Black as compared to white elderly males and females is presented.

It can be seen clearly that among the Black elderly, whether male or female, a lower percentage are married both in the young-old period and in the old-old period. Substantially more Black elderly are widowed and divorced than are white elderly.

Mindel (1979) examined multigenerational households in the U.S. population and found that a major change had occurred with respect to the multigenerational household. It appears that elderly who might have lived with their kin have gradually shifted to living alone. While it cannot be seen what the historical changes have been, Table 23.4 indicates that in 1970 the Black elderly were rather similar to the whites. It appears that among the Black elderly there is almost as great a tendency for the elderly to live by themselves as there is among the whites. It has been noted elsewhere (Hill, 1971) that four times as many families headed by Black elderly couples take younger relatives into their households than do white

TABLE 23.3
Marital Status of Black and White Elderly, 1978

Marital Status	Black		White	
	65-74	75 +	65-74	75 +
Females				
Married	40.3	17.4	49.3	23.5
Widowed	48.4	78.4	40.4	68.3
Divorced	6.2	2.6	3.6	2.1
Never marrried	5.1	1.6	6.8	6.1
Males				
Married	68.6	55.9	82.7	72.2
Widowed	18.9	31.2	8.7	21.8
Divorced	5.8	6.0	3.2	1.4
Never married	6.8	6.9	5.5	4.6

Source: Data are from U.S. Bureau of the Census statistics, appearing in Jackson, 1980, pp. 129-31.

elderly couples. The lesser probability that the children or other kin will absorb the elderly person into their household is reflected in Table 23.4. The greater likelihood that an elderly female will be a head of a household is also apparent. Cantor et al. (1979) also found that a larger number of Black elderly women were likely to be reporting themselves as household heads than was the case among white families. Cantor contends that this sharing of limited resources "on the part of Hispanic and Black elderly suggests a positively adaptive method of meeting the pressures of poverty and unemployment within a functional family system."

Kinship Relations and Family Support

Discussions of kinship in the United States usually cover three areas, affectional attachments, interaction, and mutual assistance. There is a growing literature on the Black family describing the components of the kinship system. For example, in an earlier section it was shown that the proportion of extended family households among Blacks is slightly higher than among whites, but definitely lower than for Hispanics. There is also a growing literature on the kinship interaction among Black families as well as the system of mutual aid and support that persists and exists within Black families.

Staples (1981) has claimed that it is "generally acknowledged that the Black kinship network is more extensive and cohesive than kinship bonds among the white population." It appears from the research that for Blacks the kinship network serves its members most effectively as a functional mutual aid system. Numerous studies have shown that Black relatives help

TABLE 23.4
Living Arrangements of Black and White Elderly by Sex,
65-74 and 75 + , 1970

	Black		White	
	65-74	75 +	65-74	75 +
Males				
Primary individuals	21.6	24.5	13.0	20.3
Family heads	66.5	56.0	81.1	66.0
With other relatives	7.0	14.2	4.6	13.6
Secondary individuals	4.9	5.3	1.3	0.1
Females				
Primary individuals	31.8	33.1	33.2	41.1
Family heads	17.8	17.1	7.8	9.8
Wives of family heads	31.9	15.2	45.4	21.0
With other relatives	15.7	31.3	12.2	26.3
Secondary individuals	2.8	3.3	1.4	1.8

Source: Data are from U.S. Bureau of the Census statistics, appearing in Jackson, 1980.

each other with financial aid, child care, advice, and other supports to a rather extensive degree (Aschenbrenner, 1975; Hill, 1971; Martin and Martin, 1978; Shimkin et al., 1978; Stack, 1974). Mindel (1980), in a study of Anglos, Blacks, and Hispanics in Kansas City, found that both the Blacks and the Hispanics had higher levels of interaction and exchange of aid with kin than Anglos, but that the Blacks actually had a more functional aid system than the Hispanics. Curran (1978) found that elderly Black women as compared to elderly white women had a substantially greater use of both formal and informal support systems and a larger social network.

On the other hand, there have been a number of studies that have found relatively few differences by race among the elderly in participation with family and kin. For example, Cantor (1979) found relatively minor differences between elderly Black women and elderly white women in terms of emotional ties and interaction with relatives. Rubenstein (1971) also found relatively few differences by race in terms of participation. Hays and Mindel (1973) and Mindel (1980) found that Blacks interacted with family members to a greater degree than whites, but differences were not always very large.

Two recent studies by Mindel and Wright (1982a, 1982b) have served to clarify the relationship between the informal support system as represented by the kinship group and the formal support system existing in the community with respect to aid to the elderly. In the first study on a national sample of elderly, Mindel and Wright (1982a) examined the multiple factors that predict the use of formally provided social services by Black and white elderly. Each group was analyzed separately on the same factors. It was found, contrary to some views which suggest that either one receives aid from one's informal kinship system or one receives aid from the formal support system of government and voluntary agencies, that for Black elderly, the two support systems were not alternative systems but rather they were supplements and/or complements to each other. Black elderly who tended to receive aid from family and kin groups were also the ones who needed and used the greatest number of formally supplied social services as well. Rather than serving as an alternative support system, the family appeared to be providing supplemental aid to those in greatest need. Curiously, this relationship between the informal family support system and the use of formally supplied support was not apparent in the white sample.

In the second study by Mindel and Wright (1982b), a closer examination of the types of aid that both the informal, kinship support system and the formal support system provide was examined for both Black and white elderly. In this study, conducted in Cleveland in 1976, the aid and support provided by both informal and formal support groups was measured in terms of dollars of aid, with each type of aid having a cost per unit of service. After controlling for social class, the findings provided some further insight into findings of the earlier study. It appears that formal and informal support are, in fact, complementary to each other for both Black and white elderly. The informal support system provided certain types of support for the elderly and the formal support system provided other types. Table 23.5 summarizes the specialization of support functions of the two systems. For example, for Blacks it was found that the formal support system provided substantially more of what was called basic maintenance services than it did for whites. These services included financial aid, food, and living quarters. The informal support system, on the other hand, tended to provide home and personal care services, which included checking, supervision, meals, nursing care, and homemaker services. In addition, the formal support system provided such services as physical and mental health services about equally for Blacks and whites. In addition to the division of labor between the formal and informal support systems, it was found that the differences between the Black and white elderly, once the effects of social class were removed, were not especially great. The Black informal support system supplied somewhat more home and personal care services, but the white informal support system provided somewhat more basic maintenance services. The Black elderly received more services from the formal support system than did the white elderly, but only in the basic maintenance area.

What appears to be true from the analysis of information concerning the support system of the Black elderly is that to a somewhat greater degree the

TABLE 23.5
Mean Dollars Expended on Social Services by Black and White Elderly Support Systems, Adjusted for Income (N = 1354)

Services	Formal Support		Informal Support	
	White $	Black $	White $	Black $
Home and Personal Care				
Checking	.2	.1	3.8	4.5
Continuous supervision	1.4	4.9	11.3	13.0
Personal care	122.7	162.7	725.7	593.4
Meals service	15.4	30.6	36.7	45.4
Nursing care	228.8	475.3	291.8	452.1
Homemaker	68.6	133.3	363.1	416.2
Subtotal	$437.1	$786.9	$1432.4	$1524.6
Basic Maintenance				
Financial aid	137.4	435.7	46.5	18.3
Food, groceries	25.0	62.0	16.2	8.6
Living quarters	118.2	198.5	149.5	161.3
Subtotal	$280.6	$696.2	$212.2	$188.2
Physical and Mental Health				
Medical care	806.9	852.4	n/a	n/a
Physical therapy	98.7	101.8	3.8	.0
Mental health	24.1	26.1	n/a	n/a
Psychotropic drugs	15.9	14.1	n/a	n/a
Subtotal	$945.6	$994.4	$ 3.8	$ .0
Social Support				
Transportation	6.5	24.0	195.0	159.2
Social/recreational	114.5	158.0	n/a	n/a
Administrative/legal	3.1	2.2	4.9	8.7
Escort	.7	1.5	n/a	n/a
Evaluation	.9	1.4	n/a	n/a
Relocation	.1	.1	.8	.5
Subtotal	$125.8	$197.2	$200.7	$168.4
Total expenditure	$1789.1	$2664.7	$1849.1	$1881.2

Source: The data utilized in this table were made available by the Inter-University Consortium for Political and Social Research. The data for the Study of Older People in Cleveland, Ohio, 1975-1976, were originally collected by the United States General Accounting Office. Neither the collector of the original data nor the Consortium bears any responsibility for the analyses or interpretations presented here.

informal family and kinship group of the Black elderly provides and sees to it that the elderly are helped. In addition, it is also clear that for many Black elderly it is they, the elderly, who are a main source of support for younger members within their families. In this sense, the support system is a mutual system of exchange of aid. This reciprocal nature of the exchange system within the Black family perhaps explains why the support for the Black elderly as measured in the study by Mindel and Wright (1982b) may mask the true nature of the support system within the Black family, since only the one-way exchange of aid from the support system to the elderly was examined in that study. It did not reflect the support of the elderly to other family members.

Conclusion

Much of the research on American kinship relations in past decades, though not explicit, has concentrated on the relationship between older parents and their adult children. Early on, the issue of the "isolation" of the nuclear family and by extension the "abandonment" of the elderly was debated. It has become quite clear that neither is the nuclear family "isolated" nor are the elderly "abandoned" by their children. In fact, it was discovered time and again that the American kinship system was alive and functioning and changing. Elderly parents did not live with their children quite as often as they once did, but this appeared to be less a rejection of the elderly than self-determination and greater affluence on the part of the elderly people. Care and support of the elderly in time of need still is a major responsibility of children of all races and ethnic groups.

The debate on the existence and functioning of the kinship group in the general population has had a similar sound in discussions of minority families. The Black family has been criticized as "sick" and "pathological," unable to care for its own and to produce productive, responsible members of society. An enormous amount of data and research in recent years has emerged to challenge this view. The kin group, it has been discovered, functions as a strong support system for its members, providing a whole range of services to family, frequently beyond the narrowly defined nuclear families of orientation and procreation. As a mechanism for survival in an often unfriendly world, the Black extended family, some argue, has done extremely well. Additionally, the Black elderly are, often by neccessity, more active participants in the maintenance and support of family members.

For Hispanics as for many traditionally defined American ethnic groups (such as the Poles, Italians, and Japanese), the opposite view is often held concerning the functioning of the kinship system. Hispanics have often been viewed as having strong family ties in which they "take care of their own." In large measure the data, of which there is not a substantial amount, bear this out. But there are a number of warning signs. Mexican Americans are not Mexicans, Cuban Americans are not Cubans, Puerto Ricans on the mainland are not Puerto Ricans living in Puerto Rico. Culture is not static, and social change based on cultural contact and assimilation has occurred. To describe the Mexican American family and its ties to the elderly as if transplanted out of Mexico from some nostalgic time in the past is a serious mistake. However, this is still often seen in descriptions of the Mexican American family. Warnings of the effects of social and geographical mobility, urbanization and industrialization, and acculturation and assimilation on the structure and functioning of the Mexican American family are appearing, and a more accurate picture is emerging.

Certainly what is needed is more information on minority families and their relationships with their elderly members. Each minority group brings its own unique cultural definitions and meanings to its family structure. Change is a constant feature in present-day American life constantly affecting the interplay of traditional cultural values and patterns with the demands of modern life. How minority groups cope and adapt to these forces is the subject of continuing research.

References

Adams, B.N. 1968. "The Middle Class Adult and His Widowed or Still-Married Mother." *Social Problems* 16:50-59.

Alvirez, D., and F. Bean. 1981. "The Mexican-American Family." In C.H. Mindel and R.W. Habenstein (eds.), *Ethnic Families in America,* 2nd ed. New York: Elsevier.

Aschenbrenner, J. 1975. *Lifelines: Black Families in Chicago.* New York: Holt, Rinehart, & Winston.

Bengtson, V.L. 1979a. "Ethnicity and Aging: Problems and Issues in Current Sociological Inquiry." In D. Gelfand and A. Kutzik (eds.), *Ethnicity and Aging: Theory, Research, and Policy.* New York: Springer.

Bengtson, V.L., and S. Schrader. 1982. "Parent-Child Relations." In D. Mangen and W. Peterson (eds.), *Research Instruments in Aging,* vol. 2: *Social Roles and Social Participation.* Minneapolis: University of Minnesota Press.

Billingsley, A. 1968. *Black Families in White America.* Englewood Cliffs, N.J.: Prentice-Hall.

Cantor, M.H., K. Rosenthal, and L. Wilker. 1979. "Social and Family Relationships of Black Aged Women in New York City." *Journal of Minority Aging* 4:50-61.

Clark, M. 1959. *Health in the Mexican American Culture.* Berkeley: University of California Press.

Crawford, J.K. 1979. "A Case Study of Changing Folk Medical Beliefs and Practices in the Urban Barrio." Presented at the Pacific Sociological Association, Anaheim, California.

Crouch, B. 1972. "Age and Institutional Support: Perceptions of Older Mexican Americans." *Journal of Gerontology* 27:524-29.

Curran, B.W. 1978. "Getting By with a Little Help from My Friends: Informal Networks among Older Black and White Urban Women below the Poverty Line." Doctoral diss.

Dinkel, R. 1944. "Attitudes of Children toward Supporting Aged Parents." *American Sociological Review* 9:370-79.

Gallego, D. 1980. "The Mexican American Elderly: Familial and Friendship Support System. . . Fact or Fiction?" Presented at the annual meeting of the Gerontological Society, San Diego.

Gilbert, J.M. 1978. "Extended Family Integration among Second Generation Mexican Americans." In M. Casas and S.E. Keefe (eds.), *Family and Mental Health in the Mexican American Community,* Monograph 7. Los Angeles: Spanish Speaking Mental Health Research Center.

Grebler, L., J.W. Moore, and R.G. Guzman. 1970. *The Mexican American People: The Nation's Second Largest Minority.* New York: Macmillan.

Hays, W.C., and C.H. Mindel. 1973. "Extended Kinship Relations in Black and White Families." *Journal of Marriage and the Family* 35:51-57.

Hernandez, C. 1976. *Chicanos: Social and Psychological Perspectives.* St. Louis: Moseby.

Hill, R. 1971. *The Strengths of Black Families.* New York: Emerson Hall.

Keefe, S.E., A.M. Padilla, and M.L. Carlos. 1979. "The Mexican American Extended Family as an Emotional Support System." *Human Organization* 38:144-52.

Ladner, J. 1971. *Tomorrow's Tomorrow: The Black Woman.* Garden City, N.Y.: Doubleday.

Maldonado, D. 1974. "The Chicano Aged." *Social Work* 20:213-16.

Martin, E.F., and J. Martin. 1978. *The Black Extended Family.* Chicago: University of Chicago Press.

Melville, M. 1980. *Twice a Minority: Mexican American Women.* St. Louis: Moseby.

Mindel, C.H. 1979. "Multigenerational Family Households: Recent Trends and Implications for the Future." *Gerontologist* 19:456-63.

———. 1980. "Extended Familism among Urban Mexican Americans, Anglos, and Blacks." *Hispanic Journal of Behavioral Sciences* 2:21-34.

———. 1982. "Kinship Relations." In D. Mangen and W. Peterson (eds.), *Research Instruments in Aging,* vol. 2: *Social Roles and Social Participation.* Minneapolis: University of Minnesota Press.

Mindel, C.H., and R. Wright. 1982b. "Assessing the Role of Support Systems among Black and White Elderly." Presented at the annual meeting of the Gerontological Society, San Diego.

Miranda, M. 1975. "Latin American Culture and American Society: Contrasts." In A. Hernandez and J. Mendoza (eds.), *The National Conference on the Spanish Speaking Elderly.* Kansas City: National Chicano Social Planning Council.

Moynihan, D.P. 1965. *The Negro Family: The Case for National Action.* Washington, D.C.: Office of Planning and Research, U.S. Department of Labor.

Murillo, N. 1971. "The Mexican American family." In N.N. Wagner and M.V. Haug (eds.), *Chicanos.* St. Louis: Moseby.

Rainwater, L. 1966. "The Crucible of Identity: The Lower Class Negro Family." *Daedalus* 95:258-64.

Ramirez, O., and C. Arce. 1981. "The Contemporary Chicano Family: An Empirically Based Review." In A. Baron, Jr. (ed.), *Explorations in Chicano Psychology.* New York: Praeger.

Rubenstein, D. 1971. "An Examination of Social Participation of Black and White Elderly." *Aging and Human Development* 2:172-88.

Saunders, L. 1954. *Cultural Differences and Medical Care: The Case of the Spanish Speaking People of the Southwest.* New York: Russell Sage.

Sena-Rivera, J. 1979. "Extended Kinship in the United States: Competing Models and the Case of la Familia Chicana." *Journal of Marriage and the Family* 41:121-29.

Shimkin, D.B., E.M. Shimkin, and D.A. Frate. 1978. *The Extended Family in Black Societies.* The Hague: Mouton.

Sotomayer, M. 1973. "A Study of Chicano Grandparents in an Urban Barrio." Doctoral dissertation, University of Denver.

Stack, C. 1974. *All Our Kin: Strategies for Survival in the Black Community.* New York: Harper & Row.

Staples, R. 1981. "The Black American Family." In C.H. Mindel and R.W. Habenstein (eds.), *Ethnic Families in America,* 2nd ed. New York: Elsevier.

Sussman, M.B. 1953. "The Help Pattern in the Middle Class Family." *American Sociological Review.* 18:22-28.

Wagner, R.M., and D.M. Schaffer. 1980. "Social Networks and Survival Strategies: An Exploratory Study of Mexican American, Black and Anglo Female Family Heads in San Jose, California." In M.B. Melville (ed.), *Twice a Minority: Mexican American Women.* St. Louis: Mosby.

Wake, S.B. and M.J. Sporakowski. 1972. "An Intergenerational Comparison of Attitudes Supporting Aged Parents." *Journal of Marriage and the Family* 34:42-48.

Wylie, F.M. 1971. "Attitudes toward Aging and the Aged among Black Americans: Some Historical Perspectives." *Aging and Human Development* 2:66-70.

24

Caring for the Elderly:
A Cross-Cultural View

Nancy Foner

Two conflicting stereotypes dominate perceptions of the relations between frail elderly and younger family members in nonindustrial societies.
In one view, the elderly are abandoned and left to die; in the other view, the
young faithfully carry out their caretaking duties.

Reality, however, is not so simple. Abandoning the aged can be less cruel
than we might suppose; caring for them less idyllic. In this chapter we
explore, in all their complexity, relations between old people who are in
need of custodial care and the younger ones who care for them in nonindustrial societies.[1] We examine the factors motivating younger adults to
support the frail elderly as well as the sources of strain between them, and
how the young feel about caring for the aged as well as how the aged feel
about their treatment.

Social Position of the Frail Old in Nonindustrial Societies

In nonindustrial societies, the elderly who become seriously physically
or mentally disabled face numerous social losses. They can no longer attend to their own daily existence and need custodial care, and they tend to
lose prestige, influence, and independence.

Not that physical or mental incapacity necessarily means that the old
must officially give up valued roles. For example, an old man among the
Tallensi of Ghana could be blind, deaf, and mentally incompetent and have
relinquished the management of household affairs to his sons, "but he is
still the head of the family and lineage, the hub of their unity, and the
intermediary between them and their ancestors" (Fortes 1949: 181). Nor
does physical incapacity inevitably lead to retirement from political office.
Jack Goody (1976a:127) describes a chief among the Gonja of Ghana

"scarcely able to speak, being carried into his courtroom to take part in the decision-making process." While the disabled old may do no physical labor, they sometimes still occupy supervisory positions and are respected for their expert knowledge. Even those who suffer serious mental impairments may be thought to have substantial ritual powers.

Nonetheless, the physically or mentally incapacitated old, whatever their formal powers, tend to retreat to the sidelines and become increasingly marginal in everyday affairs. In his pioneering cross-cultural study, *The Role of the Aged in Primitive Society*, Leo Simmons (1945:62) argues that respect seems to decline when "individuals become physically and mentally incompetent and socially useless in actual or imaginary terms." In general, the incompetent old must, in addition, depend on others for their very livelihood and care.

Abandonment and Killing

One solution to the problem of support for the frail elderly is simply not to provide it. Cross-cultural studies indicate that abandoning or killing the aged is actually more common than we might suppose. Glascock and Feinman (1981:25) uncovered 26 instances of killing and 16 of abandoning the elderly in 42 societies. And Maxwell and Silverman (n.d.) found evidence of younger people abandoning and/or killing the aged in 20 of the 95 societies in their world-wide sample (see also Simmons 1945: 225-228, 235-240).

One might assume that the elderly would inevitably fight against or bitterly resent such harsh treatment, yet we read of their accepting, or at least not actively resisting, their fate in many societies (Glascock and Feinman 1981:28). In some places, the disabled old were abandoned upon their request. Among the Mardudjara hunters and gatherers of Australia, for example, the incompetent old were fed and spared the difficulties of moving too often, but when frequent travel was unavoidable, some elderly asked to be left behind to die (Tonkinson 1978:83).

In some societies, being buried alive was considered an honorable way to go. In "ancient times" among the Yakut of Siberia, extremely frail elders would beg their relatives to bury them. Before being led into the wood and thrust into their grave, they were honored at a three-day feast (Simmons 1945: 237; cf. Holmes 1972: 84-86 on Samoa). Cultural attitudes toward death may soften the blow or make the aged indifferent to dying. In the past, the elderly among the Eskimo of northern Canada were willing to be abandoned when they became weak or ill because they did not believe they would really die. Rather, their name substance—"the essential ingredient of a human being which includes the personality, special skills, and basic character"—would live on, entering the body of a newborn child (Guemple 1980).

Despite this evidence, it seems likely that the old were not always so resigned to their fate. In some places and in some instances, they had mixed, if not downright hostile, feelings towards their younger "executioners" (cf. Beauvoir 1973:83-87). It is possible that abandoning or killing the elderly could, on occasion, be an indication of strained relations between the generations.

Custodial Care

Reasons for Support

But if the frail elderly have been abandoned and left to die in some societies when they became too great a burden, this is far from universal.

Many studies show children, kin, or neighbors looking after the physically incapacitated aged up until the end. This is even true in some mobile hunting and gathering societies where meeting the needs of the helpless elderly could endanger the very existence of the family or band. For example, gerontocide (killing of old people) was extremely rare among the !Kung of Botswana. The blind and crippled—long past their productive years—were fed and cared for by children and grandchildren and were respected for their technical and ritual skills (Lee 1968:36). Indeed, even in those societies where the old are, at times, abandoned or killed, they are often looked after for a long period during their helpless years.

A number of factors induce people in different cultures to fulfill their obligations to support their elderly parents. For one thing, children often feel deep affection for aged parents and look after them with loving concern. Care for parents is, in addition, frequently seen as a repayment for the gifts, provisions, and care the old people provided in the past. "When you were weak (young)," one Gonja man said, "your mother fed you and cleaned up your messes, and your father picked you up and comforted you when you fell. When they are weak, will you not care for them?" (E. Goody 1973:172).

In many societies, moreover, the son or daughter who looks after the old couple receives, in exchange, special treatment in the division of property. If sentiments of affection and obligation or the promise of economic benefits are not enough, various negative sanctions can be applied—ranging from the threat of disinheritance or supernatural punishment to community disapproval. The burden of supporting the aged is often spread throughout the community, especially in societies with a tradition of communal food sharing and food distributions (see J. Goody 1976a:121-22; Simmons 1945: 20-26). Where the sharing ethic is strong, those generous to the aged may be honored and applauded. And in some societies, the elderly are assured of certain foods because such edibles are taboo to younger people (Simmons 1945: 26-31).

Sources of Strain

Although the young may meet their caretaking obligations to the frail elderly, this does not mean that all is smooth-going. In general, there are several possible sources of tension and conflict between the old and young during this phase of their relationship.

Some adult children will resent their caretaking obligations and only fulfill them grudgingly—sometimes not at all. The old often have a hard time adjusting to their reduced status, resenting those who have taken their place and complaining of neglect and ill-treatment. These resentments and complaints are, to some extent, matters of individual variation and personal dislikes. But tensions and strains also have deeper structural roots.

Resentments of the old. From the perspective of the aged, we must ask why they should feel resentful. Their physical state often has much to do with their bitterness. Among the Gwembe Tonga of Zambia, for example, the very old "resent physical processes of aging within their own bodies and project their resentment on younger people who flourish while they suffer" (Colson and Scudder 1981: 128).

It is not only that the aged may envy the young for their physical vigor. The powers and privileges the aged once enjoyed now belong to younger adults. As the frail elderly become increasingly marginal in the community and household and as they experience other social losses, they frequently resent the young who have stepped in to replace them.

Another source of resentment among the aged stems from their dependency—a complex issue that deserves some discussion. We tend to think it is "natural" for old people to wish to maintain their independence. Yet, by our standards, the old in nonindustrial societies often have little difficulty accepting their increased dependence on others. Far from resisting the thought of asking close relatives for favors and help, they often demand such support as a right.

In our own society, the elderly, as various surveys show, want to be financially and residentially independent. They are generally even reluctant to request financial assistance from children when needed (Hess and Waring 1978: 259-260). But not all cultures put such a strong emphasis on self-sufficiency and economic independence. The elderly in nonindustrial societies tend to expect help from children, and cultural norms support their claim. Among the Igbo of Nigeria, old privileged men could demand care as a publicly acknowledged right, "without any sense of guilt, ego damage, or loss of face" (Shelton 1968: 241). The person who failed to give such care was the guilty party, subject to scorn and ridicule.

Nor is dependence so closely associated with old age as it is in industrial societies. Where government does not provide social welfare benefits and where services cannot be hired when needed, individuals must rely on kin and other associates throughout their lives in times of emergency, disaster, or danger. It cannot be said that individuals in nonindustrial societies have a dependent childhood, a completely independent adulthood, followed by a dependent old age. "Such a sequence exaggerates the independence of adulthood" (Moore 1978: 69). Individuals must depend on, and cultivate and maintain, a large array of social relationships as a resource throughout their lives.

Children are a major human resource in nonindustrial societies, and the elderly have relied on them in both good times and bad. Thus, the dramatic role reversals of later life in our own society are less of a problem in the nonindustrial world. In middle-class America, material exchanges between parents and children typically involve parents as the main givers. A startling shift may occur in late old age if aged parents must turn to adult children for support. In nonindustrial societies, adult children have usually contributed to their parents' material support for much, perhaps all, of their lives.

But old people's increased dependence can lead to problems. In many societies the old often feel, or are regarded as, useless when support and assistance become one-way. Those who become incapacitated have greater needs and are more dependent than before. Accustomed to providing services in exchange for those they got, their ability to contribute to the subsistence of the group declines and they now have little, if anything, to offer in return. "You are old, you can do nothing, you are no good for anything any more," Hopi women told their very aged mothers (Simmons 1945: 59). Old Hopi women might well take such remarks to heart. An old person's sense of worthlessness and frustration could lead to anger at the very people who supported them.

Of course, the frail old do not feel useless everywhere. In some societies they are seen as making a contribution—if they are religious specialists or political advisers, for example, or property owners letting others use what they have. Then, too, the old, as well as the young, commonly take a more long-range view of the situation and feel that the old deserve to be repaid for the services they provided to the young in the past.

Even where the old are comfortable with being cared for, however, their need for support can create difficulties. Some will feel abused or neglected, believing that the young are not supporting them properly or treating them with the respect they deserve. In many cases, such complaints are well-founded. For example, except for those elderly men who maintained a degree of control in their homesteads, very old men and women among the Gwembe Tonga whose "feet will not carry them beyond" the homestead any more "are first to suffer when conditions are hard. Sleeping alone without adequate covering, they shiver at night throughout the cold season. Restricted in their movements, they must endure the dust which sweeps through barren villages during the height of the dry season when others retreat to more sheltered areas" (Colson and Scudder 1981: 128). Given these conditions, it is not surprising that many of the very old again showed the "greed and quick anger of childhood"—openly envying the good things enjoyed by others. Nor were young children exempt from the anger of the very old, who would burst into rages when the youngsters raided their possessions (Colson and Scudder 1981: 129).

Life for the disabled Hopi sounds even more trying. As long as they controlled property rights, held special ceremonial offices, or were powerful medicine men, the aged were respected. But "the feebler and more useless they become, the more relatives grab what they have, neglect them, and sometimes harshly scold them, even permitting children to play rude jokes on them." Sons might refuse to support their fathers, telling them, "You had your day, you are going to die pretty soon." Aged Hopi were heard to remark, "We always looked forward to old age, but see how we suffer" (Simmons 1945: 59, 233-234).

Even the elderly who are relatively well cared for may feel they are not being supported properly. Where the old retain economic, political, or ritual authority, this authority gives added grounds to their demands for better treatment. Complaining, moreover, can be a conscious or unconscious strategy to ensure or maximize support—to accentuate the negative with positive consequences, as when public complaints prod the young into fulfilling their duties (see Kerns 1980: 124).

Problems for younger caretakers. If the old have grounds for dissatisfaction, so have younger people. Consider their point of view. Many, of course, are willing and devoted caretakers. But there are reasons why they sometimes perform their duties with mixed, and perhaps even hostile, feelings.

While the elderly recipients may complain of their treatment, the young givers may "feel they are being leveled excessively" (Simić 1978: 102-03). However diligent they are in caring for the aged, fulfilling these duties can be a legitimate but heavy burden which saps their limited resources, physical strength, and sympathies.

The disabled old man or woman in the house is an easy target for tired and overworked younger people's frustrations, especially if the old person cannot help in reducing their burden. Younger people are usually expected to maintain an air of respect toward the aged—particularly old parents or close kin—but cranky, demanding, or complaining behavior can try anyone's patience. "Even old women sometimes lose their kindness," a Kikuyu man said, "demanding and destroying the peace of the homestead" (Cox and Mberia 1977:9).

An inability to meet all the demands of the elderly can, often unwittingly, contribute to old people's sense of neglect. Many times younger people cannot give the old the kind of attention they demand or expect. Even with the best intentions, many are simply too busy with productive or other tasks. Often, environmental factors beyond anyone's control—drought or low food reserves, for example—require decisions that increase the frustrations of the elderly. A poor harvest among the Gwembe Tonga, for instance, could necessitate moving the very old—who were no longer essential workers—to relatives in distant and more prosperous regions (Colson and Scudder 1981: 128).

In nonindustrial as well as industrial societies, the young may also be torn between obligations to dependent old parents and to their own children. Recent changes have increased this problem as land becomes scarcer and consumer needs escalate. The young have less to spare for the old while the elderly make increased cash demands. "It is a difficult job to look after them," one Kikuyu man said about his aged parents. "They are often unreasonable as children. They forget what it is like to have nine children and little land" (Cox and Mberia 1977:9).

Thus do tensions arise between adults in adjacent generations. Do the same sorts of strains develop when very young grandchildren attend to old people's needs, which is a common situation in many societies? A grandchild may even be specifically assigned to care for an old person. Among the Chagga of Tanzania, for instance, an old woman not only expected to be looked after by her youngest son and his wife, but she could also claim a grandchild who slept in her hut and served as companion and domestic helper (Moore 1977: 67-69). In Gonja society, a young boy or girl was delegated to care for aged grandparents (E. Goody 1973: 179).

We know little about the kind of strains that arise between very old and frail grandparents and their grandchildren. Yet, I suspect that tensions of the sort described in the preceding pages do sometimes develop, particularly when the old people are difficult and demanding. Reports on the Navaho, for instance, indicate that grandchildren had ambivalent feelings towards grandparents. Grandparents, on the one hand, were affectionate and indulgent towards the youngsters. But grandchildren felt some resentment at being assigned to care for an aged grandparent and at the restrictions on their freedom that such care involved. Having to cut wood and haul water and accompanying the elders on journeys cut into the time they could spend with other children (Kluckhohn 1944: 105-06; see also Leighton and Kluckhohn 1969: 102).

Differentiation among the Frail Old: Support and Strains

Having outlined the basic sources of strain between the frail old and younger people, we now need to narrow our scope of vision. Differences *among* the elderly mean that some receive better care and have less strained relations with younger caretakers than others.

Personality, Material Wealth, and Other Differences

Obviously, personality differences affect the tone of relationships. Some of the aged are difficult, others good-tempered. Younger people who are slow in meeting their obligations or do so without warmth or generosity often simply dislike the older person they are supporting. Then there is the history of the relationship between the dependent old person and younger provider. In some instances the two have always gotten along well; in others, they have long been at odds and the old person's increased dependence may reactivate or deepen old wounds.

Additional factors can make life more or less difficult for the incapacitated aged and thus influence relations with the young. The elderly bring with them certain advantages or disadvantages accumulated over a lifetime. Some have more material wealth than others. Very old men with little land or few cattle, for example, cannot lure the young to care for them with promises of abundant inheritances. The extent of old people's political influence or family authority can also affect how they will be supported. Physical health, too, makes a difference. Older people who remain relatively vigorous place less of a burden on the young than do those who have serious disabling illness for most of their later years.

Gender Distinctions

Gender distinctions also influence the quality of relations between the incapacitated young and their younger caretakers. Whereas men often depend heavily on jural and economic authority to back up claims to support from children, women usually rely more on their children's sense of moral obligation and affection. As those who raise and care for children, women often have stronger emotional ties to children and grandchildren than do men. Indeed, these ties of affection may be nurtured with an eye to old-age support.

Yet children's affection does not ensure smooth relations with dependent mothers. Among the Tallensi, for example, sons kept old mothers in their homes out of affection and duty, but some sons complained that these women become completely egoistic, thinking only of their comfort and of having enough to eat and cursing those who crossed them (Fortes 1949: 175). Then, too, when a woman lives with a son, her daughter-in-law is likely to bear most of the burden, and little love may be lost between the two women. However, a son usually makes sure that his wife cares for his old mother, as in rural Taiwan. There, sons publicly fulfilled their filial obligations to old fathers but not much more. Sons were ambivalent towards fathers who had been aloof, authoritarian figures for most of the younger men's lives. By contrast, relations with mothers were warm and close. If a woman had trained her son well, his affection saw to it that his wife cared for her "with a gentleness that an old man might never experience" (Wolf 1970:51).

If affection sometimes guarantees old women loving care from children, the fact that women often carry out useful functions well into their later years also minimizes strains with younger caretakers. In some societies, incapacitated old men are viewed as useless when they are no longer able to do productive work. Quite frail old women, however, frequently continue to perform valuable child-rearing duties and other relatively light domestic chores. Thus, Wolf (1970: 51, 1972:227) describes how fragile old women of 80 or more in rural Taiwan, until completely bedridden, still performed domestic tasks such as washing vegetables for dinner or rocking babies to sleep that even a "revengeful daughter-in-law" found valuable. Such tasks were inappropriate for old men when no longer able to do "male" farm work.

The Childless or Sonless

The above discussion presumes that the elderly have children to look after them. Not all are so fortunate. The state of childlessness or, in some societies, sonlessness is a "biologically based feature of individual biography" (Moore 1978:73) that influences not only old people's well-being but their relations with the young. This becomes especially crucial for the physically or mentally incapacitated.

The childless or sonless are forced to depend upon more distant kin with whom they have less close bonds of affection and obligation. They have provided more distant relatives with fewer services in the past and are without the same kind of moral, jural, or economic authority over them.

To be sure, family arrangements are flexible in many societies so that couples unable to bear children can rear youngsters who will support them in old age. Formal adoption is found in many European and Asian societies and fostering, which involves no permanent change of identity, is common in Africa (J. Goody 1976b: 84). In societies where daughters are supposed to leave home at marriage, couples who only bear daughters can sometimes arrange a marriage in which the daughter and her husband remain with her parents to provide old age support (e.g. Shahrani 1981: 180; Wolf 1972). Yet the best laid plans do not always succeed. Foster or adopted—as well as natural—children sometimes die before their parents or for other reasons are unable to care for them.

In preliterate as well as industrial societies, old men are often cared for by their wives since men are typically older than their spouses; especially in societies where men have several mates, they frequently have younger wives still living with them when they need care. Even then, however, sons (or sons-in-law) may be essential for such productive tasks as herding, farming, or hunting. Indeed, in many nonindustrial societies it is a son's duty, often a particular son such as the youngest, to care for his aged parents. In cases where the frail elderly lack the expected caretaking child or children, therefore, they are likely to be in very difficult circumstances.

Elderly !Kung hunters and gatherers with no surviving spouse or children—an estimated 5 percent of old men and 20 percent of old women—were less likely to receive adequate food and care than their more fortunate counterparts (Biesele and Howell 1981: 86-87). Among the Kirghiz herders of Afghanistan, the rewards of old age could not be enjoyed by the childless who suffered from lack of proper care and attention. All sons were expected to help their aged parents, although the lion's share of the responsibility fell to the youngest or only son (and his wife and children). This son never left the parental household and, in return, inherited the tent, family herd, and camping ground when his father died. While couples who only had daughters could bring a son-in-law into their household, a few were left without any natural or adopted children in their old age (Shahrani 1981: 181-83).

To reach late old age and have no adult sons was an unfortunate state in many African farming and herding societies. Among the Tallensi, sons—own sons, or second best, proxy sons—were old men's chief economic asset (Fortes 1949: 216-17). A son was morally bound to look after and farm for his father. "Yet how can I leave him since he is almost blind and cannot farm for himself?" asked one man who had just bitterly quarrelled with his father. "Can you just abandon your father? Is it not he who begot you?" (Fortes 1970:177). Old men, no matter how incapacitated, still excercised authority over sons, who had an interest in the land still being held by their fathers.

Old men without adult sons among the Tallensi had to turn to others for help on their farms. Because they had to rely on such uncertain assistance from kin and neighbors, they were unlikely to have more than a "minimum of food and other necessaries." When they became too weak to farm at all, relatives gave them shelter and food. Although refusing gifts of food to needy kin was viewed as an offense against the ancestors, people were not bound to be overgenerous to kin who did not contribute to the common pool.

If sonless old men could be at a disadvantage, so could sonless old women. Thus, among the Tallensi an old woman's strongest guarantee of economic support was her own son. Since women did not own land, the stress was on a son's duty (felt to be in part a privilege) to care for her (Fortes 1949:216-220). Among the Gusii of Kenya, an old woman needed at least one son to care for her and whose wives would work for her. Sonlessness was a disaster second only to barrenness (LeVine 1980:94).

Lack of sons to count on for old-age support is not only a matter of biological destiny. When parents reach old age, sons may be alive and well but living far away. The younger men may be working in towns, for example. And sometimes sons are not around because they have quarrelled with their parents. Whatever the reason, the lack of children or sons, it is clear, can be a real problem for the incapacitated aged. As for relations with the younger people on whom they depend for support, it appears that strains may well occur. All the tensions described earlier between parents and offspring tend to be compounded.

The basic dilemma is that the childless or sonless must rely on kin whose obligations to them are relatively weak. Not that they are totally isolated or alone. In small-scale communities, even the elderly living on their own usually have considerable contact with kin and neighbors in the community—most of whom they have probably known since childhood. Among the Chagga, hardly any of the elderly were alone in their homesteads and all lived near relatives obligated to care for them. This sense of responsibility varied in strength, however. Those who lacked nearby sons had to depend on kin whose interest in them was "secondary rather than primary in the Chagga hierarchy of intensity of relationship and obligation" (Moore 1978:73)

Because younger people usually feel less bound to support distant kin or neighbors, help tends to be seen as a heavy burden, particularly if there is also the need to support frail elderly parents. Since the young may not give distant kin or neighbors the best of care, complaining may be a means of ensuring support. The childless or sonless old must often constantly beg for help from people who resent giving, without the strong ties of affection and bonds of reciprocity of parents and offspring. In some societies, old people who depend on distant kin or neighbors for food and other support may end up being accused of witchcraft. More often, however, the dependent elderly simply arouse resentment and ridicule (see, for example, Kerns 1980: 119).

Conclusion: Strains and Accommodation

In general, the frail old in nonindustrial societies, as we have seen, are not in an enviable position. Not only do they experience various social losses but their relations with younger people on whom they depend for support are often fraught with strain. In some places, they become such a burden that they are killed or abandoned. At this point, the elderly may be resigned to such a fate and even see death as a release from their difficulties in this world.

Such strains between the frail elderly and their younger caretakers do not mean that serious open conflicts necessarily break out. In fact, most of the time these strains remain beneath the surface of fairly stable ongoing relations. We must ask, then, what factors lessen tensions and reduce the likelihood of open conflict between the disabled old and their caretakers.

Most obviously, as already noted, the aged and their children are often bound by ties of genuine affection. There is also, frequently, a strong sense of mutual identification between them. Indeed, old people's identification with and pleasure from their children's successes can overcome dissatisfaction with their own social losses and lessen potential envy and rivalry (see Hochschild 1973: 97-111).

Then, too, the elderly may accept the legitimacy of their position, believing that their incapacity requires them to relinquish roles of power and respect. There are also compensations. In a number of societies, religious beliefs and rituals offer the frail old a sense of worth and give meaning to their misfortunes (see, for example, Ortner 1978: 53-60 on the Sherpa of Nepal). Current discontent is bearable if one expects a better life in the hereafter. There is also the knowledge that one will only become more incapacitated with time, and will soon die, reducing the incentive to struggle against the young to gain improvements.

Even under extreme provocation, young and old may think twice before acting in an aggressive manner if they believe that unfortunate consequences are likely to follow. From younger people's perspective, there is often the fear of mystical punishment and sometimes the threat of disinheritance. For old people's part, they may not want to risk revenge, in the form of worse treatment, from their caretakers. And both young and old usually want to avoid the disapproval of their fellow community members.

Such perceptions and pressures, of course, are not unique to people in nonindustrial societies—many of the same forces influence behavior in modern societies, where the fear of losing an inheritance or esteem in the eyes of others serves to motivate younger people to keep their resentments to themselves. Indeed, the introduction of old-age pensions reduces the likelihood that marked tensions will develop in the first place because the elderly become less of an economic burden.

Old-age pensions, of course, are not available to most of the rural population in developing countries and, given the high costs involved, this situation is unlikely to change for a long time to come. In the absence of extensive government welfare measures, children will doubtless be the main support of the frail old well into the future. This has important implications for intergenerational relations. Difficult as it is to foretell what lies ahead, it seems safe to say that as long as children and other kin in nonindustrial societies are the ones to shoulder the caretaking burden, then relations with the incapacitated elderly are bound to remain much as they have been described here: a complex and tangled web of attachments, reciprocities, tensions, and antagonisms.

Note

1. Nonindustrial societies refer here to those in which the economy is based on hunting and gathering, herding, or agriculture, including the nonindustrial sectors of industrial societies (Goody 1976a:117). "Younger people" or the "young" in this paper are primarily mature individuals who are not yet considered old.

References

Beauvoir, Simone de. 1973. *Coming of Age.* New York: Warner.
Biesele, Megan, and Nancy Howell. 1981. "'The Old People Give you Life': Aging among !Kung Hunter-Gatherers." In *Other Ways of Growing Old,* ed. Pamela Amoss and Stevan Harrell. Stanford: Stanford University Press.
Colson, Elizabeth, and Thayer Scudder. 1981. "Old Age in Gwembe District, Zambia." In *Other Ways of Growing Old,* ed. Pamela Amoss and Stevan Harrell. Stanford: Stanford University Press.
Cox, Francis M., and Ndung'u Mberia. 1977. *Aging in a Changing Village Society: A Kenyan Experience.* Washington, D.C.: International Federation of Aging.
Foner, Nancy. 1984. *Ages in Conflict: A Cross-Cultural Perspective on Inequality between Old and Young.* New York: Columbia University Press.
Fortes, Meyer. 1949. *The Web of Kinship among the Tallensi.* London: Oxford University Press.
———. 1970. "Pietas in Ancestor Worship." In *Time and Social Structure and Other Essays,* ed. Meyer Fortes. London: Athlone.
Glascock, Anthony, and Susan Feinman. 1981. "Social Asset or Social Burden: An Analysis of the Treatment of the Aged in Non-Industrial Societies." In *Dimensions: Aging, Culture, and Health,* ed. Christine L. Fry. New York: Praeger.
Goody, Jack. 1976a. "Aging in Nonindustrial Societies." In *Handbook of Aging and the Social Sciences,* ed. Robert Binstock and Ethel Shanas. New York: Van Nostrand Reinhold.
———. 1976b. *Production and Reproduction.* Cambridge: Cambridge University Press.

Guemple, Lee. 1980. "Growing Old in Inuit Society." In *Aging in Canada: Social Perspectives,* ed. V.W. Marshall. Toronto: Don Mills, Fitzhenry, & Whiteside.

Hess, Beth, and Joan M. Waring. 1978. "Parent and Child in Later Life: Rethinking the Relationship." In *Child Influences on Marital and Family Interactions,* ed. R. Lerner and G. Spanier. New York: Academic Press.

Hochschild, Arlie. 1973. *The Unexpected Community.* Englewood Cliffs, N.J.: Prentice-Hall.

Holmes, Lowell D. 1972. "The Role and Status of the Aged in a Changing Samoa." In *Aging and Modernization,* ed. Donald O. Cowgill and Lowell D. Holmes. New York: Appleton-Century-Crofts.

Kerns, Virginia. 1980. "Aging and Mutual Support Relations among the Black Carib." In *Aging in Culture and Society,* ed. Christine L. Fry. New York: J.F. Bergin.

Kluckhohn, Clyde. 1967. (1944) *Navaho Witchcraft.* Boston: Beacon.

Lee, Richard B. 1968. "What Hunters Do for a Living or, How to Make Out on Scarce Resources." In *Man the Hunter,* ed. Richard B. Lee and Irven DeVore. Chicago: Aldine.

Leighton, Dorothea, and Clyde Kluckhohn. 1947. *Children of the People.* Cambridge: Harvard University Press.

LeVine, Robert A. 1980. "Adulthood among the Gusii of Kenya." In *Theories of Work and Love in Adulthood,* ed. Neil J. Smelser and Erik H. Erikson. Cambridge: Harvard University Press.

Maxwell, Robert J., and Philip Silverman. n.d. "Gerontocide." Paper delivered at American Anthropological Association Meetings, Los Angeles, December 1981.

Moore, Sally Falk. 1977. "The Chagga of Kilimanjaro." In *The Chagga and Meru of Tanzania,* ed. Sally Falk Moore and Paul Pruitt. Ethnographic Survey of Africa. London: International African Institute.

———. 1978. "Old Age in a Life-Term Social Arena: Some Chagga of Kilimanjaro in 1974." In *Life's Career—Aging,* ed. Barbara Myerhoff and Andrei Simić. Beverly Hills, Calif.: Sage.

Ortner, Sherry B. 1978. *Sherpa through Their Rituals.* Cambridge: Cambridge University Press.

Shahrani, M. Nazif. 1981. "Growing in Respect: Aging among the Kirghiz of Afghanistan." In *Other Ways of Growing Old,* ed. Pamela Amoss and Stevan Harrell. Stanford: Stanford University Press.

Shelton, Austin J. 1968. "Igbo Child-Raising, Eldership, and Dependence: Further Notes for Gerontologists and Others." *Gerontologist* 8: 236-41.

Simić, Andrei. 1978. "Winners and Losers: Aging Yugoslavs in a Changing World." In *Life's Career—Aging,* ed. Barbara Myerhoff and Andrei Simić. Beverly Hills, Calif: Sage.

Simmons, Leo. 1945. *The Role of the Aged in Primitive Society.* New Haven: Yale University Press.

Tonkinson, Robert. 1978. *The Mardudjara Aborigines: Living the Dream in Australia's Desert.* New York: Holt, Rinehart,& Winston.

Wolf, Margery. 1970. "Child Training and the Chinese Family." In *Family and Kinship in Chinese Society,* ed. Maurice Freedman. Stanford: Stanford University Press.

———. 1972. *Women and the Family in Rural Taiwan.* Stanford: Stanford University Press.

25

Elder Abuse:
The Status of Current Knowledge

Claire Pedrick-Cornell and Richard J. Gelles

Child abuse emerged as a social problem in the 1960s and wife abuse was identified as a major social issue in the 1970s. Similarly, abuse of the elderly has become a topic of interest and concern in the 1980s.

Two major factors seem to help explain why the abuse of older persons became a focal point of social, scientific, and media attention in the last 12 to 18 months:

First, the discovery of a significant number of elderly victims of family violence was a natural outgrowth of intensive research on the extent and patterns of family violence. By conceptualizing the problem as one of "family violence" and not simply "child abuse" or "wife battering" researchers have been able to identify varying patterns and incidence of violence in the family (e.g. Straus, Gelles, and Steinmetz, 1980).

Second, major demographic changes have occurred over the last half century which help explain why problems of the elderly and problems of elderly abuse specifically have captured public and scientific attention. First, the life expectancy of the average person has increased by nearly 50 percent in as many years (U.S. Bureau of Census, 1978). Secondly, as a consequence of the increased life expectancy (and the population increase in general), there are growing numbers of individuals 60 years of age and older. Thirdly, the proportion of the population 60 years and older also increased (Harris, 1975).

This aging of the population has resulted in an increased need for long-term care of the elderly. Of those between 65 and 72 years of age, only one person in 50 needs long-term care. But of those over 73 years old, the chances increase to one in 15 (Koch and Koch, 1980).

Moreover, as one can see from the changing age distribution, children having the responsibility of caring for their aging parents is also a relatively new and growing aspect of family life (Laslett, 1973). The changing population and a current push towards deinstitutionalization of and home care for the elderly (Maddox, 1975) means that more adult children are providing more home care to a larger number and proportion of the older population. Treas (1977) voices concern about the impact of the increasing burden of home care on the emotional and financial resources of families, especially in light of the increased entry of women into the labor force. This could reduce time and energy for home care for their elderly relatives.

Finally, we are entering a period where the modal family situation is one of fewer children available for sharing the responsibility of providing for and caring for elderly parents. It is against this background of increased research on family violence, demographic changes in the society, and an increased concern for the problems of older persons that elderly abuse became a significant focus.

Most students of child abuse credit Kempe and his colleagues' seminal paper, "The Battered Child Syndrome" (Kempe et al., 1962), as drawing public and scientific attention to the problem of abused children. It was more than a decade from the time that that paper was published until the convening of the first National Conference on Child Abuse, held in Washington, D.C. in 1973. Congressional hearings and congressional legislation on child abuse also did not occur until 1973. While there were scattered investigations and media reports of child abuse in the sixties, concentrated scientific and media attention was not focused on this issue until the seventies.

Prior to 1973 there were but two scientific articles published on wife abuse, and virtually no articles in the popular press. However, the time period from the "discovery" of wife abuse in the early 1970's until there were national conferences, media coverage, and congressional hearings was compressed from the 10 years it took for child abuse to be widely discussed to less than 3 years. The time frame from discovery to widespread interest for the topic of elderly abuse was so short that one wonders whether there was any lag at all between discovery, media attention, and legislative initiative at the local, state, and federal level.

While the rapid diffusion of concern for the problem of elderly abuse has been helpful in mobilizing resources to deal with this problem, it has led to some significant problems in terms of identifying what knowledge is available on this subject. In the case of elderly abuse, media interest and concern outpaced the conducting and dissemination of scholarly research.

As scientific information was scarce, journalists tended to locate the same experts, cite the same facts, and advance the same theories. Certain pieces of information, based on tentative research, unpublished reports, or even educated guesses have been published, republished, cited, and repeated so often that they have taken on the status of "fact" and "conclusive evidence," more because of how often they are reported in newspapers and on television than as a consequence of the data meeting the normal scientific rules of evidence.

This chapter examines the scientific status of knowledge about elderly abuse. The first section sets the stage for this review by discussing problems of definition. Next, data and research on the rates of elderly abuse and factors found related to elderly abuse are examined. In the following section theories which have been developed to explain the abuse of the elderly are critiqued. Recommendations for research and practice draw it to a close.

Definitional Dilemmas

Perhaps the most significant impediment in the development of an adequate knowledge base on intrafamily violence and abuse has been the problem of developing a satisfactory and acceptable definition of violence and abuse. Just as confusion about "what is child maltreatment" abounds 20 years after research commenced, there is considerable variation and confusion in the definitions of elder abuse. Students of violence, abuse, and maltreatment of the elderly have stumbled down the same paths tread before by those attempting to study child abuse. The same concerns with intentionality, outcome, physical vs. non-physical maltreatment, acts of omission vs. acts of commission, and the range of acts considered abusive have been discussed in the brief period of time during which elderly abuse has been identified and studied as a social problem.

Rathbone-McCuan (1980) restricts the definition of elder abuse to the physical abuse of non-institutionalized elderly, much in the same way Kempe and his colleagues (1962) 20 years earlier restricted their definition of child abuse to medically diagnosable injury caused by physical attack. Most others in the field of elder abuse use broader definitions which include both passive and active neglect, mental anguish, material abuse, medical abuse, or self-abuse in the definition.

One can plainly see the struggles of defining elder abuse in the recent reports on the problem. Douglass, Hickey, and Noel (1980) try to make clear distinctions between passive neglect and active neglect, while also attempting to distinguish between "neglect" and "abuse." Legal Research and Services for the Elderly's (1979) definition included mental abuse as well as physical abuse. Block and Sinnott (1979) added material abuse and medical abuse to acts of abuse and neglect. Lau and Kosberg (1979) included "violation of rights" in their definition of elder abuse, which covered situations where elderly are forced out of their dwelling or into another setting, such as a nursing home.

While few would dispute that any of the acts listed by researchers may be harmful, the problem is that the concept of elder abuse has become a political/journalistic concept, best suited for attracting attention to the plight of the victims. But while elder abuse may be a fruitful political term, it is fast becoming a useless scientific concept. The variety of definitions of elder abuse in current studies makes the task of comparing the results of the research impossible. Estimates of the extent of elder abuse (as will be discussed in the next section) range from thousands to millions, depending on the definition applied. A more serious problem is that the wide range of behavior lumped into a definition of elder abuse makes it virtually impossible to assess the causal factors related to abuse. By combining behaviors and phenomena which are conceptually distinct, one loses the ability to truly determine what causes elder abuse (e.g. the generative causes of an act of physical violence are different from factors which lead to acts of omission). As long as investigators fail to separate and distinguish between behaviors which are conceptually and etiologically distinct, and as long as definitions vary from narrow to broad, we will be unable to develop an adequate and useful knowledge base in this area of study.

Operational Definitions

While there are various nominal definitions of elder abuse in use, there is nearly overwhelming agreement on operationally defining elder abuse. Nearly all research on elderly abuse has been based on samples drawn from cases officially reported to professionals or paraprofessionals in the field of adult protective services (Lau and Kosberg, 1979; Douglass et al., 1980; Legal Research and Services for the Elderly, 1979; Block and Sinnott, 1979).

Relying exclusively on cases which come to professional attention produces serious problems in assessing the conclusions and generalizability of the data generated by such research. Research on child and wife abuse clearly demonstrates that those cases which come to public attention represent a skewed and biased portion of the entire population of victims of abuse. Research has also demonstrated that social, racial and economic factors influence who is labeled as "abused" (Newberger et al., 1977; Turbett and O'Toole, 1980). Research which samples *only* from those cases that come to official attention is research which cannot partial out the factors which lead to a case being labeled from factors which caused the person to be abused. A continued reliance on samples drawn *only* from cases which come to professional attention will restrict and limit our ability to learn more about the problem of the abuse of the elderly.

The Extent of Elderly Abuse

Situations which are viewed by society as legitimate social problems are typically those which are found to be harmful to a significant number of people. There is no question that the abuse of children, women, and the elderly is harmful, but the acceptance of family abuse as a social problem has been dependent on documentation that the problem affects a large number of people. Thus, just as students of child and wife abuse first faced the question, "how common is abuse?" those who advance the idea of the abuse of older persons as a social problem have asked "how many elderly are abused?"

The most frequently cited statistics place the range of elder abuse between 500,000 and 2.5 million cases per year (see, for example, "Aging committees consider programs to curb growing problem of elder abuse," 1980). Four studies are frequently cited by those discussing the extent of elder abuse: (1) Lau and Kosberg's (1979) investigation at the Chronic Illness Center in Cleveland. They reported that 39 of 404 clients, 60 years of age and older, were abused in some manner. They estimated that 1 in 10 elderly persons living with a member of the family is abused each year. (2) A University of Maryland report (Block and Sinnott, 1973) which indicated 4.1 percent of elderly respondents in the urban areas of Maryland reporting abuse. They believe that if this rate were projected for the national population of elderly, nearly 1 million cases of elderly abuse would occur. (3) An exploratory study of professionals' and paraprofessionals' encounters with elder abuse in Massachusetts (Legal Research and Services for the Elderly, 1979). It was stated that 55 percent of the respondents (183 out of 322) knew of at least one incident of abuse in an 18-month period. (4) A study in Michigan (Douglass et al., 1980), which was based on recollections of professionals in five study sites in Michigan, concluded that many respondents reported little or no direct, regular experience with verbal or emotional abuse, active neglect, or physical abuse, while 50 percent reported contact with passive neglect. There was some confusion among respondents as to the exact definition of "passive neglect."

Analysis

It would be necessary, and fair, to say that despite the data presented in available reports, the extent and incidence of the abuse of the elderly is still unknown. There are major problems and limitations with the four major reports on elder abuse. Current estimates of the number and incidence of cases of elder abuse are based on cases which are reported to social service agencies. This is problematic because: (1) instances of child, wife, and elder abuse which are reported to public and private agencies are but a fraction of the total number of cases; (2) mandatory reporting laws for elder abuse exist in only a handful of states; thus, reported cases of elder abuse are probably a smaller proportion of the total number of cases than the fraction of child abuse reports received by agencies (due to the fact that all 50 states have enacted mandatory child abuse reporting laws); (3) the recency of concern and awareness about elder abuse means a low degree of awareness of this problem among professionals, paraprofessionals, the public, and even the victims; and (4) the number of cases reported to agencies vary by type of agency, location, title, etc., as demonstrated by the testimony before the House Subcommittee on Aging (U.S. Congress, Select Committee on Aging, Subcommittee on Human Services, 1980).

Current information on the extent of elder abuse is also limited by the fact that the research is based on small, non-representative samples. Any attempt to extrapolate incidence data from such samples to the national population of elderly must be viewed with great caution. For example, Lau and Kosberg's (1979) estimate of 1 in 10 elderly persons residing with caretakers being abused each year is based on a non-representative sample of 39 persons reported to the Cleveland Chronic Illness Center. This agency cannot be considered representative of other agencies in Cleveland, Ohio, or anywhere else.

Block and Sinnott (1979), who estimated the incidence of elder abuse nationally to be 1 million, conducted a "representative" study of "community dwelling elderly" living in the greater Washington, D.C. SMSA. Although Block and Sinnott state that the elderly they surveyed were "fairly representative" of older persons nationwide, it must be emphasized that *Block and Sinnott's response rate in their interviews was but 16.48 percent*! This extremely low response rate virtually renders meaningless their claim for representativeness of their sample. Also, there are significant inconsistencies in their printed report, such that it is impossible to determine their exact sample size.[1] Regardless of how large their sample actually was, their estimate of national incidence is based on a total of between *1 and 3 actual reports of elderly abuse*. Even if their sample was representative, the sampling error is such that the lower boundary of the actual range of the incidence of abuse is 0 percent.

Legal Research and Services for the Elderly (1979) recognized that their non-representative sampling precluded a meaningful attempt to generate a national incidence statistic. Moreover, they note that it is possible that the same case of elderly abuse could have been reported by both a professional and paraprofessional in their study. The possibility of duplication means that 183 reports do not necessarily translate into 183 different cases.

Douglass et al. (1980) also declined to speculate on the national incidence rate. They did report the mean scores for monthly occurrences of cases of neglect and abuse. Nevertheless, the overall response rate to their questions on monthly occurrence was quite low.[2] They note that their findings are not generalizable because: (1) they used a purposive sample; (2) the number of respondents in each of the occupational categories was unequal and the categories were not uniformly homogeneous; and (3) the number of respondents who answered each question was extremely small, and a single respondent with an unusually large caseload could inflate or deflate the mean scores. What was actually found in their investigation was that many respondents (the exact number cannot be determined from their report) reported little or no direct, regular experience with verbal or emotional abuse, active neglect, or physical abuse.

Based upon the methodological problems with the studies, the authors would advise that extreme caution be used when generalizing data from these studies. Due to their exploratory nature, these studies are inappropriate for generating a national incidence statistic.[3]

Factors Associated with Elder Abuse

A first step in unraveling the causes of a phenomenon such as elder abuse is to identify the major social and psychological factors associated with being an abuser or abused. The current research and reports on elder abuse offer some tentative insights into the profile of the abuser, abused, and abusive situation.

Age and Gender

Reports on elder abuse consistently identify females of very advanced age as the most likely victims. The abuser is thought to be middle aged, female, and typically the offspring (daughter) of the victim (Lau and Kosberg, 1979; "The Elderly: Newest Victims of Familial Abuse," 1980; Legal Research and Services for the Elderly, 1979; Block and Sinnott, 1979).

Physical and Mental Impairment

Students of child abuse report that children who suffer from physical or mental handicaps are the most likely children to be abused (Friedrich and Boriskin, 1976). Similarly, researchers studying elder abuse are unanimous in agreeing that older individuals with physical or mental impairments run a greater risk of being abused than those of similar age who do not suffer from major impairments (Block and Sinnott, 1979; Burston, 1975; Lau and Kosberg, 1979; Legal Research and Services for the Elderly, 1979; Rathbone-McCuan, 1980).

Stress

Investigators frequently note that the responsibility for caring for a dependent, aging parent can lead to a stressful situation for the caregiver as well as the entire family (Block and Sinnott, 1979; Legal Research and Service for the Elderly, 1979; Litman, 1971; Rathbone-McCuan, 1980; Steinmetz, 1978). Legal Research and Services for the Elderly (1979) stated that in 65 percent of the cases of elder abuse, the victim was viewed as a source of stress to the abuser.

Horowitz (1978) notes that persons who found the caretaking role the most stressful were often those who were trying to meet the needs of both their spouse and children, while at the same time trying to meet the needs of an older relative.

Cycle of Abuse

While no formal empirical data are presented, researchers believe that the use of violence to resolve conflicts runs in families, and this use of violence is passed on from generation to generation (Briley, 1979; Rathbone-McCuan, 1980; Steinmetz, 1978; U.S. Congress, Select Committee on Aging, Subcommittee on Human Services, 1980).

Analysis

Despite the consistency of factors reportedly associated with elderly abuse in the variety of articles and reports written on this subject, it is clear that the support for these claims is intuitive, speculative, and/or based only on findings from studies of other forms of family violence. There is almost no empirical evidence in the literature which supports the claims made for such associations.

The major drawback of research to date is that, with the exception of the work by Legal Research and Services for the Elderly (1979), *no comparison groups were included in the research designs*. Thus, researchers cannot report whether the factors they found present in their cases of abuse were distinctive of abuse cases, compared to other clients where no abuse was present, or compared to the general population of the elderly. For instance, the finding that abused elderly suffered from mental and physical impairments could simply be a function of the fact that agencies caring for the elderly have many clients who are physically or mentally impaired. The current crop of research reports on elderly abuse cannot answer the question, "Is the stress found in homes where there is elder abuse greater than stress found in homes of similarly aged elderly who are not abused?" Granted the number of very old victims of elder abuse may appear disproportionately high compared to the age distribution of the general population. A question which also must be addressed is, "Is the agency in which the research data have been gathered seeing a disproportionately large population of very old individuals?" The failure to employ comparison groups in the current research means that these questions cannot be answered. Moreover, without comparison groups, it is impossible to establish statistical significance of relationships of magnitude of associations.

As stated earlier, most studies gather data on cases of elder abuse by selecting cases or subjects from elderly seen in agencies which serve the elderly. Because of this procedure, these studies cannot determine if they have discovered factors related to elder abuse or factors related to an individual or family being seen or discovered by an agency.

Theories of Elderly Abuse

Even as there are precious few studies on elder abuse which can meet the minimum standards for empirical evidence, there is a corresponding lack of empirically tested propositions on the generative causes of the abuse of older persons. Much of what is offered as theoretical work on elderly abuse are actually propositions and theories which have been developed and applied to other types of intrafamilial abuse.

Working from research on child and wife abuse, researchers have proposed a number of propositions and theoretical explanations of elder abuse. The central problem with these theoretical explanations is that, in no case, has there been an empirical test of the propositions or explanations. Some propositions are similar to the conventional wisdoms frequently applied to other forms of abuse, and which were subsequently not supported by rescarch (e.g. the claim that abusers of the elderly are psychopaths). Other propositions are borrowed from research on spouse and child abuse (e.g. patterns of violence are passed from one generation to the next), while a third class of propositions is based on assumptions about the status of the elderly in society and the typical family situations of the elderly (e.g. abuse is a consequence of inadequate services available to assist families caring for an aging member). In many instances, these assumptions are of dubious accuracy, and should themselves be subjected to empirical verification or falsification.

The shortcomings in the other areas of study of elder abuse, especially the definitional confusion over what is and is not abuse, come home to roost in the preliminary theoretical work which is available thus far. Clearly, some factors are more likely to be related to acts of overt physical abuse, while other factors may be more closely related to neglect. Such distinctions are not made in the theories since the definitions fail to distinguish between types of abuse.

This critique does not mean that the theoretical propositions which have been proposed are not plausible. Rather, the problem is that there are innumerable plausible rival explanations for elder abuse. They will all be plausible until quality empirical data are generated.

Summary

There are three fundamental questions concerning elder abuse (four if one asks, "What is it?"): What is the extent of elderly abuse? Who are the most likely offenders and victims? and, What causes people to abuse elderly relatives? The state of current research on abuse of older persons is such that we can answer all three (four) questions the same way, "We do not really know."

What is truly regrettable about the current state of research on elder abuse is that the lack of quality data has lead to the widespread dissemination of myth, conventional wisdom, and in some cases, falsehood. Statements presented as facts which have no scientific foundations and are then used to frame both policy and programs to treat and prevent the abuse of older persons. Legal changes are proposed, innovative treatment programs are initiated, and recommendations are made by Congressional panels, all without so much as one piece of information which can meet normal standards of scientific evidence. Many resulting programs and policies may be misguided. At best, some might even fortuitously prove to be effective. At worst, when we base programs and policies on popularized notions about extent, patterns, and causes, we run the very real risk of doing more harm than good to elderly clients and their families.

The authors believe that programs and policies must be built on a sound knowledge base. Towards this end, the following steps must be accomplished:

Depoliticizing the Definition of Elder Abuse. Researchers must carefully construct precise, measurable, and scientifically useful definitions of elder abuse. Acts of commission must be seen as conceptually distinct from acts of omission. Violence must be viewed as different, in kind and cause, from neglect.

Study More Than Publicly Visible Cases. Research should not be limited to sampling cases of elder abuse from public and private agencies. Prior research on family violence has demonstrated that reliable and valid data can be obtained by utilizing self-reports of abuse from subjects in non-clinical settings.

A Measure of Extent Must Be Based on a Representative Sample. Multiplying the rate of elder abuse found in a pilot study by the number of persons over 60 years of age yields a large number, but a number which is no way indicative of the incidence of elder abuse. The best way to derive such an estimate is with a representative sample of subjects. The continued reliance on small, non-representative samples will continue to yield unreliable, biased data which cannot be generalized to any population.

Comparison Groups. The simple issue here is that one cannot identify factors associated with elder abuse without having some kind of comparison groups built into the study.

Theory Testing and Building. Finally, researchers need to reject the kind of *post hoc* analysis which is so evident in current work on elder abuse, and begin to conduct studies which are designed to test theoretical propositions.

Until such a program of serious and adequate research is begun and begins to yield reliable and valid data, those interested in the study of elder abuse should studiously avoid the temptation to further disseminate the current crop of guesses and notions about the extent, patterns, and causes of elder abuse. The truth is that we really do not know very much at this stage, and we need to concentrate our energies on gathering meaningful data on this important topic.

Implications for Practitioners

The implications of the current state about knowledge on abuse of elder persons for practitioners are less clear and direct than the implications for researchers.

While neither definitive nor even tentative answers are available to the major questions concerning elder abuse, it is reasonable to assume that the abuse of elder persons by family members is a significant problem and that clinicians who treat elderly clients could expect to encounter abuse victims. Practitioners face two major problems when treating victims of elder abuse. First, since there is very little in the way of sound scholarly knowledge on this topic, practitioners cannot presently locate quality research knowledge which could be informative for their clinical practice. Second, since elder abuse has only recently been identified as a family and social problem, there are few established resources, services, and treatment programs which can be adopted, copied, or applied to the problem.

Until both knowledge and services are developed, practitioners will have to cope the best they can. Towards that end, a number of steps can be taken.

Be Aware That Elderly Are Abused by Family Members. The first step for practitioners is to overcome the selective inattention which has long masked the abuse of elderly from public and professional eyes. Just as pediatricians had to learn not to take patterns of injuries in children for granted, practitioners who service the elderly must be willing to ask difficult and sensitive questions surrounding the appearance of bruises, fractures, or other untoward injuries to an elderly client.

Use Existing Domestic Violence Services. Fortunately, there has been an intensive and extensive development of services for victims of family violence. Refuges or battered wife shelters have increased from 6 in 1976, to more than 300 today. While there are still an insufficient number of such shelters to meet the needs of battered wives, these shelters do offer potential placements for female victims of elder abuse.

Support and Supporting Caretakers. Clinicians who treat victims of child abuse often find that providing support services to families, such as homemakers, visiting nurses, or home health visitors serves to alleviate family stress and reduce the risk of future abuse. Services which aid and assist those who care for elderly and/or infirm relatives could be an important asset in a treatment program for elder abuse. Just as it is unrealistic to expect that everyone who bears a child has the personal, social, and economic resources to adequately nurture that child, it is equally unrealistic to assume that all those who must care for their elderly relatives have the full resources to do that job with kindness and compassion.

Avoid Applying Myths to Clinical Practice. Clinical practice with victims of family violence can be emotionally draining and upsetting. To counterbalance these emotions, clinicians often search for simple and direct answers to the problems they must solve. Since the media has milked a few facts for all they are worth, it might be tempting for clinicians to assume that if they read facts about elder abuse often enough in the newspapers, then these are facts which can be applied to clinical practice. This paper has attempted to show that few facts exist and that clinicians should resist the temptation to apply what they read in the newspapers or magazines to their clinical work.

Notes

1. It cannot be determined if 4.1% of 73 individuals were abused (N = 3), if 4.1% of 48 individuals were abused (N = 2), or if 1 out of 48 individuals (2%) were abused. Block and Sinnott (1979) cited each of these statistics on various pages of their final report.
2. The exact numbers could not be determined because they reported mean scores for many types of abuse and neglect and the categories were not mutually exclusive.
3. This section omits reference to, and discussion of, the estimate of 500,000 victims of elder abuse attributed to the second author. The estimate, which has been widely published, is actually a figure arrived at by estimating the number of individuals 65 years old or older who married, had children, and have contact with their children. The 3.5 percent incidence statistic was based on the percentage of parents who reported being abused by teenage children in a national

survey of family violence (Straus, Gelles, and Steinmetz, 1980). Thus, the estimate has no more empirical standing than a guess, irrespective of how frequently it has been cited in popular and professional literature.

References

Aging committees consider programs to curb growing problem of elder abuse. *Federal Contracts Opportunities.* 1980, 5(15), 1.

Block, M., and Sinnott, J. (eds.). "The Battered Elder Syndrome: An Exploratory Study." Manuscript, University of Maryland, 1979.

Briley, M. "Battered parents." *Dynamic Years,* 1979, 14 (2), 24-27.

Burston, G.R. "Granny Battering." *British Medical Journal,* 1975, 3 (5983), 592.

Douglass, R.L., Hickey, T., and Noel, C. "A Study of Maltreatment of the Elderly and Other Vulnerable Adults." Manuscript, University of Michigan, 1980.

"The Elderly: Newest Victims of Familial Abuse." *Medical News,* 1980, 243 (12), 1221-25.

Friedrich, W.N., and Boriskin, J.A. "The Role of the Child in Abuse: A Review of Literature." *American Journal of Orthopsychiatry,* 1976, 46 (4), 580-90.

Harris, C. *Fact Book on Aging: A Profile of America's Older Population.* Washington, D.C.: National Council on the Aging, 1975.

Horowitz, A. "Families Who Care: A Study of Natural Support Systems of the Elderly." Manuscript, 1978.

Kempe, C.H., Silverman, F.N, Steele, B.F., Droegemueller, W., and Silver, H.K. "The Battered-Child Syndrome." *Journal of the American Medical Association,* 1962, 181, 17-24.

Koch, L., and Koch, J. "Parent abuse: A New Plague." *Washington Post,* 1980, January 27, pp. Pa14-15.

Laslett, B. "The Family as a Public and Private Institution: A Historical Perspective." *Journal of Marriage and the Family,* 1973, 35 (3), 480-92.

Lau, E., and Kosberg, J. "Abuse of the Elderly by Informal Care Providers." *Aging,* 1979, 299, 10-15.

Legal Research and Services for the Elderly. "Elder Abuse in Massachusetts: A Survey of Professionals and Paraprofessionals." Manuscript, 1979.

Litman, T. "Health Care and the Family: A Three Generational Analysis." *Medical Care,* 1971, 9 (1), 67-81.

Maddox, G.L. "The Patient and His Family." In S. Sherwood (ed.), *The Hidden Patient; Knowledge and Action in Long Term Care.* New York: Spectrum, 1975.

Newberger, E., Reed, R., Daniel, J., Hyde, J., and Kotelchuck, M. "Pediatric Social Illness: Toward an Etiologic Classification." *Pediatrics,* 1977, 60 (2), 178-85.

Rathbone-McCuan, E. "Elderly Victims of Family Violence and Neglect." *Social Casework,* 1980, 61 (4), 296-304.

Steinmetz, S.K. "Battered Parents." *Society,* 1978, 15 (5), 54-55.

Straus, M.A., Gelles, R.J., and Steinmetz, S.K. *Behind Closed Doors: Violence in the American Family.* New York: Anchor Press/Doubleday, 1980.

Treas, J. "Family Support Systems for the Aged." *Gerontologist,* 1977, 17 (6), 486-91.

Turbett, J.P., and O'Toole, R. "Physician's Recognition of Child Abuse." Paper presented at the annual meetings of the American Sociological Association, New York, 1980.

U.S. Bureau of the Census, *Statistical Abstracts of the U.S., 1978*. Washington, D.C.: U.S. Government Printing Office, 1978.

U.S. Congress, Select Committee on Aging, Subcommittee on Human Services. *Domestic Violence against the Elderly*, Washington, D.C.: U.S. Government Printing Office, 1980.

26

To Heir Is Human

Jeffrey P. Rosenfeld

Some families today are splitting heirs. Others are putting on heirs. And some are getting no heirs fast. Family patterns are changing, alternative lifestyles are emerging and, as they do, new forms of inheritance are taking shape.

A 22 year-old even won the right to adopt his 26 year-old male lover, with approval from the courts. Now, should he die, his assets will go to his "child." In its decision, the New York State Supreme Court acknowledged, "the nuclear family arrangement is no longer the only model of family life in America."

The naming of nontraditional beneficiaries is one of the most unexpected results of today's new lifestyles, and one of the most far reaching. Many of today's most popular living arrangements are based on relationships that will make direct lineal descent unimportant, or unachievable, in estate planning. The sheer number of people involved means that demographic trends in American life will alter tomorrow's trusts and estates. By 1995, almost one-quarter of all trusts and estate plans could involve friends, outsiders, and distant kin instead of lineal descendents.

The new lifestyles—childlessness, cohabitation, remarriage—are socially acceptable but rarely considered in terms of the inheritance patterns they generate. Childlessness, however, can mean heirlessness; cohabitation blurs the legal rights of spouse-equivalents; and remarriage muddles descent lines.

Children in reconstituted families can have multiple sets of parents and grandparents, and may be eligible to inherit property from them all. Even migration and settlement patterns affect inheritance by separating kin and involving people in relationships that eventually become the basis for trusts and estate plans.

There have always been people who willed property outside the family, but until recently they were less than 8 percent of the will-making population. Their number will grow as more people cohabit, remarry, and migrate in the 1980s and beyond. The interplay between demographics and inheritance patterns varies by age, considering separately Americans aged 65 and older, those 45 to 64, and those aged 25 to 44.

Traditionalists

People who are 65 and over today will likely be the last group who routinely have heirs to name and will name the heirs they have. The majority have not divorced and have grandchildren. Fifty percent of men approaching age 85 are still married to their first and only wife. Three-quarters of older Americans have living children, and of these 90 percent also have grandchildren. The conventional estate plan for people with spouse and descendents is to provide first for the spouse and then for descendents. Surveys of older people confirm that this is what they intend.

In reseaching inheritance patterns for 225 New York families, I found that elderly people, especially those with the most traditional families, had the most conventional estate plans. There was more variance in estate plans among younger people reflecting the greater range of lifestyles of young people today.

Older people's traditional attitudes toward inheritance are in keeping with the importance of kinship and family in their lives. A 1979 survey by Ethel Shanas reported in *The Gerontologist* found that 77 percent of older people visit regularly with children and grandchildren, and that three of four older parents live within a half-hour of a child.

However, these traditional bonds already show signs of weakening, especially for older people who live far from their kin, in retirement communities or nursing homes. Life on the geriatric ward has in common with places like Sun City or Leisure Village a tendency for friendship to grow more important than kinship. People who live in nursing homes deplete their wealth paying for long-term care. Those in the retirement villages that dot the Sunbelt are probably the most affluent of America's elderly. But the beneficiaries these elderly name are not a function of wealth (or poverty) so much as the lifestyles they live.

Benefactors in the Middle

Most elderly people today, however, continue making conventional bequests along lines of descent. Their middle-aged sons or daughters do not, however. The middle-aged people of today (ages 45 to 64) will be the first routinely expected to provide for both ascendents and descendents. Over one-quarter of people in their fifties have one or more parents and in-laws still living. It is common for people in their forties or fifties to bear responsibility for parents or other older kin. Estate planning has become an important aspect of this care.

Demographer Judith Treas has reviewed the social characteristics of the aging and finds that the most dependent of these people are usually widowed women, aged over 75. Their helplessness prompts growing numbers of middle-aged sons and daughters to create caretaker trusts for them. A surrogate's court judge in New York estimates that caretaker trusts for elderly people—a rare arrangement in 1960—now account for close to one-fifth of the trusts he oversees.

Trust plans of this kind reduce the estates that descendents will inherit. But though they deplete an inheritance, they do not jeopardize the principle of descent. Divorce and remarriage do jeopardize this principle, however.

One-quarter of American women aged 45 to 64 have already divorced, and an estimated 20 percent are remarried. Nearly four million children live in stepfamilies where one or both of the parents are aged 45 to 64. Who will inherit property after parents divorce and remarry? Increasing numbers of people now aged 45 to 64 will have to reconcile the claims of the three types of heirs in reconstituted families.

Assume that Joe and Mary are married, have a daughter, and then divorce. Mary now has custody of the daughter, remarries, and moves away. Joe also remarries, to a woman with a child from her previous marriage. They have a child together, leaving three heirs eligible to inherit Joe's property—an absentee heir from his previous marriage, a step heir from his second wife's previous marriage, and the reconstituted heir from the remarriage.

Middle-aged people in this situation are ambivalent about what they owe their absentee heirs—their children from previous marriages. An American Bar Foundation survey found that 98 percent of remarried people will bequeath at least half their property to reconstituted heirs, but are not enthusiastic about naming step heirs or absentee heirs even though they may have as much legal right to share in the inheritance. Twenty-three percent of respondents surveyed by ABF said they would leave nothing to children from previous marriages—which amounts to disinheriting them. An additional 29 percent would leave them between 1 percent and 49 percent of their estate.

Ambivalent as these parents are today, they may be at even more of a loss over what to do 15 or 20 years from now when they are step-grandparents. High rates of divorce and remarriage within the baby-boom generation mean that half of all parents of these baby-boomers will be step-grand-parents by 1995. Will they have to reconcile the claims of absentee grand-children, reconstituted grandchildren, and step-grandchildren?

Innovative Benefactors

Of all the baby-boom lifestyles and attitudes that will affect inheritance, the most significant are childlessness and cohabitation. Couples without children are freer to make unconventional bequests than those who feel bound by lines of descent, or who know the courts will invalidate estate plans that exclude spouse or children. Though the wills of childless people can be contested on grounds such as fraud or undue influence, they cannot be invalidated for excluding descendents.

Along with married but childless couples, the baby-boom cohorts have produced more cohabitating people than previous cohorts did. The Census Bureau estimates there were 1.9 million couples cohabitating in 1982, or about 4 percent of all couples. At least 70 percent of cohabitants have no children.

Who will cohabitants name in the trusts and estate plans they finally make? The principle in the "adoption" mentioned earlier is that cohabitat-ing couples now may have the right to each other's assets—a right once reserved for married people, or for parents and children. "The realities of present-day family life may allow many types of nontraditional families," said the New York court. Today's cohabitants, be they straight or gay, conventional or unconventional, will probably figure in each other's estate planning tomorrow.

The career plans of baby-boom women will also affect inheritance pat-terns. The Census Bureau confirms that women's participation in the work force increased steadily between 1965 and 1980, especially among single and childless women. This segment of the female labor force tends to be more predominantly white, better educated, and younger—aged 25 to 34—than working women at large. Many of these women are executives or professionals who earn more money than most working women. But they are also unusual in that they have no descendents, and are free to make unconventional bequests. This elite group of working women is still de-cades from old age. But many of today's younger professional women will not have the traditional set of heirs and beneficiaries when they make their wills.

American women of the baby-boom generation have a greater life expec-tancy than their husbands and will outlive their partners by longer than ever before. In 1920, for example, married women outlived their husbands by an average of one year whereas widows today average over seven years more than their husbands. This leaves more time to spend the estate rather than passing it along intact. It also provides more opportunities to establish new relationships that rival family and kinship and thus threaten lineal descent. In an article in *Psychology Today* (May 1980), such a pattern was called "benevolent disinheritance" because it occurs when widowed people feel they already have done enough for their offspring and are ready to use their property as they see fit. Even now cars in the Miami-Fort Lauderdale region sport bumper stickers that read, "I'm Spending My Kids' Inheritance."

Today's elderly people are products of the Great Depression and the work ethic and—bumper stickers to the contrary—they are generally reluctant to spend their life's savings. They prefer to pass along an inheritance to their offspring and kin. But will members of the baby-boom, who are products of affluence, be as motivated to hold on to their savings so that their survivors will have something to inherit?

Legal Changes

At a time when people are divorcing and remarrying more than ever before, the once sacrosanct inheritance for one's spouse is being modified both in law and in practice. Laws throughout the United States require that married people designate some assets—usually between 33 percent and 50 percent—for the surviving spouse. In theory they are free to do with the remainder as they please. In practice most married people today intend to leave the spouse more than the legal minimum. It is rare for one spouse to deprive the other of inheritance.

Antenuptial agreements are a legally binding way for married people to evade this obligation. People waive the right to one another's estate by signing a contract before they are wed. The rising popularity of antenuptial agreements parallels the rise in divorce and remarriage.

Antenuptial agreements are common among older people who marry late in life or remarry after being divorced or widowed. This kind of agreement appeals to people who remarry, because it permits them to keep estates separate for their respective grown families.

Recent changes in the Federal Estate Tax Code erode the property rights of married people even further. Prior to 1982, for example, the spouse who died first had to relinquish title to property if that property went into a trust fund for the surviving spouse. The presumption was that the survivor received trust income because she or he would someday inherit the actual estate.

The new law allows a spouse to set aside trust income for the surviving spouse while giving control of the actual estate to his or her own designee.

This arrangement, called a Qualified Terminable Interest in Property Trust (Q.T.I.P. Trust) already appeals to remarried people who prefer not to name a new spouse as major beneficiary. Q.T.I.P. Trusts, like antenuptial agreements, separate property rights from marital arrangements. They may be reshaping the rights and obligations that married people have towards one another.

Conflict Ahead?

Will contests are rare these days. Studies based on probate records throughout the United States indicate that only 3 or 4 percent of all probated wills ever reach the jury trial stage. The ones that do usually involve either enormous amounts of property, or hardly any at all. It is as though families decide to see a case through to jury trial if there are millions of dollars at stake, or so little money that they have nothing to lose by going to court.

Most families settle their differences out of court. They rely on the family lawyer, or on one another, to settle the arguments and to soothe the hard feelings which often arise during probate.

But the incidence of will contests could rise sharply as trusts and estate plans become less conventional. Inheritance has traditionally been an occasion when families reconfirm the importance of kinship ties, and one another's power and authority. The scant evidence from research on will contests shows that more than property is at stake when families go to court. There is concern that a traditional aspect of the family—a role, relationship, or the balance of power—has been violated by the terms of the trusts or estate plan. Bequests outside the family to friends, lovers, stepheirs, and so forth may never become socially acceptable, even if they are increasingly common.

Where to Turn

Estate planners are already beginning to find their job more difficult. The graying of America, the gaying of America, cohabitation, and remarriage now put estate planners in the difficult position of counseling people whose estate plans are complicated by unusual heirs or beneficiaries. It is no wonder that some estate planners are turning to family therapists and social consultants for tips on how better to serve a changing clientele.

Firms like AgeWise in New York meet this growing need in the estate-planning industry. Estate planners are usually well trained in law, taxation, and accounting. But they lack the training necessary to counsel willmakers; and more than ever before find themselves at a loss when irate families threaten to contest a will.

AgeWise, Inter-City Services in Dallas-Fort Worth, and a handful of similar consultant services around the country are strengthening themselves in these areas by teaching estate planners basic social and behavioral skills, and by developing software that estate planners can use on their own.

The result is a new set of techniques for planning trusts and estates, and for dealing with the anger and hostility that heirs and beneficiaries often harbor. If demographic projections are correct, these innovations are not a moment too soon.

27

Housing the Elderly

Anne Woodward

"Where will I live when I'm old?" Millions of graying Americans, alarmed at the fate of their parents, are starting to ask that question. With more than 400,000 men and women in the United States now entering the over-65 age group each year—most of them headed for at least another decade of life—jobs, recreation, and home and health-care services for the elderly are getting considerable attention. Government and the private sector willing, these can be rapidly instituted.

Bricks and mortar, however, are here to stay—and we must now mold the built environment to the more than 12 percent of the population who will, by the year 2000, be elderly (over 65). Given the current conservative climate, where do we start? By prodding architects out of their preoccupation with other design problems. By enlisting planners and private organizations to fight obsolete zoning regulations. And above all, by convincing homebuilders after short-term gains that people of all generations seek living options unavailable in our present inflexible housing.

The three-bedroom detached house in the suburbs, for instance, remains the typical dwelling in the United States, representing two-thirds of all our housing. More than 750,000 three-bedroom houses were built in 1980, compared to only 75-80,000 townhouses and condominiums. Whom does this ideal three-bedroom detached house—often some distance from shopping—really serve? It serves the nuclear family with two or three growing children, and one or two cars; not the one in every nine Americans now over age 65, and even less the family of three or four generations who may need, or wish, to live in closer proximity.

Recently, there has been considerable debate about whether the extended family, in the good old days, was ever as close as we have been led to believe. Certainly multigenerational living was easier to achieve in an agrarian society, and it apparently worked for many people. Also, our multiple

422

migrations—from the western movement to population shifts into and out of cities—must have pulled families apart.

In any case, it is clear that, from the 1930s on, many factors combined to isolate the elderly. That decade saw the beginning of zoning and private covenants prohibiting two-family dwellings on one lot, the proliferation of small houses—newly affordable under FHA—and a widespread ignorance of, or indifference to, the housing needs of the elderly. As Winston Churchill put it, "We shape our buildings, and then our buildings shape us." By 1950, the youth-cult and experiments in single-generational living, in communes of the 1960s, contributed to a growing apartheid, as youths warned "don't trust anyone over 30." From 1960 to 1970, while the number of persons 65 and over increased by more than 20 percent, the number of multigenerational households decreased by 10 percent. By 1978 a mere 9 percent of all older Americans lived with adult children, although 42 percent reported they "depended" on their children for other support. Figures from the 1980 census are still being analyzed. But it seems likely that in addition to younger persons who have never married or are divorced, the elderly make up a good proportion of the single-person households that now constitute nearly a quarter of all U.S. households.

In addition to solitary living, two other living arrangements for the elderly now substitute for multigenerational households: the institutionalization or "warehousing" of infirm older persons in nursing homes and homes for the aged, and, for the more affluent elderly still in relatively good health, the privately developed retirement community. Well-intended government policy may have contributed to the isolation of the impoverished elderly with legislation authorizing funding of public housing for the low income aged in 1956. That year, reflecting on the trend, Lewis Mumford was moved to declare that "probably at no period and in no culture have the old been so completely rejected as in our own country, during the last generation."

The question has been raised: Is the rejection a two-way street? Do the elderly really want to remain with the rest of society? In Mumford's day, even cities were still relatively free from violent crime. Now, faced with purse snatching on the street and violent invasions of their homes, older persons sometimes seek out the comparative safety of a home for the aged or a specially guarded retirement community as a haven from abuse and perhaps also from other hostile elements of daily life: traffic congestion and noise, haste and rudeness in public places and on public vehicles, the clamor of young children at play. It should come as no surprise, then, that some studies have shown that, contrary to expectation, many elderly persons find high-rise apartment living quieter and safer than living in a house.

For some of the relatively affluent elderly, withdrawal now means a flight to a privately developed retirement community—most often in the sun-belt—or to an apartment or apartment-hotel that provides its own restaurant and shopping facilities on a small to spectacular scale. Middle-income groups may rely on homes for the aged provided by the Veterans Administration, labor unions, churches and synagogues, or other beneficent organizations with which they are associated. But many of these homes have long waiting lists.

Despite the public protest, homes for the aged not sponsored by charitable organizations are frequently mere rooming houses in old buildings that are basically firetraps and, despite licensing and occupancy regulations, seem difficult for authorities to monitor. Against living in these poorly staffed and managed homes, many low- and middle-income elderly prefer to take their chances on their own. Nursing homes, the last resort, are generally regarded as housing only for the most infirm cases. Ironically, the Government Accounting Office (GAO) has established that between 15 percent and 40 percent of the elderly now living in nursing homes could live in a normal community if special homemaker and health-care services, and transportation, were available to them.

Challenging the Experts

There is a drastic need for experts in several disciplines to look at home and community design and ways they might function for the elderly. Safety, convenience, and ease of home maintenance are obvious, worthy objectives. But the real challenge may lie in how to achieve an ideal balance between privacy and human contact, since these depend to some extent on individual preferences. Most elderly persons seek some companionship with their peers to indulge in shared memories and common concerns over health and families. But they also desire the comforting awareness of life's continuity that comes with the mix of generations. It is clear we will need many options.

Fortunately, some forward-thinking planners are beginning to realize that services to the elderly who live independently—such as Meals on Wheels, and health and homemaker services—should be taken into consideration in locating building sites and planning traffic patterns. Other planners have suggested housing options which aim at preserving in individual communities the approximate proportion of older persons in the population as a whole. Mumford articulated this goal a quarter-century ago, but it was never pursued in any meaningful way, except in some planned new communities. Several new towns in Europe and Australia did successfully incorporate imaginative design for the elderly into development plans. And in Reston, Virginia, as in some of Britain's new towns special housing for the elderly is located on the perimeter of shopping centers, with access to nearby shops and medical clinics. The early collapse of the new-town movement in the United States in the 1970s, however, slowed any innovation here, and we are largely faced with working within existing land-use patterns.

Frank Spink of the Urban Land Institute suggests interesting but costly uses of property in city suburbs, which are gaining in elderly households while central cities are losing. The first involves adding to or converting unused space in elementary schools as service centers for the elderly. Schools could become day-care centers, or, filling an even greater need, temporary convalescent homes, utilizing existing cafeteria and nursing services to assist those unable for short periods to manage for themselves at home. Spink also recommends construction of in-fill housing—small, one-bedroom units specially designed for the elderly—on the land between existing, larger homes. This would mean higher density in low-density areas, but it would permit the elderly to own or rent homes in familiar neighborhoods, with about the right degree of isolation and privacy. Ideally, these suburban in-fill units would be situated reasonably close to suburban shopping areas or the school centers. To accomplish the transition, services now commonplace in urban areas would have to be made available farther out: delivery of or transportation to shopping, food, and medical services, as well as access to recreational opportunities. How can we achieve such radical redesign of our suburbs? Tax incentives would be vital. And other guarantees, probably similar to those instituted to permit the preservation and rehabilitation of our cities, would also have to be created.

Architects design upon demand. With 25 million Americans already over 65, it is somewhat shocking to learn that only around seventy members of the American Institute of Architects (AIA) specialize in housing for the elderly, and that no one, apparently, is clamoring for multigenerational schemes. Fortunately, the executive director of the AIA, David Meeker, a former Assistant Director for Community Development of Housing and Urban Development, is alert to the possibilities. He acknowledges that "under present economic and social pressures, the extended family may reassemble as an economic unit" and exert pressure on architects to think about houses to accommodate several generations.

And what of the home builders? Obviously, they are looking for profit and build for the market as they perceive it. And as a nation, we have only very recently begun to recognize and accept new family living patterns and the dramatic increase in the number of elderly. These developments give rise to new market demand. Who will do the innovating? Only 10 percent of all homebuilders construct more than a hundred housing units a year.

These larger firms are usually in a better financial position to take risks than the smaller, average homebuilder, who completes less than fifteen units a year. Yet the smaller firms have been more adventurous in seeking new markets. After young "homesteaders" started rehabilitating older city houses in the 1970s, smaller firms pioneered in the construction of town-houses in urban, then suburban, areas. Perhaps these homebuilders will now develop innovative designs for tomorrow's aged.

What is the incentive? First, home-buyers, mindful that a small cost-saving today could necessitate an enormous investment in changes tomorrow, should make their voices heard. They should demand that houses now being built will suit their needs in twenty or so years. This may prompt a little more social concern. However, other efforts will be needed if we are really to progress beyond the omnipresent inflexible house and the bigger and bigger home for the aged. Government may have to stir homebuilders with better carrots and sticks. As Meeker admits, "both in coordination and process, our present instruments are increasingly less important and relevant to today's housing." Some new possibilities? HUD could cooperate in the development of new housing types and financing mechanisms. FHA and the Veterans Administration regulations could stipulate a limit on loans for home building unless the product would be suitable for the new population mix. Then, with tax incentives and other logical guarantees, private enterprise should respond. Among the alternatives architects and builders might consider are: double-houses, multigenerational group-living arrangements, congregate housing of suitable size and design, and basic houses or other new structures with flexible design features.

Creative Alternatives

Seventy-one percent of all persons over 65 own their own home. Is there any way those who wish could stay there until they are too feeble to care for themselves? Their empty nests—the aging, oversized homes in cities and older suburbs—are often unsafe, too big, and awkward to care for. The average lifespan of a house is estimated to be fifty years; and half of the elderly still live in housing built before World War II. The high cost of modernization, plus increased taxes, make maintenance difficult. Present tax deductions for improvements or partially subsidized repairs are apparently inadequate. HUD admits that the present FMHA Section 504 Home Repair Loan Program, available to the elderly of low income, is rarely used because of the loan repayment schedules. If better financing could be arranged, and zoning changed to make possible remodeling to a "double," some, but not all, of the problems might be resolved. A reliable tenant in a rental unit could provide extra security, supplemental income, and even transportation in emergencies.

The "double" is also a good bet for the family worried about an aging parent or wanting parents nearby, but not underfoot. In these cases, provision of not only health and homemaker services, but some relief from the constant strain of care-taking, is essential. To preserve privacy and pursuit of special interests, an addition to the family home, or conversion of space to a completely separate "grandparents unit," is most desirable. But in most cities—Los Angeles and Houston among the exceptions—zoning regulations prohibit such conversion.

How can houses be remodeled so that there is living space for an elderly person or couple? Often there are basements in city townhouses that can be converted to living quarters suitable for renting to students or young professionals. But families hardly wish to put their aged parents in damp or dark basements. Duplex houses—living quarters that mirror-image each other side by side—are scarce but useful. One-floor "double" brick houses with three bedrooms each, dubbed "executive bungalows," have been successful with middle-income families in Dallas; they are near stores and recreation. Stacked apartments, one over another in an older home, like the "triple deckers" of Massachusetts, could be fine, except for the stairs. However, in ground-level townhouses, conversion of the lower level into an apartment for the elderly works out well, with use of the top two floors for a younger family—provided care is taken through use of thick carpets, carpet pads, and other sound-abatement devices to ensure that noise from above is not transmitted to the apartment below. Inner conversions of space are more likely and offer interesting, if costly, design challenges. But most "doubles" will have to be created out of existing housing. With land at a premium, remodeling, not new building, is the wave of the future, for at least a couple of decades.

The tax deductions for interest paid on home mortgages, and also for remodeling and repairs to rental units, are helpful but need simplifying. What is missing is any special deduction for remodeling to modernize or maintain a full-time "granny flat." (A bill to allow a credit for household expenses to any taxpayer who maintains a household with a dependent 65 years old or over was proposed in the 96th Congress—but languished in committee. This, too, might be resurrected.)

The concept of several generations sharing living space is not limited to members of the same family. A Presbyterian minister, the Reverend Dennis Day-Lower, developed in the Back Bay area of Boston a model, nonprofit "shared living project," in which fifteen unrelated persons, aged 20 to 80, have lived together since July, 1979. Day-Lower started with Title III seed money from the Administration on Aging and obtained additional funds from private sources to convert a former rooming house for primarily low-income residents (in accordance with HUD guidelines). Residents pay from $150 to $250 for private rooms, some with baths, in the Victorian row house with one large kitchen, common all-purpose living-dining space, one kitchenette on each floor, and a roof-top garden. The essential privacy is maintained. And none of the elderly residents are so disabled that they cannot contribute physically, socially, or mentally to the management of the project. The apparent success of the Boston project has encouraged Day-Lower to establish "Inter-generational Housing Services" in Philadelphia to advise on other extended "family" living arrangements. Privately supported by churches and individuals, the center expects to engage in direct consulting and technical assistance on similar shared-living projects, develop educational material for interested persons, act as a resource to local groups on the removal of legal barriers to shared-living projects, and establish a nationwide network for information exchange. Day-Lower cites at least fifty shared houses now around the country—some rented, some individually or jointly owned.

There have also been experiments accommodating a few rental units for the elderly in condominiums. In essence, the individual owners of condo units carry the older residents, who pay a flat monthly rent according to income and receive regular condo services—maintenance, utilities, etc.—free of additional charge. There are several advantages to this situation. Elderly residents receive protection and pleasant surroundings at minimum cost. And while the cost to residents who "carry" them is minimal when divided among many unit owners, the benefits of having a few elderly persons readily available for temporary child care or home management may be important.

Group living for the elderly should not be ruled out. It has worked in Scandinavian countries, and many gerontologists, including Marie McGuire Thompson of the International Center for Social Gerontology, affirm its usefulness. The Urban Institute estimates that a million Americans require this living arrangement, but this is somewhat debatable. It is necessary now because so few alternatives and home services are available. Group living is a practical solution when independent living, living with a family, or living with an extended "family" of different age groups is undesirable or impossible for physical, emotional, or financial reasons. As long as the building housing an elderly group is not too large, and as long as it is located in a community where the elderly are not completely isolated from other age groups, shops, medical centers, and neighborhood activities, this is not necessarily a bad solution. Unfortunately, new buildings for the elderly appear to be being built farther and farther out into the countryside, where land is cheap. And new or renovated buildings in the

center city—and even in some new communities like Reston, Virginia—
get bigger and bigger, also for maximum financial return.

There is some agreement that, socially, the ideal group housing for elderly occupants contains six to twelve units to a building. The ideal building is located in a mixed-age community, in pleasant surroundings, but
close to amenities; the ideal design takes into consideration regional preferences and the ethnic or other cultural differences of the occupants. In other
words, the best group living facilitates not only the necessary services to the
elderly, but also friendship formation. Peers, in such situations, add to or
substitute for the emotional and other support of the family. In most such
congregate housing in the United States, the minimum age limit is 62. In
Europe, it is often 55—which may make for a better mix.

The idea of a house as a changing process rather than a fixed object has
intrigued architects for some years. The concept was strongly advocated at
a Stanford Research Institute Conference in 1967, and since then a number
of attempts have been made to design and build both an adaptable conventional house and a more radical "core" house to which self-contained
units, requiring only furniture, could be added or subtracted according to
the needs of the occupants. The "typical" housing consumer, like the "typical" American family, is becoming more and more diverse. The press has
recently pointed out the many young persons now returning to their parents' households—for economic reasons—and the benefits and friction this
may generate. Thus, the time seems particularly ripe for developments to
accommodate changing family roles, provided home builders and the construction trades overcome their resistance to innovation.

For the most part, builders have been frightened away from experiments
as a result of an unfortunate experience with the "basic house" in 1970-71.
In an effort to keep down costs, builders constructed a dwelling without
amenities like fireplaces or dishwashers or larger rooms. The idea never
caught on; although the buying public had been asking for more affordable
homes, few purchased this stripped-down model. At the January 1981 annual meeting of the National Association of Home Builders, however, the
concept resurfaced as one way to make houses affordable despite high
interest rates. And the American Institute of Architects tends to agree. A
few initial experiments in "core" housing to which other units could be
hooked were also less successful. Olin Corporation attempted some "flexible" modular units in the new town of Jonathan, Minnesota, in 1971—
dwellings with a basic service core of kitchen, two bathrooms, and an all-
purpose area to which bedroom modules could be added on one side, and a
living-dining room on the other. (There was even talk of having rentable
units that could be added for a special need at a special, specified time.)
The cost of moving the additional modules into place, however, proved

prohibitive—at about the same cost as moving a trailer. Grumman Modular Buildings experimented with modules made with structural steel stacking frames with both fixed and movable walls and partitions, but never went into mass production. The idea undoubtedly has merit, but the ideal formula has yet to be found. And once it is found it will take a carefully thought-out public relations campaign to lure people away from their desire for the single-family detached unit built on conventional lines, the dreamhouse useful for only limited family years. Perhaps people can become educated to become less fixture-oriented—seeking only houses with rooms rigidly dictating specific functions such as dining rooms, bedrooms, etc.—and become more space-oriented.

Little has been said to date about the usefulness of flexible housing as a solution to the needs of the elderly. But it may be significant that in Japan, where families traditionally take care of aging parents, houses are made more flexible through the use of moveable screens which can open up space or close off rooms for privacy. Architects and interior designers, who in recent years have removed doors to create an illusion of greater space, might well consider installing screens, "pocket" doors, or large, hinged doors that fold back to multiply room use (and, as a side-benefit for the elderly, make the passage of a wheel chair practical). Some experiments with design of a conventional adaptable house that could accommodate the handicapped or elderly, however, are now taking place. Under contract with HUD, the National Association of Home Builders Research Foundation has recently completed two houses (one in Las Vegas and the other in Loveland, Colorado) and four apartment units (two in Bethesda, Maryland, and two in southern Florida) to show that new design standards, making the house adaptable for handicapped (or elderly) persons, would not necessarily be prohibitive in cost. Adaptations in the houses and apartments were, for the most part, available on the standard market. They included such small changes as levers rather than door knobs as handles; wider doors—36 rather than 32 inches wide—and light switches and plugs at waist level; stronger bathroom walls to accommodate bars and rails that might be added later. The largest cost was for items not now available, such as kitchen counter tops that could adjust to different heights. The counter tops had to be custom-made but, should they come into mass-production, would not be excessive in cost. HUD is currently evaluating this "adaptable" housing for new American National Standards Institute (ANSI) building standards, but from the cost aspect only. HUD reports no interest in seeing how the living arrangements work out with occupancy, despite the fact that handicapped persons have now occupied the first-completed homes for several months.

Long-Term Planning

Persons over 75 currently make up the fastest growing age group in the United States, but only about 46 percent of this group are able to function without help (as opposed to 71 percent of persons age 65-74, according to the Government Accounting Office). Despite all medical effort to prevent or alleviate loss of sensory acuity, for example, people still have to expect this physical deterioration to begin at around age 70. And even with the trend toward better general health for the aged, handicaps due to a particular illness become noticeable at this time of life. As a result, architectural and interior design features—special treatments of light, color, and texture as well as physical space—become increasingly important.

The elderly, moreover, require safety features to guard them not only from crime, but also from accidents. Accidents in the home cost the nation two and a half billion dollars annually, and the elderly are particularly vulnerable. These facts have not been ignored. The Department of Commerce has issued safety guidelines for those who want to construct homes that have the potential to be relatively accident-free. Accommodations for the handicapped, which have won wide attention, are now commonly used in reputable homes for the aged and nursing homes. This is encouraging. But it is only a beginning. If older persons are really to maintain their independence for as long as possible—alone, in a family setting, or with a surrogate family—builders must give some thought to incorporating special design as accepted practice in standard homes (and, where suitable, shops and medical clinics).

Some design elements deserve special review:

Special alarm systems. In Britain an alarm system alerts neighbors that the older person is having difficulty at home: the older person's residence contains switches in each room which turn on a bright blue light outside the front door, in plain view of neighbors and passers-by, as a signal for help. Other alarm systems, including an alarm bell that also opens the front door, are being experimented with here. Such house systems would complement Med-Alert, the device worn on the body which can signal a receiving station that help is needed.

Aid to physical movement. Awning and crank-operated casement windows (except for the arthritic) should replace double-hung windows, which are awkward and often stick. Non-slip floors, with no raised thresholds, and levers rather than door knobs would be helpful. Handrails should be installed where appropriate, and at the proper angle (Marie McGuire Thompson reports that too many handrails are now being used in homes for the aged).

Sensory aids. Changes in textures and contrasting colors for walls and floors, risers and treads on stairs, etc., would reinforce perceptions of depth and location. A proper balance of lighting—not too bright, not too dim— would eliminate glare and sharp contrasts.

Predictions for the future are mostly perilous. The Institute for the Future, for example, conducted a study in 1971 of "Some Prospects for Residential Housing by 1985." One way-off-base prediction: "A gradual lowering of the prime interest rate to 7.5 percent by 1980, followed by a rise to 8 percent by 1985 is expected." Experts, moreover, disagree. At about the same time that the Institute's report was also predicting that "building codes will undergo extensive revision emphasizing standardization mechanisms which permit a greater degree of innovation and use of mass-production techniques," architect Peter Blake was telling a Washington, D.C. audience—only half in jest—that "building costs and unemployment may be so high in the future that we will have to go back to construction with handmade bricks."

New technologies, we now expect, may offer resources in the future that will improve life for the elderly no matter where they live. Advanced and computerized communications systems seem the most obvious and promising development, since they could reduce the feeling of isolation and permit better medical and other monitoring. Developments in health fields also make us inclined to predict longer, healthier lives, with decline and death following quickly at the end.

So we have to consider several possible scenarios. And we have to be willing to risk experiments. Short-term planning does us in, in the end. The persistence of homebuilding in which energy conservation is given short shrift points out the problem of building for immediate profit, not future utility. Unless we overcome the resistance to change on the part of builders and trade unions, and the addiction of architects to design for the sake of design (and not for the sake of people), by the turn of the century we could become a nation of trailers, nursing homes, and "efficiency" apartments, with a huge inventory of obsolete, unlivable houses.

Herein lie the economic and aesthetic incentives to constructing an attractive environment that does not exclude the elderly. It deserves attention. But the emotional gain may be even greater. If in our building and planning we grasp this opportunity to show loving care for the elderly and a desire to incorporate them into our lives, the guarantee of our own future may be the biggest payoff of all.

Bibliography

Brown, David. "Housing for the Elderly: Federal Subsidy Policy and Its Effect on Age-Group Isolation." *University of Detroit Journal of Urban Law* 57:2 (Winter 1980).

Folsom, James C. "Architectural Uses of Space and Texture to Prevent Disorientation in the Elderly." Paper presented at conference on Improving the Quality of Life of the Elderly through Environmental Design, New York Academy of Medicine/AIA New York City Chapter, October 1980.

Kasschau, Patricia L. *Aging and Social Policy*. New York: Praeger, 1978.

Pastalan, Leon A. "Housing for the Elderly." Paper presented at the White House Conference on Aging, Michigan, 1981.

28

Snowbirds: Seasonal Migrants to the Sunbelt

Deborah A. Sullivan and Sylvia A. Stevens

Since 1970 the graying of the United States population and the vigorous growth of some nonmetropolitan areas and the Sunbelt region have focused attention on the mobility of older people. The origins and destinations of their moves as well as their social, economic, and demographic characteristics have been identified (Barsby and Cox, 1975; Golant, 1977; Serow, 1978; Rudzitis, 1979; Longino, 1979, 1980; Biggar, 1979; Murphy, 1979; Chevan and Fisher, 1979; Wiseman, 1979; Fuguitt and Tordella, 1980; Flynn, 1980; Patrick, 1980). The impacts of the interstate streams of highly selected long-distance movers on origin and destination have been considered (Longino and Biggar, 1981; Biggar, 1980; Lee, 1980) as has the lack of selectivity of local moves (Goldscheider, 1966; Lenzer, 1965; Lawton et al., 1973; Wiseman and Virden, 1977; Golant, 1979). A typology of elderly migration based on a decision-making process has been developed (Wiseman and Roseman, 1979; Wiseman, 1980) and the relationship between relocation and the primary social theories of aging—disengagement, activity and continuity—has been explored (Wiseman and Roseman, 1979; Wiseman and Virden, 1977; Longino, 1980; Hochschild, 1973; Jacobs, 1974).

As fruitful as this interdisciplinary research has been, it does not provide a full description of the mobility of older people. This deficiency stems from the constraints of the two primary sources for migration data—the Census of Population and Housing and the Current Population Survey (Rives, 1980). Both contain data aggregated according to politically defined geographic areas. Both allow a maximum of one move per individual over the specified period, ranging from one to five years. Both assume that the concept of "usual place of residence" is relevant to all respondents and

434

both define a move as a change in "usual place of residence." The resulting classification is limited to local movers (intracounty movers), intrastate migrants (cross a county line), interstate migrants, and immigrants. There is not only a bias inherent in the diverse size of counties and states and a bias against successive moves but also a problem with the underlying concept of "usual place of residence," which does not allow for temporary migration. This bias is particularly critical when examining the mobility of retirees who have a relatively high incidence of seasonal migration.

Seasonal migration among the retired and semiretired is not a new phenomenon. In 1954 Hoyt reported that two-thirds of the residents of a trailer park in Florida owned housing elsewhere and only 12 percent lived in the park 10 or more months per year. The median annual residence was 6.7 months. Most of the economically diverse residents were married couples from rural areas or small towns in the eastern or north central states. They had been attracted to the area primarily because of the climate (Burgess et al., 1955) and resided in a trailer park because of the "sociability" of a retirement community.

Hoyt accurately foresaw the evolution of "small cottage" retirement communities with recreation facilities similar to the early trailer parks. However, these retirement communities have not replaced trailer parks, which have multiplied in Sunbelt states. There are now two types of parks—mobile home (relatively immobile units over 8 feet wide and 40 feet long) and travel trailer.

In this report we present evidence from a variety of sources on the importance of seasonal migration among retirees. Then we examine the characteristics and lifestyle of those temporary migrants who live in travel trailers and mobile homes.

Seasonal Migration of Retirees

The number of elderly involved in cyclical streams is difficult to document. Some indirect estimates can be culled from the 1970 Census (U.S. Bureau of the Census, 1973). At that time approximately 5 percent of all households with a head age 60 or over owned a second home; 3 percent owned a mobile home or travel trailer. In view of the increased affluence, greater leisure experience and rapid growth of retirement-oriented communities, it is likely that the percentages have risen over the last decade. However, not all having access to a second housing unit use it over a sufficiently long period to be considered a temporary migrant. On the other hand, not all seasonal migrants own a second home, mobile home, or travel trailer. Some stay in resorts, hotels, motels, apartments, and other rented quarters. Some stay with family or friends. Some camp on government land or vacant private property (Bond, 1976).

Arizona is one of several states that experiences a large inflow of older winter visitors. The 1977 National Travel Study estimated that 3.8 million trips were made to Arizona by people over 55 years of age (U.S. Bureau of the Census, 1979a). Although a large majority of these trips were of too short a duration to be considered a temporary migration, some snowbirds, as they are known in Arizona vernacular, stay as long as 9 or 10 months. It is difficult to draw a line between those vacationing and those who are temporary migrants. We feel that 3 months, although arbitrary, is appropriate. Most of those who visit less time stay in hotels and motels, while most of those who stay at least 3 months rent or own housing and return to the same, or similar, location each year.

There is no statistical information available on the total number of snowbirds arriving in Arizona each year. However, the largest receiving area which includes Phoenix and the surrounding communities received at least 73,000 snowbirds who stayed a minimum of three months in the winter of 1979-1980 (Western Savings and Loan Association, 1980). This estimate is based on a stratified probability sample of small geographic units with quotas and a count of travel trailer spaces. The interviews of 5,100 permanently fixed housing units took place from November 1979 to January 1980. It is difficult to contact part-time residents, and the time frame of the sampling would have missed those who came after the holidays, went home for the holidays, or who moved in after a space or housing unit was vacated. Morever, the figure does not include the visitors who stayed in travel trailers outside of established parks or in the 25,000 rooms in resorts, motels, and hotels which are generally filled during the winter months. Neither does it include those who stayed with family or friends. Local officials in the East Mesa-Apache Junction area, one of the more popular roosts with over 11,100 spaces in travel trailer parks and 19,600 mobile homes, estimate that their winter population increases 100,000 to 125,000.

One of the rare references to the seasonal migration of retirees since the early 1950s suggests that snowbirding is an intermediate stage of migration which allows retirees to experiment with a new location (Wiseman, 1980: 148). While this may be true for some, this is not true for those who maintain two or more residences on a permanent basis. In one of Arizona's better-known retirement communities, Sun City, an estimated 12 percent of the 29,000 households are occupied on a part-time basis, 50 percent from three to six months, and an additional 42 percent for more than six months (Western Savings and Loan Association, 1980). Virtually all the males in these households are over 55 years of age (99 percent) and 88 percent are currently retired. An even larger number of part-time households can be found outside of retirement communities. In one affluent area, Scottsdale, an estimated 8 percent of the 45,000 households are occupied by part-time residents. Three-quarters of these households are only occupied three to six months. Three-quarters of their male occupants are over 55, and 62 percent already are retired or not employed. Some of the part-time households in these two communities may eventually become permanently occupied households, but it is significant to note that even in a mixed community like Scottsdale, over half the males in the part-time households are already over 65 and retired. This suggests that the maintenance of two housing units is a permanent aspect of their affluent lifestyle.

Snowbirding is not confined to the affluent who can afford to maintain two separate, permanently fixed housing units. The middle-class version relies on mobile homes and travel trailers. For the participants, it is an alternative lifestyle.

Data and Method

This project combined participant observation with a survey methodology. One of the authors is employed by a hospital in the East Mesa-Apache Junction area as a community organization worker. She developed a rapport with indigenous leaders in several parks and attended coffee klatches, potluck suppers and other activities.

There is considerable variety in the size and facilities offered by individual parks. Some of the smaller parks have limited recreational facilities, while others have large recreational complexes with saunas, swimming pools, jacuzzi pools, billiard rooms, craft rooms, dance and social halls, and golf courses. The facilities and activities in most mobile home parks, which usually have a small section of travel trailer spaces, are run by resident recreation committees. Parks exclusively for travel trailers, in contrast, hire recreation directors to coordinate and plan most activities.

In November 1980, questionnaires were distributed to all occupied spaces in one of the newer, larger travel trailer parks using centralized message boxes. One of the authors had previously announced the research project at several park functions. Although most of the information requested applied to the household, we requested that only women fill out the questionnaire in order to control for sexual differences in the answers to some personal questions such as educational levels and medical history. Of the 229 questionnaires distributed, 70 percent were completed and returned within three weeks.

Mobile home parks do not have a centralized message system, and the management of several that we contacted were reluctant to allow us to distribute questionnaires at each mobile home. Two women active in the self-government of an older, smaller park with recreation facilities similar to the mobile home park suggested that we ask for participants at a mid-March potluck supper which almost all residents attend. They also made questionnaires available to residents not attending. Questionnaires were given to both sexes since the mobile home park, unlike the travel trailer park, contained some single men as well as single women. Of all residents, 65 percent in the park on the day of the initial request for participants returned a questionnaire. Unless otherwise noted, only the responses of the women are included in this report to insure comparability with the travel trailer park data.

The questionnaire consisted of 38 structured and open-ended questions. Topics included the social, economic, and demographic characteristics of respondents, their health status, residency status, reasons for coming to Arizona in general and their park in particular, and length of stay. The questionnaire also asked about participation in activities and patterns of socializing.

Findings

Residents

Only 11 percent of the travel trailer households and 15 percent of the mobile home households claim Arizona as their primary residence. Most of the older residents in the travel trailer park come from Canada (12 percent), the north Pacific (21 percent) and north central states (32 percent). The mobile home residents come from Canada (20 percent) and the western and central Canadian border states (41 percent). The majority have spent most of their lives in rural areas or small towns (Table 28.1).

Virtually all are white and retired (99 percent of the travel trailer households and 91 percent of the mobile home households). Most are married (Table 28.1). Single men are extremely rare in travel trailer parks and almost as rare in mobile home parks catering to winter visitors (only 2 of the 57 male respondents in our mobile home survey were single). As can be seen in Table 28.1, the high incidence of marriage among the female respondents in both types of parks contrasts sharply with that of women 55 and over in the United States.

Compared to the age profile of all women 55 and over, the respondents in the travel trailer park tended to be younger. There is a noticeable dearth of women over 70 among the residents. The mobile home respondents, on the other hand, tended to have an older profile with a dearth of women in their late 50s. The age differences are in part attributable to the length of time the parks have been open; the travel trailer park opened in 1977 while the

TABLE 28.1
A Comparison of the Female Residents of Travel Trailers and Mobile Homes with Females in the United States

	Travel Trailer	Mobile Home	United States
	%	%	%
Size of Place Where Most of Life Spent (N)	(158)	(65)	—
Rural	22.9	33.8	—
Small Town 2,5000-15,000	31.8	27.7	—
City 15,000-50,000	21.6	15.4	—
Metropolitan Area 50,000+	23.5	23.1	—
Marital Status (N)	(159)	(65)	—[1]
Never Married	.6	.0	5.6
Married	91.2	78.5	52.8
Widowed	8.2	21.5	37.0
Divorced/Separated	0	0	4.6
Age (N)	(158)	(65)	—[2]
Under 56	16.3	4.6	4.7
56-60	19.5	7.7	22.6
61-65	37.7	20.0	19.5
66-70	19.5	29.2	18.3
71-75	3.8	18.5	13.8
76+	3.1	20.0	21.1
Children Ever Born (N)	(154)	(62)	—
Average number	2.8	2.4	—
Education (N)	(158)	(65)	—[3]
Grammar school or less	5.7	3.1	44.1
Some high school	16.4	18.5	16.7
High school graduate	46.8	33.8	23.4
Some college	24.2	15.4	8.8
College graduate	1.9	16.9	7.0
Post graduate	5.0	12.3	—
Work Experience Outside Home (N)	(159)	(64)	—
None	9.4	15.6	—
Usually part-time	11.9	12.5	—
Mixed	26.4	24.4	—
Usually full-time	52.2	48.4	—

TABLE 28.1 (Continued)

	Travel Trailer	Mobile Home	United States
	%	%	%
Household Income before			
Retirement (N)	(137)	(47)	—
Less than 5,000	0	0	—
5,000-8,000	20.3	30.0	—
8,000-15,000	23.9	19.1	—
15,000-25,000	37.0	35.0	—
25,000+	18.1	14.9	—
Current Household Income (N)	(135)	(48)	—[1]
Less than 5,000	9.6	12.5	12.3
5,000-8,000	20.7	25.0	46.9
8,000-15,000	45.9	22.9	
15,000-25,000	20.0	29.2	22.7
25,000+	3.7	10.4	18.1

Source: U.S. Bureau of the Census, Social and Economic Chracteristics of the Older Population, 1978. Current Population Reports: Series P-23, No. 85, 1979. Marital Status and Living Arrangements: March, 1978. Current Population Reports: Series P-20, No. 338, 1979. Estimates of the Population of the United States, by Age, Race, and Sex: 1976 to 1979. Current Population Reports: Series P-25, No. 870, 1980. U.S. Government Printing Office, Washington, D.C.
1. Noninstitutional women 55 and over.
2. Women 55 and over.
3. Women 65 and over.

mobile home park opened in 1970. Although our observations indicate that travel trailer park residents tend to be younger, older travel trailer parks do have an older age profile than the one included in this study.

The pronounced age difference between the two groups of snowbirds has consequences for a number of other characteristics including children ever born, education, work experience, and health status. The travel trailer respondents had more children on average than the mobile home respondents, who were more likely to have had their childbearing disrupted by the Depression and World War II. Neither group differs greatly from all women of a comparable age range. Women 65 to 74 in 1978 had an average of 2.4 children (U.S. Bureau of the Census, 1979b) while those 50 to 59 had 2.9 children (U.S. Bureau of the Census, 1979c).

Given the age differences, one would expect to find a higher level of education among travel trailer respondents. Instead, a much higher proportion of mobile home respondents reported graduating from college and postgraduate work (Table 28.1). The high level of education among the mobile home respondents is even more remarkable when compared to that for all women over 65 years of age. The high level of educational attainment among mobile home respondents is associated with an equally high rate of work experience outside the home. The work experience of the generally younger travel trailer respondents is only slightly higher.

Household income before retirement spans a broad spectrum in both populations (Table 28.1). This contrasts sharply with Johnson's (1971) report of a homogeneous working class structure in an adult mobile home park occupied yearround in California. Given the age difference and the high level of inflation in the last 20 years, it would appear that the majority of the mobile home residents had a higher real income before retirement. Current household income also varies considerably, with the mobile home respondents more concentrated at both ends of the spectrum than the travel trailer respondents (Table 28.1). Both groups have a lower income profile than that of all families including women 55 and over in 1977. The income of the latter group is not directly comparable, since some of the women included are not living in a retired household and women living alone are excluded.

The mobile home and travel trailer respondents have as few or fewer health complaints than noninstitutionalized women 45 and over in the United States even though both groups have an older age profile (Table 28.2). The health status of the mobile home respondents, the majority of whom are 65 or over, is particularly remarkable when compared to all women in this age range.

Lifestyle

For most snowbirds, length of stay in Arizona is partly dependent on winter weather in the north. The winter of 1980-1981 was relatively mild; parks filled later and began to empty earlier than usual. Nevertheless, most of the snowbirds in both the travel trailer park and mobile home park planned to stay three to six months (75 percent and 63 percent respectively). A slightly higher proportion of the mobile home respondents intended to stay more than six months (26 percent versus 18 percent). The flexibility of plans in this leisure lifestyle was further evident in the 4 percent of the travel trailer respondents and 9 percent of mobile home respondents who said that they were unsure how long they would stay.

Some of the snowbirds spend their summer months traveling in cooler areas, visiting family, friends, checking property and investments, and sightseeing. Of the mobile home respondents, 30 percent also owned a travel trailer for this purpose. Another 35 percent previously had owned one but are no longer willing or able to travel extensively. Older travel trailer park residents show a similar pattern. Residents are more likely to

TABLE 28.2
A Comparison of the Health Status of the Female Residents of a Travel Trailer and a Mobile Home Park on Selected Items with Civilian Noninstitutional Females in the United States

	Travel Trailer %	Mobile Home %	Civilian Noninstitutionalized		
			45 + %	45-64 %	65 + %
Heart Disease	6	5	18	13	27
Cancer	1	9	—	—	—
Diabetes	2	8	7	6	8
Respiratory Problems	8	3	13	14	11
Hearing Problems	8	18	18	12	28
Arthritis	33	32	32	25	44
Hypertensive Disease	—	26	27	21	38

Source: U.S. Department of Health and Human Services, Current Estimates from the National Health Interview Survey: U.S., 1979. Series 10, No. 136, 1981. Acute Conditions Incidence and Associated Disability, U.S., July 1977-June 1978. Series 10, No. 132, 1979. Unpublished data from the National Health Interview Surveys.

own a "park model" trailer, which they leave in the park, and use a smaller trailer for traveling.

Climate was the dominant reason for coming to the Sunbelt (Table 28.3). Other reasons mentioned included health and the opportunity to visit friends and family in the area.

Most of the people in the mobile home park moved in between 1970 and 1973, when the park first opened, and 45 percent of the travel trailer respondents had stayed in their park previously. Informal discussions indicated that most of the travel trailer respondents who had not previously stayed in this park had stayed in the area. The travel trailer respondents

TABLE 28.3
Reasons Given by Respondents for Sojourn in Arizona

	Travel Trailer %	Mobile Home %
Climate	89.9	86.2
Visit friends	28.3	36.9
Own health	22.0	35.4
Husband's health[1]	26.2	27.4
Traveling through area	8.2	4.6

1. Includes only those with a spouse.

were attracted to their current park because of its remote location (73 percent mentioned this feature), activities (55 percent), good management (53 percent), and inhabitants (39 percent). The mobile home park, which was in a remote location when it first opened, has since been surrounded by growth. Respondents from this park listed activities (79 percent), management (55 percent), and inhabitants (54 percent) as reasons for choosing the park.

There is instant comradeship among snowbirds in new parks. Residents tend to be outside much of the time, particularly in the travel trailer parks. This, along with the many activities, allows them to become acquainted easily. They quickly regard each other as close friends or "family," and the frequency of socializing is extremely high (Table 28.4). Many of the parks erect "Welcome Home" signs in the fall. There is a relaxed atmosphere which fosters numerous impromptu parties and potluck dinners. A commonly expressed attitude is that they have worked all their lives and now it is time to play. There also is a feeling of entitlement to services. In answer to an open question about additional comments, many of the respondents said that the local area should provide them more medical facilities and public transportation.

None of the travel trailer respondents and only 14 percent of the mobile home respondents were interested in volunteer work in the community. Some residents in mobile home parks do volunteer to take responsibility for self-government and specific activities in the park. They raise funds through pancake breakfasts and the like for desired facilities and equipment. This even includes providing a turkey or ham for holiday potlucks. In contrast, travel trailer residents expect the management to provide all the activities. When residents expect more services than the management is willing to supply or when there are disputes between different cliques over facilities for activities, the conflicts are resolved by either the residents or a manager suggesting that the residents "have wheels."

To live in one of these parks it is almost a necessity to be an active, outgoing, sociable person. There is an "adult camp" flavor to the lifestyle. The level of participation in group activities is extremely high (Table 28.4). A common cliché heard in the parks is that "I would rather drop dead rock hounding or playing shuffleboard than sitting in a rocking chair."

Both parks in this study contain the same recreational facilities. However, the older mobile home respondents had a higher level of participation in more activities than did the travel trailer respondents. The most popular activities for both groups of women were potluck dinners, swimming, church, crafts, card games, bicycle riding, bingo, golf, and dancing. Other activities attracting a smaller following included silversmithing, billiards, lapidary, rock hounding, swap meets, hiking, adult

TABLE 28.4
Social Interaction in Travel Trailers and Mobile Home Parks

	Travel Trailers %	Mobile Home %
Close friends in local area (N)	(156)	(64)
Less than 4	24.3	1.6
4-8	16.0	9.4
8-12	15.3	20.3
12 +	44.2	68.8
Frequency of seeing friends (N)	(144)	(63)
Daily	51.4	65.1
2-4 times per week	29.9	23.8
Weekly	9.7	7.9
3 times per month	9.0	3.2
Number of activities pursued (N)	(159)	(65)
Less than 4	13.8	0
4-5	27.0	7.7
6-7	22.0	27.7
8-9	17.0	18.4
10	6.9	16.4
More than 10	13.2	29.3
Frequency of participating in activities (N)	(153)	(64)
Daily	33.5	56.2
Weekly	58.5	37.5
3 times per month	1.3	1.5
Monthly	0	3.1
Occasionally	6.5	1.5
Visiting other places in Arizona (N)	(157)	(64)
Frequently	21.0	17.2
Sometimes	60.5	68.8
Rarely	13.4	12.5
Never	5.1	1.5
Participation in other activities in Mesa (N)	(154)	(62)
Frequently	5.2	11.3
Sometimes	16.2	29.0
Rarely	16.2	17.7
Never	62.3	41.9
Participation in other activities in Phoenix (N)	(154)	(63)
Frequently	0	8.0
Sometimes	7.1	9.7
Rarely	11.7	33.9
Never	81.2	48.4

education courses, shuffleboard, and rodeos. Men in the mobile home park were likely to participate in the same activities, excluding sewing and other arts and crafts, although at a slightly lower frequency. Men were also more likely to play billiards.

Most activities are available in the parks, although the residents go out for restaurants, church, swap meets, picnics, hiking, rock hounding, square dancing meets, golf, rodeos and "tag-a-long" tours. A fairly high proportion toured in the state during their stay (Table 28.4). Many parks sponsor trips to such places as Las Vegas or Acapulco. The participation in other activities in the local area was low (Table 28.4). The attendance at activities in Phoenix, which is only about 30 miles to the west, was extremely low.

There is little evidence that the snowbird lifestyle is an intermediate step toward permanent migration for most residents of mobile home or travel trailer parks. Only 8 of the 65 mobile home park respondents were considering becoming a resident of Arizona. Six of these were temporary residents of the small travel trailer section of the park. Only one was considering buying a house. These findings must be qualified since most of the residents have been coming to the mobile home park for at least seven years. The turnover in a newer park might be higher.

A higher proportion (25 percent) of the travel trailer respondents were considering becoming a resident of Arizona, yet few of these were considering moving to a permanently fixed housing unit. Three-quarters of these households were considering either just staying in their travel trailer or buying a "park model" trailer with "tip-outs."

For most of the travel trailer and mobile home residents, traveling is an important part of their lifestyle. Many of the older residents have been coming to the Southwest for over 25 years. One respondent said that she and her husband have been coming to the Phoenix area since 1946. Of the travel trailer respondents, 72 percent owned a travel trailer for four or more years; 65 percent of the mobile home respondents either own a travel trailer currently or have owned one. The majority of both groups have a long history of camping experience; 69 percent of the travel trailer respondents and 78 percent of the mobile home respondents went camping with their children when they were young.

Discussion

There are a number of limitations in this study. Only two types of snowbirds are considered—those residing in mobile homes and those living in travel trailers. We believe these two groups have a different lifestyle than other types of snowbirds. Data were gathered at only one of each type of park. Thus, the difference that age of park, size of park, facilities of park, or possible socioeconomic level of park might make cannot be fully explored. The two parks in this study had almost identical facilities, and the space rental fees were at the lower end of the middle range. The data were collected toward the beginning and end of the winter visitor season. This may result in an upward bias in the length of stay information, although it is similar to that reported by Hoyt in the 1950s. It also may mean that the populations contained fewer individuals experimenting with the lifestyle than would be found in January, the peak month for winter visitors. The respondents, from the travel trailer park and those in the mobile home park who volunteered to participate in the study may be healthier, better educated, and more active. Because residents were moving in and out during the data collection periods, it was impossible to follow up nonrespondents.

In contrast to Jacob's (1974) finding that the "active way of life," promoted by some retirement communities, is limited to the 10 percent visible minority, we find persuasive evidence of activity in our populations. Some of the activities such as card games and bingo are passive in terms of physical exertion; however, their popularity stems from the opportunities they provide for socializing, the most highly valued activity in this lifestyle.

The two groups we studied constitute a unique subculture among older individuals. They were very similar to the residents of the initial trailer parks described by Hoyt (1954). Both were heterogeneous in terms of age, health, education, and income and homogenous in terms of area of origin, race, and marital status. The participants in this alternative lifestyle are drawn together by their similar interests in traveling, socializing, and desire to live an active lifestyle. They are the archetype of the activity model of aging. They are disengaged only in their retirement status and choice of an age-segregated community.

Some of the differences between our two retirement communities and those described by Jacobs (1974) and Johnson (1971) may be due to the seasonal nature of the communities and the fact that most of the residents have alternative housing elsewhere. Each year participants have the opportunity to decide not to continue the snowbird lifestyle. As a result, those who return to the parks are committed to the active lifestyle. The smaller size of these communities compared to the one examined by Jacobs may also be an important factor in promoting comradeship and involvement.

The lifestyle of mobile home and travel trailer park residents is similar in many ways. However, there are some important differences. Mobile homes are rarely moved because of prohibitive costs, and residents tend to stay for a longer time. They also tend to be older and have more health problems. We also have observed a different response to incapacitating illnesses between the two groups. In travel trailer parks there is an immediate plan to go back home, while in mobile home parks there is considerable debate about what to do. Some of the residents have local doctors and some bring medical records with them. But for others, a health crisis precipitates another crisis of where to go for care. It is not easy, and sometimes not possible, to reenter a family structure in a dependent position, and family and friends back home have often died or moved away. Referring to this one person said that her neighbor had "jumped the wall for security, but only found loneliness."

There is also a belief among travel trailer park residents that mobile home residents are staid and condescending toward them. There may be some class conflict underlying this belief, since mobile home residents tend to be more highly educated and have a higher income profile. However, this explanation is insufficient, since there is a large degree of income heterogeneity in both communities. There may be some ageism in the belief, since mobile home residents tend to be older. Also, the greater commitment that mobile home residents have made to the area may be a factor.

It is our experience that mobile home owners do look askance at the more transient lifestyle of travel trailer residents. They value the security of knowing who their neighbors will be each year as well as the greater privacy a mobile home offers. Despite the lower level of activity reported by travel trailer respondents, mobile home residents regard the activity and socializing of travel trailer residents as frantic and not selective. Mobile home residents also take pride in the better quality of their recreational buildings and facilities.

There is a distinct trend in the area for the newer mobile home parks to be far larger (1,200 spaces compared to the 100 spaces in the park in this study) and have more elaborate recreational facilities. The starting price for mobile homes in most of these almost self-contained communities is currently about $45,000. This puts them beyond the reach of many middle-class retirees as second homes. The escalation of mobile home prices had played a significant role in creating adult travel trailer parks such as the one in this study. The increase in gasoline prices is now threatening this alternative. Residents of the travel trailer parks are seeking ways to adapt their lifestyle. There is much less experimentation with different areas, and increasingly residents are leaving their travel trailers in the parks. As long as there are economically independent, retired workers in good health who can maintain contact with family and friends without residential proximity, the demand for recreation-oriented retirement communities in favorable climates will continue. To assess the full impact of these communities on the redistribution of older adults, seasonal as well as permanent migration needs to be considered.

References

Barsby, S.L., and D.R. Cox. 1975. *Interstate Migration of the Elderly*. Toronto: Heath-Lexington.

Bond, T. 1976. "Variables Associated with the Winter Camping Location of Elderly Recreational Vehicle Owners in South Western Arizona," *Journal of Gerontology* 31:346-51.

Burgess, E. W., G.C. Hoyt, and C.R. Manley. 1955. "The Construction of Scales for the Measurement of Migration After Retirement," *Sociometry* 18:616-23.

Biggar, J.C. 1979. "Who Moved among the Elderly, 1965-1970: A Comparison of Types of Older Movers." *Research on Aging* 2:73-91.

_____. 1980. "Reassessing Elderly Sunbelt Migration." *Research on Aging* 2:177-90.

Chevan, A.,and L.R. Fisher. 1979. "Retirement and Interstate Migration." *Social Forces* 57: 1365-80.

Flynn,C.B. 1980."General versus Aged Interstate Migration, 1975-1980." *Research on Aging* 2:165-76.

Fuguitt, G.V., and S.J. Tordella. 1980. "Elderly Net Migration." *Research on Aging* 2:191-204.

Golant, S.M. 1977. "Spatial Context of Residential Moves by Elderly Persons." *Journal of Aging and Human Development* 8:279-89.

Goldsheider, C. 1966. Differential Residential Mobility of the Older Population." *Journal of Gerontology* 21:103-8.

Hochschild, A. 1973. *The Unexpected Community*. Englewood Cliffs, N.J.: Prentice-Hall.

Hoyt, G.C. 1954. "The Life of the Retired in a Trailer Park." *American Journal of Sociology* 19:361-70.

Jacobs, J. 1974. *Fun City: An Ethnographic Study of a Retirement Community*. New York: Holt, Rinchart, & Winston.

Johnson, S. 1971. *Idle Haven: Community Building among the Working-Class Retired*. Berkeley: University of California Press.

Lawton, M.P., M.H.Kleban, and D.A. Carlson. 1973. "The Inner City Resident: To Move or Not to Move." *Gerontologist* 13:443-48.

Lee, A.S. 1980. "Aged Migration: Impact on Service Delivery." *Research on Aging* 2:243-53.

Lenzer, A. 1965. "Mobility Patterns among the Aged." *Gerontologist* 5:12-15.

Longino, C.F. 1979. "Going Home: Aged Return Migration in the United States, 1965-70." *Journal of Gerontology* 34:736-45.

_____. 1980 "Residential Relocation of Older People." *Research on Aging* 2:205-16.

Longino, C.F. and J.C. Biggar. 1981. "The Impact of Retirement Migration on the South." *Gerontologist* 21:283-90.

Murphy, P.A. 1979. "Migration of the Elderly: A Review." *Town Planning Review:* 50:84-93.

Patrick, C.H. 1980. "Health and Migration of the Elderly." *Research on Aging* 2:233-41.

Rives, N.W. 1980. "Researching the Migration of the Elderly." *Research on Aging* 2:155-63.

Rudzitis, G. 1979. "Determinants of the Central City Migration Patterns of Older Persons." In S. Golant (ed.), *Location and Environment of Elderly Population*. New York: Wiley.

Serow, W.J. 1978. "Return Migration of the Elderly in the USA: 1955-1960 and 1965-1970." *Journal of Gerontology* 33:288-95.

Western Savings and Loan Association. 1980. *Foresight Eighty.* Phoenix: Western Savings and Loan Association.

Wiseman, R.F. 1979. "Regional Patterns of Elderly Concentration and Migration." In S.Golant (ed.), *Location and Environment of Elderly Population.* New York: Wiley.

_____. 1980. "Why Older People Move: Theoretical Issues." *Research on Aging* 2:141-54.

Wiseman,R.F., and C.C. Roseman. 1979. "A Typology of Elderly Migration Based on the Decision-Making Process." *Economic Geography* 55: 324-37.

Wiseman,R.F., and M.Virden. 1977. "Spatial and Social Dimensions of Intraurban Early Migration." *Economic Geography* 53:1-13.

U.S. Bureau of the Census. 1973. "Census of Housing: 1970." Subject Reports. HC(7)-2 Housing of Senior Citizens. Washington, D.C.: Government Printing Office.

_____. 1979a. "National Travel Survey: Travel During 1977." 1977 Census of Transportation. Washington, D.C.: Government Printing Office.

_____. 1979b. "Social and Economic Characteristics of the Older Population, 1978." Current Population Reports, series P-23, no. 85. Washington, D.C.: Government Printing Office.

_____. 1979c. "Fertility of American Women: June 1978." Current Population Reports, series P-20, no. 341. Washington, D.C.: Government Printing Office.

_____. 1979d. "Martial Status and Living Arrangements, March 1978." Current Population Reports, series P-20, no. 338. Washington, D.C.: Government Printing Office.

_____. 1980. "Estimates of the Population of the United States, by Age, Race, and Sex, 1976 to 1979." Current Population Reports, series P-25, no. 870. Washington, D.C.: Government Printing Office.

29

Ducktown: Holding On but Losing

Marea Teski, Robert Helsabeck,
Franklin Smith, and Charles Yeager

In the heart of Atlantic City, both geographically and socially, lies a concentration of people of Italian ancestry. Their neighborhood, roughly a six square block area, is nicknamed "Ducktown" (so named to refer to the ducks which used to gather in the Bay, at the neighborhood's edge). Ducktown's Italian character is rooted in at least four generations with many of the current residents mentioning grandparents who also lived in the neighborhood.

The neighborhood is a combination of private homes and businesses. Two main streets within a block of Atlantic City's main street provide the setting for the businesses and the connecting side streets are mainly residential. Many of the businesses also have residences above or behind the business itself.

The businesses are local in clientele. A famous "sub" shop seems to be the closest thing to a neighborhood "watering hole," with the local fishmarket a close second. Barber shops, a shoe repair store, a small upholstery shop, small restaurants, a beauty parlor and a drugstore are examples of the scale of businesses in this neighborhood.

It is clear to an outsider that a neighborhood exists here and that it's Italian.

Physical, Economic, and Social Changes in Ducktown

Since the Casino development has occurred a number of changes involving the use of space have occurred. Suddenly space has become quite valuable for uses which directly or indirectly serve the Casinos. The need for parking space for the Casinos, located within walking distance, and living space for Casino workers is extreme.

450

The results of the parking crunch are several. First, a parking lot may be a better business investment than almost any alternative investment. Hence parking lots are frequently replacing buildings which have stood for fifty or more years. Second, there is a scramble for Casino parking (customers and employees absorb residential parking spaces that were formerly available for local residents). This loss of one's "own" territory in front of one's residence is a point of considerable irritation among neighborhood residents.

The pressure for housing people is as strong as that of housing cars. Consequently, the rental costs are rising for persons who were accustomed to very stable rents. The elderly, on fixed incomes, are particularly hurt by this by-product of the increased value of the neighborhood space.

From the perspective of the long-time residents, these two space utilization changes are quite disturbing. A number of persons mentioned the loss of homes and business to parking lots. They see these empty lots as "holes" in a formerly complete neighborhood structure. One resident said, "It is like someone had scooped-out handfuls from a beautiful cake. It's been violated!" A randomness and chaos in the loss of structures is keenly felt.

In some cases, buildings have been boarded up for demolition but have not yet been torn down. A sense of uncertainty exists about the future use of that sort of space. As one barber put it, "If they build a high-rise apartment, my business will improve. If they lay a parking lot, I'll lose business because people used to live in that building."

The neighborhood is in a land use "trough." A number of structures are coming down but a clear picture of future uses has not yet emerged. What is emerging is that the new renters of space are not the traditional Italians, but rather are Casino "middle" to "lower level" employees. These new residents are Black, Hispanic, Oriental and other non-Italians. This transition is another disturbance in the "appearance of things" for the neighborhood.

Another major change in the neighborhood is the availability of resources needed by the residential community. It is obvious that the resources needed by Casino visitors and workers are sometimes not the resources needed by traditional residents. A basic resource for a stable neighborhood is low cost housing for elderly residents. A basic resource for a thriving, growing industry is proximate housing for younger persons (persons who are beginning a lower-level job in the Casinos or who are working to construct a Casino building). Both groups' needs cannot be satisfied fully given limited, highly demanded space.

Another resource needed to "run a neighborhood" is low cost labor—people to work in the businesses, schools, hospitals, and in local government. The Casino industry, too, needs labor and will pay what it must to acquire the needed work force. The consequence to the neighborhood enterprises is a labor shortage. A nursing home, near Ducktown, had to move from the city because it was becoming so difficult to keep its employees (as well as the fact that it could profitably build a new facility elsewhere with the profit on the land). This is a resource no longer available in the same way to local residents.

Finally, a resource which has improved for residents of Ducktown is the other side of the labor situation—the presence of jobs. Clearly, at this point, the interests of local residents, particularly those in their working years, converge with those of the Casinos. A significant number of residents have found jobs in the Casinos and are happy about these new opportunities, although few of these jobs go to the elderly residents. At the same time, however, certain indirect benefits could occur for the elderly if younger members of their extended family make extra money at the Casinos. In fact, there is little evidence from the elderly themselves that this sort of indirect benefit is occurring. It seems likely, instead, that the standard of living of the middle aged employed persons is improving at the expense of the elderly residents.

In addition to space and resource changes in the neighborhood, important changes in the social organization of the neighborhood are also occurring. Several factors are working in combination to dramatically alter the social networks. The already mentioned influx of "outsiders" to the neighborhood gives the older residents an increasing sense of alienation from their neighbors. It's not always that they feel hostile towards their new neighbors (although sometimes they do), it's more that they simply don't feel the automatic bond that stems from ethnic commonality. In addition, fewer and fewer elderly persons make up the neighborhood. As the space between elderly persons becomes greater and is filled in with non-elderly, any given elderly person is likely to feel more and more isolated and vulnerable.

Another social network which affects a neighborhood's ability to deal effectively with all sorts of problems, is access to the larger, municipal political structure. For Ducktown residents, this large political network is less and less responsive to their needs. As the Casino industry has become larger and more powerful, the competition for political considerations vis à vis the neighborhood needs become intense. Although, as Atlantic City neighborhoods go, Ducktown has been politically strong, its influence currently seems to be waning. Certainly, the portion of the neighborhood which is elderly is weaker still.

Ducktown as Political Actor

As a part of Atlantic City's Master Plan for the orderly development of the city, a large new convention center, called the Megastructure, was proposed. Residents of Ducktown, both as individual landowners and as members of the particular neighborhood most directly affected by the proposed building site, became politically involved in the defeat of the proposed project. The neighborhood united in their objection to the Megastructure and showed their political effectiveness in defeating the plan. The aftermath of the Megastructure fight and other individual fights over property rights was one of heightened emotion and open hostility.

The following transcript from a New Jersey Public Television broadcast in 1980 entitled "Atlantic City: Winners and Losers" is indicative of the sentiments of neighborhood residents toward the city government.

> Mayor, Atlantic City: We're booking a lot of conventions for the future—1982, 1983. Most of the big conventions want to come back to Atlantic City, because it's a new attraction. But we'll have to have more facilities for them. We certainly have to have more first class rooms, and improve convention facilities. But if we are able to accomplish this, certainly we'll get a lot more convention business.
>
> N.J. State Senator: But we don't want to build a gambling town. We want to build a resort and convention city that has gambling. And that difference is very substantial, although a subtle kind of distinction.
>
> Reporter: Burt S. is a businessman, with years of experience booking large conventions into Atlantic City.
>
> Burt S.: Atlantic City, at this point, has plans for what they call a megastructure, that is, a four-block convention hall, which is in excess of 700,000 square foot, in addition to the existing convention facilities of 500,000 square foot.
>
> We think that the amount of area that they are using is far in excess of what is required in this convention city, a city of 40,000 people; we cannot get every convention in the country.
>
> If you get a large convention in town, the convention requires—let's say, if you get 15,000 people, you're talking in terms of 10 to 15,000 rooms, right there. And that's just a—not a great, big convention; that's more of a medium size convention. So our problem is not so much the convention space that is required, as it is rooms.
>
> Reporter: Casino corporations must, by state law, build 500-room hotels in order to qualify for their gambling licenses. This was intended to rebuild the convention business, along with the birth of the gambling casinos.
>
> But most of the casinos are building only the legal minimum of 500-room hotels. Thus, Atlantic City may still fall far short of the number of hotel rooms it needs to compete as a full convention resort, and not just a gambling town.
>
> Burt S.: Now, the casinos are self-contained, in that they have like 12 or 14 restaurants. They have all the facilities that are necessary for people to shop. They have clothing stores—men's clothing, women's clothing.

Giftware, souvenir shops, and all of the other things associated with it. The people come into these places, and they're there like every other major hotel in the country; they have become basically resorts—self-contained resorts.

Their point is really not to further the city's business district; it's to be in competition with the city's business district.

Willie G.: A small business in—in Atlantic City—what'll happen—they are being squeezed out. And not only minority business—people—also other business, small business. They just can't handle it, because the rents are going up. People are selling—landlords are selling their building rights out from under them—too big money and big investment. And they're tearing them down, a lot of them, in Atlantic City. That's all from down Atlantic Avenue, the boardwalk, Arctic Avenue. The small businessman, he's going to have a lot of problems.

Reporter: Willie made those remarks in 1978. By 1980, he was proved to be a prophet, as he was forced to close his shop. Dozens of other businesses have also closed in Atlantic City. Of the 300 shops along the boardwalk before casinos, only a handful remain today.

In stark contrast to the casino wealth, the traditional business community is failing. Atlantic City's Chamber of Commerce is nearly bankrupt from the loss of members.

Director, Chamber of Commerce: In the short term transition of Atlantic City, there has been—basically, has hurt a lot of small businesspeople. It's an adjustment of the marketplace, of the type of economy, of the type of clientele who are coming here that has caused that, to a great extent. Our membership has dropped by 35 percent, evidencing and reflecting the fact that many small businesses who had been along the boardwalk either have lost their leases or have sold their property to casino developers.

As those new properties—new properties are built, we'll replace that. If the vote were to be taken over again, today; I think you'd see a—a significant growth in those opposed to casino gambling because it did not meet their expectations.

Reporter: For 78-year-old Louie S., expectations have not been met. One promise of gambling was to provide enough jobs to reduce crime. Yet, violent assaults in Atlantic City are up nearly 40 percent. Louis was severely beaten in front of his home, one morning—not robbed, just beaten.

Louie S., Atlantic City Resident: The month of November, I told you that I went out to buy a newspaper. Two guys grabbed me and beat the hell out of me. See? And with no reason. They didn't look for no money, nor nothing. The only thing I know—because we don't want to sell. We resent to sell them any property.

So who put them up? Somebody must have put them, because they're not going to come—because I never done nothing. I owe nobody a nickel. I never borrow anything. If I had something to spend, to spend myself, all right; but borrowing money from anybody, never did.

And this is home, I told you that. This is . . .

Olga S.: This is our home, and we don't want to move.

Louie S., Resident: We don't want to move. But, like we said before, the— when the city wants you out, it's going to get you out anyhow. So, who are you going to fight with? Who is going to fight for you?

Reporter: Louie and his wife, Olga, live in the area the city had planned to use for the new convention hall.

But the history of the city of Atlantic City as a developer has caused suspicion and anger among the residents.

Burt S., Businessman: We have determined that if they grab these four blocks of land, that they will do nothing with it, really, for maybe two or three years. And, at that point of time, the property has increased so much in value, then they can go out and borrow big money, as far as it's concerned.

Look what happened in Atlantic City to the Urban Renewal area, uptown. They took over 10 city blocks that were supposed to be developed for housing and public use. What ended up with the property? It ended up being sold to Resorts International Hotel. It's going to be a casino.

What happened to the present convention hall Urban Renewal section? That was taken over, and the front section of the boardwalk was eventually turned over to Playboy as a casino hotel.

Now, what's to stop the city from doing the same thing in this four-block area that it's done in every other area that it's grabbed up to this point?

It's a proven fact that this is the way this city works.

Louie S: And they—they want to push all the poor people that were here 60 years, now—60 years in the neighborhood, being for 60 years—they want to push us out. Don't want no poor people. Like Reese—what's his name—Reese; Reese said that, No more poor people in Atlantic City; push them all out.

Reese P., Entrepreneur: And you wouldn't expect the people who operate Disneyland to live in Disneyland. The land is too scarce. A casino hotel takes eight to ten acres, and we simply don't have the acreage.

Atlantic City Mayor: And some of the older people have made sacrifices, knowing that the young people were going to do better, and that's our future.

Barry I., Atlantic City Resident: My name's Barry I. I'm a lifetime resident of Atlantic City. My father was a lifetime resident of Atlantic City and my grandfather lived here most of his life. We've been here as long as that boardwalk's been out there. And he says, Now the Housing Authority tells me that they're taking my land from me, that I paid 70,000 dollars for, and they're going to give me 28—they told me I have 28,000 dollars in escrow and I do not own my land. My land, today, is valued at a half a million dollars.

Director Housing Authority: Our approach, in light of our new-found prosperity brought on by the advent of casino gambling, is to effect a very viable housing program; to ensure the development of middle income housing would be one of the prongs on our approach to our housing problem.

Barry I., Atlantic City Resident: I was at a megastructure meeting, at which the people were complaining about them stealing the land for houses—same Housing Authority, coming in and taking the whole center city and giving them so much for it. People have been fighting hard for it. So I went up to the megastreet—structure meeting to help them in the cause. I found out at the megastructure meeting—they said, they're taking your land, too, Mr. I.

I said, who's taking my land?

They said, The Housing Authority. There's Mr. Housing Authority, that's right in the back of the meeting.

So I went back to ask him. I says, my name is Mr. I. I said, I own the land on G-1 block. I said, I heard you were taking my land.

He says, Mr. I., we took your land. I said, how did you take my land? I bought it, I paid for it, I got deeds right in my drawer for it. He says, Mr. I., we took your land. You have $28,000.

Director Housing Authority: Mr. I. elected to purchase the property from then-the-former (sic) owner, and we merely picked it up in our tracking of the various transactions—real estate transactions, and notified him, as a matter of courtesy, that we were in the process of quick-taking that particular property.

Unfortunately, the address on record for Mr. I. was not his current mailing address, and the notices came back to us, and they were unanswered.

That did—that in no way stops the process, because we are—we are not policemen. We—we attempt to find the person by using their—the tax bill, the billing address, the County Clerk's office, the address that—that—that is indicated on the deed. Other than that—that's the best that we could possibly do, in—in an effort to locate someone.

What followed from there was that we—we, the agency, quick - quick - un—under our quick-take process, took title to the pro—to the project and deposited the 28,000 dollars in—with the Clerk of the Superior Court of New Jersey.

Mr. I.'s Mother: Now, I—I feel very, very bad, because these people feel that you're going to take their land. You al—ready say you took my son's land. You sent him a notice, stating, or somehow or other he got word of it, that his money is in escrow, that you have stolen his land. The ordinance was not passed, but you took his land. Like he's paying 70,000 plus all the interest, and you're going to give him 28,000?— 28,000 you're going to give him, for 70,000. That's a big profit.

(Laughter)

Now, 70,000 is only what is cost him, that ain't costing what he's got to pay, to—to—in order to buy the land. Now, shouldn't I feel bad? And then you call him a speculator.

I had nothing. I went to the soup house when I was child. I had nothing being raised. My children had nothing. Now, my son has a chance to buy a little bit of land and make a few dollars, and you feel that you should come and take it away from him?

I'm more so against you—I think you're lying, like you did before casino gambling. I think you lied about the Urban Renewal. The casinos got it, right?

Clearly the lines are drawn. Many neighborhood residents see the politicians as the "bad guys" out to "line their own pockets" at the expense of long-term home owners. Whether the Ducktown of today with its weakened fabric could hold its own in another major intergroup struggle is an open question.

Observations of Individual Elderly Ducktown Residents

The predominant response of the elderly respondents in Ducktown to the question "Did you vote for the Casino referendum?" was "yes." The overwhelming response to the next question, "Would you again?" was an emotional "No." They felt that the promise to bring benefits to the elderly was a fraud. (Some benefits are spread evenly over the entire state's elderly population, though the impact individually is seen as trivial.) Although the elderly acknowledge that the younger people may be benefiting, for them, the effects are seen mostly as bad. In short, they see their city and neighborhood "sold away from them" or "raped."

In the neighborhood itself, the elderly are saddened to see the disappearance of buildings which represent something in their past or had served as recent guideposts for orienting themselves and their friends. There is a sense of loss of the familiar.

There is a sense of violation by crowds of strangers. Their Boardwalk isn't their's anymore. They used to be virtually the sole occupants during the off-season. Now they must share it with millions of visitors, many of whom are in a hurry to get where they are going. The traffic violates them. It's harder to cross a street, to make their way down the sidewalk, to get waited on in stores and to feel safe in their own neighborhood at night. The familiar cop on the beat has long since been replaced by the patrol car and the elderly are afraid.

Some of the elderly (and non-elderly) residents of Ducktown feel that their Italian community is being invaded by ethnic "foreigners." There is a gradual movement of Blacks into the edges of Ducktown as Blacks are having to find new housing in the face of space pressures. In addition, the increase of crimes in Ducktown is blamed on "Blacks who make raids on the neighborhood."

In general, among the elderly, an extreme fear of street crime has developed. Most elderly no longer consider the streets safe after dark as they did 10 years ago. Much of this fear is probably characteristic of urban areas throughout America today, but in Atlantic City, the blame is placed on Casino development. Some of the elderly explain that the criminals assume everyone carries gambling money around these days and so everyone is a prime target. Just how much *real* increase in crime as compared to the *fear* of crime is occurring is difficult to tell. There is, however, enough of a real increase to fuel the fears of the vulnerable elderly.

Another frequently mentioned problem among the elderly is the difficulty of "making ends meet." Although in Ducktown, among Italian landlords, the rental costs are kept from astronomical increases, the costs *are* rising. For those whose employment has improved over the past few years, the increases in cost of living are not so bad, but for the unemployed elderly, the cost increases are acute.

Not only are they hit by increased prices for food and lodging, they also must spend more time getting to the food stores and other services. A supermarket that once was a profitable use of space is no longer so profitable when the space becomes highly valued for other uses. Hence, the store closes. Now the elderly must either pay the high prices of the efficiency— 24-hour-stores or travel on a "senior citizen bus" for an hour to get to and from a supermarket. Medical Doctors are moving "off of the Island" as office rental costs become higher and more residents move "to the mainland." The elderly feel this loss greatly. In short, the acquiring of many essential services is becoming more and more of a headache for the elderly.

When asked about their desires to move from the city, a variety of responses were given. Some wanted to leave but couldn't manage it financially. Others felt betrayed by those friends and acquaintances who chose to leave. They felt deserted. Increasingly, of late, a feeling of fatalism is emerging. They don't feel in control. When asked specifically about their future, the elderly generally saw few bright spots for themselves. In the face of an uncertain future, they choose "to take one day at a time." They don't like what they see for themselves in the future but they are reconciled to take it as it comes.

As for an Italian Ducktown in the future—they don't see one. They see property no longer passing from an elderly member of the family to a younger member. They now see the property passing out of the family and the young men and women of the neighborhood leaving the neighborhood for school and choosing not to return. "The kids can't pay these high rents even if they choose to," the elderly explain. These elderly residents are witnessing the death of an ethnic neighborhood.

Marie Costello: A Case Study

Marie Costello, a longtime, 68-year-old resident of Ducktown now lives in a neat, comfortable house in Ventnor, New Jersey. She owns and runs a business in Ducktown and many members of her family still live there. She is in the neighborhood each day and has a sense of what is happening. She is terribly worried about the changes she has seen in the past few years. She talked about the things on the minds of many of her Ducktown friends.

> Some of the older people are frightened. Frightened is the word. Or they are moving. This [Ducktown] used to be a close community regardless of age. You help each other. Say, when I was a youngster—before I got married there would be block parties. Our garden—my Dad cemented the whole yard—there was an every Saturday night occasion there. Now if you want to have something like that you have to have a thousand dollars ready to blow. Then it was all fun and everyone donated what they had. The yard was cemented and there were colored lights all around. Now . . .

> It is broken now. Lately everything is going down. I was in shock. My brother came and he said to me, "You ought to see Missouri Avenue," he said, "you know that they were tearing down the movies, they are tearing down all of Missouri Avenue." I said, "You are kidding," but it was true, it's only one house standing. Within two weeks they tore down every house except one!

There is a feeling that no one knows who is buying up the Ducktown property for sure. Marie Costello expressed this.

> Nobody seems to know who bought this all. It is a hush-hush thing. People will sell property but they won't come out and say, "I sold it and I sold it for so much." Maybe they were told not to tell. Nobody likes it. I was sort of sick when my brother drove me around Missouri Avenue. It was just coming apart in front of your eyes.

Services are less than they were in the old days. Marie Costello talked about the community stores which are increasingly rare.

> We had one little old lady—she had been living there since I was ten. She had a small store probably about 60 years. People went in there. She didn't make a lot, but it kept her going. The people helped—went there to shop because they knew it would help her. There is a bakery shop there—if that goes too . . . that is another part of it. You have the grocery store, but that's already closed. So many people are going that the money is not there any more.

People seem to move out of Ducktown because business is bad and also because they have offers to buy their property. The changes are especially difficult for the older people to cope with. We wondered whether the older people of Ducktown were using the Casinos as a new way of spending time.

> They are not interested in those things. Those people are not interested in casinos. Like myself. Big deal! I have been there twice. To these people— casinos are so far from their mind. They were happy in their own little neighborhood. If they wanted to go to a movie it was around the corner— now it's gone.

Crime is now a fact of life for the Ducktown residents. There is the sense that the neighborhood is no longer safe. Marie Costello remembered how it had been in the past.

> Everybody used to leave their doors wide open. In fact, I still have the habit and my kids scream at me! My front door is open, my back door is open. Now it's not safe. People blame this on casino development. They sure do. Really the older people—they just thought they would build casinos on the boardwalk and we will be left where we are. But really, you know, nothing worked out the way the said. The older people are not getting anything out of it. I am happy that my Dad isn't in this today. I wouldn't want to see him hurt.

Marie Costello remembered a few crimes that had occurred recently in the Ducktown area. It seems that the fear of crime is the worst thing, the feeling that the neighborhood is not what is was. Especially there was the knowledge that the neighborhood was no longer a place where the old could be safe and comfortable.

> The old people don't want to move; don't like the idea of moving. I give it five years—and then there isn't going to be any neighborhood there. The older people are being pushed out, but they don't want to go out. And it is going to kill a lot of them. A lot of those old people. When they have to move, that will be the end of them. They will be gone.

Marie Costello is one of the more fortunate older people of Atlantic City. A house in Ventnor and a business in Ducktown mean that she, at least, will be able to remain in the area. She is a bouyant person with many interests in life and a large lively family who live close enough for frequent visiting. Yet when she speaks about Ducktown there is the sense of irretrievable loss, that she sees her past disappearing before her eyes. The Ducktown community was a real center for the Italian residents of Atlantic City and the loss of its integrity is experienced as a kind of death. They know that as people disperse, move to other communities, the kind of interrelatedness that they grew up with will never return. Marie Costello said that the move from the community would kill the old people, and in a way she is right, for life in the community is the only life that many of them have known. It is hard for them to imagine living in another setting.

30

Impact of the Psychosocial Environment of the Elderly on Behavioral and Health Outcomes

Ellen J. Langer and Jerry Avorn

Epictetus once said that it is not events themselves that cause stress, but rather the views one takes of those events. That is, our own subjective reality, rather than an objective reality, largely determines the way the world impinges on us. The full age-related implication of this idea has only recently been felt in the scientific community. In the past decade, researchers have been devoting extensive study to the importance of perceived control over events in one's life. One focus of our own research has been the importance of this variable in appreciating the problems of the elderly. Much research in this area suggests that the belief that one can affect outcomes relevant to one's own life is of paramount importance to psychological and perhaps even physical health. Interestingly, this has been shown to be true regardless of whether or not such belief in fact reflects the reality of control.

There are several subtle ways in which physical and interpersonal environments lead us to believe that we have no control over our actions and our experiences. The consequences of such perceived loss of control may be devastating. In this chapter, we will describe the negative consequences of believing one has lost control over one's environment, some of the factors that lead to such a belief in institutionalized elderly adults, and possible ways of ameliorating the situation.

In 1942, the great Harvard physiologist W.B. Cannon helped make the scientific community aware of the strange phenomenon of voodoo deaths. People who, for one reason or another, are led to expect they will die, do in fact die, often despite previously good health. Autopsies often reveal no apparent medical cause. Bettelheim's (1960) descriptions of some concentration-camp victims reveal similar findings. While some victims starve to death, others die without apparent physical cause. This phenomenon has been documented in numerous other reports, particularly in the literature of sudden cardiac death (Lown et al. 1977).

Laboratory investigation confirmed the validity of these observations and suggested some clues to its physiological basis. Richter (1957) found that if he held a wild rat in his hand until it stopped struggling and then placed it in a tank of water, the rat drowned within a half hour. He repeated this with several rats and in each case found the same result. He compared this finding to another group of wild rats that swam around for approximately sixty hours when placed directly into the tank. Why did the former group drown so quickly? It was as if the rats had simply given up.

The effects of giving up are real and the consequences may be extreme. Additional evidence of the phenomenon comes from epidemiological studies that reveal a markedly increased rate of death among surviving spouses in the year following bereavement (Parkes 1964). Patients judged prospectively to have a sense of helplessness or hopelessness have been found by Schmale (1969) to have a much higher likelihood of subsequently being diagnosed as having cancer. Dr. Ellen J. Langer has attempted experimental interventions to test this hypothesis in the institutionalized elderly. Nursing-home residents were randomly assigned to two groups. The control group was told that the home's staff was there to care for them and to make decisions for them regarding their day-to-day lives—in their best interest, of course. Residents in the experimental group, by contrast, were encouraged to make their own decisions as much as possible concerning meal times, recreational activities, and so forth. The latter group was found to show significant improvement in psychological well-being and activity (Langer and Rodin 1976). A follow-up study eighteen months later suggested that the residents in the experimental group also seemed to have a lower rate of mortality when compared with controls (Rodin and Langer 1977).

The physiological mechanisms through which such learned helplessness can be transformed into physical illness are not totally clear, but some intriguing evidence exists. Some investigators invoke the notion of a parasympathetic death—death resulting from overactivity of the parasympathetic nervous system. This could be mediated, for example, through excessive stimulation by the brain of the vagus nerve, which innervates the heart as well as many other vital organs. Vagal impulses slow the heart rate; extraordinary activity of the vagus nerve can result in cardiac standstill and, consequently, death.

Recent cardiovascular research has focused on another mechanism, perhaps more important. This is the sympathetic nervous system, the apparatus responsible for the fight-or-flight emergency response that quickens the heart, constricts the blood vessels, releases adrenalin, and creates the hyperaroused state we have all experienced at times of extreme stress. Evidence from dogs and humans has shown that psychological stress that initiates this emergency response makes it likelier that the heart will become over-stimulated and go into ventricular fibrillation—a disordered and ineffective twitching of the heart muscle that pumps no blood and is therefore incompatible with life (Lown et al. 1977). Excessive activity of the sympathetic or parasympathetic nervous systems has been suggested as the means through which psychological stress can be transformed into physical illness or even death.

Of course, in daily life the physiological effects of the psychosocial environment are considerably subtler, but even when death does not result, successful living is clearly undercut by a threatening milieu, and unnecessary debilitation can result. The loss of perceived control is stressful at first; if it persists, the individual becomes passive and dependent, feels incompetent, and may display symptoms characteristic of reactive depression.

The early psychological experiments in this field focused on the effect of negative outcomes in producing these feelings of helplessness. People typically were put in situations where they were going to experience some aversive event over which they had no control. To make the appropriate comparisons, other people in these studies were made to experience the same aversive consequence, but were led to believe that they were doing so by choice. Thus, the same negative outcome was experienced by the two groups and all that differed between them was their belief about their control over the outcome. One group believed they could control the outcome, the other believed they could not. In virtually all of the studies of this type, although neither group exercised control, the group that believed that control was possible experienced less stress. In other studies, subjects were given prior experience with uncontrollable negative outcomes in which their attempts to terminate the negative consequences were repeatedly met with failure. No matter what they did, they were unsuccessful. After this experience, they were then placed in a second situation where control was possible. The prior experience with uncontrollability led people not to exercise control in this second situation even when control was possible. They have learned that responding is futile and hence they have given up and become passive. However, they were giving up in a situation in which giving up was clearly maladaptive. Comparison groups not given the prior experience with uncontrollable outcomes readily exercised control in the second situation. It would seem that much passivity and giving up in general is a result of prior experience with loss of control (Seligman 1975).

The relevance of control to the environment of the elderly becomes much clearer when we consider other factors that may lead residents of nursing homes to give up because they believe themselves to be helpless. First, there may be a discrepancy between what nursing-home residents are permitted to do and what they think they are permitted to do. Residents may indeed be able to exercise control over some aspects of their lives; however, if the subjective experience of that reality is such that the individual believes no control is available, then the negative physical and psychological consequences resulting from this belief will exist regardless of the reality. Further, Baltes and Barton (1979) have shown that the reality of nursing-home life may, in fact, not be so benign. In a study of staff and resident behavior, they found that independence-affirming behaviors on the part of residents were generally met with negative reinforcement by staff, while dependence-affirming resident activity was rewarded.

The power of the environment to induce helplessness and giving up is made even more apparent when one considers the following observation: belief in one's own incompetence may evolve even if the individual is not given direct experience with uncontrollable outcomes. Incompetence may be inferred from very subtle environmental and interpersonal cues, quite independent of a direct-failure experience. It is these subtle factors that insidiously communicate loss of control that will be considered in the remainder of this chapter.

What interpersonal aspects of nursing-home environments tell the elderly resident that he or she is incompetent and unable to control his or her environment? First is the very decision to institutionalize—usually made by families or health care professionals, and not by the elderly themselves. Ironically, the need to place a parent is often a result of the inability of society to provide adequate noninstitutional support for partially disabled elderly (Avorn 1982); yet such societal inadequacy is perceived as inadequacy of the elder to perform in that society. Even before the elderly adult takes up residence in the nursing home, staff may unwittingly communicate their belief in his or her helplessness. They do this by speaking almost exclusively to the children who are placing their parent in the home, rather than to the elderly adult who is actually moving to a new home.

Simply bearing the label "nursing-home resident" may be debilitating if the resident accepted, in younger days, a set of negative, preconceived ideas about why one goes to a nursing home. We found in our own research (Langer and Benevento 1978) that when people were assigned labels that connoted inferiority, they performed poorly on tasks that they not only could perform but in fact did perform quite well before they wore the label. Labels may also be a problem from the perspective of the staff's behavior. In other research (Langer and Abelson 1974) we asked professional psychotherapists to evaluate a person whom we called either a "patient" or a "job applicant." Both groups saw a videotape of the same person; nevertheless, their evaluation differed considerably depending on the label. The person labeled "patient" was generally seen as sick and in need of help, while the same person labeled "job applicant" was seen as well-adjusted. (Professionals who were specifically trained to observe behavior and not use labels saw the person as well-adjusted no matter what we called him, but most people do not receive this kind of training.) A great deal of social psychological research tells us that people behave differently with people for whom they have different expectations and that the latter group in turn comes to behave in a way that confirms those expectations (see Rosenthal 1971, Kelley 1967, Snyder 1978). The label instigates this process (Rodin and Langer 1980).

If those caring for the elderly expect them to be generally incompetent because they are nursing-home residents, they will unwittingly behave as if they are incompetent, and the residents, in turn, may come to believe that they are incompetent and act accordingly. In this kind of a system, all expectations may receive confirmation so no one knows that it could have been otherwise. This point of view has been documented as well in *Stigma* by Erving Goffman (1963) and in medical research. In the latter case, patients who were told that they had high blood pressure immediately began to experience more illness-related absenteeism, though their physiological condition had not changed from previous months or years—they had simply been labeled as sick (Haynes 1978).

Another interpersonal factor that may subtly lead to an erroneous belief in incompetence is one that denies what would seem to be the guiding principle of most institutions: tender loving care. Because the elderly as a group are seen as frail and vulnerable, the tendency of society in general is to treat them with special care—always being ready to "help the little old lady across the street." In this case what is true in the general population would seem to be even more prevalent in nursing homes. Here the people are pictured as more frail than average and the staff are hired primarily to help them; yet simply helping people may make them incompetent (Langer and Avorn 1982). Although well-meant, such attention may communicate belief in the inability and inadequacy of the recipient. If the person faces no difficulty, if there are no challenges, large or small, feelings of mastery are precluded and consequences such as involution, depression, and morbidity are real possibilities. Helping the resident get dressed to go to breakfast (either out of concern for the resident or to save time for the staff) may only result in feelings of incompetence and dependence for the resident and ultimately take more of the staff's time, since the individual will soon come to assume the need for such help.

A fourth interpersonal factor worth considering is the effect of uniforms. Uniforms constantly remind residents that they need to be taken care of, that they are not members of the higher-status group, and that they can never hope to join the ranks of these potential role models. Since uniforms make it easy to recognize who is doing what in the institution, they also make salient to the resident what they themselves or others in their same position are not doing. Watching someone else do things that one used to do oneself, but is no longer doing, may lead to the sense that one has become incapable of performing those activities. This can occur even when the only reason the person is not engaging in the behavior is an institutional decision based on other matters and not at all an assessment of the individual's competence. The expectation of incompetence on the part of the individual, facilitated by similar expectations held by the staff, is often so pervasive that there may be no other explanations offered for why an individual is or is not doing something. When there is a ready explanation for an event, one rarely searches for other possible causes. The lack of systematic and recurrent functional-assessment of institutionalized elderly in most settings makes it more likely that such a "lowest common denominator" approach will be used instead of a more person-specific, accurate measurement of what each individual can (or could) do.

The physical aspects of most nursing homes also nurture this belief of no control. One simply cannot feel much control over that which is unfamiliar; however, we can exercise control by making the unfamiliar familiar if the environment suggests that this is possible. In fact, it is the very process of making the unfamiliar familiar that gives rise to the perception of control and the feeling of mastery. Residents come from homes that they have lived in all their lives, that had kitchen facilities they could use, rooms with furniture and belongings that were familiar, doors that could be open or locked closed, decorations that were unique and aesthetically appealing, and so on. Obstacles were dealt with as the environment was mastered, and new obstacles were forever revealing themselves. Mastering the environment led to general feelings of mastery; however, if the individual is faced with an already-mastered environment, mastering will not take place and the positive and life-sustaining consequences of perceived control will be lost.

Attempts by professionals, family, or the residents themselves to explain disorientation in the elderly may not take these issues into consideration. This is not surprising. One typically tries to explain behavior based on what there is to be seen, rather than on what is missing; yet the disorientation could be a function of the lack of salient, easily discriminated cues. The negative effects of this misattribution would be likely to multiply and may rob the individual of the motivation to find more subtle cues to help make the discrimination (Avorn 1981a). Why bother looking if you do not think you are capable of finding?

Perhaps the biggest problem for the elderly resident is that the environment is either too easy or too difficult to negotiate. Those aspects perceived as too difficult will be ignored entirely. Those aspects that are too easy are just as problematic. Having doors that are always opened for you, food that is always served to you, ramps for entering or leaving instead of a few steps, almost preclude feelings of control. How can one feel a sense of mastery if there is nothing to master?

In a series of studies testing the illusion of control (Langer 1975), this kind of physical involvement with the environment was found to be important to people even when the situation they were trying to control was, in fact, uncontrollable. For example, in one study, subjects were face to face with an electrical apparatus with three paths displayed on it. They were told that a buzzer would sound if the correct path was traveled with a stylus. Subjects in the high-involvement group traversed their chosen path themselves while those in the low-involvement group chose the path for someone else to travel. In fact, only chance determined whether the buzzer rang; yet, even in a situation as constrained as this, where the outcome was, in fact, random, involvement mattered. Subjects who were more actively involved felt more confident and perceived greater control over the outcome. Similar effects of feeling involved with the environment have been found in other settings (Langer and Roth 1975). How many times has each of us pushed buttons on elevators that were already lit to exercise control and because doing nothing is so difficult? Thus, obstacles that are mildly to moderately difficult to overcome (but not dangerous) should not be quickly removed from the environment of the elderly; instead they should be dealt with by the residents.

Another factor that is worth examining when considering the environment of the elderly is routinization. Detailed analysis of the ways in which routinization is a problem have been dealt with elsewhere (see Langer 1978a, 1978b; Langer 1979). We will present here only the results of those analyses. If an environment is almost perfectly predictable, the hallmark of routinization, then there is nothing for the individual to think about. However, the individual must be in a mindful state to perceive control over the environment; thus, routine does not promote perception of control. We all perform many tasks (particularly the so-called activities of daily living) mindlessly; that is, in doing them we do not think carefully about what we are doing or how we are doing it. This is possible because many of these activities have been overlearned through decades of practice; we have become so adept that we can do these things without thinking. Ironically, however, it is just such overlearned tasks that are the most likely to make us feel incompetent. The reason for this paradox is straightforward: because we perform the tasks almost automatically, we have lost conscious awareness of many of the intermediary steps necessary for their completion. This explains the familiar sensation of having to perform an entire overlearned task (such as tying shoes) from the beginning in order to get it right.

Normally, when our competence is called into question, we can satisfy ourselves that we are in fact competent by mentally retracing the steps required to do such a task. For an overlearned task that is normally done mindlessly, this ability may be lost. For an elderly person in an institutionalized setting, it becomes very easy to imagine that one is not competent to perform many tasks: many self-care needs are performed by others, and it is no longer possible even to remember how one used to perform such tasks for oneself, because they were overlearned many years earlier.

Implications for the Design of Environments for the Elderly

The above experimental data and clinical observations can have immediate and far-reaching applications to the care of the elderly. These include: changes in existing institutions, alterations in policy to discourage institutionalization, the development of healthier alternatives, and the identification of potential obstacles inhibiting such developments. We will conclude by discussing each of these in turn.

Changes in the Nursing-Home Environment

The evidence we have presented argues strongly in favor of a number of specific changes in the design of nursing homes. Some are quite readily accomplished, requiring virtually no changes in the present management and reimbursement structure of long-term care; others would require more far-reaching developments. Among the more do-able changes would be architectural diversification of the nursing home, so that rooms and wings of a facility would look quite distinct from one another. It is striking how rarely variations in paint color are used in nursing homes to accomplish this end. While there may be a certain small economy in using the same institutional color throughout a facility, the cost in terms of confusion, loss of mobility, and psychological debility of residents is far greater. Permission for residents to bring in their own furniture and memorabilia would also go a long way toward reducing the institutionalization syndrome that is such a predictable apect of life in an anonymous environment. A sense of control would further be heightened if residents who are at no risk of harming themselves were allowed keys to their rooms. Where possible, the medical model of a hospital setting with four-bedded or two-bedded rooms should be abandoned; it is not a living arrangement that is ever chosen voluntarily. Being forced to share a room means, besides the endurance of loss of privacy, further exposure to the problems of partner-changing and the need to tolerate the idiosyncrasies (often irritating) of another—a constant reminder of lack of control of the environment.

It is striking how carefully nursing-home environments have been made to conform to life-safety-code provisions to guard against fire hazard. While tragic, nursing-home fires are rare and certainly do not seem to us to present the greatest threat to the health and well-being of institutionalized elderly. What is needed is a mind-safety-code enforcement, a series of environmental and behavioral standards to guard against the much more debilitating psychological hazards that form the nursing-home environment. A general guideline would require impressive and documented evidence to justify a change in the life-space or a diminution of personal control, the elements that make the institution look very different from the real world. We believe that many restrictions of nursing-home life would then be found unsupportable.

Public-Policy Considerations

Our present reimbursement system for long-term care obviously is heavily biased in favor of the institutionalization of frail elders. No matter how enlightened the institution, certain built-in bureaucratic considerations make institutional life inherently more destructive of control and of independence. There will be a limit to the extent to which nursing homes can be humanized. The needs of mentally and physically handicapped residents and the pervasive needs of staff members will constantly work toward creating a milieu that is not in the best interests of the nonhandicapped resident. The full solution to this problem awaits an enlightened public policy that will adequately fund noninstitutional services for impaired elderly as generously as it has funded nursing homes in the past. Implicit in such a reorientation is a strict limitation of the medical model for long-term care adapted so enthusiastically over the past two decades in this country. This approach, in which the recipient of care is viewed as inherently ill and incompetent, may be appropriate in the operating room or in an intensive-care unit (though probably not completely in the latter), but it is certainly not a fit way to view people who may have only slight problems with mobility or sensation, and are otherwise quite able to care for themselves.

In recent years, a number of alternatives to institutional care for the elderly have received increased attention in the United States: home care, respite care, and congregate-living facilities. A number of studies have suggested that significant numbers of the institutionalized-elderly population could be dealt with in less-restrictive, but reimbursable, alternative-care programs. It is not yet clear whether such alternative forms of care, if available, will in fact be more cost-effective than institutional care. For many nonfrail elderly misplaced in nursing homes because of inadequate housing opportunities or because of poor judgment by a referring agency, noninstitutional alternatives will save money. We are concerned here with, however, a larger issue: the saving of psychological well-being and ability for self-care that are clearly better enhanced in noninstitutional settings. From the bulk of psychological and geriatric evidence, we can now conclude with some certainty that there is good reason to favor options such as congregate housing over conventional nursing-home care.

Obstacles to Overcome

The mere preponderance of evidence, however, has never been enough to assure the acceptance of an idea. Powerful institutional and economic interests will continue to favor the nursing-home model of care for the frail elderly. There is tremendous inertia in the present system, a result of both the reluctance of people (particularly health-care professionals) to change, and, more important, the enormous economic motivation of the nursing-home industry to maintain its current hegemony over the long-term care scene. Attempts to construct a more psychologically (and medically) healthy environment for the elderly will be met, but rarely head on with considerable resistance. Of course, no discussions will take place in the language of capital investment or profit. As always, "the welfare of the patients" will be voiced as the main rationale for policy decisions that might in fact work against their interests. It will be particularly important to be certain that the proprietary (that is, profit-making) nature of the present long-term industry not be transferred to a burgeoning new alternative care industry. We make this argument on clinical, rather than on economic grounds (although persuasive arguments can be based on the latter as well). If our focus is to be upon the preservation of individual competence and sense-of-self in the elderly in whatever setting, we have an inherent contradiction between this goal and the development of a for-profit sector to serve the elderly. Concerns of business will necessarily require standardization, routinization, streamlining, and efficiency, often at the expense of idiosyncrasies, individuality, personal attention, diversity, and all of those "minor" aspects of human life which distinguish it from that of an ant colony. It will always be cheaper and "more efficient" to house elderly people four to a room instead of individually; to have staff feed them rapidly instead of letting them try it for themselves in a more time-consuming and "inefficient" manner; to design facilities, whether nursing homes or congregate-living arrangements, with the sameness and drabness that mark public-housing projects instead of the variety in private homes; to hire the cheapest available labor for the most intimate contact with residents, with predictable results.

It is evident now that the direction of public policy in the mid-1960s to excessively reimburse institutional care and nearly ignore home-based alternatives has led to a long-term care crisis in which costs have escalated out of control (Avorn 1981b). The quality of life for the elderly thus cared for has fallen into a state (at least in terms of psychological well-being) not in their best interest. In this decade, as we look ahead to patterns of long-term care that are more consistent with the variety and individuality of human life, we must base our public policies on clinical and experimental evidence that will further those goals, and not once again construct policy around misguided reliance on inappropriate commercial or medical paradigms that do not fit the people we hope to serve.

References and Additional Sources

Avorn, J. 1982. "Beyond the Bedside: The Social Context of Geriatric Practice." In *Health and Illness in Old Age*, ed. J. Rowe and P. Besdine. Boston: Little, Brown.
——. 1981a. "Studying Cognitive Performance in the Elderly: The Need for a Biopsychosocial Approach." In *Aging and Cognitive Processes*, ed. F. Craik and S. Trehub. New York: Plenum.
——. 1981b. "Nursing Home Infections: The Context." *New England Journal of Medicine* 305:759-60.
Avorn, J., and Langer, E. 1981. "Helping, Helplessness, and the 'Incompetent' Nursing Home Patient: An Empirical Study." *Clinical Research* 29:633A.
Baltes, M.M., and Barton, E.M. 1979. "Behavioral Analysis of Aging: A Review of the Operant Model and Research." *International Journal of Behavior and Development* 2:297-320.
Bettelheim, B. 1943. "Individual and Mass Behavior in Extreme Situations." *Journal of Abnormal Social Psychology* 38:417-52.
Cannon, W.B. 1942. "Voodoo Death." *American Anthropologist* 44:169-81.
Chanowitz, B., and Langer, E. 1980. "Knowing More (or Less) Than You Can Show: Understanding Control through the Mindlessness/Mindful Distinction." In *Human Helplessness*, ed. M.E.P. Seligman and J. Garber. New York: Academic.
Goffman, E. 1963. *Stigma: Notes on the Management of Spoiled Identity.* Englewood Cliffs, N.J.: Prentice-Hall.
Haynes, R.B., and Sackett, D.L. 1978. "Increased Absenteeism from Work after Detection and Labeling of Hypertensive Patients." *New England Journal of Medicine* 299:741-44.
Kelley, H. 1967. "Attribution Theory in Social Psychology." In *Nebraska Symposium on Motivation*, ed. D. Levine. Lincoln, Nebr.: University of Nebraska Press.
Langer, E. 1975. "The Illusion of Control." *Journal of Personality and Social Psychology* 32:311-28.
——. 1978. "Rethinking the Role of Thought in Social Interaction." In *New Directions in Attribution Reserch*, ed. J. Harvey, W. Ickes, and R. Kidd. Hillsdale, N.J.: Lawrence Erlbaum and Associates.

Langer, E., and Benevento, A. 1978. "Self-Induced Dependence." *Journal of Person-ality and Social Psychology* 36:886-93.

Langer, E., and Abelson, R. 1974. "A Patient by Any Other Name: Clinician Group Differences in Labelling Bias." *Journal of Consulting and Clinical Psychology* 42:4-9.

Langer, E., and Imber, L. 1979. "When Practice Makes Imperfect: Debilitating Effects of Overlearning." *Journal of Personality and Social Psychology* 37:2014-25.

Langer, E., and Rodin, J. 1976. "The Effects of Enhanced Personal Responsibility for the Aged: A Field Experiment in an Institutional Setting." *Journal of Person-ality and Social Psychology* 34:191-98.

Langer, E., and Roth, J. 1973. "Heads I Win, Tails It's Chance: The Illusion of Control as a Function of the Sequence of Outcomes in a Purely Chance Task." *Journal of Personality and Social Psychology* 32:951-55.

Lown, B.; Verrier, R.; and Rabinowitz, S. 1977. "Neural and Psychologic Mech-anisms and the Problem of Sudden Cardiac Death." *American Journal of Car-diology* 39:890-901.

Parkes, C. 1964. "Effects of Bereavement on Physical and Mental Health." *British Medical Journal* 2:274-79.

Richter, C.P. 1957. "On the Phenomenon of Sudden Death in Animals and Man." *Journal of Psychosomatic Medicine* 19:191-98.

Rodin, J., and Langer, E. 1980. "Aging Labels: The Decline of Control and the Fall of Self-esteem." *Journal of Social Issues* 36:12-29.

———. 1977. "Long-Term Effects of a Control-Relevant Intervention among the Institutionalized Aged." *Journal of Personality and Social Psychology,* 35:895-902.

Rosenthal, R. 1971. "Pygmalion Reaffirmed." In *Pygmalion Reconsidered,* ed. J. Elashoff and R. Snow. Worthington, Ohio: C.A. Jones.

Schmale, A.H. 1969. "Somatic Expressions and Consequences of Conversion Reac-tion." *N.Y. State Journal of Medicine* 69:1878.

Seligman, M.E.F. 1975. *Helplessness.* San Francisco: Freeman.

Snyder, M., and Swann, W. 1978. "Behavioral Confirmation in Social Interaction." *Journal of Experimental Social Psychology* 14:148-62.

31

Episodic Nature of Behavioral Disturbances among Residents of Facilities for the Aged

John Cumming, Elaine Cumming, Joan Titus,
Eileen Schmelzle, and Jacqueline MacDonald

There is division of opinion among health professionals about whether elderly patients are better served in specialized or in multilevel facilities. No matter what the merits of the argument there seems little doubt that the staff of many facilities exercise pressure upon their administrations to remove patients whose behavior deviates too far from that found acceptable.

In British Columbia, all facilities for the elderly are financed by the Provincial Ministry of Health where plans for establishing them are also developed. In 1979, those charged with planning were debating the advisability of building a number of 50-bedded hospital units to receive patients whose behavior was unacceptable in their current placement. We were invited to determine the magnitude of the problem.

Method

There are two parallel systems of residential care for the elderly in British Columbia. The first, the Extended Care System, is administered by the Hospital Programs Department of the Ministry. Many of its Units (ECU's) are attached to general hospitals, and the patients must meet rigid criteria of limited physical mobility. The second system, Long Term Care, is administered by a different office of the Ministry; its units (LTC's) are not usually attached to hospitals, and its patients do not have to meet criteria of reduced mobility. The ECU's are responsible to the Boards of Hospitals and most of the LTC's are run by non-profit societies although a few are still run for profit. A third care service sponsored by the Capital Regional District, which includes the City of Victoria and its adjoining municipalities, is offered to the elderly in their own homes.

Transfers of patients into and around these systems require the approval of centrally located officers of the Health Ministry, but it is reasonable to suppose that before a patient is considered for transfer, he must be brought to the attention of the appropriate officials by a member of the staff of the facility in which he is resident. Accordingly, we asked staff members familiar with the patients and their problems a carefully worded series of questions. First, they were asked which patients were causing the most trouble, and then, for each patient named, we asked the nature of the troublesome behavior, the time over which it had persisted, and what was believed to cause it, as well as the management tactics presently being used. Next, we asked which of these patients would be nominated for transfer to a new unit if one were available. Finally, when all problem patients had been described, we obtained a history of past transfers of difficult patients and informally discussed the kinds of difficult patients in the facility who would not be considered for transfer. All residential facilities in the Capital Regional District were included in this study, but only patients aged 65 and over are considered here.

At the second visit we asked an identical set of questions. We then inquired about any patients who had been named the first time but not the second. Finally, we interviewed the caseworkers responsible for the elderly in their own homes because these clients are an important source of admissions to the residential facilities.

We inquired about a population of 995 patients aged 65 and over in the ECU's, 1500 in LTC's, and approximately 1755 on the LTC caseloads. Included in these numbers were a few patients slightly under 65 years who were suffering from such premature neurological aging as Alzheimer's disease.

Findings

Two-Point Prevalence

Table 31.1 shows the numbers of patients per 1,000 at risk in the residential facilities and on the workers' caseloads nominated for transfer. The prevalence of nomination is highest in the ECU's and lowest on the caseloads, which might be expected given the admissions criteria used by these services. Between the two time points the prevalence rises slightly in the ECU's and somewhat more markedly in the LTC facilities and on the LTC caseloads. Because the survey team approached the LTC facilities at the same time that they were expecting visits from Government auditors, fear of losing patients may have depressed the original nominations. The survey team reported a more relaxed atmosphere during the second series of visits in February.

These nominations are in no sense high; they average about three per cent of those in facilities in December and only slightly more in February. Although other studies of this kind are hard to find, the rates in the ECU's are similar to the proportion of very difficult social and interpersonal behavior reported from a study of elderly patients in an assessment and treatment setting(1). A more important finding, however, is shown in Table 31.2.

In the first column of Table 31.2 it can be seen that although there were 43 ECU patients nominated in December and 46 in February, only 17, or a little more than one-third of them were the same patients. A similar proportion of the LTC patients were nominated both times. A total of 34 patients in the two kinds of facilities were nominated in December and remained in the system in February but were not named again; of these, 11, or approximately one-third, were said to have improved; 7, or about one-fifth, were said to be easier to handle because they had deteriorated; but 16, or nearly half, were described as unchanged, and probing produced neither a nomination nor a reason for the change of heart. Furthermore, of 130 patients described in December as problems but not serious enough to transfer, 26, or one-fifth, were nominated for transfer in February. In contrast, only approximately one percent of all of the 2495 residents of the facilities who were nominated in December and were still at risk in February were new nominees. These findings suggest that disturbances occur cyclically and that the less serious problems of December were either cycling into or out of the nominated group. Table 31.3 shows that there was a total of 108 patients ever nominated who were in the system in both De-

TABLE 31.1
Patients Nominated for Transfer per 1,000 at Risk in ECU's, LTC's and on Caseloads, December 1979 and February 1980

Type of Facility	Total Patients[1]	Numbers per 1,000 at risk nominated for transfer		Percent Increase
		Dec.	Feb.	
Extended care	995	43.2	46.2	6.9
Long-term care	1500	16.7	23.3	28.3
Caseloads	1755	8.5	10.8	27.0

1. Base population January, 1980

Sources: Ministry of Health; Hospital Programs, Extended Care Registry and Long-Term Care Central Registry; Capital Regional District Office, Long-Term Care.

TABLE 31.2

Two-Month Experience of Patients Ever Nominated for Transfer in Extended Care Units and Long-Term Care Facilities

| | Nominated by | | |
	ECU's	LTC's	Total
Resident December, 1979	43	25	68
(1) Separations Dec. 79-Feb. 80			
Died	3	1	4[1]
Discharged	1	0	1
(2) Remaining in the System			
Kept nomination	17	12	29
Lost nomination	22	12	34
Acquired nomination	26	19	45
(3) Entered System, nominated	3	4	7[2]
(4) Entered, nominated, separated	0	2	2[2]
Resident February, 1980	46	35	81

1. This number represents a rate of 353 deaths per annum per 1,000 at risk compared to 236 for all residents of ECU's, 109 for all residents of LTC's, 114 patients over 65 in acute care wards, and 45 for the total population 65 years and over in the Capital Regional District.
2. These numbers represent a rate of nomination about ten times that of the patients already resident.

cember and February and hence could have been named twice; of these, 29, or one-quarter, were in fact nominated twice. As Table 31.3 shows, the proportions are almost identical in the two types of facilities.

Calculated Incidence of Disturbed Behavior

From Table 31.2 it is possible to calculate the incidence of serious behavior disturbance, although it should not be forgotten that these can also be viewed as episodes of staff intolerance. As 26 new episodes emerged among the December population of the ECU's and 19 in the LTC's, it would be expected that in a year approximately 156 episodes would occur in the

TABLE 31.3

Proportion of 108 Patients at Risk of Double Nomination Named in both December and February in ECU's and LTC's

| At Risk of Double Nomination | Total | | ECU's | | LTC's | |
	N	%	N	%	N	%
Total	108	100.1	65	100.0	43	100.0
Double nominated	29	26.9	17	26.2	12	27.9
December only	34	31.5	22	33.8	12	27.9
February only	45	41.7	26	40.0	19	44.2

ECU's and 114 in the LTC's. Translating these figures into rates produces approximately 157 episodes per 1,000 patients at risk per annum in ECU's and 76 in LTC's.

Using these data it is possible to calculate the duration of an episode of disturbances. (Using the formula: $D = \frac{365P}{I}$,) where D = duration in days, P = absolute prevalence, I = absolute annual incidence. The average expected duration of a behavioral disturbance is either 101 or 108 days, depending or whether the December or February prevalence is used in the ECU's, and 80 or 113 days in the LTC's. Because these calculated durations of episodes are longer than the period of observation, a telephone check of the fate of the 29 double-nominated patients was made in April. Ten, or about one-third of the patients, had lost their nominations; two had died and one had discharged himself. Although the method of resurvey was different and hence interpretation must be cautious, these figures tend to confirm the earlier findings.

Types of Problems

The types of behavior described by staff members were similar to those reported by others(2,3,4,5). Although staff members described some patients as presenting multiple problems, they have been classified here according to what was described as the "real" cause for nomination. The problems complained of are summarized here:

Intrusive Behavior. This category includes noisiness, persistent demands, and wandering into other patients' rooms, the nursing station, and so on. One-third of the ever-nominated ECU patients and one-sixth of the LTC patients fell into this category.

Aggression. About a quarter of the nominated patients in both types of facilities were physically or verbally aggressive.

Psychiatric Symptoms. Symptoms of depression, paranoia, or neurosis were complained of in just over one-quarter of the ECU nominations and close to half of the LTC's.

Resistance to the Rules of the Facility. In both types of facility about one-twelfth of the patients were either uncooperative with care procedures, negligent in smoking habits, or intransigent about drinking, usually alcohol smuggled in by their friends.

Wilfully Unacceptable Behavior. Behavior such as exhibitionism and deliberate soiling and smearing was shown by about one-fifteenth of ECU patients and one-twenty-fifth of LTC patients.

Although there are significantly more complaints of intrusive behavior in ECU's and of psychiatric symptoms in LTC's, neither these nor any other categories predicted nomination, renomination, or death.

Discussion

It is by now a truism that the elderly are subject to dramatic fluctuations in their physiological states. Hunt(6), for example, described the kinds of homeostatic malfunctions commonly observed in very elderly patients.

It does not seem, however, that any study has been made of analogous fluctuations in behavior. Such fluctuations might result from biological or psychological swings; as Müller et al. point out, "intact bio-psychological functions are elementary tools for psychosocial functions"(7). Conversely, disruption of predictable interaction patterns might not only result in disordered behavior but also in psychological and even physiological upheavals.

This study suggests that a significant proportion of that disordered behavior which is experienced as particularly taxing by the caretakers of the elderly is not permanent, that the response to such behavior by staff members is not immutable, or both. Either explanation is supported by the adventitious finding (see Table 31.2, second footnote) that newly admitted, and hence socially dislocated, patients are nominated more often than residents with whom staff have perhaps found a *modus vivendi*. Whether or not there is a small group of patients who remain consistently difficult to manage for long periods remains an open question; it seems plausible that such a group exists.

It is not possible to relate the behavioral and interactional problems discovered in this study to diagnosis or to any existing scalar device for "measuring" behavior, which is a disadvantage both theoretically and clinically. The study was primarily designed to provide guidance to administrators, and therefore used a naturalistic method; that is, we investigated what could be expected to occur supposing that a special facility were to become available. By using this method we succeeded in answering the question originally asked, at the same time raising questions about the cyclic nature of the interactional behavior of older people.

In the debate about the relative merits of segregated versus integrated facilities(5,8), the findings of this study, and a number of others(2,9,10,11), clearly support the integrationists. Obviously all of the patients who cycled out of the nominated-for-transfer category would be better off in an integrated facility than in any special unit. The same would be true for the majority of those who cycled into the category. Furthermore, removing the most troublesome patients to a special unit would prove essentially frustrating because as soon as the facility was full, pressure for admission would be exerted by those cycling into the transfer category. In the extreme hypothetical case, the creation of limitless new units would result in emptying the existing units because among those who remained there would inevitably emerge a new group of "most difficult patients" even if under the original conditions they would never have been nominated.

There is ample evidence from this and other studies(12,13,14) that very difficult behavior can be managed successfully in a wide variety of settings including the patients' own homes, especially when there are adequate supports to those who must act as caretakers. The results reported here support the concept of assessment and brief treatment units for the behaviorally disturbed elderly such as has been developed by the British and more recently accepted and instituted in some Canadian jurisdictions, including British Columbia(11,15,16).

References

1. Keong, C.C., and Beard, O.W. "Psychiatric Findings in the Population of Geriatric Evaluation Unit: Implications." *Journal of the American Geriatric Society* 28 (1980): 153-56.
2. Trier, T.W. "Characteristics of Mentally Ill Aged: A Comparison of Patients with Psychogenic Disorders and Patients with Organic Brain Syndromes." *Journal of Gerontology* 21 (1966): 354-64.
3. Sanford, I.R.A. "Tolerance of Debility in Elderly Dependents by Supporters at Home: Its Significance for Hospital Practice." *British Medical Journal* 3 (1975): 471-73.
4. Pablo, R.Y. "The Evaluation of the Physical and Mental Impairments of a Long Term and Rehabilitation Hospital Patient Population." *Canadian Journal of Public Health* 67 (1976): 305-12.
5. Margo, J.L., Robinson, J.R., and Corea, S. "Referrals to a Psychiatric Service from Old People's Homes." *British Journal of Psychiatry* 136 (1980): 396-401.
6. Hunt, T.E. "Homeostatic Malfunctions in the Aged." *British Columbia Medical Journal* 22 (1980): 379-81.
7. Müller, H.F., Pastoor, D.P., Hontela, S., Kachanoff, R., and Klinger, A. "A Psychogeriatric Assessment Program, IV: Interdisciplinary Aspects." *Journal of the American Geriatric Society* 24 (1976): 54-57.
8. Brocklehurst, J.C. "Brain Failure in Old Age: Social Implications." *Age and Ageing* 6 (1977, suppl.): 30-34.
9. Gilleard, C.J., and Pattie, A.H. "The Effect of Location on the Elderly Mentally Infirm: Relationship to Mortality and Behavioral Deterioration." *Age and Ageing* 7 (1978): 1-6.
10. Copeland, J.R.M., Kelleher, J.M., Kellett, G.B., Cowan, D.W., and Gourlay, A.J. "Evaluation of a Psychogeriatric Service: The Distinctions between Psychogeriatric and Geriatric Patients." *British Journal of Psychiatry* 126 (1975): 21-29.
11. Pasker, P., Thomas, J.P.R., and Ashley, J.S.A. "The Elderly Mentally Ill: Whose Responsibility?" *British Medical Journal* 2 (1976): 164-66.
12. Roth, M., and Mountjoy, C.Q. "Mental Health Services for the Elderly Living in the Community: A United Kingdom Perspective." *International Journal of Mental Health* 8 (1979): 6-35.

13. Harwin, B. "Psychiatric Morbidity among the Physically Impaired Elderly in the Community: A Preliminary Report." In Wing, J.K., Häfner, H. (eds.), *Roots of Evaluation*. London: Oxford University Press, 1973.
14. Isaacs, B. "Geriatric Patients: Do Their Families Care? *British Medical Journal* 4 (1971): 282-86.
15. Brocklehurst, J.C. "Planning for Old Age." *Canadian Medical Association Journal* 122 (1980): 1235-36.
16. Gillis, J., Ho, F., and Choat, N. "A Review of the First Six Months of a Short Stay Assessment and Treatment Centre in British Columbia." Presented before the ninth scientific and educational meeting of the Canadian Association of Gerontology, Saskatoon, October 16-19, 1980.

32

Discharge Planning: No Deposit, No Return

Martin Hochbaum and Florence Galkin

In the last half dozen years, the operations of nursing homes have been examined thoroughly by legislative committees, investigative bodies, newspapers, university public policy centers, and others. In spite of all this activity, one aspect of the operations of nursing homes, their implementation of government-mandated discharge-planning policies, has received relatively little attention. This is so even though both the federal and state governments, in theory at least, have committed themselves to a discharge-planning program for nursing-home patients. On the national level, federal law requires that patient-care policies "effect awareness of, and provision for, meeting the total medical and psychological needs of patients including . . . discharge planning." Under New York law, operators are required to "maintain a discharge planning program" and "develop and document in the resident's medical record a multidisciplinary discharge plan for all residents; and review . . . the plan as indicated by change in the patient's . . . medical condition." What actually occurs is a compliance which fails to consider adequately the individual patient's potential for discharge. Once admitted to a nursing home, the patient has lost his options; he has arrived at this last residence.

Discharge planning is based on the assumption that each patient has needs and potentials which will be most effectively met by evaluating "the total person and not just his immediate medical needs," in the words of a report published by the Commission on Professional and Hospital Activities. Ideally, the process should begin at admission with an assessment of medical, nursing, social, and emotional needs. This should be followed by evaluation of the patient's rehabilitative potential and review of alternative care plans to meet his needs. Once this is completed, the patient's potential for discharge can be ascertained. Discharge planning is not, however, a one-time process. A patient's potential for discharge must be reevaluated periodically to reflect his current state, needs, and resources. For example, a newly admitted patient may have multiple medical and nursing needs which could be compounded by disorientation. This patient may only be eligible for discharge after months of rehabilitation. Recognizing this, the New York law mandates that the patient's discharge plan be reviewed and revised every 90 days "as indicated by change in" medical conditions or needs. This is obviously a time-consuming process. The discharge planner must gather information from a variety of sources to compile "a total picture of the patient's needs and his discharge potential," again in the words of the Commission on Professional and Hospital Activities report. For example, the discharge planner must be familiar with the availability and effectiveness of such community-based programs as visiting nurses, homemakers, home delivery of meals, public welfare, housing, and home visitation. He must also be able to overcome the pervasive fragmentation of services in these areas.

We concentrate here on discharges from health-related facilities (hrf) because patients in these institutions are better off physically and mentally than those in skilled nursing facilities (snf) and, therefore, stand a better chance of being discharged to their homes. Hrf patients, for Medicaid reimbursement purposes, must have scored between 60 and 180 on a New York State patient assessment scale; snf patients must have scored at least 180. In 1977, out of 17,126 patients discharged from hrfs in New York State, only 1,483 were discharged to their homes. When one discounts the 732 patients "discharged" by death, out of the 16,394 people discharged, only 1,483 (nine percent) were discharged to their homes. The others were discharged to hospitals and facilities offering other levels of care. The figures for 1978 are not very different. Out of 15,908 patients discharged from hrfs in New York, 1,296 were discharged to their homes. Again, discounting deaths, in this case 822, out of the 14,612 patients discharged, only 1,296 or nine percent were discharged home. Most of the others were discharged to hospitals and locations affording other levels of care.

In many cases, the problem begins with the admissions process itself. Most patients are admitted to nursing homes following discharge from a hospital. With hospitals under pressure to empty their beds to satisfy utilization review requirements, there is little opportunity to consider community-based, long-term care options. Moreover, even if there is interest in such alternatives, the chronic nature of the patient's condition often requires multidimensional treatment which the home-care system cannot adequately deliver. The patient is usually confronted with a host of fragmented services with diverse eligibility requirements, rather than a one-stop supermarket mechanism, to meet his varied needs. It frequently becomes simpler to arrange long-term care in a nursing home than in the community. Nursing homes therefore admit patients who lack the ability to live independently or to piece together, from an unorganized and fragmented home health-care system, a solution to their needs. Thus, even for patients who do not require institutionalization, the nursing home may represent the best solution for the individual with chronic conditions. Moreover, it frequently is, or appears to be, the only solution. Once the patient is institutionalized, there is a failure to implement an effective discharge-planning program. This results from a number of interrelated factors: government financial benefits are greater for nursing-home care than for home health care; nursing-home services are not rehabilitative, but aimed at maintaining the patient in the institution; institutionalization is not viewed as part of a continuum of care, but as the end of care; and care, including pre-admission assessment, is based on a medical model which ignores alternative long-term care possibilities.

Obstacles to Discharge Planning

Under the present system of Medicaid supplemented by Medicare, the government covers most medical expenses incurred by an elderly indigent person. If the patient lives at home, government payments meet the greatest part of the cost of doctors, nurses, drugs, and certain other medical services. If the patient is placed in a nursing home, Medicaid covers not only all of these expenses but also the cost of lodging, meals, and custodial care normally borne by the patient or his family. This creates a powerful incentive to keep an aged or infirm person in an institution even though better care might be available elsewhere. This situation is compounded by the overwhelming percentage of patients who give up their homes or apartments upon admission to a nursing home. Those on Medicaid no longer possess the financial ability to move from a nursing home to a new apartment because this requires a substantial financial outlay. As Amitai Etzioni has noted, patients become "de facto prisoners of these institutions and of the state since they no longer have . . . the option of returning to the community, even if their health permits it."

Moreover, the Medicare program, which provides little nursing-home coverage, does not provide comprehensive home health-care benefits. Medicare concentrates on skilled services for the acutely ill, rather than on health related or basic services for the chronically disabled. Personal care services are not covered. Thus, the limited home health care available under Medicare and the payment of all nursing-home costs for eligible patients through Medicaid create a powerful incentive for institutionalization. Once a person is institutionalized, the system of limited home health-care benefits plus the patient's poverty work to prevent his return to the community.

Many nursing-home patients require specialized rehabilitative services to restore them to their highest physical, psychological, and social functioning and thus bring them to a level of maximum independence. These services should enable them to function effectively within their limitations, prevent deformities, and retard deterioration. A wide variety of services can be provided to meet these goals. They include testing, motivating, and keeping patients physically, mentally, and socially active, as well as improving such functions as toileting, walking, and the use of prosthetic devices.

Three of the principal rehabilitative services for which some data are available are physical, occupational, and speech therapy. According to a national HEW study—based on a review of patients' diagnoses, observed functional status, medical records, and discussion with staff, patients, and others—relatively few patients in skilled nursing facilities receive such services (many respondents in a survey of California's facilities suggested that they "did not have the professional staff to carry out active rehabilitation efforts"). The HEW study demonstrates that, in relation to need, only 11 percent of those requiring occupational and speech therapy and 31 percent of those requiring physical therapy actually receive it. Viewed from another perspective, 89 percent of those requiring occupational and speech therapy and close to 69 percent of those requiring physical therapy were in skilled nursing facilities where they did not receive these services. The HEW study also shows that few of those receiving physical therapy had written plans which were coordinated with rehabilitation programs and that accurate baseline data with which to judge progress is nonexistent.

Where rehabilitative services are available, they are frequently little more than efforts to comply with government regulations aimed at enabling the patient to function in the institution, not in the community. One witness before a congressional committee observed that while the New York State Hospital Code requires nursing homes to provide such services as occupational therapy, this frequently consists of nothing more than "a weekly visit by the occupational therapist, with little or no follow-up between visits." Further indications of this lack of interest are the New York State Moreland Act Commission's making only passing reference to this subject and Ronald Toseland's conclusion, in "Rehabilitation and Discharge: The Nursing Home Dilemma," that the process of rehabilitation in nursing homes is not focused. Even if a patient is potentially capable of discharge, the unavailability of effective rehabilitative services, which could facilitate return to the community, will lead to continued institutionalization. Without such programs aimed at restoring patients to their maximum potential, it is easy to understand why so few are discharged.

The placement of a patient in a nursing home is not viewed as part of a continuum of care which allows for, and encourages, movement back into less restrictive environments. Rather, it is viewed as an individual's final residence or movement into a more restrictive setting. His freedom of choice and right to service in the least restrictive setting are virtually ignored. This is not surprising, given the fact that perhaps as many as fifty percent of nursing-home patients are admitted from hospitals following acute episodes of a chronic condition. Nevertheless, this view makes it virtually impossible for any effective discharge planning to take place. Almost by definition, a patient can only be discharged by death or transfer to a hospital. The fact that so few patients return to the community reinforces this view and makes it a self-fulfilling prophecy.

Further reinforcement of the view of the facility as the last residence arises from the patient's inability to maintain a domicile in the community. This, plus the Medicaid poverty requirement, makes it difficult to find an acceptable community residence. Moreover, Title III of the Older Americans Act and Title XX of the Social Security Act have not yet achieved what the Federal Council on the Aging termed a "focus on long-term care which might make such services a major element in" its delivery.

According to the General Accounting Office (GAO), it is important to prepare an assessment which "identifies the chronically impaired elderly's long-term care needs, and to match those needs to the most appropriate level of services." Such assessment must include an evaluation of the individual's potential to perform activities of daily living, his family preferences and life-styles, his financial status and psychosocial factors. The study goes on to note that what usually occurs is a medical examination which "often cannot distinguish the impaired elderly who require nursing home placement from those who have the potential to remain in the community."

Nursing-home care is based on a medical model which is delivered in a scaled-down hospital. This is often the case in spite of the fact that nursing homes contain patients whose problems are chronic rather than acute, long-term rather than transient. Moreover, nursing homes lack the hospital manpower and technical machinery; their business is treatment, not diagnosis. Nevertheless, it is the medical model with its emphasis, according to Robert and Rosalie Kane, on "staffing standards, care plans and audits of results" which prevails.

Quality care is jeopardized when the whole person is not considered. More significant for our purpose is that concentration on medical needs virtually ignores the possibility for effective discharge planning and precludes a return to the community. This is especially poignant since patients are often placed in long-term care facilities not because of medical problems but because alternative arrangements could not be worked out. Once institutionalized, the possibility of alternative arrangements that consider the patient's total needs are ignored and medical needs receive the most attention. Hence, it is precisely those factors which often precipitate institutionalization which receive the least attention.

Potentials for Discharge Planning

Many more nursing-home patients could be discharged to live in the community, in part because many patients are placed in institutions who do not belong there in the first place. One government analysis of studies concerned with appropriate placement of nursing-home patients concluded that two-fifths of residents of Intermediate Care Facilities (ICF) were receiving more care than their conditions warranted. Another analysis stated that up to one-fifth of the institutionalized could remain in the community if they received adequate services. As the GAO observed, "assessment mechanisms have not enabled Medicaid adequately to control avoidable institutionalization."

The failure to consider, and the limited nature of, community-based alternatives results in a nursing-home population which is similar to the population resident in the community. This has been documented in a number of studies. One author notes that individuals with the same characteristics as nursing-home patients continue to reside in the community. Another concludes that both nursing homes and community populations contained people whose impairments ranged from moderate to total. A third suggests that the medical conditions of elderly nursing-home patients are shared by many of the elderly in the community. Another estimates that with adequate community services, one-fifth of nursing-home patients could get by in the community.

The unnecessary institutionalization of people able to function in the community, and their retention in these institutions, ignores the many familiar reasons for their remaining in their own residences. These include their preference for doing so, avoiding the institutionalization syndrome, and, in some cases, financial savings. Older people, when confronted with the need for institutional versus home-based care, usually choose the latter. They do so to preserve their independence, dignity, and identity and because institutionalization is often viewed as a prelude to death.

People who are kept in institutions in spite of the fact that they could function in the community are deprived of an opportunity to obtain care in a setting which offers maximum reliance on individual potential and resources. They lack privacy and are insulated from the general society. Months of unnecessary institutionalization will frequently lead to the loss of the mental and physical will to handle one's own affairs. For some patients, the unnecessary reliance on others to care for them, unless caught in time, will lead to their premature dependence.

The unnecessary retention of some patients in nursing homes also leads to a waste of public funds. We are not discussing patients who will require twenty-four hours a day of paid supervision in the community. For them, home-based programs of care would probably not produce financial savings. However, for patients requiring more moderate attention—i.e., those for whom discharge is most likely—there would be financial savings. The potential savings are of two types. The first are those produced by avoiding the high cost of institutional care. According to the survey by the GAO, "in terms of public dollars, the cost of home-based long-term care is less than or comparable to the cost of the equivalent level of nursing home care." Another savings derives from the fact that hospitalized patients are often required to undergo long waiting periods of expensive hospital care before a nursing-home bed is available. By discharging increased numbers of patients from nursing homes, this waiting period would decrease and produce shorter stays and concomitant savings in public funds.

To those who are uncomfortable with increasing the discharge of patients to the community because of the fear of an increase in mortality, we would point out that the results of numerous studies on this subject appear to be contradictory. Relocated patients have been found to have mortality rates higher than, lower than, and the same as those who are not moved. Moreover, it is important to understand that we are not talking about a move from one institution to another, but from an institution back to the community. Such relocation is not proposed where there is a lack of community programs, including both formal and informal supports, to follow up with and serve the patients.

In numerous cases, because of massive, unalterable physical and psychological infirmities, the nursing home is the final resting place before the hospital and/or grave. In other cases, however, elderly residents who can function independently outside the nursing home are denied exit from the institutional setting. But because nursing homes see placement as permanent, their services are skewed toward continued institutionalization. In addition, government and institutional policies often hinder the discharge of elderly persons from long-term care facilities. This situation is incompatible with the implementation of meaningful state and national discharge-planning requirements.

33

The Aged as Scapegoat

Robert H. Binstock

And the goat shall bear upon him all their iniquities.
                                        -Leviticus 16:22

Policy issues concerning older Americans have been framed for a long time by an underlying *ageism* (Neugarten,1970)—the attribution of the same characteristics, status, and just deserts to a heterogeneous group that has been artificially homogenized, packaged, labeled, and marketed as "the aged."

From the Townsend Movement of the 1930s until about 4 or 5 years ago, several categorical stereotypes concerning older persons were axioms of public rhetoric in America. These were compassionate stereotypes. Simply put, they were:

1. The aged are poor, frail, and perceived in negative terms; hence, they are in need of collective assistance and require some positive image-building.
2. The aged are relatively impotent as a political force, so their advocates should help to develop "senior power."
3. The aged are "the deserving poor" because their disadvantaged plight is forced upon them by mandatory retirement, the frailties and disabilities of old age, and the prejudices of a youth-oriented society. Consequently, with this rationale satisfying the Protestant ethic within American political ideology, there is no reason why a wealthy American society should not do more for them.

Since 1978, however, beginning in the middle of President Carter's administration, these ageist axioms have become virtually reversed. The immediate precipitating factor seems to have been the so-called crisis in Social Security, within the larger context of a depressed economy. We now

489

find—in the media, political speeches, public policy studies, and the writings of scholars—a new set of axioms:

1. The aged are relatively well-off—not poor but in great shape.
2. The aged are a potent political force because there are so many of them and they all vote in their self-interest; this "senior power" explains why more than one-quarter of the annual federal budget is expended on benefits to the aged.
3. Because of demographic changes, the aged are becoming more numerous and politically powerful and will be entitled to even more benefits and substantially larger proportions of the federal budget. They are already costing too much and in the future will pose an unsustainable burden on the American economy.

If you have not been observing these pronouncements in scholarly journals, you have certainly seen them in weekly news magazines, *The National Journal, The Washington Post, The New York Times, The Wall Street Journal,* and your own local newspapers. Perhaps the "new wisdom" was captured most succinctly and patronizingly by *Forbes* magazine: "The myth is that they're sunk in poverty. The reality is that they're living well. The trouble is there are too many of them—God bless 'em" (Flint, 1980, p. 51).

These new axioms regarding older persons have provided the foundation for the emergence of the aged as scapegoat in American society. That is, the aged are bearing the blame for a variety of economic and political frustrations.

In the context of a depressed economy, characterized by relatively high rates of unemployment and inflation, countless editorials, "Op-Ed" essays, and feature stories are telling us that the aged are better off than most other segments of American society. The classical trade-off metaphor of political economy—"guns vs. butter"—has now been reframed as "guns vs. canes" by an Office of Management and Budget fiscal analyst writing in a scholarly economics journal (Torrey, 1982), despite the fact that federal outlays for both guns and canes continue to increase. And we are constantly being told that the political power of the aged hamstrings our politicians from undertaking reforms. *Newsweek* (1982) has characterized Social Security as "the third rail" of American politics and reports to us that the word in Congress is, "Touch it and you're dead" (p.24).

Scapegoating the aged has become an acceptable practice throughout the spectrum of American political ideology. To be sure, politicians who aspire to election and reelection try to avoid saying anything in public that will offend older persons or any other reasonably large category of potential voters. But public figures on the political left and the right who are not subject to electoral politics are not so shy. The celebrated liberal economist Lester Thurow, author of the best-selling book *The Zero-Sum Society* (1980), argues vehemently and often against President Reagan's cuts in social welfare spending. But he makes two explicit exceptions: Social Security and Veterans Administration (VA) health care for the elderly. Indeed, he urges the President to cut Social Security and to completely eliminate VA health care expenditures on older persons (Thurow, 1981).

Conservative economist Martin Feldstein, newly-appointed Chairman of the Council of Economic Advisors, often punctuates his criticisms of Social Security with hyperbolic illustrations suggesting that the program provides far more than adequate or justified income to almost anyone who is elderly. He frequently writes up a hypothetical but very atypical case of a Social Security beneficiary, implies that the case is typical, and draws a picture that portrays all older persons as sitting around getting just about as much income from Social Security benefits in retirement as they earned while working (Feldstein & Feldstein, 1982a,b).

By focusing on the emergence of the aged as scapegoat I do not intend to suggest that the aged, in the aggregate, are suffering more than other broad constituencies in American society—at least, not at present. In some ways the aged are suffering less than others. For example, because of the automatic cost-of-living adjustments in Old-Age, Survivors, Disability, and Health Insurance (OASDHI) benefits, those older persons whose money income is largely comprised of Social Security checks have been less adversely affected by inflation than other Americans.

Nonetheless, this scapegoating does have important consequences for American society in the following respects. First, it is diverting our attention from a variety of deficiencies in political leadership and public policy. Second, it is engendering intergenerational conflict which may ultimately become rather serious in its implications. Third, it is diverting our attention from longstanding issues of reform involving policies that provide benefits to older persons.

I will consider these consequences in some detail, as well as the challenges involved in attempting to avert them. But, before doing so, it is important to consider whether the axioms which blame the aged are justified and how they arose. Examining them and their origins will help us to understand their possible consequences and how they might be dealt with.

Examining the Axioms

The new axioms that have facilitated the emergence of the aged as scapegoat are classic examples of "tabloid thinking," one of the major mechanisms that Gordon Allport has identified in the process of scapegoating. Each axiom includes some elements of truth, but each is an oversimplification. As Allport (1959) notes in his description of tabloid thinking:

> Periods of social strain bring out vividly the helplessness every individual feels in the face of worldwide forces. He must seek to simplify the issues in order to make possible some understanding of this social chaos. . . .
>
> An issue seems nicely simplified if we blame a group or class of people rather than the complex course of soical and historical forces.(pp. 13-14)

In the scope of this presentation I can hardly even attempt to deal with all the complexities and social and historical forces that are simplified by the tabloid thinking represented in the new axioms about the aged. I will simply attempt to demonstrate some of the more important ways in which they distort reality.

Axiom 1: *The aged are well off; they have been lifted out of poverty.* A relatively small number of aged are very well off; many are moderately comfortable; many are extraordinarily poor. How poor is extraordinarily poor?

As we know, many approaches are used to assess the income adequacy of older persons, and each approach can involve a variety of specific measures. One approach is to use absolute standards such as the "poverty line," the "near poor line," or the hypothetical budgets for an elderly couple that are constructed by the Bureau of Labor Statistics (BLS). Another approach is to compare the income status of older persons to that of the population in general, using medians or averages. Or one can measure income adequacy by employing various replacement ratios which are constructed on assumptions regarding what a retiree needs as income in order to maintain the same standard of living that he or she had in the years just before retirement. Each of these approaches, and even the specific measures used to implement them, can yield a result that is substantially different from the others.

Consider some of the wide discrepancies in reports on income adequacy that have been produced through the use of absolute measures. In 1977, for example, the official poverty line indices used by the federal government led to a determination that 14% of persons age 65 and older were in poverty even after they had received cash transfers from government programs (Brotman, 1978). A different analysis for 1977, undertaken by the Congressional Budget Office (CBO), reduced the proportion of elderly poor to 6% by taking into account the value of non-cash or in-kind government benefits which older persons received (Congressional Budget Office, 1977).

Still another estimate of poverty among the elderly in 1976, undertaken by Molly Orshansky (the original designer of the poverty line indices), yielded an estimate that 36% of older Americans "have too little income of their own to live by themselves" (U.S. House of Representatives, 1978, p.203). Each of these widely divergent estimates was technically correct, and the discrepancies among them can be reconciled with sufficient background interpretation. But any one of them could be substantially misleading if used irresponsibly and out of context.

Perhaps the best way to gain an understanding of the economic status of older Americans is to consider a specific budget. Let us examine for a moment an example of a "poverty line budget"—a budget that is constructed on the assumption that it is adequate for sustaining a "temporary emergency diet." In 1981, the poverty line (or "threshold") for an elderly couple was $5,498; if the couple had this much income they were not classified as "in poverty" (U.S. Bureau of the Census, 1982). According to the budgetary assumptions used in constructing the poverty line, this couple would have $153 per month for shelter (either for rent or for mortgage, property tax, and home maintenance costs), and $17.62 a week, per person, for food. The remaining $76 a month, per person, would be available for clothing, transportation, utilities, taxes, personal and property insurance, recreation, and medical and dental care. The average expenditures for medical and dental care are clearly assumed to be minimal. Yet, in the same year, out-of-pocket medical and dental expenses alone averaged $4 more than $76 a month for each elderly person (U.S. Senate, 1982, pp.295-301). So even with extensive Medicare and Medicaid coverage, which accounts for 98% of the in-kind benefits attributed to older persons (Borzilleri, 1980), many couples that had made it up to the poverty line, or had even exceeded it, would have had little or no money left for clothing, transportation, utilities, and all the other items after paying their out-of-pocket health care expenses. In short, receiving in-kind benefits from the government may change the category in which one is officially classified by CBO economists, but it does not necessarily lift one out of poverty in a functional sense.

This example should provide some perspective on the exceedingly harsh statistical measure of income adequacy that is imposed by the poverty line. We have just examined the budget of a couple that has made it up to the poverty line and has the additional benefits of government-subsidized health insurance. Over 4 million older persons are below this line, and several million more are clustered just above it. With this perspective in mind, we can better interpret the current axiom of public rhetoric which glibly states that the aged are now relatively well off.

Some will argue that this portrayal of low-income older persons ignores two important sources of income that are not included in poverty line statistics or in analyses of in-kind transfers through government programs. What about intra-family transfers, the income that older persons may receive from their children and other kin? And what about the income that older persons could obtain from their assets such as home equity? After all, a great many older Americans own their own homes and have fully paid off their mortgages.

To date, very little is known about the impact of intra-family transfers. One study found that they altered the well-being of about 28% of aged families (Moon, 1977). But relatively large transfers flow *both* ways, with slightly more aged families receiving assistance than giving assistance to younger children. The net result is unclear from data currently available.

The equity that many older persons have in their homes represents a potential source of additional money for them. But converting this asset into a liquid stream of income is not as simple as it would seem (Scholen & Chen, 1980). Substantial changes would be needed in financial and marketing practices, and in statutory law, in order to unlock home equity; and, even if such changes are advisable, it will take many years to bring them about in a responsible fashion. Most importantly, under the best of circumstances, unlocking home equity would not generate a significant stream of income for poor and marginally poor persons.

In summary, there is little doubt that definitions and statistics can be generated and interpreted in a fashion that makes it possible to declare that poverty among the aged has been virtually eliminated or that, as Thurow has expressed it, we are making "the elderly richer while the average tax-paying worker is becoming poorer" (Thurow, 1981, p.56). At the same time, it is also clear that a substantial proportion of older Americans, at least a third, is functioning within a budget that none of us would like to rely upon.

Axiom 2: *The aged are a potent, self-interested political force.* The aged do constitute a large block of participating voters. They comprise from 15 to 16% of those who vote in national elections. But older persons do not vote in a monolithic bloc, any more than middle-aged persons or younger persons do. And while aging-based organizations—like other interest groups—can play a role in framing or reacting to the agenda of public policy, they have not demonstrated a capacity to swing the votes of older persons. Consider the 1980 presidential campaign in which the leaders of a number of major aging-based organizations endorsed Jimmy Carter. The *New York Times/CBS News* "exit poll" during the 1980 presidential election reported that 54% of voters 60 years of age and older voted for President Reagan; among voters 30 to 44 years old, 54% voted for President

Reagan; and among voters in the middle, 45 to 59 years old, 55% voted for the President (*New York Times*, 1980). An exit poll during the recent November, 1982 Congressional elections showed once more, despite the campaign emphasis on Social Security, an enormous divergence in voting behavior within age groups but hardly any difference between age groups (*New York Times*, 1982).

Although some empirical data have been generated to suggest that the votes of older persons may cohere somewhat in the context of a referendum (Douglass et al., 1974), when a single issue is at stake, no data have been generated to show similar cohering tendencies in the context of candidate elections, let alone a monolithic or even decisive bloc of older voters (Hudson & Strate, in press).

Candidates, not issues, run for office. In the context of choosing between candidates, a voter's response to any one issue is part of an overall response to a variety of issues in a campaign and to many other campaign stimuli that have little to do with issues at all. Moreover, within a heterogeneous group such as older Americans, responses to any single issue are likely to vary substantially. Human beings do not suddenly become homogenized with respect to their political behavior when they reach a particular birthday (Hudson & Binstock, 1976).

But don't politicians behave as if older persons vote as a bloc because of issues? Aren't they terrorized by so-called "senior power"? The answer is not so clear (Reimer & Binstock, 1978). It cetainly is evident that no politician wants to offend the aged if he or she can avoid doing so. On the other hand, the Omnibus Reconciliation Act of 1981 legislated nine provisions narrowing benefits and eligibility under OASDHI, of which at least five can be interpreted as directly affecting Old Age benefits (Board of Trustees, 1982). Or consider that Congress enacted automatic cost of living adjustments for Social Security benefits in 1972. The introduction and passage of that legislation confounded longstanding conventional wisdom regarding the stimulus-response mechanisms of the politics of aging and of other broad constituency groups. The conventional wisdom had it that Congress was very well-served politically by enacting ad hoc Social Security benefit increases every few years, thereby receiving periodic fresh credits from constituents which were translated into subsequent rewards through election returns. Then why enact an automatic mechanism that evokes no recurring credits and electoral rewards?

Innumerable examples (e.g., Derthick, 1979; Heclo, 1974; Marmor, 1970) can be cited to demonstrate that senior power does not affect legislative and administrative decisions in a fashion that is in accordance with conventional wisdom. Without elaborating upon this topic any further in the context of this discussion, let me say that the politics of aging are much more subtle and complex than conventionally perceived. I will simply state, in summary, that the axiom of public rhetoric regarding the potency of senior power is unsophisticated and inaccurate.

Axiom 3: *Demographic changes mean that the aged will pose an unsustainable burden on the American economy.* In 1978, at the same time that the stereotype of poverty among the aged was being transformed, journalists, scholars, and public officials began to recognize the economic implications of an aging population. Attention was directed to the "graying of the budget" (Hudson, 1978)—the demographic age changes and public program benefit structures which have led to a situation in which the federal government currently expends more on aging than on national defense. Moreover, on the basis of reliable predictions of increases in the number of older Americans and assumed continuity in present program benefit structures, projections were made that the 27% of the federal budget expended on the aging in 1982 (U.S. Senate, 1982) will reach 40% early in the next century (Califano, 1978) and 63% by the year 2025 (U.S. Senate, 1980). On the basis of such dramatic projections, some journalists began to suggest that American society could not afford to maintain collective public efforts to sustain the economic burden of an aging population (Samuelson, 1978).

Numbers that express the percentage of federal expenditures devoted to a single function such as "benefits to the aged" or "defense" may be important political symbols. But they do not necessarily represent unsustainable economic burdens. The pertinent question to be addressed is: Can the American *economy* afford to continue, well into the next century, the current policies through which it provides benefits to the elderly? Or, put another way: What proportion of the gross national product (GNP) will be required to sustain public benefits to the aged at various points in the future, and how do those proportions compare with the current proportion of GNP spent on the aged?

A recent analysis by economists Robert Clark and John Menefee (1981) sheds some interesting light on this issue. They have projected to the year 2025 the proportion of GNP required to maintain current benefits per older person in real dollar terms, using alternative assumptions.

One projection rests on the assumption that inflation adjustments in the level of benefits per person will be tied to the consumer price index (CPI). Using this assumption they find that the proportion of GNP needed to finance benefits to the aged in the years ahead is smaller than at present. Under this scenario it would seem that the costs of an aging population will not be at all difficult to sustain.

But an alternative projection, based on the current rate of inflation for health care costs, yields a substantially different picture. In recent years, health care costs have been inflating at nearly double the rate of the CPI. When Clark and Menefee undertook a projection which used the true contemporary rate of inflation in health care costs rather than a rate tied to the CPI, they found a consistent trend of increase in the proportion of GNP required to sustain present per person levels of federal benefits to the aged. The contemporary rate of 5.3% of GNP expended on benefits to older persons rises steadily to 10.15%, or just about doubles by the year 2025.

Judging from this study, the challenge of sustaining the costs of an aging population will lie in our willingness and ability to confront and control the causes of runaway health care costs. The problem is not, as many would have us believe, one of sustaining Social Security and other cash income transfers to older Americans.

This conclusion is buttressed by another analysis which was undertaken by the Technical Committee for the 1981 White House Conference on Aging which addressed *Economic Policy in an Aging Society*. It examined the probable aggregate economic effects of an *expanded* public income transfer program that would be used as a direct measure for alleviating income adequacy problems of the elderly through the year 2025. The Committee's analysis led to the finding that such a program of increased income transfer and taxation "would not have a significant effect on the overall economy" (Technical Committee, 1981, p. 29).

No definitive judgments can be made on the basis of either this analysis or the one conducted by Clark and Menefee. They are among the first in what will undoubtedly be a spate of serious technical studies examining the implications of an aging population for the American economy. But they do provide an early indication that the axiom concerning the unsustainable costs of an aging population is off target. What seems to be unsustainable are the spiraling costs of health care. In contrast to Old Age Insurance, the costs of health care are not determined by specifically legislated benefit and cost-of-living formulas. Rather, they are largely determined by the providers of health services, equipment, and facilities. The most critical economic implications of an aging population appear to lie in our approaches to the costs and financing mechanisms of health care.

How Did Scapegoating Arise?

I have tried to suggest in this brief discussion that the current stereotypes concerning older persons are partially unwarranted and are generated by applying simplistic assumptions and aggregate statistics to a grouping called "the aged" in order to gloss over complexities. If one chooses to compare changes in the median income of all older persons with changes in the income of other groupings, one can assert that the aged are relatively well off. If one wishes to ignore all evidence to the contrary, one can assume that the votes of older persons are determined by issues, particularly one issue above all others, that they will respond to that one issue self-interestedly, and that they will all perceive their self-interests to be the same. If one pretends that outlays for Medicare and Medicaid are determined in the same fashion as Old Age Insurance benefits, one can conclude that the aged—instead of health care costs—constitute an unsustainable burden for the American economy. This kind of tabloid thinking, which underlies the new axioms of public rhetoric, has facilitated the emergence of the aged as scapegoat.

How did this kind of thinking arise? The immediate precipitating factor seems to have been the so-called crisis in the financing of Social Security in the context of a depressed economy. But, in my view, the roots of scapegoating the aged can be traced back to the compassionate stereotypes concerning older persons that have permeated public rhetoric from the Townsend Movement until the late 1970s. This *compassionate ageism,* which Richard Kalish (1979) described several years ago under a different label, set the stage for tabloid thinking about older persons by obscuring the individual and subgroup differences among them. For four decades the friends of the elderly told us that they were poor, frail, socially dependent, objects of discrimination, and above all deserving—or, in the jargon of economists, victims of market failure, not individual failure.

The message took hold. American society accepted the notion that all older persons are essentially the same. The American polity took the next logical steps. It adopted and financed major age-categorical benefit programs and tax and price subsidies for which eligibility is not determined by need. Through Social Security, Medicare, the Older Americans Act, and a variety of other measures, older persons were exempted from the Calvinist screenings which are applied to other Americans in order to determine whether they are worthy of public assistance. Moreover, virtually every issue or problem affecting some older persons that could be identified by the friends of the aged and a growing number of aging-based membership organizations became a governmental responsibility—nutritional, supportive, and leisure services; housing; home repair; energy assistance; transportation; help in getting jobs; protection against being fired from jobs; special mental health programs; a separate National Institute of Health; and on, and on, and on (Estes, 1979). In short, by the late 1970s, if not earlier, American society had learned the catechism of ageism very well and had expressed it through a variety of ageist-based governmental programs and objectives.

Against this backdrop it is not difficult to understand how the aged, as a group, might become a scapegoat in an era of economic instability. When the precarious balance between Social Security financing and projected benefit obligations was identified in the late 1970s, it provided a simple tabloid symbol for a broad range of economic anxieties. The particular financing mechanism of Social Security, with its earmarked tax to finance defined benefits, framed a crisis in terms of two broad options: increase revenues or reduce outlays. These options subliminally reinforced the fashionable but threatening counter-Keynesian notion that all of us—individuals, families, groups, and nations—must live within our means. It should not surprise us that this primitive symbol would evoke a scapegoating of the aged. The roots of scapegoating had been developed through decades of compassionate ageism. It was to be expected that a shrinking of resources would be accompanied by a shrinking of compassion (Binstock, 1974, 1981). But the ageism that was so laboriously constructed remains intact, in both attitudes and program structures.

The Consequences of Scapegoating

Regardless of what gave rise to scapegoating of the aged or the extent to which it may be unwarranted, it does have potentially grave consequences for American society and the persons who inhabit it—young, middle aged, and old.

At the most general level scapegoating the aged diverts our attention from a host of deficiencies in political leadership and public policy, including our incapacity to manage the economy more effectively. If the aged are "busting the budget" and if their political power prevents us from cutting back their benefits, then our hands are tied and we cannot deal with macroeconomic problems. Unemployment, a poor balance of trade, the erosion of the American steel and auto industries, bankruptcies, and other issues seem to pale in the shadow of the Social Security crisis. Ironically, the shortfall in funds to finance Social Security benefits is one of the few current problems for which dozens of practicable and reliable solutions have been generated. While it is tempting to enumerate a number of other broad issues from which our attention is being diverted (Minkler, 1983), a higher priority in this forum is issues affecting age relations and older persons within American society.

One clear consequence of the emergence of the aged as scapegoat is that intergenerational conflict is being engendered. As social welfare program cutbacks began in 1981, the children's lobby immediately expressed concern that it would be pitted against the "gray lobby" in a battle to gobble up the remaining pieces of a shrinking pie. A former Assistant Secretary of Health and Human Services under President Carter, fearing that the gray lobby would win this pitched battle, proposed that parents with children under the voting age of 18 be enfranchised with an extra vote for each of their dependent children (Carballo, 1981). Someone may soon revive Douglas Stewart's (1970) proposal, made about a dozen years ago, that all persons be disfranchised ". . . at retirement or age 70, whichever is earlier"—a proposal made because the author was disgusted by his perception that the aged were responsible for the election of Ronald Reagan as governor of California.

Conflict is also being engendered between the middle aged and the old through discussions of changing dependency ratios—that is, the number of active workers it takes to support a dependent retiree. (Dependent children are not prominently featured in these discussions.) Here again we can see the role in framing the discussions which is played by the singular payroll tax financing mechanism of the Social Security system. Few people are discussing how many workers it takes to finance an aircraft carrier, a tobacco subsidy, a renal dialysis unit, or an investment tax credit. By pitting generations against each other, scapegoating the aged once again diverts our attention from other issues of significance to American society.

More immediately, scapegoating the aged diverts our attention from longstanding issues involving the reform of policies toward older persons, themselves. As Elizabeth Kutza (1981) and Gary Nelson (1982) have argued, the very structures of programs providing benefits to the aged help to ensure that life cycle inequalities of status will be perpetuated into and throughout old age. Yet, in a climate in which the aged are perceived as relatively well off and busting the budget, issues of adequacy and equity have virtually disappeared from our public agenda. To the extent that these issues are considered, attention is almost exclusively focused on private market mechanisms—savings, private pensions, and putting older persons back to work—which have proven inadequate through a long history of recurring cycles of unemployment and inflation. At a time when none of us can confidently foresee when and how our current economic instability will end, the solutions offered are private market mechanisms that can only function adequately in the context of a long period of optimum economic stability.

The crisis in Social Security has provided a rare political opportunity for substantially reforming the public mechanisms of support for older persons, which we are able to control far better than market mechanisms. Yet, because of the emergence of the aged as scapegoat, the moment is not being seized. The opportunity costs are enormous in view of the current problems of equity, financing mechanisms, and particularly the depth of the income adequacy problem which I emphasized in my earlier discussion of a poverty threshold budget.

What to Do about It

If one wishes to combat these and other consequences of scapegoating the aged—to avert intergenerational conflict; to deal with grave and long-standing issues of adequacy, equity, and financing; and to get more attention refocused on other issues of importance in American society—what challenges lie ahead? What responses are needed and from whom will they come?

Ultimately one would need to have public policy framed within a non-ageist political context in which the heterogeneity of older persons is recognized. In such a context some older persons—perhaps most older persons—would receive benefits from government, but on the basis of straightforward value premises regarding collective responsibility toward human beings within our society. Policies would not necessarily be wholly age irrelevant, but neither would age serve as a simple proxy for rationales as to why collective assistance is being provided (Neugarten, 1981). Nor would it be assumed that every issue or problem affecting some older persons should be taken on as a government responsibility.

In such a context one would be able to generate questions that would place fundamental issues of value conflict and resource allocation on our public policy agenda and have them resolved through the political process. For instance, what is our rationale for providing public income support to older persons? Do we wish to provide cash income transfers like Social Security to persons on the basis of their work histories? Or do we wish to provide income to them on the basis of their existential needs so that they can survive with some modicum of human dignity?

If our answer to the last question is affirmative, we will finally be able to face up to the issue of income adequacy and how much it would cost to provide it. If our answer is affirmative to the work history rationale, we will be equipped to face up to issues of equity by confronting them where they arise: in the labor market and in the career patterns of men and women of all races and ethnic groups. In either case, we could also be freed from the myth that the regressive payroll taxes used to finance Social Security are some form of "contributions," "insurance premiums," or "compulsory savings" which individuals have paid into the system. Many Americans no longer believe in the myth today, anyway. It would be easy enough to eliminate altogether this particular financing mechanism and along with it the intergenerational conflict that it engenders.

In a non-ageist context we can ask ourselves why we should be providing tax-free in-kind transfers and tax and price subsidies to persons on the basis of their age, without regard to financial need. We might agree that there are some good reasons, for example, in the case of Medicare, but not in the case of tax subsidies. We will not find out how we feel, however, unless we face these issues squarely. The knee-jerk cliché that "a means test makes for a mean program" is a cute slogan, but it forestalls rather than facilitates the resolution of grave problems. Perhaps we are a mean society that is only willing or able to pay for mean programs. But let us not pretend that we are a generous society while we are capping Medicare, increasing so-called co-insurance, and allowing more and more health care providers to refuse assignment of Medicare patients.

To whom can we look for leadership in bringing about a non-ageist political context for the consideration of such issues and for placing such issues forcefully on our societal agenda? Those of us who are scholars would like to assume that intellectuals can be the source of such leadership. But James Q. Wilson (1981) has sharply questioned this assumption, suggesting that intellectuals only seem influential if they happen to be articulating an idea at a time when society is ready for that idea to become fashionable. Whether or not he is right, it is surely the case that our intellectuals are currently of little immediate help on this matter. As I have illustrated briefly at the outset, those who can command mass media platforms are conforming in the scapegoating of the aging. A handful of intellectuals such as Bernice Neugarten (1979) have framed non-ageist constructs for helping us to understand age relations and age status in our society and have raised fundamental policy issues of value conflict and resource allocation. But it usually takes substantial time for radically different constructs to percolate through the various strata of society in order to have an impact (Cobb & Elder, 1975).

A seemingly more obvious place to look for leadership is the aging-based organizations, particularly the mass membership organizations. Because of the symbolic legitimacy that American interest-group liberalism (Lowi, 1969) confers upon them as representatives of a mass constituency, they have ready access to national media platforms and to public officials—to members of Congress and their staffs, to career bureaucrats, to agency and department heads, and occasionally to the White House (Binstock, 1974; Pratt, 1976). Consequently they can put forth their own proposals or work to block those of others.

Yet, judging from the response of aging-based membership organizations to the Social Security crisis and from their behavior for years before that, we can hardly look to them for leadership in framing a non-ageist context in which fundamental value issues can be put forth for consideration in isolation from the trappings of existing program structures. They have responded to the current agenda of policy issues in an ageist fashion that has reinforced the new axioms of public rhetoric that provide the foundation for scapegoating the aged. They have insisted that all programs benefiting the aged and those who make their living off of them are sacred, without regard to their distributional effects. They have fought to "Save Our Social Security" without paying much if any attention to those who are not saved by Social Security or any other program. They have threatened to exercise senior power and puffed up its image through elaborate charades at pseudo-events like the 1981 White House Conference on Aging.

One could hardly expect otherwise. As an analysis of these organizations noted some ten years ago (Binstock, 1972) the very bases, or incentive systems, on which these organizations exist dictate that they be ageist in their stance. They purport to represent or to be concerned about all older persons—the aged. To act otherwise—to emphasize differences within the constituency—would undermine their legitimacy.

It should be evident that at this point I am scapegoating aging-based organizations, including the Gerontological Society of America. I have argued that these organizations and other self-styled friends of the aged, by engaging in compassionate ageism for several decades, have planted some of the major roots which have nourished the emergence of the aged as scapegoat. I think that at least part of the blame for what is taking place today should rest with us, although there are clearly other factors at work as well.

The intention of this portion of my analysis is to have a positive consequence. Some of the aging-based organizations—including this one—are in a position to respond to the challenges of leadership by helping to frame a non-ageist context in which fundamental value issues can be posed concerning age relations and the nature and extent of collective responsibility in our society.

We can learn from looking around us at some of the other aging-based organizations. On the one hand, the mass membership organizations are unlikely to respond to the challenges of providing non-ageist based leadership; they would no longer represent the mass of the aged and would thereby lose their *raison d'être*. On the other hand, we can look at an organization like the Gray Panthers. It has a non-ageist philosophy, it is able to capture national media attention, and it has access to public officials. To be sure, when it moves from the arena of philosophy to the arena of action and policies on aging, it frequently undermines its goals by supporting ageist programs and threatening the retributions of senior power. But what I wish to emphasize is the philosophy of that organization. Its philosophy is focused on age relations in particular, and more generally on a sensitivity to the human condition in all its manifestations.

I see no inherent reason why our organization, which is presumably concerned with the phenomena of the aging process, and other organizations like it cannot refocus to be more self-consciously concerned with *age relations* rather than *the aged*. I am not suggesting that the Gerontological Society of America is an instrument for political action and social change or that it should become one. But I am suggesting that we have a responsibility and the capability to provide leadership in pointing up the heterogeneity of older persons, the issues of age relations in society, and the value conflicts involved in public policy issues.

Note

This essay was first presented at the 35th Annual Scientific Meeting of The Gerontological Society of America, Boston, Massachusetts, November 21, 1982. The author wishes to express appreciation to James H. Schulz for a constant flow of information and stimulating ideas and to Thomas D. Leavitt for critical reading and suggestions; they are not, of course, responsible for the content.

References

Allport, G.W. *ABC's of scapegoating*. Anti-Defamation League of B'nai B'rith, New York, 1959.

Binstock, R.H. 'Interest-group liberalism and the politics of aging' *Gerontologist,* 1972, *12*, 265-80.

_____. "Aging and the future of American politics." *Annals of the American Academy of Political and Social Science,* 1974, *415*, 199-212.

_____. "The aging as a political force: Images and resources." In A.J.J. Gilmore et al. (eds.), *Aging: A challenge to science and social policy,* vol. 2: *Medicine and social science.* Oxford University Press, London, 1981.

Board of Trustees, Federal Old-Age and Survivors Insurance and Disability Insurance Trust Funds. *1982 Annual Report.* U.S. Government Printing Office, Washington, D.C., 1982.

Borzilleri, T.C. "In-kind benefit programs and retirement income." *National Journal,* 1980, *12*, 1821-25.

Brotman, H.B. "The aging of America: A demographic profile." *National Journal,* 1978, *10*, 1625.

Califano, J.A., Jr. "U.S. policy for the aging: A commitment to ourselves." *National Journal,* 1978, *10*, 1576.

Carballo, M "Extra votes for parents?" *Boston Globe,* December 17, 1981, p. 35.

Clark, R.L. and Menefee, J.A. "Federal expenditures for the elderly: Past and future." *Gerontologist* 1981, *21*, 132-37.

Cobb, R.C. and Elder, C.D. *Participation in American politics: The dynamics of agenda building.* Johns Hopkins Press, Baltimore, Md., 1975.

Congressional Budget Office. "Poverty study of families under alternative definitions of income." Background paper no. 17, revised. U.S. Government Printing Office, Washington, D.C., 1977.

Derthick, M. *Policymaking for Social Security.* Brookings Institution, Washington, D.C., 1979.

Douglass, E. Cleveland, W., and Maddox, G. "Political attitudes, age, and aging: A cohort analysis of archival data." *Journal Gerontology,* 1974, *29,* 666-75.

Estes, C.L. *The aging enterprise.* Jossey-Bass, San Francisco, 1979.

Feldstein, M., and Feldstein, K. "It's time to do something about Social Security costs." *Boston Globe,* February 2, 1982a, p. 46.

———. "Social Security changes near." *Boston Globe,* March 30, 1982b, p. 46.

Flint, J. "The old folks." *Forbes,* February 18, 1980, pp. 51-56.

Heclo, H. *Modern and social politics in Britain and Sweden: From relief to income maintenance.* Yale University Press, New Haven, Conn., 1974.

Hudson, R.B. "The 'graying' of the federal budget and its consequences for old-age policy." *Gerontologist,* 1978, *18,* 428-40.

Hudson, R.B., and Binstock, R.H. "Political systems and aging." In R.H. Binstock and E. Shanas (eds.), *Handbook of aging and the social sciences.* Van Nostrand Reinhold, New York, 1976.

Hudson, R.B. and Strate, J. "Aging and political systems." In R. Binstock and E. Shanas (eds.), *Handbook of aging and the social sciences* (2nd ed.). Van Nostrand Reinhold, New York, in press.

Kalish, R.A. "The new ageism and the failure models: A polemic." *Gerontologist,* 1979, *19,* 398-407.

Kutza, E.A. *The benefits of old age.* University of Chicago Press, Chicago, 1981.

Lowi, T.J. *The end of liberalism.* W.W. Norton, New York, 1969.

Marmor, T.R. *The politics of medicare.* Routledge and Kegan Paul, London, 1970.

Minkler, M. "Blaming the aged victim: The politics of scapegoating in times of fiscal conservatism." *International Journal of Health Services,* 1983, *13,* 153-66.

Moon, M. *The measurement of economic welfare: Its application to the aged poor.* Academic Press, New York, 1977.

Nelson, G. "Social class and public policy for the elderly." *Social Service Review,* 1982, *56,* 85-107.

Neugarten, B.L. "The old and the young in modern societies." *American Behavioral Scientist,* 1970, *14,* 13-24.

———. "Policy for the 1980s: Age or need entitlement?" In National Journal Issues Book, *Aging: Agenda for the eighties.* The Government Research Corporation, Washington, D.C., 1979, pp. 48-52.

———. "Age distinctions and their social functions." *Chicago Kent Law Review,* 1981, *57,* 809-25.

New York Times/CBS News Poll. "How different groups voted for president." *New York Times,* November 9, 1980, p. 28.

———. "Party choices of voters, 1982 vs. 1978." *New York Times,* November 8, 1982, p. B11.

Newsweek. "The third rail of politics." May 24, 1982, p. 24.

Pratt, H.J. *The gray lobby.* University of Chicago Press, Chicago, 1976.

Reimer, Y., and Binstock, R.H. "Campaigning for 'the senior vote': A case study of Carter's 1976 campaign." *Gerontologist,* 1978, *18,* 517-24.

Samuelson, R.J. "Aging America: Who will shoulder the growing burden?" *National Journal,* 1978, *10,* 1712-17.

Scholen, K., and Chen, Y.P. (eds.), *Unlocking home equity for the elderly,* Ballinger, Cambridge, Mass., 1980.

Stewart, D.J. "Disfranchise the old: The lesson of California." *New Republic,* 1970, *163* (8-9), 20-22.

Technical Committee for an Age-Integrated Society: Implications for the Economy, 1981 White House Conference on Aging. *Economic policy in an aging society.* 1981 White House Conference on Aging, Washington, D.C., 1981.

Thurow, L.C. *The zero-sum society.* Basic Books, New York, 1980.

———. "Undamming the American economy." *New York Times Magazine,* May 3, 1981, pp. 38-60.

Torrey, B.B. "Guns vs. canes: The fiscal implications of an aging population." *American Economics Association Papers and Proceedings,* 1982, *72,* 309-13.

U.S. Bureau of the Census. "Money income and poverty status of families and persons in the United States, 1981." *Current population reports,* series P-60, no. 134, U.S. Government Printing Office, Washington, D.C., July 1982.

U.S. House of Representatives, Select Committee on Aging. *Poverty among America's aged.* U.S. Government Printing Office, Washington, D.C., 1978.

U.S. Senate, Special Committee on Aging. *Emerging options for work and retirement policy,* U.S. Government Printing Office, Washington, D.C., 1980.

———. *Developments in aging, 1981.* U.S. Government Printing Office, Washington, D.C., 1982.

Wilson, J.Q. "'Policy intellectuals' and public policy." *Public Interest,* 1981, *64,* 31-46.

34

The Trillion-Dollar Misunderstanding

John Myles

This spring, the Reagan administration proposed the first cuts in Social Security, cornerstone of the American New Deal. The administration justified the cuts on the grounds that the Social Security system is close to insolvency, another casualty of government profligacy. This rationale has been dutifully repeated by the press, with a remarkable lack of skeptical inquiry. As Associated Press began its May 13 dispatch, "The Reagan Administration unveiled its plan to save the nearly bankrupt Social Security system yesterday, proposing to slash benefits."

In reality, Social Security is not "nearly bankrupt" at all. By design, Social Security is a pay-as-you-go system, whose benefits are funded by payroll taxes. The level of benefits, like the level of contributions required to finance them, reflect simply a political choice. Moreover, any fair comparison makes clear that Social Security yields a far better return for workers and better protection against inflation for retirees than its private sector counterparts—pension plans and life insurance. And, as we shall see, the simplest remedy for reconciling Social Security to changing demography is to increase current taxes slightly and build up a surplus. This remedy is rejected on ideological grounds by those conservatives who profess concern for the system's soundness.

But the Reagan cuts are the culmination of conservative assaults on Social Security, spanning nearly a decade. The periodic declarations of a Social Security crisis have appeared regularly in prominent journals of commentary (*The Public Interest*), in learned volumes emanating from the think-tanks of the New Right (the American Enterprise Institute), the business press (*Forbes, Fortune, The Wall Street Journal*), and the popular news media (*New York Times, Newsweek*). What is remarkable about the attack is the extent to which its claims have penetrated American culture, both high and low. Perhaps because the left has found the conclusions congruent with their own discovery of the "crisis of the welfare state," or perhaps because of the arcane actuarial terms of the debate, there has been little in the way of critical response to these analyses.[1]

The typical critique portrays the Social Security system drifting toward bankruptcy, with the most serious crisis emerging when the baby boom generation of younger workers enters retirement after the year 2010. The result, according to supply side economist Arthur Laffer, is that Social Security "*will not only* not deliver its promises but will be *unable* to deliver its promises."[2] The press analysis of the recent Senate vote to reduce benefits was characteristic, in its unexamined acceptance of the claim that the system would soon "face insolvency," as the *Wall Street Journal* of May 12 put it, due to cost of living adjustments and the rising share of elderly pensioners in the population. Rather less restrained was *Forbes'* May 26, 1980, depiction of Social Security as the "monster that's eating our future."

A more cautious version of this theme among conservative economists unable to swallow the bankruptcy myth, is the view that for the current generation of workers, Social Security is a "bad buy." Thus Martin Feldstein, Harvard economist and president of the prestigious National Bureau of Economic Research, writes that over the next several decades the current generation's "investments" in Social Security will provide a much lower rate of return than would comparable investments in private pensions.

The not so implicit message is that Americans would be better off putting their trust in the market than in Uncle Sam. Paradoxically, however, the conservative critics insist that the first generations of Social Security recipients have actually enjoyed *windfall* profits from their meagre investments in the system (see, for example, *Fortune*, August 25, 1980). Indeed, the current generation of elders is said to be doing rather well, though they have managed to conceal their high living beneath a cloak of penury (see *Forbes*, February 18, 1980). This cannot last, say the critics, because of the changing ratio of retirees to workers.

Finally, if this is not enough, Social Security has also been blamed for the current low growth of the American economy. Here, Martin Feldstein contends Social Security is a cushion of pseudosavings, partly to blame for the low level of real private savings and investment which afflicts the American economy.[3] This is also said to be an obstacle to current and future efforts to "reindustrialize" America.

To understand the logic of these attacks it is necessary to review the history and operating procedures of the system. American Social Security was devised in the midst of the Great Depression not only to provide for the consumption needs of the elderly, but also as a mechanism that would draw older workers out of the labor market and thereby reduce unemployment.

American business had long considered older workers inefficient but was unable to create a private pension system to institutionalize wide scale retirement. Social Security addressed both problems. By the 1950s many categories of workers originally excluded were incorporated into the Social Security system and by the 1960s approximately 90 percent of the American labor force was covered.

For a variety of reasons, Social Security was designed on a "pay-as-you-go" basis. Rather than have individuals pay into a capital fund to generate interest and pay benefits, current expenditures (benefits) are paid out of current revenues (contributions). The decision not to fund Social Security had several political advantages. It enabled the system to become effective almost immediately (the first Social Security check was paid out in 1940), which was necessary in order to have the desired short term effects on the unemployment rate. Pay-as-you-go had the further advantage of preventing the build-up of huge capital funds in the program, which would have amounted to a significant transfer of economic power from the private sector to the state.

But what was once virtue is now vice. It is a mistake, so the argument goes, to consider Social Security as an insurance system in which each generation "pays its own way." Rather it is an intergenerational transfer system in which the working population supports the retired population. And because all age cohorts are not equal in size, some get less and some get more than what they have paid into the system. Demographic imbalances in the age pyramid mean that eventually the bubble must burst. When the baby boom generation retires the system will collapse, brought down in the Armageddon of what the demographer Kingsley Davis has referred to as an intergenerational "class struggle."[4] More immediately, as Feldstein claims, "pay-as-you-go" Social Security supposedly has become an endemic source of weakness in the American economy. Since pay-as-you-go fails to build up capital funds, aggregate savings are reduced and the new investment required to energize the American economy is not forthcoming.

While there is more myth than reality in such claims, myths may rest on very real concerns and may have very real consequences. Although President Reagan has not proposed to dismantle the Social Security system, only to narrow it, these assaults on the system clearly have had effect.

Is Social Security Going Broke?

It is not surprising that the neoconservative offensive should single out Social Security for special attack, since Social Security is the most important nonmarket mechanism for the allocation of income in the American economy. The fact that Social Security works efficiently, with minimal red tape and broad public support, is a continuing challenge to the supposed superiority of marketlike institutions. Indeed, the claim that Social Security is actuarily shaky is possible only by misapplying a market concept to this distinctly nonmarket program.

Especially in the popular press, however, the favored line of attack on Social Security is to declare it to be actuarily unsound. The term "actuarily unsound" means simply that projected expenditures exceed projected revenues to a degree that would be unacceptable in the marketplace. This in turn projects a failure to meet commitments to workers now contributing to the system. The figures involved are usually such as to defy comprehension, but a recent estimate puts the projected deficit in the neighborhood of a trillion dollars. The conclusion is presumably obvious. As *Forbes* put it last December, "Social Security—don't count on it."

It is doubtful that such arguments would be taken seriously in any country but the United States, where market analogies are widely and inappropriately used to analyze government practices. As Larry Smedley of the AFL-CIO points out, declaring the system to be "actuarily unsound" is simply bad economics based on a false analogy between a state system for allocating income and a private insurance scheme.[5] The "soundness" of the Social Security system depends on the state's ability to collect taxes, not on the actuarial criterion of the relationship between a firm's assets and its future commitments. Even Martin Feldstein observes that as *"long as the voters support the Social Security system it will be able to pay the benefits that it promises"* (emphasis in the original).[6]

This propensity to apply the language of the market to the outcome of a political process when discussing Social Security is in itself an interesting phenomenon. There is no comparable discourse, for example, about the "American Defense Fund" going broke by the turn of the century as a result of the billions or trillions of dollars in unfunded liabilities accumulated by long term American defense commitments. Defense expenditures involve real costs to the economy, and thus a discussion of the unfunded defense liability of the nation might indeed make more sense. In contrast Social Security expenditures are merely transfers, the economic costs of which are negligible.

The long run soundness of the Social Security system, then, rests on political not market criteria. And the critical question is how large an older population will the younger generations support and at what standard of living? At what point can we expect a taxpayers' revolt against the elderly, and the creation of a major political fault line between age strata? When placed in this context, the size of the pension obligation is quite irrelevant. What is relevant is the tax rate required to finance it.

In 1981, the combined employer-employee Social Security tax rate on covered earnings in the United States is approximately 13 percent and is scheduled to increase to 15.5 percent by 1990 under existing law.

To meet the presumed trillion dollar deficit, it would be sufficient to increase the tax rate by 1.5 percent now. This would generate a capital surplus, which would produce enough money to meet anticipated future claims without further increases in the tax rate.[7]

These are rather modest levels by current international standards. In 1978 the combined tax rate for social security was 24 percent in Italy, 20.3 percent in Sweden, and 26 percent in the Netherlands. In West Germany it was 18 percent. But the same conservative critics who are questioning the financial soundness of the system would strenuously resist this remedy, because it would increase the amount of national savings in the public sector. Thus, we can expect pay-as-you-go rates to gradually increase as the population ages. Under current legislation, tax rates are due to peak at 20.1 percent in the year 2035.[8]

What then of the capacity of the following generations to bear these tax rates? For many, the impending crisis in Social Security is an inevitable consequence of the demographic realities that are already on us. The baby boom generation is simply not having enough children to support it in its old age. As a result, the current generation is implicitly imposing an intolerable tax burden on its children and grandchildren, the taxpayers of tomorrow. As Nathan Keyfitz argues in *The Public Interest*, it is simply more difficult for a small number of children to take care of their parents than a large number.

These bleak projections of our demographic future, however, do not stand up to examination. First, the "burden" which the working age population must carry is determined not by the relative size of the elderly population but by the relative ratio of the *total* nonworking population, including the young. Declining fertility also means fewer young people for the economy to support, with the result that the total dependency ratio (number of nonworkers to workers) is projected to *decline* in the coming decades. Although public expenditures on the old are larger than public expenditures on the young, the *private* economy spends vast sums on the dependent young. Thus, the analysis of changing dependent-worker ratios must include both *public* and *private* expenditures on both *children* and the *retired*. In *The Economics of Aging*, James Schulz cites one German study that indicates the total cost of raising a child to age twenty is one-fourth to one-third higher than that of supporting someone who is over sixty for the remainder of his lifetime.

Secondly, a smaller cohort does not necessarily mean less work done or lower levels of production. Rather, labor force participation rates within the working age population are likely to increase (more women will work) and they will work more hours (more women will work full time). And, finally, other things being equal, individual productivity will tend to increase since the small cohorts which follow the baby boom generation will benefit from having more capital per capita with which to produce. Like only children they will benefit from not having to divide their inheritance. As the baby boom generation is well aware, they suffer from being under-capitalized—there are simply not enough good jobs to go around.

In contrast, the smaller cohorts of the future can expect to experience careers that begin earlier in the life cycle, more rapid progression up career ladders, and lower rates of unemployment. This means higher per capita lifetime incomes and thus greater capacity to absorb an increased tax burden. Other things do not always "remain equal," of course, and it may well be that the relative increase in the demand for labor from which a small cohort might reasonably expect to benefit will be offset by disproportionate destruction of jobs—the result of technological innovation and increased substitution of capital for labor. But this does not affect the total level of wealth produced for the "carrying capacity" of the working age population. Rather, it simply generates a political choice about the distribution of that wealth.

It is necessary to be precise about the point of the preceding arguments. There may well be crises in store for the American economy. But the aging of the American population will not be among the causes. Nor, unless the prophets of doom are successful in creating it, will American society be brought down by an intergenerational "class struggle" in this century or the next.

The most salient evidence on this point are the several Western European societies that are already "old" by demographic standards, but where the fabric of society has not been rent asunder by clashes in the streets between old and young or their economies brought to a standstill because of "excessive" pension expenditures. The elderly already constitute more than 16 percent of the populations of Austria, Sweden, and West Germany, a figure which is not far from the 18 percent at which the American elderly population is expected to peak in the next century. All three of these countries, moreover, have pension benefits that are considerably more generous than those currently provided or promised under Social Security. And all three are being financed—more generously—by populations whose standard of living is considerably lower than that which can be expected for the American population of the next century. Although a society which is aging requires economic and other institutional adjustments, the lurid images of embittered elders doing battle with their over-taxed offspring currently being painted by the soothsayers of the right hardly seem warranted in light of what is already known of such societies.

Instead, it represents a position of extreme individualism, which systematically underestimates the importance of family ties as a bond between generations.

Ironically, if there is to be a future economic crisis created by the graying of America it is more likely to result from the failure to develop national health insurance rather than from any crisis in Social Security. Countries with private medical care and fee-for-service, third-party payment, such as the United States, have experienced runaway inflation in medical prices in recent years and dramatic increases in the percentage of GNP devoted to health care.[9] In contrast, countries such as Canada, which have introduced national health insurance, have not only arrested this growth but actually brought health care expenditures down relative to GNP. Runaway prices in health care not surprisingly become critical in aging society. A recent projection of future government expenditures on the elderly in the United States finds that bringing medical prices down to the rate of inflation for all prices would reduce federal expenditures on the elderly from 10.15 percent to 8.3 percent of GNP by 2025.[10]

Is Social Security a Bad Buy?

A rather more modest line of attack is the charge that compared to plans available in the private pension market, Social Security is a bad buy. Thus, Martin Feldstein's attack informs us that the best real rate of return participants can expect on Social Security contributions in the future will be about 2 percent per year, the expected growth rate of real wages. Elsewhere, he concludes that those currently aged 24-34 can anticipate real net losses on their Social Security investment. This he compares to the real annual yield of approximately 5 percent which an investor might expect from a conservative portfolio in a private pension fund.[11] If such were the case, Social Security would clearly be an investment to avoid.

Estimating the implicit rate of return on current contributions to Social Security is, of course, a risky and uncertain exercise despite the certitude with which the results are reported in the popular media (see, for example, *Fortune*, August 25, 1980). Among other things, it requires making assumptions with respect to long term future trends in fertility, mortality, and marriage rates, wage and price changes, typical job histories and levels of taxation. Varying one's assumptions by as much as half a percentage point will make enormous differences in results when cumulated over the very long time spans in question. The best that can be said about such exercises is that they yield contradictory and inconclusive findings.[12] Thus Dean Leimer of the Social Security Administration projects typical rates of return of between 4 and 5 percent under current legislation and Martin Feldstein projects declining and ultimately negative rates of return.

If the existence of some confusion about the future of Social Security is excusable, the benign view the conservative literature has adopted with respect to the private pension fund market is not. The consistent failure of the private pension industry to offer a satisfactory pension vehicle for the elderly is among the better documented instances of "market failure."[13] From the point of view of society as a whole, the most serious and endemic shortcoming of the market is its failure to provide adequate pension coverage unless compelled to do so by the state. Both the risks and costs of establishing employer-sponsored plans deter smaller employers from establishing occupational plans, on the one hand, and discourage insurance and trust companies from marketing plans to these firms, on the other. Thus, in the United States, less than 50 percent of all private and public sector workers are covered by a private occupational plan. But for those who are covered by private plans, how do such investments compare to "investments" in Social Security? The answer is not very well. Someone is making money in the market with all those private pension funds but it is not the pensioner.

When a worker joins a firm with a pension plan, part of his or her total compensation package includes the pension credits that are accumulated on the basis of earnings and length of employment. For tax reasons, most plans are noncontributory; that is, no contributions are taken from the worker's salary and the plan is financed solely by the employer. However, irrespective of whether employees actually contribute, it is generally agreed that such pension credits constitute a deferred wage since in their contract negotiations current wages tend to be traded off against future pension benefits. Thus, a critical question with respect to "deferred wages" is what kind of return does the worker get on this investment?

The first and perhaps most significant real loss which most workers experience occurs when they lose or change jobs. Unless the pension credits have been *vested*[14] the "investment" simply reverts to the employer. Prior to the Employment Retirement Income Security Act of 1974 (ERISA), vesting was virtually nonexistant in many companies and employees lost all entitlements when they lost their jobs or changed employers. Since that time, most employers have adopted the formula of full vesting after ten years of service. Even with ERISA, the amount lost through vesting regulations is enormous. Data for 1972 (prior to the ERISA legislation) indicated that only 72 percent of retired males and 55 percent of retired females who had been covered by an occupational pension on their longest job were actually receiving benefits from a private pension.[15] In 1979, 42 percent of active workers were covered by a private pension but only 25 percent were vested.[16]

It is not just the marginal or excessively mobile worker who suffers. Simulations done by the Canadian Government Task Force on Retirement Income Policy indicate that under the ten year vesting provision common in the United States, the typical worker can expect to lose more than 25 percent of his pension credits in this fashion. The actual figure for the United States is probably higher due to higher rates of job mobility.[17] A pension fund would have to have very high rates of return indeed to compensate for such losses. In contrast, Social Security in effect provides immediate vesting and on these grounds alone is a better buy.

Secondly, Social Security generally protects against inflation far more effectively than most private pension plans. This occurs not only because Social Security benefits are fully indexed for inflation after retirement while private plans are not, but also because the formulas used by many private pension plans allow erosion in their value before retirement. The typical formula used to calculate the value of pension credits tends not to recognize inflationary increases in wages *prior* to retirement. The result is that while they are accumulating, investments in private pensions earn a zero rate of return on pension contributions at best, and more typically a loss. The very best private pension formulas base pension benefits on the earnings just prior to retirement and pay the retiree a percentage of that amount, based on years of service. But many pension formulas average ten or more years of earnings, leaving retirees with far less purchasing power than the real value of their contributions at the time they were deducted from their pay packets.

Retired workers from industries with strong labor unions to defend them have generally fared better than other retirees since inflation adjustments to pension benefits for the retired are frequently included in current labor contracts. As a result of a 1971 Supreme Court ruling, however, retirees are not mandatory subjects of collective bargaining. And employers may choose to exclude current benefits from negotiations, at their discretion. Thus, the greater the reliance on private pensions, the greater the erosion of real income over the retirement period.

The most familiar reason for this is the fact that pension plans purchased in the market are fixed in nominal dollars, while Social Security benefits are fixed in real dollars. That is, Social Security is adjusted to inflation so that over the life of the individual he or she experiences no net loss of wealth. Further, the advantages of Social Security continue even *after* the worker's death since few private schemes contain survivor's provisions which are comparable to those of the public system.

Thus, while in some few cases workers might expect to do better in the market, *on average* Social Security must be considered a "best buy." There continue to be real shortcomings in America's Social Security system, but its most serious would seem to be that it has not developed to the point where it would put the private pension industry as it currently exists out of business. The actuarial soundness of the private plans does not mean that they will return what has been *invested*, only that they will return what has been *promised*. In the case of American private pensions, what has been promised is not very much.

The market is apparently unable to provide an inflation-free investment vehicle such as an indexed bond even though such a bond would be doing no more than guaranteeing the 3 or 5 percent real rate of return being generated by the market. Irrespective of the average real rate of return being generated by the market, the private pension industry is simply not prepared to provide a pension vehicle which would reflect this rate.[18] Moreover, the money lost through inflation does not just disappear from the economy. Inflation simply redistributes real wealth, in this instance from workers and pensioners to employers and the issuers of fixed-income securities.[19]

The Myth of the Leisure Class

A further claim by the critics is that today's contributors are being duped, and that far from being impoverished, the elderly constitute a new leisure class living off a (perhaps too) generous Social Security system. In its crudest expression, *Forbes* magazine explains that the AFL-CIO and the Gray Panthers have been busy painting misleading pictures of the elderly "trapped in squalid rooms" with nothing but "dogfood to keep cold and malnutrition away." In reality according to *Forbes* writer Jerry Flint, the typical retired worker is like Joe, a retired mechanic from Detroit, who plays tennis six days a week near his mobile home outside of Tampa, or Dave, a retired West Virginia coal miner who spends his time on the twenty-nine-foot pontoon boat docked a stone's throw from his backyard. Retirees, he tells us in the February 18, 1980, issue, are even "into recreational sex."

More subtle forms of this view emerge from the official statistics of the United States government which quickly become part of both the academic and popular literature. In 1963, Labor Department economist Mollie Orshansky developed a "poverty line" for the United States based on the cost of a basic basket of goods seen as being necessary for subsistence at that time. Using price-adjusted values of this measure the percentage of the elderly in poverty can be shown to have declined from well over 30 percent in the early 1960s to less than 15 percent today. The problem of poverty and aging, it would seem, has been licked. But all that such figures tell us is that the standard of living in the United States has grown substantially in the past two decades and the elderly have shared in that increase. It says nothing about where the elderly fall in the overall income distribution or how their consumption levels fare in comparison to those in the rest of the society either then or now. The use of such absolute measures of poverty to chart changes in the economic well-being of various groups in society, such as the aged, has been abandoned virtually everywhere but the United States in favor of relative poverty measures which chart their relative status in the economy as a whole. What then are the facts?

First, it is important not to underestimate or deny the very real victories and achievements made in Social Security during the past decade and a half. From World War II to the mid-1960s, the incomes of the elderly relative to the rest of the population showed a pattern of steady decline. But, major increases in benefit levels, automatic indexing, Supplemental Security Income, and tighter regulation of private pensions (ERISA) all contributed to a turnaround in the declining economic status of the elderly so that by the mid-1970s the relative income shares of the elderly had returned to approximately the level they had been immediately after World War II.[20] Moreover, it is clear that the elderly now have a protected position in the sense that once won, the "wages of the elderly" can be less easily rolled back than those of other groups such as welfare mothers and sufferers from black lung disease. For those workers who are fortunate enough to retire not only with full Social Security benefits but also with a fully developed occupational pension, the initial postretirement period can be a period of relative affluence and leisure until such time as inflation, illness, and loss of a spouse begin to disrupt the honeymoon.

The facts, however, hardly warrant the claim that the elderly constitute a new leisure class. They continue to be highly concentrated in the lower levels of the income distribution. Some elderly people own a great deal of wealth, but most do not.

The number of elderly persons who may be counted among the relatively affluent is miniscule. In 1978 less than 15 percent of elderly couples and less than 8 percent of unrelated individuals had incomes higher than the corresponding median income levels of $22,571 and $13,860 for nonelderly couples and unrelated individuals respectively. Moreover, those who do fall above this level are likely to still be in the labor force or in the very early years of retirement. In sum, the number of the elderly (especially elderly women) in dire economic condition is still substantial, and the corresponding number cruising the Caribbean is small indeed. And nobody is cruising the Caribbean on Social Security pensions.

In view of all this, how could it be claimed that Social Security has been too generous to past and current beneficiaries? To understand such charges we must look to the intergenerational accounts once again. All beneficiaries to date, it is argued, have received windfall gains from their meagre or limited investments in Social Security.[21] The first generation of beneficiaries was particularly fortunate in this respect since they had in fact paid a trifling amount in contributions. These "windfalls," moreover, were paid for out of the contributions of the young—those currently in the labor force. The message of all this is clear. The current generation of workers is being twice burnt by Social Security. Not only will they not receive their benefits in the future but they are also being charged an unfair tax to keep the elderly on the tennis courts today.

What this inspection of the intergenerational accounts ignores is the fact that in order to receive these "windfalls" the elderly were required to forego the wages they could have reasonably expected to receive from continued labor force participation.[22] And, indeed, this was precisely the intent of the initial legislation. The elderly were offered a relatively low retirement pension in exchange for giving up their jobs to a younger generation of workers. The estimates, which abound, of the "transfers" received by the first generations of beneficiaries never incorportated these foregone wages.

The danger of becoming engrossed in such debates is that the real issues of what might constitute a reasonable income maintenance system for the elderly and how well Social Security approximates those standards are lost from sight. By international standards U.S. Social Security benefits are modest, as is the income floor assured by the Supplementary Security Income. Nor are there apparent "substitution effects" in the form of more highly developed private sector pensions. Indeed, the opposite seems to be true. Sweden, which has one of the most generous public pension programs of all the advanced capitalist countries, also has approximately 90 percent of its labor force covered by private pensions. As a result of national legislation, countries as diverse as Finland, France, West Germany, Switzerland, and the United Kingdom all have private coverage levels of greater than 70 percent, and usually much tighter regulation of private sector pensions as well.[23] In sum, it is difficult to determine by what standard American Social Security in particular or the American pension system in general might be considered extravagant or even "generous."

The Real Crisis in Social Security

Does this mean that the "crisis in Social Security" is all sound and fury; that there is nothing here which ought to concern ordinary working men and women? There is indeed a crisis but it is the crisis of confidence this massive attack has generated, not just with respect to Social Security but also with respect to the welfare state in general. Historically, Social Security has been among the most popular of welfare state reforms in this country. Unlike the various poverty programs, Social Security benefited virtually everyone; not just the "poor" but also the middle class when it encountered the poverty of old age; not just the elderly but also their middle class offspring who would otherwise have been forced to provide for their parents directly. A large portion of "intergenerational transfers" that the conservatives bewail as unfair would have occurred regardless, but not with the ease and limited financial disruption that Social Security's "pooling of risk" permitted.

Despite its popularity, however, conservatives have not bought the efforts of the Social Security Administration to present itself as just another big insurance company. Social Security is *socialized* consumption which provides a "citizen's wage" as opposed to a "market wage." It has been used to redistribute income *within* generations; it has paid out benefits on the basis of *need* and not just past contribution levels; it has attached income claims to persons and not just to their capital. Thus, from the point of view of the free market purist, Social Security is truly and certainly "out of control." The "wages" of the elderly and disabled are rendered immune to market forces and made subject to a political process in a polity where workers, in their capacity as citizens, have the right to make claims to a share of the social product that would never be recognized by the market.

That such a program should have become so popular was, if nothing else, a cultural crisis from the conservative viewpoint. And on this front at least the attack on Social Security seems to have met with considerable success. According to Henry Aaron, 80 percent of all Americans are reported to have "less than full confidence" in Social Security and the disillusionment is particularly pronounced among younger workers.[24]

But is the attack on Social Security nothing more than an exercise in cultural warfare, an attempt by the ideologues of the right to correct American wrongheadedness? While it is at best speculative to impute a hierarchy of motives to those involved, or even a consensus on what the attack is really about, there does appear to be a set of more specific economic considerations underlying it—considerations that bear directly on the more general crisis of American capitalism and the kinds of responses seen to be necessary for its resolution. These have to do with the role of private pension funds in generating the capital required to "reindustrialize" America.

While the potential economic and political power of the pension funds has been frequently overstated, there is little doubt that they have become a singularly important form of capital formation in the United States. In

1978 they owned 25 percent of all equity capital and were projected to own 50 percent by 1985. More significantly, the financial community is well aware that among the easiest ways to increase the rate of saving is encouragement of funded pension plan expansion.

Thus, for those who consider private pension funds a tool for increasing capital formation, Social Security must be restrained from expanding further and, preferably, cut back. According to Alicia Munnell, a dollar of social security contributions displaces approximately 74 cents of private pension saving.[25]

However, if "pension fund capitalism" offers corporate America new opportunities for capital formation, it also offers new risks, risks having to do with the control of that capital. The most immediate risk is that this new capital will be controlled by the state. By their own standards, the most obvious, equitable, and actuarially responsible solution to the projected Social Security deficit would be to immediately introduce the 1.5 percent increase in Social Security contributions which it is estimated would be sufficient to resolve the "crisis." But this will neither be introduced nor given serious consideration. The reason for this is not any fear of a taxpayers' revolt but rather the fact that such an increase would produce enormous surpluses in the fund until the year 2010.[26]

The initial fear, then, is that such additional capital formation as does occur will take place inside the state. From the conservative perspective, increased capital formation is desirable, but state control and the potential politicization of that capital is not. Democracy has no place in the determination of new investment flows. Here then is a dilemma. According to their accounts, the culprit in the piece is the "pay-as-you-go" method of financing Social Security. But for the state to abandon "pay-as-you-go" and move to a funded scheme is to place control over an important new source of capital inside the state. Given this dilemma, the only solutions acceptable to the conservative critics are those that involve cutting back Social Security—increasing the age of eligibility, abolishing automatic indexing, removing the transfer components of the system and the like.[27] Such changes would not only resolve the deficit problem but also have the additional virtue of encouraging the growth of private pensions.

The more remote but very real risk for corporate America is that the funds could fall under the control of organized labor. Although Peter Drucker was premature in announcing the advent of pension fund socialism, the American labor movement has become aware of the potential of such a strategy. At present this risk has been minimized by legislation restricting labor control. Furthermore, expanded private pensions entail the risk of greater state control. Politically, it is unlikely that the private pension industry would be allowed to displace Social Security without simultaneously accepting major new forms of regulation by government to remedy the many shortcomings of the private pension system. Tougher vesting rules, improved indexing formulas, and survivors' provisions would all be required to make such a shift acceptable. But more regulation of private industry is equally abhorrent in the current climate.

If capital formation and financial stability of the Social Security system are truly of concern, the obvious remedy is to raise the Social Security tax rate and fund a capital surplus inside the public sector. Obviously, this solution will not be embraced by the Reagan administration. And for now, the alternative solution of greater regulation of private pensions is almost equally abhorrent.

Thus, we have a stalemate, in which those who devalue Social Security fail to offer any remedy that serves the needs of retired people. In the meantime, the attack continues to serve its immediate political purpose. If workers can be convinced that the social wage is dangerous and unreliable, then there will be little pressure for further socialization of consumption or of savings. And the cutting and hacking in other sectors of the social wage budget can proceed apace.

The unfortunate result of these misleading attacks is that national attention is diverted from the real reforms that would facilitate adjustment to an aging population and an aging labor force. Most urgent among these is the redesign of jobs so that older workers will not feel compelled to flee their jobs at the first opportunity. Like so many institutions, the organization of work reflects the priorities of the postwar period dominated by the young, and is increasingly ill-suited to the needs of an aging society.

By dispensing with the purely ideological component of the attack on Social Security, we can get on with the serious business of adjusting the system to meet the changing demographic realities.

Notes

The basic data in this article are available in the public domain, as the footnotes indicate. Readers who wish to pursue this issue further should consult James Schulz's *The Economics of Aging* (Belmont, California: Wadsworth, 1980).
  1. An exception is James Morgan's "Myth, Reality, Equity and the Social Security System," *Challenge* (March-April 1978): 59-61.
  2. Arthur Laffer and David Ranson, "A Proposal for Reforming Social Security," in G.S. Tolley and R.V. Burkhauser, eds., *Income Support Policies for the Aged* (Cambridge: Ballinger, 1976), p. 133.
  3. Martin Feldstein, "Facing the Crisis in Social Security," *The Public Interest 47* (Spring 1977): 90.
  4. Kingsley Davis and Pietronella van der Oever, "Age Relations and Public Policy in Advanced Industrial Societies," *Population and Development Review 7* (March 1981).

5. Lawrence Smedley, "Comment on Laffer and Ranson," in Tolley and Burkhauser, p. 151.
6. Feldstein, p. 90.
7. June O'Neill, "Social Security: Fundamental Economic Problems and Alternative Financing Methods," *National Tax Journal 33, 3* (1980): 361.
8. Dean R. Leimer, "Projected Rates of Return to Future Social Security Retirees Under Alternative Benefit Structures," in *Policy Analysis with Social Security Files.* Social Security Administration, Research Report no. 52. Washington, D.C., 1979, pp. 235-57.
9. Paul Starr and Gösta Esping-Anderson, "Passive Intervention," *Working Papers* (July-August 1979): 25; and Ted Marmor, "National Health Insurance: Canada's Path, America's Choice," *Challenge* (May-June 1977).
10. Robert Clark and John Menefee, "Federal Expenditures for the Elderly: Past and Future," *Gerontologist* (April 1981): 136-37
11. Martin Feldstein and Anthony Pellechio, "Social Wealth: The Impact of Alternative Adjustments," in Colin Campbell, ed., *Financing Social Security* (Washington: American Enterprise Institute, 1979).
12. For a review of these studies see James Schulz's *The Economics of Aging* (Belmont, Calif.: Wadsworth, 1980), p. 160.
13. Perhaps the most thorough documentation and analysis of "market failure" in the area of pension policy is to be found in the report of the Government of Canada's Task Force on Retirement Income Policy. See *The Retirement Income System: Problems and Alternative Polices for Reform* (Hull: Canadian Government Publishing Centre, 1980), esp. ch. II.
14. Vested pension credits are those to which a worker is legally entitled whether or not he or she is working under the plan at the time of retirement. If a worker leaves an employer prior to vesting, the worker loses any legal claim to such benefits. The practice dates from an earlier period when pensions were seen as a gift of the employer, which could be withheld at his discretion. Much of the early enthusiasm among employers for pension plans was based on the assumption that they could operate as a form of labor control and elicit loyalty to the firm.
15. Gayle Thompson, "Pension Coverage and Benefits, 1972: Findings from the Retirement History Study," *Social Security Bulletin 41* (February 1978): 3-17.
16. President's Commission on Pension Policy, *An Interim Report,* November 1980.
17. *The Retirement Income System in Canada,* vol.2 (Hull: Canadian Government Publishing Centre, 1980), App. 8.
18. For a review of research on private pensions and inflation see Alicia Munnell, "The Impact of Inflation on Private Pensions," *New England Economic Review* (March-April 1979).
19. For a discussion of the manner in which private pension funds function to redistribute income from labor to capital and a review of the relevant American and Canadian literature see J.E. Pesando and S.A. Rea, *Public and Private Pensions in Canada: An Economic Analysis* (Toronto: University of Toronto Press, 1977).
20. Fred Pampel, *Social Change and the Aged* (Lexington: D.C. Heath, 1981).
21. See for example Douglas Parsons and Douglas Munro, "Intergenerational Transfers in Social Security," in M. Boskin, ed., *The Crisis in Social Security:*

Problems and Prospects (San Francisco: Institute for Contemporary Studies, 1978).

22. Within neoclassical economics of course one would also have to put a value on the "leisure" the elderly received in this intergenerational exchange; i.e., workers are seen as making trade-offs between labor and leisure. Given the historical realities surrounding the institutionalization of retirement, this makes little sense, but if one *were* to take it seriously the value of the leisure would simply be equal to the difference between the wages foregone and the social security benefits received. The result of such a theoretical calculation would mean that there were no intergenerational transfers of any sort and thus no "windfalls."

23. For a comparison of United States and other national pension systems see Barbara Torrey and Carole Thompson, *An International Comparison of Pension Systems,* President's Commission on Pension Policy Working Papers, March-April 1980.

24. Henry Aaron, "Advisory Report on Social Security," *Challenge* (March-April 1980). For a comparative look at the high repute in which Europeans generally hold their social security system see Stanford Ross, "Social Security: A Worldwide Issue," *Social Security Bulletin* (August 1979): 3-10.

25. Alicia Munnell, "Social Security, Private Pensions, and Saving." Paper prepared for the Conference on Public Policy Issues in the Financing of Retirement. January 16-17, Alexandria, Virginia.

26. O'Neill, p. 365.

27. See Michael Boskin's "How to Reform Social Security," *New York Times* (January 11, 1981).

35

Age, Work, and Social Security

Nathan Keyfitz

The crisis of social security, in the United States as in other industrial countries, consists in public disappointment that the cost is higher than expected. Underestimation of long-term costs has been a persistent feature of social security budgeting. "Pay as you go" systems require no initial funding and permit immediate coverage of persons who have made but a trifling contribution. They have the advantage of nearly universal participation right from the start: no one has to wait the thirty or more years needed to build a reserve on individual account. So long as population and wages continued to increase, there would be an advantage in each generation's support of the previous generation in its old age, for the supporting generation would in its turn be supported by an even larger and richer body of workers to come.

For some time the system did indeed work, but the advantage from such an arrangement is a short-term one. To count on the growth of population for an indefinite future is to neglect the reluctance of parents in a consumer society to bear enough children to replace themselves—not to mention the population-limiting finiteness of the earth. The ultimate leveling off of wages is less certain, but even here recent experience tells us that the annual 5 percent growth of the 1960s is hardly inevitable.

Paradoxically, a society that counts on a future of increasing wealth is by that very fact reducing the likelihood that its wealth will increase. For to rely on the next generation for comfortable support in our old age causes us to save less than we otherwise would, tending to diminish the capital that would be available under a more prudent policy. Feeling the bad effects of our failure to save, our descendants will be resentful and disinclined to help us, even if they have the means to do so. In this respect, at least, excessive optimism about growth helps destroy its own foundation.

Aside from this, social security has become ill-adapted to the requirements of longevity and rapid technical change. Even if we can provide every subscriber with twenty years of leisure (that is what present trends in mortality will soon give us beyond age 65), at a price we are willing to pay, do we want all that free time deferred to the end of our lives? Many would prefer to take some of it at midcareer. Some would like to change over to some other occupation, the learning of which requires two or three years of freedom from work. As it is now set up, social security undermines that dream and pushes people to drag on at their old jobs, somehow hold out until age 62 or 65, and then quit for good.

It is not only the individual who suffers. Most of the labor force now works in tertiary occupations (in office work of one kind or another, essentially processing information). Just as manufacturing was revolutionized in the 1920s with the assembly line, and agriculture in the 1950s with combines and artificial fertilizer, so will white-collar work be drastically changed in the 1980s with the computer and its offshoots. New occupations are emerging, and many old ones are becoming obsolete. It now appears that the pace of change will be too rapid to be accommodated by the turnover of generations. We have seen this before, with the abandonment of typesetting in newspapers, and many similar events can be expected. In the past, each generation could live out its working life using the methods it had learned in youth, and there was time enough for new methods to be introduced by new entrants. Today, we have both an onrush of new methods and, because of the lower birth rate, a shortage of young people. Experienced personnel retire, voluntarily or not, when their experience becomes obsolete, even though they might like to try their hands at something else. It took a Keynes to see that leisure is not all that desirable for the ordinary person, and retraining is both desired by many and needed for efficient production.

I will argue that the underestimation of long-term social security costs caused the public, through its legislators, to buy more social security than it really wanted. Moreover, the kind of social security offered is not appropriate to present-day longevity, the less rapid turnover of generations, or the pace and direction of technical change. First, though, it will be helpful to look at the two ways in which pensions for the aged can be financed.

The Chain Letter Principle

If an individual is left to provide for his own old age, he does so by saving (perhaps with monthly payments from age 20 to 65) into a fund maintained by some financial intermediary. The fund, which is invested and accumulates interest, is available to start monthly payments at age 65. The community has the use of the physical capital in which the fund was invested, both before and after the retiree starts to draw from the fund. The individual has the benefit of interest that materially reduces the amount he will be required to contribute. If many individuals do the same thing, through an insurance company or some other agency, they can take advantage of the laws of probability. Each contributor can have a life income, and no one need outlive his resources.

This is not the method used for social security, which builds up no reserve but is "pay as you go." This year's collections from the workforce are immediately paid out to this year's pensioners. The present method is designed for a rapidly growing population: quasi interest derives from the fact that the people now being supported come from an older, smaller cohort. This idea can be better understood by analogy to a chain letter.

The advantage of a chain letter to those who initiate it, and the disadvantage to those that follow, is well known. If each recipient pays his dollar to the name at the top of the list and sends the letter on to four new people, whose names he adds at the bottom and asks to do as he has done, then—provided the necessary discipline is maintained and enough new addresses are found— each participant will get the fourth power of $4 back after four cycles of mail. If there are ten persons on each list, participants will obtain $10 billion back, always provided that enough new participants willing to maintain the discipline can be found. More than twice the present world population would be required for the original sender to get his $10 billion, and a like number would be needed for each later sender. It is the same with social security on the "pay as you go" basis, except that the cycle is not the mailing time, but the length of a generation. U.S. law forbids the use of the mails for chain letters, but mandates the chain letter principle for the social security system.

All this has been said before, but the resemblance of the two processes can throw further light on social security. If a letter takes a week in the mail, then the chain letter with four names provides an interest rate of 300 percent each week; one with ten names, 900 percent each week. It can be shown algebraically that the formula for cost under a funded scheme with rate of interest r is identical with the formula for a "pay as you go" scheme with rate of increase r. Population growth works just as interest does to increase the return that the individual participant receives.

As a "pay as you go" scheme matures and the population increase slows, people get less and less for their money. If the benefits are to be maintained, then the contributions have to be increased. This has been happening in all countries where the contributions have been specifically levied for this purpose. Where the benefits are paid out of the general treasury, the same phenomenon occurs, but the cost records to reveal it are lacking. Since the drop to stationarity is sooner or later inevitable—if only because space and resources are finite—the quasi interest obtained because of population increase is necessarily temporary.

To examine the chain letter effect, individual-contribution records can be linked to benefit entitlements for the same individuals. The equivalent in the aggregate would come from the regulations on tax and benefit that existed from year to year during the history of the scheme. For each individual or for each category, one could see what interest percentage he or she effectively obtained. Early participants in the U.S. scheme could obtain a generous 7 percent or more per year in real terms, but those who retired in the 1960s and 1970s typically secured much less, perhaps 3 percent, and at least one retiree this year will get his contributions back without interest. Later participants, say in the 1990s, will balance this out with negative interest. Such a balancing out must occur, for the scheme as such does not produce anything, and at some point in the future the labor force will shrink in relation to the number of pensioners. (Though the scheme does not produce anything, its administrative costs are a creditably low percentage of the amount handled and, for my purposes, can be disregarded.) The way that early participants are favored over later ones deserves both theoretical clarification and empirical study.

In such a study one should distinguish between *open* and *closed* systems. The idea of the chain letter is that it is expected to be open, which is to say that ever-increasing numbers of people would continue to enter. All such arrangements that come to an end, in that the recruitment to the chain drops to zero, are closed and hence zero sum. In other words, such arrangements amount to an exchange, with the losses exactly equal to the gains. In an intermediate condition, the chain does not end, but drops from increase to stationarity. Under such stationary conditions, entrants just get their money back, without interest or quasi interest. Those who were in the scheme in the increasing phase have made their gains at no monetary cost to anyone else, so long as the stationary phase continues. The only sense in which their gain can be said to cost anything is that all subsequent players now must be on the ''pay as you go'' system rather than on the funded system. This is no disadvantage so long as exact stationarity is maintained in the population, but population waves arising from changes in the birth rate can rock the boat. If the scheme begins to contract, then generations later—perhaps centuries later—people must pay for the benefits provided to their ancestors who started the whole operation.

The maturing of the system need not occur once and for all. When a new group enters the labor force—for instance, married women in the 1960s—that event offers a new start, since the entrants contribute but do not yet draw benefits. Such an impulse is temporary and comes to an end when all the women who are going to enter the labor force have done so. Other groups previously omitted—farmers, the self-employed, public servants who have previously avoided incorporation—can be drawn in by legislation. Each such group enables the existing contribution schedule to be continued a little longer without any diminution of benefits.

But this is not all. The chain letter principle is sustained by another element. Rising wages have the same effect as population increase. Wages rising at 3 percent annually will enable everyone to seem to obtain a 3 percent return on contributions. This applies whether rising wages stem from inflation, in which case the 3 percent is a money return, or whether they are caused by rising productivity and real wages, in which case the participants get a real 3 percent return.

If wages fail to rise as expected by the planners, then there will have been an underestimation of costs; the same is true if contributions are lowered by greater than expected unemployment. In light of the apparent upward trend in unemployment among industrial countries during the past forty years, this is an important fact. Such elements in the long-term cost of the scheme are not easy to forecast, and their prominence today tells us that only a conservative allowance for them will avoid later fiscal imbalance and public disappointment. The need for caution in projecting costs and benefits applies especially to assumptions about retirement age.

Beneficiaries under the U.S. retirement program OASDHI (Old-Age, Survivors, Disability, and Health Insurance) rose from 13,918,000 in 1965 to 22,421,000 in 1979, and benefits paid out went from $12.5 billion to $67.1 billion. This fivefold increase was caused partly by the drop from 27.9 percent in 1965 to 20 percent in 1979 of men 65 and older who were still working. While social security benefits increase as a result of earlier retirement, however, those benefits are also a cause of earlier retirement. With each expansion of the benefits—including provisions for dependents and indexing—additional millions of people are attracted into retirement. Some of the underestimation of costs stems from this effect of social security on behavior: it is not easy to take account of such behavioral responses in actuarial calculations.

Cause is difficult to impute in the present context. One may be able to say that so much of the cost increase is explained by mortality change, insofar as this can be demonstrated with a direct numerical decomposition. One might likewise say that earlier retirement was responsible for some part of the increased cost. But when one looks more closely, one gets into trouble: there is no way of determining how much of the earlier retirement results from the social security scheme, on the one side, and how much results from changed lifestyle, lower ambition, or some other cultural change, on the other side. Such fine computations are impossible.

It is natural to think of longer lifetimes as responsible for our difficulty in supporting the old, and of lower mortality as increasing the contributions required. Elementary demography gives the appearance of confirming this. It is commonly noted that the life expectancy around 1930 was 60 years; around 1945, this had risen to 65 years; in 1960, it was 68 years; and in 1990, it will surely be 75 years. Reference to these figures alone suggests that the number of years over age 65, once null, is now rising toward ten. Surely that increase must decisively affect social security. This sort of thinking seems to underlie most popular articles on the subject. A sophisticated knowledge of demography, however, shows such reasoning to be wholly wrong. Life expectancy at birth has nothing to do with the matter, for it is affected by mortality in infancy and childhood. What counts is the fraction of workers who survive to draw benefits, the mean length of time after retirement that such workers live, and above all the supply of new workers who will pay their benefits.

A Problem in Social Choice

The oft mentioned "crisis of social security" consists in the public's expectation of more benefit from social security than plain arithmetic shows it to be capable of providing. The political dynamics by which social security was sold to the U.S. Congress, and to the corresponding institutions in other countries, enmeshed the notion's liberal sponsors in exaggerated promises of what social security could provide and in understatements about what the benefits would cost. The result was to surprise and please the public that so much could be obtained for so little. People said "Now I will be relieved of the care of my aged parents; they will have their own income at the government's expense." No one seemed to notice that setting up parents in their own homes was going to cost much more than having them live with their children, and that the same children—now collectively—were going to have to cover the increased cost.

When a commodity is underpriced people will buy too much of it. Think of being offered shoes at $20 a pair. Seeing that as a bargain, you buy a half-dozen pairs on credit; but when you get the bill, you find they cost $50 a pair. A crisis ensues. You are outraged that the apparent low price prompted you to buy more shoes than you wanted, and you are reluctant to pay the bill.

The price of social security needs to be clarified, so that in future purchases the customer will not buy more than he wants. What corresponds to "buying too much" in the matter of social security? The quantity of social insurance can be expressed in terms of the fraction of salary replaced and the age at which the pension starts, as well as such lesser matters as whether the benefit is to be subject to income tax, how much is to be allowed for dependents, and so forth. It is highly desirable to find out how much the public wants—whether people would like to replace all their income at a cost of, say, 25 percent of their wages when they are working or whether they would prefer to drop down to 50 percent replacement at a cost of 12.5 percent of their wages. Because the public has never been given a simple, understandable statement of what it will cost for a given benefit, it has not had an opportunity to say how much it wants to buy. We have suffered from a detachment of benefits from costs.

Long-term costs of the social security scheme can best be discussed with an appreciation of how population and work are going to evolve during the coming years. To start with the very simplest hypothesis, suppose that each person begins work at age 20, retires at 65, and then lives to be 80. Each hypothetical person works for forty-five years and is then on pension for fifteen years. If everyone fits this description, and if the population is stationary, with a fixed number feeding in each year—say, 3.5 million for a U.S. population of about 250 million—then the contribution each year will have to be exactly 25 percent of salary to yield a pension equal to the supposed uniform salary. For with three persons working for each one retired, the benefits would be three-fourths of salary for the retirees, and each of those working would retain three-fourths of salary; so everyone would have a lifetime income of three-fourths of the nominal salary. It is as if three full salaries were earned for every four persons in the population, and divided equally among the four. One can take account of mortality in the stationary condition by referring to a life table, and the result is not very different. For the United States' 1979 table, assuming 100 percent replacement and everyone working to age 65 and then retiring, 24 percent of salary would have to be taken in tax. Such calculations can be improved by several feasible modifications:

- Suppose that people are satisfied with 60 percent of the uniform salary on retirement. After all, a considerable portion of the expenditures of working people is directly connected with their work: many items of clothing, transport, restaurant meals, entertaining, and even some housing insofar as housing accessible to the workplace is more expensive. Aside from this, the retired person is not typically sending children to college and indeed is long past maximum financial responsibilities. Budget studies ought to be consulted to ascertain the *work-related cost* and *diminution of responsibility* in a typical family. Suppose that work-related costs are 40 percent of expenditure during working life, so that the person's own costs are 60 percent of salary; this would be the right percentage to provide a person in old age so that he could live as well as when working. There are some costs to being old, especially health costs, but I will assume that these are covered under some scheme, such as Medicare, that does not enter the present calculation. Few people, moreover, do not have some private savings, in durable consumer goods if not in money. In this situation, the premium or contribution that the person would have to make while working would be 60 percent of the 25 percent discussed above; that is to say, the premium would be 15 percent of salary, which is somewhat higher than the 13 percent now contributed by employer and employee together in the United States. It is necessary to test how realistic this 13 percent is in light of other qualifications.
- How much difference would it make if people insisted on retiring at age 60, or if they were satisfied to work until age 70? Evidently, a great deal. Re-

tirement at age 60 on 60 percent of salary, assuming zero mortality to age 80, would raise the tax from 15 percent to 20 percent; retirement at age 70 would lower it to 10 percent. It would take twice as big a bite out of the salaries of all those working to provide for retirement at age 60, versus age 70. Since a rectangular distribution, rather than the actual downward-sloping distribution, has been used, the difference that retirement age makes is underestimated. A calculation using the life table is one stage more realistic. If one averages the two sexes, one finds that a tax of approximately 24 percent is required for retirement at age 60, against 10 percent at age 70 (for 60 percent replacement). To ask the electorate whether it would prefer to pay 24 percent of salary in order to retire at age 60 or pay only 10 percent and hold off retiring until age 70 may seem like a hard choice to impose, but it is better imposed than made unknowingly. Aside from the information gained regarding public desires, the mere asking of such questions has a beneficial educational effect: it helps make clear how much must be paid for how much pension.

- Our sense of equity undoubtedly would provide somewhat more for those with family responsibilities, particularly for those with a nonworking spouse who does not qualify for a pension. Suppose that one-third of the population is in this condition, and that these persons are entitled to a 50 percent increase of pension on that account. With the standard age 65 retirement, the 15 percent premium for 60 percent replacement would go up by one-sixth ($1/3 \times 1/2$) to 17.5 percent. The need to provide some minimum pension is also apparent.

A Sufficient Reserve

With fixed birth and death rates (hence a steady increase) all generations can pay the same contributions and will draw the same benefit, for in such a population the age distribution is stable. This uniformity is not possible with the birth rate fluctuations that occur with the use of birth control. The most trouble will come from the two-generation population cycles. It is those cycles which change the ratio of the over-65 population group, say, to the 20-to-65-year-old group that are of concern. The effect will be strongest with the birth cycles of about thirty years. Such a cycle first yields a high ratio of those drawing to those contributing, and hence places a great burden on the latter; then this changes to a low ratio, and offers corresponding relief to the contributors. That we had a low birth rate in the 1930s, a high one about 1960, and now a low one again in the 1980s is going to cause some unevenness for the next seventy-five years or so if we continue present-day procedures.

A reserve serves to buffer such population waves. One technical question is how big the reserve must be in order to permit a constant charge to individuals along with a constant amount of pension. A full reserve, such as the law requires a private insurance company to set up for its annuity business, would be about six times the annual benefits paid. This would allow the insurance company to go out of business without loss to its customers. It has been estimated that one or two times the annual benefits would serve for the easier task of buffering fluctuations in births and in the business cycle.

Contrary to what the present financial problems of social security might prompt one to think, we are not now facing a difficult phase in the demographic cycle. The baby boom is coming into the labor force, while those now retiring were born around 1920. By the end of the century, the exceptionally low births of the 1930s will have retired. The ratio of retirees to workers is rising, but very slowly, and will continue to be reasonably low until about the year 2020, when those born around 1960 will begin to retire. At that time, an increase in the ratio of more than 50 percent can be expected. It is that situation against which a reserve will be needed. Present difficulties are caused by unemployment (which cuts down contributions, besides causing some premature retirement) together with other elements that can help make the price charged too low.

If the scheme is permitted to borrow when short, then a smaller reserve will suffice—the only condition being that the average balance over the long term be zero. No initial reserve would need to be built up; one would start accumulating or borrowing from a neutral point. Given the history of short-range politically influenced decisionmaking on social security, we may well question the prudence of allowing borrowing.

The fluctuation of pension costs and benefits raises larger issues of intergenerational equity. It is well to list the various components of equity and see how the pension component fits with them:

- Working people pay the pensions of those who have retired. It should not be forgotten, though, that other kinds of transfer to the aged population exist, and that these cross generations in the same way as pensions. Health insurance, whether private or public, requires heavier payments and is used less by those working than by those too old to work. Insofar as the former are healthier than the latter and current premiums do not take full account of this, some part of the premium must be considered in the intergenerational account.
- Working people pay for the upbringing, including schooling, of the next generation. This works in the opposite direction to the pensions and may be regarded as an offset. If the amounts expended were the same, then equity would be preserved in the community as a whole, just as it is in the traditional family: the parents pay for the upbringing of their children, and expect to be cared for in their old age. The balance is not so easily drawn,

though, when upbringing costs are largely in kind and, on the other side, pensions are in cash and are also mediated by the Social Security Administration. Yet, if there is any place for gratitude in the social system it is here, and if there is one virtue that traditional parents took care to instill in their children, it was a sense of gratitude and respect toward their elders. In a modern community, the pale comparison is that the same (more or less undefined) group that paid for schooling now claims pensions through the state as the intermediary. It would be too much to expect a quality like gratitude to be funneled through the government and then be transmitted to old people collectively.

- The larger generation has an easier time covering the pensions of its parents but, on the other hand, has a harder time making a living (if we accept the reasoning that a group's prosperity is dependent on that group's size). It is at least possible that the older generation did the younger one damage by bearing so many children, and to give youth an easier time in paying for the pensions of their parents is but a small offset to this problem.

- A crucial element in the exchange is the material investment by which the older generation gives the younger one a standard of living higher than its own. One can imagine a selfish group that ran its capital into the ground, aiming to leave it at net value zero by the time the group's members died. Such a group would have little claim on the one that followed, and the following group would have no means to respond if a claim were made, given the limited income that could be produced with the small and declining capital remaining. Of course material capital is not what counts most, but rather human capital, including the ability of individuals to work together, to organize themselves effectively, and to perform the required technical tasks. This returns to the question of what sort of education parents provide their children, but it does not permit total disregard of material capital. A group that educated its children well, and also gave them a generous stock of physical capital, would have a large claim on them collectively. The children, moreover, would have both the means to look after their aging forebears and the willingness to do so. This in turn relates to the means of providing pensions that arises naturally under a competitive system—that is, the purchase of actuarially calculated annuities. If the savings involved in this purchase are invested in capital goods, income—from which pensions can be paid—is produced. I have argued for partial funding on the grounds that it can even out the costs and benefits of successive generations battered by the population waves that are part of life in a contraceptive-using society. Consideration of intergenerational equity and the out-of-date virtue of gratitude leads to the same conclusion.

Yet, one may doubt the value of discussing pensions in a larger context. Usually, the subject of pensions is rightly segregated from other issues simply because, otherwise, decisionmaking is inordinately complicated. The public will be well off if it ascertains the relationship of costs and benefits in social security alone, and such a narrowing of the focus makes expert calculation sharper, as well.

The waters have been muddied by successive authoritative statements that the social security scheme was financially sound, followed by evidence that, to the contrary, the system is headed for bankruptcy. Many, therefore, find it difficult to accept reassurances that if some modification is made now, social security will be restored to health. It is widely believed that the scheme is in danger of collapse, that present payers may never collect their own pensions, and that the best hope for those worried about maintaining the system during their lifetimes is to resist any modification whatsoever as long as possible. Change, however slight, threatens to be just the opening wedge that will lead to total dismantlement. This attitude is understandable, but hardly conducive to the adaptation so badly needed, and it could well have an unintended result: the scheme might become so expensive that at some point a generation of workers simply gives up. The question is how best to bring about a healthier understanding of the relation of costs to benefits and an acceptance of the changes needed for true permanence. In addition, there are ways in which the system can be made more attractive and useful at any given level of cost.

Consideration of how social security benefits should be distributed through life is past due. Do people really want the whole benefit after they have completed their paid worklife? Given today's low mortality and improved health, a person may be part of the labor force for fifty years. He might wish to spend that time in more than one career, but that would require retraining, which could well be charged to social security. A person, for example, might agree to postpone retirement for, say, three years in exchange for drawing two and a half years of social security at age 45.

Rapid technical change places retraining demands on many. Hence, the right to choose when one will draw benefits would benefit both the individual and the economy. To offer such flexibility would constitute no burden to the scheme and would greatly increase the participant's feeling that he has some control in the process, rather than being merely a passive object. Retraining would be sought especially by women who had taken time out for raising their children and do not wish to go back to their previous jobs. Aside from some additional record keeping, this flexibility would be introduced at no cost.

The Nation versus the Family

Social security was devised to take the place of individual support of parents by their children. True, with the falling birth rate children are fewer in number, but what is more important is that children quickly develop interests outside the family, families engage in fewer activities together, and family solidarity declines. Just as parents want fewer children, so are children less eager to support aging parents. Care of old people is one of the many functions that the state has taken over from the family.

The current agitation about social security points up the fact that the solidarity of the state can also come into question. The implicit social contract by which each generation unilaterally contributes to the pensions of its parents—without hope of getting anything more back from them, but with the expectation that its children will likewise unilaterally contribute in due course—can stand only so much strain. Quite aside from any financial argument for funding, the case for it can be made solely on the evident need to place as little strain as possible on the sense of intergenerational unity and commitment.

Nothing will avoid the need for mutual support of the generations, whatever the arrangement for pensions. Whether the scheme is funded or not, perishable goods must be produced day by day by the labor force of the moment. Thus, there is no way that the old can do without the young. A working person can buy a house in which to live when he retires; he cannot buy in advance the bread he will eat as a retiree. The point of saving money in the form of contributions to a funded scheme is to increase current production and so justify the claim to later support.

Financial arrangements do not eliminate the need for social commitment. The annuity policy issued by an insurance company, or the mortgage contract if that is the instrument in which the savings have been invested, might simply be repudiated. But such repudiation seems less likely than the repudiation by some generation of its obligation to the preceding generation under ''pay as you go.'' If the burden continues to climb, it will be easy for the legislature to curtail benefits immediately in order to relieve the current contributors, unfair as that would be to the old (who have made their payments in good faith).

On the other hand, agreement to a social security modification that might start twenty or thirty years hence is an action by present payers to reduce their *own* return. Downward adjustments on benefits to be available some decades after the legislation is passed is more equitable than an immediate adjustment to contributions as well as benefits. Just as the group principle embodied in a funded scheme puts less strain on relations between generations, so will any modification place less strain on generational commitment if benefits or contributions are adjusted for a given group rather than at a given moment.

How can we be as sure as possible that, at some moment when the pensioners are many in relation to the contributors, the latter do not just give up and, through their legislators, repudiate the whole scheme or drastically and suddenly curtail benefits? In principle, the answer is simple, if politically difficult: make the scheme funded, at least in part. If full funding means holding six years of contributions in trust, then start by building up one year's contributions in trust; that is, start by working toward one-sixth funding. Such a reserve fund could be built up either by increasing taxes or by curtailing benefits with existing taxes. By subsequently running the fund up or down, as necessary, all generations could have identical returns on their contributions.

A reserve is not to be thought of as a mere manipulation of finances but, rather, as the creation of a direct *quid pro quo* by the older generation. Such reserve building corresponds to the man in his working years who builds one house for himself and another for his son, on the understanding that in old age the man will live in the house he built for himself and the son will provide his father with groceries. Every contribution that is made along this line will help strengthen the solidarity of the generations and head off the repudiation of social security that is so widely feared. It may well be that the investment of the old in their children is not adequate to ensure maintenance of the old by their children. A funded scheme is a way of enabling people to help their children more—by contributing to the capital stock—and a way of creating a more even balance between the generations. Private schemes would serve the same purpose, and they should be encouraged through income tax incentives and other provisions. The U.S. government, by indexing, guarantees the pensions of its own employees against inflation. Why should it not do the same for all employees?

Several policy recommendations suggest themselves from the foregoing discussion. It is necessary, first of all, that long-term costs be presented realistically so that the public can buy the quantity of social security (expressed as replacement fraction of salary together with age of initiation) it really wants. That would almost certainly mean a reduction from what it bought when it thought that the long-term cost was much less than it turned out to be. Needed, also, is a statement of the redistributive aspects of the plan, including categories of contributors that will get more than they put in and those that will get less, expressed in understandable terms. Clearly the public wants some redistribution, but does it want more or less than the scheme now offers? No easy question, but a conscious choice is better than a choice by default. Second, in times when the ratio of pensioners to workers is lower than it will later be, a partial reserve should be built up. Unfortunately, that time is now. Finally, there is a great need for flexibility in drawing benefits, so that a person can choose early, temporary retirement from an obsolescing occupation in order to train for a new one. Any social security plan that neglects these matters will be a patchwork job that will itself require patching within a few years.

36

Social Security Is a Women's Issue

Maxine Forman

The concerns of women were practically invisible during the recent Social Security debate. For a little over a year the nation followed the deliberations of President Reagan's 15-member bipartisan National Commission on Social Security Reform whose mandate was to find solutions to the system's short- and long-term financing problems. It was amazing how few times the subject of women was raised in discussion or in press reports of commission or congressional proposals. Clearly, few individuals recognize how important Social Security is to women or how the system affects women's lives.

In fact, most people seem to think that the majority of elderly (aged 65 and over) Social Security recipients are retired white males who enjoy good health, have other sources of income, and have a full work life of average or high earnings behind them. Like the photograph of the elderly white male chemist at work in his lab—which appeared on the covers of all three volumes of the final report of the 1981 White House Conference on Aging—this portrait ignores the problems of those who face limited options throughout their lives because of sex or race. Even a 1981 *New York Times* article, whose purpose was to show that the elderly are perceived to be more desperate than they really are, admitted as an aside in the last paragraph that within the over-65 population, there are four groups who report living a miserable, dismal existence: Blacks, Hispanics, those with incomes under $10,000—and women.[1] Even excluding overlap with the first three categories, women make up 60 percent of the elderly population and 60 percent of elderly Social Security beneficiaries.[2]

Women as Beneficiaries

Women receive Social Security benefits as workers, spouses, and survivors under the Social Security system. In all three categories, their benefits are very low. In April, 1982, the average monthly benefit for a retired woman worker was $355, as compared with $432 for men; spouses averaged $196, while widows received $351.[3] In general, women's low Social Security benefits can be attributed to low wages resulting from a lifetime of discrimination in education and employment, time spent out of the paid work force because of homemaking responsibilities, and provisions that treat divorced women and elderly widows inadequately. Actuarial reductions for taking benefits before the age of 65 also play a part in decreasing women's monthly checks.

As low as women's benefits are, they are often the primary or sole source of income. For most women, a history of low or no earnings works against building a nest egg to supplement meager Social Security benefits. In addition, few women receive pensions, either as workers or as survivors—and when they do, the amounts are small. Only 10 percent of women aged 65 and older received benefits from private pension plans in 1980, as compared with 27 percent of men over 65.[4] Women received a median income of only $1,400 from private pension plans based either on their own work experience or as survivors of working spouses.[5] For men, the median income was $3,000.[6] The median annual income for all women over the age of 65 from all sources (i.e., earnings, interest from assets, pensions, and Social Security) was only $4,757, as compared with $8,173 for men.[7]

It is not surprising, then, that the poverty rate for elderly women is higher than for the over-65 population in general—18.6 percent, as compared with 15.3 percent.[8] It is also not surprising that the loss of a husband can send an elderly woman more deeply into poverty because the event often signals the end of earnings or pensions. Only 22 percent of elderly widows receive retirement benefits other than Social Security.[9] Only 14 percent of unmarried elderly women have earnings of their own, and only 28 percent of those with earnings work full-time.[10] Of almost 16 million women over the age of 65, only 6.1 million (38 percent) are married, 8.1 million are widowed, 900,600 were never married, and 695,200 are separated or divorced.[11] Of these 9.7 million unmarried women over the age of 65, about 6.7 million (or 42 percent of all women over the age of 65) live alone or with unrelated adults.[12] (Elderly women, who have an 18-year life expectancy at age 65, seldom remarry and often remain alone for the remainder of their lives.) Over 2 million of these women are officially "poor" (income below $4,359).[13] (They comprise 85 percent of all elderly people living alone below the poverty line.)[14] Using 125 percent of the poverty level (income below $5,449), the figure for elderly women living alone at or near poverty soars from about 31 percent to over 50 percent.[15] For minority elderly women living alone, the statistics are substantially higher. It is not surprising, then, that women comprise 73 percent of elderly recipients of Supplemental Security Income (SSI), a form of welfare for the poorest of the elderly, disabled, and blind.[16]

Women have already lost much through changes in Social Security in the 1981 Budget Act. Now a widow (who is not disabled) cannot receive benefits before the age of 60 unless she is caring for a child under age 16 (previously it was age 18). In addition, Social Security dependents benefits to children over 18 of retired, deceased, and disabled workers are being gradually reduced, with total elimination planned by September, 1985. Now widowed mothers, most between the ages of 40 and 60, will have to dip into their own resources to educate their college-age children. Especially burdened will be the high proportion of older Black women who raise and educate their grandchildren. Perhaps the most controversial change was the elimination of the minimum Social Security benefit for future recipients. The Administration portrayed these beneficiaries as "double dipping" retirees with high government pensions. But the overwhelming majority are elderly women, most of whom have earned low wages during their work life. Now these women will receive Social Security benefits based solely on their wage record—no matter how low.

Saving the Social Security System: Do Women Gain or Lose?

Financing Provisions

It is against this economic scenario that advocates for women and policymakers must measure the Social Security Amendments of 1983.[17] It is easy to vacillate between viewing the legislation as a glass half-empty or as a glass half-full. After all, Congress did not tamper with or eliminate the weighted benefit formula devised to help low earners or increase the number of computation years. Such changes would have been devastating to women's benefit levels. Yet two financing provisions in the new legislation will especially hurt women: freezing the cost of living adjustment (COLA) for six months and raising the retirement age to 67 by 2027. Both provisions will mean further losses or reductions in elderly women's meager benefits. Raising the retirement age—the age at which workers would receive full benefits—is especially onerous because it is based on several faulty assumptions: that there is a solid link between living longer and living longer in good health; that those able to work to a later age are welcome in the work force; and that most retired elderly people supplement their Social Security benefits by other sources of income and, therefor, can tolerate reduced benefits if they retire early.

In view of the repercussions of these particular changes, an examination of selected provisions of the 1983 Social Security Amendments and their impact on women is instructive. Brief descriptions of some of the most important of these follow.

With respect to retirement age, the current law holds that a retired worker receives a full Social Security benefit at age 65. Also at age 65 a spouse receives 50 percent of her husband's benefit: a widow receives 100 percent of her deceased husband's benefit. If these benefits are claimed before age 65, they are reduced for life. Under the new legislation, the retirement age at which Social Security recipients can receive full benefits will be raised gradually to 66 in 2009 and to 67 in 2027. Benefits will be reduced for recipients who retire at age 62 from 80 percent of the full benefit to 70 percent. Medicare eligibility will remain the same—at age 65.

Raising the retirement age results in benefit cuts because workers, spouses, and widows who need to retire early would get even less than they do now. Seventy-nine percent of women workers and 81 percent of workers' spouses applied for reduced benefits in 1979—many because of ill health or inability to find employment.[18] With less income, many older women will find it neccessary to turn to welfare or seek employment in a workplace marked by sex, age, and race discrimination.

Concerning the cost of living adjustment (COLA), the current law states that a COLA is provided when the Consumer Price Index (CPI) increases over 3 percent from the first quarter of one year to the first quarter of the next year. Under the new legislation, the COLA would be declared from June, 1983, to January, 1984, and paid every January thereafter.

This change will greatly affect elderly women, most of whom have little or no income other than Social Security. For example, a six-month COLA freeze at a 3.9 percent inflation rate would force widows to lose an average of $80 over the six-month period. The 3 percent rule is waived for 1984 so that a COLA will be paid even if the CPI is less than 3 percent. This will offset some of the damaging effect.

Under the category of universal coverage, the current law holds that federal employment is covered by the Civil Service Retirement System—not by Social Security. Social Security participation is optional to state and local governments and nonprofit organizations. The new legislation would provide mandatory Social Security coverage to newly hired federal employees and employees of nonprofit organizations. It prohibits state and local governments from terminating employee Social Security coverage.

Spouses, elderly survivors, and divorced spouses will receive better treatment under Social Security than under public or private pension plans. The weighted formula will benefit women, the majority of whom earn low wages. Disability coverage under Social Security will be better in many respects. Social Security's portability will cover those who move between nonprofit, public, and private employment.

On the subject of self-employed taxation, the current law holds that self-employed individuals must pay 75 percent of the combined employer/employee Social Security tax and 50 percent of the Medicare tax. Under the new legislation, self-employed taxes would be increased to equal 100 percent of all combined employer/employee taxes, providing offsetting tax credits.

These increases will burden women entrepreneurs, most of whom are low earners. But tax credits for all self-employed persons will reduce some of the self-employed tax actually paid.

With regard to taxation of benefits, the current law states that Social Security benefits are not subject to taxation. The new legislation would tax Social Security benefits for recipients whose adjusted gross income, non-taxable interest income, and one-half of their Social Security benefits exceed $25,000 for an individual and $32,000 for a married couple filing jointly.

This change will not, in general, hurt elderly women, most of whom have very low incomes. But the amount of income on which couples will have to pay taxes penalizes some married people with two incomes.

As for payroll taxes, under the current law, a worker's annual earnings up to a limit of $35,700 are taxed for Social Security purposes at a 6.7 percent rate with a matching tax paid by the employer. The new legislation would accelerate payroll tax increases scheduled for the future so that the tax rate will be 7 percent in 1984 and 7.51 percent in 1988. It will allow a tax credit for employees in 1984.

Accelerating payroll tax increases will result in even less disposable income for women and others who are low earners, but it is preferable to cuts in benefits for those dependent on the system.

And finally, under the current law, Social Security provides a COLA when the CPI increases over 3 percent from one year to the next year. With the new legislation, when Social Security trust funds fall below a certain percentage of annual benefit payments, the COLA would be based on increases in prices or wages—whichever is lower. When the balance in the trust fund rises above 32 percent of annual benefit costs, recipients would receive catch-up payments.

When prices rise faster than wages, basing the COLA on wages will burden elderly women trying to live on their small incomes. Catch-up payments may be unlikely under the high 32 percent trigger.

Women's Provisions

Congress's task was to shore up the Social Security system through money-saving financing provisions, so policymakers did not explore changes that would recognize marriage as a partnership or provide women with portable protection in their roles as both homemakers and paid workers. Nevertheless, the new legislation does include modest provisions that will help small numbers of women. Brief descriptions of these provisions follow.

Within the category of divorced widows and spouses, the current law states that divorced surviving spouses who remarry after age 60 cannot continue to receive benefits; disabled widows and disabled divorced widows cannot continue to receive benefits if they remarry between the ages of 50 and 59. The new legislation would continue benefits to disabled widows aged 50 to 59, disabled divorced widows aged 50 to 59, and divorced widows aged 60 and over who remarry.

The remarriage rate for older women is very low, but this change will still help some women.

In addition, the current law holds that an eligible divorced spouse may not collect her retirement benefit until her ex-husband retires and claims his. The new legislation would allow a divorced spouse to collect her retirement benefit at age 62 even if her ex-husband has not claimed his.

This provision will help a women older than her ex-husband or one whose ex-husband continues to work. Unfortunately, it is not effective until January, 1985, and, even worse, the divorced spouse must wait two years after her divorce before she can collect her benefits.

At the same time, according to the current law, a widow's benefits are indexed according to prices from the time of her husband's death until the time she receives the benefits. A widow who becomes eligible for benefits many years after the death of her husband often receives extremely low benefits because wages usually rise faster than prices (applicable to disabled widows aged 50 to 59 and others beginning at age 60). The new legislation would index a widow's benefits by increases in wages after the death of the worker, rather than in prices as under current law—but only if a higher benefit results.

This provision is good for widows because in recent years prices have increased faster than wages, so it makes sense to index benefits to either price or wage increases—whichever produces a higher benefit.

And finally, under the current law, a disabled widow receives 50 percent of her age-65 benefit at age 50. The new legislation would increase from 50 percent to 71.5 percent the benefit a disabled widow aged 50 to 59 receives.

Although still not adequate, this change is especially helpful because it applies to all disabled widows—both current and future beneficiaries.

In addition to the provisions providing for divorced widows and spouses, there is one pertaining to earnings sharing that also affects women. Under the current law, the Social Security system does not treat marriage as an economic partnership and does not provide portable protection to women as homemakers and workers. However, under the new legislation, the Department of Health and Human Services is required to develop by July, 1984, earnings sharing legislative proposals that include data on the implementation, the costs, and the effect of each proposal on Social Security beneficiaries.[19]

This provision assures that earnings sharing receives serious attention from Congress and the Administration. Earnings sharing would regard marriage as an economic partnership where both the roles of homemaker and paid worker are recognized. The earnings sharing concept has been endorsed by the 1979 Advisory Council on Social Security, the 1980 President's Commission on Pension Policy, the 1980 Justice Department's Task Force on Sex Discrimination, and by the major women's organizations.

Meeting Women's Needs

The low cost of these measures, the desire on the part of many policymakers to "do something for women," and pressure from women's groups were factors that helped the women's provisions survive the legislative process. It cannot be emphasized enough, however, that additional women's concerns still need to be addressed. For example, women who leave the work force for homemaking responsibilities receive zeros on their earnings record for every year over five they do not work for pay; this substantially reduces their retirement benefits. A woman is often entitled to a higher benefit as a spouse than as a worker, but her spouse benefit (an amount up to half of her husband's worker benefit) is no greater than what she would have received had she never worked and never paid Social Security taxes. In addition, a worker qualifies for disability benefits only if she worked five of the previous ten years at the onset of disability. Women often cannot pass this "recency of work" test if they have been out of the labor force for family responsibilities. Upon reentering the labor force, such women must begin all over again to meet the five-year requirement.

The woman as homemaker is similarly not fairly provided for. For example, a divorced women is eligible for a maximum of 50 percent of her former spouse's Social Security benefit, but only if the marriage lasted at least ten years and her former spouse retires.[20] Further, the spouse benefit, meant to supplement the worker's benefit, is usually inadequate to maintain a separate household.

In addition, a widow has no Social Security protection during the "widow's gap"—the years between the time her youngest child turns 16 and the widow turns 60, unless she is disabled. Displaced homemakers without earning skills may not qualify for Aid to Families with Dependent Children and are too young for Social Security, yet they must survive.[21] If the benefit is claimed at age 60, it is reduced by 28.5 percent for life.

And finally, a homemaker who becomes disabled is not eligible for Social Security benefits even though her disability could cause economic hardship for her family.

Women—as homemakers, paid workers, and increasingly as individuals who combine both roles during their lifetime—must continue their vigilance to assure that the Social Security system is responsive to their needs, now and in the future. They must educate policymakers to the notion that Social Security is a woman's issue and work to eliminate the inequities and inadequacies in the system that have contributed to their disadvantaged status as elderly women in our society.

Notes

1. Binstock, Robert H., "Reframing the Agenda of Policies on the Aging." *Proceedings of a Symposium on Income Maintenance* (May 17, 1982), p. 17, citing Warren Weaver Jr., "Pollster Detects Myths on Problems of Aged," *New York Times* (November 19, 1981), p. A18.
2. *Income of the Population 55 and Over, 1980,* U.S. Department of Health and Human Services, Social Security Administration, SSA Publication no. 13-11871 (January 1983), p.11 (Social Security data) Census Bureau, 1982 (population data).
3. Social Security Administration, April 1982.
4. *Income of the Population 55 and Over, 1980,* p.11.
5. Census Bureau, current population study, 1981.
6. Ibid.
7. *Money, Income, and Poverty Status of Families and Persons in the United States, 1981,* U.S. Department of Commerce, Bureau of the Census, Current Population Reports, Consumer Income Series P-60, no. 134 (July 1982), p.13-14.
8. Ibid., p.26.
9. *Income of the Population 55 and Over, 1978,* U.S. Department of Health and Human Services, Social Security Administration, SSA Publication no. 13-11871 (December 1981), p.18.
10. Sherburne, Jane D., "Women and Social Security: Seizing the Moment for Change." *Georgetown Law Journal* (August 1982): 1576, citing *Social Security and the Changing Roles of the Men and Women,* HEW Report (1979), p. 173.
11. *Factsheet on Women,* Community Services, American Council of Life Insurance (1982), p.1.
12. *Income of the Population 55 and Over, 1980,* p.65.
13. Ibid.
14. Poverty Branch, Bureau of the Census (1982).
15. *Income of the Population 55 and Over, 1980,* p.65.
16. *Social Security Bulletin: Annual Statistical Supplement, 1981,* U.S. Department of Health and Human Services, Social Security Administration, p.236.
17. Social Security Amendments of 1983, as printed in the House of Representatives Conference Report no. 98-47 (March 24, 1983).

18. Social Security Administration (December 1982).

19. Earnings sharing is a system in which the total earnings of a married couple are divided equally between them for each year of the marriage and credited to their individual earnings record for Social Security purposes. A number of variations on this concept are possible.

20. Section 132 (a) of the new legislation strikes the requirement that her former husband must retire before the divorced woman can get her benefit. But the requirement will remain in effect until December 31, 1984.

21. A displaced homemaker is an individual, almost always a woman, who has spent a substantial period of time in the home providing unpaid household services for family members. She suddenly finds herself thrust into the job market as a result of divorce, separation, death, or disability of a spouse, or loss of public assistance.

37

Women and the Economics of Aging

Carroll L. Estes, Lenore Gerard, and Adele Clarke

Introduction

Dr. Robert Butler, former Director of the National Institute of Aging, has observed that "the problems of old age in America are largely the problems of women" (1, p. 1). This observation reflects not only demographic data predicting that there will be 10 women for every five men over the age of 75 by the year 2000, but also, and more importantly, it reflects the distressing socioeconomic conditions in which many older women experience higher rates of poverty (60 percent higher than elderly men), differential pay and treatment in the labor market (averaging 60 percent of male wages), and consequently lower Social Security benefits (about two-thirds of the average male benefit) (2, 3).

The National Advisory Council on Economic Opportunity has challenged the myth that poverty has been eradicated. This observation becomes more salient when one examines the economic status of American women. The phenomenon that "two out of three poor adults are women" has been called the "feminization of poverty" (4). For some women, this poverty is a reflection of the life-long experience of poor socioeconomic conditions. For many others, however, it is a new experience resulting from the inequities of divorce. The question has been posed whether divorce, in effect, has created a class of "new poor" consisting of women and children who previously were in the middle income bracket (5). It is likely that this "new poor" class of women will experience hardships as they grow older and seek income security benefits.

During the 1970s, families headed by women increased more than 51 percent, from 5.6 million to 8.5 million. Today, there are "9.4 million single-adult female-headed families and the number is growing ten times as fast as male-headed families" (6,p.40). Because women usually earn less than men and these families generally lack the benefit of a second income, they face economic hardships (3,7). In 1978, the median income of families maintained by women was $8,540, or less than half of the $17,640 median income of all families. Among whites, 12 percent of all families were maintained by women, while females headed 20 percent of Hispanic families and 41 percent of black families (8).

By any standard, the most critical problem facing older persons is the lack of an adequate income. Retirement from the labor force often reduces an individual's income by about one-half. After years of decline, the poverty rate of older persons is on the rise again—rising dramatically from 14 percent in 1978 to 15.7 percent (or 3.9 million people) in 1980. More significantly, there is a larger percentage of persons over age 65 whose income levels are stacked just above the official poverty threshold. Almost 35 percent (8 million) of the elderly are estimated to be poor and near poor (9).

These economic realities are compounded for elderly women and minorities (10-14) who traditionally do not achieve social or economic status in society. Women, blacks, and other minorities are the most disadvantaged, with 38 percent of aged blacks and 30.8 percent of Hispanic aged living at extreme poverty levels (15). Today, half of all the aged poor are single women (never married or widows) who live alone (16). As shown in Table 37.1, about one-fifth of elderly women are poor, with the highest rates of poverty concentrated among older black and Hispanic females.

It is important to examine the factors underlying these inequities and how they relate to the economics of aging for women. Two major structural factors affect the economics of aging for women and in the future: (a) the explosion of the fourth generation, and (b) the labor force participation of women.

Explosion of the Fourth Generation

More than 25 million people are 65 years of age and over according to the 1980 U.S. census. This represents 11.3 percent of the total population, up from less than 3 percent a century ago when the first compulsory retirement policies were introduced. The concept of the fourth generation refers to the demographic boom of the very old and is attributed not only to greater longevity but also to earlier marriages and earlier childbearing, reducing the average span in years between generations (17). The percentage of aged who are 75 years and older, now comprising 38 percent of the elderly population, is expected to grow to 45 percent by the year 2000 (17,18). It is estimated that two-thirds of those over age 75 will be women (1). The oldest group—particularly women who are unmarried or widowed and without social supports—is most vulnerable because of dependence

TABLE 37.1
Incidence of Poverty among Persons Aged 55 and Older, by Sex and Race, 1981

	Percentage of persons with income below poverty line	
	Age 55-64	Age 65+
All groups (total)	10.1	15.3
Male	7.8	10.5
Female	12.1	18.6
Whites (total)	8.3	13.1
Male	6.6	8.5
Female	9.9	16.2
Blacks (total)	27.8	39.0
Male	20.3	32.3
Female	33.7	43.5
Hispanics (total)	19.1	25.7
Male	15.9	23.6
Female	21.2	27.4

Source: U.S. Bureau of the Census. Money income and poverty status of families and persons in the United States: 1981. *Current Population Reports,* Series P-60, No. 134.

upon public resources and programs to offset social factors such as diminished finances, loss of spouse or family supports, urban relocation, and increased incidence of health problems.

Labor Force Participation of Women

Some attribute the economic plight of older women to the inadequacies and inequities of income maintenance programs. However, as the Task Force on Women and Social Security (3) cautions, "There is no magic in Social Security." Social Security payments merely reflect differential rewards and inequities in the labor market: in other words, the root of the income problem for women stems from the labor market, wherein differential pay, low-wage occupations, and episodic work participation due to familial commitments have a combined and often devastating effect on income in later years.

The social and economic inequalities experienced in old age, then, are extensions of individuals' earlier positions in relation to the labor market (19-23). The economic security or insecurity that women experience in later life will be determined, to a large extent, by the relation of women in their middle years (45-64 years of age) to the labor market. This observation was affirmed by Congressman John Burton when he commented,

"Certainly we cannot erase all the inequities in Social Security until women achieve equality in the labor force" (2, p. 12).

There has been an enormous increase in labor force participation by older women over the past 30 years (24-26) and women now comprise about 40 percent of those 45 years of age and over in the labor force, compared with 25 percent in 1950 (26). This dramatic increase in older women's labor force participation in the United States can be attributed to women's changing role in society, economic factors, the growth of the service industry, increased education, and efforts to provide equal employment opportunities (24). However, older women's labor force participation is largely in the lower paid service sectors. For example, women make up 80 percent of the employees in the health care industry (27), but they represent the lower paid workers within that industry.

Women's Roles and Social Policy

An examination of women's roles in society as caregivers, as workers, and as beneficiaries is central to a social policy perspective. These roles are neither inclusive nor mutually exclusive; they form a complex and dynamic interrelationship. Each of these social roles has corresponding institutional structures that mediate between the individual and society, schematically shown below:

Roles	Institutional Structure
Caregiver	Family/Marriage
Worker	Labor Market
Patient/Beneficiary	Public and private policy: Income and health programs

Attention is now being given to the family's and women's caregiving roles, particularly in light of growing concern about the public cost of long-term care for the elderly, disabled youth, and adults. The general thrust of recent policy proposals and political rhetoric has been to emphasize family responsibility with minimal subsidies or tax incentives. Home care and other assistance for dependents is often provided by unpaid adult women. The consequences for such caretakers in terms of their own economic and social well-being is largely ignored.

Although the family continues to be the institution that assumes primary responsibility for the young and old, the family is not a system that operates in isolation: "It is deeply enmeshed in the social, political, and economic conditions of the times" (1, pp.12-13). Interventions targeted at the family alone do not acknowledge the complexity of the problems of older women, nor do they appropriately address the need for intervention.

Few policy intervention measures are targeted at the second and probably most significant institutional structure that affects women's economic status throughout their lifespan: the labor market. Although the aged have been accused of "busting the budget" and of draining resources from the younger working population (28,29), there are few public policies that lend support to the continued and valued experience of older persons in the labor market, and virtually none address the particular labor market problems of older women.

The Age Discrimination in Employment Act[1] and the Age Discrimination Act of 1975[2] have had a very limited effect. While evidence indicates that millions of older people want to work, the Older Americans Act employment program has never employed more than 53,000 nationwide. Further, in both 1982 and 1983, the Reagan Administration requested reductions that threatened the survival of even this small program. The Civil Rights Commission has found discrimination against the elderly in federal training and employment programs, which are targeted to those seen as most employable, thus largely excluding the elderly (30). The loss of many Comprehensive Employment and Training Act (CETA) jobs through federal cuts and other reductions in public funded employment and training programs seriously exacerbates the problem. In addition, the President's economic program has reduced jobs for women in multiple ways. For example, between April and June of 1982, 46 percent of the federal work force reductions involved females although women make up only 29 percent of the force. It has been estimated that 9,500 jobs disappear for women with every $1 billion increase in the military budget (6).

Ageism, sexism, the economic climate, and specific employment policies (e.g., superannuation or retirement) undermine continued work for older persons in general and for older women in particular. Even if work can be found, there are disincentives, such as the reduction of Social Security benefits ($.50 for every $1.00 earned) above a fixed minimum of allowed earned income. Although there has been substantial discussion about maintaining the productivity of older persons in the work force, the U.S. Joint Economic Committee has observed that the U.S. government and industry are unlikely to encourage older persons to remain in jobs or to take new jobs as long as there is widespread unemployment (24).

The third major institutional structure is public and private policy as it affects income and health programs. Publicly financed income and health programs are targeted largely toward those who are retired. At retirement age, an older individual can seek income support from private savings, investments, employer pension plans, or public programs such as Social

Security or means-tested Supplementary Security Income. In addition, Medicare (Title XVIII of the Social Security Act) is designed to provide health insurance to most individuals aged 65 and over and to disabled persons under age 65 who qualify. Cost-sharing and deductible features of the Medicare program, which finances the cost of acute, episodic illness requiring hospital care and some portion of physician services, result in Medicare coverage of only approximately 44 percent of an older person's health care bill. The limitations of such income and health programs and the consequences of the Reagan Administration cutbacks have been described as severe (31).

For persons under 65 years of age, access to medical care is almost entirely tied to group insurance plans negotiated at the place of employment. The only exception to this pattern of health care coverage in the United States is the Medicaid program, which is the nation's largest publicly financed health insurance program for the poor. Access to Medicaid is tied to a state's welfare criteria and consequently not only has a high stigma associated with it, but also varies widely from state to state. While women living at the poorest economic level can seek access to health care through Medicaid, many others who are "near poor" (subsisting on an income just above the official poverty threshold) or on "moderate" incomes are caught in between without the financial means to secure adequate health protection.

There are some 30 million persons in the United States without any health care coverage. An overlooked segment of this population is women between 45 and 65 years of age who are frequently without adequate insurance coverage to protect them against the risk of acute or chronic illness. This "invisible" group of uninsured women is estimated to be around 4.5 million women in mid-life. The experience of these women is often one of dependent homemaker or part-time worker whose health insurance was lost (or nonexistent) as a result of a change in marital status. Also, midlife married women may lose family health care coverage when the older husbands retire and can no longer afford to continue the insurance on a private, individual basis of payment (32). Furthermore, many of those women who can afford to pay for private insurance will be subjected to careful scrutiny by the insurance carrier. For example, what is viewed as an "adverse health history" of a woman over 45 years of age can be the basis for disqualifying an applicant from private health insurance protection (32).

In summary, health-related policy issues for women encompass older women in mid-life as well as those over 65 years of age. Major concerns are: 1) the effects of work on health status and the effects of health on work status (33); 2) access to health care for women in mid-life living on moderate to low incomes and for women over 65 years of age; 3) the effect of women's caregiver role on poverty, health, stress, and labor participation; and 4) the inadequate and fragmented health care system skewed toward institutional services with few or no community care alternatives—a system which burdens the informal caregiving sector, the family and especially the older woman.

Sources of Income for Older Women

There are four potential sources of income in old age: 1) assets, 2) private pensions, 3) Social Security, and 4) income programs for the poor over age 65.

Assets

Although approximately half of the older population receives income from assets, many units receive only small amounts and the proportion of total income this represents is low (10). For example, the median amount of asset income for those aged 65 and over was only $870 in 1976. Evidence indicates that individuals whose lifetime income is high will accumulate more assets than will those whose incomes are lower. Thus, it is not surprising to find that men have larger assets than women, and that marital status is a critical factor in the distribution of those assets (34).

Private Pensions

Any attempt to determine the adequacy of income for the elderly must consider private pension systems as well as the public system and the inequities that characterize them. There are about one-half million pension, profit sharing, and stock-bonus plans. In 1979 it was estimated that over 30 million persons—about half of all wage and salary workers—were covered in private pensions. However, women are much less likely than men to be covered by a retirement plan (24). According to the White House Miniconference on Older Women (35), private pensions are not available to over 80 percent of retiring women workers.

Further, until 1983, it was legal for pension plans taking equal contributions from men and women to pay women retirees at lower rates based upon their greater longevity. Significantly, it was a Supreme Court decision (under the 1964 Civil Rights Act), rather than a legislatively enacted policy, that finally provided individual women pensioners with equal protection (36).

Social Security

The issues surrounding the treatment of women under Social Security have been and continue to be a topic of national importance, especially since Social Security is the major source of income for the majority of older women (2, 3, 24, 35). Of particular public policy concern are those older women in the lower economic strata. Using data from the 1981 Current Population Survey, a recent study (6, p.61) showed "that single women over age 65 with incomes less than $5,000 depend on Social Security for more than 80 percent of their income. But half the older women in this country have incomes under $5,000 and almost two-thirds of all older women in the United States are single (widowed, divorced, separated, or never married)."

Although it is estimated that Social Security preserves two-thirds of the older population from *acute* poverty, it is insufficient to keep millions of retired persons from *real* poverty (8). The 1979 *median* Social Security benefit was $290 per month (30). And, as previously noted, women's Social Security benefits are only about two-thirds those of men.

Major gaps and inadequate benefits in Social Security are particular problems for women who are divorced and who have spent most of their working years as homemakers. The major adequacy problems are 1) lack of protection for women divorced after less than 10 years of marriage, 2) inadequate benefit levels for aged divorced women, and 3) gaps in protection for women whose spouses die before retirement (37). Divorced women who have not been consistent wage earners have little or no Social Security protection in their own right. Since aged widows tend to live longer, they are likely to have little or no income other than below-average Social Security benefits computed on outdated earnings, which may be further reduced if the widow finds she must draw benefits before age 65 (2).

The major inequities in Social Security are between married couples and single individuals and between one-earner and two-earner couples. Two-earner couples generally receive lower benefits than one-earner couples with the same total earnings. Because of the differences in the benefits of one- and two-earner couples, the surviving spouse of a two-wage-earner couple generally receives less than the surviving spouse of a one-earner couple with the same total income. Moreover, married women who spend time out of the paid labor force in homemaking and child-care activities are not allowed to drop childrearing years from the averaging period used to compute benefits. (Both men and women have five drop out years.) This long averaging period generally results in lower average benefits to women than to men.

There are serious inadequacies and inequities within the Social Security system for millions of working wives, single working women, and homemakers (38). As Treas has pointed out (39,p.571): "While recognizing the family as the consuming unit in need of income, the system failed to allow for the coordinated efforts of family members in income-getting. In the case of the housewife's support services, the system has been faulted for not adequately protecting the homemaker's community property claim to husband's earned benefits, especially against a rising tide of marital disruption. In the case of the working wife's earnings, the system has been criticized for discounting the second earner's essential role in family finances."

Income Programs for the Poor over Age 65

For those individuals who have been intermittently employed and for those who have had very low lifetime earnings covered by Social Security (mainly women and minorities), a federal minimum benefit had been established. Especially significant for women are the Reagan Administration and Congressional cutbacks in 1981 and 1982 that resulted in the eradication of the minimum Social Security benefit (which then was only a bare $122 monthly) for all but those already in the program and those who would become eligible before January 1982.

In addition, Supplementary Security Income (SSI) is a cash assistance program enacted in 1972 for the poor aged, blind, and disabled persons. This federal-state program is a means-tested program, for which an individual's income and resources determine eligibility and the amount of payment. SSI provides a subsistence income to over four million needy persons, with the majority (three-fourths) of aged beneficiaries being women over 75 years of age. Of those aged families subsisting on the combined benefits provided by SSI and Social Security, 49.4 percent were still below the poverty line in 1977. For single persons in these circumstances, 59.5 percent were officially living in poverty in 1977 (24). The maximum federal SSI benefit is $265 for an individual and $397 for a couple (as of January 1982). Once the minimum federal payment level is established, states have complete discretion in determining whether they will supplement this amount, by how much, and the standards. Among the 25 states that administered their own programs in 1980, the average level of state supplement benefit varied greatly from $20 in Wyoming to $206 in Virginia for poor, aged single individuals living alone. Thus, there are substantial inequities based on such factors as place of residence and living arrangements (31).

Policy Issues Concerned with the Economic and Social Well-Being of Women

The status and resources of older women in the next two decades will be affected by the economic climate and health of the U.S. and world economy and the politically negotiated choices of how a "healthy" economy is to be achieved.

Health Policy

The two structural factors noted earlier—women's increased labor force participation and the explosion of the fourth generation—raise important questions pertaining to the issue of health and who bears the burden of its cost. We know enough to predict that the fourth generation will require a measure of family reponsibility as well as possible monetary support in the form of private income transfers among family members.

What demands will a fourth generation exert on the social and medical support system funded largely out of public dollars? How, in turn, will this contribute to or hinder the labor force participation of older women? We must keep in mind that 80 percent of the care of elders is given by family members, primarily women. Given the knowledge that differences in social class, race, and marital status are crucial in determining women's economic status, can we assume more women will be better off in their later years as a result of increased continued employment?

With the push to reduce the federal role as well as publicly funded social expenditures, increasing attention has been given to approaches in social and health policy that lower the public costs. An example is the emphasis upon the family assuming responsibility for the long-term care for family members (whether it be a spouse, parent, or child). Yet, often such words as "the family" or phrases as the "informal support system" have been euphemisms for women, with daughters and daughters-in-law being the primary caregivers (40).

Clearly, the family is an important social institution in assuming responsibility for the young and the old. We know that both the presence of a caregiver and the type of living arrangement are critical in determining nursing home entry (41, 42). Nevertheless, a key issue is whether the current policy emphasis on the family in long-term care is commensurate with other social and economic demands on women in their middle and later years, and especially for those who are single, divorced, or widowed and without adequate income. Is it realistic to assume that women (many of whom are in the work force) can still meet familial expectations and obligations assigned to them in the 19th century? The Task Force on Women and Social Security (3) has noted that the traditional belief that "women's place is in the home" has persisted into the 20th century in the face of so many contradictions and exceptions that it has become a "convenient myth." Although the historical increase of women's participation in the labor force challenges this notion, the recent resurrection of such myths is useful in supporting public policies that limit state-sponsored services for groups like the elderly, the disabled, and the young chronically ill.

Intervention strategies need to take into account these social-structural parameters so that "informal support" is not a rhetorical substitute for further inequitable burdens on women as caregivers. Consideration must also be given to the fact that a women's role as a caregiver in a family unit may be quickly transformed into that of patient or beneficiary, dependent upon the state. The purview of long-term care policy should not be limited to the poorest segments of society, but rather should encompass a larger population of *all* women who are without adequate income protection and sufficient assets to offset the possible afflictions of chronic illness, depression, loss of spouse, the necessity to support a parent, and social isolation. A woman's economic and social well-being may very well be threatened by a configuration of any one of these factors as she grows older.

Although much attention is afforded the public costs of long-term care, much less attention has been given to the financial impact on the remaining partner of institutionalizing a spouse (43). The financial problems arising from this situation may indeed be devasting, yet public policy offers little or nothing to the middle class or near poor elderly spouse in this situation. For example, as noted by Packwood (43, p. 1040), "This individual, who is usually a woman, is forced to divide one income into two parts; one portion for the payment of nursing home costs and the second for her own living expenses. This not only keeps the community-based spouse from maintaining her maximum level of functional independence, but it also increases the likelihood of her entering a nursing home."

There are several options open to a woman when faced with the dilemma of having a spouse who requires long-term care: 1) "spending-down" until Medicaid eligibility is achieved, thereby impoverishing herself; 2) getting a divorce; 3) continuing payments for long-term care (43); or 4) if she works, quitting her job to assume the role of primary caregiver to prevent the spouse's institutionalization.[3] Each of these "solutions" virtually assures poverty for the spouse. Because this is largely a hidden problem of the middle class married elderly population, very little is known about its role in the poverty of older women. A similar set of pressures and financial losses is incurred by millions of daughters and daughters-in-law in caring for older parents. This also is an understudied and ignored phenomenon by public policy.

Current public policy provides strong disincentives for community-based family support in the following ways: 1) the one-third reduction in Supplemental Security Income (SSI) for an elder's living in the household of one's children (thus depriving elderly parents of essential income if they reside with their adult children); 2) the prohibition in many states against payment through the Social Services Block Grant (formerly Title XX) to individual family members providing care to an elderly parent,[4] although homemaker help provided by non-family may be paid for; 3) the Title XIX Medicaid spend-down provision that may impoverish both the patient and spouse in order to receive nursing home care; 4) the almost nonexistent Medicaid-Medicare home health benefit coverage; and 5) the tax structure that offers no incentives (i.e., tax deductions) to family members who assume some financial responsibilty for their elders, regardless of whether they live in the same household.[5]

Income Policy

Historically, women have earned less than men—averaging 60 percent of men's earnings. Worse, the median income for women 56-64 years of age approximates *one-third* of the *median* income of males of the same age (7). The median income for older men in 1981 was $8,173; the figure for women was $4,975, or just 58 percent of men's income. Since half of all older women have incomes below or within $400 of the official poverty level ($4,359), it is not surprising that 72 percent of the elderly poor are women (44). Table 37.2 breaks down the differences in median income for three age groups: 45-54, 55-64, and 65-69. As shown, women's median income is even less than half of men's prior to age 65.

This disparity in earnings stems from "the social institutions of school, family, and economy and not within Social Security per se" (39,p.572). It is important to note that serious issues of adequacy and equity in income security benefits exist for older women because these benefits are based largely on labor market experience that is disadvantageous to women of all ages. In analyzing the effects of mid-life work history and the retirement income of older single and married women, O'Rand and Henretta (45) summarize several important features of women's participation in the labor market. First, many women experience in-and-out-of work patterns

TABLE 37.2
Male and Female Differences in Median Income (in dollars), 1977

Age and sex group	Median income
45-54 years	
Male	15,331
Female	5,670
55-64 years	
Male	12,243
Female	4,533
65-69 years	
Male	6,516
Female	3,010

Source: U.S. Bureau of the Census. *Statistical Abstract of the United States: 1979.* U.S. Department of Commerce, Washington, D.C., 1980.

(interrupted participation) over time. Second, women largely are concentrated in a few occupations such as sales, service, and clerical work, a 1 a few professions such as teaching and social services. Third, women tend to work in industries characterized by high turnover rates, low wages and fringe benefits, and the absence of a union. Furthermore, starting work after the age of 35 years can be particularly disadvantageous in terms of the level of retirement income unless work is begun in an industry with good wages and pension benefits (45). Thus, a determining factor in the adequacy of retirement benefits is whether one works in the primary labor market (characterized by high-paying jobs with stability and benefits) or the secondary labor market (characterized by low-paying jobs with instability and poor working conditions). Women and minorities are overrepresented in the secondary labor market and as a result depend largely on Social Security benefits which turn out to be quite low.

Summary and Conclusions

Social policies are shaped largely by requirements of the economy and the economic climate. The position of women workers in the economy has been and continues to be systematically unequal. By failing to address these inequities, social policies affecting older women have perpetuated their disadvantaged economic situations throughout old age. Bluntly stated, public policy has reflected the myth that women have worked only for "pin money," assuring that elderly women did not then have a right to a reasonable or even decent standard of living. The value of women's labor in the home and in creating and maintaining the family also has been ignored or minimized.

Given the politics of fiscal retrenchment and its severe impact on young and old women alike, the policy outlook for older women is grim. The bias against women and minorities of federal policy shifts, and of tax and budget cuts since 1981 has been extensively documented (46-48). Tax cuts have dramatically benefited households with annual incomes above $80,000 (augmenting their income by more than $55 billion), while households with incomes under $10,000 are losing $17 billion between 1983 and 1985 (49). Benefit reductions, on the other hand, have been taken in largest measure from the under $10,000 annual income category and next from those in the $10,000 to $20,000 income category. While 45 percent of the cuts will come from the under $10,000 group, and 25 percent from the $10,000 to $20,000 group, less than one percent of the cuts will come from the $80,000 and over group by 1985 (45,48). Because women have lower incomes, they are incurring a larger share of benefit cuts and a disproportionately small share of the tax reduction benefits. Thus, the inequities in wealth distribution have been increased as there has been an accelerated shift of resources from females to males and from minorities to whites in the United States with the policy changes imposed during the Reagan Administration (6,49).

Despite retrenchment, policies continue to be reformulated. Attention to the sources of previous socio-structural and policy inequities is needed to ameliorate their negative impact and to aid in the development of new policies in order to avoid furthering the already extremely inequitable economic situation of older women.

Notes

A modified version of this article will be included in *The Political Economy of Aging,* edited by M. Minkler and C.L. Estes, forthcoming from Baywood Publishing Co.

1. The 1978 amendments to this 1967 act extended coverage by upper limit from age 65 to 70 for private employment and nonfederal public employment, plus other changes.
2. P.L. 94-135, 1975, provides that "no person in the U.S. shall on the basis of any age, be excluded from participation in, be denied the benefits of, or be subjected to discrimination under any program or activity receiving federal financial assistance."
3. To avoid impoverishment due to an institutionalized spouse, it was found that welfare case workers in North Carolina were encouraging elderly married couples to file for divorce (43).
4. This is not the case, however, in California, which does make payment to family members in support of a poor elderly individual; many other states in the U.S. do not make this offer.
5. At the federal level, bills have been introduced in Congress that would allow a credit against tax for care of elderly family members. Currently there are tax provisions to offset some expenses incurred; but, because of rigid eligibility requirements, very few families use them. At the state level, some states have proposed tax relief legislation to help families, but few have actually enacted such legislation (30).

References

1. U.S. National Institute on Aging. *The Older Woman: Continuities and Discontinuities.* U.S. Government Printing Office, Washington, D.C., 1979.
2. Burton, J. L. "Elder women suffer frequently and severely during retirement." *Generations* 4(4): 12,1980.
3. U.S. Senate Special Committee on Aging. *Women and Social Security: Adapting to a New Era.* U.S. Government Printing Office, Washington, D.C.,1975.
4. Blaustein, A. I. (ed.). *The American Promise: Equal Justice and Economic Opportunity.* Transaction Books, New Brunswick, N.J., 1982.

5. Culverwell, M. "Are divorcees the nation's 'new poor?'" *Sheet* (University of California) 58(26): 1,1983.
6. National Women's Law Center. *Inequality of Sacrifice: The Impact of the Reagan Budget on Women.* Washington, D.C.,1983.
7. U.S. Bureau of the Census. *Statistical Abstracts of the United States,* 101st ed. U.S. Government Printing Office, Washington, D.C., 1980.
8. U.S. General Accounting Office. *Perspective on Income Security and Social Services and an Agenda for Analysis.* Washington, D.C.,1981.
9. Lehrman, P. "Poverty statistics serve as nagging reminder." *Generations* 4(1):17,1980.
10. Grad, S., and Foster, K. "Income of the population aged 55 and older, 1976." *Social Security Bulletin* 42(7):16-32,1979.
11. Abbott, J. "Socioeconomic characteristics of the elderly: Some black-white differences." *Social Security Bulletin* 40(7):16-42,1977.
12. McNeely, R.L. (ed.). *Aging in Minority Groups.* Sage, Beverly Hills, Ca., 1983.
13. Fuller, M. M., and Martin, C.A. *The Older Woman.* C.C.Thomas, Springfield, Ill.,1980.
14. Manuel, R.C. (ed.). *Minority Aging: Sociological and Social Psychological Issues.* Greenwood Press, Westport, Ct., 1982.
15. U.S. House Select Committee on Aging. *Every Ninth American.* U.S. Government Printing Office, Washington, D.C., 1981.
16. U.S. House Select Committee on Aging. *Hearing: Poverty among America's Aged, August 9.* U.S. Government Printing Office, Washington, D.C.,1978.
17. Townsend, P. *Poverty in the United Kingdom.* University of California Press, Berkeley, 1979.
18. Data Resource. *Inflation and the Elderly.* Data Resource, Lexington, Ma., 1980.
19. Walker, A. "The social creation of poverty and dependency in old age." *Journal of Social Policy* 9:49-75,1980.
20. Walker, A. "Towards a political economy of old age." *Ageing and Society* 1(1):73-94,1981.
21. Townsend, P. "The structured dependency of the elderly: A creation of social policy in the twentieth century." *Ageing and Society* 1(1):5-28,1981.
22. Myles, J.F. "The aged, the state, and the structure of inequality." In *Structural Inequality in Canada*, edited by J. Harp and J. Hofley. Prentice-Hall, Toronto, 1980.
23. U.S. House Select Committee on Aging. *The Status of Mid-Life Women and Options for Their Future.* U.S. Government Printing Office, Washington, D.C.,1980.
24. U.S. Joint Economic Committee, Special Study on Economic Change, *Social Security and Pensions: Programs of Equity and Security.* U.S. Government Printing Office, Washington,D.C.,1980.
25. Kreps, J., and Clark, P. *Sex, Age, and Work.* Johns Hopkins University Press, Baltimore, Md., 1975.
26. Work in America Institute. *The Future of Older Workers in America.* Work in America Institute, New York,1980.
27. Urguhart, M. "The service industry: Is it recession proof?" *Monthly Labor Review* 104:12-18,1981.
28. Samuelson, R.J. "Busting the U.S. budget: The costs of an aging America." *National Journal* 10(7):256-260,1978.

29. Samuelson, R.J. "Benefit programs for the elderly: Off limits to Federal budget cutters?" *National Journal* 14(40):1757-1762,1981.
30. U.S. Senate Special Committee on Aging. *Developments in Aging.* U.S. Government Printing Office, Washington,D.C.,1980 and 1981.
31. Harrington, C. "Social security and medicare: Policy shifts in the 1980s." In *Fiscal Austerity and Aging: Shifting Government Responsibility for the Elderly.* Sage, Beverly Hills, Ca.,1983.
32. Older Women's League (OWL). "Health Insurance Coverage of Women in Mid-Life." Oakland, Ca.,1983 (manuscript).
33. Fee, E. (ed.). *Women and Health: The Politics of Sex in Medicine.* Baywood, New York, 1983.
34. Friedman, J., and Sjogren, J. "Assets of the elderly as they retire." *Social Security Bulletin* 44(1): 16-31, 1981.
35. White House Conference on Aging. *Miniconference on Older Women.* U.S. Government Printing Office, Washington, D.C., 1980.
36. *San Francisco Chronicle* (July 11, 1983).
37. Munnell, A.H., and Stiglin, L.E. "Women and a two-tier social security system." In *A Challenge to Social Security: The Changing Roles of Women and Men in American Society,* edited by R.V. Burkauser and K.C. Holden. Academic Press, New York, 1982.
38. Burkauser, R.V., and Holden, K.C. (eds.). *A Challenge to Social Security: The Changing Roles of Women and Men in American Society.* Academic Press, New York, 1982.
39. Treas, J. "Women's employment and its implications for the status of the elderly of the future." In *Aging: Social Change,* edited by S.B. Kiesler. Academic Press, New York, 1981.
40. Brody, E.M. "Women in the middle and family help to older people." *Gerontologist* 21(5): 471-80, 1981.
41. Butler, L.H., and Newacheck, P.W. *Health and Social Factors Relevant to Long Term Care Policy.* Institute of Health Policy Studies, University of California, San Francisco, 1980.
42. U.S. General Accounting Office. *Entering a Nursing Home: Costly Implications for Medicaid and the Elderly.* Report to the Congress by the Comptroller General of the United States. General Accounting Office, Washington, D.C., 1979.
43. Packwood, R. "Long term care: Costs, financing and alternative services, public and private sector policy options." In *The Future of Health Care: National Journal Issues Book.* National Journal, Washington, D.C., 1981.
44. Leadership Council of Aging Organizations. *The Administration's 1984 Budget: A Critical View from an Aging Perspective.* Leadership Council of Aging Organizations, Washington, D.C., 1983.
45. O'Rand, A.M., and Henretta, J.C. "Midlife work history and the retirement income of older single and married women." In Szinovacz, M. (ed.). *Women's Retirement: Sage Yearbooks in Women's Policy Studies,* vol.6, edited by M. Szinovacz. Sage, Beverly Hill, Ca., 1982.
46. Palmer, J., and Sawhill, I. (eds.). *The Reagan Experiment.* The Urban Institute, Washington, D.C., 1982.
47. U.S. Congressional Budget Office. *Effects of Tax and Benefit Reductions Enacted in 1981 for Households in Different Income Categories.* Congressional Budget Office, Washington, D.C., 1982.

48. U.S. Congressional Budget Office. *Effects of Tax and Benefit Payments Enacted in 1982 for Households in Different Income Categories.* Congressional Budget Office, Washington, D.C., 1982.
49. Greenstein, R., and Bickerman, J. *The Effects of the Administration's Budget, Tax, and Military Policies on Low-Income Americans.* Interreligious Task Force on U.S. Food Policy, Washington, D.C., 1983.

Contributors

Arnold Arluke is associate professor of sociology and anthropology at Northeastern University in Boston. His current research focus is on the infantilization and dehumanization of elders.

Jerry Avorn is assistant professor of social medicine and health policy, Harvard Medical School, and faculty internist, Division of Gerontology, Beth Israel Hospital, Boston. His major research interests are drug use patterns and adverse effects in the elderly, and ethical and policy aspects of geriatric care.

Paul M. Baker is associate professor of sociology at the University of Victoria, Canada, and is also vice-president of the Victoria Institute of Gerontology. His current research concerns ageism, the role of grandparents in Western society, and adaptation to retirement.

Robert H. Binstock is Henry R. Luce Professor of Aging, Health, and Society, in the School of Medicine, Case Western Reserve University. His current research is focused on the implications of an aging society.

Adele Clarke is a doctoral candidate in Sociology at the University of California, San Francisco. Formerly coordinator of the Women's Studies Program at Sonoma State University, she has taught on women's issues since 1974. She is currently studying the organization of modern reproductive biology in the United States from 1900 to 1940.

Linda Evans Cool is associate professor of anthropology and chair of the Department of Anthropology-Sociology at the University of Santa Clara. Her gerontological research focuses on the role of ethnic identity in the social aging process.

Elaine Cumming has published numerous books and articles in sociology including *Growing Old; Systems of Social Regulation;* and *Closed Ranks.* She is Professor Emeritus of Sociology, University of Victoria, Canada.

John Cumming has published extensively in the areas of psychiatry and mental health. He is currently director of psychiatry at the Greater Vancouver Mental Health Service, a community service he established in the early 1970s.

Carroll L. Estes, a professor of sociology, is chair of the Department of Social and Behavioral Sciences and director of the Aging Health Policy Center, School of Nursing, University of California, San Francisco. Dr. Estes conducts research and writes about aging policy, issues in long-term care for the elderly, and the effects of fiscal crises and the new federalism. She is the author of *The Aging Enterprise* and *The Decision Makers: The Power Structure of Dallas,* and coauthor of *Fiscal Austerity and Aging; Political Economy, Health, and Aging;* and *Public Policy in Long Term Care.*

Marjorie Chary Feinson is a postdoctoral fellow in the Rutgers-Princeton Program in Mental Health Research and consultant on health and mental health policy and planning issues. Her research interests include health and mental health policy, particularly related to older adults; health and gender issues; and ethics and aging.

Nancy Foner is associate professor of anthropology at the State University of New York, College at Purchase. She has done research on aging in cross-cultural perspective, on Caribbean populations, and on migration. She is the author of *Ages in Conflict: A Cross-Cultural Perspective on Inequality between Old and Young; Jamaica Farewell: Jamaican Migrants in London;* and *Status and Power in Rural Jamaica: A Study of Educational and Political Change.*

Maxine Forman is director of policy analysis for the Women's Equity Action League. She serves on the Technical Committee on Social Security Reform for Women, a nongovernmental group which is developing a Social Security earnings sharing model. Ms. Forman also serves on the Women's Issue Committee of Save Our Security (SOS), a coalition of diverse groups formed to strengthen and protect the Social Security system.

Florence Galkin is a participant in the CORO Foundation's Public Affairs Leadership Training Program for Women. Previously, she was the founder and director of Community Action and Resources for the Elderly, a consultant to the Community Council of Greater New York's Nursing Home Ombudsman Project, and a staff associate at the United Hospital Fund. She has published several monographs on long-term care and articles in *Congress Monthly* and *New York Affairs.*

Richard J. Gelles is dean of the College of Arts and Sciences and Professor of sociology and anthropology at the University of Rhode Island. He has authored and edited five books on family violence and numerous professional articles on child abuse, wife abuse, and family violence.

Lenore Gerard is staff research associate, Department of Sociology and Behavioral Sciences, Aging and Health Policy Center, University of California, San Francisco. She coauthored *Political Economy, Health, and Aging.*

Brian Gratton is assistant professor of history at Arizona State University, Tempe. He is interested in the contemporary retirement behavior of older women, the historical labor force participation of aged men, and the origins of geriatric medicine.

Jaber F. Gubrium is professor of sociology at Marquette University. Currently researching the descriptive organization of senile dementia, Gubrium has completed a book on *Oldtimers and Alzheimer's.*

Robert Helsabeck is professor of sociology at Stockton State College, Pomona, N.J. He has published a number of articles in the areas of organizational behavior and conflict resolution. He authored *The Confound System: A Conceptual Framework for Effective Decision-Making in College.*

Beth B. Hess is professor of sociology at County College of Morris, Randolph, N.J. She is a Fellow of the Gerontological Society of America, and has served as an officer of the Section on Social and Behavioral Sciences. She has written introductory textbooks in sociology and in social gerontology, and has contributed chapters on many facets of aging to the works of others. Her most recent publications include an analysis of the *New Feminist Movement,* a volume of readings on *Women and the Family,* and the second edition of *Sociology.*

Martin Hochbaum is director of the Commission on Urban Affairs at the American Jewish Congress. He is also adjunct professor of health advocacy at Sarah Lawrence College and Chairman of the New York State Council on Shared Health Facilities. His publications have appeared in numerous journals and newspapers and he is coeditor of *Poor Jews: An American Awakening.*

Charlotte Ikels is a research associate at the Laboratory of Human Development, Harvard Graduate School of Education. Currently collaborating with Christine L. Fry and Jennie Keith on a cross-cultural project on age and culture, she spent 1982-83 in Hong Kong collecting data on people's perceptions of the life cycle and the significance of age to social participation.

David A. Karp is on the sociology faculty of Boston College, Chestnut Hill, Massachusetts. The author of numerous scholarly publications on sociology and aging, his current research interests center on the connections between work, organizational affiliation, and aging among professionals.

Nathan Keyfitz is Andelot Professor of Sociology and Demography at Harvard University. Besides articles in such magazines as *Science* and *Transaction/Society,* his numerous writings on the mathematics of population include *Applied Mathematical Demography.*

Ellen J. Langer, a professor of psychology at Harvard University, is a member of the Division on Aging of the Faculty of Medicine at Harvard. Her research interests broadly focus on psychological and physical debilitations associated with aging that may be reversible through psychological intervention.

Gary R. Lee is associate professor of sociology, associate rural sociologist, and associate scientist in the Social Research Center at Washington State University. His research and writing have focused on comparative family systems and the sociology of aging, with particular emphasis on the social integration of the elderly.

Jack Levin, a professor at the Department of Sociology of Northwestern University, is currently completing a study of mass murderers and continuing research concerning the impact of ageism on the status of the elderly.

Robert J. Lynott is a Ph.D. candidate at Loyola University of Chicago and a predoctoral fellow with the Midwest Council for Social Research in Aging. He is active in research on the social organization of senility. He recently completed papers on the decision to institutionalize Alzheimer's patients and Alzheimer's disease as biographical work.

Justine McCabe has conducted gerontological research on needs assessment methology as a research associate in the Department of Agriculture Economics at the University of California at Davis and also did extensive work as a lobbyist in the California Legislature on behalf of a consumer health group, DES ACTION. At present she is a research scholar at the Henry T. Murray Research Center at Radcliffe College where she is pursuing her main research interest in psychological androgyny in later life.

Jacqueline MacDonald, a resident of Victoria, British Columbia, is currently working at the Cubbon Geriatric Day Care Center.

Kyriakos S. Markides is associate professor in the Division of Sociomedical Sciences, Department of Preventive Medicine and Community Health, University of Texas Medical Branch, Galveston, Texas. His research interests include minority aging, aging and health, and intergenerational relationships.

Elizabeth W. Markson is director for social research, Boston University Gerontology Center; adjunct associate professor, Boston University Medical School; and research associate professor, Department of Sociology, Boston University. She has published extensively on health care of the aged, and has edited *Public Policies for an Aging Population* and on *Older Women.* She has also collaborated with Beth B. Hess on introductory textbooks in sociology and social gerontology. Professor Markson is currently book review editor of *The Gerontologist.*

Charles H. Mindel is professor, Graduate School of Social Work, University of Texas at Arlington. His current research interests concern ethnic differences in the use of social services by the elderly and the role of the family in the provision of social support to the elderly.

John Myles is associate professor in the Department of Sociology and Anthropology, Carleton University, Ottawa. He is the author of *Old Age in the Welfare State: The Political Economy of Public Pensions.* He is currently engaged in a comparative study of class structure and class consciousness in capitalist democracies.

Corinne N. Nydegger is professor of medical anthropology and psychiatry, University of California, San Francisco. Her research focus is the father's role (timing consequences, relations with adult children, interactions of career and family) and the older family in cross-cultural perspective.

Leonard I. Pearlin is professor of medical sociology and director of the Human Development and Aging Program in the Department of Psychology at the University of California, San Francisco. His research examines stress along the life course.

Claire Pedrick-Cornell is an instructor in the Department of Sociology and Anthropology at the University of Rhode Island. She has authored two books on family violence and several professional papers on child abuse, elder abuse, and spouse abuse.

Jill Quadagno is associate professor in the Department of Sociology at the University of Kansas. She is writing a monograph on the history of economic support for the aged in the United States. She is also engaged in a research project on the administration of services to the aged in Kansas.

Clarice Radabaugh is at the National Cancer Institute where she is presently involved in an evaluation of the impact of a community oncology program on the quality of treatment for cancer patients, among them an increasing number of older persons.

Matilda White Riley is deputy director of the National Institute of Aging where she directs social and behavioral research. The author of numerous books and scholarly articles, she has been elected president of the American Sociological Association for 1986.

Jeffrey P. Rosenfeld teaches sociology at Nassau Community College. He is researching the impact of aging on patterns of inheritance in American society. He works with Plan Wise, which does consultation and research in the estate planning industry.

Eileen Schmelzle is a liaison nurse at Curry General Hospital, British Columbia.

Franklin Smith is professor of sociology at Stockton State College. His last book was *A City Revitalized: The Elderly Lose at Monopoly,* and he has also written in the areas of sociology of sports and sociology of education.

Sylvia A. Stevens is director of social services at Apache Junction Medical Center, an outreach clinic of Mesa Lutheran Hospital. As a practicing social worker, she has a continued interest in the interaction of her clients and their environment.

Deborah A. Sullivan is assistant professor of sociology at Arizona State University. She was formerly affiliated with the Center for Demographic Studies at Duke University. In addition to her interests in migration and retirement lifestyles among the elderly, her recent research and publications have dealt with alternatives in maternity care.

Maximiliane E. Szinovacz is associate professor of sociology at Florida State University. Her recent research interests focus on women's roles, family power relations and decision making, as well as women's retirement. She coauthored *Family Decision Making* (with John Scanzoni) and is editor of *Women's Retirement.*

Marea Teski is associate professor of anthropology and coordinator of sociology-anthropology at Stockton State College, Pomona, New Jersey. She was instrumental in setting up Stockton's gerontology program. Her current research interests are ethnic aging and the elderly under severe conditions of social change.

Joan Titus is currently conducting research at the West Coast Savings Credit Union in British Columbia. Trained as a nurse, she has a master's degree in sociology and training in computer analysis.

Barbara F. Turner is director of the Center on Aging and professor of education, psychology, and labor relations at the University of Massachusetts at Amherst. Her research interests and many publications center on sex-related differences in aging, focusing in particular on personality and sex roles. Recent chapters and articles include "Sex-related Differences in Aging," "Mental Health in the Adult Years," "Sex Differences in Psychotherapy with Older People," and "Reported Change in Sexuality from Young Adulthood to Old Age."

Lois M. Verbrugge is associate research scientist at the University of Michigan, with the Institute of Gerontology, and the Institute for Social Research. She is a social demographer who focuses her research on sex differentials in health and mortality.

Andrea S. Walsh teaches sociology at Clark University. Her research and teaching interests focus on social gerontology, women's studies, and mass communications.

Ruth B. Weg is associate professor of biology and gerontology in the Leonard Davis School of Gerontology, Ethel Percy Andrus Gerontology Center, at the University of California, Los Angeles. She is the author of numerous publications on aging and is editor of *Sexuality in the Later Years: Roles and Behavior.*

John B. Williamson is professor of sociology at Boston College and is the author of several books on aging including *The Politics of Aging.* He is currently studying cross-national variations in social security systems and social control aspects of aging programs and policies.

Anne Woodward, an anthropologist, has been a writer in several departments of the federal government, both houses of Congress, and the United Nations. Now with the National Science Foundation, she is the author of *Learning from British New Towns* and numerous articles on housing and historic preservation.

Charles Yeager is associate professor of basic skills and political science at Stockton State College in Pomona, New Jersey. He has written in the areas of history, political science, and teaching mathematics to skill-deficient students.

William C. Yoels, with David Karp, has coauthored *Experiencing the Life Cycle: A Social Psychology of Aging* and *Symbols, Selves, and Society: Understanding Interaction.* With Gregory P. Stone and David Karp he has coauthored *Being Urban: A Social Psychological View of City Life.* Professor Yoels is currently professor of sociology and department chair at the University of Alabama in Birmingham.

Index